With You & Your Baby

All the Way

The Complete Guide to Pregnancy, Childbirth, Recovery, and Baby Care

With
You &
Your Baby

All the Way

The Complete Guide to Pregnancy, Childbirth, Recovery, and Baby Care

Jerri Colonero, RN, BS

BULL PUBLISHING

Publisher: James Bull
Developmental Editor: Nancy Evans
Production: Publication Services, Inc.
Cover Design: Lightbourne Images
Cover Photo: Michael Keller, The Stock Market
Interior Design: Publication Services, Inc.
Printer: Malloy Lithographing, Inc.

Bull Publishing Company
P.O. Box 208
Palo Alto, CA 94302-0208
Phone (650) 322-2855
Fax (650) 327-3300
www.bullpub.com

ISBN 0-923521-43-7

Distributed in the United States by:
Publishers Group West
1700 Fourth Street
Berkeley, CA 94710

This book is meant to educate, but it should not be used as a substitute for professional
medical advice or care. The reader should consult her health care provider concerning her
individual pregnancy and medical condition and her pediatrician regarding her baby. The author has done her best to ensure that the information presented here is accurate up to the
time of publication. However, as research and development are ongoing, it is possible that
new findings may supersede some of the information in this edition.

Colonero, Jerri, 1949-
With you & your baby all the way: the complete guide to pregnancy, childbirth, recovery, and baby care / Jerri Colonero.
        p.   cm.
Includes index.
ISBN 0-923521-43-7
1. Pregnancy—Popular works.   2. Childbirth—Popular works.   3. Infants (Newborn)—Care—Popular works.
4. Motherhood—Popular works.   5. Obstetrics—Popular works.   I. Title.
RG525.C684   1998
618.2—dc21
                                                                                                98-41647
                                                                                                CIP

10 9 8 7 6 5 4 3 2

This book is dedicated to
my three sons,
Craig, Curtis, and Clayton,

my future grandchildren
(God willing),

and,

in loving memory of my dad,
Dr. Olie Ohlsson,
who started this whole process by taking me along
to watch a baby delivered when I was just 16 years old.

Brief Contents

Contents

Preface

Throughout my 22 years of obstetrical nursing, I've heard these questions and comments countless times:

Now, what exactly did the doctor tell me I couldn't do?

I wasn't sure if I should call the doctor in the middle of the night or if it could wait until morning.

I didn't know this was an important symptom that needed to be reported right away.

Why isn't all of this information written down so I can refer to it at home?

If only you [the nurse] could come home with me!

Until just a few years ago, nurses had four days to teach you the things you needed to know about your postpartum recovery, basic care of your newborn, breastfeeding techniques and issues, bottle feeding and formula preparation and storage, normal vs. abnormal behavior of your baby, what to report to your obstetrician and pediatrician after your hospital discharge—all the things we worry about that are behind those questions and comments.

In today's world, you just get through labor, meet your new baby, and in 48 hours you are out the door. It's time to go home! Although you may be completely exhausted, you are responsible for the care of your newborn child, who is totally dependent on you. In addition to caring for your baby, you need to learn overnight how to monitor your infant for the complications, from jaundice to developing infections, that nurses and doctors used to watch for in the hospital.

In *With You & Your Baby All the Way*, I have drawn on my 22 years of experience to answer frequently asked questions, to prepare you for your labor and delivery as best I can, and to be your resource after you have left the hospital. I hope you'll think of this book as a way of having an experienced labor and delivery nurse along with you, from your pregnancy through the entire birthing experience, and as a friendly source of information in the first months at home with your baby.

Some nervousness about your pregnancy, your labor, and your new parenting role is certainly normal, but I believe that the better prepared you are, the more likely you are to feel relaxed and confident. My goal is to help you have the best birthing experience possible.

With You & Your Baby All the Way will help you:

- Become an educated consumer of obstetrical and newborn care.
- Eat right and stay healthy during your pregnancy.
- Deal with the normal discomforts of pregnancy.
- Know what to report to your obstetrical practitioner and when to report it. (Throughout the book, this telephone symbol, $\mathbf{C}$, alerts you to important symptoms that need to be reported to your practitioner.)
- Be a better advocate for your labor and delivery experience, participating more effectively in the many decision-making opportunities you will have with regard to your childbirth experience and your newborn's care.
- Know what to expect in the different stages of labor.
- Learn about your pain control options and how to deal with labor discomforts.

- Know what to expect if an emergency arises.
- Learn how you and your partner can work as a team during pregnancy, labor, and delivery and after you go home.
- Learn about post-delivery recovery and how to take care of yourself after delivering your baby.
- Learn about breastfeeding, bottle feeding, and all other aspects of baby care.

- Become informed on baby and child safety issues.
- Assess yourself and your baby for any developing problem after you've been discharged.

Enjoy your pregnancy, your baby's birth, and above all your baby, and thank you for allowing me to be *With You & Your Baby All the Way!*

How to Use This Book

The pregnancy, labor, pain control, and delivery expectations of women are as varied and unique as the children they produce. Not all of the subjects covered in this book need to be read by every reader. If this is not your first pregnancy, it is the author's suggestion that you use the table of contents or index to find those areas where you need information, explanations, or instructions.

Some of this book is quite detailed. In my years of nursing, I have placed many a baby into the arms of parents who have never held a baby before that moment. They need to be taught how to shift the baby from the cradle position in their arms in order to hand the baby to another person. They need to be shown how to pick a baby up safely. This type of detailed information is provided and illustrated, but readers experienced in handling an infant should just skip over it.

The table of contents for the book was made very extensive to help you easily find answers to your specific questions. The index, in addition, cross-references each item under several terms to assist you in easily finding specific information you seek. The index can also be used as a symptom index (for example, to look up headache, nausea, heartburn, and so on).

I recommend that everyone read the chapter on cesarean section births (Chapter 12) and the sections explaining spinal and general anesthesia (in Chapter 9) so that, if an emergency arises and you require an immediate cesarean section, you will feel better prepared.

The chapter on relaxation breathing is not intended to be a substitute for natural childbirth classes. These classes are informative and educational, and they are where the expectant mother and her support person begin to work as a team. Reading a book can in no way duplicate the practice sessions these classes offer. Breathing techniques and the mnemonics taught in the classes can be quite varied. There is no single correct way to do relaxation breathing. The breathing and relaxation techniques I discuss in this book are the ones that I have found work best for patients who come to the hospital without another practiced technique, or who find that their learned technique causes them to hyperventilate. At no time would I ever advise a patient to change the breathing or relaxation technique she learned in childbirth education classes if that technique is working well for her.

My chapter on breastfeeding is meant to be an introduction to the techniques needed to help you get started successfully. Learning proper techniques not only reduces your apprehension, it reduces your risk of developing sore or blistered nipples. Breastfeeding consultants are the experts who should be consulted if problems develop along the way. There are also books available about breastfeeding. The information in this book will get you started correctly, answer a multitude of questions, and share with you the helpful hints I have collected and used along the way in my many years of experience.

In the entire newborn section of this book, it became repetitious to continually say he or she in reference to the baby. Therefore, I chose to alternate the use of he and she between chapters.

Again, use the table of contents or index to find the information you need.

If you experience a miscarriage or suffer the loss of your baby, Appendix C offers some possible explanations and a discussion of the grief you and your family will experience. Professional help during this difficult time is recommended.

Technical terms used in pregnancy, labor, and delivery are defined in Appendix A at the end of the book.

The information in this book should not be a substitute for prenatal care or the advice of your obstetrician or midwife. Likewise, it is not a substitute for your pediatrician's watchful care and advice. It is meant to be their aid as well as yours. By helping you to know how to stay healthy during pregnancy and what you need to report promptly, your practitioner and pediatrician benefit, you benefit, and, most importantly, your baby benefits.

Eat well, get plenty of rest, and enjoy your reading as you get prepared for pregnancy, childbirth, recovery, and baby care.

Acknowledgments

Before I acknowledge anyone else, I want to thank our pediatrician, Dr. Richard Antonelli, not only for his professional consultation and review of the newborn and feeding chapters but also for all his encouragement along the way. In the beginning, he just listened to me as I told him about my goal of writing this book. Each time I brought one of my children to his office, he asked me how I was doing and encouraged me. As time passed, he finally said, "I don't want to hear any more about this book. Get it done; get it on my desk—it's needed and it is needed *now*." He told me about a house call he had just made: the parents of a newborn were panicked about something that was normal, something they should have been informed about in the hospital. After hearing that, I put extra effort into finishing this book.

Knowing that I had doctors like Dr. Antonelli to review my work helped me a great deal. I could not have been successful in completing this book without their help.

Dr. Thomas Beatty, Jr., a highly respected obstetrician and now Chief of Obstetrics and Gynecology at Newton Wellesley Hospital in Massachusetts, agreed to do the obstetrical consultation on my work. I appreciate sincerely the hours of time he gave to me in reviewing this material.

Dr. John Sutton, an anesthesiologist, also at Newton Wellesley Hospital, reviewed the material on pain control in labor. I thank him not only for his assistance but especially for clarifying my wording on the more technical forms of anesthesia.

My dad, Dr. Olof G. Ohlsson, did the initial review of the first material I wrote for this book. He was a family doctor in a small town—they don't make doctors like him anymore! He took care of adult medical problems and pediatrics, delivered babies, and did general surgery, with a special love for orthopedic hand surgery. After his medical edit, I felt ready to send my manuscript on to the other doctors mentioned above.

To both my mom, Gladys, and dad, I will be eternally grateful for their constant encouragement, as I grew up, to be the best that I could be. They both instilled in me the belief that I could achieve whatever I set out to accomplish as long as I was willing to work hard. Without that foundation, and the education they provided for me, this book would never have been written.

My sister Mardo Eaton is also a registered nurse with a master's degree in psychology. She reviewed the pregnancy and labor sections of this book, primarily focusing on areas where I may have been too technical or medical in my wording. Most important, she was looking for wording that may have been too frightening. Her input was invaluable. I will never be able to thank her enough for the hours and hours she spent helping me reach my goal.

Steve Glines and my sister Sandee Tyler gave me a lot of support and ideas with regard to publishing. I thank them for their help and advice.

I have watched Deborah Saviano-Mello, the daughter of our dear friends, grow up. She is now a professional advertising writer for a computer company and happened to be pregnant with her first baby at just the right time! She had a lot of questions, and I offered my book in exchange for her opinions and suggestions. She kindly reviewed the book from the standpoint of a prospective first-time parent. As questions came up in her pregnancy, she tried to find the answers in my book. If an answer wasn't there, she let me know! In addition, she offered me some format and order suggestions that were most helpful.

Her encouragement and suggestions were invaluable and most appreciated. I had the pleasure of being with Debbie and her husband Scott during the birth of their son, Jack. I was also privileged to help her off to a successful nursing experience. Jack is a beautiful little boy, and we are enjoying watching him grow up.

To Jim and Cynthia Saviano, Paul and Nancy D'Amore, and Bob and Penny McLaren go my thanks for their love and encouragement.

I appreciated the assistance of my colleagues Linda Winslow, Kathy Pellegrini, and Sue Allman-Carlo, who are all RNs and International Board Certified Lactation Consultants. They were very helpful in answering many of my specific breastfeeding questions and informing me of the latest research results. I also thank my colleagues Karen Mueller and Michelle Palmer for posing along with me for the labor position pictures that were used by the artist in rendering his drawings.

I would like to thank Sue Rose, and Mary Baker, both CNMs, who helped me to define the role of the certified nurse midwife. I appreciate the Women's Health Certified Nurse Midwife group for allowing me to take pictures of their birthing chair and Jacuzzi at their birthing center.

A special thanks to the American Cord Blood Program staff at the University of Massachusetts Medical Center, Worcester, for helping me write about their "A Gift Of Life" program.

I would especially like to thank my developmental editor, Nancy Evans, for all that her background and experience brought to this book. Not only was she a great person to work with, but she continually challenged me to make this book the best that it could be. Nancy sent me volumes to read on the effects of pesticides in our food chain and toxic chemicals in our home products and our children's toys. Nancy is relentless in teaching others that what we do today affects not only our health—it affects the health of our children and the health of future generations. Collectively, we can make a difference, even against large, powerful companies.

I never got to meet all the people at Publication Services, but I feel that I know them well. My thanks to the artist, Duane Gillogly, for his patience and willingness to make changes.

I have three babies to thank for posing for my many photos. (From these photos my artist rendered the drawings.) Colleen Laughlin is the infant daughter of Lynnann and Randall Laughlin. Lynnann was kind enough to allow me to come into her home and take many pictures: bathing, positioning, nursing positions, and many more.

Ava Saster, daughter of Bob and Tami Saster was also one of my infant models, and my neighbor, Jackie Weiler, saved me by being born at just the right time. I realized I had forgotten several important newborn pictures and her parents, Anne Marie and Pat Weiler, allowed me to use Jackie for those last remaining photo needs. Her sister Shannon also joined in the fun. Thank you all so very much. I hope it was as much fun for you as it was for me.

I would like to thank Jim Bull, my publisher. This is definitely our book. I could not have done it without you. To make it even better, you included me in all aspects of the publishing process and even made it fun for me. Thank you.

Last but not least I would like to thank my family. My husband Ben has been very patient with me as I worked fewer hours than usual, and he had to cook more than his usual share of dinners. I especially want to thank him for his support when I got nervous about the publishing process. He promised to publish it himself if he had to: his words "you just finish the book" were just what I needed at that moment.

Every day that I worked on this book, I literally took over my son Curtis's room (where the computer is located). I know it wasn't easy for him working around and putting up with my card table, papers, and books. The hole punches on the floor drove him crazy! I appreciate the patience he had with me. Hopefully the training will come in handy now that he has a roommate to live with at college!

I would also like to thank my son Craig for always asking me about my book, showing an interest, and encouraging me to reach my goal by finishing. It was such a good feeling to know that I had my sons behind me. I was proud when he had to give a speech at college and he chose to talk about me and my book endeavor. I had no choice but to finish it after that!

My youngest son Clayton is definitely, without a doubt, my biggest supporter. He has teachers who have already raised their own children signed up to buy his mother's book! If he weren't only 15, I would ask my publisher to hire Clayton to market this book!

If my three sons choose to have and are blessed with children some day, I hope they find this book helpful. I won't have to worry about being an interfering mother or mother-in-law when my grandchildren come along, now that they each have a copy of this book!

Consultants

Newborn (pediatric) editor:
Richard Antonelli, MD, FAAP—pediatrician

Obstetrical editor:
Thomas L. Beatty, Jr., MD—Chief of Obstetrics and Gynecology at Newton Wellesley Hopital

Anesthesia editor:
John A. Sutton, MD—anesthesiologist

Nutritional consultant:
Christine Berman, MPII, RD

About the Author

Jerrilyne Colonero was born in Bakersfield, California, in 1949. When she was 16 years old, her father, Dr. Olof G. Ohlsson, obtained permission from one of his patients for his daughter to view her delivery. Just as for the mother, the anticipation of this day for Jerri lasted nine months! One day, when she awoke, her Dad said, "You're not going to school today—today is the day." The rest is history! This experience obviously made a huge impression on her—at the completion of this book, Jerri has been a labor and delivery nurse for 22 years.

Jerri graduated from the nursing school at the University of California, Los Angeles, in 1971 with a B.S., and she married Benjamin H. Colonero, Jr., later that year. Together they moved to Massachusetts, where Jerri began her nursing career.

After an initial period in medical-surgical nursing, Jerri took a job teaching pediatrics and obstetrics in the LPN (licensed practical nurse) nursing school at Day Kimball Hospital in Putnam, Connecticut. The special interest she had in maternal-child nursing while she was in nursing school was reborn.

In September 1976, after spending a year at home with her first-born son, Craig, Jerri took her first part-time clinical job in labor and delivery. The script was now signed, sealed, and delivered. She spent time at home after the births of both Curtis and Clayton, but each time she was ready to work again, it was in labor and delivery, postpartum care, and the nursery.

In February 1989, Jerri accepted a job offer from Newton Wellesley Hospital, outside of Boston, Massachusetts. She had the opportunity to be part of the opening of their new, 20-bed LDRP unit. (These are the private rooms where a patient labors, delivers, recovers, and remains postpartum *all in the same room*.) For the past nine years, Jerri has worked in all areas of mother and baby care. She is a highly skilled labor and delivery nurse, as well as a trained scrub, circulating, and recovery room nurse for cesarean section patients. In her role at Newton Wellesley Hospital, Jerri also provides comprehensive postpartum care and teaching, including assistance with breastfeeding and bottle-feeding techniques. She has taught many sessions of the hospital's daily newborn care classes. Because of her knowledge and experience in maternal-child nursing, Jerri is often a preceptor instructor for college students and staff in labor and delivery and postpartum care.

In 1993 Jerri was nominated by her peers for the Newton Wellesley Hospital Excel Award, which she received in August of that year. Her role as a patient advocate and teacher and her willingness to share her knowledge with her peers were listed as reasons for her nomination and receipt of this award.

Pregnancy

When Pregnancy Begins

Am I Pregnant?

The most common sign that says "yes!" is a missed menstrual period. But periods are not always regular. Even if you have a regular-as-clockwork 28-day menstrual cycle, illness or stress can make it shorter or longer. You can also be pregnant if you have spotting or a "low-flow" (compared to your normal period) period.

Breast tenderness and a bloated feeling, especially in the abdominal area, are also common symptoms of pregnancy. Some women experience fatigue and nausea as early signs of pregnancy.

A frequent need to urinate is another common symptom of early pregnancy. For about the first 12 weeks of your pregnancy, your uterus fits neatly within your pelvis. Then, as the uterus begins to expand, it grows wider, creating pressure on your bladder and triggering the urge to urinate frequently. Relief is on the way, however. At the beginning of the second trimester, your uterus begins to rise out of the pelvis, relieving the pressure and the need for frequent urination.

Pregnancy Tests

There are now tests available that can confirm your pregnancy within about one week of a missed menstrual period. The tests work by detecting human chorionic gonadotrophin (HCG), a hormone produced by the developing placenta early in pregnancy, in either urine or blood.

There are several home pregnancy tests on the market. When using these tests, it's important to follow the directions carefully. Always use a clean container for collecting the urine, and don't reuse the same container for another test. Most tests require that you use the first urine you pass in the morning for the test. Carefully time your test according to the specific directions provided.

False negative test results (indicating you are not pregnant when you actually are) sometimes happen. Although false negative results are rare if you follow directions, no test is perfect. So if your home pregnancy test result is negative, but you still suspect that you are pregnant, you should see your doctor for a more accurate blood test.

If your home pregnancy test is positive, you need to call your doctor's office for a confirmation test. Once a positive result is confirmed, your next steps are choosing a health professional—an obstetrician or a nurse midwife—to manage your prenatal care and scheduling your first prenatal visit.

Prenatal Care

Pregnancy and childbirth are normal processes for which women's bodies are beautifully designed. Because each of us is unique and because there is some degree of risk with any pregnancy, you want to be sure that your pregnancy is proceeding normally. This makes prenatal care by an experienced health professional an essential part of every pregnancy. With regular prenatal visits, complications can be discovered early and treatment initiated when it is most likely to be effective.

You should call for an appointment as soon as you suspect you are pregnant. (See page 6 for factors to consider when choosing a maternity care provider.) Be sure to tell the receptionist if you have any medical condition, no matter how insignificant it may seem to you. Also tell her or him if you are taking medication for anything. If you do not provide this information, you may be scheduled for a visit later when in fact you should be seen right away. In addition, if you feel that your current medical condition, medication, or medical history requires immediate evaluation from a practitioner when you become pregnant, and the receptionist does not agree, please ask to speak directly to a registered nurse.

The First Appointment

Your first prenatal visit includes:

- Assessment of your medical history and your family's medical history
- A physical checkup

- A baseline assessment of your weight and blood pressure
- A pregnancy blood test
- Other urine and blood tests
- A pelvic exam to assess your cervix and uterus
- Educational information on nutrition, exercise, and other important issues
- An opportunity for you to ask questions

The practitioner will also estimate your due date at this visit. Any referrals to other specialists will be made at this time if your medical history or dietary needs suggest that specialized care is needed.

Your first prenatal visit takes more time than any other. Be prepared by bringing information on your medical history, your family medical history, any genetic conditions in your or the father's family, how old you were when you had your first period, and the date of your last period. Be honest in providing information, especially about previous pregnancies. All information is confidential, and your history in many areas is important to your current care.

Continuing Care

Later prenatal visits include urine tests, weight and blood pressure monitoring, assessment of your developing baby, childbirth education, counseling, and, possibly, referrals to other professionals (a dietitian or a diabetic counselor, for example). In addition, time should be allowed to answer your questions and address your concerns. You should always feel free to discuss all aspects of your care with your practitioner. No question is a "dumb" or "silly" question.

Informed Consent

Before undergoing any procedure, test, or treatment, you have the right to understand why it is being done, how it will be done, and what the risks are to both you and your baby. You also have the right to be informed

of your diagnosis, *all treatment options,* and the expected outcome of each treatment.

The process of obtaining this information before agreeing to treatment is called *informed consent.* For some procedures, only verbal informed consent is required; for other procedures or tests, you must sign a consent form. **It is your right to have all your questions answered and your concerns addressed before giving your verbal or written consent.**

It is also your right to refuse a treatment, test, or procedure and to know the expected outcome of refusing treatment. However, your practitioner may ask you to sign a form stating that you were informed of the recommendations and refused what was suggested.

Again, it is important to be honest when answering all questions, including those about past pregnancies, as well as past or current alcohol and drug use. Your practitioner may suggest certain tests to safeguard both you and your baby because of your medical, social, or occupational history. All information is private and confidential, and you are protected by physician/patient confidentiality laws.

Pregnant Patient's Bill of Rights

For more information about your rights during pregnancy, labor, and delivery, see Appendix B for the "Pregnant Patient's Bill of Rights."

How Do I Calculate My Due Date?

The length of pregnancy can be described in many ways:

- ❑ Ten lunar months of four weeks each
- ❑ Nine calendar months
- ❑ Three trimesters of three months each
- ❑ Forty weeks

Birth normally occurs about 266 days after fertilization, or about 280 days (40 weeks) after the first day of the last menstrual period. Most physicians calculate the due date from the first day of the last menstrual period, since the exact dates of ovulation and conception are usually difficult to identify. The duration of pregnancy is considered normal if delivery occurs between 38 and 42 weeks after this time (two weeks before to two weeks after your due date).

Estimated Date of Delivery

Back in the days when childbirth was treated like an illness and women were confined to bed for a week or more after delivery, the due date was called the *estimated date of confinement* (EDC). Today, the more positive terminology *estimated date of delivery* (EDD) is used.

Nägele's rule is the easiest and most common formula used to calculate the EDD, or the estimated date of your baby's birth. Take the first day of your last menstrual period, count back three months, add seven days, and then add one year: LMP – 3 months + 7 days + 1 year = EDD. This rule assumes a 28-day menstrual cycle with ovulation occurring on the 14th day. Because of the variations in women's cycles, only 4 to 10 percent of women deliver spontaneously on their due date. Your physician may order an ultrasound if more accurate determination of your due date is needed. (See page 76 for an explanation of ultrasound.)

What Is My Baby's Gestational Age?

Taber's Medical Dictionary defines gestation as the "period of intrauterine fetal development." When you see your practitioner or arrive at the hospital for tests or labor, your baby's gestational age is calculated at that time, based on your estimated date of delivery. If, for example, you are in labor nine days before your due date (which was based on a 40-week gestation), the gestational age would be calculated by subtracting 1 week and 2 days (9 days) from 40 weeks. Your baby's gestational age would therefore be 38 weeks + 5 days. If, on the other hand, you are having contractions and the gestational age is calculated to be only 31 weeks, this constitutes premature labor. As you can see, treatment decisions will vary based on your baby's gestational age.

To see how you and your baby grow and develop over the nine months of pregnancy, see Chapter 4, "Mother and Baby: The First Nine Months."

Choosing Your Practitioner and Where to Give Birth

Pregnancy and childbirth are among the most memorable experiences in a woman's life. The better your health and your baby's health, the happier those memories will be. Choosing a maternity care practitioner who is competent, caring, and considerate of your ideas and concerns is one of the most important decisions you will make. As you consider your choices, keep in mind that it's your body and your baby, and that pregnancy and birth are normal life processes, not an illness that demands high-tech interventions, unless you have special health considerations.

You can be an active advocate for the quality of maternity care that you receive and directly influence your birthing experience by seriously researching your alternatives and making educated and informed choices.

Know Your Insurance Options

In today's world, your health insurance may determine which group or groups of health professionals you can consider for your prenatal care and which hospital you are required to use. Even in this system, however, there is usually some degree of choice.

Call your insurance company to be fully aware and certain of all the options allowed

under your policy, and explore the choices you are given. Some of the possible options are as follows.

Maternity care practitioner

Does my insurance company specify which I must choose:

> *Obstetrician?*
>
> *CNM?*
>
> *Family Practice physician?*

Birthing place

Does my insurance specify:

> *Hospital?*
>
> *Birthing center? Based on my insurance and physical condition, is this an available option?*
>
> *Home?*

Postpartum stay

How long is my postpartum hospital stay?

Is early discharge an option?

If I elect early discharge, is a home visit from a nurse an available option?

After researching insurance options, some people choose the care provider first and then choose the place of delivery based on where the care provider has delivery privileges. Others feel very strongly about delivering at a particular hospital, a particular birthing center, or at home and choose the care provider based on this decision.

Exploring Birthing Place Options

Equipped with the information from your insurance company and having identified possible care providers, you are ready to explore the various birthing options (hospital, center, or home) available to you. Not all of the following choices may be important to you. This list is meant only to help you think about possible options.

Hospital Delivery: Hospitals provide various settings for delivery depending on the facility. Newer units tend to be built to meet patients' current desires.

Type of Delivery Setting

L = Labor room

D = Room where delivery occurs

R = Room where initial recovery occurs

P = Room for the remainder of your postpartum hospital stay

A hyphen between letters means a *change of room:*

L-D-R-P

LD-R-P

LDR-P

LDRP

If you have a normal vaginal delivery, the LDRP setting provides for your entire labor, delivery, recovery, and postpartum experience to occur in the same room. LDRPs are also referred to as *single-room maternity care.*

Currently the LDRP setting is most popular, and the LDR-P setting is the second most popular.

Programs and Facilities

Are childbirth classes available at the hospital or other convenient location?

Is a Jacuzzi available?

Is a shower available in my room or only down the hall?

Are hand controls and back jets available in the shower?

Are chairs available for the shower?

Do I have a private room?

Are special birthing beds available?

>*Do the beds have multiposition options?*

>*Are the controls within the reach of the patient?*

>*Are pushing bars available?*

Does the bottom of the bed detach for delivery?

Are follow-up appointments from a nurse available if I go home sooner than 48 hours after delivery?

What types of written information or instructions are provided to me before discharge?

Labor Options

Are partners allowed?

>*During labor?*

>*During birth?*

>*In the operating room if a cesarean birth is required?*

>*To spend the night in the room?*

At what point in my labor will I have one-to-one care from an RN?

There are many forms of labor care delivery. Your insurance may dictate the hospital you must go to for delivery. If it does not, then look for the facility that provides the earliest one-to-one care in labor. Some hospitals provide one-to-one care when you become dilated 4 centimeters or become very active and uncomfortable. Other hospitals use central fetal monitoring, in which case your monitor screen is also displayed at the nursing station, allowing one RN to evaluate several patients' fetal monitor strips at once from a central location. However, some hospitals with central monitoring, and some even with intermittent monitoring, do not provide an RN until you are very close to delivery.

Many hospitals assign two early-labor patients to one RN. One of these patients is turned over to another nurse when she becomes active, requiring one-to-one care.

Will I have to wear a hospital gown?

Is electronic fetal monitoring intermittent or constant?

Is ambulation encouraged?

Are showers or hot tubs encouraged for pain control?

Baby Care Options

Will I be allowed to hold my baby right after delivery if there are no complications?

Will I be allowed to breastfeed immediately after delivery?

Does hospital policy require immediate administration of antibiotic ointment in my baby's eyes and intramuscular injection of vitamin K, or can these procedures be delayed to allow for bonding? (Most hospitals allow nurses to wait one hour before providing these treatments.)

Are feedings on demand or on schedule in the nursery? (Most hospitals lean toward on-demand feedings except for underweight and premature babies and babies born to mothers with gestational diabetes.)

Visitors

Are there any restrictions on who can visit?

Are visiting hours restricted?

Are siblings allowed at any time?

Are grandparents allowed at any time?

Birthing Center Delivery: Birthing centers strive to make your surroundings more like home. They are family centered, meaning that all family members (grandparents and other children), as well as other people you invite, are welcome to be present and participate in the birth experience.

There are two types of birthing centers where midwives practice. An *alternative birthing center* is a separate area within or attached to a hospital. A *freestanding birthing center* is a separate building not within or attached to a hospital. It may or may not be very near a hospital.

In a birthing center you are under a midwife's care while in labor. However, since more than one patient may be in labor at the same time, registered nurses may also participate in your care. After delivery you are most often under a nurse's care.

How long you remain at the center after birth varies. However, all birthing centers will make sure you and your baby are stable before sending you home.

Home Birth: Home birth is another birthing option. In this setting the midwife comes to your home to be with you during labor and birth. You are under the care of either a certified midwife or a lay midwife, whichever you hired to assist in your birth.

Begin Writing Your Personal Birthing Plan

Once you understand your insurance and birthing place options, you can begin to write your personal birthing plan. (It would not serve any purpose, for example, to write that you want LDRP rooms and Jacuzzis for labor, if these are not available at the hospital where you later decide to deliver.)

At this early stage, write down the things that are important to you, such as a practitioner who takes time to listen to and carefully answer your questions and your desire to be allowed to walk or take a shower during labor. If you have had a previous cesarean delivery, indicate whether or not you would like the opportunity to try a vaginal birth. Specifics (such as the type of pain control options you prefer) can be added later, after childbirth education classes.

Your goal in this initial writing is to have your general ideas on paper so you will have questions in hand to ask various physicians or midwives as you choose who will become your maternity care provider (also referred to as your practitioner in this book).

Instructions for finishing the birthing plan with your support person can be found on pages 130–131.

Obstetrician or Midwife?

Regardless of how you choose your care provider, you want to be certain that the practitioner's office is an acceptable distance from your home. Next you need to ask which hospital, hospitals, or birthing centers the practitioner uses for delivery.

Obstetricians are medical doctors who have specialized training in obstetrics, the care of women from pregnancy through delivery (including both vaginal and cesarean delivery) and the six-week postpartum (postdelivery) period.

Certified nurse midwives (CNMs) are registered nurses with additional training and education in obstetrics and gynecology. They are qualified and licensed to provide primary care for (independently manage the care of) women and newborns who are considered low-risk. They also manage those considered high-risk in consultation and collaboration with a physician during pregnancy, labor, and birth and after birth. CNMs are also licensed to treat gynecological problems in women. Most states grant prescription-writing privileges to CNMs.

CNMs work in offices and hospitals and are often affiliated directly with a particular obstetrical practice. They also work in clinics under a formalized relationship with a physician for consultation and referrals. In addition, they can have their own private practices in some states, often with their own birthing centers. In these circumstances, a CNM must have a formal written contract with a particular physician that allows the midwife to hire this doctor for consultation and referral when needed. In many states, midwives are certified to attend home births.

Whether prenatal care is provided in a hospital, clinic, or private practice, and whether labor and delivery occurs in a hospital, in a birthing center, or in the home, a midwife will call in the physician if complications arise. However, if labor is taking place in a birthing center or at home and a situation arises requiring medical intervention, the patient will need to transferred to the hospital for the physician to assist in providing care.

CNMs consider birth a normal process and therefore usually take a noninterventional, family-centered approach to labor and delivery. This does not mean that a CNM will not provide pain control in the form of an injection or epidural or utilize oxytocin for labor augmentation when necessary. However, a more natural childbirth is usually the initial goal of CNMs and the patients who seek their care.

When a woman delivers in a hospital setting under the care of a CNM, the state's law and the individual protocol of the hospital determine whether the physician must be physically present in the hospital or merely available. Whether present or not, however, the physician, because of the formalized relationship, will be available to provide medical consultation, take over the care if the woman develops a high-risk problem, or provide joint care with the midwife if necessary.

Under freedom-of-practice laws, insurance companies must pay for care by a CNM. However, be sure to check with your insurance provider to be sure that it is aware of, and covers the care of, your practitioner, whether obstetrician or midwife. If your midwife practices privately, it is a good idea to check with your insurance company to be certain it also approves and pays for the care of her consulting physician, if he or she is needed.

There are educational programs available that allow a person who is not trained as a nurse to become a midwife. Such a midwife is known as a certified midwife (CM). Most states, however, presently have wording in their laws that states that a midwife must first graduate from an accredited school of nursing before being certified as a nurse midwife. These laws will have to be rewritten before CMs are fully licensed to practice in most states.

Lay midwives, or independent midwives, practice in some places in the United States. A lay midwife assists people who want a home birth or accompanies the couple to the hospital (by private arrangement with the couple) and acts as their labor coach or support person. The lay midwife's role is usually one of support to the entire family during pregnancy and birth.

Lay midwives learn by apprenticing with another lay midwife. There are now also schools for the training of lay midwives, but because training varies, it is difficult to evaluate a lay midwife's schooled competence.

A lay midwife may not have a license, because licensure requirements vary between states. Lay midwives may be members of the Midwives Alliance of North America, which requires a certification process and examination to help ensure a level of competency.

Some insurance companies will reimburse you for maternity care by lay midwives.

Making the Choice

Now you are ready to choose your care provider. How do you choose the practitioner—obstetrician, certified nurse midwife, or lay midwife—who is right for you? Begin by making a list of the things that are important to you. This list will be a starting point for the questions you need to ask as you look for the right practitioner to care for you and your baby during this important time.

If you are new to an area, talk with parents of babies and small children about their experience with local physicians or midwives. It won't take long to get an idea about the reputations of hospitals and practitioners in the area.

The following list is meant only to help you in making decisions about your care and to make you a better advocate for the quality of care that you receive. Only some of the questions will be important to you.

Evaluating a Practitioner's Philosophy of Care: You are looking here for open-mindedness and flexibility. Be wary of words like *always* and *never.*

Do you support noninterventional labor and delivery?

Will I be required to have an enema? (Most practitioners do not require this any longer.)

Will I be required to have any perineal or pubic hair shaved? (Most practitioners do not require this today.)

If I have said I want natural childbirth, will you allow me to change my mind and have pain medication or an epidural if it is safe for my baby and me?

Do you routinely rupture membranes to speed up labor? (Routinely is the key word in this question.)

Will I be in stirrups for delivery? If you have a natural labor, will the practitioner allow you to deliver without breaking down the labor bed and using the stirrups, or allow you to deliver on your side or in a squatting position? Again, you are looking for flexibility.

Will my partner be allowed to cut the umbilical cord if there is no meconium in the amniotic fluid and there is no fetal distress?

Questions for an obstetrician

Do you routinely use Pitocin to induce or speed up your patient's labor? Be sure to acknowledge that you realize that Pitocin is sometimes necessary. There are no good statistics available to evaluate the average number of Pitocin inductions or augmentations for obstetricians or midwives. The answer will vary depending on the socioeconomic status of the area of the practice and the number of high-risk patients in that area. Again, be wary of words like *always* and *never* in evaluating the answers you receive.

Do you routinely do episiotomies on your patients? The circumstances of each woman's unique anatomy and delivery should determine this decision.

What percentage of your patients have cesarean deliveries? The national average is 24 percent. Anything under 19 percent is excellent.

If I require a cesarean delivery, will you or a doctor from this group perform the procedure?

If I require a cesarean delivery for this birth, would you advise me to try for a trial of labor after cesarean (TOLAC) in my next pregnancy? (The term *vaginal birth after cesarean,* or VBAC, is sometimes used instead of TOLAC. Technically, however, VBAC means that you have had at least one vaginal birth after cesarean.) Here you are ascertaining the practitioner's open-mindedness toward your trying labor after a cesarean birth.

Do you recommend breastfeeding? If so, do you have a breastfeeding consultant (lactation consultant) to refer me to if I need help after delivery?

If the hospital where you deliver has medical residents, will you still manage my care in labor? Will I see you or one of the doctors from your group during my labor, or will my labor be monitored only by a resident? If you do not have health insurance or are being managed by a clinic, you may not have a choice here.

How often will I see you during my pregnancy? Will I have some visits with the other doctors in this group to get to know them in case they are on call when my labor begins?

Will any of my prenatal visits be managed by someone other than an obstetrician? If so, who will that be, what are that person's qualifications, and what percentage of my visits will be with that person? Many physicians have nurse practitioners in their offices. Generally, the nurse practitioner sees the patient every other visit or three to four times during the pregnancy. However, your health insurance plan or your access to health care will affect this. In some clinics, an MD sees patients only at the end of their pregnancy unless complications arise.

Questions for a certified nurse midwife

Will any risk factors that I develop be considered in deciding where I will deliver? Where you deliver—hospital, home, or birthing center—should be determined based on careful review of your risk factors. High-risk pregnancies (those women with PIH, diabetes, or meconium-stained amniotic fluid) usually require a hospital delivery. However, your health insurance plan will also affect this decision.

If I will be delivering in a birthing center and an emergency occurs, how long will it take to transfer me to the hospital?

Is medical backup available in the hospital or on call to cover your midwifery service, should an emergency arise? A physician should be available quickly.

If you have more than one patient in labor at once, is another midwife called in or do you cover both patients?

If I decide during labor that I need pain control, such as intravenous medication, an intramuscular injection, or epidural anesthesia, are you open to providing those measures? Every woman in labor deserves the right to change her mind about pain control options. If there are medical reasons for withholding medication, you deserve and have the right to a full explanation.

What Is a Doula, and Is This an Option for Me?

Female attendants during labor were popular in the past, and they are now being used again in some areas of the country. A *doula* (pronounced doo-la) is an educated person (although there is no certification), sometimes a nurse midwife, who offers encouragement, support, and massage throughout labor and delivery and assists in the care of the mother and baby into the postpartum period.

Doulas typically are hired for four hours a day for about two weeks, but this varies, as do their rates. Doulas essentially assist the mother, providing both care and special attention. They typically do housework and shopping, and babysit. Their primary goal is to help the mother feel rested and happy so she can enjoy her newborn.

If you are interested, ask your hospital or care provider for the name of a doula in your area. Doulas are not common in all areas of the country, so be aware that a nearby doula may be difficult to find.

Childbirth Education Options

Your care provider will usually recommend a childbirth class to you if you are interested in taking one. It may be offered by a private instructor or by the hospital where you will deliver. For couples having their first baby, classes usually begin around the sixth or seventh month, depending on the course schedule; however, you will need to register for a particular session earlier in your pregnancy. If you are moving to a new area in late pregnancy or need assistance in finding a program in your area, you can call the International Childbirth Education Association at (612) 854-8660. The telephone directory in most areas will also list phone numbers for the La Leche League and Lamaze Childbirth Education.

Some hospitals and private instructors offer a refresher course for those people who previously took a full course or have experienced childbirth before.

Childbirth education classes are a good way to learn about the physiology and the emotional aspects of labor. Videos and movies are generally shown to illustrate labor, vaginal birth, and cesarean birth. Some form of relaxation breathing technique is taught and pain control options are discussed. Usually, the better educated women and couples are about labor and delivery, the more active they can be in the decision-making process concerning their birthing experience. For most people, education also helps to control fear of

the unknown. Concerns are shared and discussed in class. It is often helpful simply to realize that other people have the same concerns that you have.

Childbirth education classes usually provide a tour of the hospital where you will deliver. Policies of the hospital on such things as parking, visitors, and where to go when you arrive in labor are generally covered in class.

Some programs offer preparation classes for your other children, to get them actively involved in the upcoming family event. It also helps them not to be afraid about where Mommy and Daddy will be going. Doctors, nurses, and midwives do not want children to be afraid of hospitals. A tour ahead of time helps show them a place that is not scary. They will see the kind of bed you will have and the crib the baby will use. They will see how the doctors and nurses are dressed and what a hospital looks like on the inside.

Lamaze Education

In the 1950s Fernand Lamaze introduced the Lamaze method of childbirth. A Lamaze class provides education about labor and relaxation and breathing techniques to relieve pain and help you have a more natural delivery without the use of drugs. Some Lamaze classes teach only the Lamaze breathing techniques; other classes teach a wide variety of breathing and relaxation techniques.

The Lamaze method involves specific breathing techniques and concentration on focal points (outside the body), which help to distract the woman from the pain of labor and delivery. Practice and repetition are used to teach the techniques. The father or other labor support person also attends the class and is actively involved in the labor process.

Ask whether the instructor of your class is a certified Lamaze instructor. Such certification means that they received training and passed an exam to become an instructor.

Lamaze childbirth education usually includes six two-hour classes (twelve hours of total instruction) with a maximum of ten couples per class. The cost for the class will vary. Ask questions and pick the class that seems right for you.

Bradley Education

In 1965 obstetrician Robert Bradley wrote a book on husband-coached childbirth that focused on "natural" childbirth. He emphasized good nutrition and exercise during pregnancy, both to decrease the discomforts common in pregnancy and to increase muscle tone for labor and delivery.

The Bradley method of childbirth preparation establishes the husband or partner as the primary coach. The partner learns tension-reducing techniques, especially touch and massage, to help the laboring woman. Massage, deep abdominal breathing, general body relaxation, deep mental relaxation (using focal points within the body), and the use of darkness and quiet are the chief techniques taught in the Bradley method. Medication is suggested only when complications occur.

Bradley courses begin early in pregnancy and usually go into the postpartum period. The additional class time allows for both physical and psychological preparation for childbirth.

Grantly Dick-Read Education

Grantly Dick-Read was the first organized childbirth preparation method in the United States. It was the first program to offer prenatal classes and the first to include the father in both the educational preparation and the actual labor process.

This method of childbirth preparation strives to break the fear-tension-pain cycle. It uses relaxation breathing and muscle group relaxation techniques along with prenatal education. In this technique a woman practices until she is able to relax muscle groups throughout her body. This

prenatal training and practice enable her to learn to relax completely between contractions and relax all but her uterus during a contraction.

Other Childbirth Education Options

If you belong to an HMO (health maintenance organization), it may provide its own childbirth education classes. In addition, some hospitals and cities offer their own programs. Some private instructors, certified by the International Childbirth Education Association, sponsor their own family-centered childbirth education classes.

Programs are not limited to teaching one particular method of childbirth preparation (e.g., Lamaze, Bradley, Grantly Dick-Read). Many programs teach information from several methods and base their teachings on current research.

Ask questions and find the program that feels right for you and meets your educational needs.

Choosing a Pediatrician

It is best to choose a pediatrician while you are pregnant. There is time during pregnancy to do your research, interview pediatricians, and make a decision that feels right to you. It is also advisable to have a pediatrician and pediatric office staff on board to answer your questions when you come home from the hospital with your newborn. Your obstetrician or midwife can give you names of pediatricians in your area. You can also ask other parents for recommendations.

Your insurance company may provide you with a list of pediatricians who accept your insurance (especially if you belong to a Health Maintenance Organization (or HMO)). Be sure to cross-reference this list with the names you receive from other sources. In this way, you can form an initial list of possible pediatricians. To narrow your list it may be helpful to drive to the various offices to see how accessible they are from your home and how available and convenient parking is.

Early in your last trimester, call the offices on your list. Make a note of how long it takes for your call to go through. (Great pediatricians are busy, and there will be some wait. However, you should be asked if you can hold or if it is an emergency before you are put on hold.) How friendly and helpful is the receptionist? If desired, ask for a consultation/interview and whether or not there is a fee for this service.

Questions for a pediatrician

Some of the following questions may be pertinent or important to you:

Do you have privileges at the hospital where I will be delivering? This is not mandatory. If the pediatrician you choose does not practice at the hospital where you will be delivering, you will be assigned a temporary pediatrician for your baby's hospital stay. A copy of your baby's hospital record will be sent to your regular pediatrician or will be given to you to take to your pediatrician.

What are your office hours?

How many pediatricians are in your practice?

How long do you schedule for each sick call visit? Fifteen minutes is good. Ten minutes is tight and doesn't allow much time for questions to be answered. Shorter time spans between patients may also mean longer waits. It is usually not informative to find out how long a patient waits on average after arriving for an appointment. You would not want a pediatrician who always follows an exact schedule, because she or he may not be flexible in meeting the emotional needs of children or parents, which takes time. You also would not want to always have to wait two hours because a doctor books too many patients per hour. You should be

understanding and patient, however, if you occasionally have to wait an inconvenient amount of time. If you need extra time from the pediatrician, you will appreciate having a doctor that meets your needs.

How many weekends and nights do you cover per month within your office staff? This will, of course, be determined by the number of pediatricians in the practice.

Which pediatricians cover weekends and nights for you? Check to be sure they are on your initial list, or check them out by asking neighbors and friends.

What is your opinion or philosophy about breastfeeding?

If I choose to breastfeed, how soon will you see my baby after discharge from the hospital? The usual first newborn visit is at two weeks; however, many pediatricians ask to see breastfeeding babies two days after discharge for a weight check.

If I prefer to bottle feed, do you recommend sterilization? (Refer to page 304 for more information.)

If my insurance requires me to pay in full for visits to the pediatrician, what are the usual fees?

Is there a separate waiting area where a sick child with a communicable illness can be isolated from other children when they come in?

When you leave the interview, think about the overall office environment. Did it appear organized? Was it clean? Were there clean toys available in the waiting area? Did you feel comfortable talking to the staff and the pediatrician? Did the pediatrician agree with and support things that are important to you? How did you feel about the answers you received? Which pediatrician is the best for you will become evident if you follow these suggestions during your evaluation process.

2

Living Healthy During Pregnancy and Beyond

A Well-Balanced Diet for Life

The Food Guide Pyramid

It is easy to be overwhelmed if you think of your diet in terms of protein, vitamin A, vitamin C, calcium, and so on. You may feel confused when trying to figure out how to control calorie intake and yet eat foods containing necessary nutrients. The Food Guide Pyramid (Figure 2-1) was developed to simplify daily food selection for a balanced and healthy diet. The serving numbers suggested in the Food Guide Pyramid are for men and non-pregnant women. Pregnant women, as explained later in this chapter, have increased requirements.

Each level of the Food Guide Pyramid is essential for a healthy diet. However, the pyramid shape is used to illustrate the proportions of the food serving amounts recommended in the different categories. For example, food items at the base of the pyramid have the greatest number of daily recommended servings.

The Food Guide Pyramid emphasizes breads, cereal, rice, and pasta as the basis for a healthful diet and recommends 6 to 11 servings of these foods daily. These foods provide complex carbohydrates for energy as well as vitamins, minerals, and some protein. The whole grains found in this group are high in fiber, which helps prevent constipation and may reduce the risk of several forms of cancer (including colon cancer).

Vegetables (three to five servings) and fruits (two to four servings) form the next-largest layer of the pyramid. They provide vitamins and minerals essential for helping the body fight infection.

15

FIGURE 2-1

The Food Guide Pyramid: A Guide to Daily Food Choices

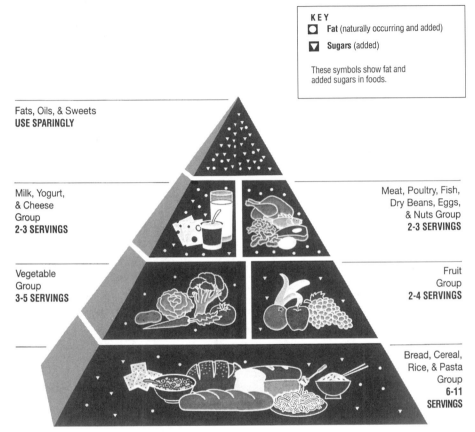

KEY
◻ **Fat** (naturally occurring and added)
▽ **Sugars** (added)

These symbols show fat and
added sugars in foods.

Fats, Oils, & Sweets
USE SPARINGLY

Milk, Yogurt,
& Cheese
Group
2-3 SERVINGS

Meat, Poultry, Fish,
Dry Beans, Eggs,
& Nuts Group
2-3 SERVINGS

Vegetable
Group
3-5 SERVINGS

Fruit
Group
2-4 SERVINGS

Bread, Cereal,
Rice, & Pasta
Group
**6-11
SERVINGS**

Source: U.S. Department of Agriculture.

Vitamins and minerals also promote healthy skin, bones, teeth, and eyes. Fresh vegetables and fruits are usually the most nutritious, but if fresh isn't an option, fresh-frozen is the next best choice.

Milk and other dairy products (two to three servings daily) make up half of the next layer of the pyramid. These foods provide protein and vitamins, as well as calcium and phosphorus, so essential to strong bones and teeth. Yogurt, cottage cheese, cheese, ice cream, and custard are all products made from milk.

Meat, poultry, fish, eggs, nuts, and dry beans (two to three servings daily) are in the second half of the same layer of the pyramid as the milk and dairy products. This food group provides protein, B vitamins, zinc, and iron essential for growth and tissue repair. Iron is necessary to prevent anemia. Because this food group can also be high in fat, it's a good idea to use lean cuts of meat, poultry, and fish, broiled or baked rather than fried.

Fats

The tip of the pyramid contains fats, oils, and sweets. The advice given is to "use sparingly." However, **do not eliminate fat from your**

diet altogether. Fats contain fatty acids that are absolutely necessary to both you and your baby. Just try to keep your calories from fat to less than 30 percent of your total calories.

Fats have almost twice the number of calories per gram as either protein or carbohydrates, so they can boost your overall calorie intake without boosting your nutrients. Therefore, it's better to choose foods lower in fat that contain two or more nutrients. For example, choose a protein that also contains a vitamin or mineral (like low-fat cottage cheese, which contains protein and calcium, or beans, which contain protein, folate, vitamins, and iron).

For your general health, remember that saturated fat is bad for your heart. It is the fat that leads to clogged veins and arteries, increasing your risk of high blood pressure, heart attacks, strokes, and many other conditions.

Saturated fat is *not* the same as cholesterol. A food can be advertised and labeled cholesterol-free and still be high in unhealthy saturated fats. (Cholesterol is only found in animal products.) Check your food labels carefully in order to avoid foods high in cholesterol or saturated fat.

When choosing cooking oils and margarine (or products such as potato chips cooked in them), look for oils higher in mono-unsaturated fat. Olive oil and canola oil are the best choices. Oils that you should avoid include coconut oil, cocoa butter, palm kernel oil, and palm oil.

Fiber

Benefits: Every day we seem to be learning more about the benefits of fiber. Fiber appears to reduce the risk of colon cancer and is known to lessen the symptoms of hemorrhoids and diverticulosis. It is useful in controlling weight gain and reducing high cholesterol levels. In addition, fiber in the diet helps prevent constipation—especially important during pregnancy.

Keep to the recommended amounts of fiber: 20 to 35 grams per day. Eating excessive amounts can interfere with the absorption of many vitamins and minerals, including iron and zinc, and can cause bloating and gas.

Dietary fiber comes from plants and is not digestible. The outside layer of a grain is where fiber is found. When grains are refined and processed, this outer layer containing the fiber is removed, along with beneficial antioxidants.

Food Sources: Whole wheat cereals, whole wheat breads, and brown rice are good sources of fiber. Some breads and cereals made from white flour may be "enriched" to give them vitamins, but they lack the fiber you need.

It is difficult for a consumer today to know what is actually whole wheat and what is refined. Labels can be confusing. Look for products that list a whole grain first in the list of ingredients. Also, dietary fiber should be listed and also presented in grams under "percent of daily value." "Wheat flour" and "unbleached wheat flour" are *not* whole grain.

Whole grains and legumes (beans and peas) are packed with fiber, as well as vitamins (especially B vitamins) and minerals. They also contain complex carbohydrates essential for your health and for your baby's growth and development. Whole grains include whole wheat, rye, barley, corn, brown and wild rice, and oats. Cooked whole grain cereals include (to name a few) oatmeal, Wheatena, Ralston, Roman Meal, and Quaker Multi-Grain. Oat bran is not technically a whole grain, but it is high in fiber. Ready-to-eat whole grain cereals such as Shredded Wheat, Cheerios, Raisin Bran, and Wheaties (to name only a few) are also made with whole grains (be sure to read the labels). When buying hot cereals, the ones you have to cook on the stove are more nutritious than the instant variety.

All cooked beans and peas add fiber to your diet. Other foods high in fiber include berries, unpeeled pears and apples, prunes, raisins, bananas, grapefruit, oranges, air-popped popcorn, broccoli, corn, white potatoes with the skin left on, sweet potatoes, and raw vegetables.

Enjoy a variety of high-fiber foods—try to eat one with each meal. Substitute whole grain breads for white flour varieties. Eat whole grain and bran cereals instead of low-fiber cereals. Eat fruits and vegetables with skins on instead of peeled. Whole fruits lose most of their fiber when made into juice.

Caution: If you are not used to eating a high-fiber diet, increase your fiber intake gradually so that your digestive system can adjust. Too much fiber too fast may cause cramps, gas, and diarrhea.

Fiber absorbs water. To prevent constipation, drink extra water with increased amounts of fiber.

If You Are Planning a Pregnancy

Eating a healthful diet—a variety of foods that provide a balance of carbohydrates, proteins, and fats, with enough essential vitamins, minerals, and trace elements—is never more important than during pregnancy. Research has shown that women eating a healthful diet are more likely to give birth to babies with excellent health. In contrast, fewer women with extremely poor diets have babies with excellent health. So if you are pregnant, or planning to become pregnant, now is the time to shape up your eating habits, as well as those of your family. You'll all be healthier as a result.

Folic Acid

Folic acid (also called folate) is one of the B vitamins. It is necessary in the formation of genetic material (DNA, RNA) and red blood cell production. It is also needed in order for our bodies to metabolize or utilize the amino acids (proteins) in our diet.

You should take folic acid daily *before conceiving*, because it decreases the risk of neural tube defects. It cannot be stored in the body and therefore must be consumed daily. If folic acid

intake is deficient during pregnancy, anemia and infant neural tube defects can result. Your practitioner will guide you in the amounts needed.

Folic acid is found in many raw vegetables, especially broccoli, spinach, and other green leafy vegetables, yellow fruits and vegetables, and avocados. It can also be obtained from yeast, liver, kidney meat, and beans, peas, and nuts. Fortified cereals and whole grain breads also contain folic acid.

Folic acid is lost in overcooking and processing. Eat cut-up raw vegetables, and add raw spinach leaves to your salads.

Eating Disorders

If you have an eating disorder of any kind, it would be best to seek help to get it under control before you become pregnant. The vital organs and the nervous system of your baby develop during the first three months of pregnancy. Adequate nutrition during this time and throughout pregnancy is essential to both you and your baby. Therefore, speak openly and honestly with your practitioner about your eating disorder in order to get help before pregnancy. Nutritionists, counselors and medications can help safeguard you and your baby.

If you are already pregnant and you did not obtain help for an eating disorder before you became pregnant, you need to ask firmly for a prompt appointment *before* the first normally scheduled prenatal visit to discuss your eating disorder with your practitioner. Ask to speak with the nurse if you are uncomfortable discussing the reason for the early appointment with the receptionist. (What you discuss with a doctor, midwife, or registered nurse is confidential information.)

Chronic Health Conditions

If you have a chronic health condition, inform your medical doctor when you are thinking about having a baby. It is best to learn about controlling your condition during a pregnancy before the pregnancy begins. You are already two weeks pregnant when you miss your first menstrual period, so if you take routine medication it is essential to determine its safety during pregnancy before conception occurs. An alternative medication, one that is safe in pregnancy, may need to be ordered.

Isotretinoin (Brand Name Accutane)

Isotretinoin is an oral prescription medication used to treat acne. The *Physician's Desk Reference* states in bold type, "Accutane must not be used by females who are pregnant or who may become pregnant while undergoing treatment. There is an extremely high risk that a deformed infant will result if pregnancy occurs while taking Accutane in any amount even for short periods. Potentially all exposed fetuses can be affected."

If this medication has been prescribed for you and there is any chance that you may be pregnant, discontinue the medication at once and consult your doctor.

All Medications—Prescription and Over-the-Counter

If you have prescription medication for occasional use when needed, discuss the safety of its use during pregnancy with your care provider before conception. If you are of child-bearing age and are not using birth control, you should be certain that any medication that you take, including over-the-counter medication, is considered safe for use during pregnancy.

A Well-Balanced Diet During Pregnancy

When you're pregnant, your baby depends on you for the nourishment he or she needs to grow and develop normally. Producing new cells and growth requires protein and other nutrients;

carbohydrates alone simply aren't enough. The National Academy of Sciences Recommended Daily Allowance (RDA) of calories is 2200 for *nonpregnant* women over 18 years of age. You will need to increase your calories to 2500 per day after your first trimester. The necessary 300-calorie increase is small—your job is to make those calories count. Choose foods from all levels of the Food Pyramid that provide the added calcium, iron, and other nutrients needed during pregnancy, not "empty" junk-foods. For instance, by having a bowl of cereal with one cup of skim milk and a banana, you have added 300 calories, as well as 10 grams of protein and necessary vitamins and minerals. Another example would be two ounces of turkey on two slices of whole grain or enriched bread, topped with lettuce, tomato, and sprouts (300-calorie examples from *The American Dietetic Association's Complete Food and Nutrition Guide*).

Healthy snacks can also provide extra calories. Carbohydrates, fats, and proteins are all sources of calories, but not all calories are equally nutritious. Understanding a few facts will help you make your calories count for you and your baby, and not just for your hips.

It is important for both you and your developing baby that you eat at regular intervals. **Do not fast during pregnancy.** If nausea or heartburn have depressed your appetite, try eating six or more small, nutritious meals rather than three large meals. If this does not help, please consult your practitioner. **Don't wait until your next prenatal visit to tell your practitioner that you are having difficulty consuming a balanced diet.**

Not eating enough or consuming the wrong kind of calories can delay growth in your developing baby. Research has shown that inadequate protein and calories in the last three months of pregnancy can adversely affect the baby's brain development. Poor nutrition during pregnancy can also lead to anemia and premature births.

Try not to become overwhelmed by the amounts of nutrients you will find listed in grams, milligrams, micrograms, and International Units. In reading about calories and amounts, it is easy to become overly focused on the details. The recommended amounts are given in this book only for those people who like a lot of detailed information. If you follow the recommended servings suggested in the Food Pyramid, increase the number of servings containing protein and calcium, and take your prescribed prenatal vitamin-mineral supplement and any additional iron that may be ordered for you and you are gaining an appropriate amount of weight, you will meet your pregnancy requirements.

Don't worry if you skip a meal or have a special high-calorie dessert once in a while—it is really no big deal. Exercise care, but keep your diet and the occasional deviations from the norm in the proper perspective. If you eat a well-balanced diet as described above, don't worry or feel guilty if you splurge once in a while.

Weight Gain

Your eating right helps ensure a healthy birth weight for your baby. Low birth weight puts your baby at risk for many complications.

Research has shown the importance of gaining weight throughout the entire pregnancy according to the **recommended pattern and rate of weight gain.** If you have poor weight gain early in pregnancy, your baby will be at risk for being small for its gestational age. If you have poor weight gain at the end of your pregnancy, it puts you and your baby at risk for preterm labor. You cannot cancel out these risks by eating more at another time in your pregnancy. Research has proven that the pattern of weight gain is important *throughout* pregnancy.

Weight gain in the first and second trimesters results mainly from growth in the mother's tissues. Her blood volume and overall fluid volume increase, and her uterus and breasts grow in size and weight. During the third trimester, weight gain is mainly the result of growth in the baby and placenta and the added weight of additional amniotic fluid.

According to Lowdermilk, Perry, and Bobak, if your weight is average for your height, you should expect to gain about 25 to 35 pounds during pregnancy. It is recommended that a person of average height and weight gain 2 to 5 pounds during the first trimester. During the second and third trimesters you should gain approximately 0.8 pound per week if you are of normal weight. Overweight women are usually told to hold weight gain to 0.66 pound per week, and underweight women are usually advised to gain about 1.1 pounds per week. These recommendations will be adjusted by your practitioner to meet your and your baby's unique needs.

Pregnant adolescents have special nutritional needs. They need to eat for their own growth, as well as the developing baby's growth. A practitioner may refer an expectant adolescent to a nutritionist for assistance. In addition, **if you are overweight, or expecting twins, your calorie intake will need to be adjusted.** (If you are carrying twins, your total weight gain should be around 40 pounds.) Your practitioner will be able to guide you or may refer you to a nutritionist with special training in pregnancy nutrition and the above special circumstances.

If your practitioner thinks you should gain additional weight, look for snacks or additional foods that are high in calories but also contain nutrients (such as nuts and dried fruits). Don't stuff yourself with things like popcorn or salad that make you feel full but don't add many calories. If you are having difficulty maintaining weight during pregnancy, you may be advised by your practitioner to increase your fat intake (since fat is high in calories).

If you are gaining more than the amount recommended for you in the second and third trimesters, decrease your intake of simple carbohydrates (such as refined sugar, white bread, cake, and cookies), but do not eliminate unrefined or complex carbohydrates. Whole grain breads, potatoes, whole grain cereals, brown rice, dried beans, peas and other vegetables, and fruit provide essential nutrients, protein, and fiber. They also help you feel full and thus keep you from consuming empty calories in sugary snacks. If you have a sweet tooth, go for natural sugars in fruit, which also provides vitamins! Of course, you will need to cut back on fat, also. Try to switch to skim milk and use less butter, salad dressing, mayonnaise, and so on.

Purposely losing weight during pregnancy is not recommended. Weight loss elevates ketone levels in the blood. (Ketones are given off as a by-product in fat breakdown). Since ketones cross the placenta, this results in fetal ketonemia—elevated ketones in the baby's blood—which is associated with mental retardation.

Protein

Benefits: Every cell in your body requires protein for growth, reproduction, and repair. Protein is the building block essential for growth and for the body's production of hemoglobin, the blood cells that carry oxygen. Protein also maintains and repairs all body tissues and helps produce antibodies to fight infection. Although protein is an essential nutrient, only 8 to 12 percent of the calories from a balanced diet need to come from protein.

Requirements for protein amounts vary with a person's age, weight, and health. It is generally recommended that nonpregnant women 19 to 24 years old consume about 46 grams of protein daily. Women 25 to 50 years old should consume about 50 grams per day. (Teenage requirements are higher.) You should increase your protein intake to 60 to 65 grams daily in pregnancy and lactation.

Proteins are made up of 22 chemicals called amino acids. Thirteen of the amino acids needed for good health and growth are produced by the body. The other nine amino acids are called the *essential amino acids,* and they must be supplied by the food you eat.

Food Sources: Protein can be obtained from milk, cheese, eggs, red meats, pork, chicken, and fish. These are *complete proteins* because they contain all of the essential amino acids.

Nuts, grains, and legumes (peas and beans) are also sources of protein. These plant products are called *incomplete proteins* because they lack some of the essential amino acids. When eaten with a small amount of animal protein source (such as milk meat, or cheese) or plant proteins with complementary amino-acid profiles, they become complete proteins.

Processed meats should be off limits, or eaten only occasionally, during pregnancy; they provide less nutrition than fresh meats and often contain many chemical additives.

If you suffer from headaches in the afternoon, now or even when you are not pregnant, it may help to increase your protein intake at breakfast and lunch. You may also want try a small high-protein midafternoon snack such as a few unsalted peanuts and raisins, low-fat peanut butter on low-fat crackers, a few ounces of skim milk, or low-fat cottage cheese and pineapple.

Calcium

Benefits: Calcium is needed for more than strong bones and teeth; it is also vital to the heart, muscles, nerves, and metabolism. Even your blood needs calcium to clot correctly. If you don't consume enough calcium for both you and your baby during pregnancy, your baby will call on the calcium reserves in your bones. Depleting your calcium reserves puts you at greater risk for osteoporosis in later life. Despite the old saying, "For every child, a tooth is lost," decalcification of the teeth does not occur in pregnancy. (Poor dental hygiene and inflamed gums are more likely the cause of cavities and tooth loss during pregnancy.)

Dietary Reference Intakes (DRI), which are updating and replacing Recommended Daily Allowances (RDA), place greater emphasis on calcium intake during the 9- to 18-year-old range. This reference is stressing the importance of calcium intake early in life. The new scale lists calcium requirements for nonpregnant, pregnant, and lactating females age 14 to 18 at 1300 mg/day, and for 19- to 50-year-old females at 1000 mg/day.

The National Research Council has put an upper limit on the amount of calcium that is safe to consume in one day. This upper limit is 2500 milligrams. Higher doses can cause constipation and, in people with kidney disease, kidney stones. Doses of 5000 milligrams per day can cause kidney failure and vision defects.

Food Sources: Milk is high is calcium; one quart contains 1200 milligrams. Other foods that contain calcium are milk products such as cheese, cottage cheese, and yogurt. If you don't like to drink milk, you can add nonfat dry milk or evaporated milk to recipes to increase their calcium content. If you can't tolerate milk or milk products, consult your practitioner and increase the amounts of other foods that contain calcium.

Calcium is found in canned sardines and salmon (if you eat the soft bones). Collards, kale, turnip greens, fresh broccoli, dried figs, tofu that contains calcium sulfate, and calcium-enriched processed orange juice are good calcium sources. Many soy and rice milks are now fortified with calcium, as well as some cereals, and some mineral waters contain calcium.

Both the calcium and the magnesium levels in your prenatal vitamins are lower than the necessary amounts if the supplement also contains iron. This is because calcium and magnesium can interfere with iron absorption. Take your prenatal vitamins with your meal and any additional iron supplements between meals. Do not take additional calcium supplements unless told to do so by your practitioner. Instead, concentrate on eating foods high in calcium.

Iron

Benefits: Eighteen milligrams of elemental iron are recommended daily for nonpregnant females. During pregnancy, an additional 30 to 60 milligrams should be consumed daily depending on the results of your hemoglobin and hematocrit blood testing.

During pregnancy, you need more iron than at any other time in your life. Iron is absolutely essential for the production of hemoglobin in your blood supply and the developing blood supply of your baby. Iron prevents anemia and increases your resistance to infection. Anemia in early pregnancy increases your risk of having a low-birth-weight infant.

Food Sources: Iron is found in small amounts in most fruits, vegetables, meats, and grains. To meet the added demands of pregnancy, try to choose foods with high iron content, such as lean red meat, ham, pork, and veal. Organ meats, such as liver, tongue, heart, and kidney, are very high in iron. Other good sources of iron include eggs, sardines, shrimp, clams, oysters, duck, poultry, enriched cereals, prune juice, collard greens, spinach, pumpkin, potatoes with skins, kale, turnip greens, soybeans, soy flour, dried beans, lima beans, lentils, peas, dried fruits (apricots, dates, prunes, and raisins), and almonds.

Supplements: Iron is usually prescribed in pill form in addition to prenatal vitamins. Whether you're getting iron in food or in a supplement, some form of vitamin C (such as in fruit juices, tomatoes, strawberries, cantaloupe, broccoli, or cabbage) will help your body absorb more of this mineral. It's best to take iron supplements *between meals* with some form of vitamin C because milk, coffee, and tea inhibit the absorption of iron.

If you are taking iron, add extra fiber (salads and bran) to your diet to help counteract the constipating aspect of iron. Prunes and prune juice are very helpful in preventing constipation. (Go easy on these at first and increase the amounts until your stool is soft. If you are not used to taking them, you may get diarrhea if you begin with eight ounces of prune juice.)

Sodium

Sodium is necessary to maintain the body's water balance. In the past, sodium was restricted in pregnancy to control swelling in the hands and feet. However, doctors now understand that a small amount of swelling in the hands and feet is due to elevated levels of estrogen in pregnancy. (Estrogen causes fluid retention.) If sodium is restricted in pregnancy, the kidneys and adrenal glands must work harder to retain it, and women may have difficulty obtaining an adequate diet, because many nutritious foods contain sodium. Therefore, unless you have chronic hypertension or a kidney or liver condition, sodium will not be restricted in your pregnancy. If you have pregnancy-induced hypertension, low-salt diets are *not* recommended. Your practitioner will advise you.

Table salt (sodium chloride) is the biggest source of sodium. Salt is not usually restricted during pregnancy, because it is needed to maintain blood volume and placental blood flow. However, it is not necessary or advisable to add extra salt to food. It is advisable to avoid or limit foods and snacks low in nutritional value and excessively high in sodium.

Other Minerals

Phosphorus, zinc, iodine, and magnesium requirements increase in pregnancy, but deficiencies are rare in pregnancy if you are eating a well-balanced diet. Because iron interferes with zinc and copper absorption, these two minerals are added to your prenatal vitamins. Addition supplements should not be taken, unless you are instructed to do so by your practitioner.

Vitamin Requirements

Vitamin requirements also increase in pregnancy. Most practitioners prescribe prenatal vitamin and mineral supplements to cover these additional needs. However, even if you are taking prenatal vitamins, your daily diet should include a wide variety of fruits and vegetables. Your prenatal vitamin and mineral supplement is just that—a supplement. It is not intended to replace a healthy variety of fruits and vegetables in your daily diet.

When cooking vegetables, lightly steam or stir-fry them so as not to destroy many of the beneficial vitamins.

Some vitamins dissolve in water; these include vitamin C and the B-complex vitamins (including folic acid). Water-soluble vitamins cannot be stored in the body and must be consumed frequently. Any excess of these vitamins is excreted in the urine. Other vitamins dissolve only in fat and can be stored in the body; these include vitamins A, D, E, and K. Fat-soluble vitamins are stored in the liver, so excessive amounts of them can be toxic to you and your baby. Do not take megadose vitamins or any vitamin supplements except those recommended by your practitioner.

Vitamin C

Benefits: Vitamin C cannot be stored in your body for later use, so you need to eat foods containing vitamin C every day. Vitamin C is essential to your health because it helps prevent infections and promotes healing of wounds. It also helps iron to be absorbed into your system. Vitamin C is essential for the developing bones and teeth of your fetus and also promotes the formation of connective tissues and blood vessels. The normal dietary requirement for vitamin C is 60 milligrams. It should be increased to 70 milligrams during pregnancy.

Food Sources: Vitamin C is found in citrus fruits (oranges, grapefruits, tangerines, lemons, and limes). Other sources are cantaloupe, strawberries, raspberries, melons, papayas, tomatoes, cabbage, kiwi, bell peppers, broccoli, cauliflower, kale, raw spinach, potatoes, and collard greens. Orange and grapefruit juice from concentrate and some other fruit and vegetable drinks also contain vitamin C, but if you rely on fortified foods you may miss out on some of the other compounds that come in foods naturally rich in vitamin C.

B Vitamins

Benefits: B-complex vitamins are essential and perform many functions within your body. They cannot be stored in the body and therefore must be consumed every day. Do not take any B vitamin alone unless recommended by your doctor.

Vitamin B6 is needed to help your body metabolize and use the protein and carbohydrates that you eat. It is also essential for normal nerve function and the formation of of red blood cells and antibodies. B6 is often used to treat early-pregnancy nausea; however, again, do not take additional vitamin B6 unless told to do so by your care provider. The normal nonpregnant requirement for B6 is 2.0 milligrams. Just 2.2 milligrams of vitamin B6 will meet your pregnancy requirement. It is included in your prenatal vitamins.

Sources: Milk, cheese, beans, and meat are all good sources of B vitamins. B6 can be obtained from spinach, potatoes, soybeans, meat, poultry, fish, bananas, prunes, enriched and whole grains, and whole grain cereals. Add bananas to your whole grain breakfast cereal for two sources of this vitamin.

Folic Acid (Folate):   Because folic acid should be taken daily (400 micrograms) *before* conceiving to reduce the risk of neural tube defects, it was discussed in the section "If You Are Planning a Pregnancy." If folic acid intake is deficient during pregnancy, anemia and infant neural tube deformities can result. (Refer to page 18 for more information on and sources of folic acid.)

Vitamin A

Benefits: Vitamin A (a fat-soluble vitamin) is necessary for cell growth (especially in the skin, gastrointestinal tract, and nervous system), for healing, and for normal vision (especially vision in dim light). It is essential for normal healthy eye development in the fetus and also plays a role in carbohydrate and fat metabolism. Like vitamin C, vitamin A increases resistance to infection.

The normal daily requirement of vitamin A for women aged 18 to 50 is 800 micrograms. Normally, this requirement does not increase during pregnancy.

Food Sources: Vitamin A is found in leafy green vegetables, as well as yellow vegetables and

yellow fruits: carrots, spinach, sweet potatoes, yams, winter squash, broccoli, kale, mustard greens, turnips, escarole, cantaloupe, fresh and dried apricots, mangoes, nectarines, yellow peaches, and papayas. Whole milk, egg yolk, fortified margarine, and liver also provide vitamin A.

Choose fresh fruits and vegetables whenever possible: organic varieties are best but are often expensive. Fresh-frozen vegetables are an acceptable alternative when fresh supplies are limited, lacking, or very expensive. Fresh-frozen vegetables are frozen immediately after harvest to reduce vitamin loss. When cooking vegetables, lightly steam or stir-fry them so as not to "boil away" all the vitamins.

 Caution: Too much vitamin A can be toxic to you and your baby. Therefore, do not take additional supplements of Vitamin A.

Vitamin D

Benefits: Vitamin D is absolutely essential in the formation of bones and teeth and is required for the proper absorption of calcium and phosphorus. Based on adequate intake of vitamin D of 200 IU daily, the authors of *Dietary Reference Intakes* now believe that vitamin D should be maintained at 200 IU daily and does not need to be increased during pregnancy. (They do add, however, that the 400 IU presently included in prenatal vitamins is not harmful.) Because recommended amounts are being revised as this book goes to press, please follow your care provider's instructions. Do not take additional vitamin D supplements above the amount in your prenatal vitamins.

Sources: Fortified milk is the main source of vitamin D for most people. Sun exposure also causes the formation of vitamin D in the skin. However, it is not necessary, or medically advised, for you to bake in the sun! For most people, only short exposures several times a week of their hands, face, and arms are needed for vitamin D production in the skin. Fish-liver oils, yo-

Pregnancy

gurt, butter, egg yolks, herrings, and sardines also contain vitamin D. Vitamin D supplements may be ordered for strict vegetarians.

Special Considerations

Vegetarian Diets

If you are on a strict vegetarian diet, please discuss pregnancy nutritional needs with an obstetrical care provider. If you do not eat dairy products or you avoid eggs and fish, you may not be getting all the nutrients you will require. Supplements of calcium, zinc, vitamins B12 and D, and folic acid, carefully planned with the help of your care provider or nutritionist, may be necessary. Vegetarians often need to take extra measures to get enough zinc. (In addition to milk, meat, liver, shellfish, and eggs, zinc is found in wheat bran, whole grain cereals, and whole grain breads.) You may also need assistance in learning how to obtain enough calories in order to achieve optimal weight gain as recommended for your pregnancy.

If your diet includes milk and milk products, seeds, nuts, and a variety of grains, vegetables, and fruits and you plan carefully, you should be able to obtain all the nutrients you require during your pregnancy. The standard prenatal vitamin-mineral supplements and iron may be prescribed.

Teen Pregnancy

Pregnant adolescents have special nutritional needs. An adolescent needs to eat for the growth taking place in her own body, as well as for the growth of her developing baby. Teens are often referred to a nutritionist for assistance.

If you are a teen and think you may be pregnant, please seek the assistance of an obstetrical care provider immediately. It is important that the nutrition issue be addressed promptly.

Multiple Pregnancy

Extra babies need extra calories and extra nutrients. When you discover that you are pregnant with more than one fetus, your practitioner will discuss dietary adjustments with you.

Drink Plenty of Fluids

Most of your body and the body of your developing baby is made up of water. Body fluids increase during pregnancy, and you need to drink extra fluids to maintain the proper balance. Fluids help bring nutrients to cells and carry away waste products. They also help to decrease your risk of constipation and urinary tract infections.

Drink at least two quarts of fluid every day while you are pregnant. Here are some conversions to help you know how much you are drinking:

1 cup = 8 ounces

4 cups = 32 ounces = 1 quart

(which is almost the same as 1 liter)

Spread your fluid intake out over the entire day. Water is not the only thing that meets your fluid requirement. Natural fruit and vegetable juices and soup are nourishing ways to increase your fluid intake. Soda also counts, but it does not provide any nutrients and can add many empty calories. Ask your practitioner about his or her feelings about diet sodas' artificial sweeteners. Avoid excessive amounts of caffeinated soda, coffee, and tea—caffeine dehydrates you.

If you are retaining fluid, *do not* restrict your fluid intake (but *do* decrease your *added*-salt intake). Fluids are actually necessary to relieve swelling (edema); the fluids you drink help flush cellular fluid out of your tissues and back into your circulatory system, from which it is eventually excreted. ✆**Any swelling should be reported to your practitioner promptly because it**

may be a sign of pregnancy-induced hypertension.

Exercise

Regular exercise during pregnancy helps you feel better physically and emotionally and helps minimize many of the common discomforts of pregnancy. The right exercise program for you depends on how active you were before you became pregnant and your exercise schedule and your routine before pregnancy. Early in your pregnancy, consult your care provider about exercise that is appropriate for you during pregnancy. She or he will review your medical and pregnancy history and your current level of exercise and fitness to establish an exercise program that is within safe limits for you and your baby.

Keep your care provider informed about your exercise program at your regular prenatal visits; you should not assume that she or he knows what you are doing. Keeping your care provider informed enables both of you to devise an exercise program that is right for you and safe for your baby.

Keep well hydrated with water before and during exercise. Drink 16 to 24 ounces of water after exercising to replace the fluids lost through perspiration. Caloric intake may also need to be increased to cover exercise requirements.

Wear a supportive bra to adequately support the added weight of your breasts during pregnancy. Good supportive shoes, appropriate for exercise, are also important, and not only for comfort. During pregnancy, your natural center of gravity is shifted due to the weight of your growing uterus and baby, which often makes you feel off balance. Good shoes can help to prevent injury.

With any exercise program, use common sense. For example, it is best not to exercise when you are ill. Schedule your exercise for times of the day when the temperature is not too high—very hot temperatures can cause overheating and dehydration. It is best to limit exercise to a maximum of 35 minutes, and perhaps even less if the weather is hot and humid. Never allow your body temperature to go above 100.4°F. (Body heat is transmitted to the fetus, and elevations can be dangerous to it.)

Always begin with a five-minute slow walk or stationary bike ride to warm up your muscles. Next do some stretching exercises to lessen the risk of muscle or joint injury. Take a few minutes of rest every 10 to 15 minutes while you are exercising. Likewise, end your exercise period with a cool-down walk, followed by a 10-minute rest period on your left side. (Lying on your left side helps to promote return circulation from your legs and muscles back to your heart. In turn, this increases the blood flow to your placenta and therefore to your baby.)

Do not push yourself to increase your aerobic capacity during pregnancy; instead focus on maintaining aerobic muscle tone. It is generally better to get moderate exercise several times a week rather than go all-out occasionally. Try to exercise regularly—strive for three times per week. This will increase your muscle tone and make you feel more energetic.

If you are in good physical shape, you should be able to continue your exercise routine during pregnancy with a few exceptions. You may be asked to decrease weight-bearing exercise and focus on non-weight-bearing exercise instead. Swimming, bike riding, and stretching exercises are considered non-weight-bearing. However, if you are accustomed to running, you may be allowed to continue, although your care provider may ask you to decrease your time and distance and, during your last trimester, to walk. Likewise, women who before pregnancy regularly used stairmasters, treadmills, and weight-training machines may be allowed to continue, in moderation, depending on their total medical and pregnancy history. (Weight-training weight limits may be decreased to prevent injury to your lower abdominal and back muscles, which are softened by your increased pregnancy hormones and stretched by your expanding uterus.)

Avoid any exercise that puts a heavy demand on your lower abdominal muscles or lower back. Full sit-ups and double leg raises can strain back and abdominal muscles in pregnancy. Of course, additional limitations will apply as you enter your last trimester, or before if you have complications.

Avoid contact sports and sports in which you may get hit in the abdomen by a ball or fall on your abdomen (such as skiing and surfing). Ask your practitioner for advice about your participation in a specific sport. Avoid high-impact exercise and bouncing. Change your motions slowly so as not to throw yourself off balance.

After about 20 weeks of pregnancy, you need to avoid exercises that require you to lie flat on your back. Lying flat compresses the vena cava, a major blood vessel, reducing blood flow to your heart and lowering your blood pressure (hypotension). In addition, after lying down, sit up slowly and remain sitting for a short period before slowly standing up. This will help prevent dizziness and fainting caused by a drop in blood pressure from standing up too rapidly.

When you are not pregnant, you should not exceed your target heart rate. To calculate your target heart rate, first find your maximum heart rate. Your maximum heart rate is 220 minus your age. Your target heart rate is 60 to 75 percent of your maximum heart rate. For example, if your age is 27:

$$220 - 27 = 193$$
$$193 \times 0.60 = 116$$
$$193 \times 0.75 = 145$$

Thus, at age 27, if you are *not* pregnant your target heart rate during exercise ranges from 116 to 145.

During pregnancy, it is generally recommended that you not exceed a pulse rate of 140. If your pulse is above 140, slow down your exercise program until your pulse returns to 90 and then continue. Check your pulse every 10 to 15 minutes to keep it within the safe range. There is some evidence that women who have a high level of physical fitness can sustain their pulse rates at a higher rate than stated above. However, you should consult your care provider, and together, considering all of your history, you should come up with a pulse rate during exercise that is safe for you.

*©***If you experience pain, dizziness, tingling or numbness, shortness of breath, or pain of any kind, stop exercising immediately.** Of course, if you experience uterine contractions of four per hour or vaginal bleeding while exercising, stop exercising immediately and call your care provider.

Appropriate Exercises for Pregnancy

If you are not accustomed to regular exercise, you will need to begin slowly. The following exercises are a good way to begin to increase your muscle tone and level of fitness. Depending on your level of physical conditioning from exercise before pregnancy, there may be many more exercises that you will be allowed to do. Pregnancy water aerobics near term is wonderful.

Head Circles: Stand or sit and rotate your head slowly in all directions.

Shoulder Circles: Stand or sit and rotate your shoulders forward and backward. See page 243 for further explanation of this exercise.

Arm Raises: See page 243 for an explanation of arm raises.

Arm Reaches and Arm Circles

Stand or sit.

Stretch each arm upward, alternating left and right.

"Swim" the freestyle and the backstroke with your arms.

Hold your arms out to the sides and make forward and backward circles.

Bend Forward

Stand with your feet apart and knees bent.

Reach slowly toward the floor. Stop when you begin to feel pressure on your uterus.

Come back up slowly; "uncurl" your back one vertebra at a time.

Pelvic Tilt: See Figure 2-2.

Begin on your hands and knees with your back relaxed, your head extended, and your chin forward. (See Figure 2-2A.)

Breathe in.

Breathe out and tuck your buttocks inward and forward. This movement also brings your pubic bone forward and upward in the direction of your chin. Your head is turned down and your neck is tucked near your chest. (See Figure 2-2B.)

Hold for a count of three and then breathe in and relax.

Do this exercise in sets of five.

Side Leg Raises: See Figure 2-3.

Lie on your side with your head supported by a pillow.

Use your upper arm on the floor for balance and support.

Raise your upper leg slowly as you breathe in.

Lower your leg slowly as you breathe out.

Work up to a set of 10 on each side. Add sets as tolerated.

Leg Stretch: See Figure 2-4.

Sit on the floor with one leg out to the side and the other bent at the knee.

Lean your upper body over the outstretched leg, bringing the opposite arm up over your head.

Hold the stretch.

Think About Feeding Options

There are very few decisions in life as personal as how you will feed your newborn. Both breast-

FIGURE 2-2

Pelvic Tilt

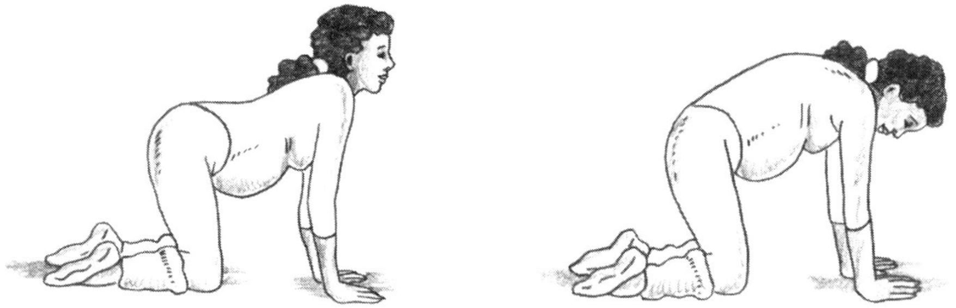

A   B

FIGURE 2-3

Side Leg Raises

FIGURE 2-4

Leg Stretch

feeding and bottle feeding have advantages and disadvantages. Only you can make the decision that feels right for you. Don't let others make you feel guilty. Whether your decision is based on emotional or medical reasons or convenience doesn't really matter. You don't owe anyone an explanation for your decision.

To eliminate last-minute confusion, it is best for you to decide on your method of feeding before your due date. However, like most decisions in life, this decision can be changed. If you start with bottle feeding and during the first week after birth you begin to regret that you didn't try breastfeeding, you can begin nursing and slowly wean from the bottle as your milk comes in. Be sure to make your pediatrician aware of your change in order that your baby's weight gain can be monitored more closely. This is a more difficult way to begin nursing, but usually not an impossible one. On the other hand, if you begin nursing and, for any number of reasons, decide you'd rather bottle feed, that is okay too.

If you are undecided about your method of feeding, review the following pros and cons for both breastfeeding and bottle feeding. Then decide, remembering that you can change your mind later.

Advantages of Breastfeeding

Breast milk is nature's perfect food for babies. It is easier to digest than formulas made from cow's milk. It changes as your baby changes. For example, if your baby is premature, your breast milk at this point in your pregnancy is right for a premature baby. Because it is nature's ideal food, breastfed babies are less likely to have colic.

Constipation, diarrhea, and diaper rash are rarely problems with breastfed babies. Breast milk contains a natural laxative that keeps stool soft. An added advantage is the absence of odor in the stools of babies who are totally breastfed.

Breast milk is lower in both salt and protein than cow's milk, and this puts less stress on a newborn's kidneys. In addition, the calcium in breast milk is easier to absorb than the calcium in cow's milk.

The "hind" milk (the milk that comes down after the baby has nursed for a while on a breast) is richer in calories and fat and thus tends to make your baby feel full. When your baby stops nursing, the feeding is ended. Because the breastfeeding mother cannot see how many ounces are taken, she is less tempted to stimulate the baby into taking more and more. The baby gets what his or her metabolism is demanding without excess calories.

If you are from a family with a history of many allergies, your pediatrician may strongly encourage you to nurse. About 10 percent of all babies will develop some intolerance to formulas based on cow's milk. If this occurs, nonmilk formulas (such as a soy-based formula) must be substituted. Nonmilk formulas are even less like breast milk in their chemical structure.

Breastfed babies tend to be healthier because they receive a constant supply of antibodies from the mother. When they do get sick, they tend to recover more quickly. Bacterial meningitis and intestinal and respiratory disorders occur less frequently in breastfed infants. New research is showing a reduced risk to many teenage and adult illnesses in people who were breastfed as infants.

Breastfed babies have greater sucking satisfaction. First, they must suck harder to get milk from a breast than from a bottle. Also, they may continue to suck after emptying a breast, just to satisfy their tremendous sucking need.

These are all advantages for the baby, but there are also advantages of breastfeeding for you. First and foremost, you always have a convenient, made-to-order, correct-temperature feeding available instantly! No bottles to prepare or warm in the middle of the night. Breast milk is a bargain: baby's ideal food, always ready in the right amount, at the right temperature, and the right price—almost free. Minimal costs include the purchase of two or three nursing bras, cloth or disposable breast pads if untimely leaking is a problem, a manual or electric breast pump if one is needed, and a nutritious, well-balanced diet for you. No breast milk goes to waste; it is produced in the quantity demanded.

Breast milk can be pumped and frozen in order to have a supply to be given by another family member or baby-sitter, so that Mom may have some time away.

Putting a baby to breast immediately at birth stimulates the uterus to contract and decreases bleeding. This advantage continues throughout the postpartum period, helping your uterus return more quickly to its prepregnancy size. Breastfeeding also gives you much-needed rest periods (you must sit or lie down to nurse) throughout the day. Most women find breastfeeding a very satisfying experience, especially the skin-to-skin contact with their infant.

Women who have breastfed have a reduced risk of breast cancer before they reach menopause and a reduced risk of osteoporosis after menopause.

Disadvantages of Breastfeeding

Breastfeeding is the only part of infant care that no one else can share; being "on call" for feedings, you have less freedom. To get away during a feeding time, you must pump and store your breast milk ahead of time, which takes extra time and effort.

Although there are few dietary restrictions when nursing, some foods may irritate your nursing baby. It is difficult to predict which, if any, foods will be problematic. However, caffeine, chocolate, spicy foods, acidic foods, and foods that are known to often produce gas seem to be repeat offenders. (Common gas-producing foods are fatty foods, dried beans, kidney beans, dried peas, lentils, soybeans, onions, cabbage, broccoli, cauliflower, and Brussels sprouts. Too many carbonated drinks and apple juice bother some women also.) This is a disadvantage for some women who find it difficult to live with a food restriction.

Breastfeeding in public may be difficult if privacy is a major concern to you. Depending on what you wear, breastfeeding can be done discreetly in many settings. Button-front shirts and blouses and nursing bras are essentials in every nursing mother's wardrobe. One-piece outfits that do not unbutton in the front make nursing and pumping difficult.

If your future includes returning to work, you will need to take a breast pump and breast milk storage equipment to work with you if you plan to continue nursing.

Some breastfeeding mothers notice vaginal dryness caused by the hormonal changes that occur with nursing. This condition, and sometimes sore nipples and leaking breasts, can create concerns in your sexual relationship.

Is Nipple Preparation Necessary During Pregnancy?

"While there are still some types of nipple preparation a mother can do during the last few weeks of pregnancy, nipple preparation is no longer considered a major prerequisite to successful breastfeeding" (La Leche League International, *The Womanly Art of Breastfeeding*, p. 28).

You may wish to apply a moisturizer to your breasts and nipples during pregnancy, although this is not absolutely necessary. You can use your regular skin moisturizer during pregnancy or special lanolin, which has been used for years to moisturize the nipples. Lansinoh, which is purified lanolin (with the alcohol removed), is used by some women. Some major drug store chains now carry Lansinoh. If your pharmacist cannot order it for you, it is available through La Leche League and the Nursing Mothers' Council. Lansinoh has also shown great success in promoting the healing of sore, cracked nipples after nursing begins.

Avoid soap and any product that contains alcohol. Years ago, vitamin E obtained from inside vitamin E pills was used by many women as a nipple lubricant. It was discovered, however, that because vitamin E is not water soluble, the vitamin built up to toxic levels in the infant. Therefore, do not use vitamin E on your nipples when nursing.

Nipple stimulation during lovemaking serves as a natural form of nipple preparation. Friction to the nipples using towels is no longer recommended. Studies today show that sore nipples result from improper positioning and a failure to rotate positions during breastfeeding, not from a lack of nipple preparation during pregnancy.

Advantages of Bottle Feeding

Seeing how much your baby has eaten is considered an advantage by some mothers. Also, bottle-fed babies tend to be full and satisfied longer, making for longer breaks between feedings.

Mothers who bottle-feed have more freedom and can leave the feedings to other family members or baby-sitters without having to take time to pump breast milk. The father or another support person can take care of those middle-of-the-night feedings while you get some badly needed sleep.

Privacy is not an issue when the baby needs to be fed in public, nor does bottle feeding place any dietary or clothing restrictions on you. Another advantage is that you do not have to deal with sore nipples or leaking breasts.

Disadvantages of Bottle Feeding

Although bottle-fed babies tend to go longer between feedings, formula is not as easily digested as breast milk. Thus they generally experience more colic, gas, constipation, and spitting up than breastfed babies, making them more restless between feedings. Diaper rashes are also more common in formula-fed babies.

Rather than feeding based on metabolic demands or the baby's sense of fullness, parents often encourage a baby to finish all of the bottle or at least to take the usual amount.

Formula is expensive and requires equipment to prepare and store, and leftover formula may be wasted. Bottles must be prepared and stored properly to prevent bacterial growth. Some babies also prefer a bottle to be warmed before feeding. These storage and warming needs can be inconvenient when traveling. (There are ways to avoid these problems, however. See page 303, Chapter 17, for more information on traveling with formula.)

The American Cord Blood Program—A Gift of Life

After your baby is born, his or her cord blood can save the life of another person. The blood in every umbilical cord and placenta contains stem cells that are necessary for the production of healthy blood. When matched with a person who has leukemia, Hodgkin's disease, or other cancer or blood disease (including sickle-cell anemia and aplastic anemia), these cells offer a second chance to live a healthy life.

Until recently, cord blood has typically been discarded after birth, but blood from the umbilical cord can easily be extracted in a simple, noninvasive procedure that takes a few minutes, poses no risk to the mother or infant, and doesn't interfere with the normal delivery process.

About 9000 transplant candidates, a third of them children, die each year before a suitably matched bone marrow donor can be found. Suitable matches are now found for fewer than 30 percent of patients who initiate searches for unrelated bone marrow donors, and the percentages are even lower for African Americans, Asian Americans, and other ethnic minority groups. Use of cord blood stem cells as an alternative to bone marrow stem cells will greatly improve the chances of locating a good match for patients who need a life-saving transplant.

Most cord blood transplants have been used to help children with cancer and blood diseases. However, an increasing percentage are being performed on adults.

Presently there are fewer than a dozen cord blood donor banks throughout the world. In the United States, cord blood donor banks are located in Arizona, Massachusetts, Missouri, and New York. The American Cord Blood Program, located at the University of Massachusetts in Worcester, is of special note, since it is combined with the Caitlin Raymond International Registry of Bone Marrow and Cord Blood Donor Banks. In addition, the University of Massachusetts program is a nonprofit charitable corporation developed to make cord blood available to all patients worldwide in need of transplantation from unrelated donors.

There is no cost to be a donor. If you are interested in learning more about how you and your baby can participate in this program, please talk to your obstetrician, family practitioner, or

midwife. If they do not have the information for you, call the American Cord Blood Program at the University of Massachusetts Medical Center in Worcester, Massachusetts, at (508) 756-3076, or fax it at (508) 756-6181. You do not have to live in Massachusetts or any of the eastern states to use this site. Most of the cord blood programs accept cord blood from anywhere.

Avoid Anything That Can Harm You or Your Baby

Medications

If you are taking regular prescription medication when you begin to suspect that you may be pregnant, it is important to consult a physician promptly because some medications can be harmful to your baby. The physician can make any necessary adjustments in your medications.

It is equally important *not* to stop a routine medication without consulting your practitioner. Stopping a medication that you need may be more harmful to your fetus than continuing your treatment. Only your maternity care practitioner can answer this question safely—don't make the decision on your own.

Don't use *any* over-the-counter medication when you are pregnant without approval from your practitioner. She or he can recommend a medication and the proper dosage that will help relieve your symptoms and at the same time be safe for your developing baby.

Alcohol

Alcohol can harm your developing baby, so if you're pregnant or hoping to become pregnant, don't drink alcohol. Experts know a lot about what happens to babies of mothers who are heavy drinkers. Drinking five to six glasses of wine, beer, or other alcoholic beverages per day during pregnancy is associated with *fetal alcohol syndrome,* a group of severe birth defects that includes mental retardation, growth retardation, heart and nervous system defects, malformed facial features, deformed limbs, and coordination and behavior problems. Babies with fetal alcohol syndrome never catch up; they are damaged for life. In the United States, alcohol use in pregnancy is the leading cause of mental retardation.

Three to four drinks daily or occasional binges during pregnancy have been shown to be associated with an increased risk of miscarriage, low birth weight, and premature birth. Behavioral and developmental problems after birth can also occur from this level of drinking.

What experts don't know is whether any level of alcohol consumption is safe during pregnancy. Even moderate alcohol use during pregnancy has been associated with hyperactivity, nervousness, and learning disabilities in children.

When a pregnant woman drinks alcohol, it crosses the placenta and enters the baby's bloodstream in the same concentration as in the mother. However, it takes the fetus twice as long as the mother to eliminate the alcohol from its system. Thus, when a pregnant woman is drunk, her baby's alcohol levels may already be at toxic levels.

The risks to your baby increase with increased alcohol intake and increased frequency of alcohol consumption. The most severe damage can be done in the first three months, when all of the major organs and the nervous system are developing. If you commonly drink every day or have occasional binges and you plan to become pregnant, it would be wise to seek help prior to your pregnancy.

From the information available today, it appears that the wisest choice is to stop drinking once you suspect that you are pregnant. This does not mean that you cannot have a small glass of wine (taken with food to reduce absorption) to celebrate a special occasion—occasionally!

Caffeine

Anyone who has to have that morning cup of coffee can attest to the power of caffeine addiction. For people hooked on caffeine, being without it can mean headaches, fatigue, and mood swings. This, coupled with the normal mood swings of pregnancy, can make life very difficult for you and those around you. Since abrupt withdrawal is difficult, try to slowly reduce your caffeine consumption before you become pregnant.

Caffeine crosses the placental barrier and enters the baby's circulation. In addition to the normal wakefulness it produces in you, the added activity of your baby stimulated by caffeine can further prevent you from getting rest.

Caffeine acts as a diuretic. During pregnancy, when added fluids are needed, this diuretic effect can deprive both you and your baby of fluid and necessary electrolytes. In addition, it can cause you to be up and down all night using the bathroom, further inhibiting your rest.

Coffee intake has been linked to an increased risk of miscarriage.

Caffeine is found in coffee, tea, chocolate, and some sodas. All of these not only contain caffeine but also fill you up and may prevent you from eating the nutritious diet that you need during pregnancy.

If you are cutting down on caffeine before or during pregnancy, eating small frequent meals that contain protein and complex carbohydrates will help keep your blood sugar up and help to minimize withdrawal symptoms. Get exercise and plenty of rest and substitute naturally decaffeinated drinks or, better yet, vegetable or fruit juices for the caffeine drink. The caffeine withdrawal symptoms will not last forever. Both you and your baby will be feeling better soon!

Smoking

Smoking is hazardous to everyone's health, but it is particularly hazardous to your baby, before, during, and after pregnancy. When you or anyone around you smokes, carbon monoxide crosses the placenta, decreasing the amount of oxygen available to your baby. Nicotine also crosses the placenta, constricting blood vessels and further reducing the baby's supply of oxygen and nourishment.

Smoking during pregnancy is associated with miscarriage, stillbirth, low birth weight, premature birth, and high blood pressure (hypertension) in the mother. Infants of parents who smoke are more likely to suffer from respiratory problems such as asthma and bronchitis. The risk of SIDS is twice as great for infants whose parents smoke.

If you cannot stop smoking, you need to cut down as much as possible. Every cigarette you *don't* smoke gives your baby a better chance at health. Because it is so difficult to stop smoking, it would be wise to seek help in kicking the habit before you become pregnant.

Recreational Drugs

While you are pregnant, every pill you take and everything you inhale or inject finds its way to your developing baby. Any use of recreational drugs can have disastrous results.

Like many prescription and over-the-counter drugs, marijuana, cocaine, crack, LSD, heroin, methadone, amphetamines, and other controlled substances (narcotics, diet pills, tranquilizers, and sleeping pills) can complicate your pregnancy and cause serious, permanent damage to your baby. Please speak openly and honestly with your care provider (anything you tell them is confidential) about any illicit drug use or addiction that you may have. Seek professional help in stopping drug abuse. See "Other Resources" in Appendix D for help hotlines.

Marijuana, the most frequently used "recreational" drug, has been associated with poor weight gain during pregnancy, as well as both rapid and prolonged labors and increased incidence of meconium-stained amniotic fluid. Its use during pregnancy has also been associated with low-birth-weight infants, tremors in the newborn, and increased need for resuscitation at birth.

Because marijuana smoke contains carbon monoxide, it adversely affects the developing baby's oxygen supply. The United States Surgeon General warns that marijuana use in pregnancy may be hazardous to the health of the developing baby.

There is no documented evidence that marijuana use prior to pregnancy adversely affects a later pregnancy. However, more long-term studies need to be done. It will be years before all the evidence is in and evaluated. If you are a marijuana user and plan to get pregnant, seek help to end your habit before pregnancy. Otherwise, you and your baby will be part of the experiment to see exactly how marijuana affects a pregnancy and developing baby, beyond what we already know.

Cocaine use during pregnancy can lead to the death of both mother and baby. Whether snorted, smoked, or injected, cocaine can cause heart attacks, strokes, seizures, and death in the mother. In the infant, cocaine crosses the placental barrier, damaging the placenta. It can cause miscarriage, premature birth, small size (for gestational age) at birth, microcephaly (small head), abnormal fetal heart patterns, and stillbirth. It is also known to cause other birth defects and developmental delays, visual disturbances, irregular sleep patterns, diarrhea, poor feeding problems, and addiction withdrawal in the baby. Cocaine-addicted infants can be very irritable, overly sensitive to noise and other stimuli, hyperactive, and extremely difficult to calm.

As with any drug, the risk increases with the frequency of exposure. However, with cocaine, even occasional use can have disastrous effects.

As a nurse, I find nothing more difficult than seeing a newborn baby going through withdrawal from the drug or drugs his or her mother used during pregnancy. It is very difficult to control any addiction without help. If you use drugs, get help before you get pregnant, or, if it is too late, as soon as you suspect that you are pregnant. There is professional, confidential help available for you and your baby.

Physical Abuse

Are you a victim of physical abuse? Unfortunately, many women are. According to FBI statistics, a woman is beaten by her husband or lover every 15 seconds. Physical abuse is estimated to affect one in three marriages; it occurs at every level of society and in every cultural and ethnic group.

Sometimes pregnancy triggers or increases physical abuse, especially if the father is unemployed or sees the baby as competition for his partner's time or affection.

Physical abuse during pregnancy can injure you and your baby, leading to miscarriage, stillbirth, premature birth, and low birth weight. If you are being abused, your child is also at risk for abuse after birth.

No one deserves to be abused or battered. Free and confidential counseling is available to help you better understand what is happening to you. Counseling helps you learn to not blame yourself, to recognize the signs of impending abuse, to plan for a safe, fast escape, and where to obtain legal aid services and shelters. Ending the violence begins with talking to someone you can trust.

Special Concerns

Emotions During Pregnancy

Whatever you call it—emotional lability, fluctuating emotions, moodiness, irrationality, or mood swings—it is nearly always present in pregnancy and is considered normal. This emotional roller coaster is common even in pregnant women who wanted to get pregnant and have a general feeling of well-being. One minute a pregnant woman can be happy and the next minute be angry and crying. The cause of this erratic behavior is thought to be the hormonal changes of pregnancy; however, a mother's fears for her own and her child's well-being, fatigue, and sexual concerns may also play a part.

In addition to fluctuating moods, even women who want to be pregnant may experience ambivalent feelings toward the pregnancy and the baby. These are all normal experiences.

Avoiding mood triggers like chocolate, caffeine, and sugar may help to relieve these symptoms. In addition, eating a balanced diet with small frequent meals that include protein will help maintain blood sugar levels, which may help prevent hypoglycemic lows. Adequate rest is also important in helping to keep mood swings within a normal range.

Fears and anxieties may also be expressed in dreams. Especially as their pregnancies reach term, you commonly hear women talk about dreaming about such things as taking curtains off the wall to use as diapers because the baby came before the mother was "ready"! In addition, as they approach full term, mothers often dream about having a deformed baby. These dreams are common and normal.

If you are feeling blue or experiencing depression, please try the suggestions on page 233. If you are not feeling better within a few days, call your care provider. You may benefit from a referral to a professional who can help you work through your feelings.

Don't Forget Me: Father's Having a Baby Too!

Although today's childbirth education classes, labor, and delivery include the father, he often feels left out and forgotten, especially during the pregnancy. Jealousy often is the end result, both toward the mother and later possibly even toward the baby.

Whether it is the mother, father, or culture that precipitates this problem, it is important to recognize that this is happening, talk about it, and take active steps to include the father in all aspects of the pregnancy, the delivery, and the postpartum period.

Today, most obstetricians and midwives encourage fathers to come to prenatal visits. This allows them not only to participate but also to receive education along the way. When only the woman receives the education, she is forced to be the teacher of her partner—thus beginning to set up the female as the primary caretaker of the children and in some cases prompting feelings of inadequacy or inferiority in her partner.

If you are a partner, read books on pregnancy and childbirth, attend classes, and talk to other couples about their experience during pregnancy, childbirth, and the first few weeks at home. The more prepared you become, the more confident you will feel.

The mother definitely has the advantage of getting to know the baby before birth. The baby is in her body and she feels its movements and hiccups and even a sense of its daily activity routine. Fathers have to work harder at this one, but it is not out of their reach. Touch your partner's abdomen and feel your baby's movements and kicks. Talk and sing to your baby. (I have seen many a baby after birth calmed down by Dad's familiar voice!)

Take part in shopping for your baby's crib and first clothing, and help paint and prepare the baby's room for the new arrival.

Have a little fun being pregnant along with your partner. Some partners give up habits like smoking, caffeine, alcohol, or excessive sweets along with the mother, thus supporting her through these worthwhile changes. Other partners follow an exercise routine of their own, or the same one as the mother, making this a special time together.

The weight gain of pregnancy is a very difficult issue for many women and their partners. Eating healthfully and avoiding empty calories together can be very helpful. The woman feels supported and the partner has more understanding of how difficult dietary changes can be. If you must splurge, do so out of her sight. It is difficult to stick to healthful eating habits when those around you are having cake and ice cream every night.

Fathers have many concerns during pregnancy. They worry about hurting their partner or the baby during intercourse, and about their partner's health and her changing body. By participating in the prenatal visits, you will have the opportunity to hear reassurance directly from your care provider. With a few exceptions, and a few alterations in positioning in later pregnancy, sexual intercourse is safe during pregnancy. (See page 54 for more information.) Sexual intercourse provides both emotional and physical closeness, something both of you need during this time. Please talk openly about your concerns both with your partner and with your care provider.

Moodiness is part of pregnancy. From the changing hormone levels in early pregnancy to the fatigue and discomforts of later pregnancy to the new adjustments and altered sleep patterns after delivery, plan on and expect mood swings in the mother throughout pregnancy and the postpartum period. If you can remember that pregnancy is a temporary condition, it will help you to be more patient and understanding. Think of this as training for the patience and understanding you will need later for your child and teenager! Offer a shoulder to cry on, and most of all, listen. Crying and expressing her feelings is sometimes all that the woman needs. If you are feeling impatient while your partner cries and complains, think of how much easier it is to listen to this than to deal with built-up anger that finally explodes from being held in too long. Perhaps, at especially vulnerable times, a dinner brought in, a dinner out, or a thoughtful bouquet of flowers may help. At other times she may just need to hear how beautiful she looks when she's pregnant.

Between 10 percent and 60 percent of fathers (depending on the study) suffer from some form of pregnancy symptoms: nausea, vomiting, weight gain, dizziness, food cravings, bowel changes, leg cramps, fatigue, and mood changes. Theories trying to identify a cause for these symptoms vary: sympathy, jealousy, or identification with the pregnancy partner; a guilty feeling for having caused this condition; stress from dealing with moodiness; fear of or changes in sexual activity; and financial fears and fears over becoming a father. Of course, you are also perfectly normal if you do not have these symptoms—it does not mean you do not care.

Again, talking with your partner, care provider, and other parents about how you are feeling may help. Of course, you should also see your doctor to rule out illness if symptoms persist. If you are feeling jealous and left out, talk about this and take action to correct it. If you have financial fears, talk to a financial adviser. If you have fears about your wife's pregnancy, or sexual anxiety, talk to your maternity care provider.

All of these feelings and symptoms are normal. If they don't go away during the pregnancy, they will go away after it.

When labor begins, expect anything from your emotions. Most partners surprise themselves in some way during the process. You may take much more control than normal for you, or you may fall apart. You may feel very emotional, feel overly protective, cry, or even faint. You may feel very fearful, or you may surprise yourself by being totally calm. Pregnant women and babies come in all sizes, shapes, and forms, and so do expectant fathers!

Some fathers really do not want to be in the labor or delivery room. Because it is "the thing to do" today, they feel pressured to be there. If your partner feels strongly about your being there, perhaps you could agree to go to childbirth education classes and then make an educated and informed decision after classes. If you do decide not to be present during labor or delivery, rest assured that studies have never been able to prove ill effects in the bonding process or future parent/child relationships from dad's not witnessing the birth. If you decide to attend the labor or birth, don't feel ashamed if you need to leave the room at times, or even for the duration. Talking about this ahead of time will help you not to feel guilty if you feel the need to leave, and it will help your partner not to feel deserted. You made the effort and did your best.

The best preparation is education. Read about labor, attend childbirth education classes, talk to your care provider, and take the hospital tour ahead of time. More important, express your thoughts, concerns, fears, and expectations to your partner and ask her to do the same with you. Then, most important, recognize—and talk together about—the fact that labor is not a pass/fail experience. She may not deal with pain as she thought she would; you may not be the perfect coach. You will, however, be together and have the experience together, and that is the important thing.

Sexual Relations

Unless your practitioner advises restricting sexual relations during pregnancy, you should not be afraid to enjoy this normal part of your life. Intercourse will probably be restricted in early pregnancy if you have a history of miscarriages. During the last three months of pregnancy, intercourse is restricted if you are carrying twins or if you have previously had a preterm birth.

If you experience pain or vaginal or urinary infection, or your amniotic sac breaks or begins leaking fluid, your practitioner will request that you stop having intercourse. Bleeding during late pregnancy may indicate that the placenta is attached near or over your cervix (*placenta previa*). Thus, if bleeding occurs, intercourse will be restricted.

If the above restrictions do not apply to you, simple adjustments in position can make intercourse more comfortable. To avoid putting too much weight on your enlarged uterus, the man should *only* be on top *if* he is off to the side with his arms supporting his weight. It may be more comfortable for both of you if you are on top. You can also experiment with other positions such as the side-lying position or the hands-and-knees position (for vaginal rear entry).

Travel

If you are not experiencing any pregnancy complications that require close supervision by your practitioner, travel is generally safe and permitted. If you plan to be some distance away from your practitioner, it would be wise to discuss your travel plans with her or him and obtain a copy of your prenatal record to take with you.

If you are traveling by car, be sure to wear a seat belt. **To wear a seat belt safely during pregnancy, place the lower part of the belt as low as possible under your abdomen. The upper shoulder belt should be positioned above your uterus and between your breasts.** Your belt should be snug—belts worn too loose or too high on the pregnant uterus can cause injury to both you and your baby.

Long car rides are usually discouraged after 35 weeks for two reasons. First, they take you some distance from your care provider. Second, the large uterus and the weight of your baby put pressure on your groin veins, leading to pooling of blood and swelling in your legs and feet. If you do travel by car, take frequent rest stops for walking to help prevent this problem.

If you would like to travel abroad during your pregnancy, discuss your plans with your practitioner. She or he should be familiar with diseases prevalent in foreign countries. She or he will be able to advise you whether travel to a particular country would be safe for you and what advance precautions should be taken. Vaccinations are required for travel to certain countries; some vaccines are safe during pregnancy, but others (such as rubella vaccine) are not.

Organisms in food and water in some countries can produce severe diarrhea in individuals not accustomed to them. You may need to bring bottled water and paper cups along with you (to avoid glasses that may have been washed in contaminated water). You may also need to avoid certain fruits or vegetables or peel them before eating them.

If you will be traveling to parts of the world where malaria is common, a medication that is safe to take during pregnancy will be prescribed to prevent this illness. However, certain countries have malaria strains that are resistant to this medication. Your practitioner can best advise you.

Flying in unpressurized small planes is discouraged during pregnancy. The reason many practitioners discourage air travel after 35 weeks is not low air pressure (pressurized planes are acceptable) but being away from the care provider who knows you best.

Dramatic altitude changes are discouraged during your last month of pregnancy. It takes your body time to compensate for the decreased oxygen levels at high altitudes. Your body's slow adjustment could lead to decreased oxygen for your baby. Consider this issue before traveling to high-altitude locations and when hiking and driving there.

Planning Ahead for Returning to Work

Unfortunately, maternity leaves from work are often very short. In addition to recovering from labor and childbirth, getting to know and enjoy your new baby and caring for it, you don't need the added stress of making arrangements for returning to work. While you are pregnant is a better time to think about all your options and plan ahead.

Consider All the Issues: Deciding whether or not to work involves complex issues and mixed feelings. You may find it helpful to go to your local library or bookstore and read some of the many books addressing this subject. There are many issues to be considered, such as the mother-child relationship, separation anxiety, careers, and finances, to name only a few.

Plan on having very mixed feelings about going back to work. Most women feel guilty no matter which decision they make. Remember, however, that no decision is irreversible. If the decision you make doesn't work out for you or the others involved, it can always be changed.

For some people, taking a temporary leave from a job is financially out of the question. For others, setting new priorities allows them to live on one income for a while. Still others may work for companies where job sharing is allowed and encouraged.

Ask for Help: In speaking with mothers returning to work, their advice was, "Don't be afraid to approach your boss about options. You may even want to come prepared with information about the maternity leave and work return policies at other similar or competing companies."

As you think about your options, avoid the common superwoman phenomenon. Don't try to do it all—work full-time and be a mother, wife, cook, and housekeeper. Experience has taught many women that it just doesn't all fit into a day. Something will suffer—your health, your job, your marriage, or your child.

Consider your top priorities, and then ask for help in the other areas. This may mean fewer hours at work, a less strenuous or time-consuming job, or more help with shopping, cooking, and housework. It may also mean full- or part-time child care. Include your partner in setting priorities and making choices. Your partner will have to help and be actively involved in order to make any system work; partners have feelings, choices, and priorities too.

Parents should be partners in child care as well as at play time. Changing diapers, bathing, soothing a fussy infant, going to well child office visits—all are part of forming a bond that grows stronger every day between a parent and child. If you are a single parent, then plan ahead to arrange assistance on a regular basis. Grandparents, relatives, friends, church organizations, play groups, and child care centers are all resources that can be tapped for help and much-needed time to yourself.

Child Care Options: If returning to work is necessary or a top priority and you don't have family to care for your infant, seek out quality child care that meets your and your baby's needs. The best time to plan for this child care is during your pregnancy. Talk to parents who have young children, ask your local library for a list of local child care resources, and use the yellow pages of your phone book to come up with a list of local child care centers or private care providers. Visit each site without an appointment first to get a

sense of how things are run on a daily basis when parent visits are not expected. Once you have narrowed your list, you will want to check with your state's agency to be certain that the centers or private care providers you are considering are licensed and in good standing in their reviews. The agency in your state that can provide this information can be located by calling information and asking for the Office for Children or, in some states, the State Human Services listing. From there you will be referred to a child care referral agency in your area.

When you are interviewing at a center or with an individual for child care, prepare your questions ahead of time. Be sure to ask if you will be free to enter *without knocking* at any time when your child is in their care. A red flag should go up if a care provider or center does not allow a parent this right.

Also, a word of advice from a mother who recently went through this process: "I was looking for the perfect place that met all my standards and I didn't find it. No place is perfect . . . no place will meet every one of your standards. The place I chose had toys that were a little old and not quite as clean as I would like them to be, but it was very strong in the areas of top priority to me. Safety is a top priority at this center. I actually had to bring my husband and let them meet him in person before he would be allowed to pick up our son! The overall environment was clean. The people who work there were friendly, they laughed and smiled a lot. They encouraged us to make spontaneous visits and come and have lunch with Jack whenever possible. They also requested parent participation for special events, and that was very important to me. Finally, I made sure they were licensed and had no complaints against them."

What About Breastfeeding? Mothers who work outside the home can successfully continue to breastfeed. In fact, for many mothers, continuing to breastfeed helps to make up for the time apart. If you plan to breastfeed and go back to work, ask your employer if you can return gradually, beginning with several hours a day part-time, then full days part-time, to make the transition to full-time easier on both your infant and your breasts. Also think about the clothes you normally wear to work. If you will need nursing bras or more blouses or dresses that open in the front, purchase them now. It is also a good idea to have a supply of breast pads to take care of leaking breasts until your milk production adjusts to the new schedule. Purchase supplies that you will need now, while you have more time.

If you plan to pump your breasts at work, you will need a breast pump and a cooler for storing and transporting your breast milk. Before purchasing a breast pump, explore your work environment for a private place you can use for pumping. Check for the availability of an electrical outlet *before* deciding on purchasing or renting an electric pump. Look for models that provide a double collection option so you can save time by pumping both breasts at once. (See pages 292–297 for more information on purchasing a breast pump, pumping your breasts, and safely storing and transporting breast milk.)

Take some time to make the decision about when to go back to work. You cannot go back and regain that year you missed in climbing the corporate ladder—but you also cannot go back and relive a year in your child's life.

Planning Ahead for Newborn Supplies

During your last trimester, you will need to begin planning for the arrival of your baby. In addition to the furniture items you may be getting, you'll need diapers, linens, clothing, and a car seat.

For suggested items to have on hand, see the following.

Bed linen, diapers, outerwear, and other clothing basics for baby at home: Box 18-1, pages 324–325

Bath and bottom supplies: Box 18-2, pages 326–327

Essential medications and safety items to have on hand in case of emergency: Box 18-3, pages 328–329

3

Possible Discomforts of Pregnancy

Most women who are generally healthy also enjoy good health during pregnancy. After all, pregnancy is not an illness but a normal life process for which your body is perfectly designed. However, that normal life process involves many changes—both physical and emotional—and some of these changes can cause discomfort. Shifting hormones, gaining weight, and changing body contours are among the realities of pregnancy. This chapter is intended to help you understand why these discomforts occur and to help you deal with them.

Nausea or Vomiting ("Morning Sickness")

Nausea alone or with vomiting occurs in about half of all pregnancies to some degree. If it oc-

curs, it is present during the first three months of pregnancy and is probably caused by increased levels of hCG (the pregnancy hormone human chorionic gonadotropin). Increased estrogen levels also play their part in causing this discomfort, as do stress and fatigue.

Although it is called morning sickness, the nausea and vomiting of pregnancy can occur at any time, day or night. In a few rare cases it persists into the second or third trimester.

What Can Help:

❑ Open the windows and get some fresh air.
❑ Elevate your head and shoulders on pillows when you lie down.
❑ At night, place dry toast, crackers, or dry cereal on your bedside table. When you awake in the morning, don't jump right out of bed, but slowly eat your crackers, dry toast, or cereal. Eating fruit or drinking a sweet fruit

41

juice just before getting out of bed also helps some women. Allow extra time in your schedule so you can move slowly and avoid rushing.

❑ Eat as soon as you begin to feel hungry. Eating small frequent portions throughout the day, rather than three big meals, decreases nausea. A totally empty stomach can lead to increased nausea. Having a snack at bedtime or if you wake up during the night may help. Increase the amounts you eat slowly as your nausea eases later in your pregnancy.

❑ Eat slowly and chew your food well.

❑ High-carbohydrate foods like fruit, fruit juices (other than citrus juices), breads, cereals, potatoes, pasta, and rice are easily digested. They are also high in calories and therefore help to keep your calorie count up when you feel like eating less.

❑ If you are vomiting, eat foods high in potassium (avocados, bananas, citrus and dried fruits, legumes, tomatoes, whole grains, and many vegetables) and magnesium (almost any food) to replenish these vital nutrients.

❑ Drink fluids an hour before or an hour or two after eating rather than with your meals. This prevents an overdistended stomach, which may trigger nausea and vomiting. Skim or low-fat milk, unsweetened low-acid fruit juices, herbal teas, and ginger ale are good choices. Sipping noncola carbonated beverages and carbonated water may help. Avoid coffee, tea, whole milk, citrus juices, and beer and other alcoholic beverages. Even plain water can be problematic for some women, so experiment to find out what works best for you.

❑ Avoid fatty foods. They are hard to digest and may produce more nausea. Also avoid foods cooked in oil or other fat and trim all visible fat from meats. Limit your use of butter, margarine, gravy, sausage, bacon, mayonnaise, and oily or creamy salad dressings.

❑ Highly seasoned foods cooked with onions, garlic, pepper, chili, and other spices may also cause problems. Avoid eating or drinking any food or beverage if you don't like the smell; odors can increase nausea.

❑ Avoid acidic foods, which may also add to nausea.

❑ When you are feeling nauseated, eat whatever you think your stomach will tolerate. If solid foods won't stay down, you may want to try beverage supplements such as instant breakfast drinks.

❑ As morning sickness ends (generally by the end of the 12th–16th week), you can increase the variety of foods you eat to get all the nutrients necessary for a healthy baby. Begin with bland carbohydrates such as dry toast, dry cereal, crackers, mashed potatoes, plain bagels, and plain English muffins. If you can tolerate these foods, try low-fat proteins such as turkey, chicken, and hard-boiled eggs with the yolk removed. Low-fat cheeses, egg yolks, and skim or 1 percent milk may be added to your diet as nausea decreases. As your condition improves, add bland, low-fat foods such as applesauce, carrots, peaches, and winter squash. Fats and fluids (juices) are added last.

❑ Take your iron pills with meals; taking them on an empty stomach may increase nausea.

Emergency Call
Nausea or Vomiting (Morning Sickness)

If nausea and vomiting have made it impossible for you to eat a healthy diet for two or three days or if you are vomiting excessively, report this to your practitioner immediately.

Emergency Call

Excessive Vomiting (Hyperemesis Gravidarum)

Hyperemesis gravidarum **is severe and persistent vomiting. It can produce weight loss, dehydration, starvation, and profound disturbances in metabolism and body chemistry.** Thankfully it is rare, occurring in only about 1 percent of pregnancies. If it continues untreated, the profound chemical changes that can occur in your body from this condition can lead to organ damage and even death in the mother, baby, or both.

If you are vomiting excessively, report this to your care provider immediately. Hyperemesis gravidarum is not a discomfort of pregnancy—it is a condition that requires treatment. It is discussed here because the dietary progression used for morning sickness is also helpful in treating hyperemesis gravidarum. You and your baby cannot receive adequate nutrition if vomiting makes it impossible to retain your food.

In severe cases of hyperemesis gravidarum, hospitalization may be required, as well as intravenous nutrition therapy. Although this type of therapy is started in the hospital, it can be maintained at home through patient education and follow-up supervision and care by visiting nurses.

All of the suggestions regarding nausea and vomiting earlier in this section also apply for hyperemesis gravidarum.

Indigestion

Indigestion, commonly called heartburn, is a burning sensation felt anywhere from the stomach area to the throat. It is caused when the stomach acids that digest food get pushed upward into the esophagus (the tube that connects your throat to your stomach).

Many factors in pregnancy increase your chances of heartburn. The most obvious is the upward pressure that your growing uterus places on your stomach. However, indigestion can occur in pregnancy even before your uterus is greatly enlarged. Changing hormone levels decrease your gastric motility and relax your stomach muscles, resulting in slowed digestion and a slower emptying of your stomach. In addition, *gastrin*, a hormone produced by the placenta, raises the acid,

chloride, and enzyme levels in your stomach during pregnancy far above their prepregnant levels. All these factors also increase the risk that stomach acids will be forced up into your esophagus.

What Can Help:

- ❏ Eat sitting up.
- ❏ Do not exercise after meals.
- ❏ Try to avoid bending down at the waist.
- ❏ Do not lie down for at least two hours after eating, avoid eating before going to bed, and sleep with your head elevated.
- ❏ Instead of eating three large meals a day, try five or six smaller meals.
- ❏ Avoid spicy foods, any food known to cause gas (fatty foods, fried foods, dried beans, kidney beans, dried peas, lentils, soybeans,

onions, cabbage, broccoli, cauliflower, and Brussels sprouts), and any food that usually causes you to have indigestion.

❑ Do not take antacids without checking with your practitioner, who may also be able to offer further assistance.

Backache

As pregnancy progresses, the normal support structures (ligaments) in your abdomen and back are softened by pregnancy hormones and stretched by the growing uterus. This softening and stretching, along with your changed posture, can lead to backache.

What Can Help:

❑ If you have a soft bed, have someone put a bed board between the mattress and the box spring for added firmness.

❑ Sleep on your side with a pillow between your knees and another large, full pillow to hug (which keeps your upper shoulder from rolling forward). (See Figure 12-11, page 220.)

❑ Do not lift your children or any heavy object.

❑ When you bend over to pick up light objects, do not bend at the waist. Instead, bend your knees, pick up the object close to your body and use your leg muscles to stand up again. (See Figure 12-12, page 221.)

❑ Wear good supportive shoes. Low-heeled shoes are often more comfortable than completely flat shoes. For safety as well as comfort, do *not* wear high heels.

❑ Work at countertops that are the correct height for you. You should be able to work standing straight and not be required to bend forward.

❑ Try to avoid standing or sitting for prolonged periods of time. If you must stand, elevate one foot on a low stool. When sitting, use a straight-backed chair with arms

and a firm cushion, and elevate your feet slightly on a low stool. Never cross your legs.

❑ Your practitioner can give you pamphlets on back-strengthening exercises. Follow the instructions carefully. Begin slowly and increase the number of exercises and the repetitions for each as tolerated.

❑ See page 28 for a pelvic tilt exercise that can help relieve backache.

❑ Ask your care provider if a maternity girdle may be helpful in providing support and in lessening back strain and pain.

Sciatic Nerve Pain

The sciatic nerves run down the middle of the buttocks and the back of the thighs on both sides. During later pregnancy, the growing uterus may put pressure on the sciatic nerves, causing intense discomfort or pain. Some women experience sciatic nerve pain only when sitting, some only when walking. An unfortunate few have it almost all of the time. Women experiencing this discomfort often complain that they cannot find a comfortable position to relieve the pressure on this nerve.

What Can Help:

❑ Inform your care provider about sciatic nerve discomfort.

❑ Try the measures to relieve backache listed above; they can also be helpful for sciatic nerve pain.

Shortness of Breath

Your respiratory system must make adjustments during pregnancy to meet your needs and the needs of your infant. In addition to the added responsibility of providing oxygen to the fetus, your own oxygen requirements increase because of your increased weight and metabolism.

As you approach full term, your oxygen consumption will increase up to 25 percent over your nonpregnant levels. The baby and the placenta use about half of this added oxygen; your heart, lungs, kidneys, uterus, and breasts use the other half.

In late pregnancy, your diaphragm has been pushed up about one and a half inches by your expanding uterus, limiting the ability of your diaphragm to expand. This may cause shortness of breath, breathlessness on exertion, and increased awareness of the need to breathe. But even though you feel short of breath, you can be sure your fetus is getting enough oxygen.

What Can Help:

❑ Use good posture and sleep propped up with extra pillows.
❑ Avoid overfilling your stomach.
❑ Avoid smoking and alcohol.
❑ Do deep-breathing exercises: inhale deeply and slowly through the nose, and then exhale slowly through pursed lips.
❑ Try to do less and do what you do more slowly to reduce your oxygen demand.
❑ Ⓒ**If the symptoms worsen, report the problem to your practitioner to rule out anemia and other more serious but treatable problems.**

Dizziness

Postural Hypotension

Postural hypotension is dizziness on standing up quickly. Our bodies are made to compensate quickly when we suddenly stand up after lying flat or sitting. This compensatory mechanism constricts veins in our legs and prevents blood from suddenly pooling there. However, during pregnancy, this compensatory reaction may not be able to restore circulation quickly enough to prevent lightheadedness, dizziness, and sometimes fainting.

What Can Help:

❑ After lying down, sit for several moments before standing. When you do stand, stay close to the bed or couch for a moment in case dizziness occurs.
❑ After sitting for a long period of time, rise slowly and stay next to the chair until the lightheadedness passes.
❑ If lightheadedness persists, put your head lower than your knees or lie flat on your left side.
❑ Low blood sugar in your first trimester can make you feel shaky and lightheaded. You can avoid this problem by eating small frequent meals that include protein and eliminating high-sugar desserts from your diet.

Dizziness Occurring When Lying Down

Some women also develop fainting symptoms (nausea, dizziness, pale skin, rapid pulse, and sweating) when they lie flat on their back. This reaction is caused when the heavy uterus compresses both the aorta and the inferior vena cava, causing blood to pool in the legs and decreasing the amount of blood that returns to the heart. This in turn causes cardiac output and blood pressure to drop.

When blood pressure drops anytime in anyone, pregnant or not, the body's fainting defense mechanism kicks in. It is the body's way of saying "lie down flat" so more blood and therefore more oxygen will reach your heart and brain. This defense mechanism kicks in when a pregnant woman's blood pressure drops because of compression of the aorta and inferior vena cava from lying flat on her back.

What Can Help:

❑ The solution is simple: sleep on your side, or when on your back, place a small pillow wedge under your hip to wedge the weight of the uterus off to one side. (If swelling of the feet or ankles or hemorrhoids is also a problem, the left-side position is preferred.)

Paresthesia

Paresthesia is numbness and tingling of the fingers and toes. As your body adapts to your growing uterus, your posture shifts to maintain balance. This leads to a curving of the lower spine, and often a bending forward of the head and neck, with slumping of the shoulders. When this upper curvature occurs, pressure and traction are placed on the nerves leading to your arms and fingers. Aching, numbness, and generalized weakness in the arms or fingers can occur. Tingling in the hands and fingers can also be caused by hyperventilation (rapid breathing with forceful exhaling).

You may feel this same aching, numbness, and weakness in your legs, feet, and toes when the weight of your growing uterus puts pressure on the femoral nerves and veins in the groin. Circulation is impaired by this pressure and so the symptoms occur.

What Can Help:

❑ Stand straight and tall.
❑ Sleep on your side.
❑ Avoid prolonged sitting or standing.
❑ Avoid hyperventilation.

Carpal tunnel syndrome can develop if edema (swelling) in the peripheral nerves of the arms and hands compresses the median nerve, which runs beneath the carpal ligament of the wrist. Tingling, numbness, and pain can radiate all the way to the elbow when this occurs, although it is often restricted to the thumb and index through ring fingers. Carpal tunnel syndrome usually affects the dominant (most-used) hand in people who perform repetitive hand and wrist actions such as data entry or typing, but it can occur on either or both sides since it is caused by swelling during pregnancy. Carpal

tunnel syndrome usually goes away without surgery after pregnancy.

What Can Help:

❑ Wrist braces are often prescribed to allow the nerves to rest (see your practitioner).
❑ Do not sleep on your hands.
❑ During painful episodes, dangling and shaking the hand helps some people.

Insomnia

Insomnia can be caused by fetal movements, muscle cramps, urinary frequency, or other discomforts. Anxiety and stress can make matters worse, but it's important to know that insomnia won't harm you or your baby.

What Can Help:

❑ Take a walk or get other exercise during the day, but don't exercise too close to bedtime.
❑ Take short periods of rest during the day, but don't nap.
❑ Avoid heavy dinners or spicy foods that can cause indigestion.
❑ Take a warm shower and drink warm milk before going to bed. Avoid sugary snacks.
❑ Lie on your side with pillows supporting all body parts. The pillow under your head should be thick enough to keep your neck and spine in straight alignment. Place a pillow between your legs to keep your hips from rolling forward. (This will also prevent lower backache by keeping the lower spine in proper alignment.) Place a thin pillow or towel just under your abdomen for support. Next, if you have one more thick pillow, you will find it very comfortable to place it slightly under your upper arm and across your abdomen to support your upper arm and prevent your upper shoulder from rolling forward. I call this a "teddy bear" or "hug" pillow. Again, this proper body align-

ment will help prevent backaches and shoulder aches. See Figure 12-11 for this sleeping position.
❑ Try relaxation breathing and other relaxation techniques for labor described later in this book.

Headaches

Minor Headaches

Minor headaches are a common complaint during the first six months of pregnancy. They are normally mild and located in the front of the head. Although headaches can be caused by stress, emotions, and eye strain during pregnancy, they are also thought to be caused by pregnancy hormones. During pregnancy, as at all times, headaches are more common and more severe if you are tense or upset.

What Can Help:

❑ Get adequate rest.
❑ Do relaxation exercises.
❑ Be sure to eat nutritious foods, with frequent small meals that include protein (hypoglycemia can also cause headaches). Carry snacks with you when you go out to prevent hunger and long periods without food.

❑ Avoid noisy places if they bring on headaches for you.
❑ Concentrate on good posture when walking and sitting.
❑ Prevent yourself from getting overheated. Wear layers of clothing that can be removed to keep you cool.
❑ When headaches occur in the sinus area, try alternating hot and cold compresses while resting quietly.
❑ Tension headaches often respond to neck and temple massage or cold packs applied behind the neck (10 minutes on, 10 minutes off).
❑ **Get approval from your practitioner before taking any medication. There are medications that are safe for use in pregnancy to treat headaches that persist despite the above measures; however, always let your practitioner be your guide on any medication.**

Migraines

If you had migraines before pregnancy, they will probably occur during pregnancy also. Be prepared and try to prevent them.

What Can Help:

❑ Avoid what normally brings on your migraines.

Emergency Call
Headaches and Pregnancy-Induced Hypertension

After 20 weeks of gestation, severe headaches can occur if you are developing pregnancy-induced hypertension. When you have pregnancy-induced hypertension, your veins constrict, causing cerebral (brain) swelling, which results in severe headaches. Severe headaches after 20 weeks of gestation must be reported immediately to your doctor, even if it is a holiday or the middle of the night.

These headaches may occur even before you have been told that you have pregnancy-induced hypertension, so don't assume that it is just a bad headache because you have not yet been diagnosed with pregnancy-induced hypertension.

- Avoid foods that commonly trigger your migraines. Common culprits are chocolate, coffee, cheese, and wine (especially red wine).
- If you feel a migraine coming on, treat it immediately by resting in a dark room free from noise and television.
- **ⓒEarly in pregnancy, consult with your practitioner about what medication you may take safely for a migraine when you are pregnant. If you have never had migraines and now suddenly in pregnancy have a headache that feels like a migraine, consult your practitioner. This could be a symptom of pregnancy-induced hypertension. See the accompanying emergency call box and pages 108–110 for more information about pregnancy-induced hypertension.**

Fatigue

Feeling tired during pregnancy is normal. You're carrying another person around all the time, so why shouldn't you be tired?

What Can Help:

- Expect that you will require extra sleep while you are pregnant. Plan for adequate rest and sleep.
- Don't overload your schedule. Take a few days or hours off from work if possible when this symptom is particularly bothersome.
- Accept help from friends and family. Lower your housecleaning standards and use less time-consuming recipes until this feeling passes.
- Naps can be very beneficial. Listen to what your body is telling you—you need more rest. Pamper yourself a bit!
- Keep your evenings as schedule-free as possible. Enjoy reading or watching movies,

with your feet up, or use this time to play quiet games or read with other family members.
- Use pillows for extra support while you sleep. (See examples for pillow use under "Insomnia," above, or see Figure 12-11, page 220.)
- During the last trimester, it is best to avoid lying on your back. When you are flat on your back, your heavy uterus decreases the flow of blood returning to your heart by pressing on the inferior vena cava (the principal vein returning blood from your legs and abdomen back to your heart). Lying on your back also tends to make the baby more restless because this position places the weight of the uterus, and of the baby, directly on your spine. If you enjoy sleeping on your back, place a pillow or wedge of some kind under your right side. This will tilt you slightly toward the left side and shift the weight of your uterus off of your spine.

Leg Cramps

This very painful problem can interrupt your day and also interfere with sleep. Leg cramps have many causes, including compression of lower-extremity nerves by your growing uterus, fatigue, poor peripheral circulation, and pointing your toes when you stretch your legs and walk. Sometimes leg cramps are caused by calcium and phosphorus imbalances.

What Can Help:

- Stretch your cramped leg muscle until the spasm relaxes (Figure 3-1A).
- Stand on a flat surface and lean forward over your toes (Figure 3-1B).
- **If these spasms occur frequently, report them to your practitioner.** He or she may recommend an oral supplement of calcium carbonate or calcium lactate tablets or the

FIGURE 3-1

Relieving Leg Cramps

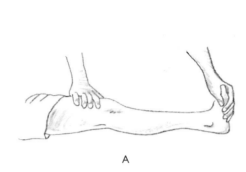

A   B

Adapted from Lowdermilk DL, Bobak IM, Perry SE, editors: Maternity & Women's Health Care, ed 6, St. Louis, 1997, Mosby, Inc.

use of phosphorus-absorbing gels. Do not take supplements unless your practitioner recommends them.

Inflamed Gums

Pregnancy hormones and an increase in the pH of your saliva tend to cause swelling in all mucous membranes, including your gums. They also increase the incidence of dental caries (cavities) during pregnancy, and your gums may become inflamed and bleed more frequently. Some women also experience increased salivation during pregnancy.

What Can Help:

❑ Eat a well-balanced diet with plenty of protein and fresh fruits and vegetables.
❑ Avoid refined sugars; they contribute to tooth decay and gum disease.
❑ Get plenty of calcium and vitamin C from your diet. Calcium is needed to keep teeth and bones healthy, and vitamin C strengthens gums.

❑ Practice good dental hygiene. Brush gently with a soft toothbrush, floss regularly, and get regular professional dental cleanings. This not only will remove plaque but will also provide prompt recognition of any developing gum problem. **Be sure to inform your dentist that you are pregnant. If possible, delay any dental X-rays until after your baby is born.**

Perineal Discomfort and Pressure

Your growing baby and enlarging uterus put added pressure on the muscles, nerves, and circulation in your lower abdomen and perineum (the area between the vagina and the anus). This can make sitting or standing uncomfortable.

What Can Help:

❑ Good posture is very helpful. Stand up straight.
❑ Sit in a chair that supports and aids good posture.

Emergency Call ☎

Cervical Pain

During the last month of pregnancy, some women report sharp, stabbing, infrequent pains in the cervical area. This is usually just a sign that either the presenting part of your baby has engaged in the pelvis or that effacement of the cervix is beginning. However, if this pain is frequent, occurs before the end of the 36th week of pregnancy, or is accompanied by bright red bleeding or thick, dark mucus, call your practitioner immediately.

Emergency Call ☎

Abdominal Pain

If you experience abdominal pain any time during your pregnancy, report it to your practitioner. He or she will want to rule out labor and possible complications.

❑ Be sure to get plenty of rest.
❑ A maternity girdle can be useful for additional support. Maternity girdles are needed more often in subsequent pregnancies than in the first.

Braxton Hicks Contractions (False Labor)

It is normal to have some uterine contractions throughout the day. During a contraction, the uterus becomes firm and then relaxes. These irregular, mild, and usually painless contractions are called Braxton Hicks contractions. They are also called false labor contractions.

Braxton Hicks contractions often occur when you change position, but, they can occur at any time, even when you're resting.

Braxton Hicks contractions usually begin at about the 12th week of gestation; however, early in pregnancy they last only a few seconds, and most women are not aware of them. It is usually around the 20th week of pregnancy, when they become more frequent and last longer, that most women feel them. You may be aware of Braxton Hicks contractions earlier if this is not your first pregnancy.

Although Braxton Hicks contractions may be uncomfortable, they are not painful (until perhaps your ninth month). They are usually described as a tightening of the uterus that progresses from the top of the uterus to the bottom. They normally last about 30 seconds but can last up to two minutes. They are more intense if you have a fever or a urinary tract infection, and during orgasm. (Please refer to page 114 for the importance of reporting early symptoms of urinary tract infections in the prevention of preterm labor.)

These contractions are signals that mean your uterus is rehearsing for labor. As you near your last month of pregnancy, they may be felt more often and may even be painful. This is why it is sometimes difficult to tell the difference between true and false labor contractions without a vaginal exam to assess your cervix.

Emergency Call

Contractions Before the End of Your 36th Week of Pregnancy

It is not normal to have frequent contractions (every 10 minutes or more frequently, lasting for one hour) before 36 weeks' gestation.

It is also not normal for these contractions to occur at regular intervals or to cause back or abdominal pain.

If contractions are frequent, painful, or regular or are accompanied by increased vaginal discharge or bloody show (bleeding from the vagina), report them to your care provider immediately.

Do not confuse the normal, occasional, painless contractions of pregnancy with premature labor. Refer to "Signs and Symptoms of Premature Labor" in Chapter 7 (page 115) for more information.

Although Braxton Hicks contractions are not strong enough to deliver your baby, they may begin the process of *effacement* (thinning out of the cervix). Any work these contractions get done before labor begins is helpful!

What Can Help:

❑ For normal contractions, rest. Use breathing techniques if the contractions are bothersome.

❑ Change your position. Lying down, standing, or walking may help at different times.

❑ Try drinking fruit juices. The uterus can become irritable if you are dehydrated or have low blood sugar from not eating.

❑ A gentle, fingertip touch massage of the abdomen called *effleurage* may help relieve the discomfort. To perform effleurage, place the fingertips of one or both hands on the abdomen. With the lightest touch possible, follow the arrows in Figure 3-2.

FIGURE 3-2

Effleurage

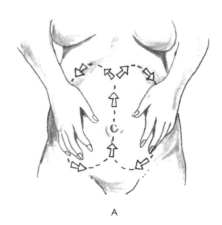

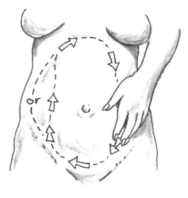

A

B

Adapted from Lowdermilk DL, Bobak IM, Perry SE, editors: Maternity & Women's Health Care, ed 6, St. Louis, 1997, Mosby, Inc.

Emergency Call

Pitting Edema

If you push in the skin on your feet and a depression remains (pitting edema), report this to your physician. It may signal the beginning of pregnancy-induced hypertension.

Also report fluid edema that is generalized over your body (overall bloating, swelling, or puffiness of your face, hands, and feet.)

Many women also use effleurage to help relieve the discomfort of true labor contractions.

Swollen Feet and Ankles (Edema)

As your pregnancy progresses, your heavy uterus places added pressure on veins in your groin area, causing your ankles and feet to swell (edema). Swelling is made worse by prolonged standing or sitting, poor posture, lack of exercise, constrictive clothing, and hot weather.

Other factors also contribute to swelling of the legs and ankles. Pregnancy hormones that cause dilatation of the veins and increased blood volume contribute to the relaxation of the veins. All of these factors further promote pooling of blood in the legs, ankles, and feet.

What Can Help:

❑ Drink plenty of fluids for natural diuretic action (urination to eliminate fluid).

❑ Wear support stockings or support pantyhose and put them on before getting out of bed in the morning. Do not wear anything that binds your legs.

❑ Rest occasionally during the day with your hips up on a pillow and your legs up against a wall. If this is not possible, elevate your legs when sitting.

❑ Sleep on your left side with a pillow between your knees.

❑ Practice good posture when sitting and standing.

❑ Exercise moderately and regularly.

Varicose Veins

As your growing uterus presses on the veins in your groin, you may develop varicose veins in your legs or on your perineum, around the vagina. Although this is not a serious condition, it can cause some discomfort.

What Can Help:

❑ Do not wear garters or stockings or socks with tight upper bands.

❑ Try to avoid sitting or standing in one spot for long periods.

❑ If your job requires sitting, take frequent short walks.

❑ Elevate your legs whenever possible.

❑ Lie on your back (with a pillow wedged under one hip to keep you from lying too flat) and elevate your legs on several firm pillows, a stool, a chair, or a wall. In this position, gravity will help your veins to drain and help relieve the discomfort when your legs are aching.

Emergency Call

Pain and Burning on Urination

If you experience pain or burning on urination, report this to your practitioner promptly. These symptoms may indicate the beginning of a urinary tract infection, a common cause of premature labor. Urinary tract infections can be treated with antibiotics, so prompt diagnosis and treatment are important.

Urinary Frequency and Urgency

Your kidneys must work overtime to handle your increased metabolism, additional blood volume, and elimination of the baby's waste products. In addition, the kidneys must do their regular jobs of keeping the electrolytes in your body in balance, controlling the acid-base balance, eliminating fluid overload, and conserving all the essential nutrients we need for health. To do this additional work, up to 1200 milliliters of blood flow through the kidneys every minute. This is an increase of 25–50 percent over your nonpregnant state. The kidneys also produce about 1500 milliliters of urine every day. So don't be surprised when you have to get up in the middle of the night—as you can see, your kidneys are working very hard for you and your baby!

When a baby "drops," or engages in the pelvis, women often experience less shortness of breath (due to less upward pressure on the diaphragm) but greater urinary frequency and urgency (due to more downward pressure on the bladder). Your bladder capacity is smaller because of your enlarging uterus and the pressure caused by the presenting part of your fetus (the part of your baby that enters the birth canal first) as it engages, or drops, into your pelvis. This decreased capacity of your bladder to hold normal volumes of urine will require you to urinate more frequently, and the urge to urinate may come on suddenly.

What Can Help:

- Limit fluid intake before bedtime.
- Do Kegel exercises. (These exercises are explained under "Beginning Toning Exercises," page 240.)
- Wear a pantyliner or sanitary pad if you lose bladder control when sneezing, coughing, or laughing.
- Urinate immediately when you feel the urge. Do not try to hold your urine for a long time.

Constipation

The tone and motility of the entire gastrointestinal tract are decreased during pregnancy. The hormones of pregnancy slow down digestion and slow the movement of wastes through the intestines. Adding to this, the pregnancy hormone progesterone causes more water to be absorbed from the colon, producing dryer and therefore firmer stools.

In later pregnancy, the enlarged uterus puts added pressure on the intestines and rectum. Iron, taken in prenatal vitamins or separately, also tends to promote constipation. All these factors cause constipation to be a very common discomfort of pregnancy.

What Can Help:

Prevention of constipation is the key:
- Eat plenty of raw fruits (with the skins) and vegetables, as well as bran and whole grain

cereals. These high-fiber foods prevent constipation. (See pages 17–18 for more information on high-fiber foods.)

❑ Drink at least eight glasses of fluids daily, especially fruit juices.

❑ Prune juice is very effective in preventing constipation. Start with two ounces in the morning with breakfast and find the amount that is right for you. It's important to keep your stools soft without causing diarrhea.

❑ Exercise daily.

Gas (Flatulence)

Flatulence is a common discomfort during pregnancy.

What Can Help:

❑ Avoid known gas-forming foods like beans, cabbage, Brussels sprouts, and broccoli. Onions, fried foods, and sweets can also increase gas production.

❑ Avoid overeating. Because your bowel motility and tone are decreased during pregnancy, small frequent meals are tolerated better than large ones.

❑ Eat and drink slowly to avoid swallowing added air.

❑ Get plenty of exercise.

❑ Avoid constipation.

Hemorrhoids

Hemorrhoids are varicose veins in the rectum. The increased blood volume and pelvic congestion occurring during pregnancy, as well as the increased pressure of the growing uterus, which slows venous return, all contribute to developing hemorrhoids. Hemorrhoids often accompany constipation—they become more severe and may protrude from the rectum if you repeatedly strain to pass constipated stools. Preventing constipation is the key to preventing hemorrhoids during pregnancy.

A long pushing stage in labor can also exaggerate existing hemorrhoids or produce them for the first time.

Hemorrhoids are painful and may cause you to pass small amounts of blood with your stools. *✆***Black stools or bright red blood in your stools should be reported promptly to your practitioner.** Bleeding that occurs high up in the intestines causes your stools to be black. Bleeding low in the rectum, as with hemorrhoids, shows up as bright red blood.

What Can Help:

❑ Prevent or promptly treat constipation. (See the above section on constipation for more information on prevention.)

❑ Sleep on your side or wedged off your back.

❑ Avoid prolonged standing or sitting.

❑ Treat hemorrhoids with warm sitz baths and topical anesthetics made for hemorrhoids. (See pages 228–230 for information on sitz baths.)

Intercourse During Pregnancy

Unless your practitioner advises you otherwise, you should not be afraid to enjoy intercourse during pregnancy. Simple adjustments in position can help eliminate excessive weight on the enlarged uterus. The male superior position should be used *only* if your partner is off to one side with his arms supporting his weight. Other possibilities include female superior, hands-and-knees, or side-lying, rear-entry positions.

If you have a history of miscarriages, intercourse will probably be restricted in early pregnancy. If you are having twins, have a history of premature births, or are having symptoms of preterm labor, intercourse will be restricted during the last trimester.

Intercourse will also be restricted if you have any vaginal bleeding, if ultrasound examination has shown that your placenta is partially or completely covering your cervix, or if your membranes have ruptured.

Mood Swings

Expect mood swings during pregnancy. They just happen—so don't blame yourself if you sometimes feel down. Changing hormone levels during pregnancy and added fatigue during the first three months and again during the last two months can make you more irritable and unpredictable.

What Can Help:

❑ Eating a balanced diet and taking an extra nap may help you smooth over a particularly bothersome time. A warm, relaxing bath may also be helpful.

❑ Try not to take on added responsibilities or activities if you are feeling tired and grumpy. Let some of the housework go undone or ask your partner for help.

❑ Pregnancy offers a wonderful learning opportunity for your older children. If you share your feelings with them, they learn that parents have moody times too. They also learn how to help someone who is feeling down. Explain to them how rest helps people feel better when they are tired, and let them know how much it would mean if they dusted or vacuumed for you (if they're old enough) or just played quietly for awhile. Remind children about how they are often sent to bed when they are cranky—and right now Mom needs to be "sent to bed." Tell them how much they will be helping you if they behave well for the person watching them while you rest. When you get up, be sure to give them a special hug and thank them for helping you to feel better. If you do not have someone to help with the children while you rest, at least put your feet up and ask them to play a quiet game near you. Also, plan ahead so you can rest when your children are napping.

Anxiety

A small amount of anxiety is normal in pregnancy. Prospective parents worry about how pregnancy and a child will change their lives, as well as the actual labor and delivery. However, if you are spending a lot of time feeling anxious and worried, you should discuss it with your practitioner. She or he may be able to relieve your concerns, suggest counseling, or offer medications (in severe cases) to help.

Breast Changes

By the end of your second month of pregnancy, your breasts will appear larger from the increased thickness of the fat layer and the increased number of milk glands, and they will also feel more tender. Because vascularity of the breasts increases during pregnancy, you may be able to see veins under the skin.

During the first three months of pregnancy, the nipple and *areola* (the circle of darker skin around the nipple) darken and become larger. As the areola enlarges, small glands beneath the skin that produce an oily, lubricating substance may appear as small bumps on the areola. (These are called *Montgomery glands*.) All of these changes may cause your breasts and nipples to tingle, feel full, and be more sensitive.

If you plan to breastfeed, your practitioner should check your nipples early in your pregnancy. If they appear to be inverted, there are steps you can take to help draw the nipples out. (See the section on inverted nipples in Chapter 16, "Breastfeeding," pages 289–290.)

Around the 14th week of pregnancy, your breasts may begin to produce *colostrum*, the easily digested, nutritious fluid that precedes the production of breast milk. (Breast milk comes in around the third day after delivery). Colostrum is high in protein, minerals, and vitamins and contains antibodies that protect your infant from infection. It is thick and yellow in early pregnancy and becomes lighter in color later on.

Colostrum may leak from your breasts occasionally, especially during sexual excitement or when your breasts are massaged. Although your breasts are ready for lactation by the end of your second trimester, hormones suppress lactation until after delivery of the placenta.

What Can Help:

❑ A good supportive bra is essential not only for support but also to help relieve the discomfort of the added weight of the breasts.

Skin Changes

Pregnancy hormones and stretching of the skin around the enlarging uterus and breasts may cause normal skin changes. Increased skin pigmentation is thought to be caused by the increase in the pituitary hormone MSH (melanocyte stimulating hormone). After the second month of pregnancy, increases in estrogen and progesterone levels also contribute to these skin changes, which may include linea nigra, mask of pregnancy (chloasma), and stretch marks.

Linea nigra is a black pigmented line that commonly appears and extends down the middle of the abdomen (from the sternum to the pubic bone) in pregnancy and fades after the birth. Linea nigra is especially prominent in brunettes. Not all women experience this skin change. There is nothing you can do to prevent linea nigra.

Mask of pregnancy (chloasma) is dark brown, irregularly shaped discolorations over the cheeks, forehead, and nose and around the eyes. Their masklike pattern gained them the nickname *mask of pregnancy*. Not all women experience chloasma. There is nothing you can do to prevent it, but exposure to sunlight does seem to worsen this condition and make it less likely to fade after delivery. Therefore you may want to limit your exposure to direct sunlight and use a sunscreen when outdoors. Chloasma generally fades after the birth, but it may reappear if you are exposed to excessive sunlight or take birth control pills after pregnancy.

Stretch marks are shiny white lines on the skin of the abdomen, breasts, and thighs that look like surface scars and are caused by the skin stretching to accommodate the growing uterus and breasts. There is no way to prevent stretch marks, but you can help reduce them by rubbing your abdomen, breasts, and thighs daily with baby oil or skin cream. Stretch marks are usually permanent; however, they do fade after pregnancy.

4

Mother and Baby
The First Nine Months

From the moment you suspect you may be pregnant, your curiosity is probably intense. What is happening inside my body? What does my baby look like at this stage of development? The following section is intended to help you see and understand the many changes that occur throughout pregnancy and the importance of every week in the development of your baby.

The *numbered weeks* in the following sections are based on a 40-week gestation, which begins on the first day of your last menstrual period, not the date of conception. Your due date and gestation are calculated by this same method, and therefore this is the number your practi-

tioner will tell you at each of your prenatal visits. Because conception actually occurs approximately two weeks after the first day of your last menstrual period, it occurs in week two of the gestational scale, and fetal development occurs throughout the remaining 38 weeks.

When reading this chapter look for the heading corresponding to the gestation week number you were given at your prenatal visit. The fetal development pictures under that heading are approximations of fetal development occurring at that gestation week number. They are not true to life-size at that time.

Two Weeks' Gestation: Conception

Fetal Development

Fertilization, the joining of the egg and the sperm, takes place around the 14th day after the first day of the last menstrual period. The fertilized egg is called a *zygote.* The zygote takes about three to four days to travel down

57

the fallopian tubes, and then it implants on the uterine wall.

By one week after conception, three cell layers have formed that will later develop into every organ of the body. After the zygote implants in the uterine wall, cellular division continues very rapidly. The cells form a small ball called a *blastocyst*. The thick, blood-rich uterine lining provides nourishment for the blastocyst.

Maternal Changes

At the site where the egg follicle was released, the ovaries increase production of progesterone, which is known as "the pregnancy-sustaining hormone."

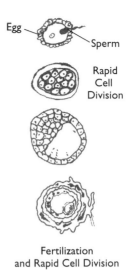

Egg   Sperm

Rapid
Cell
Division

Fertilization
and Rapid Cell Division

Four Weeks' Gestation

Fetal Development

From the second to the eighth week of fetal development (4th to 10th gestation week), the developing baby is called an *embryo*. By four weeks the first cells appear that will later develop into the spine, the spinal cord, and the brain.

Maternal Changes

The first menstrual period is missed. Early pregnancy blood tests can confirm pregnancy. Some home pregnancy urine tests can detect pregnancy two weeks after conception.

The breasts may begin to feel tender. Fatigue may begin, and morning sickness may occur. If you are going to have morning sickness, it generally occurs between the 4th and 12th weeks. (See pages 41–43 for more information on morning sickness and Chapter 3 for other possible discomforts of pregnancy.)

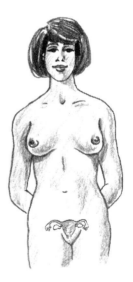

4 Weeks

Self-Help

See pages 41–42 on how to decrease morning sickness symptoms.

This is the time to contact your doctor for pregnancy confirmation.

Avoid any medication unless prescribed, and check with your doctor about the safety of any medication that you take for any chronic illness.

Get adequate rest and exercise (see pages 27–28 for appropriate exercises during pregnancy).

Wear a good supportive bra.

Eat a balanced healthy diet that includes foods from the entire food pyramid (see pages 15–25 for more nutritional information). Vegetarians, please consult your care provider to be sure your diet includes enough protein intake for your pregnancy.

Five Weeks' Gestation

Fetal Development

The heart and blood circulation system are beginning to form: two chambers of the heart, the aortic arch, and major vessels are already present. **The heart begins to beat.** The digestive tract begins to take form, and arm and leg buds are apparent. The fetus is one-fifth of an inch long, with the head tipped forward at a right angle, forming the body into a C shape. The head occupies one-third of the total length at this stage of development.

An ultrasound can be performed to confirm pregnancy.

Maternal Changes

Urinary frequency (the need to urinate often) may begin, because the uterus widens before it grows upward and thus puts side-to-side pressure on the bladder. Urinary frequency is more commonly present, however, between 6 weeks and 12 weeks of gestation.

Self-Help

Explore your maternity insurance options concerning location, practitioner, and newborn care.

If you have not done so already, select your maternity care practitioner. See pages 6–11 for options and assistance on exploring and choosing a maternity care practitioner.

Increase your fluid intake to two quarts per day. Increasing fluid intake during the day and decreasing intake in the evening helps to reduce urinary frequency during the night.

See Chapter 3 for suggestions on how to deal with individual discomforts of pregnancy that you may encounter.

Six to Seven Weeks' Gestation

Fetal Development

During this early stage of development, the baby is not ready to produce its own blood cells. A yolk sac develops and attaches to the embryo for this purpose, until the baby is ready to make blood cells on its own.

The nervous system is developing very rapidly at this point. Cells are forming the neural tube. By the end of the seventh week of gestation, one end of this tube is developing into the brain.

At six weeks, the arms and legs are mere buds. By the seventh week, they are much more defined. At seven weeks the eyes begin to form and the ears are just a tiny fold in the skin.

A stem connects the embryo to the developing placenta. This stem will later become the umbilical cord. At seven weeks, the exchange of nutrients and wastes begins to occur across the attachment site of the placenta to the uterus.

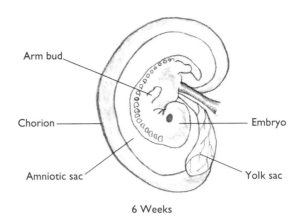

6 Weeks

Maternal Changes

The endocrine, pituitary, thyroid, and adrenal glands increase their hormone production during pregnancy, and the developing placenta produces several important hormones. However, progesterone, the main pregnancy-sustaining hormone, still mostly comes from the ovaries.

Self-Help

Call for your first appointment with your maternity care practitioner.

A healthy amount of weight gain in pregnancy is important. How much is right for you depends on your prepregnancy height and weight. If you are a teenager, or if you are having a multiple gestation (twins or more), your necessary weight gain will be different from the normal averages for a woman of average age, height, and

weight. **Therefore be sure to get specific information from your practitioner on what the normal expected weight gain is for you.** The expected weight gain during the first three months of pregnancy for a woman of average height and weight is two to five pounds. Please consult your practitioner if you are not keeping within your expected weight gain range.

Eight Weeks' Gestation

Fetal Development

Rapid development continues. The eyes are complete, but they are still spaced far apart. The lips and tongue are developed, but the nose is still flat. Evidence of teeth begins to appear. Inner ear bones and the system for hearing have developed.

Small bones and muscles can be seen through very thin skin. The testes or ovaries can

be detected, but sex cannot be determined by the external genitals at this point.

The diaphragm can now be seen separating the heart and liver. The liver begins to take over blood-cell production from the yolk sac, and the yolk sac begins to disintegrate.

Toes and fingers are formed.

The main blood vessels are almost completely formed.

The baby is now three-fourths of an inch long and is protected as it floats in amniotic fluid. The head and neck make up one-half the total length of the body. The spinal cord still runs the entire length of the body.

8 Weeks

Maternal Changes

There is still very little if any weight gain.

The uterus is still within the pelvis.

White or yellow vaginal discharge may increase.

The breasts may have enlarged and may feel tender.

Morning sickness may or may not be present. If present, it usually lasts until about 12 weeks.

Some women experience an ambivalent feeling toward their pregnancy at this point, even if the pregnancy was planned.

Self-Help

See the suggestions on pages 41–43 for treatment of nausea and vomiting. Be sure to report nausea or vomiting to your practitioner if self-help measures do not bring relief or if you are unable to get adequate nutrition and fluids.

Wear a supportive bra.

Nine to Ten Weeks' Gestation

Fetal Development

From eight weeks of fetal development (which is 10 weeks of gestation) until term, the baby is called a *fetus* in scientific terminology.

By 10 weeks, all of the major organs are formed. The face takes on a more normal human appearance. The fetus is now approximately one inch long.

The placenta now occupies one-third of the inside lining of the uterus.

The figure on the next page shows the actual size of the embryo at nine weeks of gestation.

Between 10 and 17 weeks, your care provider may be able to pick up heart tones from your baby using an amplifying device or special stethoscope. However, because it is difficult and time-consuming to locate the right spot (and not necessary if the pregnancy is progressing normally), and because not locating the heart beat may cause you needless concern, listening for the

9–10 Weeks

baby's heart rate is usually deferred until 16 or 17 weeks of gestation.

Maternal Changes

The mother's blood volume has increased by about 25% and up to 45% by 34 weeks.

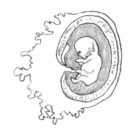

Actual size at 9 weeks

Twelve Weeks' Gestation

Fetal Development

The fetus is now approximately two inches long and half an ounce in weight. The head is more upright and is still large in proportion to the rest of the body. The lower body is developing and growing rapidly.

Nails are beginning to appear. Some bones have formed, and blood is now being produced in the baby's bone marrow. The lungs are starting to take their normal shape, and the kidneys are beginning to secrete urine. External sex organs are evident on a male fetus.

The sucking reflex has developed. Other movement is also beginning, although it is not usually felt by the mother. Some women at this point describe a feeling like that of bubbles being blown in their pelvis.

12 Weeks

Maternal Changes

The uterus now rises above the pubic bone and can be felt through your lower abdomen.

You may begin to feel Braxton Hicks contractions.

The risk of urinary tract infection (UTI) increases and remains throughout pregnancy.

You may experience fatigue.

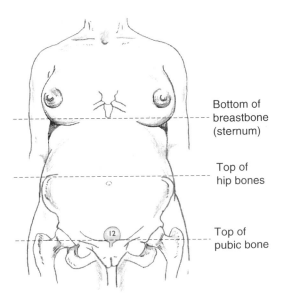

Bottom of breastbone (sternum)

Top of hip bones

Top of pubic bone

Self-Help

Drink two quarts of fluid daily.

Get regular exercise and adequate rest. Accept help from others.

Eat a healthy diet and avoid empty calories.

To help decrease the risk of UTIs, always wipe from front to back and empty your bladder frequently and after intercourse.

Bathe regularly. Be aware that perspiration increases at this time.

Begin to explore childbirth education class options. Register early.

Fourteen Weeks' Gestation

Fetal Development

At 14 weeks, the head is still one-third the body's total length. Bones are appearing, the nose and ears have formed, and hair is beginning to appear.

The baby is growing rapidly, and its arms and legs are moving, even if you do not yet feel it. By 13 weeks, your baby has learned to suck and swallow. On ultrasound it may even be seen sucking its thumb!

Maternal Changes

The placenta is now fully mature. It serves as your baby's lungs, providing oxygen to the baby and getting rid of carbon dioxide. It also serves as the digestive tract, carrying nutrients from you to your baby, and as your baby's kidneys, returning waste by-products to you for elimination. In addition, the placenta carries out many of the functions of the liver for the baby (such as the elimination of bilirubin, released as red blood cells disintegrate), since the baby's liver is still immature. The placenta also provides for the exchange of valuable antibodies to protect the baby against viral illnesses to which you are immune. This is valuable protection against illness in the first three to six months of life.

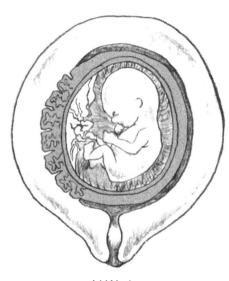

14 Weeks

Self-Help

Consult your practitioner if your weight gain is more than 0.8 pound per week (or the limits given to you by your practitioner) from now until term.

Sixteen Weeks' Gestation

Fetal Development

Your baby now weighs about seven ounces. The ears, eyes, and nose look much like they will look at birth. The hands can grasp. The muscles and bones have matured but still have growing to do.

Thick black meconium stool is forming in the baby's bowel.

The lungs are still underdeveloped, with the bronchioles only just now appearing.

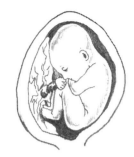

16 Weeks

Maternal Changes

At about this point, a woman with average abdominal tone, having her first baby, begins to see her tummy protrude. As the fundus (the top of the uterus) rises, pressure on the bladder is relieved and urinary frequency decreases.

If this is not your first pregnancy, Braxton Hicks contractions may begin. The fetal heartbeat can be heard with amplification.

A woman's energy level usually increases from now through the seventh month.

Vaginal discharge usually increases; however, any pain, itching, or odor needs to be reported to your practitioner.

Self-Help

Daily hygiene is essential due to increased perspiration and vaginal discharge.

Loose, comfortable clothing and good supportive shoes are imperative. Low-heeled shoes are usually better in preventing backache than flats or high heels.

Refer to Chapter 3, "Possible Discomforts of Pregnancy," for ways to minimize any discomfort that you may have. Also carefully read Chapter 7, "What to Report to Your Practitioner."

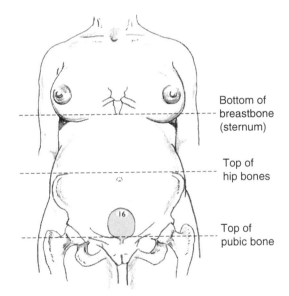

Bottom of breastbone (sternum)

Top of hip bones

Top of pubic bone

Eighteen Weeks' Gestation

Fetal Development

Your baby is 6 inches long, and he or she is actively sucking and swallowing.

Maternal Changes

Any time after 16 weeks of gestation, Braxton Hicks contractions begin.

Self-Help

Get adequate rest, exercise, and nutrition.

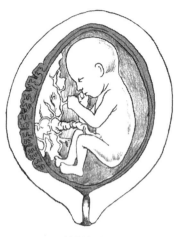

18 Weeks

Twenty Weeks' Gestation

Fetal Development

Your baby is now nine inches long and weighs about 10 ounces. Body proportions are now normal.

Vernix, the white cheesy substance that covers the skin, and *lanugo,* downy hair covering the body, appear. Head hair, eyelashes, and eyebrows begin to show, and fingernails and toenails are evident.

Very early respiratory movements start and are evident on ultrasound. Your baby is kicking and turning somersaults.

Maternal Changes

The top of your uterus is just below your navel.

Your breasts begin internal secretion of colostrum; however, it may not be externally apparent. The areolas darken in color.

Constipation and leg cramps may occur.

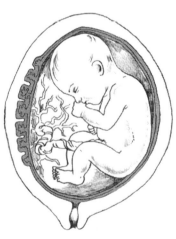

20 Weeks

Quickening, the first fetal movements felt, usually occurs between 18 and 22 weeks. (The range considered normal is 14–26 weeks.) You are especially likely to feel your baby move when you are resting.

Self-Help

See pages 53–54 and 48–49 for how to treat constipation and leg cramps.

From now until the end of your 36th week, report any frequent, regular contractions (10 minutes apart or closer, or farther apart but very regular) that are felt as contractions or as periodic cramps or backache.

Know the signs and symptoms of preterm labor. (See pages 115–118 for this information.)

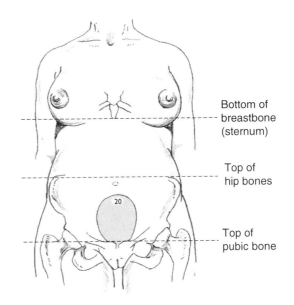

Bottom of breastbone (sternum)

Top of hip bones

20

Top of pubic bone

Twenty-Two Weeks' Gestation

Fetal Development

The baby has well-established sleep/wake cycles that are evident to you. Sucking and all kinds of movement are occurring.

Bones are developing rapidly.

At 21 weeks the placenta now occupies half of the uterine lining.

The age of viability (when the fetus is able to survive outside of the womb) continues to change with advances in neonatal intensive care. Presently, the age of viability is considered 22 to 24 weeks of gestation (20 to 22 weeks postconception). The ability of the fetus to live at this point depends on the maturity of the lungs (their ability to oxygenate the blood) and the development of the central nervous system. The accuracy of your dates can also be an issue if your infant is born early. Of course, the staff and technology immediately available to assist an infant born this prematurely are important. This is why women in premature labor are often sent to a high-risk facility when it becomes clear that their contractions cannot be controlled.

Maternal Changes

Leg and perineal varicosities may develop.

Your feet and ankles may swell.

You may experience dizziness and/or lightheadedness when standing or getting out of bed.

Self-Help

Avoid standing or sitting for long periods.

Avoid tight clothing and stockings with calf or thigh bands.

Elevate your legs as often as possible throughout the day.

Support stockings may help reduce swelling.

Do not lie directly on your back.

Eat a well-balanced diet and drink plenty of fluids.

Get adequate exercise.

Sit for a few moments before getting out of bed. Stand up slowly from a chair and wait for lightheadedness to pass before walking away from the chair.

Twenty-Four Weeks' Gestation

Fetal Development

Your baby's body is now well proportioned but lacks fat. It weighs about one pound, five ounces.

The skin is red and wrinkled and covered with vernix. Veins and arteries can still be seen through the thin skin. The bone marrow is now producing more blood, and bone growth is rapid. In a male fetus, the testes begin to descend into the scrotum.

Your baby can open and close its eyes and can hear!

24 Weeks

Maternal Changes

The fundus (the top of the uterus) is at about the same level as the top of your hips.

Backache and leg cramps are common.

Stretch marks may begin to appear, and abdominal itching may be experienced as the skin stretches.

Nosebleeds may occur.

Weight gain should be approximately 0.8 pound per week if you are of normal weight.

Self-Help

See page 44 for treatment of backache and page 28 for an exercise to relieve backache.

Be extra careful to maintain good posture when sitting and walking.

Lubricate nostrils to help prevent nosebleeds.

Lubricate breast and abdominal skin with lanolin creams.

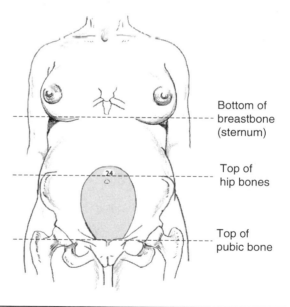

Bottom of breastbone (sternum)

Top of hip bones

Top of pubic bone

Twenty-Eight Weeks' Gestation

Fetal Development

The baby weighs approximately two pounds, seven ounces and occupies most of the space inside your uterus.

Downy hair covers the head, shoulders, and back. It is lost between 36 and 40 weeks and is therefore usually seen only on premature infants.

Your baby could already hear at 24 weeks; at 28 weeks it can now hear voices and music. Although your voice sounds like it's under water, newborns do seem to recognize familiar voices after birth. The main sound your baby hears is your heartbeat. This is why babies are often soothed after birth by tapes of heart sounds.

Fingernails and toenails are present, as are muscles, but the muscles have poor tone. If the baby is born now, its cry is weak or absent. The sucking reflex may also be weak at this time.

Lecithin is forming on the alveolar (airway air sac) surfaces. The presence of this substance, in adequate amounts, indicates lung maturity.

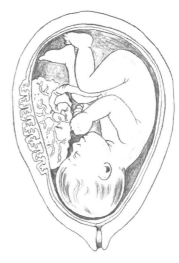

28 Weeks

Maternal Changes

The muscular breathing efforts of the infant and "hiccups"—a rhythmic jumping—are felt occasionally.

As the fundus begins to push upward on the diaphragm, shortness of breath and heartburn may develop.

Hemorrhoids, as well as leg and perineal varicosities, may develop.

Self-Help

Eat smaller, more frequent meals. Do not lie flat immediately after eating.

Sitz baths and topical ointments for hemorrhoids may bring temporary relief. Eat adequate dietary fiber and roughage to avoid constipation.

See page 44 for suggestions on helping backache and page 52 for suggestions on helping leg and perineal varicose veins.

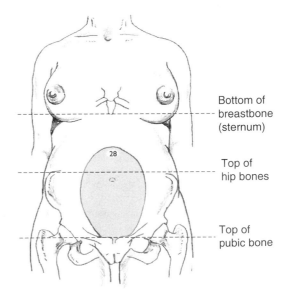

Bottom of breastbone (sternum)

Top of hip bones

Top of pubic bone

Rest on your left side.

Attend childbirth education classes with your support person. Read the labor and delivery sections and the cesarean delivery chapter of this book—being prepared helps to reduce anxiety if an emergency delivery occurs.

If you have not done so already, begin to learn about baby care. *Being prepared builds confidence!*

Thirty to Thirty-Two Weeks' Gestation

Fetal Development

At 29 weeks, the baby is about two-thirds grown and about 14 inches in length. At 31 weeks, it weighs approximately four pounds and is 16 inches long.

Body fat is increasing, but babies born now are still very thin and their veins can be seen through their skin. Muscle tone is still weak. The skin is wrinkled, but less so than before, and is no longer red. In male fetuses, testes are usually descended by 31 weeks. Permanent teeth are present in the gums.

If the baby is born after 30 weeks of gestation where neonatal intensive care is available, the survival rate without complications is good.

Maternal Changes

Fetal activity may awaken you at night.

Breasts are tender and may leak.

Self-Help

Wear a supportive bra.

Finish writing your birthing plan with your support person.

Review signs and symptoms of preterm labor, pages 115–118, and "Rupture of Membranes" and what to report, page 119.

If you will be returning to work after a maternity leave, begin to formulate plans for this now while you have time. Finding, looking at, and choosing child care is an important process. It is easier to do now than when you have a newborn to care for. (See pages 38–40 for thoughts on "Planning Ahead for Return to Work.")

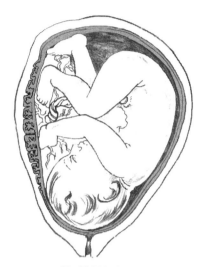

30–32 Weeks

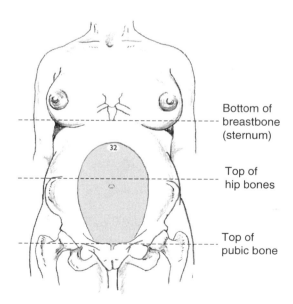

Bottom of breastbone (sternum)

Top of hip bones

Top of pubic bone

Thirty-Six Weeks' Gestation

Fetal Development

Your baby is certainly "getting there." At 36 weeks, weight varies from just under five pounds to around six and one-half pounds. Average length at this point is 18 inches. If your gestational dates are correct, your baby could do very well holding his or her own, if born now.

Muscle tone is much improved. By this point your baby can even lift his or her head.

At 36 weeks, the vernix is disappearing, but some will still be present. The skin is much less wrinkled as muscles and fat "grow into" and smooth out all that skin!

The nervous and respiratory systems continue to mature, as they do even after birth.

Sleep/wake cycles are very evident. There is not much room for tossing and turning, so your baby's movement is somewhat restricted. You can pretty much see all the stretches, kicks, and punches on the outside of your abdomen. It's fun to try to identify the bottom, knees, and so on.

Maternal Changes

Antibodies against viral illnesses to which you are immune are transferred to the baby across the placenta. This provides valuable, immediate protection to your infant against these illnesses. Antibodies are also transferred through the colostrum in the first few days of breastfeeding. These two forms of passive immunity only provide protection for three to six months, however.

Shortness of breath and indigestion peak at this time, as the fundus reaches its highest point (just below the breastbone). You will not have relief from these symptoms until lightening occurs (your baby drops). (See page 122 for more information on when lightening can be expected to occur.)

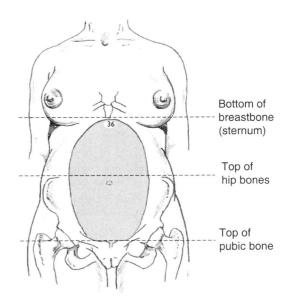

Bottom of breastbone (sternum)

Top of hip bones

Top of pubic bone

Self-Help

If you have other children, make arrangements for child care for when labor occurs. Make plans for how you will get to the hospital and who will drive you if your primary support person is not available.

Make a list of items to pack for the hospital. (See pages 132–133 for suggestions.) Pack the baby items to be brought to the hospital for discharge and set them aside. (See page 132 for suggestions.)

Thirty-Eight to Forty Weeks' Gestation

Fetal Development

Technically, 40 weeks is full term, but delivery at any time between 38 and 42 weeks is considered normal and full term.

Your baby now takes up all the "living space" inside your uterus! He or she is ready for life outside the womb. Muscle tone is good, and the baby proves this to you often by kicking, stretching, and moving about.

Between 38 and 40 weeks, weight can range from six and one-half pounds to eight pounds. The baby is, on average, 19 to 21 inches long.

There is very little vernix remaining on the skin. Downy hair, if still present, is usually only seen on the shoulders and upper back.

The sucking reflex is strong.

The baby most commonly assumes a head-down position in preparation for birth.

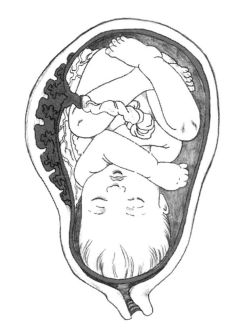

38–40 Weeks

Maternal Changes

Lightening, the dropping down and forward of the baby in the uterus, generally occurs about two weeks before delivery with your first baby and at the onset of labor with subsequent babies.

After lightening occurs, there is more pressure on the bladder and urinary frequency returns. There is now less pressure on the diaphragm and therefore shortness of breath is somewhat relieved after lightening.

Backache increases.

Braxton Hicks contractions are frequent and very noticeable.

Most women feel impatient for delivery, and some mothers experience a burst of energy.

Self-Help

Do not neglect your rest. It is best not to go into labor exhausted, with emotional reserves at a low from fatigue.

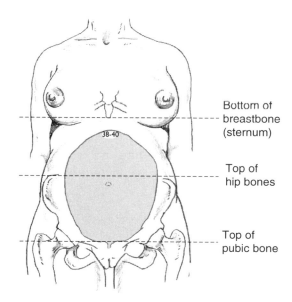

Bottom of breastbone (sternum)

Top of hip bones

Top of pubic bone

Pelvic-tilt exercises may help reduce back-ache. In addition, wear low-heeled shoes and avoid standing or sitting for long periods of time.

Sleep on your left side. Your baby will be less restless in this position, and your placenta will receive a better blood supply.

If you want to be prepared, at 38 weeks pack your suitcase. (See pages 132–133 for a list of items you may want to take with you. **Don't forget your camera, extra film, and the list of names and phone numbers for calls after delivery!**)

Arrange for a tour of your birthing place if you have not done this already.

Continue to gather information to help you to make a decision about breastfeeding or bottle feeding, circumcision, hepatitis B vaccines for the baby after birth, and family planning.

Read and learn about your postpartum care and needs, and continue to read and learn about infant care.

Be prepared. It helps to reduce your anxiety and boost your confidence.

5

Prenatal Monitoring

Monitoring Your Baby's Well-Being at Home

Because you are physically closer than anyone else to your developing baby, your own observations of the baby's movements and changes in your own condition can provide your practitioner with valuable information. You should feel confident about sharing any observations with your practitioner, as well as providing answers to specific questions about fetal movement, contractions, and vaginal discharge.

Feeling Your Baby Move

Once you know your pregnancy test was positive, you wait to feel the presence of this new life within you. *Quickening* is the term used to describe the first time you feel fetal movement.

Although the embryo begins to move by the seventh week, you cannot feel movement until much later. Quickening normally occurs between the 18th and the 22nd week of pregnancy. However, it may occur as early as 14 weeks or as late as 26 weeks. In your first pregnancy, it is difficult to know what quickening feels like. This early movement is not like the baby's later kicks, which you can actually see! Most women describe the first movement as something like a flutter. Early movement can therefore be mistaken for a gas bubble or a nervous stomach.

Women who have had other pregnancies feel movement earlier, perhaps because they know what to expect. Also, uterine and abdominal tone is decreased with subsequent pregnancies, making it easier to feel movement.

Your practitioner will want to know when you first feel your baby moving. You do not need to make a special call, however—just make a note of the date and bring the information to your next prenatal visit.

Many practitioners encourage pregnant women to monitor their developing baby's movements on a regular basis. Lots of activity generally

73

means all is well, whereas a lack of activity can indicate a problem that should be evaluated at once. During the last three months of pregnancy, decreased fetal movement can be a sign that the placenta is aging earlier than normal. A decrease in the usual amount of fetal movement at any time during pregnancy can indicate a developing problem.

In assessing your baby's movement, consider the entire day. Is there an *overall* change from what is usual? Remember that short 20-minute periods without fetal movement are just nap times for your baby. Many factors can affect your baby's activity level, including drugs, cigarette smoking, your blood glucose level, and the time of day—after all, your growing baby needs sleep too!

There is no need to count your baby's movements unless you are noticing a decrease in movement or your practitioner has instructed you to do a daily count. If you believe there is a change, pick a period of time when there will be no or few distractions. It is best to pick a time of day when your baby is normally active. Babies are usually active after you have eaten a meal, so this is usually a good time to do fetal movement counts. Sit or lie down (left side is best), and place your hand on your uterus. Record your starting time. Count every movement that you feel. You can count your baby's kicks, hiccups, even twinges of movement, but whatever you count, be consistent when you are counting again another day.

If you suspect that your baby may be sleeping, drink cold fluids. This usually awakens a sleeping baby.

Count until you feel 10 movements and then record the time again. **A general rule is that you should feel 10 movements within two hours.** (You will see conflicting time periods listed for 10 movements in various books. Some references state 10 movements in two hours, some state 10 movements in three hours, and I have even seen 10 movements in four hours on one patient handout.) It is important to remember two things here. First, the intent of fetal movement counting is not to make you obsessed

with counting the movements of your baby. The intent is for you to be aware of the significance of decreased fetal movement and report it promptly. Second, **what is important is an overall change in your baby's normal movement.** Your practitioner will tell you what counting standard she or he wants you to use as your guideline.

(C)*If one hour passes* **with fewer than five movements, drink cold fluids and then repeat the counting procedure. This is to wake your baby in case the decrease in movement was just due to its sleeping. Then, if you do not feel 10 movements within the next two hours, call your care provider's office.**

(C)**Also report to your care provider if the time it takes to feel 10 movements is getting longer each day, because, again, this is an overall change in your baby's normal activity level.**

Feeling Braxton Hicks Contractions

Beginning as early as your second trimester (months 4 to 6), you may feel contractions (tightening or hardening of the uterus) at infrequent and irregular intervals. Some women never feel these contractions; others experience them daily throughout pregnancy. These contractions are called *Braxton Hicks contractions,* and they are a normal part of pregnancy. They are also referred to as "false labor contractions." Unlike labor contractions, however, Braxton Hicks contractions do not bring about effacement (thinning) or dilatation (opening) of the cervix. (See Figure 5-3 for an explanation of effacement and dilatation.)

Braxton Hicks contractions are brief and felt mainly in the front of the lower abdomen. They may occur every 10 to 20 minutes as pregnancy reaches full term. Experts believe that these contractions are a response to the baby's growth and the resulting expansion of the uterus.

To learn what a contraction feels like, lie down and place your fingertips on top of your uterus. If your uterus is contracting, you can feel your abdomen getting tight or hard, and then feel it relax or soften when the contraction ends.

Note that even Braxton Hicks contractions can be frequent and very intense during the last month of pregnancy. However, if your contractions do not produce cervical effacement and dilatation, they are not real labor contractions. (See Table 7-1, page 124, for a comparison of true and false labor.) **True labor can be diagnosed only by noting cervical change over a period of time.** This assessment can only be made by a physician, midwife, or nurse trained in assessing cervical dilatation.

Preterm labor occurs after the 20th week but before the 37th week of pregnancy. The onset of preterm labor can be very subtle. **Learn the warning signs of preterm labor listed in Chapter 7, "What to Report to Your Practitioner," pages 115–118.**

Early-Pregnancy Tests

Prenatal care includes periodic tests to monitor the well-being of you and your baby. These tests help detect any potential problems early, when treatment can be most effective. These tests include *screening tests,* which assess your risk for a specific problem, and *diagnostic tests,* which determine whether the problem is present or not.

You will be asked to sign a consent form before any test is done. You should feel free to discuss your thoughts, feelings, and concerns about the test with your practitioner. Before signing any form, be sure your practitioner has clearly explained the purpose of the test, what the risks of the procedure are to you and your baby, what risks may be involved if you refuse to have the test, and what the results will indicate. Without this information, you cannot give *informed consent.* You have the right to refuse a procedure if no good reason can be given to you about why the test or procedure is being requested.

If your prenatal tests indicate the presence or increased risk of an abnormality, you will be given the opportunity to meet with genetic counselors. Couples who have a known family history of genetic disorders may want to seek genetic counseling before conception.

Alpha-Fetoprotein (AFP) Test

Between the 15th and the 18th week of pregnancy, all expectant mothers receiving prenatal care are offered a screening blood test for AFP, *maternal serum alpha-fetoprotein.* AFP is a substance (protein) produced by the fetus, peak levels of which occur in the mother's blood at around 13 weeks and then decrease as the pregnancy progresses.

Purpose: AFP is not a mandatory screening test but is performed to assess the risk of birth defects.

Procedure: A blood sample is taken from your arm for analysis of the AFP level.

Risks: None for the mother or baby.

Results: Elevated levels of AFP in the mother's blood may be associated with defects of the fetus's spinal column (neural tube defects) such as spinal bifida (having an opening in the back that exposes the spinal cord) or absence of all or part of the brain (anencephaly). Low levels of AFP indicate increased risk of Down's syndrome or other chromosomal abnormalities. (In women under age 35, this test will identify about 25 percent of fetuses with Down's syndrome.)

A negative AFP test is comforting, but it is not an absolute guarantee that no problem exists. Although the test is 80 to 85 percent accurate in detecting neural tube defects, this means that 15 to 20 percent of neural tube defects are not detected with the AFP test. Likewise, there is a 10 percent nondetection rate of anencephaly (lacking a brain) and a 25 percent nondetection rate of spina bifida.

Only 4 percent of women with an initial high AFP reading will later have an affected infant.

Through further testing, the other 96 percent will show other reasons for the elevated AFP (multiple gestation, such as twins or triplets; miscalculated date of conception, making their gestation farther along than previously thought; or an inaccurate first reading).

Many physicians order additional blood tests at the same time as the AFP is done to give more information about the risk of having a baby with open neural tube defects or Down's syndrome. These tests are called *multiple marker screening tests* or *triple marker screening tests*. The results of these tests, along with your AFP test results, are available in about one week.

Next Steps: If your AFP or multiple marker tests results are abnormal, your practitioner may recommend more definitive diagnostic tests such as ultrasound or amniocentesis. Genetic counseling may also be advised.

Ultrasound

Ultrasound is a painless diagnostic test that uses sound waves to produce an image of the fetus (called a *sonogram*) without the dangers of X-rays. It is not a mandatory test in a normal healthy pregnancy. You are certainly within your rights to ask your practitioner why she or he is recommending an ultrasound. However, many practitioners prefer to do an early ultrasound to determine whether or not you are pregnant with twins. They want to know early on if you are carrying twins so that adequate nutrition can be started early and closer monitoring of your pregnancy can be provided.

Purpose: Ultrasound has many uses. It can be used to verify pregnancy, determine the age of the developing fetus, estimate or verify the actual due date based on the baby's size, determine the cause of abnormal bleeding in pregnancy, and confirm multiple gestation (twins or more). Some birth defects can also be seen on ultrasound.

Later in pregnancy, ultrasound is used to *verify presentation* (the position of the baby as it enters, or *presents,* into the pelvis) if vaginal examination and evaluation of the abdomen indicate the possibility of breech or other abnormal presentation. Ultrasound also shows the amount of amniotic fluid present and the location of the placenta. In the third trimester, ultrasound is used frequently to verify fetal well-being, especially in cases of pregnancy-induced hypertension or gestational diabetes. (Refer to "Biophysical Profile," page 87, for more information.)

If you have previously had a cesarean delivery, you may be offered an ultrasound in the last trimester to estimate fetal size and other factors, especially if your previous cesarean delivery was for failure to progress or CPD (cephalopelvic disproportion: the shape, size, or position of the baby's head did not allow it to fit through your pelvis). However, ultrasound examination is not mandatory for every woman prior to a trial of labor after cesarean delivery.

Procedure: You may be asked to drink several glasses of water an hour before your ultrasound (this is not always required) because a full bladder will help produce a clearer picture. Cold, wet gel will be placed on your abdomen. An instrument that looks like a microphone, called a transducer, is gently placed on your abdomen and moved around. Sound waves are directed inward toward your uterus through the transducer. The image seen on the monitor is created by sound waves rebounding from various internal organs and then being converted into images. Sound waves rebound differently from water than from soft organs like the placenta and hard structures like bone. Thus the images created depend on size, density, and other characteristics of the anatomic structures.

Risks: There is no evidence in the present literature of any harmful effects of ultrasound in pregnancy. However, most practitioners limit its use to when it is clinically indicated.

Results: The results are available immediately. How long the test takes to complete depends on the reason it was ordered. Your care provider may be looking for one specific thing, such as the size and presentation of the fetus, or the ultrasound may be only one part of an assessment of fetal well-being (see "Biophysical Profile," page 87).

Next Steps: The results will provide answers to specific questions or provide the total score on a biophysical profile. This information will help the care provider to decide whether the pregnancy can be continued or induction or immediate cesarean section is required.

Amniocentesis

Amniocentesis is a diagnostic test in which a small amount of amniotic fluid is extracted and analyzed. The fluid contains fetal cells, as well as proteins, enzymes, and other chemicals, that give the practitioner a great deal of information about your developing baby. The accuracy of results for detection of chromosome abnormalities from amniocentesis is 99.4 percent. AFP testing of the amniotic fluid rules out spinal bifida with 98 percent accuracy.

Purpose: Amniocentesis may be recommended if you have an abnormal AFP blood test result. However, amniocentesis is done most often for mothers over the age of 35 to detect chromosome abnormality, the risk of which rises with increased maternal age. The most common chromosome abnormality in babies born to women over 35 years old is Down's syndrome, but 80 percent of babies with Down's syndrome are born to women under 35. (Amniocentesis is rarely done in women under age 35, and AFP only detects 25 percent of the Down's cases present in women under the age of 35.)

Amniocentesis may also be recommended when one or both parents are carriers of a genetically linked disorder. It may be offered to couples who have had a previous child with a chromosomal abnormality or who have close relatives whose children have genetic disorders.

Although amniocentesis can be done as early as the 14th week, it is usually done between the 14th and the 18th week of pregnancy. It can also

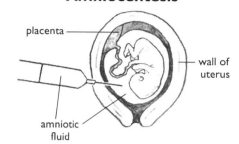

FIGURE 5-1

Amniocentesis

placenta —

wall of uterus

amniotic fluid

be done in the last three months to determine fetal lung maturity if an early induction is necessary.

Procedure: Amniocentesis is done in the ultrasound department. The entire procedure takes about a half-hour. You will be asked to empty your bladder and then be positioned on your back. An ultrasound examination will be done to determine the position of your baby and the location of the placenta. Your abdomen is then cleansed with an antiseptic solution and your lower body draped with sterile towels, leaving only your abdomen exposed.

After you are given a local anesthetic, a long, thin needle is inserted through your abdomen and uterine walls, into a pocket of amniotic fluid (Figure 5-1). Your doctor will avoid both the baby and the placenta by using ultrasound to guide insertion of the needle and the rest of the procedure. A small amount of amniotic fluid (only a few teaspoons) is obtained for evaluation. This part of the procedure takes only about a minute. Most women compare the discomfort they feel from this part of the procedure to that of having a blood sample drawn from the arm.

Your body continually replenishes amniotic fluid, so the small amount of fluid withdrawn will soon be replaced. The fluid obtained is sent to a lab, where the fetal cells are separated from the amniotic fluid and grown in a special culture for later analysis. Occasionally the cells fail to multiply and repeat amniocentesis is necessary.

Risks: You may experience a few hours of mild cramping after the procedure, for which acetaminophen, a nonaspirin pain reliever, is usually recommended. You should avoid heavy lifting, strenuous activity, and sexual intercourse for 24 hours following an amniocentesis. Other than these restrictions, you may resume normal activity.

Only about 1 percent of women undergoing an amniocentesis will develop leakage of amniotic fluid or blood from the vagina following the procedure. ✆**Contact your practitioner immediately if these symptoms do occur.** Although these symptoms usually go away, your practitioner may recommend bed rest for a few days until this complication is fully resolved. ✆**In addition to leakage of amniotic fluid or blood from the vagina following an amniocentesis, also report any signs of infection such as chills or fever.**

The risk of pregnancy loss after an amniocentesis performed around 16 weeks is approximately 1/400. However, because of even this small risk, amniocentesis should not be performed unless necessary. If you are at an especially high risk for chromosome abnormalities, an early amniocentesis, done between 12 and 14 weeks, may be recommended. The risk of miscarriage when amniocentesis is done at this earlier gestational age increases to 1/200.

Rh-negative mothers are given Rhogam after an amniocentesis because of the possibility of the mother being exposed to even a small amount of fetal blood during the procedure.

Results: Information concerning some genetic disorders can be determined almost immediately (neural tube defects, Hunter's syndrome, and Tay-Sachs disease). However, results from other genetic tests and cultures, which must be grown in the lab over a period of time, may take 8 to 10 days or even as long as 35 days to obtain. Chromosome analysis reveals the gender of the baby, but some parents prefer not to know the gender ahead of time; the choice is up to you.

Next Steps: Choosing to have amniocentesis does not automatically mean terminating the pregnancy if the results show an abnormality. Although some couples may choose to have an abortion if a genetic disorder is detected, many other couples at high risk for a genetic disorder decide to continue the pregnancy, fully willing to accept the outcome. For these couples, amniocentesis provides the opportunity to plan ahead.

Genetic Counseling: You will be given the opportunity to meet with genetic counselors if your prenatal tests indicate the presence or increased risk of an abnormality. This service is also available as a risk assessment prior to pregnancy for couples who have a known family history of genetic disorders.

Chorionic Villus Sampling (CVS)

Chorionic villi are microscopic, fingerlike projections that develop on the outside of the chorion, which is the membrane surrounding the amniotic fluid. Some of these villi will develop into the fetal side of the placenta during the second and third months of pregnancy. Because the villi develop from the same fertilized egg as the fetus, they reflect the genetic profile of the fetus.

Purpose: Chorionic villus sampling (CVS), also called chorionic villus biopsy, is a diagnostic test used to detect fetal abnormalities earlier in pregnancy than amniocentesis. The test is usually done between the 9th and 11th weeks of pregnancy. The complete results are more quickly available—usually within 10 days—than those of amniocentesis.

Procedure: CVS testing can be done through a vaginal or an abdominal approach. Both procedures are associated with mild to severe discomfort. The abdominal approach carries less risk of uterine infection.

In the vaginal approach, which is the most common, a long tube is inserted through the vagina and cervix and into the uterus. Ultrasound guides the placement of the tube between the uterine wall and the chorion, the part of the fetal membrane that will later become the fetal side of the placenta. A sample of the chorionic villi is then gently suctioned off for study.

CVS by abdominal approach is done in the hospital and is similar to amniocentesis. You will be asked to empty your bladder before the procedure begins. After you and your baby are assessed and your abdomen is cleansed with an antiseptic solution, you are given a local anesthetic. Ultrasound is used to guide a needle through the abdominal and uterine walls to the chorionic villi surrounding the chorionic membrane. A smaller needle is inserted into the larger needle and moved up and down several times to obtain samples of cells.

Risks: CVS does have a slightly greater risk of causing miscarriage than an amniocentesis, increasing the normal risk of miscarriage by an additional 1 percent. Vaginal bleeding, rupture of membranes, and infection of the amniotic fluid, although rare, can also occur. In addition, babies born to mothers who had a CVS done between the 56th and 66th days of gestation have a higher incidence of limb malformations, especially of the toes and fingers. This suggests that CVS should be performed only after 10 weeks of gestation.

CVS is not performed as often as amniocentesis. If this procedure is recommended for you, ask to have it done where the physicians are experienced in performing the procedure.

You may have some mild vaginal bleeding after a CVS. ✐**Although your practitioner will not be concerned at first, this symptom should be reported.** She or he will want to follow you to be certain the bleeding stops. **Also report any fever or severe abdominal pain in the days following the procedure, which could be signs of a developing infection.** Although there is only a slight risk of infection from CVS, any infection requires prompt treatment.

You should plan to have someone drive you home after this procedure, and rest for the remainder of the day.

Results: Some results may be available in 48 hours. The full-study report takes 10 to 14 days.

Next Steps: One disadvantage to CVS is that it does not show all abnormalities, and therefore it is not as complete a screening as amniocentesis. For example, it does not show neural tube defects, so if your AFP blood test at 16 weeks is abnormal, you would still require an amniocentesis for more information.

Many genetic abnormalities can be detected through CVS. If abnormalities are detected, your options and resources available for support will be discussed with you.

Blood and Urine Glucose Levels

At each prenatal visit, your urine will be tested for the presence of glucose (sugar). During pregnancy, extra circulating glucose is needed to ensure that there is enough for both you and the growing baby. Insulin is the hormone that allows sugar to be absorbed from circulation and utilized by the body's cells. There is a normal pregnancy mechanism that blocks insulin from being totally used up by your cells, thus leaving extra insulin available for your baby's use. Sometimes this mechanism works too aggressively and leaves more glucose circulating in your bloodstream than either you or your baby needs. Your kidneys filter out some of this excess glucose and "spill" it into your urine.

Most women's bodies sense this extra glucose and produce more insulin in response, and by the next prenatal visit there is no longer glucose in the urine. But if you are a diabetic or have tendencies toward diabetes, this correction is not made and high levels of glucose remain in your blood and your urine at your next office visit.

Purpose: In addition to the urine glucose test at each prenatal visit, between 24 and 28 weeks of gestation your practitioner will order a **one-hour glucose tolerance test** to screen for the presence of glucose in your blood. This is routinely done on all women, because 70 percent of the women with gestational diabetes do not have the classic diabetes symptoms of excessive thirst, hunger, frequent urination, or weakness and fatigue. There are many risk factors that would prompt your obstetrician to screen you even earlier for gestational diabetes: see pages 110–111 for a description of gestational diabetes.

❑ Personal or family history of diabetes.
❑ Age older than 35 (the risk increases with age).
❑ Whether you have had a previous baby over nine pounds at birth or were yourself over nine pounds in weight at birth.
❑ Glucose in your urine repeatedly in early pregnancy.
❑ Intolerance for sugar when you are not pregnant.
❑ Obesity.
❑ History of unexplained miscarriages or babies with abnormalities.
❑ History of high blood pressure during pregnancy, previous gestational diabetes, many urinary tract infections, or other pregnancy complications.

Procedure: In the one-hour glucose tolerance test you will be asked to drink a 50-gram dose of glucose. One hour later your blood will be drawn and the glucose level remaining in your blood measured. If your blood glucose level is high on this test, you will be rescheduled for a three-hour glucose tolerance test (see below for further information).

If you test positive for glucose in your urine, don't be too concerned. A small amount of glucose in the urine, especially during the second trimester, is not uncommon. However, if your one-hour glucose tolerance test result is high, you will be scheduled for the **three-hour glucose tolerance test**, which will more clearly show how your body responds to sugar in your bloodstream.

You will be asked to drink a 100-gram dose of glucose. Your blood will be drawn at one, two and three hours after drinking the glucose. You should therefore plan to remain at the laboratory for three hours.

Results: The results of this test will help your doctor determine whether you have a diabetic state brought on by pregnancy. **If you were not a diabetic before pregnancy but now maintain a high blood sugar level, you are said to have *gestational diabetes*.**

Next Steps: As many as 10 percent of all pregnant women develop gestational diabetes; it is the most common complication of pregnancy. Today, diabetes in pregnancy can be closely monitored and controlled, thus preventing potential complications for you and your baby. You will be given a special diet that you must follow closely. If diet and controlled exercise alone do not control the high blood sugar readings, you will be taught how to give yourself extra insulin for the remainder of your pregnancy. You will also be taught how to do a finger-stick blood glucose test and given a monitoring unit that will measure the results. You will have written and very specific instructions on the normal, expected range for your blood sugar level. ✆**You will need to report abnormal results to your practitioner immediately.**

Gestational diabetes is a very serious condition. Refer to page 111 for a list of the possible complications that can result from gestational diabetes if it goes untreated. ✆**The list of potential complications underscores why it is very important to follow your practitioner's orders carefully and call for help if you do not clearly understand your diet or instructions.**

Most women with gestational diabetes (98 percent) return to normal blood sugar levels after delivery without further need for diet or insulin control. However, you have a slightly greater risk of developing diabetes in later life if you have had gestational diabetes.

Later Monitoring of Your Baby's Well-Being

True Labor Contractions

True labor contractions occur at regular intervals. In the beginning, they may be 20 to 30 minutes apart. They gradually get closer together, longer

FIGURE 5-2

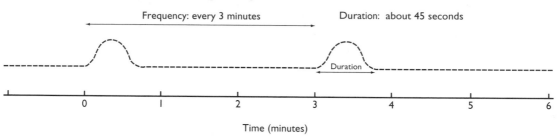

Evaluating the Frequency and Duration of Contractions

Frequency: every 3 minutes   Duration: about 45 seconds

Duration

Time (minutes)

in duration, and more intense. You feel pain in both the back and the lower abdomen. Some women even experience true labor pain in their thighs.

True labor contractions are accompanied by effacement and dilatation of your cervix. If you believe you are having premature labor (labor prior to 37 weeks of gestation), or if you are full term and think you are in labor, you should evaluate and record your contractions: their *frequency, duration, intensity,* and *location.*

Contraction frequency is timed from the beginning of one contraction to the beginning of the next (Figure 5-2). (See "Signs and Symptoms of Premature Labor" in Chapter 7 for information on how long to count premature contractions before calling your practitioner, page 116.)

Also note the duration—how long the contraction lasts, from the beginning until you no longer feel it. Describe the intensity of the pain and its *location.*

While you are timing your contractions, **continue to drink clear liquids (water, cranberry juice, apple juice, or ginger ale or other clear soda without caffeine)** unless you are specifically instructed not to do so by your practitioner. Lack of fluids and glucose can cause a painful, irritable contraction pattern that is not true labor. Because your uterus is a network of muscles, it requires fluid and calorie nourishment for energy to function effectively. Whether these are premature contractions (before 37 weeks) or true or false full-term contractions, continue to drink clear fluids.

Occasional Sharp Cervical Pains

As you enter the last month of your pregnancy, you may experience *occasional* sharp, stabbing pains in the area of your cervix. These pains last only a second and are *not* felt in the abdominal area. This discomfort is probably caused by the beginning of effacement of the cervix or engagement of the fetal head (also called lightening; see below). Think of it as labor progress being made without your being in labor!

If sharp cervical pains occur prior to your last month or if these cervical pains are very frequent at any time, notify your practitioner immediately. You may need to be assessed for premature labor or for the location of your placenta.

Lightening: When Your Baby Drops Lower into Your Pelvis

For most of your pregnancy, your baby has moved all around your abdomen. During the final weeks, however, most babies begin to prepare for their grand entrance into the outside world, ideally a head-first experience. When the head or other presenting part (the part of the baby closest to the cervix) enters ("drops") into the pelvic cavity, this is called *lightening,* or *engagement.*

First babies usually drop lower into the pelvis two to four weeks before delivery; subsequent babies usually don't drop until labor begins. Of course, there are exceptions to the rule—your first baby can drop early and still deliver late, or never drop until labor begins.

Lightening relieves the pressure on your ribs and diaphragm, so you feel as if you can breathe easier and eat bigger meals. Heartburn normally decreases. Because the baby is lower, however, the uterus increases pressure on the bladder, pelvic muscles, and joints. You feel the need to urinate more frequently. Increased perineal pressure after lightening makes varicose veins in the legs and perineum more common at this time. Lightening also shifts your center of gravity, making you now feel as though you are losing your balance more easily.

Passing the Mucus Plug

As the cervix thins, the mucus plug that sealed the cervical opening throughout pregnancy has nowhere to go but out. The mucus plug may be washed out as your membranes rupture, or it may emerge gradually or as one big chunk of mucus. It has a distinctive appearance: thick and dark (tan, yellow, or almost brown) with perhaps a small amount of blood in it. The mucus plug is thicker than normal vaginal discharge.

If you are full term, there is no need to promptly report the passing of your mucus plug. Simply make a note of the date and inform your care provider at your next visit. **℃However, if you are not yet full term (before 37 weeks), notify your care provider immediately if you pass your mucus plug, even if you are not experiencing contractions.**

When Your Membranes Rupture

℃Any trickle or gush of vaginal fluid is significant. Note the time, color, and amount and report it to your practitioner immediately. Do not wait until your next office visit.

The risk of infection to both you and your baby increases after your membranes rupture. Your care provider would like you to deliver within 24 hours after your membranes rupture in order to reduce the risk of infection. You can understand,

therefore, why it is important that you report the rupture of your membranes, or any suspicion of such, immediately. If your labor does not begin naturally within 12 hours after your membranes rupture, your practitioner may recommend inducing labor to reduce the risk of infection.

℃If you are unsure whether your membranes have ruptured, call your practitioner. There are two simple, quick and painless tests that can be done in the office to determine this. The first is a *nitrazine litmus paper test*. A small piece of this test paper is touched to the outer opening of your vagina. If the paper turns dark blue, amniotic fluid is present.

Sometimes the results of this test are unclear (called *equivocal*), in which case a second, more definitive test called a *fern test* can be done. Using a speculum, your practitioner obtains a small amount of fluid from around your cervix. This fluid is then examined under a microscope. Amniotic fluid is easily distinguished from normal vaginal secretions when viewed under a microscope. The results of this test will be given to you immediately.

For additional information see the section "When Your Membranes Rupture" in Chapter 7 (page 119).

Late-Pregnancy Tests

Vaginal Examinations

During the final weeks before your delivery date, your practitioner will want to see you each week. Weekly visits will include an internal vaginal examination to evaluate the effacement and dilatation of your cervix, the presentation of your baby, and the station of the presenting part. These terms are discussed below.

Effacement and Dilatation of the Cervix: Two processes are involved in the preparation of your cervix for labor and delivery: *effacement* and *dilatation* (Figure 5-3). With first babies, as the delivery date approaches, the thick, firm cervix gradually thins out and becomes softer. This process, called effacement of the cervix, allows the cervix to stretch sufficiently for the baby to be born. Effacement status is described as a percentage. For example, if your cervix is 70 percent effaced, it is 70 percent shorter than it was earlier in your pregnancy. For subsequent births, effacement normally occurs simultaneously with dilatation, the gradual dilating, or opening, of the cervix.

During pregnancy, the cervical opening, called the *cervical os,* points backward toward the rectum. This is called a posterior cervix in early labor, not to be confused with a posterior presentation (described later on this page). As true labor becomes established, the cervix tilts forward, placing the os directly at the top of the vagina. When the cervix moves into this position, vaginal examinations become much less uncomfortable because the examiner no longer has to reach so far in and back to touch the cervical os.

Many women dilate to three centimeters before regular contractions begin. With normal, irregular, Braxton Hicks contractions, considerable dilatation of the cervix can occur before labor begins.

Presenting Part and Presentation: The *presentation* is the part of the baby's body "presenting," or leading the way into the pelvic inlet opening and birth canal. If the head is coming down first, this is called a cephalic presentation, which is the most common presentation, occurring

96 percent of the time. If a shoulder is coming down first, this is called a shoulder presentation, which is considered an abnormal presentation or malpresentation, because it only occurs in 1 percent of all births. If the buttocks are coming down first, this is called a *breech presentation,* which occurs in 3 percent of all births and is considered a malpresentation. There are three classifications of breech presentation. In *frank breech* presentation, the legs are both straight up and the buttocks present. In *complete breech* presentation, the buttocks present and the legs are crossed in a sitting position. In *footling breech* presentation, one or both feet present. (See Figure 12-5, page 209.)

The part of the baby presenting and felt first on vaginal exam is called the *presenting part.* In a cephalic presentation the back, lower part of the baby's skull, the occiput, is usually the presenting part. However, the brow or the face can also sometimes present. Presentation and the presenting part can be confirmed with ultrasound.

Many women ask about *posterior presentation* when they come into labor. They have heard that back discomfort in labor is usually more severe with this presentation, so they want to know if this is the way their baby is presenting. In this presentation, the head is presenting (cephalic presentation), but the occiput (the lower back bone of the skull, which is used for position reference) faces the mother's back, or "posterior," not her anterior, or the pubic bone in the front. The nickname "sunny side up"

FIGURE 5-3

Effacement and Dilatation

In effacement the cervix thins; in dilatation the cervix opens.

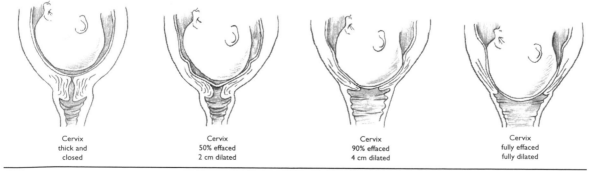

| Cervix thick and closed | Cervix 50% effaced 2 cm dilated | Cervix 90% effaced 4 cm dilated | Cervix fully effaced fully dilated |

can be confusing, because it refers to the "sunny smiling face" as a reference instead of the occiput. *Posterior* and *sunny side up* both refer to the same position. In posterior presentation the back or base of the baby's skull (occiput) is toward the mother's back or posterior side, and the "sunny" face therefore faces up toward her abdomen.

Waiting at the Station: Once your baby is engaged in the pelvis, your practitioner measures the *station* of the presenting part. *Station* refers to the position of the presenting part of the baby in relation to the mother's ischial spines, which are bony structures that can be felt during vaginal exam on each side of the mother's bony pelvis (Figure 5-4). If the presenting part is at the level of your ischial spines, your baby is described as being at zero station. If the presenting part is above the spines, your baby is described as being at –1 to –5 station (–5 indicating a presenting part that is still high and not well engaged in the pelvis). If your baby is +4 or +5, you are close to delivery! Therefore, the station refers to the level of descent of the presenting part into the pelvis. (Some practitioners still use an older scale for evaluating station, which ranges from –3 to +3. A –3 indicates that the presenting

part is not engaged. A +3 indicates that the presenting part is at the vaginal opening.)

As your baby descends far enough into the pelvis so that the presenting part is lower than your ischial spines, your station becomes +1 or +2. If you are carrying your baby low during pregnancy, you may be at +1 or +2 before labor begins, but +2 station usually occurs during the late stages of cervical dilatation or the pushing stage of labor. When the mother is pushing, the top of the baby's head is visible at the vaginal opening at +3 and +4 station. Delivery is imminent at +5 station.

If the presenting part is not engaged, your practitioner refers to it as *ballottable*. That means that the presenting part floats upward out of the pelvic cavity when pushed gently during a vaginal examination.

Evaluation of Your Nipples

If you are planning to breastfeed, pregnancy is the time to have your nipples evaluated by your care provider to determine whether they are normal, flat, or inverted. Normal nipples become erect when stimulated, whereas flat nipples do not protrude. Inverted nipples sometimes look pushed in all the time. An inverted nipple retracts into the breast when the areola is squeezed (Figure 5-5). Inverted nipples usually respond to care. If your nipples are flat or inverted, you may be asked to begin wearing cuppies for short periods during your last trimester of pregnancy (Figure 5-6).

New research indicates that during pregnancy, sleeping in cuppies or wearing them for long periods can cause nipple stimulation and lead to preterm labor. Therefore, if instructed to use them during your last trimester, do not sleep in them, and watch for signs and symptoms of preterm labor when wearing them. (See pages 115–118 for signs and symptoms of preterm labor.) Discontinue their use if symptoms of preterm labor occur. Your practitioner may prefer that you not wear cuppies until you are 37 weeks along.

FIGURE   5 - 4

Stations of Labor

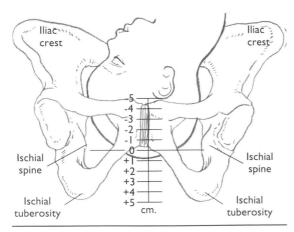

Used with permission of Ross Products Division, Abbott Laboratories, Columbus, OH 43216

FIGURE 5-5

An inverted nipple retracts more when the areola is compressed.

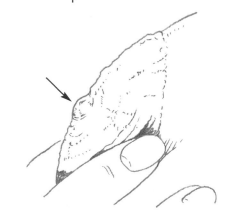

FIGURE 5-6

Cuppies for Treatment of Inverted Nipples

(A) The bottom section has a small opening for the nipple. (B) The top section is a vented plastic dome (with multiple air holes) that snaps over the bottom part to shield your nipple from clothing and allow for air circulation. (C) The two parts put together.

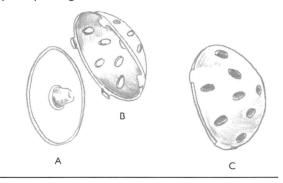

Wearing cuppies helps to pull your nipples out. If your nipples have not been assessed by the middle of your eighth month of pregnancy, ask your maternity care practitioner to do so.

Cuppies are available in most maternity stores and large drug stores. Be sure to buy a brand that is well vented with multiple air holes. Cuppies are also available through the La Leche League.

There is a surgical procedure in which the adhesions that cause inverted nipples are snipped. Many insurance companies will pay for this to be done, but not all surgeons are experienced in this procedure. If you choose to have this surgery and there is a surgeon in your area experienced in the procedure, you should have it done before you become pregnant.

Evaluation of Your Pelvis Size

Estimation of your pelvis size is a clinical judgment made by your obstetrician through a series of measurements and examination of your pelvis during vaginal exam. These are estimates only. Because of the danger of exposing your baby to radiation, X-rays are not used to determine pelvis size during pregnancy. Because these are estimates only, trial labors are normally allowed even if your pelvis appears to be narrow.

Nonstress Test (NST)

The first test ordered to evaluate fetal and placental well-being is called the nonstress test (NST). It is done with the same monitors used to evaluate your contractions and your baby during labor (Figure 5-7).

The old saying that "the apple falls from the tree when it is ripe" is true in most cases when applied to delivery. However, diabetes, high blood pressure, and certain other conditions (even if only present during pregnancy) can cause the placenta to age much more quickly than normal. Early aging of the placenta could cause stress to the growing fetus. In addition, if you are overdue or experiencing decreased fetal movement, special tests including a nonstress test may be ordered to evaluate your baby. A nonstress test is ordered any time your practitioner needs to evaluate how your baby is doing. It shows primarily whether the placenta is still healthy and functioning at optimal level.

You may be asked to come in for one or more of these tests every week, every few days, or daily during the last month of pregnancy. The frequency of the tests will be determined by the extent of your pregnancy complications and your previous test results. The results will determine whether labor induction or cesarean delivery is needed at this time.

If induction of labor is recommended after evaluation is completed, this does not guarantee a vaginal birth. If your baby shows signs of stress at any time during the induction, a cesarean delivery may be required. Also, these tests do not determine the adequacy of your pelvis size for vaginal birth.

Procedure: The nonstress test takes about 20 to 30 minutes, or longer if your baby is sleeping and needs to be awakened. The NST evaluates the baby's heart-rate response to fetal movements.

This is why the baby needs to be awake. Drinking cold fluids, gentle abdominal massage, and, if necessary, a device placed on the abdomen that makes a loud noise are used to awaken a sleeping fetus.

A nonstress test is not painful in any way. Two devices will be strapped on your abdomen with a belt. One, an ultrasound device, will monitor the baby's heart rate. The other, a tocotransducer, commonly called a *toco,* will detect contractions if they are present. Both the baby's heart rate and the uterine contraction pattern will be graphed on recording paper (Figure 5-7). You will be asked to push a button or tell the nurse each time you feel the baby move during the test. Fetal movement is then automatically or manually marked on the monitor strip. A healthy fetus's heartbeat will accelerate after fetal movement.

Risk: There are no harmful effects of ultrasound in pregnancy. However, its use should be limited to when it is clinically indicated.

FIGURE 5-7

Electronic Fetal Monitor Used for Nonstress Test

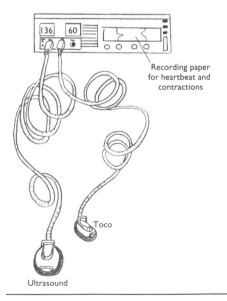

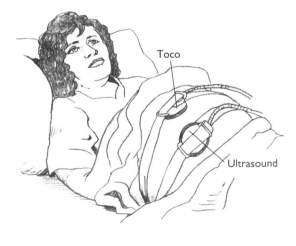

Results: Your test will be called *reactive* if it meets the criteria for fetal movement and fetal heart-rate accelerations. A reactive pattern is associated with fetal well-being. If your test is reactive, nothing further may be done for a few days.

If your nonstress test is nonreactive or questionable, or if further information is needed to evaluate your baby, your practitioner may refer you for a biophysical profile.

Biophysical Profile (BPP)

The *biophysical profile* (BPP) is an ultrasound test that assesses the well-being of your baby on the basis of five factors: breathing movement, body movement, muscle tone, amniotic fluid volume, and fetal heart rate. The first four factors are assessed with ultrasound. Together with the NST, which measures fetal heart rate, the BPP provides your practitioner with detailed information about your baby. In scoring the BPP, each of these five factors is given a possible score of zero to two. See Table 5-1.

Procedure: Same as for ultrasound.

Risks: None.

Results: Based on the total score, your practitioner may recommend one of the following: no treatment, repeat testing at a later date, or induction of labor to protect the health of your baby.

External Version

If you are at 37 weeks gestation and your baby is found to be in a shoulder or breech presentation, an obstetrician can attempt to turn the baby into a normal head-down (vertex) presentation. This procedure, called an *external version,* is successful about 70 percent of the time in turning your baby to a more favorable presentation for labor.

Before an external version is attempted, an ultrasound must be done to rule out the possibility of *placenta previa* (the placenta being attached over the cervical opening). Because a vaginal birth cannot occur with placenta previa, it makes no sense to do a version if it is present. In addition, the ultrasound will be used to determine whether you have adequate amniotic fluid, because this is a requirement before a version is attempted. The results of the ultrasound will also confirm that you are at at least 37 weeks gestation and rule out any other abnormalities. A version will not be attempted if you have twins, if you have an abnormally shaped or double-chambered uterus, if you have an abnormally small amount of amniotic fluid, or if you have had a previous cesarean delivery.

Your practitioner will also require that a non stress test be done to verify fetal well-being before attempting an external version.

You will be asked not to eat for at least six hours before your external version is scheduled. You will have an IV inserted and be given medication to relax your uterus. The physician will place his or her hands in certain positions on your abdomen and, through a series of maneuvers, will attempt to move your baby into the head-down position. Your baby's heart rate will be monitored intermittently during the procedure and for about 20 minutes after it is completed to be certain that your baby is tolerating it.

An external version usually takes less than 10 minutes, but it can be uncomfortable. You may

TABLE 5-1

Biophysical Profile

Test	Factor	Possible score
From NST:	Fetal heart rate	0 to 2
From ultrasound:		
	Fetal movements	0 to 2
	Fetal muscle tone	0 to 2
	Fetal breathing movements	0 to 2
	Amniotic fluid volume	0 to 2
Total score		0 to 10

experience cramping and a sensation of pressure. Relaxation breathing techniques are usually helpful. The medication commonly used to help relax your uterus for an external version also increases your pulse rate. It may cause you to have heart palpitations and feel as though your heart is racing. In addition, you may experience nervousness, headache, sweating, nausea, vomiting, and dryness of the nose and mouth from the medication. These symptoms may last up to four hours.

If an external version is successful, you will be asked to avoid lying flat for 24 hours. If an external version is unsuccessful, some physicians will perform a vaginal breech delivery (when you go into labor) after careful assessment of several factors. Such things as the length of your pregnancy, the size of your baby and your pelvis, and the type of breech presentation influence whether or not a vaginal delivery will be attempted. Other physicians will not consider a vaginal delivery with breech presentation and will insist that you have a cesarean delivery.

Following an external version, whether it is successful or not in turning the baby, report any signs of decreased fetal movement, spontaneous rupture of membranes, or signs and symptoms of labor.

Contraction Stress Test (CST)

Based on the information provided by your NST, ultrasound, or biophysical profile, your practitioner may feel more information is needed. She or he may order a *contraction stress test* (CST) to evaluate whether your placenta and baby can tolerate the stress of labor.

Do not be concerned if a CST is not ordered for you; it is not a routine test. Normally, enough information is obtained from the NST, ultrasound, and BPP to determine how your practitioner should best direct your care.

In the CST, contractions are initiated either by nipple stimulation (nipple-stimulated contraction stress test) or with the use of oxytocin (oxytocin-stimulated contraction stress test, or OCT)

until you have three contractions, each lasting from 40 to 60 seconds, within a 10-minute period. (Oxytocin and Pitocin are two names for the same medication.)

Procedure

Nipple-Stimulated Contraction Stress Test: If spontaneous contractions are not occurring, warm moist washcloths are applied to both breasts. You are asked to massage or roll the nipple of one breast for 10 minutes. If contractions do not occur, you are asked to stimulate both breasts for 10 minutes and to restimulate them as long as necessary to maintain uterine contractions. If contractions do not occur with nipple stimulation, an OCT will be done.

Oxytocin-Stimulated Contraction Stress Test (OCT): An OCT requires that an intravenous (IV) line be started because oxytocin, the drug used to bring on contractions, is diluted in an IV solution for this test. This solution is then inserted into the tubing of a mainline IV that contains no other medication. An electric pump is used to accurately deliver very small, controlled amounts of medication. The dosage is very slowly increased at 15- to 20-minute intervals until three uterine contractions are observed within a 10-minute period. The fetal heart rate pattern is then interpreted. This test is done to assess whether your baby can tolerate the natural stress of uterine labor contractions.

Results: Contractions temporarily decrease the rate of blood flow through the placenta. A healthy, active fetus has plenty of reserve, and the heart rate will not change with contractions. This would be defined as a negative CST result. A negative CST result provides reassurance that your baby will tolerate labor if it occurs within the next week.

A *compromised* fetus will exhibit a decreased heart rate for a short time after a contraction. These late decelerations are reason for concern, indicating that the relationship between your uterus and placenta is no longer healthy. When late decelerations occur with more than half of the contractions during your CST, the result is said to be positive. A positive CST result suggests that your baby would not tolerate labor well. In this case, your doctor will try to correct any contributing problems or proceed directly to a cesarean delivery.

Risks: Overstimulation of the uterus, causing prolonged contractions, can occur. This usually subsides when the nipple stimulation is stopped or oxytocin is discontinued. Medications can be given to help relax the uterus if needed. If contractions do in fact cause fetal distress that does not resolve quickly, a cesarean section would be necessary.

Today we are not seeing as many nipple-stimulated contraction stress tests as before. Usually, if there is enough concern to order testing, the mother is admitted for induction and the beginning of the induction serves as the oxytocin-stimulated contraction stress test. In the early stages of induction (as well as throughout it), the baby is evaluated for its tolerance of contractions. If the baby tolerates contractions, the induction is allowed to continue according to protocol. If the baby shows signs of fetal distress with contractions, a cesarean delivery will be necessary.

Cordocentesis (PUBS)

Cordocentesis, or percutaneous umbilical blood sampling (PUBS), is used both to obtain fetal blood samples and to give fetal transfusions. It is done during the second and third trimesters to diagnose inherited blood disorders, allow for more definitive chromosome tests of malformed fetuses, and determine whether fetal acid-base status is imbalanced or fetal infection is present.

Cordocentesis is also used to assess and treat the complications to the fetus resulting when an Rh-negative mother previously had an Rh-positive pregnancy, miscarriage, or abortion and was not treated with Rhogam. In this case, in addition to obtaining the baby's blood type and red cell counts, the sample will show if the baby's blood contains the maternal antibodies and the degree of anemia (or breakdown of the baby's

red blood cells) caused by these antibodies. (To further understand the Rh incompatibility condition see pages 94–95). PUBS can also be used to administer a life-saving intrauterine blood transfusion to a fetus who is severely affected with this condition.

Procedure: Guided by ultrasound, a very thin needle is inserted through the abdominal wall into a fetal umbilical cord vessel. One to four milliliters of blood are removed for testing (Figure 5-8).

A blood transfusion with the PUBS procedure can be done five weeks earlier than with the procedure previously used for intrauterine transfusions.

Your baby will be monitored for about an hour after the procedure, and then an additional ultrasound will be done to ensure that bleeding did not occur from the puncture site.

Risks: Although the needle goes through the amniotic sac membrane to reach the umbilical

FIGURE 5-8

PUBS Technique Guided by Ultrasound

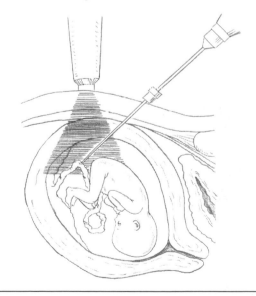

Adapted from Lowdermilk DL, Bobak IM, Perry SE, editors: Maternity & Women's Health Care, ed 6, St. Louis, 1997, Mosby, Inc.

Pregnancy

cord, premature rupture of membranes has not occurred with this procedure. Complications that can occur are bleeding from the umbilical cord puncture site, fetal bradycardia (decrease in the baby's heart rate), and infection within the amniotic fluid and surrounding membrane. Fetal loss is estimated at 1.6 percent from this procedure.

Results: PUBS is often done when time is important. The results are obtained faster than with amniocentesis. Karyotyping (chromosome studies) from a direct fetal blood sample can be obtained in two to three days.

6

When Pregnancy Means Special Care and Attention

With good prenatal care and a healthy diet, most women are well on their way to a healthy pregnancy and a healthy baby. For some women, however, special circumstances intervene, which can include multiple pregnancy (twins, triplets, or more!), a preexisting chronic health problem such as heart disease, or an acquired infection such as rubella (German measles). Special circumstances demand special care for you and your baby to help ensure the best possible outcome of your pregnancy.

Multiple Pregnancy

When you are pregnant with more than one fetus, you are said to have a multiple pregnancy. Twins are the most common multiple pregnancy. The tendency to have twins is genetic and is passed from mother to daughter. Twins occur in approximately 2 percent of all pregnancies.

Identical twins come from one egg that has been fertilized by a single sperm. For reasons that are unknown, this fertilized egg splits in

91

early pregnancy into two separate fetuses. Identical twins share one placenta, but each normally has its own amniotic sac. Identical twins share identical genetic material and therefore are the same sex and look exactly alike.

Fraternal (nonidentical) twins come from two separate eggs, each fertilized by a separate sperm and each having its own placenta. These two babies are as different as any other brothers or sisters would be. They can be two boys, two girls, or one of each, depending on the genetic makeup of each egg and sperm (as in any fertilization). You are slightly more likely to have fraternal twins if there is a family history of fraternal twins on the mother's side of your family tree. Approximately 66 percent of all twin pregnancies are fraternal twins.

The incidence of multiple births is increasing due to several factors. More women are waiting until later in life to have children, and women over 35 may have irregular ovulation and are more likely to ovulate more than one egg at a time. In addition, more couples are seeking treatment for infertility, which includes the administration of drugs to stimulate ovulation. These drugs increase the chance of multiple births, as does in-vitro fertilization.

There are factors that may cause your practitioner to suspect that you have a multiple pregnancy. See Box 6-1.

Diagnosis

Ultrasound can confirm a multiple pregnancy very early. Rarely is a couple surprised today with an unexpected "extra bundle" at birth. With early detection, prenatal care can now be adapted to better safeguard you and your babies. You will be instructed in precautions you should take to reduce your risk of multiple pregnancy complications and therefore to have a greater chance of carrying these babies to near term. You should expect to see your practitioner more frequently if you have a multiple pregnancy. Between the 20th and the 30th weeks of gestation you will most likely be seen by your doctor every other week, and thereafter every week. It is very important for the optimum health of both you and your babies to keep these appointments.

Maternal Risk

You are at greater risk for pregnancy-induced hypertension (high blood pressure) if you have a multiple pregnancy. It is very important to keep all of your prenatal appointments, so that any elevation in your blood pressure can be detected early and treated promptly.

Fetal and Newborn Risk

You are more likely to have preterm infants if you have a multiple pregnancy. Review the section in Chapter 7 titled "Signs and Symptoms of Premature Labor," pages 115–118. ©Report these symptoms promptly if you experience them.

BOX 6-1

Factors for Suspecting Multiple Pregnancy

- ❑ Weight gain more rapid than normal
- ❑ Uterus larger or higher than gestational age would indicate
- ❑ Two heartbeats detected
- ❑ Family history of twins
- ❑ Use of fertility drugs
- ❑ Hyperemesis (more common in multiple pregnancies)
- ❑ High alpha-fetoprotein (AFP) result

Anemia is also more common with twins, so supplemental iron is always given to women with multiple pregnancies.

You should expect to gain more weight during a multiple pregnancy. The average recommended weight gain for twins is 35 to 45 pounds, unless you are overweight when you become pregnant. This additional weight is not "your weight." The extra baby, placenta, and amniotic fluid all contribute added pounds. Low birth weight is a serious complication of multiple pregnancies. Listen to your doctor and take his or her advice. Gain the weight you are advised to gain. This will go a long way in helping your babies to be healthy at birth.

Prevention of Complications

The perinatal period is defined as the period from 20 weeks' gestation to one month after birth. It is estimated that 14 of every 1000 babies die during the perinatal period. In populations that are well nourished and receive good prenatal care, this number is reduced by 50 percent. In poorly nourished populations with poor prenatal care, the percentage of perinatal deaths is almost double the average.

For twins, perinatal death occurs in 65 to 100 of every 1000 births, and in triplets, 300 of every 1000. This information is not meant to frighten you. It is included here to further encourage you to seek prompt prenatal care when you become pregnant. It is also a clear reminder of the importance of nutrition, health, and prenatal care in pregnancy. **Close observation, and the education you receive through good prenatal care, can greatly reduce the risks of preterm labor and preterm delivery in any pregnancy.**

Prenatal vitamins plus additional iron are always prescribed during multiple pregnancies. Do not neglect to take the additional iron. If constipation becomes a problem, do not just stop the iron—ask your practitioner for help with this side effect. (See the section in Chapter 3 titled "Constipation," page 53, for helpful hints for preventing constipation.)

If you have a multiple pregnancy, you may be given steroid injections before 34 weeks' gestation to increase the rate of fetal lung maturation.

Nutrition

You must be extra conscious of your diet and be certain to eat adequate protein and calories. Eating foods high in iron, as well as taking your prenatal vitamins and iron, is important in treating the anemia that is always present in multiple pregnancies and in preventing more severe anemia. New research is being done every year in the field of nutrition and multiple pregnancies, so consult your practitioner. He or she will guide you in any additional dietary needs you or your babies might have above the normal needs for pregnancy. Your practitioner will individualize your nutrition plan and may also refer you to a dietitian.

Eating six smaller meals and nutritious snacks each day will help reduce indigestion and heartburn during a multiple pregnancy. Make each calorie count by trying to eliminate empty calories.

Activity, Rest, and Exercise

Expect to need extra rest if you are carrying twins. You and your babies will be better off if you don't fight this need. If at all possible, reduce your work hours or stop working earlier than expected if you need or are advised to do so. At around 24 weeks' gestation, many care providers will ask you to reduce your work hours and get one hour of rest in the morning and one and a half hours of rest in the afternoon. This added rest helps to reduce your risk of delivering too early.

Most care providers will recommend that you stop exercise after 20 weeks if you are carrying twins.

Almost every woman feels clumsier than usual when pregnant. You can double this feeling for twins. Take a few moments to sit upright before getting out of bed. Turn slowly and watch your footing—you may feel off balance. Be sure to hold handrails when using stairs.

Discomforts

You can expect an increase in the normal discomforts of pregnancy if you are carrying twins or triplets. Review the chapter on the possible discomforts of pregnancy and what can be done to help relieve them. Be sure to discuss with your practitioner any discomfort that is particularly bothersome, especially if it is preventing you from obtaining adequate nutrition or rest.

Labor and Birth

Your practitioner will assess the position of your babies when your due date nears and again when you enter the hospital in labor or for induction. If both babies are head down, your practitioner may allow you to have a vaginal delivery. If the first baby is head down and the higher baby is in another position, the practitioner may choose a vaginal delivery for the first baby and then attempt to turn the second. (See the section in Chapter 5 titled "External Version," page 87, for an explanation of this procedure.) If turning is unsuccessful, cesarean delivery may be necessary for delivery of the second baby. This is why mothers with twins (or other multiples) usually give birth in the cesarean section delivery room. A vaginal delivery of both twins can be done here; however, if needed, a cesarean delivery can be done immediately without moving or transporting the mother. A neonatologist (a specialist in high-risk newborns) or a pediatrician is usually readily available when a twin delivery is occurring.

Sometimes, after the first baby is born it is necessary to administer Pitocin to increase the frequency and strength of the contractions to facilitate the delivery of the second baby. It may also be necessary to use a vacuum extractor or forceps to help bring down the second baby. Your doctor will explain the reasons for his or her interventions whenever possible.

Under certain circumstances or when risk factors are present, your practitioner may feel that it is safer to deliver both babies by cesarean, regardless of their positions. You can expect a full explanation of his or her decision. Feel free to ask as many questions as you need in order to feel comfortable about accepting your practitioner's decision.

Rh-Negative Mothers (Rh−): Do I Need Rhogam?

At an early prenatal visit you will have a blood test to determine your blood type and Rh factor. Your Rh is a separate factor from the A, B, AB, or O blood type. It is an antigen that is either present (Rh positive) or not present (Rh negative) in your blood. Most people (85 percent) are Rh positive. Only 15 percent are Rh negative.

The Rh factor *only* creates a problem when an Rh-negative mother is pregnant with an Rh-positive baby, a condition called *Rh incompatibility*. This condition does not occur when an Rh-positive mother is pregnant with an Rh-negative baby. If you are Rh negative and you know for *certain* that the father of this baby is also Rh negative, then the Rh factor is not an issue.

The mother's and baby's blood circulation systems are separate and do not mix. Sometimes, however, antigen and antibody factors in the blood cross the placental barrier. An Rh-negative mother lacks the Rh-positive antigen. If she is pregnant with an Rh-positive baby, some of the baby's Rh-positive antigen may cross the placental barrier. If this occurs, the mother's system reacts to it like any other foreign agent: her system produces antibodies to attack the Rh-positive antigen. Although this does not harm this fetus, the next time this mother is pregnant with an Rh-positive baby, these antibodies are ready and waiting to cross the placenta and attack the baby's blood cells. The baby could die in utero or be born very ill, requiring an immediate blood transfusion. Rhogam prevents this antibody reaction in the mother from ever occurring, **if it is given during *every* pregnancy, after the birth of every Rh-positive baby, and after *every* miscarriage or abortion.**

Rhogam is given automatically at 28 weeks of pregnancy to all Rh-negative mothers (unless it is known without a doubt that the father of this baby is also Rh negative). You will receive Rhogam now because at this point, it is not known whether your baby is Rh positive. It is a preventive measure in case your baby is Rh positive. By receiving Rhogam now, your body is blocked from producing antibodies against the Rh-positive factor.

A specimen of blood from your baby's cord is obtained at birth. (There are no nerves in the cord; that is why it can be cut without any anesthetic.) The specimen is obtained from the cut end of the cord before it is clamped. If you are Rh negative, this specimen is sent to the lab to determine the blood type and Rh factor of your infant. If this test shows your infant also to be Rh negative, nothing further needs to be done. If your baby is Rh positive, however, you will be given another intramuscular injection of Rhogam within 72 hours of your delivery.

Rhogam is also given to Rh-negative mothers as a preventive measure after *any and every* miscarriage or abortion. In these cases, your practitioner is unsure of the baby's Rh status. **The secret to preventing this problem is never allowing the mother to build up her own antibodies against the Rh-positive factor.** If Rhogam is given after every pregnancy, miscarriage, or abortion, the mother never builds up her own antibodies. Every pregnancy is then like the first—that is, the baby is not affected. ✆**Therefore, if you are Rh negative or do not know for sure, call an obstetrician if you have a miscarriage or an abortion. A simple blood test will determine your blood type and whether Rhogam is needed.**

For mothers who are known to already have developed antibodies against the Rh-positive factor, you will need to be followed very carefully during your pregnancy. Intrauterine blood transfusions can be done on the baby (fetus) during pregnancy, if necessary. (See the section in Chapter 5 titled "Cordocentesis (PUBS)," page 89.)

This can prevent the anemia and cardiac problems that develop from this condition.

Chronic Health Problems in Pregnancy

Having a chronic health problem does not mean that pregnancy will be difficult or impossible, but it does mean that you need to understand how your health problem will affect the pregnancy and your baby and how the pregnancy will affect your health problem.

Chronic health problems are long-term conditions that may require continuing medications or other treatment. A woman with any chronic health problem should consult her medical doctor prior to conception to learn how her illness will affect her pregnancy and what the additional risks may be and to be certain that the medication she is taking is safe during pregnancy. (For example, in the case of chronic hypertension some medications are safe to continue during pregnancy and others are not.)

Some of the most common chronic health problems are diabetes, heart disease, epilepsy, asthma, lupus, arthritis or other autoimmune disorders, thyroid disorders, lung disease, and kidney disease. Some chronic conditions are easily managed during pregnancy and pose no risk to your developing baby. Other conditions will need to be closely managed and pose some increased risks to the baby. For example, chronic hypertension increases the risk of your developing pregnancy-induced hypertension (which is called "superimposed" pregnancy-induced hypertension when you already had chronic hypertension). By asking questions before you conceive, you will be able to make an informed decision about pregnancy.

If you have a chronic health problem and you suspect that you are pregnant, you need to inform your practitioner promptly. Be certain to make it **very clear** to the person in the office who receives your call that you have a special health problem and will need to be seen by the doctor promptly.

Don't assume that the receptionist knows you, knows that you have a chronic condition, or understands the importance of your having a prompt appointment. Be very specific, and ask to speak with a registered nurse if you are booked into the regular time for the first prenatal visit.

Feel free to ask your practitioner if she or he has experience in handling pregnancies of mothers with your specific chronic health condition. If she or he does not have this experience, you need to ask for a referral to a practitioner who routinely handles high-risk pregnancies. Your chances of remaining healthy throughout your pregnancy, and therefore reducing risks to both yourself and your baby, are much better with close monitoring of your pregnancy by an obstetrician with experience in high-risk pregnancies. You can expect information, teaching, guidance, close monitoring of your pregnancy and condition, and follow-up care when under the care of an experienced practitioner.

Urinary Tract Infections

Urinary tract infections are common in pregnancy. The usual symptoms are pain or burning on passing urine, urinating more frequently than usual, and a feeling that you still need to go immediately after finishing urinating. Discomfort and pressure in the lower abdomen may also be present. Urinary tract infections can also occur without symptoms. If a urinary tract infection has spread upward to your kidneys, you may experience chills, fever, nausea, and vomiting.

Urinary tract infections are a frequent cause of premature labor. ⒸTherefore, if **you have any of the following symptoms, contact your obstetrician or midwife promptly:**

- **Pain or burning when you urinate**
- **A need to urinate frequently, even right after you finish urinating**
- **Discomfort or pressure in the lower abdomen**
- **Chills, fever, nausea, and vomiting**
- **Uterine contractions**

Your practitioner will ask you to obtain a clean-catch urine specimen (in a sterile container provided by practitioner). Before obtaining this specimen, you need to clean your perineum. With your nondominant hand, hold the folds of your perineum apart. With your dominant hand, clean your perineum **from front to back** three times, using a new antiseptic wipe each time. First clean one side. Then take a clean wipe and clean the other side. With the third wipe go directly down the middle. Still holding the folds of your perineum open, begin to urinate into the toilet and then "catch" a midstream specimen in the sterile container. It is important that you do not touch the inside of this container or the inside of the lid with your hands. Follow all directions carefully so as not to contaminate the specimen with germs from your hands or an improperly prepared perineum.

Your urine specimen will be sent to a laboratory for analysis. If bacteria are present, this indicates that you have a urinary tract infection. The test will also identify which organism is causing the infection, so your practitioner can determine which antibiotic will be effective against it.

With the correct antibiotic, most patients recover from the symptoms of urinary tract infection within two days. **However, you must take the entire prescription to kill all the bacteria present.**

TORCH Infections

Some infections can adversely affect a developing baby. Many of these infections can be prevented by immunization; others can be prevented by avoiding exposure to infected individuals. It's important to understand these infections, how they happen, and whether they are communicable from one person to another.

TORCH is an acronym developed to make it easier to remember the infections that may affect pregnancy. These infections include **T**oxoplasmosis, **O**ther infections (hepatitis A, B, and C), **R**ubella, **C**ytomegalovirus (CMV), and **H**erpes simplex viruses (HSVs).

Toxoplasmosis

Toxoplasmosis is an acute infection caused by a parasite. Humans are exposed to this parasite through infected cat stool and the litter box of an infected cat. (Rodents are the reservoir that infects cats. If your cat lives indoors and does not come into contact with rodents, raw meat, or outdoor cats, it is unlikely to be infected with this parasite.) Humans and cats can also become infected by eating raw or undercooked lamb, beef, or pork.

Symptoms: This parasite produces only a mild illness in 80 percent of adults it infects. Symptoms, when present, are swollen lymph glands and mild viral symptoms that mimic symptoms of many other viral illnesses. Sometimes there are no symptoms at all. If you have had cats for some time, you may have already been exposed to this parasite and developed immunity to it. There is a test to determine whether you have immunity to toxoplasmosis, and your cat can be tested to see if it has an active infection.

Fetal Risk: For women who are *not immune* to toxoplasmosis, exposure to this parasite just prior to or during pregnancy may cause the fetus to be infected. The point in the pregnancy at which the initial infection occurs is important—the fetus is at greatest risk of serious damage if the infection occurs in the first three months of gestation. However, the likelihood of an infant's becoming infected from a mother's infection is the smallest during the first three months. On the other hand, during the last three months of pregnancy the fetus is at greatest risk of becoming infected, but the risk of serious damage to the fetus from an infection in these last three months is small.

If symptoms are present, the effects on the infant's central nervous system can be devastating. Effects on the baby include abortion, death, prematurity, low birth weight for gestational age, fever, jaundice, abnormalities of the retina, mental retardation, abnormal head size, convulsions, and brain calcification.

Prevention: Some, but not all, maternity care practitioners routinely screen for toxoplasmosis immunity before pregnancy or during the first prenatal visit. If immune, you do not have to worry. If not immune, you can protect your fetus by means of the following precautions.

To protect yourself during pregnancy if you are not immune to toxoplasmosis avoid contact with unfamiliar cats and with all cat litter boxes. Have someone else empty the litter box daily. (Cat feces are not infectious during the first 24 hours. They become infectious as time passes.) If you must empty the litter box yourself, wear gloves and wash your hands thoroughly immediately afterward.

Wear gloves when gardening where you might also come in contact with cat feces. Wash your hands thoroughly after gardening outdoors where cats may have been. (Remember, the transmission is from the infected cat's stool to your hands and later up to your mouth. Good handwashing is imperative to prevent transmission.)

Remember to wash all garden vegetables after touching them and before eating them. Be certain that all red meat (lamb, veal, beef, and pork) you eat is adequately cooked. The internal temperature at the center of your cooked meat should read at least 140 degrees. When eating out, order your meat well done. Do not give your cat raw meat.

Treatment: If you have been exposed, as proven by a blood test, your practitioner will discuss your options with you. Amniocentesis and cordocentesis can determine whether infection of the fetus has occurred; however, these are not options in very early pregnancy. If toxoplasmosis infection is present during pregnancy, treatment with antibiotics will be given for several months to reduce the risk of severe damage to the baby.

Hepatitis A

Hepatitis A, B, and C fall under the **O** in the acronym TORCH. They represent three of the **O**ther infections that can affect pregnancy.

Hepatitis A virus, also known as infectious hepatitis, is spread through the fecal–oral route. It is initially picked up from the stool (feces) of an infected person and, through poor hand-washing practices, passed to the mouth. Hepatitis A can be spread through the water supply in underdeveloped countries where water is contaminated with feces. It can also be spread in restaurants if employees do not use good hand-washing technique before handling or preparing food.

Hepatitis A is very common in children under five years old. The symptoms in children are usually very mild, and sometimes no symptoms are present. In adults, two to six weeks after exposure, flu-like symptoms appear. Hepatitis A can cause mild to severe liver disease. It is an uncommon complication of pregnancy in developed countries with monitored water supplies. If it occurs in pregnancy it can lead to miscarriage, and if the mother is not treated with Υ-globulin, fetal transmission can occur, although it is extremely rare.

Fetal Risk: If transmission does occur in the first three months of pregnancy, it can cause fetal developmental abnormalities, premature birth, fetal death, and hepatitis in the fetus or the development of hepatitis after birth. However, transmission to the fetus and these complications are very uncommon.

Prevention: Proper hand-washing after defecation is the best protection against hepatitis A transmission. Hepatitis A vaccine is available and can be given during pregnancy to meet travel requirements if necessary.

Hepatitis B

Of the three hepatitis viruses, hepatitis B is of primary concern because it can have lifelong effects on your developing baby. Hepatitis B virus is transmitted through contaminated blood transfusions, the sharing of contaminated needles, and sexual contact with an infected person. (Donated blood is screened today for this virus.) A blood test can confirm the diagnosis of hepatitis B.

People who abuse intravenous drugs or have multiple sexual partners are at greater risk of contracting hepatitis B. In addition, certain professionals who come into contact with blood and body fluids are at increased risk for exposure (doctors, nurses, and lab technicians).

All women are now screened for hepatitis B at an early prenatal visit. Women at risk for hepatitis B who test negative can still be given three doses of hepatitis B vaccine, which are safe during pregnancy. Increasing numbers of women are being vaccinated against hepatitis B earlier in life, before pregnancy. In an unvaccinated woman, the above vaccine can be given along with hepatitis B immune globulin (HBIG) within two weeks of exposure to prevent infection.

During pregnancy, common symptoms of a hepatitis B infection are fever, nausea, vomiting, rash, decreased appetite, fatigue, and possibly pain over the liver (just under the bottom edge of the rib cage on the right side). Hepatitis B can eventually cause cirrhosis of the liver or liver cancer. Up to 10 percent of infected persons become permanent carriers of this disease.

Hepatitis B can be transmitted to the fetus across the placenta and during childbirth through contact with contaminated urine, vaginal secretions, and feces. The risk of transmission to the fetus is greatest if the mother contracts the virus close to the time of delivery.

Fetal Risk: As mentioned above, all pregnant women are given a blood test (normally at the first prenatal visit) to determine whether they have been exposed to hepatitis B in the past, whether they are carriers, or if they have the active illness. About 90 percent of infants whose mothers have chronic hepatitis B will become infected. Premature birth and all the complications associated with it are only part of the risks to the infant. If not treated, about 90 percent of infected infants will become chronic carriers of this virus. They are also at risk of developing hepatitis, which may later lead to serious liver inflammation and chronic liver disease, including cirrhosis and cancer of the liver.

Prevention: In the United States, the Centers for Disease Control recommends that all pregnant women be screened for hepatitis B early in pregnancy. If you test positive for hepatitis B virus (antigen), your baby will be treated with intramuscular injections of hepatitis B immune globulin and the first of three hepatitis B vaccine injections at birth. Although the hepatitis B virus can be found in breast milk, you will be allowed to nurse your baby as long as she or he is treated with the above-mentioned injections.

If you test negative for hepatitis B antigen, you will be offered the option of hepatitis B vaccine for your infant. The vaccine is given in three doses over a six-month period. Your pediatrician will discuss the vaccine series with you prior to your discharge from the hospital and will ask you to sign a consent form if you choose to have your infant receive these vaccinations. The first dose of vaccine will be given in the hospital, and you will be given a record of this vaccination. You will need to follow up with your pediatrician for your baby to receive the remaining two vaccinations in the series.

Vaccination against hepatitis B is recommended for anyone with high-risk behavior, including drug users who share needles. It is also recommended for people in professions that have contact with blood (such as lab technicians and health care workers).

In some states, vaccination against hepatitis B is required for all children who attend day care, and it will soon be a requirement for entry into kindergarten. Many states are now providing the vaccination series to middle school students, and many pediatricians are suggesting it before teenagers leave for college. All of this is being done in the hope of wiping out this serious illness.

Hepatitis C

Hepatitis C is another form of hepatitis found primarily among intravenous drug users and individuals who have had blood transfusions. Hepatitis C is becoming more of a concern, because the virus has been thought to affect fetuses in a few cases. There is presently no prevention available other than to avoid the modes of transmission.

Rubella (German Measles)

Symptoms: Symptoms are usually slight: low-grade fever, drowsiness, sore throat, swollen glands, and a mild rash that develops on the first or second day and vanishes in two to three days. The rash begins on the face and spreads to the whole body. It vanishes quickly in one area even before it appears in other areas.

Fetal Risk: When mothers develop German measles during pregnancy, their babies may have birth defects, including heart malformations and irreversible vision and hearing disorders. Some of the effects are delayed and don't show up until years later. If the mother is exposed to the virus and does not develop symptoms of the illness, the fetus is not at risk. The risk of malformations to the fetus is highest when the mother develops the illness during the first month of pregnancy. By the third month of pregnancy the risk, although still significant, is greatly reduced. Because nothing can be done during pregnancy to protect an exposed baby, every attempt should be made to establish the mother's immunity prior to pregnancy.

Prevention: Most women have either had German measles, usually during childhood, or been immunized against the virus. Either method provides permanent immunity. If you're not sure if you've had it or been vaccinated, a simple blood test can show if you are immune to German measles. If you have been receiving annual checkups, this issue has probably been addressed prior to your conceiving. If you are not immune, a vaccination can be given to you, and you will be advised not to get pregnant for three months following your vaccination. Vaccinations have not been proven, however, to cause the birth defects that can occur with the actual illness. This fact should help you rest better if you received a vaccination for German measles and then found you were pregnant.

At one of your early prenatal visits, your practitioner will order a blood test to determine whether you are immune to German measles. If you are not immune, a vaccination will be recommended following your delivery. (Vaccinations against German measles are not given during pregnancy.)

If you are pregnant and not immune to German measles, every attempt should be made to avoid contact with children and adults who have been exposed to this virus. The incubation period for German measles is two to three weeks. It can be transmitted to others from one day before symptoms begin to at least one day after the rash disappears. If you are pregnant and believe you have been exposed, contact your practitioner.

Cytomegalovirus (CMV)

Up to 60 percent of all children are infected by cytomegalovirus (CMV) before the age of five. This means that you may have had this illness as a small child.

Cytomegalovirus is present in urine, stool, semen, vaginal secretions, and saliva. It is not known exactly how it is spread; however, it can be passed from one individual to another through close contact such as kissing (through the saliva), through contact with urine and stool (diaper changes), or through sexual contact. It is not very contagious, however.

Symptoms: Cytomegalovirus is hard to diagnose because it often occurs without symptoms. When symptoms do occur, they are similar to mononucleosis symptoms: fatigue, fever, sore throat, and swollen lymph glands. You probably aren't certain whether you had CMV as a child, but a test can be done during the prenatal period to determine past exposure.

Fetal Risk: If you had CMV as a child, the virus may be activated again by a new exposure, but this reactivated virus is unlikely to be passed to your fetus. Among mothers infected for the first time with CMV during pregnancy, the virus will infect about 50 percent of their fetuses. Only 10 percent of these fetuses will show signs of the disease, however. CMV can be transmitted to an infant during pregnancy through the placenta,

during delivery through the vagina, or after delivery through breast milk.

About 1 percent of all infants are born with CMV, but only a very small percentage of these infants show any of the adverse effects of being exposed to this virus while in utero. Possible symptoms from exposure to CMV in utero are deafness to high-frequency sounds, vision problems, and jaundice. In severe generalized infections, anemia, hydrocephaly (abnormally large head), microcephaly (abnormally small head), mental retardation, inflammation of the lungs, and fetal death can occur.

Prevention: If your blood test shows that you have never been infected with CMV, your practitioner may recommend that you avoid regular or daily contact with large numbers of preschool children during the first 24 weeks of pregnancy, when the risk to the fetus is the greatest. (Not all practitioners agree with this restriction.)

Use good hand-washing technique when caring for small children. Wearing gloves during diaper changes or practicing diligent hand-washing afterward is a good way to avoid exposure to CMV. It is also advisable to avoid eating leftover food from children's plates. Because immunosuppressed individuals (cancer patients on chemotherapy, persons with HIV/AIDS) often have this virus, if you work with them or with dialysis patients, a temporary leave of absence may be recommended.

All health care workers are required to use Universal Precautions on all patients. Health care workers who are pregnant should be certain that they are practicing Universal Precautions at all times of contact with blood and body fluids.

Herpes Simplex Viruses

Herpes simplex virus type 1 (HSV-1) causes cold sores and fever blisters and is transmitted primarily by contact with oral secretions, especially through kissing. This virus is not cause for concern during pregnancy.

Herpes simplex virus type 2 (HSV-2) infections are transmitted primarily through sexual contact, including external genital contact with genital secretions. (Teenagers need to be informed that HSV-2 can be transmitted with external genital contact even without internal intercourse.)

Symptoms: Painful blisters on the cervix, in the vagina, or on the external genitals occur, rupture, and then disappear (taking two to six weeks to complete this process). During the initial exposure to HSV-2, systemic symptoms of the illness are much like those of the flu: chills, fever, headache, fatigue, and generalized aches for several days. In addition to flu-like symptoms, pain and itching in the genital area occur, as well as pain on urination. Other symptoms may include vaginal discharge or discharge around the urethra (the opening from which urine is passed) and swollen glands in the groin. External blisters are sometimes seen on the genitals or buttocks; however, lesions may all be internal.

The blisters take up to three weeks to heal, during which time an infected individual can give this illness to others. Intercourse should be avoided when either you or your partner have lesions. Keep lesions clean, dry, and exposed to air (loose cotton clothing is best), and always wash your hands after using the bathroom.

During the course of the initial infection, the virus migrates to one or more sensory nerves, where it lies dormant indefinitely or until stress causes another lesion outbreak. The precipitating stress can be from another infection, fever, emotions, or a positive event like a marriage, a new baby, or a new job.

Fetal Risk: ℰ**If you believe that you have been infected with HSV-2 since you became pregnant, or you experience the above symptoms, notify your obstetrician.** It is the mother's first exposure to genital herpes that poses the greatest risk to an unborn child. A primary infection early in pregnancy increases the chances of miscarriage and premature delivery. Infection through the placenta is rare, but the effects are serious. Small brain, mental retardation, and car-

diac abnormalities are possible consequences to the fetus. The greatest risk to the infant results when the primary infection occurs late in pregnancy and the baby is delivered vaginally when vaginal blisters are present.

Symptoms of an infection acquired during the birth process (from exposure of the baby to cervical, vaginal, or external lesions) occur within four to seven days after birth. They include lethargy, poor feeding ability, jaundice, bleeding, pneumonia, convulsions, opisthotonos (arched position of the body), bulging fontanels, and lesions on the skin and in the mouth. Newborns infected with the systemic disease have an 82 percent mortality rate. Those who survive suffer central nervous system damage, which may include mental retardation and blindness, and the infection usually recurs during the first five years of life.

If this is not your first herpes outbreak, your baby has only a 2 to 3 percent chance of infection. Secondary infection symptoms in the mother are mild in comparison with those of the initial infection. Lesions are present without the more generalized systemic symptoms. Recurrent outbreaks are sometimes preceded by a burning feeling in the genital area or itching. Some women also report tingling in the legs and a slight increase in their normal vaginal discharge before recurrent outbreaks of HSV-2.

Prevention: If you become infected with HSV-2 prior to pregnancy, good medical care can greatly reduce the risks to your infant. Many doctors test pregnant women only when they develop genital lesions near the time of their due date. If the culture is positive, repeat cultures will be done closer to delivery. If a recent culture is positive or you still have genital lesions when you go into labor or rupture your membranes, a cesarean delivery is usually performed because babies can contract HSV-2 by passing through an infected birth canal.

ℰ**It is always very important to tell your obstetrician if you believe your membranes have ruptured.** If you also have an active herpes genital lesion and your fetus is mature enough for delivery when your membranes rupture, cesarean delivery is performed within four hours. (Once the protection of the sac is no longer present, the risk of HSV-2 exposure to the fetus increases.)

Mothers who have an active HSV-2 lesion can still care for their infants and breastfeed, as long as the lesion is covered and hands are washed thoroughly after using the bathroom and before handling the baby.

Treatment: Newborns who may have been exposed to HSV-2 infection during a prolonged period in utero after rupture of membranes or during vaginal birth over blisters are usually isolated from other infants. If infection occurs, treatment with an antiviral drug will reduce the severity of the infection. *There is no cure for HSV-2;* therefore, symptomatic treatment is all that is available.

Additional Infections That May Affect Pregnancy

Chickenpox (Varicella)

Many people have been infected with chickenpox as children and have developed antibodies as a result. You can be tested prior to pregnancy to verify whether or not you have antibodies against chickenpox.

Fetal Risk: Although newborn effects from maternal chickenpox are rare (about 2 percent), miscarriage or fetal death can occur. The fetus is most at risk if exposure occurs during the first half of pregnancy, but even this risk is low: only 2 to 10 infected fetuses out of 100 will develop defects in the skin, bone, muscle, and eye, as well as hydrocephalus (fluid on the brain with enlarged head). If the mother develops chickenpox in the last five days of pregnancy, her body does not have time to develop antibodies and pass them to the fetus (a process that takes one to two weeks). However, these infants have about a 15 to 30 percent chance of being infected at birth and devel-

oping the chickenpox rash about a week later. Because newborn varicella can be serious, varicella zoster immunoglobulin (VZIG) is usually given by injection to the baby after birth.

*(Ⓒ)***If you have not had chickenpox and believe you have been exposed during your pregnancy, contact your practitioner promptly. A medication (VZIG) can be safely given *post-exposure* to decrease the risk of your contracting the disease. It should be given within 96 hours of your exposure to chickenpox.**

Prevention: A vaccination against chickenpox has recently been approved for use in the United States. It is recommended that you avoid pregnancy for three months after receiving this vaccination. Once vaccination against chickenpox becomes routine, it will no longer be an issue during pregnancy.

It is difficult to prevent exposure to chickenpox, because a person is infectious before the characteristic blisters appear, as well as during approximately the first week after the blisters appear (or until two days after new pox have stopped appearing). The completely dried scabs are not infectious.

Fifth Disease

There is a group of six diseases that cause fever and skin rash in children. Fifth Disease (parvovirus B 19) got its name by being the fifth of this group. Fifth Disease is not as well known as others in the group (such as chickenpox) because the symptoms are mild and may even go unnoticed. However, it is a very common childhood disease—half of all adults have antibodies to this illness, proving that they had the illness in the past.

Symptoms: Up to 30 percent of cases are associated with fever. The rash begins on the cheeks and spreads in a lacelike pattern to the chest, abdomen, buttocks, and upper legs. The rash comes and goes and seems to appear when the body is exposed to a heat source such as the sun or warm water.

Fetal Risk: If you have your first exposure to parvovirus B 19 during your first four months of pregnancy, you are at a slightly increased risk of having a miscarriage (about 1 to 2 percent higher than the normal miscarriage rate, which is approximately 20 percent of all pregnancies). Exposure in later pregnancy may cause the fetus to be born with anemia, which can be treated. Once you have had parvovirus, you are immune, so future pregnancies would not be at risk for Fifth Disease.

Prevention: Casual contact with children does not pose a great risk of exposure to parvovirus. However, if you are pregnant, you should avoid caring for a child who is sick with this illness and avoid working in a school during an epidemic of Fifth Disease.

Treatment: Although it happens very rarely, parvovirus can cause a type of anemia in the fetus. If you have had parvovirus during your pregnancy, your fetus will be monitored with ultrasound to detect the characteristic swelling caused by this form of anemia. Treatment for the fetus is available if this rare condition occurs as a result of your illness with Fifth Disease.

Group B Streptococcus

In recent years, group B streptococcus infection (GBS) has become more recognized as an important factor in maternal and newborn infection and infant death. As a result, new treatment strategies decrease the risk of these complications.

About 10 percent of the population are carriers of this organism. (Group A streptococcus, which causes strep throat, is not the same bacteria as group B streptococcus.) Group B streptococcus commonly thrives in the gastrointestinal tract, rectum, vagina, cervix, and urethra. *To be a carrier means that you have the bacteria, but no symptoms are present.* However, this organism does have the *potential* to cause serious illness in women during and after pregnancy. In addition, it can infect the infant by traveling up the vagina into the uterus after the membranes have rup-

tured. The baby can also be exposed during vaginal birth and from direct contact with an infected person after birth (due to poor hand-washing). Group B streptococcus infection is the most common bacterial infection causing illness and death in newborns. According to the Centers for Disease Control and Prevention there are about 8000 cases of GBS disease in newborns annually, and 5 to 15 percent of these infants die.

Maternal Risk: A carrier of GBS may develop an active infection with signs and symptoms of illness if the bacteria spreads outside of its original site. In other words, if the organism spreads from the rectum or vagina to the bladder or the amniotic fluid, active infection occurs.

Several conditions increase the risk of the dormant GBS bacteria spreading outside of its original source and therefore converting to an active infection. It is apparent that if you have had an infant who developed a GBS active infection, each infant after that is at increased risk. There are also several things that your lab results can tell your practitioner that would indicate increased risk (large amounts of the bacteria found in your culture, bacteria found in your urine, and low levels of certain antibodies in your blood).

One study showed that the longer the labor and the longer the time from rupture of membranes to delivery, the greater the risk. Internal monitoring of the baby's heartbeat and the mother's contractions also increased the risk. In addition, the risk of active infection increased with each vaginal exam done during labor. Obstetrical practitioners should consider these risk factors in the care they provide to women who test positive for group B streptococcus.

If active infection occurs during pregnancy, it can lead to miscarriage, stillbirth, preterm birth, urinary tract infection, inflamed kidneys, scarlet fever, fever, and wound infections. If active infection occurs during labor, the most common results are chorioamnionitis (inflammation of the fetal membranes—the amniotic sac and placenta attachment site) and endometritis (inflammation of the lining of the uterus). Overwhelming infection (septic shock) and meningitis can also occur with any active GBS infection.

After delivery, a developing active GBS infection in the mother usually begins with fever, chills, tenderness over the uterus, and a general feeling of lethargy (drowsiness and feelings of indifference). These infections usually respond quickly to intravenous antibiotics; however, although rare, very serious and possibly fatal complications can occur. (C)Therefore, **it is important to report the above symptoms promptly to your care provider if they occur in the postpartum period.**

Fetal Risk: According to the Centers for Disease Control and Prevention, an infant whose mother is positive for GBS *and is not treated with intravenous antibiotics during labor* has a 1 to 2 percent chance of developing *early-onset GBS disease.* This infection occurs in the first week of life, most commonly near the end of the first 24 hours after birth. It begins with symptoms of sepsis (infection), with the characteristically associated symptoms of respiratory distress. These symptoms include a rapid respiratory rate, grunting noises, nasal flaring, and chest retractions. (Refer to pages 363–364 for further description of these symptoms.) In addition, these infants will often show little interest in feeding, may be excessively sleepy, may have a rapid heart rate, and may have difficulty maintaining a normal temperature (their temperature drops and their body cannot bring the temperature back into a normal range). Their skin may be jaundiced or pale in color. Meningitis and pneumonia may also be present in early-onset GBS disease. Early-onset GBS disease is treated with intravenous antibiotics. The length and outcome of the treatment depend on the site of the infection (blood infection or meningitis).

A second type of active GBS infection that can occur in infants is *late-onset GBS infection.* It most commonly occurs when the organism is transmitted to the baby from the mother, or other carrier, after delivery (transmission is usually the result of poor hand-washing). Only 20 percent of all GBS

infections are late-onset infections. The reason that an infant exposed in this way converts from being a carrier with no symptoms to active infection is still uncertain. Late-onset GBS infection can also occur from exposure during vaginal birth.

Late-onset GBS disease begins between eight days and three months after delivery and usually presents itself as meningitis. Symptoms characteristic of meningitis are seizures, sudden fever, poor feedings, a very irritable infant, a characteristic high-pitched cry, and rapid breathing. The diagnosis is confirmed through a culture of spinal fluid obtained from a lumbar puncture. Intravenous antibiotics are given for several weeks. Surviving infants usually develop long-term disabilities.

Prevention: Because of all the risks involved with this organism, and through the efforts of a nonprofit organization called the Group B Strep Association, the Centers for Disease Control and Prevention (CDC), the American College of Obstetricians and Gynecologists (ACOG), and the American Academy of Pediatrics (AAP) have developed standards for the prevention and management of neonatal (infant) GBS disease. These organizations give maternity care providers two acceptable choices in their approach for preventing GBS disease. Your practitioner will discuss his or her views and recommendations with you.

One strategy is for practitioners to do vaginal cultures on all women in late pregnancy (about 35 to 37 weeks' gestation) to determine the presence or absence of the GBS bacteria. This culture is a simple swab of the external vagina and the rectum, and results are available in 48 to 72 hours.

Women who test positive are treated with intravenous penicillin G antibiotic (or an acceptable alternative) during labor. It is also recommended that the same treatment be initiated during labor for all women delivering prematurely, less than 37 weeks' gestation. Treatment is recommended in premature births because cultures have not yet been done to determine whether the mother is a GBS carrier. Also, a premature infant, with immature defenses against illness, is more likely to develop an infection if exposed than a full-term baby. It is recommended that once you have been identified as a carrier of GBS you be *permanently* considered a carrier and always be treated during subsequent labors.

The other approach is not to do routine cultures on all patients but to base treatment on an evaluation of risk factors. Treatment in labor is recommended for all women who have the following risk factors: a previous infant who had GBS disease, premature delivery (before 37 weeks' gestation), a maternal temperature greater than or equal to 100.4°F, premature rupture of membranes, or rupture of membranes more than 18 hours before delivery. In this method, intravenous antibiotic is administered in labor only to women who have these risk factors. (In addition, if these risk factors are present but the results of a culture are unknown, treatment is recommended.)

Treatment of the Baby: According to CDC, ACOG, and AAP standards, in order for antibiotic levels in the amniotic fluid to reach the levels necessary for preventing neonatal GBS disease in the newborn, treatment with the intravenous antibiotic must begin at least four hours before delivery. If this requirement is met, a full blood-screening workup and antibiotics are not required (unless the baby was under 37 weeks' gestation or has symptoms of illness). These infants, whose mothers were adequately treated in labor, need only to be observed in a hospital for 48 hours after delivery.

If the time requirement for intravenous antibiotics (administered for at least four hours before delivery) was not met, it is recommended that the infant have a complete blood count and blood cultures done within an hour after birth to determine whether infection has occurred. Of course, if signs and symptoms of illness occur, a full workup is required and intravenous antibiotics are given.

Whenever GBS is an issue in a labor, hospital protocol will be followed and your pediatrician, or the one covering your infant while it is in the hospital, will be notified promptly after delivery.

He or she will use the above guidelines and a review of your individual case to determine what should be done next. Depending on the results of any blood tests done on your baby, your pediatrician may order antibiotics for your baby.

A hospital's protocols are developed based on the above recommended standards and the prevention and treatment methods preferred by the practitioners and pediatricians at that particular hospital, so there may be some variation.

Scientists are now working on developing a vaccine against group B streptococcus, and the future looks promising for a safe and effective vaccine.

All the above screening and prevention methods are intended to reduce GBS infection and illness in the newborn. All you need to be concerned about is that you are either cultured to determine whether or not you have GBS or you are evaluated for risk factors. In addition, if you test positive for GBS or you have the risk factors listed in this explanation, be certain you receive intravenous antibiotic treatment when you are in labor. It is also imperative that you report to your practitioner when you have or think you may have ruptured your membranes. Be certain that the person you are reporting this information to knows that you are positive for group B streptococcus.

You and your baby will be watched while you are in the hospital for signs and symptoms of any infection and treated if symptoms appear. By reviewing Chapter 19, "Identifying and Reporting Illness," you will be better prepared to assess both yourself and your baby for any developing infection after discharge from the hospital.

Chlamydia

Chlamydial infection (caused by *Chlamydia trachomatis*) has reached epidemic proportions in the United States. It is the most common form of sexually transmitted disease, many times more prevalent than gonorrhea or syphilis. An estimated

20 to 40 percent of all sexually active women have been exposed to chlamydia at some time.

Sexually active females under the age of 20 have a higher incidence of infection than those in the 20-to-29 age group. Women and men with multiple sex partners are at greatest risk. Those who do not use a condom, diaphragm, or spermicide are also at greater risk.

Symptoms: In about 50 percent of cases, chlamydial infection is present without symptoms. If symptoms are present, they include swelling of the genitals, burning and itching, vaginal discharge, painful intercourse, painful or frequent urination, and vaginal bleeding. This infection may spread to the uterus, fallopian tubes, and ovaries and progress into pelvic inflammatory disease. Chlamydial infection that spreads to the fallopian tubes may also result in ectopic pregnancy (a pregnancy outside of the uterus, usually implanted in a fallopian tube).

Fetal/Neonatal Risk: Infection of the fetus is common. Stillbirth and neonatal death occur 10 times more commonly than in pregnancies of noninfected women, and premature birth is also a risk.

A newborn can acquire chlamydial infection when passing through the birth canal. Like gonorrhea, chlamydia can cause blindness in the infant. It can also lead to pneumonia in the newborn.

Prevention: A standard antibiotic eye ointment is administered to *all infants* at birth to prevent the blindness that can result from both gonorrhea and chlamydial infections. (This is a prophylactic treatment because both gonorrhea and chlamydia can be present in the mother without symptoms.) Infants at risk for chlamydial pneumonia are treated with antibiotics.

For all of the above reasons, a cervical culture is often taken early in pregnancy to determine whether infection is present. Antibiotics are available for the effective treatment of chlamydial infections. Sexual partners must also be treated.

You can limit your risk of exposure to chlamydia by limiting your number of sex partners and using barrier forms of contraception (such as condoms and nonoxynol-9 spermicide).

Gonorrhea

Pregnant women are routinely screened early in prenatal care for gonorrhea because it is such a prevalent sexually transmitted disease (STD) in the United States. Because it often coexists with chlamydia, vaginal cultures are performed for both diseases early in the pregnancy. If you are at high risk for sexually transmitted diseases, you will be cultured for gonorrhea again later in your pregnancy.

Symptoms: Like chlamydia, gonorrhea can be present without symptoms. Any symptoms present are usually mild and may include minor pelvic pain, genital irritation, and a slight vaginal discharge.

Although gonorrhea is a sexually transmitted disease, self-inoculation can also occur through the hands. In addition to infection of the genitals, this organism can cause infection in the urinary tract, rectum, mouth, and throat, as well as systemic infection.

Maternal Risk: Gonorrhea during pregnancy can lead to miscarriage or infection of the fallopian tubes. Left untreated, it may progress to pelvic inflammatory disease, infertility, and arthritis.

Fetal Risk: Gonorrhea can cause conjunctivitis, blindness, and systemic infection in the newborn delivered vaginally by an infected mother. Because it can be present without symptoms in the mother and therefore be undiagnosed, an antibiotic eye ointment is administered to all infants at birth as a precaution.

Prevention: You can reduce your risk of gonorrheal infection by avoiding multiple sex partners, using barrier forms of contraception (such as condoms and nonoxynol-9 spermicide), and avoiding oral sex.

Treatment: Gonorrhea is effectively treated with antibiotics. Sexual partners must also be treated. Repeat cultures are taken to ensure that the organism is no longer present after treatment.

Syphilis

Syphilis, another sexually transmitted disease, is caused by the spirochete *Treponema pallidum*. Because of the devastating, progressive nature of this disease and the fact that it can cause congenital syphilis in the developing baby, all women are routinely screened for syphilis at their first prenatal visit.

Symptoms: Syphilis begins after sexual transmission from an infected partner. A sore, called a *chancre,* marks the site of infection. This sore may be inside the vagina, where it cannot be seen. The chancre disappears without treatment, but the spirochete is not gone—it begins to spread throughout the body.

Maternal Risk: Untreated syphilis can cause heart disease, nervous system disorders, blindness, insanity, and death.

Fetal Risk: Congenital syphilis occurs when the spirochetes cross the placental barrier around the 16th to 18th week of gestation. This can cause fetal bone and tooth deformities, brain damage, and stillbirth.

Treatment: Treatment with antibiotics before the fourth month of pregnancy will almost always protect the unborn baby from the above symptoms associated with this progressive disease. Treatment also spares the mother any further progression of the disease (but does not reverse any damage that has already occurred in her body).

Genital Warts (Condyloma Acuminatum)

Genital warts are a sexually transmitted disease caused by the human papilloma virus (HPV). They have been associated with abnormal Pap smears and a higher risk for cervical cancer. They can be passed to another person by skin-to-skin contact during vaginal and anal intercourse. Genital warts are highly contagious and can be passed to your baby. They are three times more common than genital herpes.

Symptoms: The human papilloma virus has a long latency period; thus warts may not appear until one to three months after exposure. They may be very small, soft, flat bumps or a large multisurfaced growth that looks like cauliflower; they grow and spread rapidly during pregnancy. There may be one or multiple warts present on the vulva, vagina, cervix, or rectum; the color ranges from pale to light red. Other symptoms include chronic inflammation of the vagina, itching, vaginal discharge, and pain during intercourse.

Fetal Risk: Newborns infected with genital warts can develop *respiratory papillomatosis,* a respiratory condition that causes chronic distress and requires multiple surgeries.

Prevention: You can reduce your risk of genital warts by avoiding multiple sex partners and using condoms when having sexual contact. It also appears that smoking and oral contraceptive use may increase your risk of infection with this virus (probably due to their suppressive effect on the immune system).

Treatment: **Do not use over-the-counter wart medication during pregnancy.** Instead, ask your practitioner to prescribe an appropriate treatment. There is an acid that can be applied to warts during pregnancy. Your practitioner may provide you with the name of this acid and instructions for its use, once diagnosis of genital warts is confirmed. If the warts become large enough to actually block the cervical opening, they can be removed by freezing, laser treatment, or electrical heat.

Human Immunodeficiency Virus (HIV) and Acquired Immunodeficiency Syndrome (AIDS)

Many practitioners today offer an HIV test to all their patients because the incidence of HIV infection is increasing among pregnant women, so do not feel insulted if an HIV test is offered to you. You must sign a consent form if you choose to have an HIV test.

People at risk for HIV/AIDS include intravenous drug users, homosexuals and bisexuals, and anyone who has anal intercourse (because the lining of the rectum can be injured and bleeds more easily than the vagina); anyone who has sex with the above individuals is also at risk. Hemophiliacs and people who had blood transfusions before 1983 (when blood began to be routinely screened for HIV) and their sexual partners are also at risk. There is presently an increase of HIV being seen among heterosexual populations, especially among heterosexual women.

If you test positive for HIV, first you will want to have the test repeated—false positive results are not uncommon. If the second test is also positive, your physician will discuss treatment and counseling options with you. Pregnancy may speed up the disease process in the mother.

Symptoms: Women experience different symptoms of HIV infection than men; in some cases, there may be few or no symptoms. Chronic vaginitis and yeast infections (candidiasis) are common among HIV-infected women. Other possible symptoms include flu-like symptoms such as fever, muscle aches, headache, sore throat, and swollen lymph glands. In addition, night sweats, rash, nausea, diarrhea, and weight loss can occur.

Fetal Risk: Up to 65 percent of infants born to mothers who test positive for HIV develop AIDS themselves within their first six months of life. Infected babies usually die within three years. About one-third of the time, the virus from an infected mother is passed to the fetus through the placenta. Infection can also occur during passage through the birth canal or after birth through breast milk.

Prevention: You can reduce your risk of HIV exposure by avoiding multiple sex partners, anal sex, and shared IV drug needles. In addition, barrier contraception—use of condoms and nonoxynol-9 spermicide—provides added protection against HIV.

Treatment: If you are already pregnant when you discover that you are HIV positive, your practitioner will discuss medication treatment options that can reduce the chances of the virus being transmitted to your baby.

Pregnancy Conditions

Pregnancy-Induced Hypertension (PIH)

Pregnancy-induced hypertension (PIH) is a form of high blood pressure that can develop during pregnancy. Approximately 1 to 2 percent of pregnant women develop PIH. It is different from chronic hypertension in that it was not present before pregnancy and goes away after delivery.

During your first prenatal visit, your practitioner will measure your blood pressure. It may be up slightly if you are nervous, but this pressure, along with the ones measured over the next few visits, will give those responsible for your care a baseline blood pressure that is normal for you.

Normally, your baseline blood pressure drops slightly during the first several months of pregnancy and then in the last two to three months goes up slightly. If your top blood pressure number (your systolic pressure) goes up 30 mm Hg or the bottom number (your diastolic pressure) goes up 15 mm Hg *over your normal baseline,* your practitioner will want to monitor you more closely. In addition, depending on how much your blood pressure is elevated and the presence of other symptoms, certain dietary restrictions and left-sided bed rest may be ordered.

©Additional **early symptoms of PIH that you need to report promptly to your practitioner are:**

- **Excessive weight gain:** Rapid weight gain, defined as more than two to five pounds per week in a single-baby pregnancy, is usually due to fluid retention in your tissues and may be associated with pregnancy-induced hypertension.
- **Swelling of the hands, face, feet, and ankles in conjunction with weight gain:** Some swelling of the hands and feet *not associated with excessive weight gain* is normal during pregnancy.

When women receive regular prenatal care, PIH is generally diagnosed and treated early before it progresses to include more serious symptoms like protein in the urine, blurred vision or spots before the eye, severe or constant headaches, ringing in the ears, dizziness, pain in the upper abdomen under the ribs that feels like indigestion, and hyperreflexia (knee, foot, and arm reflexes that overreact).

Early, mild PIH is treated and often controlled with left-sided bed rest. The effects on the mother and fetus are reduced if this measure alone is successful in keeping the blood pressure within safe levels for the patient. If bed rest successfully controls the blood pressure, the pregnancy is usually allowed to progress until the baby is mature enough for early delivery to be safe.

In addition to left-sided bed rest, a woman with early PIH will be instructed to keep a daily weight record. She will be taught how to check her urine for protein and count fetal movements. These records should be taken to all prenatal visits. It is very important for a woman with early PIH symptoms not to miss any of her prenatal visits. If an appointment needs to be rescheduled, make it very clear to the receptionist that you have PIH and must be seen at a time very close to that of the appointment that you needed to change. Don't assume that a receptionist knows your situation.

Women with PIH are usually instructed to eat a high-protein diet and avoid added table salt and foods very high in salt. However, low-salt diets are not recommended and salt is not restricted, because salt is needed to maintain blood volume and placental perfusion. (The one exception to this rule is the case in which you have chronic hypertension and have been successfully treated with a low-salt diet before pregnancy.)

Some researchers think that inadequate intake of calcium, magnesium, vitamin B6, and protein may increase the risk that a woman will develop PIH. However, more research is needed in this area.

Untreated PIH can progress into what is called *eclampsia,* which is pregnancy-induced hypertension that includes convulsions and possibly coma and death. If bed rest is not successful in controlling your blood pressure and other symptoms of PIH begin to occur, you may need to be hospitalized and treated with intravenous medication to further control your blood pressure and reduce your risk of convulsions.

Tests can show whether your baby's lungs are mature and ready for life outside of the uterus. If your practitioner is comfortable with your blood tests and blood pressure, she or he will allow your pregnancy to progress until your infant's lungs are mature. (If you are under 35 weeks of gestation, you may be given intramuscular injections of a steroid that helps speed the process of lung maturity in your baby.) At the point where tests indicate your infant's lungs are considered mature, you will be delivered by cesarean section or induction of labor, depending on the circumstances. If your condition is too severe to wait for fetal lung maturity before delivery, your baby may need the assistance of a respirator for a while after birth.

Keep in mind that, when it is diagnosed and treated early, pregnancy-induced hypertension can usually be controlled with bed rest and dietary adjustments. In addition, early induction of labor is usually recommended. If these measures do not control the PIH, intravenous medications can be administered in the hospital that offer further control of the blood pressure elevation. **The important thing is that you receive prenatal care in order that this potentially serious but rare condition can be diagnosed and treated early.**

Gestational Diabetes Mellitus

Gestational diabetes mellitus is a glucose (sugar) intolerance that is first diagnosed during pregnancy.

To understand any form of diabetes, think of the body as a car. A car needs fuel—gasoline—to run. Without gasoline the car would not move. However, even with a full tank of gas, the car doesn't go anywhere without something to help it utilize the fuel. That something is the ignition key, which starts the whole process that allows the car to run.

Our body also needs fuel. Our fuel is food, and glucose is a major part of this fuel. However, just like a car, our bodies need something else to help us utilize that glucose. The "key" for us is insulin—without insulin, glucose cannot be utilized by the cells.

A normal pregnancy mechanism blocks insulin from being totally used up by your cells, thus leaving extra insulin available for your baby's use. Sometimes this mechanism works too aggressively and leaves more glucose circulating in your bloodstream than either you or your baby needs. Your kidneys filter out some of this glucose and "spill" it into your urine.

Most women's bodies sense this extra glucose and produce more insulin in response. By your next prenatal visit there is no longer glucose in your urine. But if you are a diabetic or have tendencies toward diabetes, this correction is not made, and high levels of glucose remain in your blood and your urine at your next office visit.

When your blood and urine glucose levels are high, further testing is indicated. See pages 79–80 for an explanation of the one-hour and three-hour glucose tolerance tests. The results from these tests will clearly indicate whether you have gestational diabetes mellitus.

As many as 10 percent of all pregnant woman develop gestational diabetes; it is the most common complication of pregnancy. Today, diabetes in pregnancy can be closely monitored and controlled, thus preventing potential complications for you and your baby.

There are many risk factors that would prompt your practitioner to screen you earlier than usual for high blood glucose. These risk factors include:

- Personal or family history of diabetes
- Age older than 35 (the risk increases with age)
- Obesity
- History of unexplained miscarriages or babies with abnormalities
- History of high blood pressure or other pregnancy complications

If you develop gestational diabetes, you will be given a special diet that you must follow closely. A full, detailed explanation of the diet and its purpose will be given to you. If diet and controlled exercise levels alone do not control the high blood sugar readings, you will need extra insulin for the remainder of your pregnancy.

If insulin is needed, you will be taught how to give yourself injections. In addition, you will be taught how to do a finger stick blood glucose test and be given a monitoring unit that will measure the results. You will have written and very specific instructions on the normal, expected range for your blood sugar level. **Abnormal results need to be reported immediately so that your insulin dose can be adjusted accordingly.**

Gestational diabetes mellitus is a very serious condition. Uncontrolled high glucose levels increase your risk of other pregnancy complications (such as PIH) and include the possibility of coma and death. High blood glucose levels can result in malformations in your baby, as well as many other serious complications. All of the following conditions have been associated with uncontrolled diabetic states (high blood sugar) during pregnancy:

- Miscarriage
- Pregnancy-induced hypertension (PIH)
- Macrosomia—babies over nine pounds
- Hydramnios—larger than normal amounts of amniotic fluid
- Birth defects
- Stillbirths
- Respiratory difficulty in newborns due to immature lung development
- The development of hypoglycemia (low blood sugar) in infants shortly after birth.

The last condition—hypoglycemia in the newborn—occurs because the baby has grown accustomed to high glucose levels from the mother throughout pregnancy. After birth, the glucose from the mother's blood is no longer there, but the infant's pancreas does not get this message quickly enough. The infant's pancreas keeps producing large amounts of insulin, causing the infant's blood sugar to drop to dangerously low levels. **This is why all babies over nine pounds, all babies under 37 weeks of gestation, and all babies of diabetic or gestational diabetic mothers have their blood sugar levels checked several times during the first 24 hours of life,** even if the mother's blood sugar levels were well controlled during pregnancy.

The above list of potential complications underscores why it is very important to follow your practitioner's orders carefully and call for help if you do not clearly understand your diet or instructions.

Most women with gestational diabetes (98 percent) return to normal blood sugar levels after delivery without further need for diet or insulin control. However, you have a slightly greater risk of developing diabetes in later life if you have had gestational diabetes.

Vein Thrombosis

Vein thrombosis is a blood clot that develops in a leg vein. During pregnancy, blood clots occur because the heavy uterus impedes return blood circulation from the legs back to the heart. In addition, a pregnant woman's body prepares for the bleeding at birth by increasing the blood's ability to clot. These two factors together cause *thrombophlebitis* (clots in the superficial veins), which occurs in about 2 percent of all pregnancies.

The symptoms of superficial thrombophlebitis are tenderness and inflammation in the calf or thigh near the surface of the skin.

Deep vein thrombosis (DVT), a blood clot in a deeper vein, can also occur. If untreated, DVT can be life threatening, because an untreated clot can move from the legs to the lungs.

*C***The classic sign of DVT is pain in the calf when you flex your foot (bend your toes and upper foot toward your head). In addition, you may experience**

- **Pain in the leg**
- **Tenderness in the calf or thigh**
- **A heavy feeling in the leg**
- **Swelling in the leg, ranging from mild to severe**
- **Visible vein distention**
- **Fever**
- **Increased pulse rate**

Report these symptoms promptly to your prenatal care provider.

*C***When a clot moves to the lungs (pulmonary embolus), chest pain, coughing, frothy blood-stained sputum, cyanosis (bluish lips and nails), racing pulse, and rapid and difficult breathing may result. These are life-threatening symptoms.** *Call 911 immediately.*

Placenta Previa

If the placenta is attached so low on the uterine wall that it touches or partially or completely covers the cervical opening, it is called a placenta previa.

Symptoms: Ultrasound makes it possible to diagnose a low-lying placenta, often before labor begins, but not all women need or have an ultrasound during pregnancy. Painless, bright red vaginal bleeding is often the first symptom of placenta previa, usually occurring between the 34th and 38th weeks of pregnancy, as the lower uterine wall begins to stretch. Bleeding can be spontaneous and intermittent; it may follow sexual intercourse or straining with coughing or constipation.

Heavy vaginal bleeding can be caused by either a low-lying placenta, *placenta previa* (in which the placenta partially or completely covers the cervical opening), or *abruptio placentae* (partial or complete separation of the placenta from the uterine wall). ℂ**Report any bleeding immediately to your practitioner.**

Treatment: If you are diagnosed with placenta previa, your activity may be restricted after 20 weeks of gestation, even if you are not bleeding. If you are bleeding, you will be hospitalized on bed rest, and you and your baby will be carefully monitored. The goal is to safely maintain the pregnancy until around 36 weeks, when your baby's lungs will be mature enough that he or she can survive after cesarean deliv-

ery. If bleeding cannot be controlled by bed rest and is severe enough to compromise the safety of you or your baby, the baby will be delivered by cesarean procedure prematurely. With advances in neonatal intensive care units, it is safer for a baby to receive care and oxygen in such a unit than remain inside the mother, dependent on a placenta that can no longer deliver adequate oxygen.

If placenta previa is present and undiagnosed before labor begins, bleeding occurs as the cervix starts to dilate. If the placenta blocks the cervical opening, cesarean delivery will be necessary. If only a small margin of the placenta is near the cervix, close monitoring of the baby as labor progresses will be necessary.

Preterm Labor (Premature Contractions)

Please refer to Chapter 7, pages 115–118.

7

What to Report to Your Practitioner

For most women, pregnancy progresses in a normal and healthy manner. Occasionally, however, complications arise that you need to report to your practitioner. For the health and safety of yourself and your baby, it is important to know the signs and symptoms of possible complications. This information is included not to frighten you but to help you recognize these signs and symptoms.

In addition, there are many normal occurrences in pregnancy—such as the beginning of labor—that also must be reported. This chapter is designed to help you decide which symptoms need to be reported immediately, even in the middle of the night, and which symptoms can wait until morning. However, because many symptoms often occur in combination, you will need to use your own judgment. When in doubt, call your practitioner.

Excessive Vomiting

(*C*)**Excessive vomiting at any time in your pregnancy must be reported promptly to your practitioner.**

Excessive vomiting places a stress on both you and your baby. Vomiting depletes your body's fluid reserves and, if excessive, "washes away" electrolytes such as sodium and potassium that are essential to your health and well-being.

Severe vomiting is treated with intravenous fluids. See "Nausea and Vomiting (Morning Sickness)" in Chapter 3 (page 41) for more information on how to treat nausea and vomiting that is *not* excessive.

Temperature Above 100.4°F

*(C)*Any elevation in your temperature above 100.4°F should be reported to your practitioner. A call in the morning is usually sufficient unless the elevation is above 101°F or you are having chills (or other symptoms), in which case you should call immediately.

Do not take any medication without first getting it approved by your practitioner.

During pregnancy, a slight elevation in your body temperature is normal (low 99° range). Any increase above 100.4° (temperature taken orally) may indicate serious infection that could damage your baby.

In order for an oral temperature to be accurate, you should not have had anything to eat or drink for at least 20 minutes. (See page 355 for further instructions on taking your temperature, if needed.)

Excessive or Inadequate Weight Gain

The average weight gain for healthy women of normal height and weight is 2 to 5 pounds during the first trimester (the first three months) and 0.8 pound per week during the second and third trimesters. If you are a teenager or are above or below normal average weight, or you are pregnant with twins, the recommended weight gain is different (see "Weight Gain" in Chapter 2, page 20).

*(C)*Notify your practitioner if you are gaining weight above or below either the average weight gain or the weight gain recommended for you by your practitioner. This weight gain can be reported during normal office hours as soon as you notice it. However, if other symptoms of pregnancy-induced hypertension are also occurring (see pages 108–110 for PIH symptoms), then report all of your symptoms *immediately to your practitioner.*

Notify your practitioner if you are a vegetarian. Nutritional assistance is available to ensure that you receive adequate protein for yourself and your developing baby. Nutrition recommendations for pregnancy, including increased protein, calories, calcium, iron, and other minerals, are covered on pages 19–25.

Signs and Symptoms of Urinary Tract Infection

*(C)*Any of the following symptoms must be reported to your practitioner:

- **Urinating frequently in small amounts**
- **Burning, pain, or difficulty urinating**
- **Blood in the urine**
- **Cloudy urine**
- **Low back pain**
- **Muscular pain**
- **Chills and fever**
- **Increased feeling of pressure in the bladder area or lower abdomen**

If your symptoms begin during normal office hours, call that day. If they begin during the night, call in the morning, regardless of the day of the week.

Cramps or contractions may occur if you have a urinary tract infection, which is a common cause of premature labor. *(C)*If premature contractions occur, *call immediately,* even if in the middle of the night.

How to reduce your risk of urinary tract infection

- **After urinating or passing stool, wipe *from front to back* only,** and use a clean piece of toilet tissue for each wipe. *Do not* wipe from back to front; this can bring bacteria from the rectal area to the urethra (the external opening that leads to the bladder), which can contribute to urinary tract infections.
- **Use soft, white, unscented toilet tissue.** Many women become irritated from the

BOX 7-1

Precautions About Antibiotics

- Do not skip doses.
- Follow dietary directions or restrictions.
- Take the prescribed dosage at the frequency ordered.
- Spread dosages as evenly as possibly over 24 hours.
- Finish all the medication prescribed even if symptoms go away.

harsh chemicals used to make extra-soft, scented, or colored toilet tissue.

- **Always urinate when you have the urge.** Holding urine increases the time bacteria have to multiply in the bladder.
- **Wear comfortably fitting cotton underwear** to allow for better air circulation. Tight clothing, pantyhose, and synthetic fabrics do not allow air circulation, thus keeping the area between your legs warm and moist. This warm, moist environment facilitates the growth of bacteria.
- **Urinate before and after sexual intercourse, and drink additional fluids to promote more urination.** Intercourse can introduce bacteria to the urethral area or aggravate existing infections.

Urinary tract infections are diagnosed by microscopic examination and cultures of your urine. A special sterile cup is needed for collection of the specimen. The nurse at your practitioner's office will instruct you in the proper collection technique for obtaining this urine specimen.

Urinary tract infections are treated with a specific antibiotic taken in frequent doses by mouth. Be precise about how often you take it: if it is prescribed two times a day, take it every 12 hours; if it is prescribed three times a day, take it every eight hours; if it is prescribed four times a day, take it every six hours. **This is true for antibiotics taken for any purpose (especially strep throat).** Antibiotics work by maintaining a certain level of the drug in your blood for 10 days. If you take all your doses during your normal waking hours, your antibiotic blood level will drop during

the night. When you skip doses or take them at very irregular intervals, the organism may not be killed and may regrow. Taking an antibiotic at precise intervals is ideal, but this may not be possible if you need to take your specific antibiotic with food. In this case, try to space your doses as close to the ideal schedule as possible.

It is especially important to finish the entire 10-day prescription of your antibiotic. If you don't, the organism may mutate (change its cell structure) and become immune or resistant to the antibiotic you were using. This is dangerous not only to you but also to others who may become infected with this mutated organism. (See Box 7-1.)

Drink at least two quarts of fluids per day. Cranberry juice is especially good because it is more acidic than other fluids; it lowers the pH of the urinary tract, making it more difficult for bacteria to grow there.

Eating yogurt may also be helpful in preventing urinary tract infections. Yogurt also reduces the bowel irritability caused by many antibiotics.

Avoid alcohol, coffee, and tea; they irritate the bladder.

Signs and Symptoms of Premature Labor

You are at increased risk for premature (preterm) labor if you have any of the risk factors listed in Box 7-2. Any regular contraction pattern that begins before the end of the 36th week of pregnancy is a possible beginning of preterm labor. Contractions can be very subtle. If this is your first pregnancy, you may wonder if what you are feeling are contractions at all. Lie down and place a pillow behind your back on one side to tilt you from being directly flat on your back. Place your fingertips over the top part of your uterus. If you are having contractions, you will feel your uterus get very firm and then get soft again. You may feel a tightening in your abdomen, or you may feel a backache that occurs along with the firmness of the uterus. You may also notice nothing more than the periodic firmness you feel with your fingertips.

Uterine Contractions: Irregular, mild, occasional uterine contractions are normal (they are Braxton Hicks contractions). These irregular contractions help the uterus to maintain tone and also aid blood perfusion between the uterus and placenta. **However, contractions that occur every 10 minutes (or more often) for one hour are not normal, even if they occur with or without other signs. They should be reported immediately.** If contractions are occurring before the end of your 36th week, empty your bladder and drink several glasses of water or other clear liquids (cranberry juice, apple juice, clear uncaffeinated soda), then count your contractions for one hour. (See Figure 5-2 on page 81 for instructions on how to count contractions.)

*(C)*Report to your practitioner immediately if the contractions are occurring every 10 minutes or more often for one hour. This is a *general* guideline. If you are having *regular, uncomfortable* contractions *at any interval* you should inform your practitioner.

If the following symptoms occur for one hour, *regardless of whether contractions are present*, **report them immediately:**

- **Menstrual-like cramps:** These cramps are like those felt before or during your menstrual period. They are felt in your lower abdomen and are significant if they are constant or intermittent for one hour.
- **Any abdominal cramping** with or without diarrhea for one hour.
- **Dull ache in the lower back:** This symptom is usually described as a backache felt below the waist, either constantly or intermittently, and is significant if it occurs for one hour.
- **Thigh pain,** either constant or intermittent.
- **Pelvic pressure:** Pelvic pressure is lower abdominal or low back pressure that feels as if the baby is pushing down constantly or intermittently. This is a significant symptom if it occurs for one hour.
- **A change or increase in vaginal discharge:** If your vaginal discharge is heavier

BOX 7-2

Risk Factors for Premature Labor

You are at risk for premature labor if you have:

- A history of preterm labor or birth
- A twin or other multiple pregnancy
- Fibroids of the uterus or any abnormality in the shape of your uterus
- Premature rupture of the membranes
- A chronic illness
- Chronic high blood pressure or pregnancy-induced hypertension
- Dehydration
- A urinary tract infection
- Placenta previa: The placenta is implanted near and partially covering the cervix (*partial placenta previa*) or completely covering the cervix (*complete placenta previa*).
- An incompetent cervix

than usual or changes in consistency or color, this is a significant symptom. It can be a symptom of cervical effacement, even without contractions. Please report this symptom to your practitioner.

- **Any spotting of blood or leaking of fluid from the vagina:** Even a small amount of blood or a small trickle of fluid is significant and must be *reported immediately.*

*(C)***If you are having any of the above symptoms, notify your practitioner promptly.** She or he will want to examine you right away to see if your cervix has begun to change.

A fetal monitor will be used to evaluate your contractions and your baby's heart rate, and an ultrasound test may be ordered to obtain additional information. To be called labor, or in this case preterm labor, cervical change (softening, effacement, or dilatation) must occur. The goal of treatment is to stop preterm labor before cervical change is advanced.

If you are under 37 weeks' gestation and your contractions are frequent and regular, an intravenous line may be started to provide you with rapid hydration. A urine specimen is usually ordered and sent to the lab to rule out a urinary tract infection. **Urinary tract infections and dehydration are common causes of preterm labor.**

A vaginal swab test called FFN (fetal fibronectin) can detect the presence or absence of fibronectin, a protein, in vaginal secretions. If fetal fibronectin is found in your vaginal secretions between 24 and 34 weeks' gestation, it means that **delivery may happen within two weeks** (according to this test). This test is used as a *predictor* of whether your contractions will lead to premature delivery. Other factors are also taken into consideration to decide whether treatment, bed rest, and medications are warranted to stop your contractions. Because this test is not 100 percent reliable, some practitioners choose not to perform it because the results would not alter their course of treatment. If your practitioner orders this test for you, your results are negative, and no treatment is prescribed, be sure to report any

change in the intensity, frequency, or duration of your contractions. The test results indicated your risk only at the time of the test; any new or different symptoms warrant additional evaluation.

Medication may be given to you first by a series of three injections (20 minutes apart) to stop your contractions. If this is successful, you will then be given the same medication in pill form to take by mouth approximately every four hours. You will be on this medication and bed rest, or bed rest with bathroom privileges, until your baby is considered full term (usually 37 weeks).

It is important for you to know the common side effects of terbutaline sulfate, the most common medication used to stop preterm labor. Knowing that these symptoms are common may help you to not be frightened by them. Terbutaline increases your pulse rate, and many women also experience heart palpitations. They describe their heart as "racing" or "trying to jump out of my chest." Nausea and vomiting can occur, as well as a flushed feeling and sweating. Headaches and complaints of dryness in the nose and mouth are also side effects. Perhaps the most bothersome side effects are the feeling of nervousness and possibly even tremors that can occur.

These side effects are most evident when the medication is first given by injection to get your contractions under control. Twenty minutes later, before a second dose is given, your pulse will be checked. (The next dose is not given if your pulse is over 120 beats per minute.) If a second injection stops the contractions, a third dose is not necessary. Whether your contractions are stopped after the first, second, or third dose, a pill form of the same medication will be given to you at the same time as or soon after the last injection. You will then continue to take the pill form of terbutaline sulfate every four hours until your doctor tells you to stop. As time goes on you will develop a tolerance for this medication, and the side effects will decrease.

It is very important not to miss your medication. If you forget a pill, take it as soon as you remember and then not again for four hours. Do not double up to catch up. It is helpful to wear a watch with an alarm to help you remember to take your medication on time.

Many doctors instruct their patients not to set an alarm to get up in the middle of the night to take this medication; however, this advice takes into consideration many individual factors. Please clarify this point with your practitioner. If you wake up on your own in the middle of the night and it is after four hours, should you take the pill then or wait until morning? Follow your practitioner's instructions.

If your pulse is over 120 beats per minute, do not take the medication, but notify your practitioner immediately.

✒ **It is imperative that you notify your practitioner** *immediately* **if your contractions return or even if you have the slightest question that you may be contracting.** Carefully review again all the possible symptoms of preterm labor. Remember that many of the symptoms can be very subtle. No matter how subtle, if they are occurring, report them to your practitioner.

If the oral medication is not successful in controlling preterm labor, you may be placed on a terbutaline pump (terb pump). A home health nurse will bring this equipment to your home, set it up, and teach you how to use it and how to change the syringes in the pump.

If you are having preterm labor before 35 weeks of gestation, your practitioner may want to administer a steroid medication to you by two injections (12 to 24 hours apart) to help your baby's lungs more rapidly develop surfactant, a coating that naturally occurs later in pregnancy and helps breathing after birth.

It is very important to understand that your preterm labor does not have a good chance of being controlled unless you comply with your bed rest restrictions. This is a difficult and uncomfortable time for you to have such limited activity. You will need to have someone else prepare meals and do housework. If you have other children, you will need assistance in supervising and caring for them if they are young. *Through this difficult time, try to keep in mind that the long-term rewards and benefits of having a healthy, full-term infant are worth the short-term investment of bed rest.* Check with your health insurance company to see if it provides home or child care assistance to you while you are on bed rest.

Around 37 weeks, when your infant is sufficiently mature for delivery, you will be taken off the medication to stop the contractions and allowed to come off bed rest. Labor will be allowed to begin on its own.

You are at risk for preterm delivery if you have an *incompetent cervix*. An incompetent cervix opens or dilates during the second trimester of pregnancy under the weight of the growing uterus. This occurs without pain or contractions and thus is usually diagnosed only after the loss of a pregnancy.

During the next pregnancy, the cervix is watched closely, and often a *cerclage*, a surgical stitch that closes the cervix and prevents it from dilating, is done to prevent another miscarriage. It is done in the hospital between the 12th and the 16th weeks of pregnancy. You are normally put on complete bed rest for 12 hours and then have an additional 12 hours of bed rest with bathroom privileges before resuming normal activity (although sexual intercourse may be restricted for the remainder of the pregnancy). After having a cerclage done, as in any pregnancy, you need to report painful pressure in the pelvis or abdomen, fever, vaginal discharge, rupture of membranes, or a feeling of something being in the vagina. The sutures will remain in place until a few weeks before your due date, or (depending on the technique of closure used) they may be removed when you begin labor.

Decreased Fetal Movement

A decrease in the usual amount of fetal movement at any time during pregnancy can indicate a developing problem. During the last three months of pregnancy, decreased fetal movement can be a sign that the placenta is aging more rapidly than normal. (See pages 73–74 for information on counting fetal movements.)

✆Immediately report any decrease in fetal movement from your baby's normal activity or fewer than 10 movements in two hours or the time reference given to you by your practitioner.

When Your Membranes Rupture (Your "Water Breaks")

✆Any trickle, leak, or gush of fluid should be reported promptly to your practitioner, including the time it occurred and the amount and color of the fluid.

Because there is a slightly increased risk of infection to both you and your baby once the protective amniotic membranes have ruptured, your practitioner may choose to induce labor if it does not begin on its own within a reasonable amount of time. If you have reached full term, most practitioners will induce labor within 24 hours after your membranes rupture (your "water breaks") if you do not go into labor on your own.

Membranes rupture prior to beginning labor in about 15 percent of pregnant women. Labor usually begins on its own within several hours afterward.

When your membranes rupture, it may or may not be a large gush of fluid. Sometimes it is a trickle or small leak; other times there are large gushes with every contraction.

Often, after the initial gush or leak the baby's head moves farther down into the pelvis and seals the cervical opening. No further fluid may escape until later in labor or sometimes until the baby is born, so don't think you were wrong about the initial gush or leak. Other times you feel a gush, and the gushing continues intermittently. (You continue to produce amniotic fluid until your baby is delivered. That is why it seems to be in endless supply!) ✆Call your practitioner immediately if you suspect your membranes have ruptured, regardless of whether you felt a small leak, a one-time gush, or a continuous

leak of fluid. Your practitioner will want to assess your condition accurately. Your job is to report what you felt; it is your practitioner's job to determine whether or not it was amniotic fluid. Rupture of membranes is an important symptom whether you are preterm or full term. **The time of rupture is important and should be accurately noted and reported.**

To accurately assess the color of the fluid, put a white washcloth or sanitary pad between your legs. *Amniotic fluid is clear.* You may see a few strands of white vernix (which looks like white cheese), which comes off your baby's skin. It may also be slightly blood-tinged from blood that washes out from around the cervix. Amniotic fluid that is clear but that contains vernix or small amounts of blood is normal. Amniotic fluid may be sweet-smelling or odorless—it does not smell like urine. (See "Meconium in the Amniotic Fluid," pages 120–121, for further assessment of color.)

Prolapsed Umbilical Cord

The umbilical cord is the lifeline through which your baby receives oxygen and nutrients and eliminates waste products. If the cord becomes compressed, shutting off the flow of blood, severe fetal distress or death can occur. Compression can result from cord prolapse, knots in the cord, or wrapping of the cord around the baby's neck or body.

Cord prolapse occurs when the umbilical cord falls (prolapses) into the cervix or vagina as the amniotic sac (bag of waters) ruptures. This can occur when the membranes rupture before the baby's head is engaged in the pelvis or before the baby is big enough to fill the pelvic space. It can also occur if the baby is presenting foot first, because the tiny foot leaves room for the cord to prolapse and then be compressed.

Symptoms: Although the umbilical cord may prolapse so far that it is visible outside of the vagina, this is not always the case. Usually the

FIGURE 7-1

Knee-Chest Position for Avoiding Compression of Prolapsed Cord

The knee-chest position causes the baby to drop toward your chest and takes the compression off the prolapsed cord.

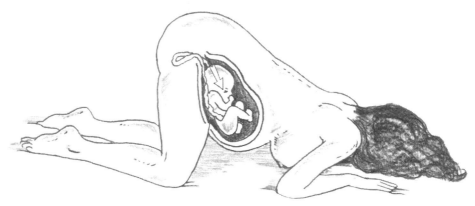

mother just experiences a feeling of something inside her vagina. If your membranes have ruptured before your baby was known to be head down and well into your pelvis, or if you experience premature rupture of membranes, remember that cord prolapse is a possibility.

Ⓒ**If your membranes have ruptured and you see anything protruding from your vagina or feel anything inside your vagina, immediately get into the knee-chest position (Figure 7-1) to take pressure off the cord, and call 911 or your local emergency medical service for immediate transport to the hospital. Do not waste time trying to call your practitioner first. Prolapsed cord is a life-threatening emergency for your baby. Someone else can notify your practitioner after 911 has been called.**

Treatment: If the cord has prolapsed, you must be immediately transported to the hospital while in the knee-chest position. If an emergency medical technician is present, he or she may insert a gloved hand into your vagina and gently push the baby's head upward to further relieve pressure on the cord. An emer-gency cesarean delivery will be done on your arrival at the hospital.

Meconium in the Amniotic Fluid

Amniotic fluid may also contain *meconium*, the greenish-black, oily-looking first stool of the baby. **It is very important that your practitioner know whether the amniotic fluid contains meconium.** When meconium has been present in the amniotic fluid for some time, it completely dissolves and the fluid turns light green or light brown. If the meconium stool was recently passed, the fluid will have particles of green, brown, or black meconium throughout. In cases of severe fetal stress, the fluid can look like pea soup.

The presence of meconium in the amniotic fluid means that some form of fetal stress has occurred, but it is not often cause for serious concern. Meconium-stained fluid is quite common, and most babies with this symptom are born vigorous and healthy. Even a very minor stress to a healthy baby, such as the baby's knee

Pregnancy

compressing the cord for a short time, can cause the baby's heart rate to drop briefly and set up a physiological response that causes the baby to have a bowel movement. If the stress causing the passage of meconium was minor, recovery for the healthy baby is immediate and there is no long-term effect.

When your practitioner learns that meconium is present in the amniotic fluid, this information is evaluated along with the fetal heart rate tracing (obtained from the fetal heart monitor) and your current stage of labor to determine what intervention, if any, is needed. If the stress causing the passage of meconium was severe, that will be reflected in the fetal heart rate tracing. These three things, evaluated together, will help your practitioner decide whether your baby can tolerate further labor or whether cesarean delivery is necessary.

If your amniotic fluid contains meconium, additional personnel are required in the delivery room. Hospitals with single-room maternity care (in which the mother stays in the same room for labor, delivery, recovery, and postpartum) have LDRP rooms designed to accommodate meconium-stained births; other hospitals may require the birth to occur in the delivery room.

When your baby's head is delivered, his or her mouth and nose will be suctioned by the doctor or midwife before the rest of the body is delivered. The goal is to prevent your baby from aspirating, or breathing, meconium into the lungs with the first breath. Once fully delivered, your baby will not be stimulated to breathe. Instead, he or she will immediately be handed to a neonatologist (a doctor who specializes in newborn care) or a pediatrician, who will place an instrument into your baby's mouth and throat in order to view the vocal cords. Any meconium in the area will be removed with a special tube or catheter that fits inside the viewing instrument. As soon as suctioning has been completed, the instruments will be removed and your baby will then be stimulated to breathe and cry.

If your baby has meconium below his or her vocal cords, **he or she will be watched very closely for signs of respiratory distress and**

infection, because meconium in the lungs causes pneumonia. Depending on how much meconium is found below the vocal cords, how thick it is, and the total assessment of your baby's respiratory function, a chest X-ray may be ordered. Your baby may need to go to the special care unit for oxygen, intravenous fluids, and antibiotics until his or her lungs are no longer stressed.

Remember, meconium in the amniotic fluid is very common—in most cases, nothing more than the initial clearing of meconium from the mouth and throat by the neonatologist is necessary.

Vaginal Bleeding

C)**Any bleeding during pregnancy must be reported to your practitioner.**
Bleeding or cramping before the beginning of your 20th week of pregnancy may be a sign of miscarriage. Even though bleeding often resolves without progressing to miscarriage, *C*)**Report any bleeding immediately to your practitioner.** (See Appendix C, beginning on page 391, for further information about miscarriage.)

Small amounts of blood are normal both after vaginal examinations by your practitioner and with passage of your mucus plug. Once labor has begun, a small amount of vaginal blood, called *show,* is typical. Both passing of the mucus plug and show are normal if you are at 37 weeks and therefore considered full term. *C*)**If they occur before the end of your 36th week, report either of these symptoms immediately.**

C)**If your vaginal bleeding fills a sanitary pad with bright red blood, call your practitioner immediately.** Sometimes the placenta separates at the edges and bleeds bright red in abnormal amounts. You will need to be monitored closely if this occurs.

Acute Abdominal Pain

C)**Immediately report sharp abdominal pains that cause your abdomen to be tense,**

hard, or very tender to touch in the area of the pain. There are many possible causes of abdominal pain; your physician will need to assess you and monitor you closely.

Symptoms of Pregnancy-Induced Hypertension

Pregnancy-induced hypertension (PIH) is a form of high blood pressure that can develop during pregnancy. Approximately 1 to 2 percent of pregnant women develop PIH. It is different from chronic hypertension in that it was not present before pregnancy and it goes away after delivery. (For a further explanation of pregnancy-induced hypertension, see Chapter 6, pages 108–110.)

Early Symptoms: Either of the following symptoms must be reported to your practitioner:

- **Excessive weight gain:** Rapid weight gain, defined as more than two to five pounds per week in a single-baby pregnancy, is usually due to fluid retention in your tissues and may be associated with pregnancy-induced hypertension.
- **Swelling of the hands, face, feet, and ankles in conjunction with weight gain:** Some swelling of the hands and feet, if it is *not associated with excessive weight gain,* is normal during pregnancy.

Your practitioner may find an elevation in your systolic blood pressure (the upper, or first, number) of 30 mm Hg, or an elevation in your diastolic blood pressure (the lower, or second, number) of 15 mm Hg above your normal baseline and lasting for two readings taken six hours apart.

Progressing Symptoms: These symptoms of PIH need prompt intervention from your practitioner. Report them immediately.

- **Severe or constant headaches**
- **Blurred vision or spots before the eyes**
- **Ringing in the ears**
- **Dizziness**
- **Pain under your ribs that feels like heartburn or indigestion:** This pain is more severe and more persistent than normal heartburn.
- **Decreased fetal movement:** See pages 73–74 for information on counting fetal movement.

Your practitioner may find:

- **Protein in your urine:** This is diagnosed by a simple urine test done in your doctor's office.
- **Hyper (or overreactive) reflexes:** These are tested in the same way that reflexes are usually checked in your doctor's office. A small reflex hammer is tapped on specific nerves below your knee and on your arms and wrists. Your reflex reactions are noted.

Signs and Symptoms That Labor Is Nearing

These *prelabor* signs may occur as long as a month before labor begins, or as little as a few hours before. As labor nears, your practitioner may confirm the beginning of cervical effacement (thinning) or cervical dilatation (opening), but these processes may not start until labor begins, especially in subsequent pregnancies. In addition, there are many other signs that you may notice on your own.

- **Lightening (engagement):** In a first pregnancy, the presenting part of the baby (normally the head) usually drops into the pelvis (engagement) two to four weeks before labor begins. This event is called lightening. In subsequent pregnancies, engagement of the presenting part usually does not occur until labor begins.
- **Two- to three-pound weight loss (or no further weight gain)**

- **Increase and thickening of vaginal discharge**
- **Braxton Hicks contractions becoming more frequent and more uncomfortable**
- **Passing of the mucus plug:** As thinning of the cervix occurs, the mucus plug that sealed the cervical opening during pregnancy may be passed. It may be washed out unnoticed if your membranes rupture or be passed as a thick chunk or as several small, thick strands of dark mucus. The mucus plug may or may not contain streaks of blood. It can be passed one to two weeks before labor begins, several days before it begins, or just as it begins—or you may never see it at all. (Consider yourself warned: Labor comes in many ways, shapes, and forms! That is why even women who have been through this before ask, Is this labor?)
- **Loose stools:** Many women have loose stools just prior to the onset of labor. Because of this common symptom, the practice of giving enemas to women in early labor has mostly been discontinued—nature has a way of emptying out the lower intestine on its own.

  If you do not experience loose stools, do not be concerned. Your first few pushes, in the second stage of labor, will eliminate any stool in your lower intestine. (Labor nurses and doctors are used to this, so don't hold back pushing for fear of passing gas or stools. If that bothered us, we wouldn't be in this profession.)
- **Sudden burst of energy: scrub-the-floor syndrome!** Some women, however, experience more fatigue instead of this often-described burst of energy.
- **Increasing pressure in the lower abdomen, bladder, and rectum**
- **Bloody show:** A small amount of blood passed through the vagina usually indicates cervical change. Labor normally begins within about 24 hours after pink or bloody show occurs; however, it may not begin until several days later.

Signs of Labor: True or False?

How will I know when I am in labor? When should I go to the hospital? What happens if they send me home? These are common, normal questions that all women ask—even women who have been through labor before! See page 74 for how to tell if you are having contractions. See pages 80–81 for an explanation of how to count the frequency and duration of contractions.

The comparison in Table 7-1 may help you answer the above questions, but until active hard labor begins, you may continue to ask, "Is this the real thing or not?" So don't feel bad if you guess wrong and get sent home. It happens all the time, even to labor nurses themselves! Final confirmation of whether labor is true or false often comes down to this: if you are having painful, frequent contractions, the only way to know for sure that it is labor is to have an experienced person assess your cervix. It may take two vaginal examinations, one to two hours apart, to determine whether cervical change is occurring.

You may come to the hospital and be found to be dilated one to three centimeters (remember, especially for your first baby, it is not uncommon to be well effaced and dilated three centimeters before labor begins), but this does not mean that you are in real labor. **Only the analysis of cervical change over time can determine whether this is true or false labor.**

Nature provides a kind of "labor amnesia" that makes women forget what their labor was really like. (Dads or other support persons can "undo" this amnesia by giving every detail to Mom after labor.) This is nature's way of ensuring that a woman will want to have other children! So even with subsequent pregnancies, during the early stages of labor you may still wonder and ask, "Is this the real thing?"

Don't feel guilty about calling your practitioner or hesitate because of the time of day or night. There are nurses at the hospital every hour of the day and night, seven days a week, who are trained to assess your cervix and determine

TABLE 7-1

Comparison of True and False Labor

True Labor	*False Labor*
Contractions occur at regular intervals and increase in frequency, intensity, and duration.	Contractions are irregular and do not get stronger or closer together.
Contractions last about one minute.	Contractions rarely last more than 20 to 30 seconds.
Contraction discomfort or pain begins in the back and radiates to the front. It may also radiate to the legs.	Contraction discomfort or pain is felt mainly in front, in the lower abdomen.
Contractions intensify with walking and activity and are not relieved by a change in position.	Contractions become less intense if you walk or change position.
Pink or bloody show may appear. Spontaneous rupture of membranes may occur, releasing amniotic fluid (this occurs before labor begins in about 15 percent of pregnancies).	Normal vaginal discharge is unchanged, except that after intercourse or vaginal exam it may be slightly brown in color.
Contractions produce cervical dilatation and effacement.	Contractions do not produce cervical change.
Contractions may be accompanied by stomach upset, vomiting, or diarrhea.	Contractions are not normally accompanied by gastrointestinal upset.

whether your labor is true or false. And don't hesitate to call because you are afraid of looking silly if you are not actually in labor. It is better for you, your baby, and the doctors and nurses that you err on the side of coming to the hospital in false labor instead of risking giving birth on the way to the hospital or as you arrive at the hospital door.

If this is your first baby, your practitioner will most likely advise you to call when you are having regular contractions every four to five minutes, each lasting about one minute, over a duration of one to two hours.

If this is not your first baby, call your practitioner when you feel that you are having regular contractions every 6 to 10 minutes or follow the specific instructions given to you by your practitioner.

If you have had a previous rapid labor, you will have specific instructions unique to your circumstances.

If you live more than 20 minutes away from the hospital, your practitioner may change the guidelines on contraction frequency for when you are to notify her or him.

Contractions That Do Not Relax

*C*Once you have reached full term, 37 weeks, and begin what you think may be labor, report to your practitioner if your uterus is not resting between contractions.

After the tightening of your abdomen during a contraction, your uterus should relax and feel soft again. Until advanced labor, you should have at least a minute of rest between contractions (from the end of one contraction to the beginning of the next).

Unexpected Home Delivery

Of all the millions of babies born every year, very few are delivered unexpectedly at home or in the car on the way to the hospital, and those that *are* delivered so rapidly probably would never have made it to the hospital for delivery no matter what, unless labor had been induced early.

If you are one of the few women for whom labor and delivery progress so rapidly that your baby is born at home or on the way to the hospital, rest assured that complications are rare. Just in case it happens to you, you and your partner should know what to do.

What your support person does:

1. As you see the baby's head begin to appear, if the amniotic sac (bag of waters) is still present, tear the sac and remove the membrane from the baby's face.
2. Apply gentle resistance to the baby's head (toward the vagina) to prevent it from popping out rapidly.
3. Have the mother *gently* push to slowly deliver the head. Short gentle blows (like gently blowing out candles one by one on a birthday cake) will help to reduce the urge to push forcefully.
4. Once the head is out, check behind the baby's neck for the umbilical cord. If it is there, try to gently slip it up and over the head. If this cannot be done, *very gently* pull it to get some slack so it will go over the baby's shoulders as delivery continues.
5. Wipe any visible secretions from the baby's mouth and nose. A bulb syringe would be ideal for removing secretions, but one is rarely available during an unexpected home birth. Any clean cloth, your clothing, the mother's clothing, or even your clean hands could be used to remove secretions.
6. The baby's upper shoulder (closest to the mother's pubic bone) usually delivers first. *Gentle* downward pressure applied to the neck assists the delivery of the upper shoulder.
7. Cradle the baby as the baby's lower shoulder is delivered. The baby will be slippery, so be prepared for this.
8. Rub the baby's back to stimulate a cry.
9. Keep the baby at the level of the mother's uterus until the cord no longer has a pulse, or, if you have a clean shoe lace, tie the cord several inches from the baby's abdomen. Either of these methods prevents your baby

from bleeding out through the cord. *Sterile* cutting of the cord should be done once you get to the hospital.

10. Dry the baby with a clean, soft towel. Once the pulse in the cord has stopped or the cord is tied, you can place the baby on the mother's abdomen and cover him or her with a *clean, dry* towel or the mother's clothing. Cover the top of the baby's head, if possible, to prevent heat loss.
11. Once the placenta has been delivered, place it in a clean plastic bag or towel. It is best to allow the hospital to actually cut the cord with sterile scissors. Place the placenta under the baby, and wrap them together for added warmth.
12. Call the mother's practitioner and let her or him know you're on the way to the hospital. When you get there, the mother will be evaluated for any tears in her perineum that may need to be repaired. The baby, of course, will also be evaluated.

What you do:

1. Rub the baby's back to stimulate a cry.
2. If the cord is long enough to allow the baby to be put to breast, do so immediately. Putting the baby immediately to your breast will help the placenta to separate and reduce bleeding. If the cord is not long enough to allow the baby to reach your breast, or if you prefer not to nurse, gentle nipple stimulation will serve the same purpose.
3. Massage the top of your uterus in a downward direction to help deliver the placenta. Wait for it to separate naturally; do not pull on the cord. Signs of placental separation are a sudden gush of dark blood and the cord moving downward out of the vagina. Separation occurs with a contraction; push gently to help deliver the placenta. Have your support person place the placenta in a clean plastic bag or towel.
4. **If you seem to be bleeding heavily** in large continuous gushes, continue to massage your uterus at the top, pressing downward firmly as

you massage. Heavy bleeding is often due to a retained clot; once you massage the clot out, the flow usually returns to normal. Nursing your baby is the natural way to promote the contractions that help control bleeding after birth, but gentle nipple stimulation can be substituted for nursing for the same purpose. In addition, a full bladder prevents the uterus from contracting hard enough to control bleeding, so empty your bladder if necessary.

Childbirth

8

The Team Leader
Your Support Person

Pregnancy and childbirth hold less anxiety and more satisfaction if the laboring woman has the support of her partner or another caring person in her life. In most cases, the support person is the father of the baby; however, some fathers are unable or unwilling to accept this role. When this happens, some women choose a family member or a close friend or hire someone (such as a childbirth education instructor, lay midwife, or doula) to act as a support person. Whoever the support person is, that person and the pregnant mother form a team and together attend childbirth classes, practice relaxation and breathing techniques, and prepare for the big day ahead.

The Role of the Support Person

As the team leader, you, the support person, can coach, support, comfort, and assist in the following ways:

- Finish writing the birthing plan *together* with your partner
- Instill confidence by being prepared
- Provide reassurance and emotional support
- Keep your partner informed of her progress
- Redirect your partner's attention and energy away from pain and toward control

129

- ❑ Provide comfort measures throughout labor and delivery
- ❑ Be an advocate for your and your partner's personal, desired birthing experience

If the support person is the father of the baby, he may have felt he has been on the sidelines during all that has been taking place (except for conception, of course), but Dad has an opportunity to play a very active and crucial role in the labor and delivery as a team leader!

Finish Writing Your Birthing Plan Together

I can think of no better way to show your partner that you want to be actively involved in the childbirth experience than to attend childbirth education classes with her and write your personal birthing plan together.

It is becoming increasingly common for partners to arrive at their hospital or place of birth with a birthing plan in hand. As a labor nurse, I personally appreciate and enjoy birthing plans. They help me to know the couple or partners better right away—what the two of them hope their ideal labor and delivery experience will be, as well as the options that they desire to have available when possible.

Taking the time to write a birthing plan clearly establishes you as a team that wants to actively participate in the birthing process with informed choices and collaborative decision making. In writing it, however, you must realize what the doctors, nurses, and midwives already understand: that it is not written in stone. Decisions in labor and delivery have to take into consideration two patients: both the mother and the baby. In addition, as a team, you are both free to change your minds based on current circumstances at any time. If everyone involved with the birthing plan understands these important points, the plan can be very useful.

A birthing plan should help you feel more in control at a time when you may feel vulnerable.

It will also reduce the chance that you will be disappointed with your birthing experience and help to avoid conflict when you are in active labor or delivering, when explaining and discussing your desires would be difficult.

You can put anything that you wish in your birthing plan. It can be handwritten or typed. It can be addressed to the obstetrician, the midwife, your labor nurse, or to all persons involved in your care.

Typically, the birthing plan expresses your hopes or wishes for your labor and delivery experience, as well as some of the fears that you have. In addition, it states your preferences for pain control options and how flexible you plan to be or not be with this option.

If you want to have "natural" childbirth, please define what you consider natural. It is also always helpful to me, and I'm sure to other labor nurses, to know how hard you want us to work to help you reach this goal. Many women want to be encouraged to keep going without pain medication (if medically okay) and offered additional comfort measures and positive reinforcement if they become discouraged. Other partners want no questions asked when they say they want something to help with the pain. You can see where it would be especially important to those involved in your care to know which of these extreme options, or perhaps an option somewhere in between, you prefer!

You can also include in your plan your preferences about walking, showers, and Jacuzzis during labor. If you have not discussed this with your care provider prior to labor, you can include things like preferences for or against enemas or pubic and perineal hair shaving (two things no longer done routinely in most places).

If you have cultural restrictions that apply to the labor, delivery, or postpartum period, please clearly define them in your birthing plan. Sometimes special needs can be accommodated if they are known ahead of time. (For example, if no man other than your husband is allowed to see your perineum, different arrangements would need to be made if the anesthesiologist on duty or the neonatologist who would come on that particular day in an emergency is a man.)

Preferences on fetal monitoring, intravenous infusions, Pitocin administration for induction or augmentation, pushing positions, and delivery positions can also be included. However, please state your understanding that in some circumstances you will not have a choice in these matters. This helps your care providers and labor nurses know that you are well informed and do recognize that there are circumstances that can develop during labor and delivery that warrant their immediate decision to ensure either your or your baby's health and safety. We appreciate knowing that you understand that in these instances, there may be no time for discussion, and questions will have to be answered later.

If you would like certain measures (application of warm towels, massage, or creams to the perineum) taken to help prevent an episiotomy, indicate this on your plan. Most hospitals do not supply perineal massage cream. If you purchase one, be certain that it does not contain petroleum (which breaks down the latex gloves used by the staff for their protection).

It will be beneficial to you and your partner if you include in your plan your preferences about having your parents or other family members in the room during labor or delivery. When well-meaning parents arrive, you may feel uncomfortable asking them to leave or telling them that you prefer they not see your delivery. (Hopefully, you have discussed this openly with both sets of parents prior to labor, but this is often not the case. Even if you have, some people think you will magically change your mind during labor and want everyone there.) I have found it helpful to establish a secret sign that the woman or her partner can give to the nurse to mean, "Please, ask everyone to leave now." I am always happy to provide this service to my couples at any time, during labor or even the postpartum period, and it takes the blame off of you.

Your plan can also include your desire to videotape or take no pictures at all and the partner's wish to cut or not to cut the umbilical cord.

Any preferences that you have concerning the immediate care of your baby should be specified in your plan. This is very important, because many hospital staff often have their own personal routine after delivery. If you have preferences about immediately holding your infant after delivery, you need to clearly express them. **No one's routine should prevent you from being the first to hold your baby, unless meconium staining, respiratory distress, or other unforeseen complications make immediate attention necessary.** How soon vitamin K and eye ointment treatments, weights, and initial baths are done can also be stated as preferences. Hospital policy will dictate this to some degree, but usually there is an hour of flexibility for most of these standards. Your desires should be honored over a nurse's usual routine. You also, however, need to be flexible if your labor nurse is being pulled quickly to another labor patient and vitamin K and eye ointments must be administered by her before she leaves.

Your infant-feeding decision should be included in your plan, as well as how important it is to you to nurse right away (if you have chosen to breastfeed) if your baby has no respiratory or other complications.

So far I have focused on a birthing plan for the labor and delivery, but your plan can also include pregnancy options (such as special exercises) that you would like to have considered, as well as your preferences about the type of birthing center or hospital for your labor and delivery.

Birthing plans can also include postpartum preferences about rooming, circumcision, discomfort control, visitor restrictions, and any desire you may have for an early discharge. Also include a request to be present during the baby's physical exam by the pediatrician, if this is important to you. (You may want to ask your labor nurse to include your postpartum requests on the postpartum nursing care plan or kardex. Otherwise your postpartum nurse, who does not routinely read birthing plans, may not be aware of your requests or desires.)

Childbirth

Instill Confidence by Being Prepared

Pack for the hospital ahead of time. That way you don't have to rush at the last minute and risk forgetting important things like your camera and film! Prepare a list of last-minute items to take along. By doing these things, you are showing your partner that you plan on this being a *team* effort and you plan on being as prepared and in control as possible. Box 8-1 includes a checklist of things to pack for the hospital for both you and your team leader. It also lists things you will need at the hospital in order to bring the baby home; set these aside in a special place to be brought to the hospital at the time of your discharge.

BOX 8-1

Checklist for Hospital Packing

For Mom:

Nightgown, if you desire to change out of the hospital gown. If you plan to breastfeed, a nursing gown would be best.

Nursing bra, if applicable.

Slippers.

Several pairs of socks.

Bathrobe for walking in the halls.

Toiletries:

    Comb and brush.

    Toothbrush and toothpaste.

    Shower cap.

    Shampoo.

    Your favorite soap, unless you want to use the little bar provided by the hospital.

    Hand lotion.

    Makeup.

    Lip lubricant.

Hair dryer.

Cloth-covered rubber bands or clips to hold back long hair.

Glasses. (Soft contact lenses may be worn during labor; hard lenses should be removed for pushing.)

A copy of this book for reference during labor and your remaining hospital stay.

Set aside for bringing Mom and baby home:

Baby's car seat, along with instructions for reference. (You should read the instructions and know how to set the car seat up in your car and how to use it before discharge day.)

Going-home outfit for your baby.

Baby hat and baby blanket.

Diaper bag, diapers, and baby wipes.

Two changes of clothes for Mom for discharge day. (Two just in case the baby spits up on the clothes you intended to wear home—it happens more often than you would think!)

For the support person:

One change of clothes.

Shorts or pajamas appropriate for spending the night, if applicable. (Remember that nurses will be coming into the room.)

Warm socks.

Slippers: some form of footwear is required in the hospital—socks qualify.

Toiletries.

Watch (with second hand if possible).

Usual headache medications: Many support persons need headache medication at some point during the labor experience. Nurses are not allowed to dispense medications (and this includes Tylenol) to any individual without a doctor's order, and they cannot obtain an order for you because you are not an admitted patient, so bring along your usual pain reliever.

Other essentials to pack:

Paper and pencil.

Your insurance card: Have insurance company phone numbers with you in case you have questions or concerns.

Camera (loaded) and extra film: remember, gift shops are not open during the middle of the night! If you are bringing a video camera, charge and pack the battery. Also bring an extra tape, and, if you have a backup battery, charge it and bring it along too.

Bring or know your calling card number.

Do *not* bring a cellular phone—they are not allowed in most hospitals.

A quick reference list of people (and their phone numbers) to call after delivery.

Cash: Mom should have no more than approximately 10 dollars on her person at admission, to avoid a tedious process of putting larger sums in the safe. A small amount is needed to cover television charges in some hospitals.

Dad or other support person will need to have additional cash on hand for meals, including take-out foods. Many hospitals do not provide meals for the support person. Bring some change for vending machines for the middle of the night! Cash may also be needed for parking, because many hospitals do not provide free parking.

Snacks for mom in labor: bring hard-candy lollipops on a stick (no chocolate or chewy centers, please). Small hard candies are not appropriate in active labor because of the choking danger. Clear lollipops on a stick are approved if clear liquids are allowed. If you have a small cooler, bring popsicles. Because creamsicles contain ice cream, they are not considered a clear liquid and are therefore not allowed. The hospital will provide clear fluid drinks if appropriate.

Favorite snacks for the support person: it's important to eat to keep up your strength, calm your nerves, and keep yourself happy and supportive!

Provide Reassurance and Emotional Support

By taking childbirth classes and reading about childbirth, you learn what is normal in labor and what to expect during the different stages of labor. You can therefore reassure your partner that what she is experiencing is normal and expected and that she is in no danger.

Praise is always helpful. Words such as, "You are doing so well," "I know this is the tough part," and, "You are doing great by keeping so focused" can go a long way in helping the laboring woman to hang in there.

Remind her that you're a team. Keep reminding your partner, "We will do this *together,* one contraction at a time."

Keep the Laboring Woman Informed of Her Progress

Tell the laboring woman how much progress she's making.

Discuss options presented to you, if time allows. However, if she is in active labor, keep discussions short. Remember that a laboring woman needs to focus inward and concentrate.

Help make decisions. If your partner is in very active labor or in a lot of discomfort, you may need to make some decisions for her. In other words, if your partner is asked, "Would you like to try the shower or pain medication at this time?" and you see question or uncertainty in her eyes, try making the decision for her. She will protest if she does not agree or if she wants to discuss it!

Childbirth

Redirect the Laboring Woman's Attention and Energy

Any form of relaxation breathing is a beneficial distraction. Concentrating on a breathing technique relaxes muscles, lowers blood pressure, and, along with visual focal points, has proven to be a beneficial way of reducing and tolerating the discomfort of labor.

A woman can memorize and practice every relaxation technique in the book, but when she is in pain, she may be unable to apply them without the help of a knowledgeable coach. The support person is there to redirect her attention and energy away from pain and toward control. When the expectant mother and her support person have learned and practiced relaxation breathing together, they form a team that is truly a pleasure to see.

Watch for early signs of tension:

- ❑ Legs moving tensely during contractions
- ❑ Fists clenched or gripping the bedding
- ❑ Tense facial lines
- ❑ Statements like, "I can't do this anymore," indicating a feeling of losing control

When Mom becomes tense and can no longer relax with the technique she is using, it is time for you to direct her back into control and then lead her to another relaxation technique. (For example, "You no longer look relaxed in the shower; let's go to the rocker and try slow rhythmic breathing," or, "With your next contraction let's change to the hut-hut-who breathing technique.")

Speak softly and slowly to redirect early signs of tension. Do not attempt to give instructions during a contraction—wait until it is over. Some women respond well to a very gentle touch, like placing your hand on her upper chest or arm while giving instructions.

If she is not focused and appears panicked, try taking her chin firmly in your hand, looking her squarely in the eyes, and giving instructions in a firm yet calm tone. (Be sure that your tone does not sound angry.) This technique usually helps in regaining focus. Keep instructions simple and specific. (For example, say, "With your next contraction, breathe this way with me," demonstrate what you want her to do, and then add, "We will do it together.")

Provide Comfort Measures Throughout Labor

Coaching in Breathing and Relaxation Techniques

Be an active coach in assisting your partner to use whatever methods of breathing and relaxation are familiar to the two of you.

Massage

Touching in labor is a very personal thing. Many women will push your hand away if you attempt to touch or massage them in any way during a contraction but will want to be massaged between contractions. Other women want to be left alone between contractions but be massaged vigorously during contractions. *Get to know your partner's needs* and respect her preferences.

Many women, especially those experiencing a lot of lower back discomfort, find direct, localized, **firm pressure over the coccyx area** (the lowest part of the spine) comforting. The support person can use his or her fingertips or the ball of one hand to apply firm pressure in a localized circular motion (see Figure 9-3 for an illustration of four lower-back, deep-pressure massage techniques, page 145).

Counterpressure—deep pressure without massage—may be comforting to some women. (The four techniques shown in Figure 9-3 can also be used without motion to apply counterpressure.)

Leg stretching and massage help relieve the painful knot during a leg cramp. Straighten the cramped leg by gently pushing down on the knee and pulling the ball of the foot toward the head. Next, vigorously massage the knotted muscle as you pull back on the ball of the foot. (See Figure 3-1, page 49.)

Ice Chips and Fluids

These are important for hydration. In addition to water, be sure to offer your partner drinks of clear liquids (if allowed) such as cranberry juice; apple juice; clear, noncaffeinated soda; and popsicles.

Petroleum Jelly or Lip Gloss

The lips become very dry during labor. Offer petroleum jelly or lip gloss to soothe dry lips.

Cold or Iced Face Cloth to Forehead, Face, and Back of Neck

A cool or cold face cloth is usually a welcome comfort measure.

Pillow Support

Extra pillows are important for support and comfort (Figure 8-1). It is a good idea to bring two extra pillows from home in bright pillowcases (so they will not be mistaken for hospital pillows). When on her side, a laboring woman should have one pillow under her head, one pillow (covered with a waterproof pad) between her knees, and one soft pillow rolled up behind her back for support. I also like to add what I call a "teddy bear" or "hug" pillow. This pillow goes across the chest and under the upper arm for support. A small towel folded and placed under the abdomen provides support and comfort.

Hot Water Bottle for Back or Thighs

If it sounds comforting to Mom, ask your nurse for a hot water bottle or hot pack. Use pillows or towel rolls to keep it in place. (Some hospitals,

FIGURE 8-1

Pillow Support for Comfort

unfortunately, do not allow hot water bottles or hot packs of any kind because of the risk of burns, especially to patients under the effects of epidurals and pain medications.)

Relaxation Music

Bring a tape player and soft relaxation music along with you to the hospital. Some hospitals provide this service, but it's safer to plan for yourself. Music that is relaxing for one person may not be right for you.

Support During Pushing

Provide support for your partner's head as she puts her chin against her chest and "curls around" her baby for pushing. Use your hand under a pillow, so you don't put too much pressure on the nerves and muscles in the back of her neck. Providing this head support saves your partner a great deal of energy and effort.

Sometimes, toward the end of the pushing stage, you may be asked to help hold your partner's legs up and out to the side to help "open the pelvis" and make more room for the baby in the birth canal. If so, support the legs by the top of the knee and the heel. Do not hold legs from behind the ankle or knee; you could damage nerves in these sensitive areas.

See "Positions for Pushing and Birth" in Chapter 10 (pages 172–180) for more information on how you can help.

Have fun and enjoy being a labor support coach!

Childbirth

9

Pain Control Options

Each person perceives and experiences pain in a unique way. What some people label discomfort or mild pain, others perceive as intense or unbearable. Some women begin their first labor having experienced intense discomfort or pain from another source, others with only preconceived ideas of what labor will be like. Occasionally a woman begins labor without having even thought about discomfort or pain. Some enter labor fearful of the unknown, not knowing what to expect. However, today more women are reading about labor and going to childbirth classes, so they understand more about labor and come prepared with coping techniques.

Fortunately, there are many pain control options available to you, ranging from relaxation techniques (used with help from your support person) to medications administered by your nurse to anesthetic agents administered by an anesthesiologist. In all situations except extreme emergencies, you can choose the pain control method you prefer at the time or be actively involved in the decision-making process. For these reasons it is important for you and your support person to know and understand your pain control options.

Why Labor Can Be Uncomfortable or Painful

The discomfort or pain of labor comes from several sources. First, the uterus is a muscle, working hard to contract. If you contract and relax your leg or arm muscles several times, you can feel the muscle tension and the fatigue and discomfort in the surrounding tissue. Second, the cervix has a vast blood supply and many nerves. The presenting part of the baby puts pressure on the cervix, causing it to stretch and open, resulting in part of the discomfort of labor. Your six- to nine-pound baby is the largest, heaviest thing to ever pass through your pelvis or vagina. The bulk and weight of the baby is certain to produce a lot of pressure. In addition,

137

some of your abdominal, pelvic, and back nerves and muscles are compressed periodically during the course of labor.

As you anticipate and experience labor, *keep in mind what is happening to produce the discomfort.* Remembering that **discomfort in labor usually means progress** will help you maintain a more positive attitude toward the experience of discomfort. Remind yourself (or be reminded by your support person), "My uterus is working hard, my cervix is opening to allow my baby to be born. Wow, with all this pressure, my baby must be much lower in my pelvis and therefore that much closer to being in my arms!" Knowing what is happening can influence your pain threshold, your tolerance, and even whether or not you label your sensations as pain.

Each Body and Labor Is Unique

The size and shape of your pelvis, the size of your baby, and the way your baby presents into the pelvis (head down, breech, face up or face down, and so on) also influence the degree of discomfort in any particular labor experience. *These are factors over which you have no control,* so you should never feel you are a failure if you need assistance in coping with pain. A woman with a wide pelvis who delivers a seven-pound baby in the perfect presentation without pain control intervention might require pain medication and an epidural if the baby were eight and a half pounds and in a less than ideal presentation.

It is important to alleviate pain during labor using some relaxation technique or other pain control option because, for most women, what shapes their feelings about the birth experience is not the amount of pain they experience but how they cope with it. Having a tool to help deal with labor discomfort and pain can be what helps women live up to their own expectations. Likewise, it is important that your nurse and

practitioner know what you would like your pain control tool to be. With this information they can work very hard to control discomfort by your expected and desired method or help you to understand why a change in plan might be beneficial to you or your baby.

Your Goals for Coping with Labor Pain

Some women come in knowing they want an epidural as soon as possible. If your maternity team is aware of your wishes, your IV can be started early to promptly begin building up the required pre-epidural intravenous fluid volume. If your nurse is not aware that you want an epidural, later initiation of your IV will delay your obtaining pain relief. Likewise, if you have made it clear that it is extremely important to you *not* to use medication unless absolutely necessary, the team will try every pain-reducing technique at their disposal to help you reach this goal. Therefore, inform your nurse on admission what your goals are for pain management. (See pages 130–131 for information on writing your personal birthing plan.)

There are times when, for a variety of reasons, a woman is so tense during her contractions that dilatation does not occur. If your practitioner feels that this is the case, she or he may recommend that you receive an injection, or even an epidural, for pain. These medications reduce pain and relax muscles. They allow better relaxation between as well as during contractions. Often this is all that is needed for dilatation to begin or resume.

If you are trying for childbirth without pain medication, please do not feel that you have failed if pain medication is recommended to you. *The decision* about whether you need pain medication for pain relief is *your decision. The recommendation* to consider the use of pain medication to facilitate dilatation *comes from your practitioner.*

If dilatation stops progressing, the first step is to try deep relaxation through pain medication and/or an epidural. Next, Pitocin augmentation is attempted. If these approaches are not successful, cesarean delivery will be necessary. In this "failure to progress" situation, you need to keep an open mind and try all the options available to help facilitate dilatation and increase your chances of a vaginal birth.

Learning to Relax Your Muscles and Your Mind

Before beginning instruction in relaxation breathing, you need to learn to locate and relax specific muscles or groups of muscles. This is helpful not only in labor but anytime to control stress, tension, anger, and anxiety.

Lie in bed on your back. Tighten the muscles in your toes and feet and hold this squeeze for about five seconds. Now relax your toes and feet until you are almost unaware of their presence. Feel your toes and feet sink into the mattress as they relax.

Progressing upward, do the same to your

Entire right leg

Entire left leg

Pelvis (groin to waist)

Chest and shoulders

Right arm

Left arm

Neck

Jaw

Face

Lie quietly and try to maintain this totally relaxed feeling for four or five minutes. Unless you are generally a very relaxed person, you will find this to be the hard part. Up until now, you were doing something; now you must lie still, quiet, and relaxed. It is your mind (your thoughts) that makes this part difficult—your active thoughts want active muscles!

Now you need to learn a valuable skill that will help you in dealing with any stress, not just

the stress of labor. You need to learn and practice to control your mind—how to keep out the thoughts that make you tense, nervous, or unable to relax. There is a tremendous feeling of power and accomplishment in learning to control your mind, thoughts, anxieties, and emotions.

As you do the above exercise, visualize "pushing" the stress up and out from your feet through your head. When you get up to the point of relaxing your jaw and face, talk silently to your brain, telling it that a certain stressful thought is not allowed in, you are resting now.

Learning to control your muscles and your thoughts can go a long way in helping control labor muscle tension and effectively learning to use a relaxation technique to control labor pain.

Relaxation Breathing Techniques

There are many forms of relaxation breathing. Lamaze breathing is one method or style commonly taught in childbirth classes. Today, many childbirth courses teach one specific method; others combine many relaxation breathing techniques, as well as other relaxation techniques. (See pages 12–13 for more information on choosing classes that are right for you.)

Over the years I have adopted what I liked from several styles (especially Lamaze) and modified techniques from my experience. Relaxation breathing as described here is the form I prefer because it is easy to learn and it discourages hyperventilation. This is not meant to be a substitute for childbirth classes. By all means, use the form you are taught and have practiced in class if you are comfortable doing it and it does not make you dizzy.

In this form of breathing (adapted from the Lamaze technique), you begin with a very easy technique when you start to have mild labor discomfort and progress to more advanced breathing techniques when muscle tension becomes evident.

Signs of Muscle Tension

Here are signs of muscle tension that mean it is time to move to a more advanced form of breathing:

> Facial tension, especially deep lines in the forehead
>
> Holding on to the sheets or clutching your support person's hand tightly
>
> Inability to hold your legs still
>
> Making statements like, "I cannot do this any more"
>
> Inability to remain relaxed or feeling out of control when using the current technique

It is the support person's job to watch for these signs and, *between contractions,* give instructions to advance to the next breathing method or alternative relaxation technique.

Slow Rhythmic Breathing

In early labor, all that is usually needed is slow rhythmic breathing. Breathe in and out slowly. Some people like to breathe in through their nose and out through pursed lips. As you breathe in, let your stomach muscles expand, as if you were filling your stomach, as well as your lungs, with air. As you exhale, pull in your stomach muscles as if pushing the air out. This form of breathing is known to lower blood pressure.

Once you or your labor support coach begins to feel that slow rhythmic breathing is no longer keeping you relaxed during contractions, it is time to change to the following technique (or another form that you have learned and practiced).

Cleansing Breaths

All of the following breathing techniques begin with a cleansing breath (as the contraction begins) and end with another cleansing breath. See Figure 9-1. To do a cleansing breath, breath in slowly through your nose and out slowly through pursed lips. At the end of the contraction, visualize blowing the contraction away with your last cleansing breath. As you do this, allow your muscles to relax, and feel them sink into the mattress if you are in bed. If you are sitting, standing, or in the shower, feel your muscles go limp and relaxed as you did in the muscle control exercise described above.

3-1 Breathing

After your cleansing breath, inhale fully, and say "hut-hut-hut-who" or "hot-hot-hot-who," whichever you prefer. (I always preferred saying "hot," but many of my patients say "hot" makes them think about their "burning" pain. Therefore, these women prefer "hut.") Form the *t* in "hut" or "hot" by placing your tongue at the roof of your mouth. Making the *t* sound as you slowly exhale helps you not to exhale too forcefully, which can lead to dizziness.

I have also found it best to inhale deeply and say your three "huts" and your "who" as you slowly exhale *once.* Then take another *deep* breath and exhale again slowly as you say the 3-1 mnemonic again. Finish exhaling fully on the "who." Continue until you feel that your contraction discomfort can be controlled by switching back to slow rhythmic breathing or until the contraction subsides. Always end your contraction with another cleansing breath.

Some breathing techniques teach you to inhale and exhale as you say each "hut" and "who." I find that my patients who do this tend to get lightheaded, dizzy, numb around the mouth, and tingly in their fingers. These symptoms are from breathing out forcefully and rapidly and therefore blowing off too much carbon dioxide (which can be counteracted by breathing into a paper bag or cupping your hands over your mouth, thus rebreathing your exhaled air). The technique of saying the entire mnemonic slowly as you exhale once, in my experience, works better and causes fewer of the above symptoms. However, if you have been taught and have practiced another technique, you are comfortable with it, and it does not make you feel dizzy, then use it. It is always best to use a technique that you and your support person have practiced. I offer these instructions only as an

FIGURE 9-1

Relaxation Breathing Pattern

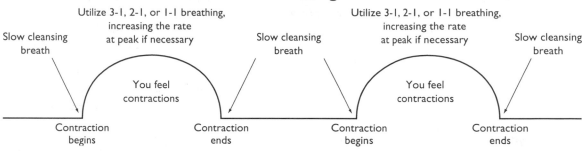

alternative if the method you have been taught makes you feel dizzy or lightheaded.

Between contractions, relax and allow all your muscles to go limp. Allow yourself to sink into the mattress or chair or feel the soothing water of the shower.

2-1 Breathing

When you begin to show the early signs of tension while using the above breathing technique, it is time (between contractions) for your support person to tell you to drop to two "huts" instead of three.

Now, after taking a cleansing breath at the beginning of a contraction, breath in fully and say "hut-hut who" slowly as you exhale fully. Repeat "hut-hut-who" until your contraction is over. (At the peak of the contraction, you may find it helpful to increase the rate at which you say it.) At the end of the contraction, take another cleansing breath ("blow that contraction away") and relax. Feel your shoulders sink into the mattress. Feel the muscle and mental relaxation.

It is helpful for your support person to remind you occasionally, "Together, we will do this one contraction at a time."

1-1 Breathing

During transition, or during the peak of an especially difficult contraction, switch to 1-1 breathing. This breathing is also helpful while you are in a curled-up position for your epidural and must remain still during a contraction.

To do 1-1 breathing, take a cleansing breath at the beginning of a contraction. *Breathe in* and say "hut" or "hot" as you exhale. (Try not to exhale too forcefully, or you may become dizzy.) *Breathe in* and say "who" as you exhale *gently* through slightly pursed lips. Note the difference: in 1-1 breathing, a breath is taken before the "hut" and again before the "who."

You may go fast at the peak of your contraction, but slow the rate as soon as possible so you don't become dizzy. Breathing too fast and breathing out too forcefully can both cause dizziness. If you do become dizzy, just cup your hands over your mouth in order to rebreathe exhaled air; this usually corrects the problem.

End the contraction with a deep cleansing breath.

Pant or Blow Breathing When Necessary to Resist Pushing

There are times when you may feel like pushing but are instructed by your practitioner or labor nurse not to. It is difficult to resist the physiological urge to push, but pant or blow breathing can help. Here is an example. If you are nine centimeters dilated or have a swollen section on your cervix, you may have the urge to push, but doing so may cause additional cervical swelling. Sometimes the cervix that remains is loose and soft enough to be pushed back over the baby's head during a vaginal exam. Your practitioner or labor nurse may attempt to do this procedure during a contraction while you push. If the remaining cervix cannot be pushed back over the baby's head, it is very important for you not to push against it. Doing so will cause the remaining cervix to swell, increasing your discomfort and slowing your progress. Pant or blow breathing can be used in this type of situation to help resist the urge to push.

In addition, some women have a strong urge to begin pushing when they are only slightly dilated. This is usually due to a baby that is at a very low station, lower than average for the dilatation. (See page 84 for a description of station.) Therefore, the nerves that produce the bearing-down reflex, the same ones compressed when you need to have a bowel movement, are being activated even though you are not fully dilated.

After your baby's head is delivered, your practitioner may want time to suction his or her nose and mouth and will therefore ask you to stop pushing. Because of the tremendous pressure, it is very difficult not to push unless you have a breathing technique to help you. Pant or blow breathing is that technique.

If you are instructed not to push and the urge is great:

Visualize a birthday cake in front of you. You must blow each candle out individually—one candle at a time.

Take a *small* breath, and *gently* blow out one candle.

Take another small breath, and blow out another candle.

Continue to do this until the contraction is over or you are instructed to push.

End all contractions with a cleansing breath.

As an alternative to blowing out candles, you may instead "pant like a puppy dog" to resist the urge to push. Patients seem to feel the effects of hyperventilation more quickly with this technique, but you should use the technique that *you* are most comfortable with.

Alternative Relaxation Techniques

The following alternative relaxation techniques are for use during all stages of labor.

Tightening and Relaxing Muscles

Some women do not like to concentrate on any breathing technique. Instead they prefer to tighten their muscles and relax them, beginning with the neck and progressing downward or from the legs upward. They do this with each contraction.

Other women use just one arm, tensing and relaxing it, beginning at the shoulder and progressing to the fingertips. Focusing attention on one muscle group helps you distract yourself from the discomfort of contractions and, if done effectively, helps to prevent overall muscle tension.

Visualization

Using visualization, the labor support person verbally creates a mental image during your contraction and leads you through the scene. The support person's voice should be soft and slow. Nothing is said between contractions.

The scene may be a walk in the park, with each flower, each bend in the path, and the children playing described in detail. Your support person may create an image of the beach where you and your children, or child to be, are building sand castles. Listening to the description of the temperature and texture of the sand, the architecture of the castles, and the reactions and faces of the children, you see yourself in this pain-free setting.

Poetry or other readings can also be used to aid in visualization.

Singing, Humming, or Listening to Taped Music

In early labor, you may find it comforting and distracting to softly sing or hum during contractions. If you are walking, hold on to a rail along the wall (provided on many maternity units), or hold on to your support person and hum as you slightly bend your knees and gently rock through the contraction.

Many relaxation music tapes are available to suit varied musical tastes. Other relaxation tapes focus on a sound in nature such as the ocean or a running brook. A trip to a nature store or music store where you are allowed to preview the tapes prior to purchase would be ideal. Remember, you are looking for gentle, soft sounds *that relax you*, not fast, loud music that stirs your emotions or makes you feel like dancing! Just as a lullaby soothes a baby, singing, humming, or listening to taped music can help relax and distract a laboring woman.

Walking

Many women in labor are more comfortable while standing and walking than while sitting; others prefer to be lying down. Walking usually has the added advantage of speeding up the labor process, which does get you to your goal faster! Walking by itself or in combination with holding on to a rail and rocking (rhythmic bending of knees), humming, squatting, or relaxation breathing throughout contractions may be helpful.

Showers

Some hospitals now provide showers with chairs so you can alternate between standing and sitting. In addition, many showers have hand controls that allow you to stream the water directly on your abdomen or thighs during the contraction. Back water jets are another helpful feature.

If you use a shower for pain control, it may take time to take effect (usually 5 to 10 minutes). Be willing to be patient for a few minutes and wait for the muscle relaxation to set in. There is no limit to the amount of time you can stay in the shower. However, you may be asked to turn the temperature of the water down or step out for a few minutes if your temperature elevates too much.

The force of the water spray on the abdomen and back provides a stimulus that can distract you from the discomfort of the contraction. In addition, the force and buoyancy of the water provide added support for tired and tense muscles. Many women stay in the shower for hours during labor, once its therapeutic effect sets in. For them, the shower provides natural pain relief without the need to use medications.

A chair outside the shower will be provided for the support person, but it is also acceptable for the support person to put on a bathing suit and get into the shower with you. **Be forewarned, however, that the stream of the water must go directly over the mother's abdomen during contractions and that the back jets must go on her back to keep her from getting chilled. Thus, the support person who goes into the shower often gets chilled from lack of direct warm water!**

The support person can provide lower-back massage during contractions or hold and direct the hand-held water control if desired by the mother. In addition, because the warm water can increase the mother's temperature and thereby increase the baby's heart rate, the support person can provide whatever fluids the mother is allowed (ice chips, water, or clear liquids and popsicles). (A cold cloth applied to the forehead is also helpful in controlling temperature elevation if it is comfortable to the mother.)

While you are in the shower, the fetal heart rate can be periodically checked using a small, portable hand-held device called a *doptone*. Because of the smaller contact surface of this device, it is important to realize and expect that it may take a little longer to find the fetal heartbeat when using it.

Childbirth

Bathtubs and Jacuzzi Baths

Many birthing centers and some hospitals offer Jacuzzi baths (Figure 9-2) as a soothing labor relaxation option. These tubs have several advantages, including that of allowing the support person to go into the warm bath along with the laboring woman.

Water therapy works because the pain relief and muscle relaxation it provides also have the added benefit of reducing anxiety. When anxiety is decreased, adrenalin production is reduced. This in turn increases the mother's production of the hormone that stimulates labor and the hormones that decrease pain. The friction of the water and bubbles (from jet therapy) on the nipples also increases the mother's production of the hormone that stimulates labor.

F I G U R E   9 - 2

Jacuzzi Baths for Labor Pain Control

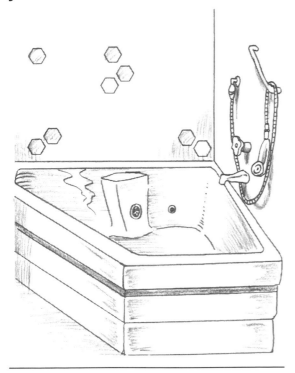

In addition, water therapy in a bath or Jacuzzi has been shown to increase the rate of dilatation, increase urination, and decrease blood pressure, and most labor baths or Jacuzzi tubs are large enough to allow the woman to get on her hands and knees if necessary to facilitate the rotation of the baby into a more ideal position for delivery.

An order from your practitioner is required for use of water therapy of any kind during labor. Therefore, it is important to explore this option when choosing a practitioner to provide your care. Not all hospitals have private showers in private rooms for laboring patients. Likewise, bathtubs or Jacuzzis are not available in all settings. (See pages 6–8 for things to consider when choosing an obstetrician or midwife to provide your care and when choosing a place for your delivery.)

In addition to your having an order from the practitioner, your vital signs (temperature, pulse, respirations, and blood pressure) must be within normal limits. Amniotic membranes can be intact or already ruptured, but, if ruptured, they must have been ruptured for less than 24 hours and the fluid should be clear (or only lightly meconium-stained).

Labor should be well established before you begin water therapy, because it is so relaxing to the muscles that it can actually slow progress if it is initiated in the early (latent) phase of dilatation (one to three centimeters of cervical dilatation). Most practitioners want you to be in the active phase of labor (four centimeters) before beginning water therapy. However, if you have been at two or three centimeters for a long period of time without progress and are having close, difficult contractions, water therapy can be started to promote comfort and relaxation.

Any increase in your temperature increases your baby's heart rate. Therefore, if your temperature starts to climb too much during a bath, either the water will be cooled somewhat or you will be asked to step out for a few minutes. Taking fluids and ice chips and applying a cold cloth to the face during a bath can help prevent this unwanted side effect of warm water therapy. The support person can assist by providing and encouraging you to take these things.

Bouncing Ball

The bouncing ball is the newest thing to hit the labor pain control market. It looks just like a big beach ball. When you sit on it, the diameter of the ball affords a comfortable sitting height.

You will need to hold on to something secure, such as your support person or a bed with locked wheels. Don't hold on to anything that can roll or be pulled over.

A gentle bouncing motion during contractions on this flexible, soft surface provides both distraction and comfort. Besides that, it can be fun, too!

Lower-Back, Deep-Pressure Massage and Counterpressure

During a contraction, the labor support person uses the ball of his or her hand, a clenched fist, or the soft part of the fingers to apply **deep pressure with a slow circular motion** over the lowest part of the spine for massage or **deep, still pressure** for counterpressure (see Figure 9-3A, B, C, and D).

FIGURE 9-3

Lower-Back, Deep-Pressure Massage and Counterpressure

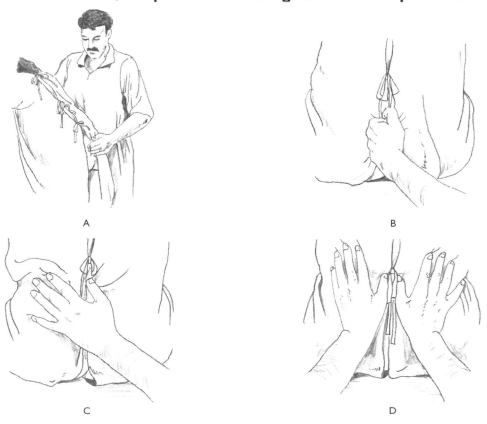

A

B

C

D

Childbirth

Tennis balls can also be used to apply a rolling counterpressure. Wooden devices (with rolling wooden balls) made for massage purposes are very comforting to many women in labor.

Deep-pressure massage and counterpressure are usually very helpful when a woman is experiencing back pain with contractions.

Effleurage

Effleurage is a very light stroking touch with the fingertips on the abdomen during a contraction (see Figure 3-2, page 51). A woman can do this herself, or it can be done by the labor support person.

Hot Water Bottle or Hot Pack

A hot water bottle or hot pack applied to the back, lower abdomen, and hips can aid relaxation. All hot water bottles must be covered with a towel to help prevent skin burns. Many hospitals have policies against the use of hot water bottles or hot packs because of the possibility of local skin burns. *Never put boiling water into a hot water bottle;* the bottle may rupture, causing severe burns. Hot water bottles and hot packs are *not recommended* and are usually not needed by women with epidurals. The epidural decreases the skin's sensitivity to pain, and therefore if the bottle or pack is too hot, the skin could be burned without the patient being aware of it.

Pain Medication

Many different medications can be used to relieve pain. Narcotics or synthetic narcotics given by intramuscular injection or directly through an intravenous line (by your nurse) decrease your awareness of pain and help you to relax between contractions. Local anesthetics (administered by your practitioner) decrease your sensitivity to pain and touch in a small area, and there are several forms of anesthesia (administered by an anesthesiologist) that can be used for pain control. **Which medication or form of anesthesia used for you depends on your needs and preferences, as well as your caregiver's judgment.**

Intramuscular and Intravenous Medication for Pain Control

Pain medication is given through an intravenous (IV) line if one has been previously started, or by intramuscular (IM) injection. Medication injected directly into your intravenous line works immediately because it does not have to be absorbed into circulation as does medication injected into a muscle. Therefore, if you are close to delivery, a *small* dose can be administered intravenously to help you immediately without making the baby sluggish at birth.

Intramuscular injections take 10 to 20 minutes to be absorbed into circulation and become effective. IM doses are larger than IV doses. They take longer to take effect but will last longer. Intramuscular injections are usually not preferred by the practitioner in rapid precipitous labors or advanced phases of dilatation because they take longer to take effect and because of the sleepy, sluggish, and decreased respiratory effort effects they may cause in a baby born within two hours of their administration.

Whether or not medication is given at all, and what dose is given to you, will depend on your weight, how dilated you are at the time, and how soon delivery is anticipated. Narcotics do cross the placenta and enter the baby's circulation. Your caregivers want to ensure that you will feel better but that the medications won't make your baby too sleepy or cause the decreased respiratory effort at birth that is common when intramuscular medication is given to the mother within two hours of birth. **Remember, both patients must be considered!**

If medication is given to you and you deliver more quickly than expected, a drug can be given to your baby if necessary to reverse the respiratory depression induced by the pain medication.

You will feel the medication in your head first, as a feeling of lightheadedness, before you feel pain relief. Remember, pain medication will not take away all the discomfort. It will lessen your awareness of the pain and help you to better relax completely between contractions. You may feel as if you have taken a nap between contractions.

After pain medication is given, the support person should dim the lights and stop talking between contractions unless the woman initiates the conversation. Pain medication puts a person into a lower state of consciousness (or awareness). If conversation or massage continues between contractions, the medication has less chance of achieving this lower state of awareness and therefore may be less effective. Talking, touching, and massaging are helpful during the contraction unless the woman is almost sleeping through her contractions or she prefers that talking or touching not be done at this time.

If the woman has gone to sleep between contractions, gently awaken her as the contraction begins so that she will be able to gain control over it. You can note the beginning of a contraction by gently placing your hand on the mother's abdomen and sensing the beginning tightening of the uterus or by watching the monitor, if one is being used.

Constant monitoring of the fetal heart is often used after administering medication so that the effects of the medication on the baby can be observed without having to awaken the mother for intermittent checks. Also, because medication may slow down the frequency of contractions, the monitor helps detect this effect if it occurs. This reduction in contraction frequency does not always mean slowing of progress in dilatation—relaxation can have very beneficial effects on the cervix during labor. However, if your membranes have been ruptured for a long time, you are starting to get a fever, or your baby's baseline heart rate is beginning to go up, oxytocin augmentation will be considered if your contractions become less frequent after medication.

Pudendal Block

A pudendal block is useful in the late second stage of labor because it relieves vaginal and perineal pain during episiotomy and delivery. It also relieves the pain around the vagina and rectum as the baby descends through the birth canal. It is rarely used, because a pudendal block does not relieve the pain of uterine contractions, and the natural urge to bear down and push is decreased and sometimes even lost after it is given.

Injection of the anesthetic agent into the pudendal nerve is usually done from inside the vagina.

Local Anesthesia

Local anesthesia only relieves pain in the small area surrounding the injection. It is used when the doctor has to make or repair an episiotomy (an incision in the perineum) or needs to do a stitch repair of a laceration (a natural tear in the perineum caused by delivery).

Local anesthesia is also injected in the back before epidural and spinal anesthesia to numb the area before beginning the actual procedure.

Epidural Anesthesia

An epidural involves continuous or intermittent injection of anesthetic medication into the space just outside the dural sac that surrounds the spinal cord. The nerves that transmit sensation from the lower body (including the uterus and cervix) pass through this space on their way to the spinal cord. If pain is blocked before reaching the spinal cord, then the pain "message" is never sent to the brain.

Prior to giving you an epidural, the anesthesiologist will ask you questions relative to anesthesia and answer any questions and concerns you might have about the procedure. Although the overall risk is small, the anesthesiologist will inform you of all the possible risks involved with the procedure prior to obtaining informed, written consent. Don't be overly frightened by this discussion—this information is legally required to be provided to you prior to your giving consent. The

Childbirth

anesthesiologist is also under legal obligation to adequately discuss the procedure with you, taking the time to answer your questions, prior to obtaining informed, written consent.

Because an epidural takes time to administer and to take effect, it is not used for cesarean deliveries unless an effective epidural is already in place when the decision is made to do a cesarean. (In this case an additional dose, large enough to adequately control pain during a surgical procedure, is added to the existing epidural catheter.)

Preparation: An IV line will be inserted prior to your epidural. The medications used in an epidural can cause your blood pressure to drop, so to counteract this side effect, it is common to administer approximately one liter of IV fluid prior to the procedure.

Some anesthesiologists order a liquid antacid to be taken to neutralize the stomach acids before the epidural.

You will need to empty your bladder before the epidural procedure begins. Once the epidural takes effect, you will not be allowed out of bed (unless you are given a walking epidural) and you may experience difficulty urinating. During the pushing stage of labor, the bladder usually empties on its own. However, if your bladder gets too full before you begin pushing, a straight catheter will be inserted through your urethra (the external opening through which urine passes) to empty your bladder. Because you are numb, this procedure is unlikely to cause discomfort. After the catheter is inserted, the urine is allowed to drain out and the catheter is removed.

If this is your first baby and your labor is progressing normally, your epidural will usually not be given until your cervix is dilated about four to five centimeters. This is because epidurals often slow contractions, and your practitioner wants to be certain that your labor is well established first. An epidural may be given before four to five centimeters dilatation if you have remained at a lesser dilatation without progress in the presence of strong contractions for an abnormally long period of time. Sometimes the overall muscular relaxation produced by an epidural helps to promote dilatation. If your contractions decrease in frequency after the epidural is given, labor augmentation may be required. (To augment labor means to increase the strength and frequency of contractions.) Oxytocin (trade name Pitocin) is the same hormone your body produces to promote labor. In labor augmentation, oxytocin is added to an intravenous solution and given to you in small and controlled amounts through your IV line. The amounts are increased until you are having regular and strong contractions without any fetal distress. Once contractions are strong and regular, augmentation is maintained at that level.

You will be either in the sitting position with your legs dangling over the edge of the bed or lying on your side (the left side is preferred) for your epidural placement. In either position, your chin should be against your chest and your back pushed *out* like a cat's—rounded and making the shape of a C. This position opens up the spaces between the bones in the spine and makes the procedure quicker and easier for the anesthesiologist, and thus for you.

If you are on your side, your back should be close to the edge of the bed and your knees must be drawn up against your abdomen as far as they will go. Try pulling your bottom shoulder forward (rounded) and placing both your hands together between your knees. Visualize "hugging" your baby with your whole body!

Whether you are sitting or on your side, the position for epidural insertion is a difficult one to maintain during contractions. Keep telling yourself that if you hold still and maintain good position, the procedure will be completed in just a few contractions. Work with your support person and nurse or midwife to use the relaxation technique that you prefer to get you through these few contractions.

If the anesthesiologist allows the support person to remain in the room, he or she should sit on the side of the bed that Mom is facing. The needles used in both epidurals and spinals are about six inches long. Just the sight of them bothers most people. *Remember, only the very tip of this needle is inserted.* The rest of the needle is held by the anesthesiologist's other hand for stability.

Procedure: The anesthesiologist will tell you what to expect as he or she proceeds. The most difficult part is staying in the curled-up position during a contraction. Your nurse will help you. Together you will get through the few contractions you will have during the procedure. Keep reminding yourself that relief is on its way!

After getting you into the correct position, the anesthesiologist will clean your back with an antiseptic solution, which usually feels cold. Then he or she will numb the area with a local anesthetic prior to placement of the epidural needle. I tell my patients that the local anesthetic is the most uncomfortable part of the procedure. It feels somewhat like a bee sting.

It is important that you follow the anesthesiologist's instructions carefully and tell him or her if anything bothers you during placement of the epidural. He or she will tell you when you *might* feel a certain sensation.

Once the epidural space is located, the anesthesiologist threads the catheter through the needle *and removes the needle.* Occasionally, some people experience a nerve response as the catheter is threaded. This nerve response is often described as a momentary electric shock sensation or a burning down one leg. Again, it is important to hold still and communicate everything you are feeling to the anesthesiologist.

The anesthesiologist will perform some tests to help verify the catheter position and your tolerance of the medications used. The catheter will then be securely taped to your back, and the end (which looks like a thin wire) will be taped on your shoulder or on your gown near your shoulder.

There are two ways to administer epidural doses: the *intermittent method* and the *continuous infusion method.* In the intermittent method, a full medication dose (*bolus dose*) is given to achieve comfort, and then the catheter is left in place but clamped off. In this case, the capped end of the catheter will be visible to you over your shoulder. When you begin to have pain again, the anesthesiologist is called to give you another bolus dose. The disadvantages of this method are the highs and lows in your pain level and the delay that may occur if the anesthesiologist is tied up when another bolus is needed.

In the continuous infusion method, an initial bolus dose of medication is given during the epidural insertion procedure, and then the catheter is attached to a continuous slow-drip pump (whose rate is set by the anesthesiologist). This is usually the preferred method because it provides more *even* pain relief. If your pain does break through the anesthesia level of the continuous drip, the anesthesiologist can be called to give you an additional bolus dose. It is important to bring the return of discomfort to your nurse's attention promptly.

As mentioned previously, epidural anesthesia may cause the mother's blood pressure to drop, decreasing placental perfusion (blood flow) and fetal heart rate. If this occurs, you will be turned onto your left side, the intravenous fluid rate will be increased, labor augmentation will be stopped if it is being given, and oxygen will be administered by mask. If these measures do not immediately produce an increase in blood pressure, the anesthesiologist can and will be called to administer a medication through the intravenous line that immediately raises the blood pressure and usually also corrects the decreased fetal heart rate.

It is important for you to be aware of this common side effect of epidural anesthesia and the measures taken to counteract it so that you will not panic if these measures are taken. I always advise my patients ahead of time of the possibility of this happening, especially within 20 to 30 minutes after the bolus dose. As I tell them, don't get nervous unless the flight attendant gets nervous! If all of the above measures do not succeed in

bringing the fetal heart rate back up into the normal range, an emergency cesarean delivery will need to be performed. (See pages 206–211 for more information on emergency cesarean deliveries.)

If your epidural anesthesia level is so deep that you are unable to even lift or move your legs, it increases the likelihood that an episiotomy will be performed and that vacuum or forceps assistance may be needed for delivery. However, with continuous-drip dosing, if the baby is tolerating labor well and time is not an issue, the epidural dose can be decreased and, usually, the patient is then soon able to push more effectively.

In some rare cases, epidural anesthesia is not effective and the procedure must be repeated or another form of anesthesia given. If labor is progressing rapidly, delivery may occur before pain relief is achieved from medications or anesthesia. Remember that delivery is the ultimate pain control!

What You May Feel: It will take about 10 minutes after the initial bolus dose before you begin to feel relief. Remember, this means you will feel approximately three to five contractions *after your epidural* before your legs begin to feel tingly or heavy. After 10 minutes, the goal or expected outcome is that pain sensation will decrease slowly over the next several contractions. Although many women are without pain after an epidural, this is not always the case. Many factors influence the degree of relief you receive.

When you first get your epidural, your blood pressure will be taken every 5 minutes for about 20 minutes, then every 15 minutes after that. This is the normal protocol because, as indicated above, the medication can cause your blood pressure to drop, which is also why you receive hydration intravenously prior to and during administration of epidural anesthesia. The anesthesiologist commonly advocates the use of a *hip wedge* (generally composed of pillows placed under your shoulder and hip on one side), because lying flat on your back, even without anes-

thesia, can affect your blood pressure and placental perfusion.

You may or may not still feel pressure in the rectal area as the baby descends during pushing—these nerves are not always well covered by an epidural.

When you have an epidural in place, you can still elevate your head; spinal headaches rarely occur. You can also lie completely on your side. If you do, place a pillow between your knees for support and change sides occasionally to prevent the medication from all running (by gravity) to one side and creating a "window" of pain on the top side. Lift your back when you are moving so that you don't drag against the catheter. (This is just a precaution to be taken even though the catheter is well taped in place.) Your legs will feel very heavy, so you may need help with them when turning. How well you can control and move your legs depends on the depth of anesthesia you received.

If you are pushing or it is nearing time to begin pushing and your legs are extremely heavy and difficult to control, discuss with your nurse whether to call the anesthesiologist to turn down the continuous-drip dosage rate. You will be able to push more effectively if you do not have a deep level of anesthesia.

Side Effects: *Shivering and shaking of the whole body* are common side effects of epidurals. These physiological shivers are commonly seen after epidurals, after cesarean deliveries, and when one is in active labor that is progressing quickly. They are not from being cold or from infection or fever, and they will pass on their own without treatment. Warm blankets and a few liters of oxygen administered by face mask may help the "shakes" to pass more quickly. Knowing that these sometimes fierce shakes are normal and not harmful is helpful to most people.

Itching, especially on the chest and arms, is also common after epidurals. If it is especially annoying, your practitioner will consider medication to help alleviate this side effect.

Urinary retention is common during and immediately after an epidural. This is why you should empty your bladder just before getting your epidural. Your nurse will watch and palpate your bladder while your epidural is in effect. (The bladder sits in front of the uterus and therefore can be seen or felt when it is full.) After delivery and removal of the epidural catheter, control over fine muscles like the small muscle that controls your ability to release urine usually returns a short time after your ability to use large muscles like those in your legs. Therefore, you may be able to get out of bed and still not be able to empty your bladder for a while. Your nurse will continue to watch your bladder and your vaginal bloody show after delivery. (A full bladder prevents the uterus from clamping down properly to control bleeding.) If necessary, your nurse will insert a sterile catheter into your urethra, drain the urine, and remove the catheter. Usually, by the time your bladder fills again, you will have regained fine motor control and be able to urinate on your own.

After Delivery: The epidural catheter is removed after delivery. It takes about one and a half to two hours for your legs to function normally. **Do not get out of bed without assistance *from your nurse:*** your legs may feel normal but still not hold your weight, and people who have had an epidural are more likely to get dizzy and faint their first time out of bed. This is because the veins in your legs may not yet have regained their ability to constrict, and therefore blood pools in your legs when you stand up. When this happens the brain doesn't get a large enough blood supply. The body corrects this by causing you to faint. (After you faint, you are lying flat and blood flows more easily to the brain.)

The first few times you get out of bed, your nurse needs to be there. You are not helping her, or yourself, by getting up alone or with the assistance of a family member. A nurse can assess whether your legs are ready to support you and is qualified to assist you properly if you

become faint. In addition, she or he needs to assess your vaginal flow at this time.

Walking Epidurals

The procedure for the walking epidural is the same as for regular epidural. Instead of an anesthetic medication being used, however, a narcotic is placed through the catheter to relieve pain. Contractions are felt but pain is not, and the mother's blood pressure usually does not drop. Because motor control is not lost, the walking epidural has the advantage of allowing better pushing control and muscle strength.

The reason walking epidurals are not used more often in labor is that they do not provide adequate pain control during pushing, episiotomy, and birth. Local anesthesia or a pudendal block can be added to help with the pain during these stages, but neither one can be given until very close to birth.

Narcotic walking epidurals are more commonly used for postoperative cesarean delivery pain. A dose that lasts approximately 24 hours can be administered and the catheter then removed, or the catheter can be left in place in case additional medication is required. With either method, once the catheter is removed and the last medication wears off, pain medication will have to be taken in another form. Usually by the time the walking epidural catheter is removed, the patient can tolerate a pill form of pain medication.

Spinal Anesthesia

Spinal anesthesia is most often used for cesarean deliveries because it is quick to administer and takes effect immediately (in one to two minutes).

Spinal anesthesia is *not* used for control of labor pain. Although its effects are immediate, it lasts only one to three hours. There is no catheter left in place to add additional medication. A spinal is a one-time procedure, and it creates anesthesia so deep that the mother cannot move her legs or push effectively. It is therefore used during vaginal delivery only if forceps or vacuum extraction is known to be necessary and there is not time to place an epidural instead. (For an explanation of vacuum or forceps delivery, see pages 182–183.) If a spinal is going to be done for this purpose, the mother will be taken to the operating room where caesarean deliveries take place. A spinal cannot be done in the birthing room.

Procedure: You will have the same preparation for spinal anesthesia as described for epidural anesthesia. You will have an IV inserted, take an antacid, and empty your bladder, if time permits. You will be asked by the anesthesiologist to sign a consent form, or, in an emergency, verbal consent only is obtained before the procedure and the signature can come later.

If the spinal is being done for a cesarean delivery, a Foley catheter will be inserted into your bladder. This is done by your nurse as a sterile procedure. A small balloon at the end of the catheter is inflated after the insertion. (The balloon inflates inside your bladder and prevents the catheter from falling out.) The Foley catheter remains in your bladder, draining urine to a collection bag for 24 hours after your cesarean delivery. (See pages 204–205 for a more detailed description of Foley catheter insertion.)

You will be in the same curled-up position as for an epidural, either sitting or lying on your side. In spinal anesthesia, the needle is inserted into the spinal fluid in your lumbar 3-4 or 4-5 space. Medication is injected into the subarachnoid space, where it mixes with spinal fluid. Numbness of the lower half of your body occurs within about two minutes.

Immediately after spinal anesthesia is administered, you will be assisted onto your back and your head will be elevated only slightly, if at all. A wedge will be placed under your right hip and side to tilt you slightly toward the left to increase placental blood flow (perfusion).

If the spinal was done prior to a cesarean delivery, your skin will be tested to ensure that you are not able to feel anything before the procedure begins.

Side Effects: Side effects include headaches, decreased blood pressure, difficulty urinating, respiratory paralysis, and rarely, drug reactions and infections (if respiratory paralysis occurs, respirations will be assisted and medications will be given to help reverse it). Urinary retention may occur and is treated in the same manner as described above under epidural anesthesia. (If the spinal was done for a cesarean section, a Foley catheter will be in place for 24 hours after delivery to automatically drain your urine.)

Spinal headaches can also occur after spinal anesthesia; they are believed to result from leakage of the spinal fluid from the insertion site. However, they are rare today due to the very fine needle used for the procedure. The likelihood is increased if it was a difficult procedure with multiple attempts at insertion. If a spinal headache does occur, it is usually only when the head of the bed is elevated or the person is standing.

It used to be thought that keeping a woman flat for eight hours after spinal anesthesia would prevent spinal headaches. Controlled studies have not proven this to be helpful, but recent evidence shows that placing a person on his or her abdomen after spinal anesthesia reduces the incidence of spinal headache and prevents further leakage of spinal fluid once a headache occurs.

If a spinal headache occurs, initial treatment usually includes pain medication, caffeine, lots of fluid intake, and flat bed rest. An abdominal support girdle or binder may also be ordered for treatment of the headache. If these measures are not effective on their own in stopping the headache, an *epidural blood patch* will be administered by an anesthesiologist. In this procedure a few milliliters of the woman's blood are taken in a tube and then injected in an epidural-type procedure at the site where the spinal was given. It is hoped that a clot will form and cover the hole, thereby preventing further leakage of spinal fluid from the site. Sometimes this procedure has to be repeated before it is effective.

General Anesthesia

General anesthesia puts you completely to sleep. It is done for an emergency ("crash") cesarean delivery in the case of severe fetal distress or maternal hemorrhage, when time does not allow for administration of spinal anesthesia. It may also be done during a cesarean delivery if the epidural or spinal anesthesia is not adequate to control pain.

If an emergency occurs, things will be moving quickly. If this happens to you, please remember that just as you are trained to do your job safely, so are the members of the maternity care team. Trust them and try not to panic; do slow rhythmic breathing to help yourself relax. They are moving quickly for the safety of both you and your baby and will not take a lot of time for explanations or reassurance. (See pages 206–210 for further explanation of obstetrical emergencies.)

Procedure: You will be given medication through your IV to put you to sleep. As with any patient having general anesthesia, monitors will be used to assess your blood pressure and pulse at all times. The anesthesiologist will never leave you. Your breathing will be assisted by the anesthesiologist by means of a tube that is placed in your throat after you are asleep. Although this tube is removed before you are fully awake, it may cause you to experience some throat discomfort in your early recovery.

What You May Feel: When you wake up your throat may be sore and you may feel nauseated. Medications will be given to you for these discomforts if they occur. Continue to try to relax.

Depending on the protocol of your hospital, if your baby was born without requiring any respiratory assistance, he or she may still be in the delivery room when you awaken. You may now see and hold your baby if you wish and feel able to do so. In some hospitals, the baby born to a mother

under general anesthesia is immediately tagged with two bracelets, which match the one placed on your arm, and taken to the nursery.

You will go to a recovery room for about two hours, where you will have leads to a cardiac monitor attached to you. An automatic blood pressure cuff will be on your arm, inflating every 5 minutes for awhile, then every 15 minutes. In your early recovery, a nurse will closely monitor your blood pressure and pulse, which serve as clear indicators of your heart, lung, and blood circulation status after surgery. They also show early clues for when pain medication is needed.

A small clamp that looks like a clothespin may be attached to your finger or toe. This is a *pulse oximeter*, and it tells the percentage of oxygen in your blood at the tip of your finger or toe. It assures the nurses that your oxygen status is adequate until you are fully recovered from the effects of anesthesia. By showing them your actual oxygen levels, a pulse oximeter also helps them to judge how much pain medication can be given to control your discomfort without depressing your respirations and thereby affecting your oxygen saturation.

You may be given oxygen by mask for a short period of time. Don't let this make you nervous. The monitors tell what you need, and you may need more oxygen until the effects of anesthesia have fully disappeared.

It is important for you to know in advance what to expect during your recovery time. That way when you wake up attached to cardiac and blood pressure monitors, with a clip on your finger and an oxygen mask on your face, you will not panic and think something is wrong. This is *normal* recovery-room protocol.

Reading about cesarean deliveries ahead of time is an important part of labor preparation. In the event that cesarean delivery is required, you will feel a greater sense of control, already having an understanding of what will occur and what you can expect. (Refer to Chapter 12 for a full review of what you and your support person can expect during and after a cesarean delivery.)

Childbirth

10

Labor and Birth

Every birth is both unique and universal. Although the physiological process of labor and birth has been the same since human life began, each woman and her baby experience the process in a different way. For some, labor moves quickly and the baby is born within a few hours of the first contraction. For others, the process is long and tiring and may require extensive medical intervention. Although usually longer for first babies and shorter for subsequent babies, labor may be the other way around. "Truly unpredictable" is the best description I have found for labor!

Stages of Labor

Practitioners describe three stages of labor: the first stage is dilatation and effacement of the cervix, the second is pushing and the birth of the baby, and the third is delivery of the placenta. Understanding what happens in each stage can help you work with the natural forces of labor and help relieve your anxiety and fear and the added discomfort they can cause.

First Stage: Dilatation and Effacement

In the first stage of labor, the cervix opens from its closed state to 10 centimeters dilated (fully dilated). Dilatation is also described as the number of "fingers" dilated. Each finger of dilatation equals two centimeters. Therefore, if you are two fingers dilated, your cervical opening is four centimeters. (See pages 82–83 for an explanation of dilatation and effacement.)

The first stage of labor consists of physiological changes. Other than walking, changing positions, keeping well hydrated, and emptying your bladder frequently, there is nothing you can do that will help your cervix dilate faster—your uterus does all the work in this stage of labor.

Second Stage: Pushing and Birth

The second stage of labor, also called the pushing stage, begins when the cervix is fully dilated and ends with the birth of the baby. It is a team effort requiring both strong contractions of your uterus and your forceful pushing efforts.

Third Stage: Delivery of the Placenta

The third stage of labor begins after the birth of the baby and ends with delivery of the placenta (see pages 183–184 for more about the placenta), sometimes referred to as the *afterbirth*.

What Is Considered Normal Labor?

"Labor is considered 'normal' when a woman is at or near term, no complications exist, a single fetus presents by vertex, and labor is completed within 24 hours."[1]

The process of labor is *very* variable. When average time limits are given for each stage, one must remember that as in all averages, there are extremes at both ends. Some women who have had more than one pregnancy may reach full dilatation in one hour, and others may take many hours. Likewise, some women in their first pregnancy may arrive at the hospital fully dilated, complaining only of gas pains; other women may take 24 hours to deliver their first baby.

In general, the average length of time it takes a woman having her first baby to dilate from a closed cervix to three centimeters is 6 to 10 hours. However, it can take up to 20 hours for first babies and 14 hours for subsequent labors and still be considered normal. (The reasons for this lengthy amount of time in the early phase of dilatation are further explained on page 162.)

Once active labor is achieved (at four centimeters of dilatation) a woman having her first baby continues to dilate on average about one centimeter per hour, thus making this active phase three to six hours in length for first babies. In subsequent labors, dilatation (after four centimeters) usually advances more quickly, at an average rate of about one and one-half centimeters per hour.

For the second stage of labor—the pushing stage—up to two hours is considered normal for the first baby. (Three hours is considered normal and acceptable if there are no signs of fetal distress.) In general, the pushing stage for subsequent labors is much shorter than for the first baby, but it can vary from a few pushes to two hours because it depends on the size and presentation of your baby, which vary with each pregnancy. The second stage can even be longer if the woman has received epidural anesthesia.

The third stage of labor—delivery of the placenta—is considered normal if it occurs anytime during the first hour after delivery of the baby, as long as bleeding is within normal limits during the waiting period. Usually, strong contractions occurring within seven minutes after delivery cause the placenta to separate.

Prolonged Labor

Labor is considered *prolonged* when it lasts longer than what is considered the normal upper limit of time in either the first (dilatation and effacement) or second (pushing) stage of labor. It is important to remember, however, that the first stage of labor is divided into the early (also called latent) phase (closed cervix to three centimeters dilated) and the active phase (four centimeters to full dilatation of the cervix). The early (latent) phase can last up to 20 hours in a woman having her first baby, and up to 14 hours in a woman having subsequent births, before it is considered prolonged. Once four centimeters of cervical dilatation is reached (at which point the labor is considered active), it is expected that a woman having her first baby will continue to dilate at a rate of about one centimeter per hour. Subsequent labors would be expected to progress at about one and one-half centimeters per hour.

[1]D. L. Lowdermilk, S. E. Perry, and I. M. Bobak, *Maternity and Women's Health Care*, 6th ed. (St. Louis: Mosby, 1997), p. 293.

There are many causes of prolonged labor. Some of these factors, such as the size of the baby or the size and shape of the mother's pelvis, cannot be changed. Other factors, such as the position of the baby, may be changed by the mother changing her position.

Ineffective uterine contractions can also prolong labor. If your contractions are two to three minutes apart and are painful but do not change the cervix, your practitioner may administer oxytocin (Pitocin) to help make them more effective.

The size and shape of your pelvis are important factors in labor. If the pelvis is too small or too narrow for the size of your baby, prolonged labor results and culminates in a cesarean delivery. A cesarean delivery can also be necessary if you have a normal-size pelvis, but an exceptionally large baby that is too big for your pelvis.

Prolonged labor can also be caused by abnormalities in the way the baby presents into the pelvis. Breech (buttocks first), footling breech (one or both feet first), shoulder presentation (shoulder presents), and face presentation (head is extended to present the face rather than flexed to present the crown of the head) are examples of abnormal presentations.

The *transverse position* (baby's back faces the woman's side) and the *posterior position* (the back of the baby's head faces the mother's back instead of the mother's abdomen) both cause more difficult, painful, and prolonged labor. In addition, if the baby is presenting in the normal head-down presentation (*vertex presentation*), just a slight cocking or tilting of the head off center (*asynclitic presentation*) can cause more prolonged labor.

Sometimes it is not evident until a woman is fully dilated that, due to one or a combination of the above factors, vaginal delivery is not going to occur during this labor or is no longer safe for you or your baby. If this is the case, your baby will need to be delivered by cesarean procedure.

Although a prolonged labor is difficult and tiring, it is important to keep in mind that the outcome for both mother and baby in the vast majority of cases is positive.

Inducing Labor

Labor is sometimes induced artificially to hasten delivery before spontaneous onset of labor. The many reasons why your practitioner may recommend induction are summarized in Box 10-1.

BOX 10-1

Reasons for Inducing Labor

- ❑ You are diabetic.
- ❑ You have gestational diabetes (a diabetic state brought on by pregnancy).
- ❑ You have hypertension (high blood pressure).
- ❑ You have pregnancy-induced hypertension, which is high blood pressure brought on by pregnancy.
- ❑ You are overdue (commonly called post-term).
- ❑ A nonstress test (see page 85 for explanation of this test) shows that your baby is under minor stress or your placenta shows signs of degenerating or aging more rapidly than normal.
- ❑ Your membranes have ruptured and you haven't gone into labor after a reasonable amount of time on your own. (There is no consensus of opinion that induction increases your chance of having a vaginal birth when done for this reason, because the length and thickness of the cervix vary at the time of membrane rupture. If the cervix is long, thick, and closed at the time the membranes rupture it is less likely to respond to induction than a partially thinned-out, soft cervix. Your cervix will be more likely to respond to induction the closer you are to full term.)
- ❑ You are close to but not yet full term, but your baby is large for gestation age (LGA), or you are full term with an LGA baby and not yet in labor.

Childbirth

Types of Induction

If your practitioner determines that labor needs to be induced, he or she may recommend either prostaglandin therapy or oxytocin induction. The method chosen depends on the condition of your cervix. If your cervix is still thick, long, and hard, prostaglandin therapy may be suggested to soften it and make it more favorable for induction. If your cervix is already soft and effaced, or once it has been softened by prostaglandin therapy, oxytocin induction will be ordered to induce labor.

Prostaglandin Therapy (Cervical Ripening)

Prostaglandin therapy softens the cervix and makes it more favorable for successful induction (thus it is known as cervical ripening), Prostaglandin is a hormone that comes in several forms. Depending on the specific type ordered by your doctor, it will either be inserted into your cervical canal, put inside a diaphragm to be placed against your cervix, or inserted as a vaginal gel.

You will be in the hospital with an intravenous line or heparin lock in place. (A heparin lock is an intravenous catheter inserted in a vein in your hand or arm but not immediately attached to an intravenous fluid. Instead, the catheter is capped and injected periodically with a saline solution to keep it from clotting. It allows immediate access to your vein whenever intravenous fluids become necessary.) Access to a vein may be required if the prostaglandin used to soften your cervix causes uterine contractions that do not relax. This "tonic" contraction is a rare side effect of prostaglandin therapy. Because a contraction that does not relax is dangerous to your baby, the intravenous line is necessary to give your doctor immediate access to a vein to administer medication to reverse this side effect.

Side effects of prostaglandin therapy are unusual, but, when they do occur, cramping and contractions are the most common. Nausea and vomiting are rare side effects.

You will be on bed rest for one to two hours after receiving prostaglandin and then allowed out of bed. You may have to lie flat for one hour, depending on the type of hormone used. In four to six hours, again depending on the hormone form used, your cervix will be reassessed. A second identical prostaglandin treatment may be recommended at this time. It takes up to 24 hours for prostaglandin to work, so you will usually go home after one or two treatments and return for oxytocin (Pitocin) induction the next day.

When you go home, try to relax as much as possible—you will want to be well rested for your induction. A warm bath or a hot water bottle may help you relax and may relieve cramping. *If cramps or contractions do not decrease in intensity or become painful and reach a frequency of one every three to eight minutes, call your practitioner.* Some women go into labor after treatment with prostaglandin therapy alone. You don't want to misinterpret this positive "side effect" of cervical treatment as just cramps or contractions; if in fact they become regular and frequent, you may be in labor. *If your membranes rupture, call your practitioner promptly.* Note the time, color, and amount of fluid. Pink or blood-tinged mucus discharge is normal after prostaglandin therapy. *If you are bleeding as you do during a menstrual period, call your practitioner.*

Sometime in the evening after you go home, count your baby's movements. (See page 73 for instructions on how to count fetal movements.) Ten fetal movements within two hours indicate that your baby tolerated the contractions brought on by the gel. *Call your practitioner if you count fewer than 10 movements in two hours,* or follow the specific instructions of your practitioner regarding decreased fetal movement.

Oxytocin (Pitocin) Induction

Once the cervix has softened (which is considered a favorable cervix), oxytocin induction can begin. Oxytocin is the exact hormone the body naturally produces to begin and sustain labor. It is often called by the common brand name *Pitocin*. Oxytocin is given through an intravenous line with the amounts carefully controlled by a pump (Figure 10-1).

Pitocin is started slowly and increased in very small amounts every 10 to 30 minutes, depending on your hospital's protocol. The goal of oxytocin induction is to achieve contractions every two to three minutes with complete uterine relaxation between contractions. Of course, this must occur without any distress to your baby, which is why your baby's heartbeat and your uterine contractions are carefully monitored during induction by means of a monitor placed on the side of your abdomen (see Figure 5-7, page 86).

If cervical dilatation has not progressed after 8 to 12 hours of oxytocin induction and your baby is tolerating the procedure well, the oxytocin is discontinued overnight so that you can sleep. The following day, the induction will be repeated. It is

not uncommon for oxytocin induction to take two days to produce cervical dilatation.

Keep in mind that inductions are done when delivery is required early (for medical reasons), when membranes have ruptured and the woman hasn't gone into labor in a reasonable amount of time on her own, or when the patient is overdue and not in labor. (See page 157 for further information on inductions.)

You should expect the induction process to take some time—remember, you are starting from *square one*. (This is different from labor augmentation, in which oxytocin is used to augment an already progressing labor or one that stops progressing at a certain point along the way.) Try not to be discouraged: once labor becomes well established and dilatation begins, you can expect to progress as described below. Although inductions are occasionally unsuccessful and cesarean delivery is required, the vast majority of inductions result in vaginal births.

Oxytocin augmentation may be used in a labor in which the contractions are weak, short, irregular, or infrequent (long periods between contractions) and are not producing normal progression in cervical dilatation. In labor augmentation, oxytocin is administered in the same way as in an induction. Small doses are given via a controlled intravenous infusion regulated by the same pump as in Figure 10-1. The dosage is increased *slowly* until the contractions are regular and approximately two to three minutes apart.

FIGURE 10-1

IV Pump

Beginning the Labor Experience

Each woman experiences labor in her own way, influenced by many factors, both psychological and physiological. Learning about normal labor, knowing what to expect, and using effective relaxation techniques can help you and your support person feel more relaxed and less anxious.

Childbirth

When Should I Call My Practitioner?

Your maternity care practitioner will have specific instructions for you about when you are to call him or her. The instructions will be individually determined by many factors, including your medical and obstetric history (both past and present). Be certain that you are clear on your instructions.

For a woman having her first baby, without medical or obstetric risk factors, the *usual instructions* are to call your care provider whenever your membranes rupture or, if your membranes have not ruptured, to call when contractions are regular and about 5 to 10 minutes apart. For multiparas (women who have previously had a labor), instructions will be affected by the above factors, especially the length of your previous labors.

Your contractions do not have to be perfectly regular for you to call. If they are irregular or infrequent but very painful, you should call. Contractions can be regular without pain, and you should still call.

Remember what I said before: labor is totally unpredictable. *If you are uncertain, call.* (See Chapter 5, page 81, for more information on timing contractions.) Your practitioner can assess much more by hearing your voice and asking you specific questions. Your practitioner and the nursing staff at the hospital would much rather you err on the side of too many calls than arrive at the hospital with delivery imminent.

What Will Happen When I Arrive at the Hospital?

Most hospitals have you register on arrival, either in the regular admitting area or an area specifically for labor patients. (You should find out the correct location during a tour of your delivering hospital.) Once registered, you will be directed to the maternity unit or maternity evaluation unit. **If you arrive at the hospital having rectal pressure or feeling that delivery is imminent, enter through the emergency room area and inform someone immediately of your situation. You will be taken directly to maternity, and registration can be completed later.**

If this is not your first baby and you are obviously in active labor, you will most likely be admitted directly to a labor room. Otherwise, you will be taken to an area where you, your contractions, your baby, and your cervix can be evaluated. If you are still in early labor, many hospitals will have you ambulate for a while and then reassess your cervix. True labor is determined by cervical change. Once you are having regular contractions that are producing cervical change, you will be admitted.

Do not feel discouraged if you are only two or three centimeters dilated when you arrive at the hospital for your first baby. Your cervix must soften, efface (thin out), and pull forward before significant dilatation begins. *Lots of work has already been accomplished* once the cervix has done these things.

If this is your first baby, your contractions are infrequent and mild, and your cervix is not dilated over three centimeters, you may be asked to go home until your labor is more active. Many things are taken into consideration before making this decision, including how far away you live. Many people are sent home a couple of times before being admitted, so don't feel bad if this happens to you, although it can be frustrating. Do not hesitate to go to the hospital if you think you are in labor just because you want to avoid the possibility of being sent home. It is much worse to arrive at the hospital with no time to get settled before delivery than to be sent home once or twice in false or early labor.

If this is not your first baby and you arrive with active contractions, you may be evaluated promptly in the evaluation unit or admitted directly to a labor room. If you arrive with mild to moderate contractions and have not yet begun to dilate, you may be asked to ambulate until the contractions are stronger or for a specific period of time and then return for reevaluation.

If you are asked to ambulate or return home, regardless of whether this is your first or your fifth baby, please remember that the decision was made at a specific time because of specific symptoms. If your symptoms change, you may need to return for evaluation sooner than instructed or call your practitioner again. Labor is unpredictable and can change quickly.

The type of room you are admitted to depends on what your hospital offers and what is available at that time (which is affected by patient census). (See page 7 for an explanation of LDRP rooms—in which labor, delivery, recovery, and postpartum stay all take place in the same room—and other types of rooms.) When you arrive at the hospital, you should certainly state your preference if various options are available at your hospital. In some hospitals there are only a few LDRP rooms and they are subject to availability at the time of your admission.

If your hospital has only LDRP rooms, the room to which you are admitted is where you will remain for your labor, delivery, birth, and postpartum stay. (Of course, if you require a cesarean delivery, you would be moved to the delivery operating room, taken to a separate recovery room, and then returned to your birthing room or another room for your postpartum stay.)

If your hospital does not have LDRP rooms available, then the room you are admitted to may be just for labor (L), or just for labor and delivery (LD). Or perhaps it will be what is called LDR-P, which means the initial room is for labor, delivery, and initial recovery (one to three hours) only, followed by a move to a postpartum room (for the remainder of your hospital stay).

Once you have been admitted to a labor room, your labor nurse will assess your contractions and the baby's heartbeat on a fetal monitor for a short period of time. During this time, admission history questions will be asked and you will have the opportunity to discuss your birthing plan. In addition, your admission blood work will be drawn and an intravenous line may be started if you prefer an epidural for anesthesia. Once it is established on the monitor that your baby is doing well and tolerating labor at this point, you

will be allowed to ambulate or shower depending on your hospital's policies.

What About Rupture of Membranes?

Sometime during the first or second stage of labor, the amniotic sac will rupture on its own (spontaneous rupture of membranes, or SROM) (Figure 10-2), or your practitioner will choose to rupture your membranes for you (artificial rupture of membranes, or AROM). If the membranes are not ruptured during labor, the sac will be cut at delivery as the baby's head is being delivered.

To artificially rupture the membranes, a plastic device with a small blunt hook on the end is used during a vaginal exam. If you are four or more centimeters dilated or if the amniotic sac is bulging through the cervical opening, this procedure will not be any more uncomfortable than a regular vaginal exam. If you are only two to three centimeters dilated the procedure may be more uncomfortable—use slow rhythmic breathing or 2-1 breathing to help you with the discomfort. (See pages 139–142 for an explanation of relaxation breathing techniques.)

Labor normally progresses more quickly after the membranes have ruptured. This is because

FIGURE 10-2

Rupture of Membranes

the fluid cushion between the cervix and the baby's head is eliminated and the firm head is now well applied to the cervix. Therefore, contractions may be experienced as more painful after the amniotic sac has ruptured.

If rupture of membranes occurs before labor starts (which happens in 15 percent of pregnancies), contractions usually begin within several hours. If contractions do not begin within 12 to 24 hours, oxytocin induction will be started.

Your practitioner will give you specific instructions about what to do if your membranes rupture prior to labor. (🖑)**Your job is to report rupture of membranes to your caregiver. He or she will also want to know the amount (a slow trickle or a gush) and the color of the fluid.** (See page 119 for more information on reporting rupture of membranes and evaluation of the fluid amount and color.)

It is sometimes difficult to know if what you are experiencing is a slow amniotic fluid leak, increased vaginal discharge, or loss of urine control. In general, amniotic fluid is clear to straw-colored and may contain specks of vernix (the white substance that looks like cheese that covers the baby's skin before birth). It may, however, be green, greenish-yellow, or light brown if it contains meconium. Amniotic fluid either has no scent or may be slightly sweet smelling. It does not have the ammonia scent of urine. Vaginal discharge, on the other hand, is usually thicker than amniotic fluid and may feel like mucus. You are *only* asked to make good observations and report your findings. From the information you give, your care provider will decide whether you need to be seen for assessment and evaluation at this time.

First Stage: Cervical Dilatation and Effacement

The first stage of labor has three phases: the early (also called latent) phase, the active phase, and the transition phase. The entire first stage may last up to 24 hours for first babies. During this time your cervix thins and dilates to 10 centimeters. Full dilatation (10 centimeters) must be achieved before the second stage (pushing) begins.

Early (Latent) Phase

The early phase, also called the latent phase, is characterized by zero to three centimeters of cervical dilation.

It lasts an average of 6 to 10 hours. For your first baby, usually long before dilatation occurs, the long, thick, firm cervix thins out and becomes softer. This is called *effacement* of the cervix, and it is stated in percentages. If you are 70 percent effaced, 70 percent of the length of your cervix is gone. For subsequent births, effacement normally occurs simultaneously with dilatation. (Refer to Figure 5-3, page 83.)

During pregnancy, the cervical opening, called the *cervical os*, points back toward your rectum. This is called a "posterior cervix" in early labor. (This has nothing to do with a posterior presentation, described on page 83, which refers to the baby's position.) As real labor becomes established, the cervical os moves forward (more anterior) until it is directly at the top of the vagina. (When the cervix comes into this position, vaginal exams become much less uncomfortable because the examiner no longer has to reach so far in and back to examine the cervical os.)

Many women progress to three-centimeter dilatation before beginning regular contractions. In women having normal irregular Braxton Hicks contractions, cervical dilatation can be well under way before real labor begins. In other women, when regular contractions begin, early labor changes the cervix from closed to three centimeters dilated.

The early (latent) phase of labor is *very variable* in how long it takes. Although the average length of time is 6 to 10 hours, it may last longer—even as long as 20 hours—or it may be shorter. "Totally unpredictable" is a good description of this early phase of labor!

A woman can have what is called *prodromal labor* for days in this phase. Prodromal labor is diagnosed when a woman has uncomfortable contractions over 24 hours that do not change her cervix. Treatment for prodromal labor usually consists of an injection or two of morphine to promote sleep therapy and allow the woman to rest. On awakening, if normal labor does not begin and the woman is near term, oxytocin labor augmentation may be given. See page 159 for an explanation of labor augmentation.

Figure 10-3 shows the baby in the normal head-down presentation with the amniotic sac still intact. The cervix is not effaced, and dilatation is approximately one to two centimeters. The figure also shows the frequency and duration of the contractions during this phase of labor.

What You May Feel: During the early (latent) phase of labor, contractions are usually mild and

FIGURE 10-3

The Early Phase

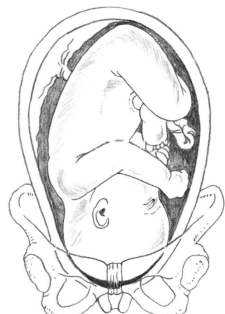

Dilatation of Cervix:
Closed through three centimeters

Effacement of Cervix For Your First Labor:
Full effacement may be completed before dilatation begins.

For Subsequent Labors:
Effacement and dilatation usually occur at the same time.

This illustration shows:
The head-down position (vertex presentation)

The amniotic fluid sac still intact (membranes intact)

The cervix thick (not effaced) and approximately one to two centimeters dilated

Contraction Pattern:

Duration

Frequency

Frequency of contractions: Ranges from every 5 to 30 minutes
Duration of contractions: 30–40 seconds

Childbirth

irregular and are from 5 to 30 minutes apart. They last from 30 to 40 or sometimes 45 seconds. You will feel the contractions but will generally be comfortable enough to talk during them.

Most women feel discomfort or cramping in the lower front of the abdomen during contractions in the early phase of labor. Show (vaginal discharge) will be scant during this phase. If present, it may consist of a brownish discharge, pink mucus, or your mucus plug.

You will feel excited and perhaps nervous. In this early phase of labor, your labor education pays off: relaxation breathing techniques can help keep your nervousness at bay.

What Your Support Person Can Do: In this phase of labor, the woman's thoughts center on herself, her labor, and her baby, and the labor support person needs to understand this. This is no time to try to make plans for upcoming family events or to discuss travel accommodations for arriving relatives. The support person needs to take conversation cues from the laboring woman.

What You Can Do: Once labor begins, digestion of your stomach contents stops. Therefore, **it is best not to eat solid foods once your contractions are regular** and you are fairly certain that you are in labor. **But do not stop drinking.** Your uterus is a muscle and it needs calories for energy. **Drink clear liquids** such as water, cranberry juice, apple juice, and noncaffeinated clear soda. **Do not drink only water.** You, your uterus, and your baby need sugar. (If you are a diabetic or have gestational diabetes, use diabetic clear liquid drinks.)

Avoid caffeine. Coffee, tea, cola drinks, Mountain Dew, and chocolate all contain caffeine, which is a stimulant and may make you feel more nervous or unable to rest between contractions. In addition, caffeine acts as a diuretic, making your body get rid of fluid more rapidly. Because you need good hydration during labor, drinks containing caffeine are not a good choice.

Walking increases the frequency and intensity of real labor contractions in all phases of dilatation. Walking during early labor is encouraged

unless your membranes have ruptured and on vaginal exam it is noted that the presenting part is still very high up in your pelvis (not well applied to the cervix). Because there is a risk of umbilical cord prolapse in this situation, your baby will be checked with an external fetal monitor until he or she comes down farther into the pelvis and the presenting part rests against your cervix. Once the presenting part is well applied to (up against) the cervix, you will be allowed to ambulate with ruptured membranes.

Changing positions can help you relax during labor. Standing, sitting in a rocking chair, and lying in bed on your side are all helpful position changes. Figure 10-4 shows additional positions that may help you relax during labor.

Slow rhythmic breathing during contractions may also be helpful. See page 140 for an explanation of slow rhythmic breathing.

Active Phase

The active phase of labor is marked by four to seven centimeters of cervical dilatation. It lasts an average of three to six hours for first babies. Dilatation on average occurs at a rate of about one centimeter per hour for first babies and one and one-half centimeters per hour in subsequent labors.

What You May Feel: During the active phase of labor, contractions are moderate to strong in intensity and regular in frequency, generally three to five minutes apart. However, they may be as close as two minutes apart in this phase. They generally last from 40 to 60 seconds, but they may last as long as 70 seconds (Figure 10-5). Most women experience pain with contractions in this phase. Pain is usually experienced in the lower back and may also be felt in the lower abdomen. Some women feel all of their labor discomfort in their thighs.

During the active phase of labor, vaginal discharge or show increases to a moderate amount and appears as a pink-to-bloody mucus.

You may feel much more serious in this phase of dilatation, becoming more apprehensive and ex-

FIGURE 10-4

Positions That May Help You to Relax During Labor

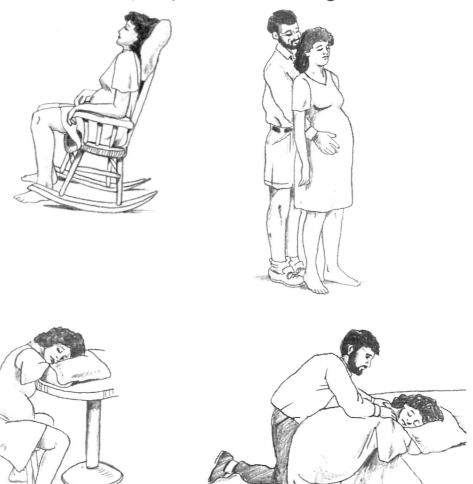

pressing doubt that you will be able to remain in control. Your attention will remain focused inward on yourself, and fatigue will be evident. This may be the first time you have experienced something happening to your body that you could not stop or control. *Tension and nervousness are natural and expected responses.* The presence of a labor sup-

port person is very helpful at this time. Words of encouragement are needed and welcomed.

Assessing Contractions and Fetal Heart Rate: The midwife or nurse caring for you may need to assess your contractions and the baby's heart rate more frequently now that your

FIGURE 10-5

The Active Phase

Dilatation of Cervix: Four to
  seven centimeters dilated

**Effacement of Cervix
For Your First Labor:**
Full effacement is often completed before dilatation begins. If not fully effaced, effacement ranges from about
60 to 90 percent.

For Subsequent Labors:
Effacement and dilatation
usually occur at the same
time. As you become more
dilated, you become more effaced.

This illustration shows:
  The head-down position
  (vertex presentation)

  The amniotic sac still intact
  (membranes intact)

  The cervix about 60 percent
  effaced

  The cervix about four centimeters dilated

Contraction Pattern:

Duration

Frequency

Frequency of contractions: 2 to 5 minutes apart
Duration of contractions: 40–70 seconds

labor is more active. An electronic fetal monitor
(Figure 5-7) is used for these assessments.
Although statistics have shown that use of the fetal monitor doesn't improve the outcome for
women who have had normal pregnancies, occasional assessment does tell the nurse and practitioner how your baby is presently tolerating
labor.

Many factors will be considered in determining whether intermittent, constant, or no monitoring will be done. Hospital policy also influ-

ences the frequency of monitoring. You may see
many variations in how often laboring women are
monitored. Feel free to ask questions—you have
a right to know why constant monitoring or no
monitoring at all is being done on your baby.

The fetal monitor continually measures the
frequency and duration of your contractions and
the baby's heart rate so the relationship between
contractions, fetal activity, and fetal heart rate can
be assessed. If you are in the shower or walking, a
Doppler ultrasound—a small, portable handheld

instrument—can be used to listen to the baby's heart rate, but it does not assess contractions.

External Monitoring of Contractions.
The toco, the part of the electric fetal monitor used to evaluate contractions, is held on your abdomen by a belt or soft girdle and contains a disc that responds to pressure. The height seen on the graphic display for contractions depends on the location of the toco (whether it is over a firm or soft area on your uterus) and the tightness of the belts holding it. The external toco evaluates the frequency and duration of contractions only; it cannot evaluate the quality or actual strength of your contractions. (See Figure 5-7, page 86.)

Internal Monitoring of Contractions.
At any point in your labor from here through the pushing stage, if you have had uncomfortable contractions for several hours but your cervix has not dilated further, or if your pushing has not brought the baby down, your practitioner may want to assess the actual strength of your contractions. If your amniotic sac has already ruptured, an internal uterine pressure catheter (IUPC) may be inserted through your vagina into and along the inner wall of your uterus. This instrument is designed to tell your caregivers the actual pressure of each of your contractions. It is used to determine whether your contractions are strong enough to cause dilatation or to bring your baby down when you push. If your contractions prove to be strong enough, then other causes of "failure to progress" (baby too big, or pelvis too small) must be considered. If your contractions are in fact determined by use of the IUPC to be too weak to bring about cervical change, oxytocin augmentation can be started. (See page 159 for an explanation of oxytocin labor augmentation.)

Some IUPC catheters allow for an *amniotic fluid infusion,* a procedure done only under certain conditions. A warm normal saline solution is infused at a specific rate through the catheter into the uterus. (Normal saline is a salt water solution with a salt concentration equal to that of your blood.) This fluid infusion may help alleviate some conditions that are causing minor stress to your infant. Amniotic fluid infusion is never used to treat severe fetal distress, because the procedure takes time to set up and take effect.

External Monitoring of the Fetal Heart.
The part of the fetal monitor used to assess the baby's heart rate is called the *ultrasound.* The relationship between the baby's heart rate, your contractions, and the baby's activity is very important. It helps your caregivers evaluate how well your baby is tolerating labor. The ultrasound picks up the baby's heart rate through the abdomen of the mother. (See Figure 5-7, page 86.) It works best when sound waves given off and then picked back up by the instrument are angled through the baby's back. If the baby or mother changes position, the ultrasound location on the abdomen will need to be adjusted.

Cord Compression: The umbilical cord can become compressed if the cord is knotted or wrapped around the baby's neck or body, in which case the knots or wrapping are usually loose enough that the blood flow inside the cord is not completely obstructed.

Symptoms: During labor, the external fetal monitor will pick up a distinct pattern in the heart rate if any cord compression occurs. As long as the fetal heart recovers quickly with position change, and the monitor strip appears otherwise normal, labor is allowed to progress. However, if the knot tightens or the cord around the neck becomes further compressed, this distinct pattern on the monitor tracing will not correct with position changes and an emergency cesarean delivery will be performed. Of course, if a knot in the cord became so tight as to completely shut off the flow of blood, fetal death would occur.

Treatment: Intermittent monitoring of the baby's heartbeat can usually detect early signs of fetal distress due to cord compression. It is important to note, however, that not all cord compression causes fetal distress. Sometimes a position change for the mother is all that is necessary to relieve the compression. At other times, especially if the umbilical cord is wrapped loosely

Childbirth

around baby's neck or body, position changes may not totally relieve the compression, in which case the signs on the monitor strip will appear intermittently and go away rapidly. If your baby's heartbeat quickly returns to normal, labor will be allowed to progress. However, your baby's heartbeat will be monitored very closely.

When cord compression is suddenly severe and is not relieved by position changes, an emergency cesarean delivery is required.

Internal Monitoring of the Fetal Heart.
If a more accurate and continuous evaluation of the baby's heart rate is needed, an internal electrode will be placed. To do this, the amniotic membrane is ruptured and an internal device (a small, spiral-wire electrode) is placed on your baby's head and turned slightly so that the wire attaches to the skin. The reading from this electrode is very accurate and gives your doctor much more information about your baby's well-being or stress. It can help your practitioner determine whether you need immediate cesarean delivery or if your baby can tolerate further labor.

Parents often ask if the baby experiences pain from the internal electrode. When the small wire is placed on the baby's head, an increase in the baby's heart rate for several seconds is normally seen. The heart rate goes back to the normal pattern quickly, however, which implies that the baby does not continue to have discomfort from the electrode after the initial attachment.

What You Can Do: You need to empty your bladder frequently. A full bladder takes up space, and emptying it gives your baby more room to come down in the pelvis and prevents bladder irritation, as well.

Continue to drink lots of clear fluids. Ice chips may also be satisfying.

Labor impulses travel from the cervix to the lower spinal nerves and then up the spinal column to your brain. If you allow your brain to focus on pain, you may become nervous, tense, and anxious. Relaxation breathing techniques and many other relaxation techniques work by mental distraction—as you focus on one of these techniques or another form of distraction, you help to "distract," or break, the pain pathway to the brain. When the pain pathways are interrupted in this way, you usually experience less muscle tension and less nervousness.

If you have been using relaxation breathing up to this point, then, as soon as you are no longer able to stay relaxed during a contraction, change from slow rhythmic breathing to the next form of breathing that you learned. (See pages 139–146 for an explanation of breathing techniques and other relaxation techniques that can be utilized.)

A shower during this stage of labor can do a great deal to relieve tension and reduce pain. It is especially beneficial if a shower chair is available along with a handheld shower head. While sitting, allow warm water to run over your abdomen during a contraction.

What Your Support Person Can Do: During this phase, the laboring woman may be very demanding and difficult to please (for example, the cloth used to wipe her forehead is too cold or too wet, the drink handed her has too much ice or not enough, the back rub is too hard or not on the right spot, and so on). It is important for the labor support person to understand that these attempts to control the environment and those around her are a *normal coping mechanism* when one feels a loss of control over one's own body. It is just a laboring woman's way of regaining some needed control, so expect that her behavior and attitudes may change during labor, and don't take offense. Allowing a woman in labor these small areas of control may be just what she needs at this time, and it is considered a form of helping.

Most women in this phase of labor have difficulty following instructions. Labor support persons may have to join the mother in a breathing technique to help keep her focused. In addition, most women find it easier to stay in control if they keep their eyes opened and focused on an object or on the face of their support person. Closing one's eyes tends to make one focus inward on the pain.

During the active phase of labor, gentle touch and massage are generally helpful, especially counterpressure or deep massage to the lower back over the coccyx area. (See Figure 9-3, page 145.) Effleurage may also be helpful. (See page 51 for a description and Figure 3-2, page 51, for an illustration.) Hot water bottles applied to the lower back and thighs may also be comforting to some women.

It is important to note, however, that some women do not want to be touched when they are in pain. No one knows how they will respond to pain until the time comes. Support persons must watch for clues to see what is helpful and what promotes relaxation. Don't continue to stroke or massage a woman who pushes your hand away. Some women want lower-back rubs during contractions and want to be left alone between contractions. Others want it the other way around. For some women, any touch while they are in pain adds to their discomfort and distracts them from their focus. **A helpful support person pays attention to nonverbal behavior clues, as well as verbal statements, to determine the effectiveness of whatever pain-reducing technique is being tried.**

Transition Phase

The transition phase of labor is characterized by cervical dilatation of 8 to 10 centimeters. It lasts about 20 minutes to two hours for first babies.

What You May Feel: Contractions during this phase are regular, strong, and two to three minutes apart, although they may be as close as every one to one and one-half minutes apart. They last 45 to 90 seconds, which allows only short rest periods between contractions.

Figure 10-6 shows full effacement and dilatation of eight to nine centimeters. The amniotic sac has ruptured, but further engagement of the baby's head has prevented remaining amniotic fluid from being released.

There is a large amount of bloody mucus show during transition. Nausea and vomiting are likely, especially if you are hyperventilating (which can be caused by breathing too fast or breathing out too forcefully).

Shaking of the thighs or the whole body is common. These are physiological tremors and have nothing to do with body temperature; warm blankets may make you feel better but will not stop the shakes. Oxygen administered for a short period of time through an oxygen mask helps this shakiness to pass more quickly, although the shaking is not caused by lack of oxygen.

What You Can Do: Make your labor nurse aware of your goals for childbirth. Whether your goals are written or expressed orally, *if your dilatation and labor are progressing within normal limits*, an experienced labor and delivery nurse or your midwife can do many things to help you reach your goals.

None of your goals is written in stone. If you are experiencing an unusually long or difficult labor, your labor nurse, midwife, or doctor may encourage you to consider assistance from pain medication. Pain medication reduces muscle tension and anxiety, which helps you to relax between contractions. Likewise, if you have reached a point in dilatation but are no longer progressing, they may recommend an epidural anesthetic. An epidural provides total muscle relaxation and may be all that is needed to complete dilatation. In labors that fail to progress, when there is no evidence of fetal distress, an epidural may be tried before your practitioner decides on a cesarean delivery. (See Chapter 9, "Pain Control Options," for further information.)

Many women make it very clear in their initial birthing plan or statements that they want to be given pain medication if they request it. Any time that your practitioner considers an order for pain medication, ***it will be ordered only if it is safe at this time for your baby.*** Please try to remember that your caregivers are dealing with *two* patients—*you and your baby*—and *both* must be considered in *all* decisions.

If you are progressing rapidly or are already in transition, pain medication may be withheld to prevent sluggishness and respiratory depression in the baby. Remember that pain usually changes

FIGURE 10-6

The Transition Phase

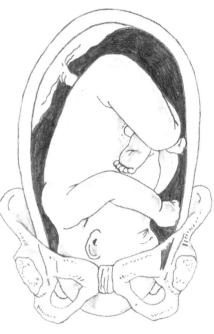

Dilatation of Cervix:
From 8 to 10 centimeters. 10 centimeters is fully dilated.

Effacement of Cervix For Your First Labor:
Since effacement usually occurs before dilatation, your cervix is usually already fully effaced by transition. If not, effacement would usually be about 90 percent.

For Subsequent Labors:
At this point you are likely to be fully effaced; however, effacement may not be totally complete.

This illustration shows:
The amniotic sac (membrane) has ruptured; however, further engagement of the baby's head has prevented all the amniotic fluid from escaping at this time.

The cervix is approximately nine centimeters dilated.

The cervix is fully effaced.

Contraction Pattern:

Duration

◄─────Frequency─────►

Frequency of contractions: 2 to 3 minutes apart
Duration of contractions: 45–90 seconds

to a much more tolerable intense pressure during pushing. Your practitioner is making an educated guess that you will very quickly pass through this difficult time and soon be fully dilated. If medication is administered to you at this late time, you will be too weak and sleepy for effective pushing, and the baby will not have time to metabolize the medication before birth and may therefore need assistance in taking his or her first breaths. If you are denied medication, ask for an explanation, but consider the above if you are late in the first stage of labor.

With the help of your support person, advance to another level of your relaxation breathing when the current method no longer helps you relax. (See pages 139–142 for more information on relaxation breathing techniques.)

During transition, you may have a very strong urge to push. The baby's head is now so low that it is pressing on the same nerves that are activated when there is stool in your lower bowel. You feel tremendous rectal pressure, as if you need to have a bowel movement, and are receiving an involuntary message to bear down. Your nurse or midwife may reevaluate your cervical dilatation at this time. **It is very important to not push until you are fully dilated or until the involuntary urge to push is strong**. If you push before the cervix is fully dilated, the cervix remaining may become very swollen. In the long run, this impedes your progress; it prolongs your first stage of labor by preventing your baby from descending into the vagina, at which point the pushing stage can begin.

Special breathing techniques can be very helpful in assisting you to resist this strong urge to push if your cervix is not yet fully dilated. (See Chapter 9, "Pain Control Options," pages 139–142.) It is sometimes possible for your nurse, midwife, or doctor to push the rim of remaining cervix over your baby's head as you push. You may be rechecked after a few pushes to be sure this rim of cervix has not slipped back.

What Your Support Person Can Do: A woman needs assistance during this stage to remain focused on whatever relaxation technique she is using. Stay close and look her directly in the eyes as you do the breathing technique along with her. Do not give new instructions or change breathing or relaxation techniques during a contraction—give all instructions *between* contractions.

It is not uncommon for a woman to have "twilight sleep" (short naps) between contractions, even if there is less than a minute's respite. It is helpful to watch the monitor or feel her abdomen and gently awaken her as a contraction begins. This allows her time to get ready for the contraction and therefore helps her to remain in control during it. If she doesn't awaken until the contraction becomes intense, it is often very difficult or impossible to begin a breathing or other technique to help control the pain.

During the transition phase of labor, the mother may display behavior that looks like panic. She may feel she cannot go on and often may say, "I cannot do this any longer." It is helpful to remind the laboring woman that these feelings of panic and anxiety are normal and expected and that the first stage of labor is almost over. It is also helpful to remind her that, once

she is fully dilated, her cervix will be gone and therefore the cervical pain will end. Pushing is a completely different sensation, usually described as intense pressure instead of pain.

Knowing that increased anxiety is normal in transition helps the labor support person to get through transition too. Without this knowledge, he or she might bend in response to the woman's anxiety and change mutually established goals during this late stage of labor, or he or she may feel angry at medical or nursing staff for not "doing something."

It is also helpful for the support person to remember during this time that nature has a wonderful way of making a woman forget what labor was like—a form of natural amnesia. This is why so many women still arrive at the hospital for their second and third babies not knowing whether they are in real labor! It is also why when they hit the active stage of labor on their second and third births, they often turn to their support person and ask, "Why didn't I remember what this was like?"

Suggest position changes if muscle tension is pronounced. Often, changing from one side to the other or raising or lowering the head of the bed may help. (See Figure 10-4 for further suggested positions for comfort during labor.)

A cold cloth applied to the forehead, face, and neck may be comforting.

Massage and lower-back counterpressure may be helpful. Take your cues from the laboring woman. If she seems bossy, allow her this control, for it may be just what she needs at this moment to stay in control herself. Offer praise and accept her behavior, and do not react to expressions of anger.

Second Stage: Pushing and Birth

The second stage of labor begins when the cervix is fully dilated and can no longer be felt on vaginal examination. If this is your first baby, this stage normally lasts one-half hour to two hours, but you may be allowed to push for up to three hours, if there is no sign of fetal distress.

If this is not your first baby, the pushing stage may last anywhere from one push to two hours, depending on the size of your pelvis, the size of the baby, and the way that the baby is presenting into the pelvis. The pushing stage is usually much shorter for subsequent labors, but this is not an absolute rule. I had three children and never had a pushing stage shorter than two and a half hours, and the pushing stage for my second baby was longer than that for my first.

Other factors also influence the length of this stage. If you have an epidural with complete anesthesia, it may take longer to push your baby out. This is because you must learn and practice how to put the push into the right muscles, which you may not be able to feel. Likewise, if your baby is presenting in any position other than the "ideal" (head down, face toward your back), this may extend the length of the pushing stage. As long as your baby is tolerating labor well, an extended pushing stage due to these special circumstances is acceptable.

The baby's presenting part (the part that enters the pelvis first) descends with each push and then recedes slightly between contractions. As it gets lower in your vagina, your perineum and anus will distend with each push.

As the baby descends to the lower part of the vagina, the *introitus* (the outer vaginal opening), begins to open slightly with each push. The opening is oval at first but becomes circular when the fetal head is exposed.

Until now, your labor has been physiologically involuntary. Other than walking, changing positions, keeping well hydrated, and trying to relax, *there was nothing that you could do to make your labor progress more quickly.* **In the second, or pushing, stage of labor, the work becomes a joint effort between you and your uterus.** You may be a champion pusher, but you will be unable to push your baby out if your uterine contractions are weak or your uterus has lost strength due to dehydration or multiple previous births. Likewise, your uterus might be contract-

ing at full force, but it cannot push your baby out alone. It needs the help of your other muscles. **Therefore it is very important for you to understand how to push effectively.**

Whether you are standing, squatting, sitting or lying flat or on your side, **it is important to work with the entire contraction.** If you have an epidural, it is important for your support person or your nurse to watch the monitor (or place a hand on your abdomen) in order to tell when a contraction is beginning. You need to work with the entire contraction, and the electronic monitoring or hand palpation ensures that you will not miss the beginning of it. When you feel the contraction beginning or are told it is beginning, follow the breathing sequence in Box 10-2.

Once you have experienced the pushing stage, you will understand why this is called *labor*—it is hard work. Your support person needs to remember to use the comfort measures!

What You May Feel: At this point there is an increase in bloody show and often an involuntary bearing-down effort. Shaking of the extremities may also occur.

Vomiting may occur in transition and during the pushing stage of labor. As mentioned previously, digestion stops when active labor begins, so if vomiting does occur, normally one or two episodes clear the stomach contents and the nausea ends. If nausea or vomiting continues, an intramuscular injection of medication can be ordered to help control it.

Positions for Pushing and Birth

There are many positions appropriate for pushing and birth. For thousands of years, long before obstetricians and labor beds, women used the birthing position that felt most natural for them, usually some form of squatting, standing, or sitting. Although these are very effective positions for delivery, they often require the person assisting the delivery to get on hands and knees both to see what is happening and to assist with the delivery. You can understand why many obstetri-

Breathing When Pushing

When you feel a contraction beginning or you are told it is beginning:

1. Take a cleansing breath.
2. With your hands, hold your thighs from the back. Avoid the back of the knee. There are veins and nerves close to the surface in this area. Holding the lower half of the thigh is best.
3. Pull back on your legs, pulling your thighs toward your abdomen but open and out to the sides.
4. Take a huge deep breath and *hold all of it in*.
5. Put your chin on your chest.
6. Bear down as if you were trying to have a very constipated bowel movement.
7. Visualize curling around your baby with your legs and upper chest (Figure 10-8).
8. Push, utilizing all your abdominal and chest muscles.
9. If you keep in your lungs all the air you took in from your deep breath, your diaphragm muscle goes to work for you. Try hard not to allow air to escape from your mouth while pushing. Any air released from your mouth means less downward pressure applied by your diaphragm.
10. Hold your push for a slow count of seven.
11. Exhale quickly and take another very deep breath.
12. Push again to a slow count of seven.
13. Exhale quickly and take another very deep breath. Fill those lungs for you and your baby!
14. Push again to a slow count of seven. This is your third push with one contraction. Always try to push three times with each contraction.
15. Take a cleansing breath, close your eyes and rest.

Note: Effective breathing during labor comes from dedicated practice throughout pregnancy *before* labor begins.

cians do not actively advocate this position for delivery! However, the experienced labor nurse with you during your labor and pushing stage should allow you to try any position that you prefer (unless you are restricted by an epidural and cannot stand up or control your legs) and even suggest positions to you that may assist your pushing efforts. Even if the obstetrician prefers you to be lying in bed for delivery, you will have been able to take advantage of other positions right up until delivery is imminent.

Midwives are trained to adapt to any position that feels right for the patient, and that may assist the pushing and delivery effort. Experienced labor nurses are also able to assist you in this way. Either will recommend the best pushing position for you, considering the position of your baby. Oftentimes your nurse or midwife will ask you to

get into a particular position to help the baby turn to a more ideal position—the baby also makes changes in position while moving down the birth canal, helping adapt its position to the shape and width of the pelvis. The largest diameter of the head moves into position to pass through the widest part of the pelvis, and then the shoulders must present to pass through it next.

The following is a description of many positions that can be used for pushing. If a position is also appropriate for delivery, it will be stated.

Sitting in Bed: Pushing in this position is necessary when you are restricted to bed because of an epidural or in bed because of fatigue. Pushing in bed is also necessary if internal leads are being used to monitor the fetal heart or your contractions.

You are in bed, are now fully dilated, and have just been instructed to push. The baby is still at the top of the birth canal. If you elevate the head of the bed to a 45-degree angle and place a pillow with the long edge vertical behind your back for support, gravity can assist your pushing efforts. **Although this position is most often used for early pushing, it can also be used for delivery.**

Place your heels together and drop your knees out (Figure 10-7A), or open both your legs and feet, dropping your knees as wide open as is comfortable (Figure 10-7B). It is helpful to have rolled-up pillows or blankets to support your knees as they are dropped to the sides. The pil-

FIGURE   10-7

Sitting in Bed to Push

A

B

lows are not only a comfort measure—if you have an epidural and therefore lack pain sensation, the knee supports prevent your knees from dropping out farther than what is normal for you and thereby pulling on the hip joint. Dropping open your knees is important because it opens and stretches your pelvis, giving the baby as much room as possible. Pull yourself forward, chin on chest, and curl around your baby as you push (Figure 10-8).

Lying on Your Back, Legs Up: When you are restricted to or choose to be in bed, this position is useful when the baby is lower in the vaginal canal and begins to come under the pubic bone. It allows the baby to have a "straight road" to come under the bone, rather than the sharp right angle that would be there if you remained sitting upright. **This position can be used both for pushing and as a delivery position.**

Lie flat and have your support person and nurse hold your legs up. You will hold your thighs (from the back) and bring your knees as far toward you and dropped as far outward as possible (Figure 10-9A) to widen your pelvis.

Your support person and nurse can now take turns helping you hold your head up, chin against your chest, while you push. *Do not* support the head from behind the neck. Support the head it-

FIGURE   10-8

Curling Around Your Baby as You Push

self with your hand, or use a pillow (Figure 10-9B). (You lose a lot of energy holding up your own head. You will need some help here!)

Side-Lying Position: This position is invaluable both **for pushing and as a delivery position, especially on the left side** (Figure 10-10). Although the placenta receives blood (and therefore oxygen) when you lie on either your left or right side, the left is preferred, especially if the baby's heart rate drops for more than 30 seconds. This is because when you lie on your left side, the weight of the uterus and baby rests on the de-

Side-Lying Pushing and Delivery Position

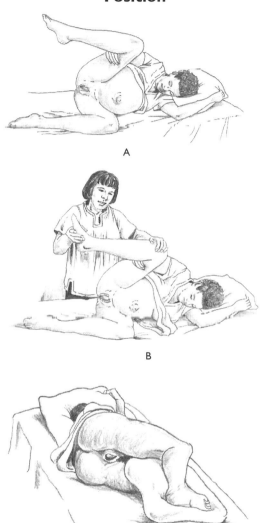

A

B

C

FIGURE 10-9

Lying on Your Back, Legs up, to Push

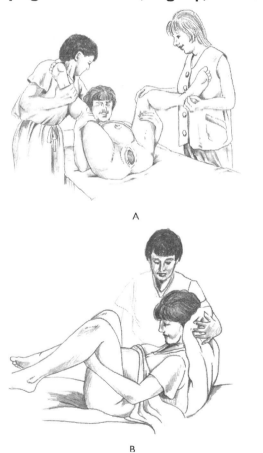

A

B

scending aorta, but because the heart is forcefully pumping blood through this artery, it is not obstructed, and blood flow to the placenta is not restricted. When you lie on your right side, however, the weight of the uterus and baby rests on the inferior vena cava, which returns blood back up to the heart and lacks the forceful pumping motion of the aorta.

The side-lying position is also very comfortable, especially if you are very tired. When you curl around your baby to bear down, you don't have to use extra energy to raise your head. You can put your chin to your chest and still be resting your head on the mattress. To open your pelvis, only the upper leg needs to be raised in this position. Bend your lower leg and draw it up near your abdomen. You can raise your upper leg without assistance, as shown in Figure 10-10A. However, to minimize fatigue, your support person can assist you in lifting the upper leg during contractions (Figure 10-10B). Even if your support person is supporting your upper leg, holding it yourself from behind the thigh and pulling it up and out as you bear down to push helps you to direct the push into the correct muscles. I have found that women who hold onto something else often put the force of their push into their hands instead of into the rectum and perineum.

It is also acceptable to push on your side without lifting your upper leg. This is especially beneficial as the baby's head begins to be visible at the perineum, because it prevents rapid expulsion of the baby and allows for slow stretching of the perineum and vaginal opening (Figure 10-10C), which helps to prevent tears.

As the baby reaches your lower vagina, the perineum begins to bulge during pushing and soon the top of the presenting part is visible with each push. At this point, each push is stretching the vaginal and perineal walls, as well as the vaginal opening. When you are taking breaths between pushes during one contraction, try to maintain a positive pressure downward against your buttocks with your muscles. This helps to prevent the baby from slipping back while you take a breath (that is, maintain positive downward pressure, exhale quickly, inhale deeply, and continue your push). You don't want to redo the same work; you want to maintain and advance the stretch and therefore advance the baby. Between contractions, of course, you should relax completely.

Visualize rocking the baby down and under your pubic bone until the nape of the baby's neck goes under the bone and the baby can then extend its head. Once this happens, which is called *crowning* (see Figure 10-15), the baby will not slip back—it is time to deliver your baby!

Sitting, Standing, Squatting, and Hands-and-Knees Positions:
If you do not have an epidural that prevents standing or squatting, which require leg strength, and the fetal heart or contractions are not being monitored by internal leads, there are many other pushing position options that you can try. (Walking epidurals do allow for standing and squatting.) As mentioned earlier, the baby's position, the mother's pelvis, the strength of the uterine contractions, and the strength of the mother's pushing efforts are all factors that affect the pushing stage of labor. All of these except for the size of your pelvis and the strength of your contractions themselves can be altered by your position. (Labor augmentation with oxytocin can be used to strengthen the contractions if necessary.)

A particular position can help or hinder your pushing efforts by the way it alters the baby's position in relation to your pelvis and how it utilizes or does not utilize gravity. A given position can also be helpful at one point in labor and not bring about progress at another point, again depending on where the baby is at that point in relationship to the pelvis. Certain positions may also lead to greater discomfort at different stages. **This is why frequent position changes are important and helpful during the entire pushing stage.**

Both sitting and squatting facilitate the baby's passage down the birth canal during pushing and therefore shorten the pushing stage of labor. Likewise, the hands-and-knees position is invaluable in helping a baby in the posterior presentation (head down but with the occiput bone at the base of the back of the baby's head facing posterior, toward the spine) turn to the more desirable anterior position. (See page 83 for a further explanation of posterior presentation.)

Hospitals are now returning to more physiologically appropriate methods for birth with multi-position birthing beds and birthing chairs. Because of these options and increased education and awareness in couples, sitting, standing, squatting, and hands-and-knees positions are all being used both for pushing and for delivery.

Sitting in a Chair.   This position is good for *early* pushing, but the firm seat and rocking motion make the rocking chair a difficult place for crowning and delivery.

Sit in a rocking chair with your feet elevated slightly and spread apart on two stools, or spread apart on the ground if stools are not available (Figure 10-11A). If you use stools, put a soft pillow or towel over them and place one pillow behind your back and another behind your head for comfort. Open your knees wide while pushing .

Bean-bag chairs and birthing chairs (Figure 10-11B) or stools are also used in some settings to facilitate the mother obtaining a comfortable position for pushing and birth, with good support.

Standing.   Pushing can be done in the standing position; however, the mother usually will need to hold on to something for support. I have found it useful for her to stand next to a bed with the bed elevated to a point where she can lean over several stacked pillows on it for rest between contractions. During the contraction she can then stand, with her feet spread apart and knees slightly bent, and hold on to the bed for support as she pushes (Figure 10-12). In addition, if she feels the need to squat farther (as in Figure 10-13A), she has the bed for support.

Squatting.   Many women feel that some form of squatting helps them "put their push in the right place." When squatting, be sure to open your knees out to the sides as wide as possible to open your pelvis. It is also important to have a firm and sturdy surface to hold on to for support.

The following squatting position (Figure 10-13A) is useful if you are more comfortable standing between contractions but feel the urge to squat during contractions. Stack several pillows

Sitting in a Chair for Pushing
(A) Rocker. (B) Birthing chair.

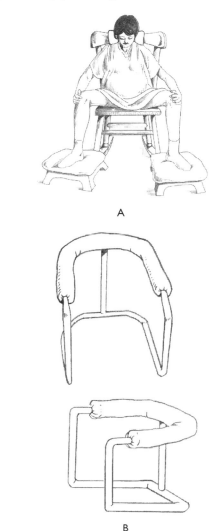

A

B

Childbirth

on top of the bed and adjust the height of the bed to allow you to lean over the pillows and rest between contractions, if you need to, at a height that is comfortable for you. During contractions, hold on to the bed for support and squat, keeping your legs open and knees as far apart as possible. **This squatting position is not usually chosen as a** delivery position because it is awkward for the practitioner, and the mother lacks solid physical support for balance during delivery.

A woman can use the squatting pushing position while in bed by coming forward with the

FIGURE 10-12

Standing for Pushing

help of two people. This is a tiring position for both the woman, who continually has to move up for the contraction and back down after the contraction, and the support people, who must help her into the squatting position and support her weight throughout the push. In addition, this may lead to back strain in the support people. For this reason, many labor nurses do not allow their patients to use them as a support for this position. See Figure 10-13B.

Figure 10-13C shows an effective squatting position that can also be used for delivery if your practitioner is willing to deliver from the floor. (If it is used for delivery, sterile drapes are placed below the perineum to create a clean delivery area.)

Some of the new birthing beds come with a squatting bar that fits into the frame of the bed and allows the woman to bring herself into the squatting position and provides support during the push (Figure 10-13D). **This position can be used for delivery if it is comfortable for the mother.**

Hands and Knees.   The hands-and-knees position (Figures 10-14A and B) is a nice alternative when you are feeling tired and can help turn a baby into a better position for delivery. It is espe-

FIGURE 10-13A

Squatting Next to Bed to Push

FIGURE 10-13B

Squatting in Bed with the Help of Two Support Persons

FIGURE 10-13C

Squatting on the Side of the Bed with the Help of One Support Person

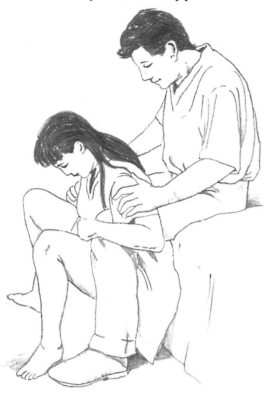

FIGURE 10-13D

Squatting Bar for Pushing

FIGURE 10-14A

Hands-and-Knees in Bed with a Foot Rail
Resting

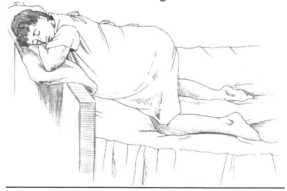

cially **useful in helping a posterior presentation turn to the more desirable anterior presentation.** In addition, if the baby is having difficulty coming under the pubic bone, this position may be helpful in facilitating the descent. **The hands-and-knees position is an acceptable position for delivery.** See Figure 10-14D.

If you are using a multiposition birthing bed, kneel on the foot of the bed, which is lowered. Spread your knees as far apart as you comfortably can. Put a towel or waterproof pad on the bed between them. Between contractions, lean over several stacked pillows for rest (Figure 10-14B); place a sheet over your back and bottom if desired for comfort or privacy .

During a contraction, come up onto your arms, rock back onto your bottom, and push (Figure 10-14C).

Crowning

The most difficult part of this stage of labor is bringing the baby's head under and around the

FIGURE 10-14B

Hands-and-Knees in Multiposition Bed

Resting between contractions

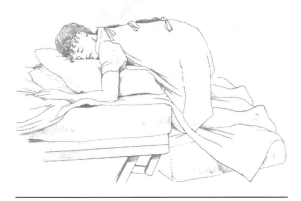

FIGURE 10-14C

Hands-and-Knees in Multiposition Bed

Pushing during contraction

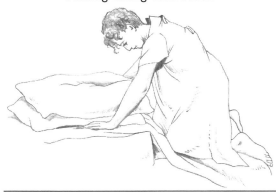

FIGURE 10-14D

Hands-and-Knees Position for Delivery

FIGURE 10-15

Crowning

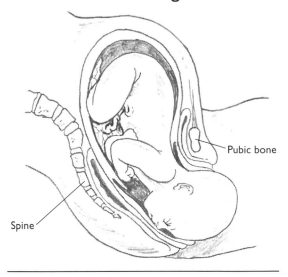

Pubic bone

Spine

pubic bone. The back of the baby's flexed head and neck rocks under the pubic bone with each push and recedes slightly between contractions. Finally the baby is advanced far enough to rock completely under the pubic bone and extend its head. Now the back side of the neck and the slightly extended head prevent the baby from slipping back between contractions. The widest part of the fetal head (crown) is now visible out-

side the vaginal opening. This is called *crowning* (Figure 10-15).

Be aware that for *your first baby* unless you are having an excessively rapid second stage, your nurse will probably not call the doctor into the room for delivery until crowning is just about to occur. At this time, if mirrors are available, you will be able to see a three- or four-inch circle of the top of your baby's head.

What Your Support Person Can Do: Massaging and applying warm towels to the perineum at this point are comfort measures that also help the perineum to relax and stretch more fully.

Episiotomy

An *episiotomy* is an incision made in the perineum (the area between the vagina and rectum) by your practitioner to enlarge the vaginal opening. (See Figure 10-16.) If you feel strongly about being allowed time for your perineum to stretch on its own, without an episiotomy, please discuss this with your practitioner during your pregnancy **and have your support person remind your caregivers now.** As long as your baby's heart rate is within the normal range and the normal drops in fetal heart rate with contractions (during the pushing stage) come up immediately after the contractions, there is no danger to your baby in allowing time for your perineum to stretch naturally. Of course, if your baby is showing signs of stress, an episiotomy will facilitate a quicker delivery.

Despite what was previously thought, a recent study has indicated that natural tears are less likely to extend into the rectum than tear extensions off of an episiotomy. However, if your perineum has a tough band of tissue that does not stretch well, your obstetrician or midwife may think that an episiotomy is advisable.

An episiotomy is done just before or during crowning. Local anesthesia is usually given prior to the incision if you do not have an epidural. However, please note that when the baby's head is crowning, the perineal tissue is so stretched that the nerves are not well perfused with blood. The nerves therefore lose sensitivity so local anesthesia is not mandatory for an episiotomy. (If you have an epidural, local anesthesia is not usually necessary, but your practitioner will test the area to evaluate your ability to feel sensations prior to doing the episiotomy.)

Your Baby Is Born!

The baby's head continues to extend and fully deliver. You will be asked not to push or to push only gently at this time. Slower delivery of the head allows the tissues in the perineum to stretch and prevents sudden expulsion, which can cause significant tearing. If the membranes have not ruptured, they will appear now like a hood covering the baby's head. Your practitioner will rupture the membranes at this time and peel the membrane away from your baby's face.

Your practitioner will check to be certain the umbilical cord is not around your baby's neck. If it is (which is called a *nuchal cord*), it is slipped gently over the head if it is not too tight. Otherwise it is clamped in two places and cut between the clamps.

The baby's mouth and nose are suctioned with a bulb syringe to clear mucus from them, which helps prevent the baby from breathing blood, amniotic fluid, and mucus into its lungs during the first breath.

The largest diameter of the baby's head is delivered first through the largest diameter of the pelvis. Nature then automatically has the baby rotate a quarter turn in order that the broad shoulders present to the largest diameter of the pelvis. This is called *internal rotation* of the shoulders.

FIGURE   10-16

Location of Episiotomies

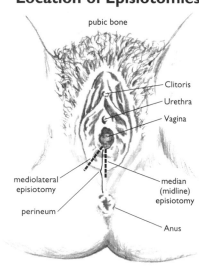

pubic bone

Clitoris

Urethra

Vagina

mediolateral episiotomy

perineum

median (midline) episiotomy

Anus

Childbirth

The baby's shoulders are now in the anterior-posterior diameter of the pelvis. This is seen on the outside as external rotation of the head. The head changes from facing down to facing sideways.

Your practitioner will now put gentle downward pressure on your baby to help the anterior, or top, shoulder come under the pubic bone and be delivered. You will be asked to push to aid in delivery of the anterior shoulder.

Open your eyes and watch now if you want to see your baby born. The physician or midwife will lift your baby upward to deliver the posterior shoulder, and complete birth will occur!

Common Complications of the Second Stage of Labor

Vacuum or Forceps Delivery: Sometimes, for any one of the following reasons, you may have difficulty bringing the baby fully under and around your pubic bone. This may be due to weak contractions, fatigue, the size of your pelvis or baby, or the position of the baby. When adequate time has been allowed for pushing or when pushing is causing fetal distress, your practitioner may decide to use a vacuum extractor, which looks like a small plunger (Figure 10-17), or forceps to help bring the baby's head under the pubic bone.

FIGURE   10-17

Vacuum Extractor

Unless you have had an epidural, you will be given a local anesthetic in your perineum. The vacuum head is lubricated, put inside your vagina, and positioned on your baby's head. You will feel discomfort while it is being put into place. The vacuum is then attached to a mechanical or electrical suction device. Suction is only applied during a contraction. As you push, you will feel the usual intense pressure as vaginal and perineal tissues stretch, but it is intensified because the vacuum brings the baby down faster. If you have an epidural, you will feel added pressure but the procedure will not be too uncomfortable. You must concentrate and try to visualize pushing through any discomfort or burning sensation during a vacuum attempt. Keep telling yourself that it is a choice between this procedure or many more pushing attempts without help. In addition, a vacuum-assisted delivery may prevent a cesarean section, which is necessary if you are unable to bring the baby's head under and around the pubic bone. Work with your practitioner and give this your very best effort.

There is normally a reddened area on the baby's head at delivery where the vacuum pressure was applied. If used within protocol by a skilled practitioner, the vacuum does not harm your baby, and the reddened area will go away in a few days.

Forceps delivery may be attempted rather than vacuum extraction. A local anesthetic, pudendal block, or existing epidural is necessary before performing this procedure. *Forceps* are long, open, spoon-shaped instruments that are applied one at a time and made to fit around the baby's head. They are then locked together to prevent excessive squeezing of your baby's head (Figure 10-18).

Forceps are applied one at a time around your baby's temples between contractions. As with the vacuum, pulling traction is applied by the physician only during and with your contractions and your pushing. Hospital personnel will have the operating room ready for an immediate cesarean delivery if the attempt to deliver with forceps fails.

Forceps in the hands of a practitioner trained in their use can make the difference between a

FIGURE 10-18

Forceps

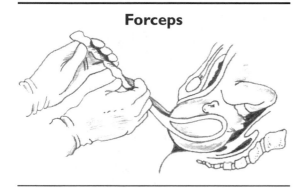

vaginal delivery and a cesarean delivery. There may be some temporary redness at the application site. Risks are minimal but possible and will be discussed with you prior to the use of forceps.

If downward movement and advancement are not achieved on the first three vacuum or forceps attempts, it is unlikely that they are going to be helpful, and a cesarean delivery will be performed.

Meconium-Stained Amniotic Fluid: For an explanation of meconium-stained fluid and its significance, see pages 120–121 in Chapter 7. If meconium is seen in the amniotic fluid at any time during your labor, special precautions will be taken at birth to ensure that meconium is not breathed into your baby's lungs during its first breaths. These precautions are also described in Chapter 7.

Shoulder Dystocia: Sometimes the baby's shoulders get stuck on the pubic bone after the baby's head has been delivered; this complication is called *shoulder dystocia.* It can occur even in a labor that has progressed normally to this point.

Your physician and nurses have specialized training in how to deal with this emergency. **You need to listen and do exactly as instructed. Nurses will assist you in pulling your legs way up over your abdomen and dropping your knees outward as far as possible,** which opens your pelvis to its greatest degree. An episiotomy is almost always done to provide a larger opening for this difficult delivery.

Your physician will place his or her hand inside your vagina and attempt to rotate your baby's shoulder away from the pubic bone. If these initial maneuvers do not work, a nurse may be asked to press down firmly just above your pubic bone. This will be very uncomfortable for you (if you do not have an epidural), but your cooperation will be necessary.

A shoulder dystocia is an emergency, and you need to concentrate, focus, and work with your caregivers as best you can. You may be asked to change positions and get on your hands and knees. If you are, you *must* move quickly.

If the above measures fail, the physician will try to deliver the posterior (lower) arm to make room to deliver the upper shoulder. Occasionally the baby's collarbone is fractured in this process. Once the shoulder is dislodged from the pubic bone, the baby can be delivered. If your baby's collarbone was fractured during delivery, his or her arm will be placed in a soft sling-type support and strapped in the proper position to prevent shoulder movement until healing occurs. (Do not position your infant on the side of the broken collarbone until this position is approved by your pediatrician.)

There is no greater sigh of relief than the one that follows a shoulder dystocia delivery.

Third Stage: Delivery of the Placenta

In most cases, once your baby is born, he or she will be placed on your abdomen and you will be so busy getting acquainted that you will pay little attention to this stage of labor. You will think your labor over! However, it is not technically over until the placenta (sometimes called the afterbirth) is delivered (Figure 10-19).

Once the baby is delivered, uterine contractions cause the site where the placenta is attached to shrink. This shrinking causes the *anchor villi,* which attach the placenta to the uterine wall, to break, leading to placental separation. Normally

FIGURE 10-19

The Placenta

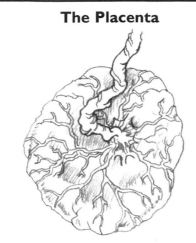

the first few strong uterine contractions five to seven minutes after the birth of the baby cause this process to occur. However, it may take as long as an hour and still be considered normal.

Putting the baby to breast immediately after birth stimulates uterine contractions and helps in delivery of the placenta. Nipple stimulation can be used to stimulate contractions in a mother who is not breastfeeding. Massaging the uterus from the top downward may also help stimulate placental separation. Usually none of these contraction-stimulating techniques is necessary, however. Given time, in the majority of cases, the uterus will contract and placenta separation will occur on its own.

If you do not have an epidural, you will experience a lot of cramping and perhaps some pain during separation of the placenta. Your physician or midwife may ask you to push as separation is occurring. Just follow his or her instructions, and hang in there—you are almost finished!

If spontaneous separation of the placenta does not occur, or if you are bleeding heavily, your practitioner will attempt manual extraction of the placenta. To manually separate a placenta, the physician or midwife uses a gloved hand to reach inside the uterus and remove the placenta.

Manual extraction of the placenta is an uncomfortable procedure if you have not had an epidural. Use relaxation breathing to help you through the discomfort of this procedure.

Once the placenta is completely removed, the uterus should be able to contract and control the bleeding. If this does not occur, however, medications may be injected both intravenously and intramuscularly to promote uterine contractions. If these measures fail to control bleeding, you will need to have a D & C (dilatation and curettage). A D & C is done under a form of anesthesia called *conscious sedation,* which controls pain, makes you sleepy, and usually causes you to have no memory of the procedure.

Keeping Your Baby Warm

Please understand that your infant will be given to you immediately if it is at all possible. Some physicians and midwives prefer to wait until the cord stops pulsating before clamping or cutting it. When the baby is placed on your abdomen, be sure the cord has been cut before pulling the infant too far up onto your chest to prevent tugging on an attached umbilical cord.

The nurses will quickly dry your infant to help prevent loss of body heat. (This is very important because newborns are especially susceptible to heat loss and cannot bring their temperature back up on their own.) The warmth of your skin and a heated blanket covering your dry baby are usually sufficient to keep your baby warm.

You may begin to breastfeed immediately if you so desire. If, however, your baby has meconium-stained fluid, slow respiratory response, a low heart rate, or blue or very pale color, he or she will not be placed on your abdomen. Instead the baby will be placed immediately in a warmer, located in your room, for assessment and, if necessary, assistance. Once stabilized, your infant will be given to you to hold and bond with.

Figure 10-20A shows a state-of-the-art newborn warming unit with full resuscitation capabilities. In this unit, a thermometer probe is taped to the baby's abdomen to regulate the amount of heat produced by the warming lights. Your baby will be undressed while under the lights. Figure 10-20B shows an incubator, which is used at a delivery only if a baby needs transport to a special-care nursery for further assistance and care.

Seeing Your New Baby

For nine months you have thought about this baby. Will it be a boy or girl? Who will it look

FIGURE 10-20

Infant-Warming Unit (A)
and Incubator (B)

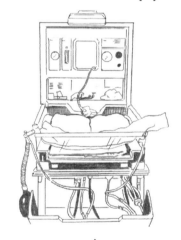

A

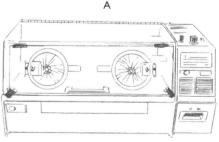

B

like? Will our child have Dad's dimple? Will our baby have lots of hair or no hair at all? Now the big moment has come. You need to know that newborns have gone through labor too, and in most cases they look like you feel!

Skin

The normal skin color of your ethnic group may not be apparent immediately at birth. Light skin may at first appear pale, red, or blue, and dark skin normally appears lighter in color at birth.

Premature babies may be covered in soft, downy hair and *vernix*, a white, thick substance that looks like cheese. We call vernix nature's lanolin. Your baby has been floating in water for nine months—think of what your skin would look like if you stayed in the bath tub that long! Vernix protects the fetus's skin. The earlier you deliver, the more vernix you will see. By full term, most of it has been absorbed and has disappeared, but even then you may still find some in skin folds such as under the arms, in the groin area, and within the folds of the female's genitals.

Babies are also born covered in blood. *This is the mother's blood, not blood from the baby.* Although the delivering practitioner does a good job of quickly wiping off most of this blood, people who are not prepared for this can become frightened or even faint.

If there was no meconium-stained fluid, your practitioner will take a second to wipe blood off your infant before placing him or her on your abdomen. However, if there was meconium in the amniotic fluid, your infant will be placed on the warmer without being stimulated to breathe or wiped clean (see page 121).

Most full-term infants' skin begins to peel a few days after birth. If born overdue, your baby may already have peeling skin at birth. This is the normal process for skin that has been in water. Beautiful new skin will soon replace the peeling, flaking skin.

If the amniotic fluid contained meconium, your baby may have a yellow-green color, resulting from the mixture of the black meconium with the amniotic fluid and vernix. Don't worry—it will wash away at the first bath!

Milia look like small white-head pimples. They can be found anywhere on the baby's body but are mainly found on the cheeks and nose. They disappear on their own.

"Stork bites" are pink areas of skin, mainly on the upper eyelids, nose, upper lip, the lower back part of the head, and behind the neck. When pressed, the red blanches to a normal skin color and then returns to red. These spots fade on their own by the second year of life.

Unlike stork bites, *port wine stains* are red to purple in color, can vary in size, and may be found anywhere on the body. They are not raised and do not blanch when pressed. Port wine stains do not disappear on their own.

Mongolian spots are bluish-black areas over any surface of the body. They are most commonly seen on the lower back and buttocks and occur primarily in dark-skinned babies of Mediterranean, Latin American, Asian, and African descent. They gradually fade over time.

Last, but certainly not least, you need to know about normal newborn rash (*erythema neonatorum*). It is often called "flea-bite inflammation of the skin." It got this nickname because it appears suddenly, anywhere on the body, and looks like little flea bites. It can be red and flat, or red and raised, and have fluid or no fluid inside the bumps. Premature infants do not get this rash; it is a rash found in infants at least 36 weeks in gestation and can be seen *coming and going* throughout the first three weeks of life. It can appear and disappear so quickly that by the time you get the baby to the doctor it is gone! Although it looks serious, it is not harmful to your baby and requires no treatment.

Head Shape

This seems to be the hardest part for new parents to accept. Although most parents know about molding (cone heads), they still ask, "Will this go away?," or, "Is this okay?"

Molding is the elongation or pointing of the head that occurs as the head narrows to allow its passage through the birth canal (Figure 10-21). The skull is made up of several bones that are joined together by *suture lines*. In an adult these suture lines are fused, but they are not in an infant; this allows the skull bones to "reshape" during delivery. They can separate and shift slightly or even overlap at the edges. This is nature's way of making vaginal births possible. Remember, babies come in all shapes and sizes and so do female pelvises and birth canals. Molding allows for variation and that little adjustment that may make the difference between a vaginal birth and a cesarean delivery.

Molding is a normal consequence of the second stage of labor. It takes some time for molding to occur, so if you push for less than half an hour, little or no molding will occur. If you push for two or three hours, however, be prepared for a molded head. Within hours after birth, you can see improvement in the head shape, and after several days, the head begins to look more "nor-

FIGURE 10-21

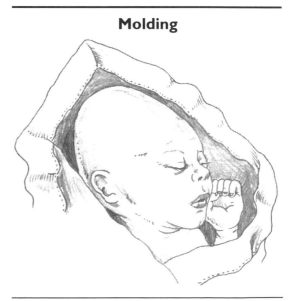

Molding

mal." Molding may take up to two weeks to disappear completely.

Caput is a swollen round bump that occurs when the baby's head sits on your partially dilated cervix for a long time. The small section of the head over the dilated opening of the cervix swells through that opening. At birth it appears as a fluid-filled bump on the head. It occurs mainly when dilatation occurs slowly, or when it stops progressing for a long period of time. This slow progression in dilatation provides the time necessary for the swelling to occur.

Caput is not harmful to your baby in any way. It will resolve without treatment within several days. You will notice a big improvement even after 24 hours.

Give your baby a few hours before you try to decide who he or she resembles. Just as the head molds, the nose often gets pushed to one side, and both the nose and ears get compressed during delivery. Your baby will be beautiful in just a few hours!

Bruising

It is hard to imagine your newborn being born with its first "boo-boo," but it does happen. Sometimes, but certainly not always, if vacuum assistance is used for delivery, the area under the vacuum head becomes bruised. This bruise resolves on its own within a few days.

If you progress from full dilatation to birth within minutes, we call this a *rapid descent*. Babies that have a rapid descent are often born with what is called *facial suffusion,* in which part of the skin on the face appears blue. This is not harmful to your baby and will resolve without treatment on its own within a few days.

Genitals

Parents are often concerned that their new son has a disproportionately large scrotum and perhaps even some swelling around the breast and nipple area. Parents of little girls are shocked to see such large labia (outer folds around the female genitals) and also swollen breasts. These enlargements in both boys and girls are due to the baby being exposed for nine months to Mom's high levels of pregnancy (female) hormones. After birth, when the newborn is no longer attached to Mom's blood supply, these hormone levels will drop off in the infant, and the swelling of the genitals and breasts will go away.

As these hormones drop off in an infant girl, you may observe small amounts of blood in her diaper. Don't be alarmed if this occurs several days after you deliver and it is only a small amount. When exposed to your high levels of hormones the inner lining of your baby's uterus may have increased in thickness and blood supply just as it will later in life before each menstrual period. After birth, when the hormone level drops off in the baby, a small amount of bleeding may occur as the extra lining in her uterus sloughs off. On a very small scale, this is similar to the menstrual period, which also occurs because of changing hormone levels.

After Delivery of the Placenta

After the delivery of your placenta, your uterus contracts to control bleeding. The top of your uterus can be felt now midway between your pubic bone and your belly button. Your caregiver may massage the top of your uterus in a downward direction to expel any accumulated clotted blood and to facilitate the clamping down of the uterus.

If you are bleeding heavily and do not have an IV (intravenous) line running, an intramuscular injection of oxytocin will be administered to make your uterus contract. If bleeding is not promptly controlled with massage and intramuscular oxytocin injections, an IV line will need to be started. If you had an intravenous line prior to delivery, oxytocin will be added to the intravenous fluid and infused rapidly to promote uterine contractions and therefore to control bleeding.

In the rare case that the above measures fail to control excessive bleeding, a D & C (dilatation and curettage) is performed. In most hospitals, you will be taken to the operating room for your D & C (the same operating room where cesarean sections are done). Sedation is administered through your intravenous line, and an instrument is used to scrape the inside lining of the uterus, removing any remaining placenta or membrane fragments, which are the usual cause of excessive bleeding.

Your obstetrician or midwife will examine your perineum (the area between your vagina and rectum) for any lacerations in need of stitching. If you had an episiotomy it will be repaired now.

Repair of Episiotomy or Lacerations

Even if you did not have an episiotomy, you may still require stitches. Tears in the perineum that occur on their own are called *lacerations*. They are classified as first-, second-, third-, or fourth degree lacerations. They can occur with or without an episiotomy.

In simple terms, a first-degree laceration involves the skin on the perineum and the underlying fatty tissue. Second-degree lacerations extend deeper, and the tear also involves a muscle. A third-degree laceration includes all of the above and the anal sphincter muscle (the muscle at the anal opening that you can voluntarily open and close). A fourth-degree laceration continues into the wall of the rectum.

The suture material used to repair the episiotomy or laceration dissolves on its own and therefore does not have to be removed later.

After all repairs are completed, an ice pack will be applied to your perineum if you had stitches, did excessive pushing, or have hemorrhoids. You and your support person will now be given some time to enjoy your new baby. Your nurse will routinely check your blood pressure and pulse during the first several hours after birth. In addition, he or she will routinely feel for the location of the top of your uterus and massage it if it is not firm.

Newborn Care During the First Hours of Life

If your baby is born without respiratory or other complications, then after an initial period of bonding a birth weight will be taken. In some hospitals the measurement of the length of your baby is delayed until the admitting physical by the pediatrician, which usually is done the following morning. By then molding of the head is already reduced, and it is easier to get the infant to stretch out to his or her full length (after being curled up for nine months!). Therefore, the measurement is considered more accurate.

Before ever leaving your presence, your infant will be given **two identification bracelets. The mother will have a matching bracelet.** These three identical bracelets will have a matching number, your last name, the sex of the baby, and the date and time of birth. **The father may be given a tag or some other form of identification in order that he too will be able to remove his baby from the nursery.** If it is not on a bracelet, a tag is usually attached securely to the back of his driver's license, making it possible for the nursery staff to photo-identify the father, as well as match the number and name to the correct baby.

It is the *responsibility of the maternity staff* to check the name and number on the baby's identification bracelet against the mother's or father's identification, to be certain that the baby is being given to its parent.

It is the *responsibility of the parents* to be certain that any person who comes into the room and requests to take your baby to the nursery:

Has on a hospital identification badge.

Is the person on the photo of that badge.

Is a member of the maternity staff—your obstetrician, your midwife, or a nurse or nurse's aid from the maternity or nursery staff. (Staff from other sections of the hospital are not allowed to take your baby for any reason.)

It is also your right to know why your baby is being taken to the nursery and to accompany your baby, if you prefer. If all of these above precautions are taken, they go a long way in guarding against infant abduction.

If your baby has no respiratory distress, you should be allowed to initiate nursing promptly after birth. If you are bottle feeding, the initial feeding will be given when the baby shows signs of readiness, usually within the first few hours of life.

Premature babies, babies under five and one-half pounds, those over nine pounds, and those born to diabetic or gestational diabetic mothers will need to have their blood sugar levels evaluated about one hour after birth and then several times thereafter. (The timing depends on your hospital protocol.) This is done with a heel stick to obtain one drop of blood for testing. In addition, these infants will be encouraged to nurse or bottle feed every three hours. (See page 111 for further detailed explanations of why this is done.)

Sometime during the first hour of life your infant will be given the standard eye treatment mandated by law for all newborns. Because there are several venereal diseases that can be present in a mother without symptoms and that can cause blindness in the infant if the eyes are exposed to the organism, state laws mandate a prophylactic eye treatment for all newborns. This is not done because we think you have a venereal disease but because it is the law and because it prevents blindness if the organism were present. If you choose not to have this given to your infant, you must sign a form absolving the hospital of responsibility if your infant does contract the organism or develop blindness.

Also during the first hour of life, your infant will be weighed and a dosage of vitamin K (based on the weight of your baby) will be administered by intramuscular injection into your baby's thigh. Giving this vitamin, which is a clotting facilitator8, helps to reduce the incidence of cerebral hemorrhages, which used to be common before vitamin K was administered routinely.

The initial bath is usually given to your baby between the first and second hours of life. Waiting at least an hour helps the baby get accustomed to life outside the uterus. The sponge bath is done under a warming unit, and after the bath the baby will remain under the warmer until his or her temperature is in the 98°F range.

Childbirth

11

Recovery After Vaginal Birth

Immediate Postpartum Care

In the four hours immediately after you give birth, a nurse will be monitoring your recovery closely, particularly the areas discussed in this chapter.

Blood Pressure and Pulse Rate

Your vital signs (blood pressure and pulse rate) tell your doctor and nurses immediately if you are hemorrhaging (bleeding excessively) from your delivery. If this complication develops, your pulse rate will increase and your blood pressure will drop. Sometimes bleeding pools inside your uterus or in the vaginal wall before it can be seen externally. That is why it is important that we

take your vital signs every 15 minutes for the first hour. By detecting these complications early, we can rapidly administer intravenous fluids and medication to help contract your uterus, control the bleeding, and treat other complications.

Temperature

Your nurse will be checking your temperature in the postpartum period. You can expect it to be in the 99°F range after delivery—you have worked hard! This slight elevation means that you are in need of some extra fluids, so drink lots of liquids!

A temperature of 100.4°F or higher should be reported to your doctor. Certain bacteria can cause serious systemic infections when present in the reproductive organs. Some take days and others weeks to show themselves after delivery. Any rash or temperature above 100.4°F must be reported at once—these infections are curable if treated promptly with the appropriate antibiotic.

Vaginal Bleeding (Lochia)

Lochia is the normal vaginal blood flow after delivery. A firm uterus keeps bleeding within normal limits. If you press in on your abdomen, your fundus (the curved top of your uterus) will feel like a grapefruit midway between your pubic bone and belly button. It should be firm and round. After delivery, your nurse will palpate (feel) your fundus often, which will cause you some discomfort; however, it is necessary to ensure that your uterus is remaining firm.

The uterus must contract and be firm in order to pinch off the blood vessels where the placenta was attached to the uterine wall. This contraction, or pinching off, stops the bleeding from the site. Sometimes your doctor or nurse may massage your uterus if it has become "boggy" (soft) to return it to a firm state. This procedure can be uncomfortable and may require some slow rhythmic breathing on your part.

If your vaginal bleeding is excessive, your fundus will need to be compressed for the expulsion of possible clots inside the uterus. A large blood clot inside the uterus can prevent the uterus from clamping down. This procedure is a forceful downward pressure applied to the top of your uterus (fundus) from the outside. It is uncomfortable unless you have an epidural that has not yet worn off. Relaxation breathing is very helpful in controlling the discomfort.

On the day of delivery, your lochia will be heavy and dark red. The first time you get out of bed, blood will probably gush down your leg. This is *not* hemorrhaging. It is just blood that pooled in your uterus after delivery and is coming out now with the aid of gravity.

On the day after delivery, your lochia will continue to be dark red or reddish brown. By this time, one sanitary pad at a time is normally sufficient.

❢At no time should you saturate a sanitary pad completely in fifteen minutes. That is considered excessive bleeding and should be reported promptly to your nurse, if you are in the hospital, or to your doctor if you are at home. It would also be considered excessive bleeding if you are consistently saturating one pad in one hour. If this occurs, notify your nurse or your practitioner.

Once you are up walking, you may pass a large clot of old blood. Clots can be very small or as large as four to six inches in diameter. (Some women who don't know about clots are frightened by this and call to say their practitioner forgot the placenta and it just fell out!) *During the first several days postpartum, a few occasional clots, even if they are very big, are normal as long as they are not followed by bright red blood.* **❢If clots are excessive in number, or followed by bright red blood, they should be promptly reported.**

Your Uterus—Involution

Immediately after delivery, the fundus of your uterus can be found midway between the belly button and pubic bone. Your uterus is now about seven inches long and weighs about two and one-half pounds. Within about 12 hours, the fundus rises to about the level of the belly button. Thereafter, it goes down at about one finger-width per day. By around the 10th day it can no longer be felt above the pubic bone. It takes about six weeks for your uterus to return to its nonpregnant size, about three inches long and weighing about two ounces. The process of the uterus returning to its original nonpregnant size is called involution.

Bladder

A full bladder interferes with the ability of the uterus to contract and remain firm. If your bladder is full, the uterine fundus will be up high, above the umbilicus and off to one side. You will be assisted out of bed at this time to use the bathroom, or, if you had an epidural and the effects have not yet worn off, you will be helped onto a bedpan.

Urinate often, especially on the first day. If you are having difficulty urinating on your own, try running water in the sink. The sound of running water often helps! Or try squirting warm water over your perineum using the peri bottle (the plastic squirt bottle given to you in the hospital). (Peri bottles are discussed further under "Care of Your Stitches," on page 197 in this chapter.)

Your nurse will want to measure the volume of your first few urinations. It is important for your nurses to know that you are fully emptying your bladder, especially if you had an epidural.

Commonly, because the epidural is still in effect in the perineum or because of a local anesthetic for stitches or swelling in the area, you will be unable to urinate on your own. Your nurse will palpate (feel) the fullness of your bladder from the outside of your abdomen. She or he will use this information, the volume of your vaginal bleeding, and the firmness and location of the top of your uterus to determine whether more time can be allowed for you to urinate on your own. If your uterus is being pushed off to one side because of a full bladder, causing your vaginal flow to be excessive, you will need to have a straight catheter inserted to empty your bladder.

Straight catheterization is a very quick procedure in which your nurse inserts a small sterile catheter into the urethra (the natural opening to your bladder) and allows the urine to drain out. The catheter is then removed. If you are still numb from your epidural or local anesthetic, you will not feel very much. If you are not anesthetized in that area, you will feel some discomfort. The most uncomfortable part of this procedure is the nurse's fingers separating the skin folds (labia) in order to see your urethra. You are very sore right now, and the nurse realizes that this sensitive area is tender to even a gentle touch. When the catheter is inserted, you may feel a slight burning or pressure sensation.

Emptying your bladder promptly in this way will allow the uterus to again clamp off and control the bleeding. It will also prevent overdistention of your bladder. Normally, by the next time your bladder is full, you will have regained control of your perineal muscles (epidural and local anesthetics will have worn off and local swelling decreased) and you will be able to urinate on your own.

Prompt attention to a full bladder also prevents overdistention of the bladder, which can cause a loss of bladder tone. Patients who lose bladder tone because of overdistention wind up having to have a Foley catheter inserted to allow the stressed bladder to rest. (A Foley catheter is a tube placed into the bladder through the urethra, secured in place, and connected to a drainage bag.) The Foley catheter remains in place for about 24 hours, allowing the bladder to rest. When it is removed, you will be given time to urinate on your own. This is an unfortunate complication and is usually avoidable if the bladder is emptied often and completely during labor and the early postpartum period.

Remember, always empty your bladder before epidural anesthesia is administered. If your nurse is not monitoring the status of your bladder during your labor, remind him or her. You can actually feel the rim of a full bladder on top of your uterus. After delivery, if the top of your uterus is up above the belly button and off to one side, be sure to get assistance out of bed or onto a bedpan promptly. If you are unable to urinate and your nurse thinks you should be catheterized, allow her to do so. The risk of a bladder infection from catheterization done by a skilled nurse is far less than the risk of complications from loss of bladder tone caused by an overdistended bladder.

Fluid Retention

A certain amount of fluid retention is normal during pregnancy. Your body rids itself of all this extra fluid during the first two to five days after delivery. You will urinate frequently in large amounts, you will wake up at night to urinate, and you may wake in the night soaked in perspiration.

Some women also experience increased swelling in their hands and feet for the first few days after delivery. Keep your feet elevated as much as possible. Drink plenty of fluids and limit your salt intake. This temporary swelling is an annoying but normal inconvenience!

Cramps

A certain amount of cramping is normal in the postpartum period. Cramps are often called "afterpains." Women having their first baby do not suffer from afterpains as intensely as in subsequent births. Because nursing increases uterine contractions, you may experience an increase in cramping while nursing. Afterpains will gradually subside in the days following your delivery. However, some woman do continue to experience mild cramping until their uterus returns to its nonpregnant size, about six weeks after delivery.

Ibuprofen and acetaminophen (the chemical names for two nonaspirin pain relievers) are commonly prescribed for cramps and both are considered acceptable medications for nursing mothers. In my experience, ibuprofen relieves cramps after delivery better than any other medication, including narcotics. A heating pad or hot water bottle wrapped in a towel and applied to the lower abdomen may also help decrease the discomfort of cramps, but **do not use an electric heating pad while sleeping.** If cramping is particularly bothersome while nursing, take ibuprofen one half-hour before nursing (but not more frequently than is recommended by your practitioner).

Severe or persistent cramps in the first 24 hours may indicate clots in your uterus. Be sure to bring this to the attention of your nurse. If you are already home, sit on the toilet and massage the top of your uterus *firmly* (in the downward direction). This should expel any clots and help alleviate cramps. Dark clots are not abnormal *unless* they are followed by bright red bleeding or are excessive in number. If the above measures do not relieve your severe or persistent cramps, consult your practitioner.

If your pain is not controlled by nonnarcotic medication, narcotic medication is ordered by your practitioner to be given every three to eight hours, depending on the dosage, on an "as needed" basis. This means that it will not be automatically given to you. **You must request this pain medication.** It is best to take medication for pain or cramps *as the discomfort begins.* Do not wait until the pain is intolerable—any pain medication is most effective when taken early.

Getting in and out of Bed Safely

To protect your weakened and stretched tummy and back muscles after delivery, take these precautions when getting into and out of bed.

To Get out of Bed: See Figure 11-1A.

From your back, turn as one straight unit onto your side. Put your heels over the edge of the bed (Figure 11-1B).

Use your upper arm to push yourself into the sitting position (Figure 11-1B, C).

Give yourself a few moments to get used to the sitting position before standing. This will help to reduce dizziness (Figure 11-1D).

To Get into Bed: This is the reverse of the procedure for getting out of bed. Sit on the side of the bed. Staying on your side, go down onto your elbow and then your shoulder. Bring your

FIGURE 11-1

Getting out of Bed Safely After Delivery

(A) From your back, turn as one straight unit onto your side. (B) Put your heels over the edge of the bed. (C) Use your upper arm to push yourself into sitting position. (D) Give yourself a few moments to get used to the sitting position before standing. This helps reduce dizziness.

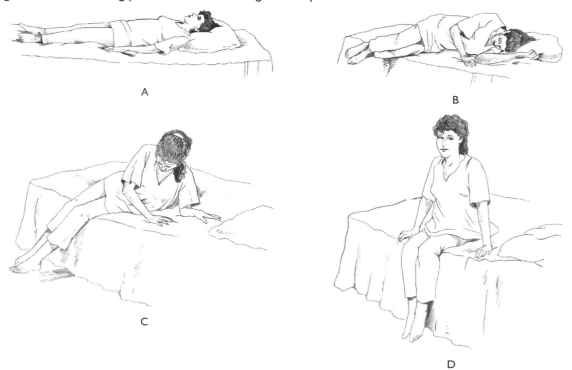

A

B

C

D

feet up onto the bed. Now with your entire body as one straight unit, turn onto your back.

Another method is to get into bed on your hands and knees and then rock over gently onto your hip. This prevents you from sitting directly on your bottom (Figure 11-2), and is often preferred by women who have an episiotomy or laceration of the perineum.

Postpartum Recovery with PIH

It is true that the cure for pregnancy-induced hypertension (PIH) is delivery. However, the risk of

seizure is still present during the first 48 hours after delivery. This is why the intravenous medication used to help prevent seizures before delivery (usually magnesium sulfate) is continued for 12 to 24 hours after delivery (depending on the severity of your symptoms and how quickly your blood pressure and blood tests begin to return to normal).

It is very difficult for a new mother to have to stay in bed, limit visitors, keep noise and lights low, and have less time with her newborn than desired. It is helpful to remember that this is for your safety and is a restriction usually limited to between 24 and 48 hours after delivery.

FIGURE 11-2

Getting into Bed

(A and B) Get into bed on your hands and knees. (C and D) Rock gently over onto your hip. This prevents you from sitting directly on your bottom and is often preferred by women who have an episiotomy or laceration of the perineum.

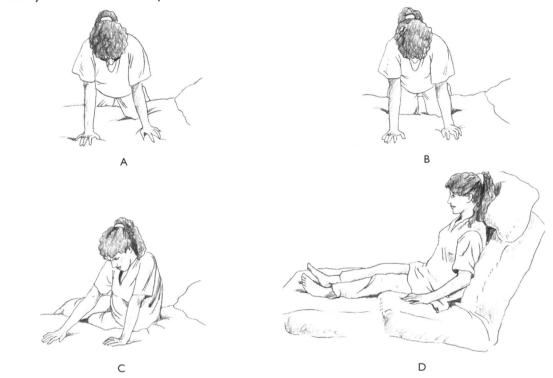

A

B

C

D

If you were planning to breastfeed, you will be allowed to do so. The use of magnesium sulfate is not a contraindication to breastfeeding. Bottle feeding is also allowed. In fact, increased contact with the baby has been shown in studies to reduce the postpartum stress of mothers who are under close observation with activity restrictions.

Ask your nurses and doctors to explain everything being done to you. Also be sure that you understand the reasons for any restrictions. This will help you to realize that they are temporary and help to ensure your return to good health after pregnancy-induced hypertension.

Perineal Care After Delivery

The perineum is the skin-covered area between the vagina and the rectum. (Refer to Figure 10-16, page 181, for an illustration.) After delivery, you will be given a *peri bottle* (a plastic squirt bottle) and taught how to use it. Every time you urinate or have a bowel movement, wash your perineum with one full bottle of warm water. **Always squirt the water from front to back.** Never squirt the water from the back, because you will bring bacteria from your rectal area toward your vagina and thereby increase your risk of infection. Gently pat yourself dry with toilet paper. **Always wipe from front to back to avoid bringing bacteria from the rectal area into the area of your vagina or urethra** (the opening that leads to the bladder). Continue to do this washing until you feel 100 percent healed. It removes old lochia discharge, which could be a source for bacterial growth if not washed away, and cleanses the area to promote better and faster healing.

Care of Your Stitches or Hemorrhoids

As explained in Chapter 10 under "After Delivery of the Placenta," your practitioner will repair any episiotomy or lacerations. (An *episiotomy* is an incision made by your practitioner in the area between your vagina and rectum in order to enlarge the vaginal opening (Figure 10-16, page 181). A *laceration* is a natural tear that occurs in this same area during delivery.) Your repair stitches may be on the outside or on the inside where you cannot see them. All stitches are done with suture material that dissolves on its own, so you will not need to have them removed.

Ice Packs: After your practitioner has finished with your delivery and made any necessary repair stitches, your nurse will clean your perineum and apply an ice pack directly to it. Most nurses apply an ice pack intermittently for several hours after delivery for comfort and swelling control even if you do not have stitches, because the force of pushing can also lead to swelling.

If you have stitches, ice packs are used intermittently on your perineum *for the first 24 hours* whenever you are in bed. To safeguard your skin, ice is usually applied for 20 minutes, followed by a 20-minute "intermission." Often the perineal ice packs used after delivery are made with a latex or plastic glove filled with ice and covered with gauze to prevent direct skin contact. Unlike other ice applications, these ice packs do not have to be removed every 20 minutes. Because

of their small size and your body heat, the packs melt quickly. By the time your nurse or support person makes a new ice pack, your skin will have had a sufficient break to prevent skin damage from prolonged contact with ice. However, if a larger ice pack is used or if you are making ice packs at home after a home delivery, you will want to remember the skin safety rule of 20 minutes on followed by 20 minutes off.

Ice packs are very important to use. Be sure that ice is applied immediately after your stitch repair is complete. This also makes it easier for you to empty your bladder, because swelling around the urethra makes it difficult for you to urinate on your own. It is to your benefit to use ice packs!

Medications: A narcotic or acetaminophen (such as Tylenol) or ibuprofen (such as Motrin or Advil) may be ordered to reduce pain in the stitch area. Nonnarcotic medication is usually sufficient after the first 24 hours (unless you have a third- or fourth-degree laceration). (For further information on lacerations, see page 188.)

Sitz Baths: After the first 24 hours, your practitioner may suggest the use of sitz baths as an additional comfort measure. Sitz baths are discussed in Chapter 13, "Taking Care of Yourself at Home."

Peri Bottle Rinsing: In addition to ice, cleansing with a peri bottle full of warm water after each urination helps to keep the stitch area clean. You may use regular toilet paper to wipe. Gentle patting to dry is best.

If you have an episiotomy or laceration, the stitches begin to dissolve about 7 to 10 days after delivery. You may feel a return of the burning sensation when you urinate (as you felt initially). Continue to use your peri bottle and sitz baths. This burning sensation will pass in a day or two. (**©Note: Burning with urination associated with fever must be reported to your practitioner.**)

Witch Hazel Pads: Most doctors allow small witch hazel pads to be applied as needed to the

Childbirth

stitch area. Most hospitals supply the first container, and you may purchase more from any drugstore after you go home. Witch hazel pads feel cool when applied. They are only a comfort measure, so use them only if they are helpful to you.

Topical Foams or Creams: Some practitioners order topical foams or creams to be applied to the stitch area. Unlike witch hazel pads, topical foams and creams *are medications.* They are usually ordered for use three to four times a day. An easy way to remember when to use them is to apply them after breakfast, lunch, and dinner and before bedtime. They can be irritating if overused, and therefore some practitioners do not order them at all. Please follow your practitioner's specific orders carefully. **A small amount (the size of a green pea) applied on a witch hazel pad is sufficient. Be sure to pick up and place the witch hazel pad so that the medication is directly on the stitches.**

Topical creams are also ordered if you have hemorrhoids. These creams also contain medication and are usually ordered to be applied three to four times a day. They can be applied directly to your hemorrhoids using your clean fingers or be applied on top of a witch hazel pad and then placed so that the cream is directly on the hemorrhoids.

Hemorrhoid creams can be purchased over the counter in any drugstore after discharge. However, when purchased over the counter, they come with an internal applicator for treatment of internal hemorrhoids. **If you had a fourth-degree laceration, do not use any rectal suppositories or internal hemorrhoid applicators until your practitioner says it is okay to do so.** A fourth-degree laceration extends into the rectum and must be allowed to heal. **Only external application of hemorrhoid cream is allowed if you have a fourth-degree laceration from giving birth.**

Foam "Doughnut" Pillows: Foam doughnut-shaped pillows (Figure 11-3) are available to make sitting more comfortable while stitches and hemorrhoids are sore. Many hospitals give these

FIGURE 11-3

Foam Doughnut Pillow

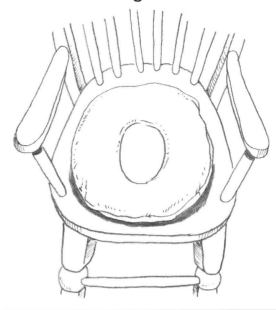

out to all their vaginal delivery patients. If a doughnut pillow is not available at your hospital, it can be purchased at many drugstores. A clean pillowcase can be used to cover and protect the pillow.

Try pinching your buttocks muscles tightly together before sitting. This technique seems to put less pulling sensation on the tender, uncomfortable perineum while sitting.

Bowel Care After Delivery

Your First Bowel Movement After Delivery

I have found bowel function to be one of women's biggest concerns after delivery. *Will it hurt? Will I pull out my stitches? When will I go?* Yes, you will go, usually in a day or two. It is common for women to have loose stools a day or two before going into labor, and while you are in labor you are not eating solid foods, so it is expected that it will take a day or two for you to have another bowel movement (BM). This is nothing to worry about.

Most doctors prescribe a stool softener to be taken twice a day while you are in the hospital. A stool softener is just that; it is not a laxative. You may continue your stool softener at home until after you have had a BM or for about 10 days to two weeks, if you prefer. Stool softeners are over-the-counter medications available at drugstores.

If you had a fourth-degree laceration, milk of magnesia and mineral oil may be prescribed for you or available on request the day following delivery.

Drink plenty of fluids, especially juices. Eight to twelve glasses per day are recommended. Prune juice is a natural laxative—have a small bottle at home if you are concerned about constipation. Remember, though, a few ounces usually does the trick. If you drink a whole glass of prune juice you may get diarrhea. Eat foods high in fiber and bulk, such as salads and bran.

No, you will not pull out your stitches when you have a BM, and if you keep your stool soft, it will not be painful. Some women say it is helpful to put light pressure over the stitch area with a clean piece of toilet paper while having your first BM. This is not necessary, but use this technique if it makes you feel more relaxed.

If you have not had a BM in three days, try a laxative such as milk of magnesia or Senekot tablets. For prevention, stool softeners like Colace or Pericolace and bulk laxatives like Metamucil may also be helpful. All of these products and other similar ones are available over the counter at most drugstores. Follow the directions on the medication box.

Hemorrhoids

Hemorrhoids are swollen, often painful, varicose veins in the rectum and anus. During pregnancy you can try to avoid this problem by not allowing yourself to get constipated—straining to have a constipated BM can make hemorrhoids bigger.

Eating a diet high in fiber, drinking plenty of fluids, and exercising all are known to help prevent constipation.

Many women also develop hemorrhoids during labor and delivery. Ice packs, witch hazel pads, and over-the-counter external ointments specific for hemorrhoids may be helpful. Sitz baths (Figure 13-1), which are covered in detail under home recovery on pages 228–230, are also useful in the treatment of swollen hemorrhoids. Hemorrhoids that develop during pregnancy or labor gradually decrease in size after delivery and most eventually disappear.

See pages 197–198 under "Care of Your Stitches or Hemorrhoids" for more information about comfort and treatment measures.

Rh-Negative Mothers: Do I Need Rhogam?

See pages 94–95 for an explanation of Rh incompatibility.

If you are Rh negative, your baby's cord blood will be sent to the lab to determine his or her blood type and Rh factor. If your baby is Rh positive, you will receive an injection of Rhogam within 72 hours of birth.

If you are Rh negative and you do not hear anything, please *don't* assume that your baby is Rh negative. **Ask for confirmation of your baby's Rh factor.** You need to double-check to be certain that Rhogam is administered to you if your baby is Rh positive.

Birth Certificate

During one of your prenatal office visits, your obstetrician or midwife will give you a *birth certificate worksheet.* You will fill this out, being careful to be accurate, and send it to the medical records department at the hospital where you will be delivering. After your delivery and before your discharge from the hospital, someone from the medical records department will visit you. At this time you will have the opportunity to add the name you have chosen for your baby. If you are still undecided on a name, you can sign the birth certificate and have 10 days to call and add the legal name.

The medical records department at your hospital obtains your practitioner's signature on the birth certificate. It then sends your baby's birth certificate to the town hall in the town or city where the hospital (of your delivery) is located. The birth certificate is a triple form. After three months, the town hall office in the town where you delivered sends a copy to your state vital statistics office. Another copy goes to your town clerk's office. (Some states may send a copy to the county vital statistics office instead of to your town.) You may want to check on the specifics of this procedure in your own state.

Birth certificates can be obtained from the town clerk's office in the town where you live (or in some states, from the county offices). Remember, your town or county will not receive its completed copy of your baby's birth certificate for about three months.

Laws in some states make birth certificates public record. In these states, you or anyone else can obtain a copy of your child's birth certificate. (Many people are working to get this law changed.) You can get a copy in person or by writing a request. Fees vary by town or county.

The copy you purchase will have a *raised seal* and therefore can be identified as an original—photocopies, of course, do not have this raised seal. If you need an original copy for some purpose, it must have the raised seal. Originals must be obtained from your town or county clerk's office. If you need an original copy of your baby's birth certificate for any purpose *immediately* (that is, you cannot wait three months for it to arrive in your town or county office), speak with the medical records department at the hospital where you delivered about the proper procedure to obtain one immediately in your state.

Discharge from the Hospital

After you deliver, two bracelets are placed on your baby and one on you as the mother. All three of these bracelets have matching numbers. In addition, the sex of your baby, your full name, and the date and time of birth are included on the bracelets. You or your support person should verify all of the bracelet information and the matching number on all three bracelets before they are put on you and your baby.

It is legally verified that you are taking home the correct infant by matching your baby's and your bracelets. At discharge, one bracelet is removed from your baby and attached to a legal document that remains part of your hospital medical record. You must sign to verify that you have the correct infant. Your bracelet and the remaining baby bracelet become your keepsakes.

In most states, an infant car seat is legally required and, of course, very important. Be sure that whoever comes to take you home brings the car seat along. Hospitals in most states are legally required to verify, in writing, that a car seat was available for the baby's discharge. Nurses are usually legally advised, however, not to teach you how to use your car seat and not to place the infant into the seat for you. **It is your responsibility to bring the car seat and know how to properly use it.**

Some hospitals have a policy that requires a car seat test be done, before discharge, on any baby born before 37 weeks' gestation and any baby weighing less than five and one-half pounds. You will be required to bring the car seat you will be using to the hospital the day before discharge. Your baby will be placed in the car seat for approximately an hour and attached to a machine that monitors oxygen saturation. A small wire is attached to your baby's toe. It does not penetrate your baby's skin or cause any discomfort; it feels like a Band-Aid. Your baby's oxygen level will be monitored for one hour to ensure that he or she can breathe well while sitting in your style of car seat. If you will be traveling longer than one hour to reach home, you will need to inform the nurses of this fact. Your infant should be tested for the length of time of your trip home.

Childbirth

12

Cesarean Birth

A*cesarean birth* is delivery of the baby through a surgical incision in the abdomen and uterine wall. Cesarean deliveries are performed for various reasons related to the health and safety of the mother and baby. Sometimes cesarean deliveries are scheduled, and other times they are performed on an emergency basis.

From 1960 to 1990 the incidence of normal pregnancies that required cesarean births increased from less than 5 percent to 24 percent. (Cesarean delivery rates for high-risk pregnancies such as multiple births, pregnancy-induced hypertension, and diabetes have to be evaluated by different standards.) Many factors could have contributed to this increase. Women were having their first babies at an older age, and there were more first pregnancies. Also, during this period, if you had one cesarean delivery, repeat cesareans were routinely done for subsequent deliveries. Electronic fetal monitoring has also been blamed as a possible cause for part of this increase. (Once fetal distress is detected on the monitor, practitioners feared lawsuits if they waited to see if the distress would pass.) Currently, with the safety of vaginal births after cesarean delivery well established (when low cervical horizontal incisions are used on both the skin and uterus), the cesarean section rate is dropping again.

When you are evaluating the cesarean delivery rate for a hospital or an individual practitioner, anything under 17 percent is considered very good.

Scheduled Cesarean Delivery

Most decisions to perform a cesarean delivery are made during labor. However, there are some reasons why you may be scheduled for a cesarean delivery prior to going into labor.

❑ You have had one or more cesarean deliveries in the past and you and your doctor have decided that a trial of labor after cesarean is not appropriate.

❑ Your baby is breech, and either *external version* (an attempt to externally, manually turn the baby) was unsuccessful or your physician does not recommend a vaginal breech delivery.

❑ If you have diabetes or gestational diabetes (diabetes only during pregnancy), the baby is often large (in weight) due to the high glucose levels in your blood. In addition, in diabetes the placenta often begins to lose its ability to function at full potential before

203

pregnancy reaches full term. For these reasons, early delivery is often recommended, although induction generally is tried before a cesarean delivery is scheduled.

❑ You have a multiple gestation (twins, triplets), and the positions of the babies are not conducive to vaginal birth.

❑ If you have *essential hypertension* (high blood pressure all the time) or pregnancy-induced hypertension, early delivery may be necessary. High blood pressure in pregnancy can lead to convulsions. It also prematurely ages the placenta. This makes early delivery necessary for your and your baby's safety. Cesarean deliveries normally would be done in these cases only after an unsuccessful induction attempt or if your pregnancy-induced hypertension is severe enough to make delivery necessary immediately.

❑ Ultrasound has shown that the placenta is attached directly over your cervix (placenta previa) or partially covering your cervix (partial placenta previa).

❑ If you had a previous cesarean delivery for cephalopelvic disproportion, better known as CPD (in which because of its size or presentation, the baby's head did not fit through your pelvis), you may be offered an ultrasound in the last trimester. Fetal size and other factors will be evaluated for the possible need for another cesarean section. (Please note that an ultrasound examination is not mandatory for every woman prior to a trial of labor after cesarean if the previous cesarean was done for reasons other than CPD.)

There are many other possible reasons that a scheduled cesarean delivery may be necessary. You can expect a full explanation from your physician if a cesarean delivery is recommended for you.

Preoperative Visit to the Hospital

Most hospitals have you come in a day or two before your surgery for routine blood tests. (If not,

your blood will be drawn on admission.) An anesthesiologist will meet with you at this time. After asking you some questions about your physical health and any previous surgeries, the anesthesiologist will explain the type of anesthesia you will be given and any risks involved. You will be asked to sign an informed consent for anesthesia after all your questions have been answered.

Preparation at Home

If you have a scheduled cesarean delivery, you will be instructed not to eat or drink after midnight the night before. Your stomach needs to be empty prior to surgery. This reduces the risk of choking on solid food particles or aspirating (taking into the lungs) liquids from the stomach if you were to vomit during or immediately after surgery. You may brush your teeth on the morning of surgery, but don't swallow any water.

Preparation at the Hospital

You will be instructed when to arrive at the hospital on the day of your scheduled cesarean delivery. Most hospitals ask you to arrive about two hours ahead of the time of your surgery. When you arrive, you will be asked to put on a hospital gown. Your blood pressure and temperature will be taken, and your baby's heart rate will be monitored for a short period of time.

An intravenous line (IV) will be started on admission. It is required for all surgeries to keep you well hydrated until you can drink adequate fluids on your own. An IV is also an immediate line for administering fast-acting medications if required during your surgery.

Your bladder lies in front of your uterus. If your bladder were full, it would be directly under the area where the "bikini" cut low horizontal incision is made. To ensure that the bladder is empty and remains so throughout surgery, your nurse will insert a Foley catheter when you are admitted. A Foley catheter is a sterile tube inserted into your urethra (the outer opening where urine is passed from the body). The bladder now remains empty and therefore does not fill and expand into the surgical area.

Before the catheter is inserted, the area around the external urethra opening is cleansed with an antiseptic solution. This will feel cold. When the catheter is inserted, you will feel some discomfort—do your slow rhythmic breathing and try not to tense your muscles.

Once the internal end of the catheter is in the bladder, a very small balloon is inflated near that end. (The nurse inflates this internal balloon by injecting sterile water into an adapter on the outside end of the catheter. You should not feel this part of the procedure.) Once inflated, this balloon prevents the catheter from slipping out of the bladder.

For a short period of time following the insertion of your Foley catheter, you may feel a pressure or burning sensation in your urethra that makes you feel like you need to urinate. This is an annoying immediate side effect that will pass within a short time. (Most people no longer complain about this feeling after surgery.) The feeling is caused by the catheter pressing on the many nerves in the bladder and urethra.

Abdominal and Uterine Incisions

Most doctors require that only the top three-fourths of an inch of your pubic hair be shaved prior to surgery. This is done so that the low "bikini" horizontal cut in the skin and abdominal wall can be made. (This is the most common skin incision made for cesarean birth.) When the pubic hair grows back, you will hardly be able to notice the incision line.

The *skin incision* made for a cesarean delivery does not predict the type of internal uterine incision. Cesarean incisions may be:

1. **Low cervical horizontal incision:** this is the most common incision. *Both the skin and uterus have the same low horizontal incision.* See Figure 12-1.

2. **Low cervical horizontal incision of the skin and a low *vertical* incision of the**

Low Horizontal Incisions

(A) Low cervical horizontal skin incision ("bikini" incision). (B) Low cervical horizontal uterine incision. (C) Cesarean delivery through a low cervical horizontal incision. (D) External closure of a low cervical horizontal incision with staples.

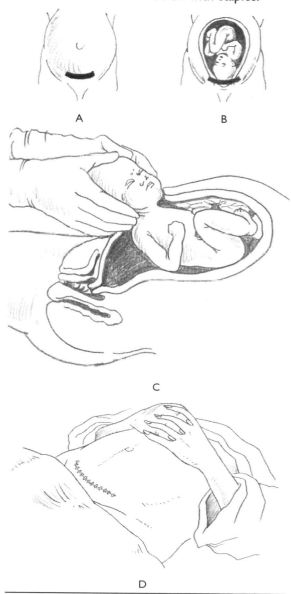

A   B

C

D

Childbirth

uterus: see Figure 12-2. This incision is rarely used today.

3. **Classic high vertical incision:** see Figure 12-3. This type of incision is also rarely used today. It is done occasionally in some cases of shoulder presentation and placenta previa. The baby can be removed faster with this type of incision, however, so you may see it used in a severe emergency.

Trial of Labor After Cesarean

When labor is allowed to occur (or is induced) in a pregnancy that follows a cesarean delivery, it is called a TOLAC (trial of labor after cesarean). The term *trial* simply means that your practitioner is going to allow you to try labor (spontaneous or induced) to see if you can have a successful labor (contractions that bring on continuous cervical dilatation without fetal distress) and a successful vaginal birth (your pelvis is of adequate size for delivery). (It is important to note that there is insufficient evidence to prove that inducing labor early increases the chances of a successful vaginal birth after a cesarean delivery.)

It is safe to labor and deliver vaginally after having a cesarean delivery in which the low cervical horizontal incision was used on both your skin and the uterus. Trials of labor are even safe if you have had two previous cesareans with this incision type. Because we now know this and because there are

FIGURE 12-2

This approach combines (A) a low cervical horizontal incision of the skin and (B) a low vertical incision of the uterus.

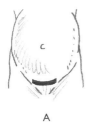
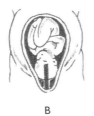

A   B

FIGURE 12-3

Classic Vertical Incisions

(A) Classic vertical skin incision. (B) Classic high vertical uterine incision.

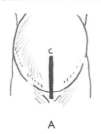
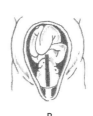

A   B

more risks involved in a surgical (cesarean) delivery than a vaginal delivery, it is common today for practitioners to advise a trial of labor following cesarean.

Trial of labor after cesarean delivery is not safe if a classic incision was made on any previous cesarean delivery. The risk of rupture of the uterine scar during a future labor is greater with this type of incision. Unfortunately, you cannot tell from looking at the outside scar what type of uterine incision was done. Be sure you know this information or have access to your previous cesarean delivery medical records when planning a future vaginal birth.

Vaginal Birth After Cesarean (VBAC)

VBAC is an acronym used to identify a mother who has had a vaginal birth after a cesarean.

Emergency Cesarean Delivery

The term *emergency* warrants some clarification. If your cesarean delivery is decided upon during the course of your labor, it is termed an *emergency cesarean delivery*. Not all "emergency" sections require a frantic dash to the operating room—the term simply means that labor was in progress or being induced when the decision was made that a cesarean section was required.

In an emergency cesarean delivery, your caregivers will explain as much as possible, depending on the severity of the situation. Your signature is obtained on a consent form, if time allows. If not, verbal consent is obtained from you or your spouse. If you do not already have an IV, one is started now. In the delivery room, the anesthesiologist will either give you additional medication (a surgical dose) through your epidural, if you have one, or give you a spinal. General anesthesia will be used in extreme emergencies (crash cesarean sections, discussed later) if it is felt that it would not be safe (for you or your baby) to take the time needed to administer spinal anesthesia. General anesthesia would also be administered during your cesarean if your epidural or spinal is not effective in keeping you totally pain free.

See the section in Chapter 9 entitled "Pain Medication" for more information about epidurals, spinals, and general anesthesia.

Failure to Progress

Ineffective Contractions: One form of failure to progress occurs when *contractions are ineffective in producing cervical dilatation, even after labor augmentation with oxytocin has been attempted.* Many women progress normally to a certain point in their labor and then stop dilating. Sometimes they stay at one point for several hours and then begin dilating again. At other times *Pitocin augmentation* is attempted to try to increase the strength and frequency of contractions and therefore encourage further dilatation of the cervix. If labor fails to bring on progress in cervical dilatation, and augmentation also fails, the diagnosis is "failure to progress" and cesarean delivery is the only option.

Just because a cesarean delivery was required for one baby *does not* mean you will need one if you become pregnant again. If you require a cesarean because of ineffective contractions, your next labor may be perfectly normal and lead to a vaginal birth.

Cephalopelvic Disproportion (CPD): Failure to progress can also be due to *cephalopelvic*

disproportion (commonly called CPD). CPD simply means that *this* baby is too big for your pelvis. In CPD there is no other option than a cesarean delivery. I emphasized the word *this* in the above definition because it is important to note that the size of the baby can be different with each pregnancy. A normal labor and vaginal delivery may occur next time if the baby is smaller.

Malpresentation: Failure to progress can also be due to the position of the baby and how it presents itself into your pelvis. Normally the biggest diameter of the baby's head presents itself into the biggest diameter of your pelvis. Later, the baby naturally (on its own) internally rotates to pass the broad shoulders through this opening. Variations in the normal pattern, however, can make the baby unable to descend farther.

Sometimes failure to progress is caused by *malpresentation.* Instead of the normal presentation (Figure 12-4A) the baby enters the pelvis shoulder-first (Figure 12-4B) or face-first. These malpresentations may or may not correct themselves as labor progresses. If the baby's presentation is such that it cannot descend and cause the cervix to dilate, cesarean delivery will be required.

Luckily, your next baby may present normally (head down) and a vaginal birth will be possible.

Breech presentation is also considered a malpresentation. Figure 12-5 shows various types of breech presentations, which occur in about 25 percent of preterm births and up to 4 percent of full-term births.

Some practitioners will consider doing a breech vaginal delivery; others will always recommend a cesarean delivery for a breech presentation; still others will recommend that an external version be attempted (as explained below). What will be considered for you depends on your practitioner's preference, the length of your pregnancy, the apparent size of your pelvis, the size of the baby, and the type of breech presentation.

If your baby is found to be breech **before you go into labor,** in some cases the baby's presentation can be changed to the normal head-down presentation by a procedure called *external*

FIGURE 12-4

Normal Presentation and Abnormal Presentation

(A) Normal presentation. (B) Shoulder presentation.

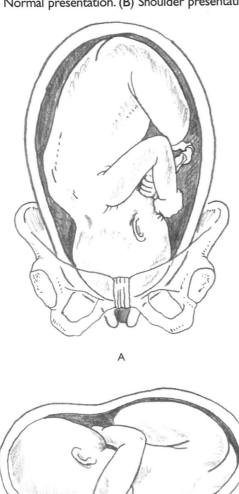

A

B

version. This is done in the hospital, but it will not be attempted if you are already in labor. (See Chapter 5, page 87, for a description of the external version procedure.)

Crash Cesarean Delivery

Crash is the term often used to describe a cesarean delivery that must be done without delay to save the life of the baby or the mother. There are many possible situations that would warrant an emergency crash cesarean delivery. A few examples follow.

Fetal Distress

Fetal Heart Rate: Your baby's heart rate drops and does not come back up into the normal range within a reasonable amount of time. The following measures will be tried to speed the recovery of the fetal heart. If these measures fail, a cesarean section will be done.

> *Maternal position changes* will be tried (to relieve possible pressure on the umbilical cord).
>
> *An IV fluid bolus* will be given to help increase placental perfusion and maternal blood pressure.
>
> *Oxygen will be administered to the mother* via a face mask to increase the oxygen saturation levels in the mother, making greater oxygen concentrations available to the baby.
>
> *Oxytocin will be discontinued,* if it is being administered.
>
> *IV medication to raise blood pressure will be given to the mother* if she has recently been given an epidural or an epidural bolus dose of medication and her blood pressure has dropped.

Cord Prolapse: Your baby's umbilical cord prolapses below the baby's presenting part or into the vagina and becomes compressed. The most common time for this to occur is when the membranes rupture before the presenting part has engaged in

FIGURE 12-5

Breech Presentations

(A) Frank breech. (B) Complete breech. (C) Incomplete breech. (D) Footling breech.

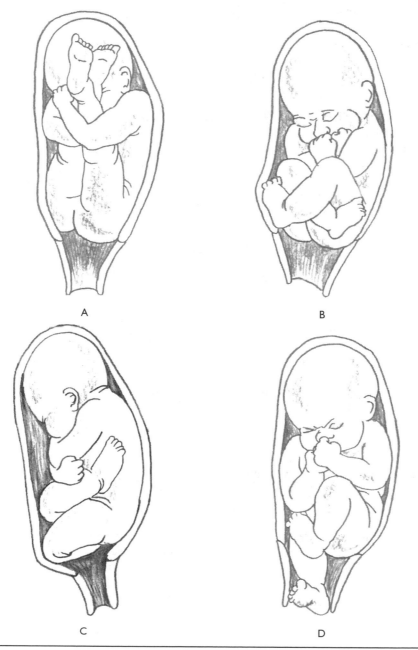

A

B

C

D

the pelvis. (See pages 119–120 for further discussion of cord prolapse.)

Abruptio Placentae

Complete Abruptio Placentae: The placenta completely separates from the uterine wall and the mother is hemorrhaging internally. Although this is a rare complication of labor, complete abruptio placentae is a life-threatening emergency for both mother and baby. Immediate cesarean delivery is required.

Partial Abruptio Placentae: Only a part of the placenta separates from the uterine wall. If fetal distress does not occur, your physician may allow you to continue to labor under close observation. If a fetal distress does occur, an immediate cesarean section will be performed.

Uterine Rupture

This is a *very rare* complication of labor. If the uterus ruptures, the mother hemorrhages internally. Of course, an immediate cesarean delivery is required. Following cesarean delivery of the baby, a hysterectomy (surgical removal of the uterus) may be required in order to stop the hemorrhage. However, this is not always necessary.

Unfortunately, in these emergency situations there is little time to provide long explanations or extra emotional support. This is when trust in your choice of physician is imperative. (If you are under a midwife's care, the backup physician who works with your midwife takes over at this point.) Explanations can and will be given later, after surgery.

In a crash cesarean delivery, lots of people will come into the room and you will feel that they are coming at you from all directions. All the things listed above (IV line, abdominal shave, Foley catheter insertion) as done prior to a scheduled birth, with the exception of explanations, will be done now. However, more people will be helping to complete preparations in a shorter amount of time. You will be placed on a stretcher, and people will *run* you to the operating room. Remember, we

are only trying to reduce the amount of time you and your baby are exposed to whatever stress is necessitating this cesarean delivery. Understanding this now can help you feel less threatened and scared if you require a crash cesarean delivery.

You will be moved onto the operating table. If you do not have an existing, effective epidural into which additional medication can be added, general anesthesia will be required because time cannot be taken to insert a spinal during this type of an emergency.

Slow rhythmic breathing or any other form of relaxation breathing technique may be helpful in reducing your tension. The presence of your support person during the rushed preparation is very reassuring. Although you are both very frightened, it may be helpful to remember that you are in experienced hands; the staff has done this many times before.

Operating Room Routines

Your husband or support person will be given a hospital gown or a scrub suit to wear into the operating room. He or she will also be required to wear shoe covers, a cap, and a mask. The mask is made of paper and permits normal breathing.

In most hospitals the support person must wait outside until the spinal is given and the sterile drape is placed over the patient. There are several reasons for this. First, this is an operating room with strict sterile procedure. While equipment is being prepared and large drapes are being opened, it is important to keep them sterile. Trained and experienced personnel know how to properly move around inside an operating room without compromising the sterile environment. There are even strict rules for how to pass a person dressed in a sterile gown! Second, many lay people become faint if they watch a spinal being done. We want the support person awake and sitting up to enjoy the birth of the baby! Your support person will not be forgotten—about 10 minutes after you enter the operating room, he or she will be shown in and seated near your head!

If you have an existing, effective epidural, after you are taken to the delivery/operating room and transferred to the operating table, it is reinforced with a surgical dose of medication; if not, a spinal is given (for scheduled or emergency deliveries). General anesthesia would be used in a crash delivery. General anesthesia is also necessary if your spinal or epidural proves ineffective for full pain control during delivery. (Most anesthesiologists do not allow support persons in the operating room if general anesthesia is administered.)

Your abdomen is prepped with betadine (a dark-colored solution that temporarily stains the skin). Next, the large sterile drape is opened. The end of the drape near your head will be placed over a metal rod that goes above your shoulders. This keeps the drape off your head and provides a shield so that you cannot see the surgery. This drape also serves as a visual shield for your support person, if he or she does not want to view the surgery. He or she is now allowed in the room to sit near your head.

When your baby is about to be delivered from the uterus, your doctor will tell you that you will feel pressure. During every cesarean birth, a surgeon and an assistant surgeon perform the surgery. The assistant will press down on the top of your uterus, helping to push the baby out of the small incision. You will feel like someone is sitting on your stomach. This is heavy pressure, not pain, so don't be frightened—your baby is about to be born!

During scheduled, nonemergency cesarean births, your doctor can hold up your baby for you to take a quick look. During emergency deliveries, however, your baby will be handed immediately to a neonatologist (a doctor who specializes in newborn care), pediatrician, or nurse for immediate assessment and any needed treatment. If fetal stress was the cause of your cesarean section, the specialist is there to be sure your baby receives immediate assistance with breathing or any other need.

Once your baby has been assessed, the mucus has been cleared, and she or he is breathing within normal limits, the nurse will wrap up your baby to keep him or her warm. The support person can

then be given the baby to hold. You can both enjoy meeting your baby for the first time while the repair part of your surgery takes place. Closing the uterus and abdomen usually takes another 30 to 45 minutes.

If your baby is suffering from respiratory distress or other conditions warranting close observation and assessment, he or she will be taken immediately to the special care nursery. The personnel in this nursery will visit you in the recovery room to keep you informed of your baby's condition. Dad, or your support person, will usually be allowed to go see your baby at this time.

What Is Different About a Cesarean Baby?

Appearance

As in a vaginal birth, your baby will be covered with blood—your blood. Vernix, the white thick substance that looks like cheese, will also cover your baby if you are early. In addition, he or she may have blue hands and feet, which is normal for all newborns.

If this was a crash delivery for fetal distress, your baby may be quite blue at birth, due to decreased oxygen. He or she may need assistance in taking the first several breaths, which is why specialists are called to attend the delivery in an emergency. We *expect* your baby to need a little help in the beginning, sort of a "jump start." So don't panic if you don't hear a vigorous cry right away. The neonatologist needs time to give the help that is needed. Remember, if your baby is not crying it doesn't mean he or she is not getting oxygen. Positive pressure breaths or "bag" breaths are providing oxygen to your baby's body and brain. It sometimes takes time to clear the lungs of fluid and stimulate your baby to begin breathing on his or her own.

It is often said that babies born by *scheduled* cesarean delivery are always beautiful! This is because their head shape is nice and "normal" looking—they do not have molding of the head or *caput* (the swollen round bump that occurs as a small section of the head sits on the cervix for a long time and swells through the partially dilated cervical opening). Of course, if Mom has labored or pushed for several hours prior to a cesarean delivery being done, then molding and caput should be expected. (Remember, molding and caput are nature's way of making vaginal births possible. They are normal consequences of labor and cause no harm at all to your baby. Within hours after birth, you can see improvement in the shape of the head. Within a few days the head returns to its "normal" shape and size.)

Breathing and Mucus

If you have had a cesarean birth (or a rapid pushing stage), please expect that your baby will have more mucus. He or she has not been squeezed and compressed while coming down the birth canal. The lungs that were filled with fluid in utero during pregnancy have not had labor's compression to help begin clearing those air sacs of fluid before birth. These babies often need a few positive pressure breaths or bag breaths to help them clear fluid from the air sacs. Expect this so that you won't be frightened if your baby does not cry right away or if you see the doctor using a bag to deliver breaths to your baby.

Cesarean babies have more mucus throughout their first few days of life. Babies drink amniotic fluid while they are growing inside the uterus, so the esophagus (food tube) develops a lot of thick mucus. Although it has never been scientifically proven that an adequate pushing stage "squeezes" this mucus out of the baby, it certainly seems that way to those of us caring for newborns. Cesarean babies and babies from rapid pushing stages tend to have more mucus after birth. You will notice them gagging or acting like they are chewing on a huge wad of bubble gum. The location of this mucus interferes with swallowing, so they will have difficulty feeding until they get this mucus up and out.

Babies have wonderful and amazing gag, cough, and sneeze reflexes—they are experts at clearing their airways. However, new parents get scared as they watch their baby try to rid himself of this annoying mucus! Eventually the baby will gag and vomit a lot of thick mucus, which may contain old blood. This is okay—it is good for the baby to get this up. It may take some time for the baby to cough or vomit all the mucus up.

How You Can Help: First, don't panic. Babies can be frightened by their gagging, and if you pick them up suddenly and with fear, they may panic and hold their breath. Then they really turn blue and scare you all the more! Remember, babies have not eaten anything solid and thus there is nothing to completely block their airway. They are just struggling with thick mucus and may need a little help getting it up.

Until you are able to get up and do this yourself, have your support person pick the baby up calmly and talk softly. Place him or her in the football hold, on the side with the head slightly lower

FIGURE 12-6

Positioning the Baby for Removal of Mucus

than the chest (Figure 12-6), which puts gravity to work. Hold him or her on your left side if you are right-handed or on your right if you are left-handed. This way you will have your dominant hand to reach over and gently pat the baby's back. Gravity, the vibration from gentle back pats, and gagging help move the mucus up and out.

Once your baby spits up the mucus, you will have your dominant hand free to use a bulb syringe (see Figure 12-6) to clear the mucus out of his or her mouth and nose. Squeeze the bulb syringe and place it inside the baby's cheek on the side that is down (closest to the floor). Release the pressure on the bulb, allowing it to fill with mucus. Remove the bulb syringe from the mouth and squirt the mucus out. Squeeze the bulb again and place it into one of the baby's nostrils. Suction the mucus, remove the bulb, and squirt out the mucus. Repeat the procedure in the other nostril. *Always* suction the mouth first and then the nose. (Doing the nose first may cause your baby to startle and bring mucus down from the mouth into the airway or cause him or her to reswallow the mucus already brought up.)

It is okay to use the same bulb syringe in both the mouth and the nose—it is for use on this baby only. You can rinse it out with warm water when you are finished. The bulb syringe is made so that you cannot put it too far into the nose if *gently* inserted, so don't be afraid to use it. It is a wonderful and very helpful little tool!

The Recovery Room

After surgery, you will be moved to the recovery room. You can expect to be here approximately one to two hours. Your pulse and blood pressure are early indicators of any internal bleeding, so they will be closely monitored. An automatic blood pressure cuff will be placed on your arm. It will tighten to take your blood pressure every 5 minutes at first and later every 15 minutes. The cuff will loosen on its own once the reading registers. An oxygen mask will be placed over your

mouth and nose for a short time. This is supplemental oxygen that is given for a short time until you are breathing deeply on your own.

The cardiac monitor leads that you had on your chest during surgery are still there in the recovery room. The medical and nursing staff need to closely monitor your cardiac (heart) status in the early postoperative period. You will also have a pulse oximeter clip on your finger or toe. This little device tells us the concentration of oxygen in the cells in the very tip of your finger or toe. Both of these monitors assure us that your heart and circulatory system are functioning normally and that you are breathing deeply and frequently enough to well perfuse all your cells with oxygen. They also help us regulate how much pain medication to give you without compromising your respiratory status. If the cells at the tips of your fingers are above 94 percent oxygen perfused, we know that your heart and brain are even better perfused, since vital organs are given even higher priority by your body's circulatory system! If your oxygen level drops below 94 percent, an oxygen mask will be applied to your face until the level rises.

You will have your IV, Foley catheter, oxygen mask, blood pressure machine, cardiac monitor, and pulse oximeter (see Figure 12-7) attached in the recovery room. These are all used regardless of whether you received an epidural, spinal, or general anesthesia for your delivery. This is standard procedure after any surgery and does not mean that anything is wrong. Knowing this ahead of time helps you not to worry when you find yourself attached to several pieces of equipment.

Pain Control After Cesarean Delivery

For pain control after your cesarean, your doctor has many options. Some doctors ask the anesthesiologist to continue an existing epidural on a postoperative-drip dose for pain control in recovery. Walking epidurals are also popular in some

FIGURE 12-7

Monitoring Equipment in the Recovery Room

Cardiac monitor.   Blood pressure, pulse, and pulse oximeter.

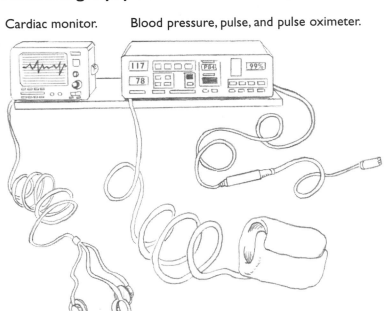

hospitals for postoperative pain control. (See page 151 for an explanation of walking epidurals.) Other doctors will leave orders for you to receive either intravenous medication (PCA—patient-controlled analgesia) or intramuscular (IM) injections (given every three to four hours).

The pain medications used for recovery after cesarean delivery are all safe for breastfeeding mothers. Some medication does go through to your breast milk and may make your baby slightly sleepy. You will have to work harder to keep him or her awake for complete feedings. Be assured that we will not give you anything that would harm your baby, but do not hesitate to discuss your questions and concerns about breastfeeding and pain medications with your physician or nurse.

If you are planning to breastfeed, you will be able to hold and nurse your baby once you are in the recovery room if your baby does not require immediate care in the nursery. Once he or she

has ensured that you are stable, your nurse can assist you with nursing if you so wish.

Patient-Controlled Analgesia (PCA)

Many hospitals use patient-controlled analgesia (PCA) pumps for pain control for the first 24 hours after a cesarean. Figure 12-8 shows a PCA pump. (The narcotic syringe is held within a covered, locked section of the pump.) In this method of pain control, your nurse in the recovery room gives you the initial IV bolus doses of the medication ordered by your doctor. Bolus doses will be given until your postoperative pain is controlled. It is important for you to understand that you should be comfortable and able to sleep but will not be 100 percent pain free. Most pain medications can cause respiratory depression—we must find that balance where you are comfortable but still breathing deeply. We need for you to be able to move, cough, and breathe

FIGURE 12-8

Patient-Controlled Analgesia (PCA) Pump

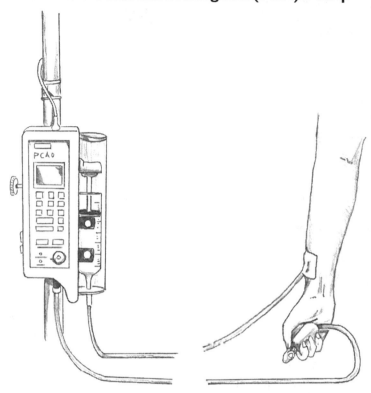

Childbirth

deeply. Some discomfort is to be expected when doing these things.

Once the nurse completes your bolus, the pump is programmed to administer a specific dose of the prescribed medication when you request it by pressing a button—thus the term patient-controlled analgesia (PCA). The pump is programmed to lock out for a specific amount of time, normally 8 to 10 minutes after each dose. (During this lockout time no medication will be delivered if you press the button.) The pump is also programmed with additional safeguards. For example, it will only allow you to administer a prescribed and programmed total amount of medication during a one-hour period of time, and the program can only be changed by your nurse,

who must use a special key. All of these safeguards prevent you from taking an unsafe amount of medication. The number of times you attempt to take a dose is recorded by the pump. This helps your nurse know if you are requiring or requesting more medication than the pump is programmed to deliver. She can then discuss this with your doctor and have the dose increased if appropriate.

The advantage of a PCA pump over IM injections is the more even level of medication in your bloodstream, offering more continuous pain relief. With IM injections, once you experience pain you must call for your nurse and she must take the time to check your order, see when you last received medication, and then draw up the medication. This all takes time, and meanwhile, your pain may be increasing. About 10 minutes after receiving an IM injection, you begin to feel the effects and you become very sleepy. There are therefore peaks and valleys in your pain and alertness (Figure 12-9A).

With the PCA pump, the loading dose gets you into your comfort level. You control the amount and timing of your doses, keeping yourself in the comfort zone *without* peaks and valleys of pain and sedation (see Figure 12-9B).

Intramuscular Injections

There are times when the PCA pump is not ordered or is discontinued and replaced with IM injection pain medication, for example, if you are allergic to the medications used for PCA. IM injections are also oftentimes ordered simply because some physicians prefer them for pain control in their patients. They are also used when the PCA medication has been tried and for various reasons is not effective in controlling pain.

Oral Pain Medication

Within 24 hours after cesarean delivery, a nurse or your practitioner, listening to your abdomen with a stethoscope, will be able to hear sounds of fluid and gas moving in your bowel. This is an indication that you should now be able to tolerate solid foods. In addition, because taking solid foods reduces the risk of stomach upset from pills, you can now try pain medication in pill form. Your PCA pump or intramuscular injections will be discontinued, and you will be switched over to oral pain medication.

Oral pain medication is usually one of the several choices of narcotic pills available. In addition, ibuprofen (common name brands Advil and Motrin) and acetaminophen (common brand name Tylenol) are also options. The majority of women still need the help of a narcotic in the immediate period after IV or IM medication is discontinued. However, within a day or two many women are comfortable switching to nonnarcotic pain pills like ibuprofen or acetaminophen.

FIGURE 12-9

Comparison of pain levels with (A) intramuscular injection and (B) patient-controlled analgesia (PCA).

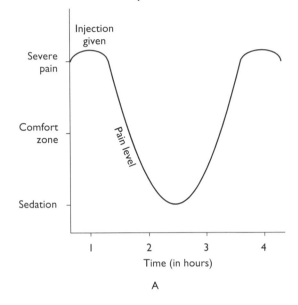

IM Injection Pain Control

A

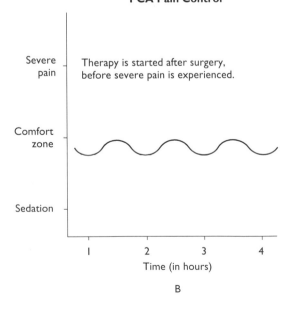

PCA Pain Control

B

Many practitioners allow ibuprofen to be given along with the PCA or IM injections for better control of the pain caused by cramping.

Postpartum Recovery After Cesarean Delivery

Average Length of Hospital Stay

The average postpartum hospital stay after cesarean delivery is three to four days, depending on your recovery and the limits imposed by your insurance company.

Activity

You will be in bed for about six to eight hours before being assisted to get up. (See Figure 11-1, page 195, for the best way to get out of bed to reduce pain and the risk of abdominal and back strain.) Some doctors require longer periods before their patients are allowed out of bed. At first, you may only stand, turn, and sit in a chair directly next to your bed. Each time you get out of bed, you will be asked to do more and walk farther.

Even though you may feel like staying in bed, you'll recover much more quickly when you get moving. Walking helps prevent such postoperative complications as pneumonia and leg and groin blood-clot formation. The importance of getting up and moving cannot be emphasized enough. Your nurses are not being mean—they are only doing what they know will help you best achieve a quick and complication-free recovery. Help us to help you!

Using Your Pain Medication

All medication, regardless of whether it is delivered through an intravenous line, injected into your muscle, or taken in pill form by mouth, works most effectively if taken when the pain is first coming on. Do not wait until the pain is intense or unbearable.

If you are using a PCA pump for pain control after a cesarean, you will still have it when you get out of bed the first time. Press the button and take a dose immediately before getting up, before doing coughing and deep-breathing exercises, and as needed to keep yourself in the comfort zone. (See pages 218–219 for an explanation of coughing and deep-breathing exercises.)

If your pain medication is administered by intramuscular injection, or you have advanced to pill-form pain medication, it is a good idea to take medication about one-half hour before getting up. You should not expect to be completely pain-free, but you should be comfortable enough to stand up straight, walk, and take deep breaths. By the second day, getting out of bed will be much easier and less uncomfortable.

When you are advanced to oral pain medication, you will most likely be started off with a narcotic pill. After two or three days, you may be ready to try a nonaspirin, nonnarcotic pain reliever.

Foley Catheter

Your Foley catheter (the catheter in your urethra that is draining urine) will be taken out in approximately 24 hours, sometimes sooner. Once it is removed, you will be watched to be certain that you urinate on your own within eight hours. The amount that you urinate will be measured to ensure that you are adequately emptying your bladder.

Intravenous Line

The IV will be removed after you are drinking adequate fluids or after you no longer need PCA medication. This is usually about 24 hours after delivery.

Routine Postpartum Needs Immediately After Delivery and at Home

Regardless of the fact that your baby was born by cesarean procedure, you have all the same postpartum needs (except for care of perineal stitches)

Childbirth

as the woman who had a vaginal delivery. In addition, you have many recovery issues specific to cesarean delivery. Please see Chapter 11, "Recovery After Vaginal Birth: Immediate Postpartum Care," to understand the assessment and needs immediately after delivery. Also please review Chapter 13, "Taking Care of Yourself at Home: The Postpartum Period," for a full explanation of *lochia* (vaginal bleeding after delivery), breast care, hemorrhoid treatments, activity and rest, diet, and other postpartum issues.

Dietary Restrictions

Most doctors allow patients to begin taking clear liquids fairly soon after cesarean delivery. Clear liquids are water and clear sodas and juices that you can see through that do not contain sediment. It is best to stay away from carbonated drinks unless you remove the fizz by stirring them or passing them back and forth several times between cups. Carbonation and ice, if taken too early or in too large amounts (before bowel sounds are present) can lead to excess gas, which causes painful distention (bloating) of the abdomen. Milk products should also be avoided until you are allowed solid foods. You may be given only clear liquids until your doctor or nurse, using a stethoscope, can hear bowel sounds in your abdomen and you are passing gas rectally. When bowel sounds can be heard and you are passing gas, this generally indicates that your bowel is ready to handle solid foods, so be sure to inform your nurse when you begin to pass gas rectally.

Some physicians allow a full, regular house diet immediately after a cesarean delivery, instead of beginning with clear liquids until bowel sounds are present. There have been successes and failures (abdominal gas distention) with both dietary approaches. Feel free to discuss your options with your surgeon.

Gas Pains

You will experience some gas pain after surgery. Avoid large amounts of ice and carbonated drinks, which tend to increase gas distention. Walking and placing a heating pad or hot water bottle over your abdomen may help if you have gas pain. Drinking warm fluids helps some people. If these treatments don't help you, try the following approach.

You will probably not be comfortable enough to try this procedure until several days after surgery. Think of the anatomy of your bowel: in order to expel the gas you must first get it from the small intestine into the large intestine. **Follow these steps in order:**

1. Lie on your left side for two to three minutes. This allows the gas to "rise up" and into the beginning of the large intestine, which travels up the right side of your abdomen.
2. Sit upright for two to three minutes. This allows the gas to advance up to your transverse colon, the part of the large intestine that crosses your body just below the waist.
3. Lie on your right side for two to three minutes. This moves the gas along to the descending colon on the left side of your abdomen.
4. Get on your knees in bed with your knees opened slightly. Turn your head to the side and place your head and shoulders flat on the mattress with your bottom up in the air. This allows the gas to rise to the lower rectum.
5. Relax and breathe deeply. You will feel the gas moving to the rectum, where it can be expelled.

These position changes work because gas rises to the top of a column of fluid. They facilitate the advance of the gas all the way to the rectal opening, where it can be eliminated.

There are anti-gas pills sold over the counter in drugstores. If you are suffering from excessive gas, take one before each meal. **If you are breastfeeding, please consult your care provider for an appropriate brand before choosing an anti-gas medication.**

Coughing and Deep Breathing

Your nurses will be asking you to cough and deep-breathe frequently. Any surgery can cause fluid to build up in the base of your lungs. You need to cough and deep-breathe to keep the air sacs in the base of your lungs well inflated and so prevent postoperative pneumonia. We know these exercises may be painful for you to do during the first 24 hours, but they are essential. **Take enough pain medication to make it possible for you to cough, deep-breathe, and move.** Your recovery will be faster, and you will have fewer postoperative complications. Do not be afraid of becoming addicted to a narcotic. If you have had no prior addiction, this will not happen in your short postoperative stay; you will most likely be off IV or IM medication and on something by mouth after just 24 hours. **Take the pain medication and move.**

To do your coughing and deep-breathing exercises, follow these instructions.

First place your hands on your *lower* rib cage and take a *deep* breath. You should feel the rib cage expand outward and feel the spaces between your ribs widen. If you do not feel this, you need to take a deeper breath. In the first 24 hours after delivery, you may need to do these exercises after receiving pain medication and during the time you are most comfortable. Exhale through pursed lips. Repeat deep breaths three or four times.

Take a firm pillow and "splint" your incision (Figure 12-10). You will not rip open your incision when you cough—the pillow splint support is only recommended because it seems to make it easier for many people to cough and deeply breathe more effectively.

Now take a deep breath and clear your throat gently. This gets upper respiratory secretions moving. Take another deep breath and cough several times. Relax.

Repeating this series of coughing and deep breathing exercises every two hours is one of the most helpful things you can do for yourself after any surgery.

While in bed, change positions often. This prevents fluid congestion from localizing in one area of the lung and helps to reduce the risk of other postoperative complications.

FIGURE 12-10

Splinting Abdomen with a Pillow

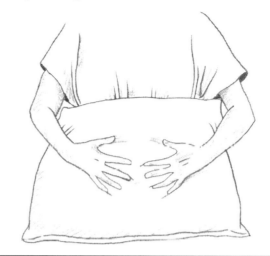

Pillow Support

Good pillow support can greatly reduce your discomfort when you are in bed. When on your back, keep your head slightly raised and your knees slightly bent (use a soft pillow under your thighs). These two measures take the stretch off your lower abdomen and groin area that occurs when you are lying completely flat.

When you rest or sleep on your side, turn *all the way* onto your side—it is more painful to be only partway there. Then use four pillows for support in the following manner (Figure 12-11). The pillow under your head should be of a size that keeps your neck in a straight line with your spine. (Your head should not be slanted up or down.) Place a firm pillow between your knees and ankles. This prevents your upper hip from rotating forward and causing lower back pain. Have someone roll a soft pillow into a roll (the long way) and have him or her tuck it in behind your back. Finally comes what I call "the teddy bear hug pillow." Tuck the narrow end of a fluffy pillow slightly under your tummy. Pull the other end up and tuck it under your upper arm. This hug pillow prevents your upper shoulder from rotating forward and

Childbirth

FIGURE 12-11

Proper pillow support can help you achieve maximum comfort and correct body alignment.

causing upper back or shoulder discomfort in the morning. (You may still want an additional small towel folded and placed under the side of your abdomen to keep it from pulling downward and tugging on your stitches.)

You will also feel that it takes less energy to stay on your side with all this pillow support. **Proper body alignment while sleeping goes a long way in reducing morning discomfort.** This works at all times, not just after surgery.

Care of Your Incision

The dressing will be removed from your incision the day after surgery. You may shower at this time and clean the incision area with soap and water. If there are small, clear adhesive strips (Steri Strips) covering your incision, pat them dry after your shower. They will gradually loosen and fall off on their own. You may remove any remaining strips after two weeks. The external stitches or staples closing your incision will be removed before you leave the hospital.

*C*Prior to leaving the hospital, or as soon as you get home, call your practitioner's office to schedule your follow-up visit. A two-week visit is commonly scheduled to check your incision and a six-week visit to check your overall postpartum recovery.

If your incision *begins* to look red or has dried blood on it, wash it two or three times a day with hydrogen peroxide. *C*If there is no improvement in the redness the next day or if you develop a fever, call your practitioner. **If the incision becomes increasingly red or begins to ooze any discharge, do not wait. Call and report these symptoms to your practitioner immediately.**

*C***Call your physician if you develop a fever above 100.4°F or have severe abdominal pain. Also report any redness or swelling with pain around the incision.** Oozing and redness around the incision are signs of infection. Please report any of the above symptoms promptly to your practitioner.

Proper Body Mechanics

When you go home, do not lift anything heavier than your baby for four weeks. To prevent back strain or injury, use good body mechanics when lifting anything. For example, bend your knees to pick up an object (Figure 12-12A), bring the object close to your body (Figure 12-12B), then stand up using your leg muscles (Figure 12-12C). Always use your strong leg muscles for lifting. Do not lift from a bent-over position.

When getting in and out of bed, do not depend on your abdominal and back muscles for support. They have been softened and stretched by pregnancy hormones and are more easily injured immediately after delivery. Do not rely on them until you have toned and strengthened these muscles through exercise.

When getting into bed, sit on the edge of the bed. Lean down onto your elbow and then your shoulder. Bring your legs up on the bed. Now turn onto your back, keeping your back straight.

When getting out of bed, turn on your side. Drop your heels over the edge of the bed and use your upper arm to push yourself up to a sitting position. (See Figure 11-1, page 195, for an illustration.)

FIGURE 12-12

Proper Body Mechanics for Bending and Lifting

(A) Bend to pick up item. (B) Bring item close to body. (C) Stand up using your leg muscles.

A   B   C

Driving After Cesarean Delivery

Do not drive as long as you are taking pain medication. Prescription pain medications can produce drowsiness, as well as pain relief. This, plus your weak abdominal muscles, makes it unsafe for you to drive. Often doctors will advise no driving for two weeks, and then only if you are completely off of narcotic pain medications.

Resuming Sexual Intercourse After Cesarean Delivery

Most women are advised not to put anything into their vagina for six weeks following vaginal or cesarean delivery. (This means no tampons, no douching, and no intercourse.) Recommendations vary as to when sexual intercourse can be resumed, however. Some practitioners allow intercourse once bleeding has stopped, *if* the woman desires to have intercourse and can do so without pain. Ask your practitioner for advice on when you can resume intercourse and what form of birth control is recommended (if you prefer to prevent pregnancy).

Remember that your flow after birth is not your period. **When you resume ovulation is a very individual and unpredictable matter.** If you are breastfeeding totally without supplements, ovulation is usually suppressed. However, this is not 100 percent foolproof and should not be depended on as a means of birth control.

What to Report to Your Practitioner

Please refer to Chapter 13, pages 236–237 for this very important information. All items except the one involving an episiotomy also pertain to cesarean delivery.

Exercising After Cesarean Birth

Coughing and doing deep-breathing exercises, changing positions in bed, walking, and exercising after cesarean birth help to restore your muscle tone and strength. In addition, they speed your recovery and prevent postoperative complications.

While in the hospital, change position often while in bed. Do your coughing and deep-breathing exercises every two hours while you are awake. This helps prevent any lung congestion from settling in one spot. It also keeps congestion and secretions moving upward to where you can cough them out.

While in bed, do foot and groin exercises frequently to reduce your risk of forming blood clots.

Foot Exercises

While lying on your back, pull your toes back as far as you can toward your head. Next, point your toes downward as far as you can. Feel the stretch in both positions. Now, make big circles with your feet from the ankle. Repeat this exercise 10 times in a row.

Groin Exercises

Follow the directions for bent-knee leg-slide exercise, page 242, which helps prevent postoperative complications after abdominal surgery.

Kegel Exercises

Begin these exercises as soon as your Foley catheter is removed and you are able to urinate on your own. (See page 240 for an explanation of Kegel exercises.)

Abdominal Breathing

Follow the directions for abdominal breathing in the postpartum exercise section, page 240.

After Two Weeks (or When Approved by Your Physician)

When you can do these without pain, you may add the postpartum tone exercises, described beginning on page 240, that are noted below:

Pelvic tilts or pelvic rocks

Buttocks lift and squeeze

Head lifts

Pelvic tilts

Single and double knee rolls, when you can do them without incisional pulling or incisional pain

Single knee to chest

Arm raises

Shoulder circles

Stop any exercise that causes pain, and wait another week before trying it again.

Try to do your postpartum exercises twice a day. **Begin exercising and building up your tone gradually. Do only three repetitions for each exercise to begin.** Increase repetitions gradually when you no longer experience signs of muscular weakness from doing the previous number of sets. **Muscle weakness is present if you experience muscle burning, discomfort, or shaking during any exercise. Follow your care provider's specific instructions and restrictions.**

After Six Weeks

After a cesarean delivery, do not do weight-bearing exercises until after six weeks. Also, do not do any exercise that requires the use of abdominal or back muscles until you have toned and strengthened those specific muscles.

Recovery

13

Taking Care of Yourself at Home

The Postpartum Period

The postpartum period is the six weeks from the birth of your baby to the time your reproductive organs return to their normal nonpregnant state. During this time your uterus returns gradually to its former size, your body rids itself of the additional fluid volume of pregnancy, your hormones level off and return to normal, and the birth trauma to your vaginal and perineal tissues heals. This chapter will help you take good care of yourself at home while you get to know your new baby.

The postpartum period is a very important time. Although your new baby needs love, care, and attention, you also have these same needs. Fatigue and fluctuating hormones interfere with your normal coping mechanisms. You may feel overwhelmed, frustrated, and weepy, crying more easily than usual. It's important to talk to your family about your feelings and needs. Let them know that a small bouquet of flowers, a picture drawn by your older child, a dinner cooked and served to you, and especially extra hugs may be just what you need. Words of praise and support go a long way in making this challenging time a positive one.

Once you're feeling better, some time out may be just the ticket. Treat yourself to a new hairdo, a facial, a massage, lunch with friends, or merely time away from home to do whatever you please. When friends and family ask, "Is there anything I can do?" tell them what you'd like.

225

Rest and nutrition are essential after delivery and during the postpartum period. This is not the time to have hot dogs and cold cuts. It is much easier to cope with a new baby, the baby's fussy times, and other children who also need extra attention at this time, if you are rested and well nourished. This is especially important if you're breastfeeding.

As you recover from labor and delivery, both your body and your psyche go through many changes. This chapter helps you understand what signs and symptoms are normal and what to report to your practitioner.

Normal Vaginal Bleeding After Delivery (Lochia)

Lochia is the term used to describe vaginal bleeding after delivery. This bleeding is not a menstrual period because it does not result from the normal monthly cycle of your hormones. Instead, it is bleeding from the placental site and the sloughing off of the inner lining of your uterus.

A few hours after delivery, your lochia changes from bright red to dark red or reddish brown. Continue to use two sanitary pads at a time until the lochia decreases in volume.

Three to four days after delivery, the lochia becomes paler and changes to a pink or brownish color. About 10 days postpartum, the discharge becomes yellow or white. This color continues for four to six weeks after delivery.

The volume and color of lochia are variable. When you first go home, you may see your lochia discharge increase and change back from dark red to brighter red for a short time. You have been resting in the hospital and now you are probably climbing stairs and doing much more walking. Try to avoid stairs as much as possible (especially if you have stitches) and rest as much as you can with your feet up. The more active and overtired you are, the heavier your flow will be and the longer it will last.

(✆**At no time should you saturate a sanitary pad completely in 15 minutes. That is considered excessive bleeding and should** be reported promptly to your practitioner. It would also be considered excessive bleeding if you are consistently saturating one pad in one hour. If this occurs, notify your practitioner.**

During the first few days you may pass old blood clots when you are out of bed or sitting on the toilet. These clots can be very small or several inches around and look like liver. This can be very frightening if you do not expect it, but it is just old blood that pooled and clotted in the uterus and is now coming out with the help of gravity. As long as the clots are *not* excessive and *not* followed with bright bleeding, they are nothing to worry about. (✆**If clots are excessive or followed by bright red bleeding, notify your practitioner immediately.**

In summary, lochia discharge gets lighter in color and less in amount over two to six weeks postpartum. It should smell like a menstrual period and never have a foul odor. (✆**Report any foul odor or thick greenish yellow discharge immediately to your practitioner.** Sometimes around two weeks, a woman whose lochia has been light in color may suddenly experience a day or two of brown discharge. The placental attachment site scabs over just as any other wound. This brown discharge is just the scab area sloughing off. As long as there is no foul odor, bright red bleeding, or thick greenish discharge, this is nothing to worry about.

Emergency Call: Urgent Problems to Report

If you have any of the following symptoms, please contact your practitioner promptly:

❑ **Fever above 100.4 or chills**
❑ **Vaginal flow consistently heavy enough to saturate one pad per hour**
❑ **Passing of many large clots or any clots followed by bright red blood**
❑ **Lochia that develops a foul odor, or a thick greenish discharge**

Breast Care

Breast milk usually comes in around the third or fourth day after delivery. Your breasts will feel swollen, full, very firm, warm, and painful. This initial overfilling of the breasts with milk is called *engorgement*. Because breast milk production works by supply and demand, your decision about feeding your new baby determines what happens next.

If You Are Not Breastfeeding

If you have decided not to breastfeed, you will still become engorged. Do not empty or pump your breasts—without stimulation, your breasts will stop producing milk, and the discomfort should disappear in about 24 to 36 hours.

Most doctors recommend that you take acetaminophen or ibuprofen for engorgement discomfort. In addition, wear a well-fitting bra, and use cold compresses for short periods of time, to relieve this short-lived discomfort. (Use ice packs covered with a towel, 15 minutes on and 45 minutes off. If applied for too long, or without adequate break time, rebound swelling can occur.) Believe it or not, cabbage leaves wrapped around each breast, held in place by your bra, and left there for twenty minutes will also help reduce the swelling more quickly.

There are breast milk suppressants that can be given to inhibit engorgement. However, most doctors do not prescribe this medication because it must be taken for two weeks, it may not work, and it has some potentially serious side effects. The most commonly used medication (Parlodil) can cause sudden drops in blood pressure, resulting in light-headedness or dizziness. People with normally low blood pressure have fainted after taking this medication.

Leaking from the breasts is common during engorgement. Wearing breast pads will help by creating a tighter-fitting bra. In addition, they protect your clothing.

If You Are Breastfeeding

Nursing immediately after delivery has many positive effects. Not only does nursing cause the uterus to contract, facilitating the separation of the placenta and controlling bleeding, it also causes the release of hormones that tell your body to begin to produce breast milk.

Initially your breasts produce colostrum, a thin, yellow fluid. Colostrum is very nutritious, high in protein, and easy for your baby to digest. It is also high in antibody protection.

When your breast milk comes in (on the third or fourth day), nurse every two hours, if possible, while your breasts are engorged. Massage your breasts and manually express a little milk before nursing (see page 293 for instructions in manual expression of breast milk). This, along with *applying warm compresses or taking a warm shower just before nursing,* will help soften the nipple to make latching on easier for your baby during engorgement. While your breasts are engorged, use a breast pump to remove more milk for added relief if necessary after nursing. Also try the cabbage-leaf trick mentioned above to more quickly reduce the swelling. Acetaminophen or ibuprofen may also be needed to help with discomfort of engorgement. (Most practitioners approve these for use while breastfeeding.)

The discomfort of engorgement should pass in about 24 to 36 hours. After this, your breasts will be softer and more comfortable even when full.

Wear a supportive nursing bra. Your breasts will be heavy and will need the added support.

To avoid sore nipples, change nursing positions with each feeding (see pages 270–276 for instructions in various nursing positions). Be sure your baby is latching on properly. The baby should latch on to most of the areola, which is the brown or pink area around the nipple. (Review Chapter 16, "Breastfeeding.") To remove your baby from the breast, place your finger gently into the corner of his or her mouth to break the suction. Avoid pulling the baby abruptly off the nipple.

Recovery

Air-dry your nipples after each feeding, and avoid nursing pads as much as possible. Rub a drop of colostrum or breast milk into your nipple frequently to help prevent sore nipples. Use Lansinoh ointment to soothe them if they become sore.

Do not use creams or vitamin E to soften your nipples or to treat sore nipples. Vitamin E oil used to be recommended, but it is now known that it builds up in the baby's system to levels that are too high if it is used frequently on the nipples. Lansinoh purified lanolin or a drop of your own colostrum or breast milk is the best treatment to soften or soothe your nipples.

Wash your nipples with water only. Do not use soaps.

*C***Call your practitioner if you get a temperature above 100°F that is associated with redness, pain, or a hard, painful lump in your breast.** This may indicate *mastitis*, an inflammation of the breast, usually due to infection. **Mastitis requires antibiotic treatment. Do not delay in reporting these symptoms.**

You may also develop a tender lump in your breast not associated with fever. This most likely is a plugged milk duct, which can be caused by not getting enough rest, wearing your nursing bra or other clothing too tight (or pulling a regular bra up or down to nurse), improper positioning of the baby at breast, or long periods between nursings.

At the first notice of any tender lump in your breast, loosen your clothing and get extra rest. Apply wet or dry heat to the area and be sure the nipple is free of secretions. (The best way to apply moist heat is to soak in the tub with your breast underwater.) Nurse the baby on the affected side every two hours if possible. Gentle downward massage on all four sides of each breast may also be helpful in getting the milk to flow through the plugged area. Check for proper positioning of the baby on the breast, and alternate the nursing positions at each feeding. **A plugged duct can develop into mastitis.** *C***At the first sign of fever, call your practitioner.**

There is a general rule to help you know whether your baby is getting enough milk. If, after five days, your baby is soaking his or her diaper six or more times a day and having three or more small bowel movements, then he or she is getting an adequate volume of milk. If your baby is continually fussy, however, even with adequate wet diapers, call your pediatrician. He or she will want to weigh your baby and determine the possible cause for the excessive fussiness.

Breastfeeding is a learning process for both you and your baby in the beginning. Don't get discouraged. Get the help you need and have your questions answered. There are also breastfeeding support groups and lactation specialists who can assist you if problems, frustrations, or difficulties arise. If you truly want to breastfeed, don't give up without first seeking assistance from those who specialize in helping nursing mothers. There are very few nursing problems that can't be solved with help! (See Chapter 16 for how to obtain help with breastfeeding.)

Stitches and Hemorrhoid Care

Many practitioners recommend the use of sitz baths to further care for your stitches and hemorrhoids, usually starting 24 hours after delivery. You no longer apply ice once sitz bath treatments are started.

Ice packs are applied initially to reduce swelling or prevent further swelling. After 24 hours, the therapeutic effects of ice packs cease. Instead, heat is needed to dilate the blood vessels to bring added circulation to the area in order that swelling in the tissues can be drawn away. After 24 hours, heat reduces swelling and promotes healing

While in the hospital, you may be given a sitz bath unit that fits into the toilet (Figure 13-1). This unit should be taken home with you. The purpose of a sitz bath is to soak your perineal area in warm water for 10 to 15 minutes. This soaking dilates your blood vessels and thereby helps your vascular system draw the swelling out of the cells in the area. Swelling and bruising will be reduced more quickly if sitz baths are used.

Sitz baths are not a substitute, however, for routine perineal rinsing with your peri bottle after every urination and bowel movement. Also continue to use topical creams as instructed by your practitioner.

Sometime between one and two weeks after delivery you may feel like your stitch area is burning again when you urinate, or you may feel a pulling sensation or just feel sensitive again. This is caused by the stitches beginning to dissolve. Continue to use your sitz bath and do your peri care; the sensitivity will pass in a few days.

If you were told that you had a tear into your rectum from the delivery (a fourth-degree laceration), keep taking your stool softener and continue sitz baths for two weeks or longer until you feel completely healed.

Sitting on a pillow or rubber doughnut helps to reduce pain. Squeezing your buttocks together before sitting may reduce discomfort in the area of your stitches. Sleeping on your side with a pillow between your knees may also be helpful.

How to Use Your Sitz Bath Unit

See Figure 13-1. First, clamp off the tubing from the bag. Fill the bag with hot tap water (but not hot enough to burn your skin). Follow the instructions with your unit to attach the tube to the bottom of the sitz unit, and fill it with warm tap water (just warm enough to be comfortable to sit in). Lift *both* the lid and the seat of your toilet and place the sitz unit in the basin of the toilet. The area on your unit marked *front* goes to the front of the toilet. Hang the bag above your shoulder level. I tell people to place a tiny nail behind their bathroom curtain and hang the bag there if it will reach. If you have nowhere to hang the bag that will hold the weight of the water, place a towel over your shoulder and hold the bag there (the towel will prevent the hot water bag from being uncomfortable on your shoulder) or place the bag on the top of the toilet tank.

FIGURE 13-1

Sitz Bath Unit

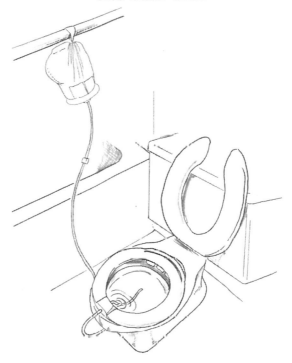

Now sit down *very slowly* into the sitz unit. The water volume you displace will go out through the back holes into the toilet if you sit down slowly. If you sit down quickly, you will soak your bathroom floor and have a mess to clean up!

After you have been soaking for about five minutes, the water in the basin will begin to feel cool. This is when you open the clamp on the tube and let the hot water mix in. A whirlpool effect is created. The water level in the sitz basin rises to the top and goes out into the toilet through the back holes. If the water starts to get too hot, use a clean cup and add cold water, or shut off the clamp and allow the water to cool down on its own. When the bag is empty, you will have had about a 15-minute sitz bath, an ideal soak. This is enough time for your blood vessels to dilate and do their work!

Recovery

It is recommended to do sitz baths three to four times a day. Doing a sitz bath when you get up, at lunch time, at dinner time, and at bedtime is a good way to remember. If this frequency is impossible, remember that any soak is better than none. A tub bath counts as a sitz bath. Be creative—while in the shower, allow the water to run over your perineum (front to back direction only) for as long as possible for a mini sitz. Then do a real sitz bath at another point in the day, and you have tended to your needs twice! *Remember that taking care of yourself is important.*

Activity and Rest After Delivery

You will be very tired after labor and delivery and you will need lots of rest. You should plan to care only for yourself and for your new baby for the first few days. It is helpful to have someone else around the house to take care of other children, cook, and do the laundry.

Try to take it easy for the first two weeks at home. Plan to rest when your baby is napping. You will be better able to cope when your baby has a fussy time if you are rested. Return to your normal level of activity gradually. Learn to let nonessential things go until you are feeling stronger again.

After two weeks, slowly return to your normal activity level. If you do too much too fast, your bleeding will increase significantly.

Driving

Your practitioner will discuss specific recommendations with you. In general, you may drive when you are comfortable walking and sitting **and are off all pain medications.** You must be sure that you can react quickly behind the wheel.

If you had a cesarean birth, you will be restricted from driving for two weeks and then allowed to drive only if you can drive without pain **and are off all pain medication that can produce drowsiness.**

Lifting

Try to avoid lifting for several weeks after delivery or until you have time to tone your weakened abdominal and back muscles. **Do not lift anything heavier than your new baby.** When you are able to lift, do so safely. (See Figure 12-12, page 221.) Have older siblings climb into your lap for holding or, if you had a cesarean delivery, have them sit next to you. Kneel down at eye level to talk to your other children instead of lifting them up. Accept help for shopping and laundry needs that involve lifting.

Tub Baths

Many practitioners do not restrict tub baths. Others will ask you to wait, generally for two weeks or until you are comfortable with your vaginal flow. Follow your practitioner's recommendations.

Swimming

You may need to wait until your flow has diminished enough to safely go into a swimming pool. This will usually take around two weeks. However, not all practitioners restrict swimming initially, especially if you will be using your own private pool. Your practitioner may have specific instructions for you in this area.

Diet

Rest and good nutrition are the two most important things you can provide for yourself in the postpartum period. A well-rested and well-nourished mother is much better equipped to handle whatever comes her way during the day or night than a tired mother who has neglected good eating habits.

Be certain to eat from all food groups in the Food Guide Pyramid. (See page 16.)

You will lose about 18 to 20 pounds naturally within 10 days of your delivery. If you continue to eat a well-balanced diet appropriate for your weight, you will return to your normal weight about two months after delivery. It is tempting to rush this process by dieting, but now is not the time. You need adequate nutrition for healing and to rebuild your strength right now.

If you are breastfeeding, please refer to the section on nutritional needs of breastfeeding mothers (pages 276–278). You need extra calories, fluids, protein, and calcium while you are nursing.

If nursing, it is best to avoid all drinks with caffeine (coffee, tea, caffeinated cola drinks, other sodas containing caffeine, and chocolate). In large amounts, caffeine will keep your baby awake. It will increase fussiness and may upset your baby's tummy and bowel.

Some nursing babies are sensitive to certain foods that the mother eats. This can only be determined on a trial-and-error basis. A food that commonly causes gas in adults may be the offender if a problem develops. Common gas-producing foods are beans, broccoli, cauliflower, and cabbage. Tomato sauces, heavily spiced foods, or chocolate may also be irritating to nursing babies. The general rule is that anything in moderation is okay, except smoking and alcohol—both off limits while you are breastfeeding.

Anemia

Most obstetricians order a blood test the day after delivery to determine whether or not you need extra iron supplements. Normal blood loss at delivery causes a small decrease in your hemoglobin and hematocrit (your red blood cells and their oxygen-carrying capacity). However, heavier bleeding at delivery can drop your hemoglobin and hematocrit to such low levels that you feel weak and light-headed. Iron, in addition to vitamins, will be needed in this case to more quickly restore your blood counts to normal.

If iron is ordered, please remember to take it—it is important. Iron can cause constipation, so eat plenty of fruits, bran, and salads. If constipation continues to be a problem, add prunes or a small amount of prune juice to your diet. You may also want to continue taking stool softeners if you are taking large doses of additional iron and constipation is a problem. In addition, eat foods high in iron. (See page 22 for a list of foods high in iron.)

Hair Loss After Pregnancy

Anywhere from two to six months after having your baby, or when you stop or decrease your nursing, you may experience hair loss. (Just because it happens after one pregnancy, it doesn't mean it will happen again.) Don't panic! These hairs were suppressed from falling out at the normal rate during pregnancy and breastfeeding and they are now just catching up.

Being extra gentle in your hair care will help. Avoid tangles by using conditioners and gentle shampoos. Avoid excessive heat to your hair. Use your hair dryer on a cooler setting or allow your hair to air dry. Consult your hairdresser before using chemicals on your hair during this time.

Once begun, hair loss after pregnancy may last up to three months. If the condition lasts longer, you should bring it to the attention of your practitioner, because postpartum thyroid problems can also cause hair loss.

Menstruation

If you are not nursing, your normal menstrual period usually resumes about six to eight weeks after delivery. Nursing mothers may not have a period until they stop nursing or until they begin to wean from breastfeeding. **It is important to note, however, that ovulation occurs before menstruation, so you may become pregnant before you resume your period, even if you're still nursing. Do *not* consider nursing a safe form of birth control.**

Recovery

Contraception (Family Planning)

If you do not plan to become pregnant right away and birth control is an acceptable option for you, discuss contraception with your practitioner before being discharged from the hospital.

If you normally use the rhythm method of birth control, remember that your period resumes at variable times if you are not nursing. Therefore, ovulation time prior to your first menstrual period after delivery is difficult to predict.

If you used a diaphragm for birth control prior to your pregnancy, it will have to be refitted. Diaphragms need to be refitted after every pregnancy, miscarriage, or abortion due to changes in the size and shape of your cervix.

Do not consider nursing a form of birth control—some women do become pregnant while nursing. Discuss your options with your practitioner.

Sexual Relations

Your practitioner may have specific instructions in this area that take into consideration any lacerations you may have had during your delivery. The general rule is that intercourse can be resumed when you are not having any bright red bleeding, your stitches feel healed, and you have the desire to have intercourse. Uncomplicated stitches normally feel healed in about four weeks. **Most physicians and midwives will recommend not putting anything into your vagina until after your postpartum visit, which is usually six weeks after delivery. This means no intercourse, no tampons, and no douching.**

It is not unusual for you not to be as interested in sex right now as you were before birth. Fatigue, fear of pain, and fluctuating hormones all cause this very normal disinterest in sex. Talk openly to your partner about your feelings and your fears. When you are ready, proceed gently.

You may feel more vaginal dryness than is normal for you. This vaginal dryness is especially noticeable in nursing mothers and before the first resumed menstrual period. A water-soluble lubricant will help correct this problem. (Water-soluble lubricants are available at your local pharmacy.) **Never use Vaseline or any other petroleum-based product as a lubricant for intercourse.** (Health note: In addition to being a barrier and not allowing air penetration, petroleum products break down latex condoms, rendering them ineffective both as birth control and as a barrier in the prevention of spread of sexually transmitted diseases, including AIDS.)

Your Emotional Needs

Don't feel guilty if you feel like you want your needs met after delivery. Labor is very exhausting, and many women turn inward for awhile and even become demanding.

Faced with a new baby, possibly other children who need extra love and attention, friends and relatives who can't wait to see the new baby and give advice, you may feel pulled in a dozen directions. Talk to your partner or other support persons about how you are feeling.

Sometimes women may seem not to want anything to do with their new baby for a while after delivery. Many women and their support persons are surprised by this reaction. They expected an overwhelming flood of love and a desire to bond with the new baby, to be together with their infant and begin to get acquainted.

All of these feelings, from wanting to bond with and nurture your infant to wanting to put the baby right into the nursery (for care by others), are normal. Don't be frightened by them. Allow yourself time if that is what you feel you need. Your support people also need to recognize this as a normal reaction after labor. Whether this is a first baby or not, a new mother doesn't need criticism—*she needs attention.* This reaction will pass, and usually by the second day the mother is ready to nurture her baby. Of course, if this feeling does not pass, other family members will need to bring this information to the attention of the mother's practitioner.

Normal Postpartum Blues

It is not abnormal to feel sad, confused, overwhelmed, alone, afraid, or angry after giving birth. As many as three-quarters of new mothers experience some of these feelings in a mild form, called *postpartum blues.* These confusing feelings begin between the first and fourth day after delivery. Moms suddenly cry easily, feel moody, and don't really understand why they feel this way. They commonly say, "I have so much to be happy about. I don't know what is wrong with me."

Well, nothing is wrong! Your pregnancy hormone levels come crashing down after delivery. This is what precipitates all those mixed-up emotions. Understanding that this is normal helps most couples to get through this challenging time. Postpartum blues usually last only a short time, from one to four days to a week at most, and go away without treatment.

Postpartum blues can last longer, however, and may progress into postpartum depression. **(✆If postpartum blues last more than one week, or at any point become intense as described in the following section "Postpartum Depression," call your practitioner. (Dad, or support person, this is your job since the woman may be unable to realize her problem or take action to help herself.)** Your nutritional intake will need to be assessed and referral for help discussed and made if needed.

Postpartum Depression

Sometimes postpartum blues don't go away but instead intensify, developing into serious postpartum depression. Intense feelings of sadness, anxiety, or despair interfere with the new mother's ability to function. **(✆After you receive initial medical help for prolonged post-**partum blues, if your symptoms do not resolve within another week, or more severe symptoms of depression occur at any time, it is essential to consult your practitioner immediately. It is important to note that the mother may be unable to identify the problem herself and will need her partner or other support person to notify the practitioner and accompany her to the appointment.

(✆In addition to depression, sadness, and a feeling of hopelessness, there are other more subtle and extreme signs of depression that must be reported *immediately* when they occur:

- ❑ Inability to sleep or sleeping most of the time
- ❑ Appetite changes from what is normal for the mother
- ❑ Extreme worry and concern about, or lack of any interest in the new baby
- ❑ Lack of feelings for other family members
- ❑ Panic attacks
- ❑ Fear of harming the baby
- ❑ Thoughts or statements about suicide

If you develop these serious symptoms of depression, it does not mean that you are a failure as a woman or as a mother. These symptoms mean that you and your body are experiencing serious difficulty while trying to make all the hormonal and other adjustments after birth. They do not mean that you are mentally ill. This is a serious postpartum complication, and there is help for these symptoms. **(✆Please consult your practitioner immediately.**

Bonding (Attachment)

The words *bonding* and *attachment* are used a lot today, but basically they mean spending time getting to know and love your baby. Bonding is sometimes experienced as a special feeling toward the new infant. Others say bonding includes the development of the desire to nurture and care for the new baby.

Sometimes this special feeling does not occur right at the time of birth. Some babies don't look so special right away, with their molded and pointed heads and flat noses! Others may be premature and not look at all like what you expected. Perhaps the baby was not the sex that was secretly desired, and initially you feel disappointed. Sometimes you are just too tired to bond. Don't panic if bonding doesn't occur spontaneously. In a few days at most, Mom, Dad, and baby will have had time to get to know one another and develop a loving relationship.

Much is written about the importance of immediate bonding. Certainly the ideal is to hold and cuddle your baby right away, and if you are nursing, it is certainly best to start as soon as possible after birth. However, if for circumstances beyond your control this immediate time together is not possible, please do not feel you have lost something you cannot regain. There are millions of stable and wonderful parent-child relationships in the world that flourished even though bonding did not occur immediately after birth. *Remember that bonding is an ongoing process.*

Emotional Needs of Older Children

Unless your older children are ill, do not prevent them from coming to see you and the new baby at the hospital. This is the beginning of the process of making this baby, who has only been talked about for nine months, real—real in person, and real as a part of the whole family.

Use the baby's name frequently when talking about him or her, but if you don't know which name you are going to choose, don't confuse young children by calling the baby one name and then another.

Holding and touching foster bonding. Many, many years after my youngest son was born, my oldest son talked about how his baby brother reached up and grasped his finger the very first time they were together. After all those years, he still remembered that experience and that "big brother" feeling it gave him.

A mother once shared with me that throughout her pregnancy she taught her children that they would be allowed to hold the baby if they followed three simple rules: "Ask, wash your hands, and sit down." When the baby arrived, her young daughter went to the sink, washed her hands, sat down and said "Mommy, I washed my hands, and I am sitting. Can I hold the baby please?"

Older children should be allowed to hold their baby brother or sister, if the rules above are followed. Use pillows to help support their arms. This arm support and your direct supervision will make them feel more secure. This is a wonderful way to get to know and bond with a new member of the family, and definitely a Kodak moment!

Involve older children in the care of the baby as much as possible. At the very least, explain to them what you are doing and why. If you are comfortable allowing them to help with some aspects of baby care, here are some suggestions: have older children dry the baby's bottom during diaper changes or put the new diaper under the baby (while you lift the legs). They may also want to hold the towel during the bath and help you dry the baby.

Teach your children to be loving and gentle with the baby. Stress the safety of never putting anything into the baby's mouth without asking Mom or Dad first. Explain to them that poking at the baby may hurt the baby or make the baby afraid. **Make your other children feel included in helping the baby feel safe and in providing a safe environment for their new brother or sister.**

Never leave young children alone with a baby. Angry or jealous feelings are normal, and you may not see them coming. Your children need to know that you will *always* supervise them. Reassure them of this and of your love for them.

When you arrive home, plan to spend some private time alone with each of your children. A small gift from you or from the new baby to each of your other children may be helpful. However, don't allow a gift to be a substitute for private, one-on-one time. Although you are very busy and tired, this special time helps to reinforce the fact that the other children still have their place and are still very special and loved.

During this busy time when you may feel pulled in all directions at once, you have to learn to be creative in finding time to spend with your other children. Read to them, play a game with them, or just listen to them while nursing or bottle feeding your baby. This may help them to not feel so jealous of the special closeness and time you are giving to the baby. Try things like singing songs together while sponge bathing the baby. All this may take a lot of effort, but it will pay off.

Hopefully, relatives and friends know to fuss over older children when they visit or perhaps bring a small gift for them, too. All these measures help the children not to feel displaced from their position of importance!

A special outing with a grandparent may be just what the child needs at some point to have a break from all the "baby fuss." However, if the outing away comes too early, your child may feel that he or she is being sent away, further exaggerating the feeling of being replaced! You will know best when the right time will be for your child.

This is not a good time to try new things like a new bed or potty training. Allow your child to make the big adjustment of having a new brother or sister before taking on other changes.

Within a few days of arriving home, show your other children pictures of their homecomings when they were the new babies. Talk about what they were like and, if applicable, what their older brother or sister felt like when they were brought home. (For example, "I think your brother was a little jealous of all the attention you got when you first came home. But it didn't take long for him to understand that Mom and Dad and Grandma and Grandpa still loved him too

and that there was still plenty of love to go around. Pretty soon, he felt it was pretty special being the *big brother*.")

Don't Forget the Third Person in This Trio!

Just as your partner or support person could feel left out during pregnancy, he or she can feel passed over now in all the fuss over the new baby and meeting the emotional needs of other children. In addition, your partner may be feeling overwhelmed by the new responsibility, doubting his or her abilities to meet financial and personal needs, and confused by conflicting sexual feelings.

As is not the case with the woman who has experienced life within her for nine months, it is very often the first moment of holding his baby when the reality of this human life, so dependent, sets in for the father. In this case, there doesn't seem to be time to feel and enjoy the relief that labor and delivery are over, and that baby and mother are okay, before new anxieties and concerns flood in. It is important for the woman, family, and friends to understand this when watching, and perhaps judging, the actions of a new father or support person at this time. Just imagine the questions that flood a new father's mind:

What will happen to our lives? How will our relationship change? Will we be able to get away or even go out with our friends again? Who will take care of this child if we do get away? Who will take care of this child every day? Will I be a "hands-on" father?

Will I be a good father? Will I be able to provide financially for my child and family? Will I be able to educate this child?

What about sex? I saw a child come out of there. Will I ever feel the same about sex again?

You can see how the questions snowball, one leading to another and another. No wonder he feels overwhelmed, confused, and perhaps scared.

What can you do to help the father or support person through this time? Don't forget that he has needs, too. He's being pulled in a million directions: remember how that feels? We have all experienced this feeling. If both partners recognize that they each have needs, that each needs special love and attention at this time, and that both feel tired and overwhelmed, this understanding will go a long way in their helping each other not to just get through these days but to enjoy them.

By all means share your thoughts and feelings with one another. Talk about feeling pulled in a million directions and doubting your ability to meet all these needs. Try to come up with some creative solutions that will make you both feel better. You are building foundations here; do your best to make them strong foundations. The patterns of communication you set today will either aid you or, perhaps, keep you stuck in the same place in the future.

Once things fall into place and you see that you can go out socially again, can both be good parents, can make it financially, and can enjoy physically expressing your love again, you will be able to look back on these days with a little humor.

I still tell my oldest son that if he had been able to see us in our first few days as parents and realize how little we knew and how insecure we felt, he would have packed his bags and left! Thank goodness babies are durable little creatures that survive despite our floundering in those first few weeks!

Planning for Return to Work

If you did your planning during pregnancy as suggested, you have already completed your arrangements for return to work. Follow-up calls can be made now to confirm your plan and your actual starting date.

If you intend to return to work and you have not made arrangements to do so, you will need to get started. See pages 38–40 for things to consider when planning to return to work after delivery.

If you are breastfeeding and you plan to pump and provide your baby with breast milk in a bottle or give formula while you are away, you will need to introduce the bottle slowly. Please allow time for this important adjustment. See pages 292–298 in Chapter 16 for suggestions on pumping, safely storing breast milk, weaning to the bottle, and handling engorgement from missed nursings.

Emergency Call: What to Report to Your Practitioner After Discharge from the Hospital

- ❑ Any fever greater than 100.4°F.
- ❑ Bright red vaginal bleeding, soaking one sanitary pad within 15 minutes or consistently one pad per hour.
- ❑ Any foul odor to your vaginal discharge. It should smell like a normal period or old blood and should not have a foul odor.
- ❑ *Continuous* passing of large clots, or any clots *followed by* bright red bleeding. In the first

two to three days, an occasional clot is normal, *unless* it is followed by bright bleeding.
- ❑ Continuous severe cramping unrelieved by ibuprofen (Motrin or Advil).
- ❑ Increasing pain with a feeling of pressure in the perineum.
- ❑ Pain, burning, or itching on urination. Also report a feeling of urgency, as if you won't be able to make it to the bathroom on time,

or a heavy feeling after urination as if you still need to urinate more.

❑ Severe, persistent, abdominal pain.

❑ Pain, redness, swelling, or tenderness in one leg. Severe pain in the back of the calf when the leg is straight and the foot and toes are drawn up toward the body.

❑ A firm area on a breast that persists and is painful or red or is associated with fever. Also report any colored discharge from the nipple.

❑ Severely cracked, sore, or bleeding nipples, if you are breastfeeding.

❑ Postpartum blues lasting more than a week or symptoms of postpartum depression (see page 233 for signs of depression).

❑ Redness or discharge from your episiotomy or laceration stitches.

❑ If you had a cesarean delivery, any persistent pain in the incision not relieved by medication. If you have treated slight redness in your incision with hydrogen peroxide for one day and it has worsened, or if oozing develops from your incision at any time, also report these symptoms to your practitioner.

❑ Severe pain, firmness, or redness in the groin following cesarean delivery.

Recovery

14

Getting Back in Shape

Pregnancy hormones soften and weaken the muscles around your back and pelvis. You must do toning exercises to get these muscles back in shape before you depend on them for support and work.

Even getting in and out of bed can strain your abdominal and back muscles if you do it incorrectly. See pages 194–195 for a description and illustrations of getting in and out of bed properly until your abdominal and back muscles are toned and strong again. If you follow this procedure, your upper back and lower back move as a unit. This method prevents strain on your stomach and back muscles, which have been stretched and weakened by pregnancy.

If you had a cesarean delivery, a complicated birth, or postpartum complications, check with your doctor or midwife before beginning an exercise program. See Chapter 12, pages 221–222, for beginning toning exercises and a timetable for further exercise suggestions. In addition, you should begin with fewer repetitions of an exercise (for example, 3 instead of 10). Stop an exercise *immediately* if it causes you pain, and wait another week before trying that exercise again. Build up your exercise program gradually.

After a vaginal birth, you may gradually begin exercising when you feel up to it. If you didn't exercise during your pregnancy, start with walking and then progress to easy exercises. If you start with the more difficult exercises you may injure yourself.

Even if you exercised during pregnancy, you still need to begin again gradually. You cannot begin at the same level and intensity you were at before delivery.

If you are very athletic, or if you exercised frequently before and during pregnancy, your care provider may allow you to progress more rapidly through your exercise recovery program.

Check with your physician to find out how soon after childbirth he or she permits swimming.

Recovery

Exercise Guidelines

❑ Regular exercise promotes both physical and psychological health.

❑ Begin your exercise program gradually, and exercise regularly for the most efficient progress.

❑ Try to exercise twice each day.

❑ If you had a cesarean birth, a complicated vaginal birth, or a postpartum complication, check with your care provider for specific exercise guidelines.

❑ Stop any exercise that causes pain. Wait one week before trying that exercise again.

❑ Increase repetitions slowly over time.

❑ Do toning exercises for your abdominal and back muscles before attempting exercises that require abdominal and back muscle strength or support.

Beginning Toning Exercises

Kegel Exercises

These exercises strengthen the muscles of the perineum and around the reproductive organs and improve muscle tone. They should be done prior to and during pregnancy and begun again immediately after delivery, and women should continue to do them for the rest of their lives.

The muscles used to start and stop the flow of urine are the same voluntarily controlled muscles that we use in Kegel exercises. If you can stop the flow of your urine, these muscles have good tone.

1. Tighten the muscle, hold for the slow count of three, and relax. Repeat 10 times.
2. Tighten and relax the muscle rapidly 10 times.
3. Tighten the muscle and try to lift it upward; then push or bear down on the muscle as if

trying to push something out of your vagina. Repeat 10 times.

It is best to do the above sequence three times a day. Make it a habit to do these exercises while you are in the bathroom, driving a car, or watching TV.

Abdominal Breathing

This exercise is like slow, rhythmic breathing. It is known to lower blood pressure, as well as strengthen abdominal tone.

1. Lie on your back with your knees bent.
2. Breathe in and allow your abdomen to expand outward. (Think of your abdomen as a balloon that you are filling.)
3. Exhale and pull your abdominal muscles inward. (Deflate the balloon.)
4. Hold your exhale for several seconds.

Do one set of 10. Build up to three sets.

Pelvic Rocks

1. Lie on your back with your knees bent and feet on the floor (Figure 14-1A).
2. Tighten your stomach and buttock muscles. Roll your pelvis upward and flatten the small of your back against the floor (Figure 14-1B).
3. Attempt to place a hand in the small of your back to be sure that there is no space between your back and the floor.
4. Do not push with your feet. Lift your buttocks only off the floor.
5. Hold to a slow count of 5 or 10. Relax.

Repeat the sequence 10 to 15 times.

You can also do this exercise on your hands and knees or standing against a wall with your knees bent slightly.

Pelvic Tilt

Pelvic tilt uses the same motion as pelvic rock, but it is done on your hands and knees. This exercise

FIGURE 14-1

Pelvic Rocks

(A) Starting position. (B) Pelvis up, small of back against floor.

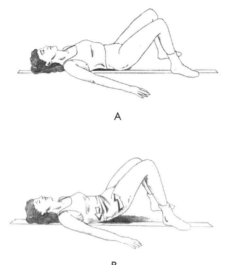

A

B

FIGURE 14-2

Buttocks Lift and Squeeze

(A) Starting position. (B) Lift, squeeze, and hold.

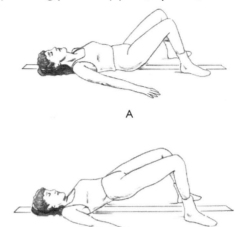

A

B

strengthens your abdominal muscles and helps relieve lower backache. See Figure 2-2, page 28.

1. Begin on your knees with your back relaxed and your knees shoulder-width apart.
2. Breathe out and tuck your buttocks inward. This movement also brings your pubic bone forward and upward toward your chin and makes your back curve upward. Tuck your chin toward your chest.
3. Hold for several seconds and then breathe in and relax.

Do this exercise in sets of five to begin with, and add more sets as tolerated.

Buttocks Lift and Squeeze

1. Lie on your back with your arms at your sides and palms down on the floor. Bend your knees and keep your feet flat on the floor. See Figure 14-2A.

2. Keeping your buttocks and waist in straight alignment, lift both off the floor to a 45-degree angle. (Your weight will be resting on your head and shoulder blades. See Figure 14-2B.)
3. Squeeze your buttock muscles together. You should feel the stretch across your waist and in your buttocks.
4. Hold to the count of three and *slowly* return to the floor. Try to feel every vertebra in your back slowly and separately touching the floor as you lower yourself.

Do this exercise in sets of 5 or 10.

Bent-Knee Leg Slides

This exercise is for your leg and abdominal muscles. It also reduces pain and tension in the lower back.

1. Lie on your back with your knees bent (Figure 14-3A).

Recovery

2. Breathe in and slide one leg very slowly out straight (Figure 14-3B and C).
3. As you lower the leg, press your lower spine against the floor. There should be no space between your back and the floor. Check by trying to slip your hand under your back—if you can get your hand between your back and the floor, your back is not flat enough (Figure 14-3D).

FIGURE 14-3

Bent-Knee Leg Slides

(A) Starting position. (B, C) Lower one leg, press lower back down. (D) Check back position.

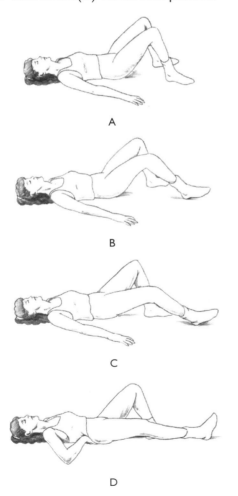

A

B

C

D

4. Exhale and bend your leg up again.
5. Repeat with the other leg.

Do sets of 10, adding sets as tolerated.

Knee Rolls, One Leg at a Time

After a cesarean, do not do this exercise until you can do it without incisional pain.

1. Lie on your back with your right leg straight on the floor.
2. Bend your left leg as in Figure 14-4A.
3. Keep your shoulders flat on the floor at all times.
4. Slowly roll your left knee over to the right side until it touches the floor (Figure 14-4B).
5. Bring your left knee back to the starting position.
6. Straighten your left leg and bend your right leg.
7. Roll your right leg over to the left side until it touches the floor.
8. Return to the starting position.

Progress in sets of 10.

FIGURE 14-4

Knee Rolls, One Leg at a Time

(A) Starting position. (B) Touch knee to floor on opposite side.

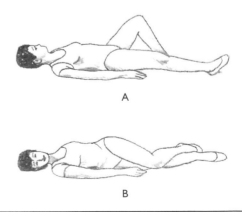

A

B

FIGURE 14-5

Knee Rolls, Both Knees Together

(A) Starting position. (B) Roll both knees to side.

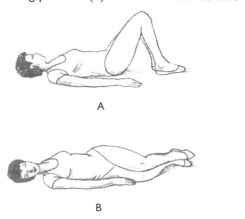

A

B

FIGURE 14-6

Arm Raises

(A) Starting position. (B) Raise arms.

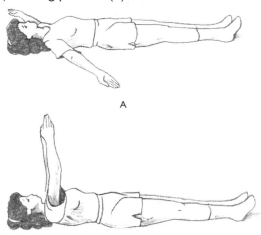

A

B

Knee Rolls, Both Knees Together

1. Lie on your back with your arms at your sides and your knees bent as in Figure 14-5A. Keep both shoulders flat on the floor and your knees bent at all times during this exercise.
2. Slowly roll both knees together over to the right until they touch the floor (Figure 14-5B).
3. Now roll both knees together slowly to the left until they reach the floor.

Start with five rolls right to left and work up to a complete set of 10. Add sets as you gain strength.

Arm Raises

1. Lie on your back with arms out at a right angle to your body (Figure 14-6A).
2. Keeping your arms straight, raise them straight up until your hands touch over your head (Figure 14-6B).
3. Lower both arms slowly back to the ground.

Add light arm or hand weights gradually as tolerated. (You can begin adding weight by holding cans of soup, or by using the lightest hand or arm weights commercially available.)

Another Variation

1. Lie on your back with your arms straight at your sides.
2. Keeping your elbows on the floor, raise your lower arms up to a right angle.
3. Raise both arms directly above your shoulders.
4. Lower to the right-angle position and then back to the starting position.

Add light arm weights as tolerated. Begin with one set of 10 and add sets as tolerated.

Shoulder Circles

1. Sit on a chair with your feet flat on floor. Extend your arms out to the sides at shoulder height.
2. With your palms facing down, make forward circles with your arms, progressing from small circles to bigger circles. See Figure 14-7. Begin with one set of 10 and increase sets as tolerated.
3. Repeat this exercise with palms facing up.
4. Repeat with circles in the opposite direction.

Recovery

FIGURE 14-7

Shoulder Circles

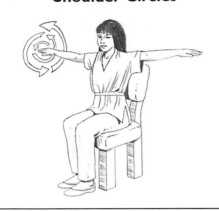

Single Knee to Chest

1. Lie on your back with knees bent and feet flat on the floor.
2. Do a pelvic tilt.
3. Raise one knee up to your chest. See Figure 14-8.
4. Hold your knee and pull it gently toward your chest. Hold for a count of 5.
5. Return your leg to the starting position. Work up to a set of 10.
6. Repeat with the other knee.

Double Knee Raises

Do not do this exercise until you have strengthened your lower back.

1. Lie on your back with your knees bent and feet flat on the floor.
2. Do a pelvic tilt.
3. Keep your back flat and raise both knees over your chest. See Figure 14-9.
4. Hold your knees or lower legs (not your thighs), and pull them toward your chest until you feel a *slight* stretch to your lower back.
5. Hold for five seconds.
6. Bring your legs back to the starting position.
7. Relax your pelvis.

Side Leg Raises

This exercise works the outer thighs.

1. Lie on your right side with your head supported by your right arm or a pillow. Use your left hand on the floor in front of you for balance and support.
2. Raise your left leg slowly while you breathe in. See Figure 14-10.
3. Lower your leg slowly as you breathe out. Work up to a set of 10 and increase slowly to three sets of 10.

FIGURE 14-8

Single Knee to Chest

FIGURE 14-9

Double Knee Raises

FIGURE 14-10

Side Leg Raises

FIGURE   14-11

Head Lifts

FIGURE   14-12

Reach for Knees (Shoulder Lifts)

4. Repeat on the other side.

While you do this exercise, try pretending that you are resisting a downward force as you raise your leg and resisting an upward force as you lower it. Light ankle weights can be added as tolerated.

Head Lifts

This exercise strengthens your abdominal muscles.

1. Lie on your back with your arms at your side, your knees bent, and your feet flat on the floor.
2. Start with a pelvic tilt. Exhale and lift your head off the floor, bringing your chin as close to your chest as possible. See Figure 14-11.
3. Inhale and lower your head back to the floor.

When you can do 10 of these without discomfort, progress to the reach-for-knees exercise.

Advanced Exercises

As you gain tone, and as tolerated, advance to these exercises.

Reach for Knees (Shoulder Lifts)

Do not do this exercise after cesarean birth until given the okay. Then, when you do begin, start by placing three pillows under your head and shoulders.

This exercise strengthens abdominal muscles.

1. Lie on your back with your knees bent.
2. Begin with a pelvic tilt.
3. Breathe out slowly and reach for the tops of your knees with your hands. See Figure 14-12.
4. As you reach for your knees, lift your head and shoulders off the floor.

   Begin by raising your shoulders only a few inches off the floor, and work up to a maximum of eight inches. Your back near your waistline should remain in contact with the floor.
5. Inhale as you lower yourself slowly back to the floor.

When you can do ten of these without difficulty, and without pain or shaking of your abdominal muscles, progress to modified sit-ups.

Modified Sit-Ups

If you had very good abdominal muscle tone before pregnancy, you can begin this exercise (coming up only slightly off the floor at first) about four weeks after delivery. Otherwise, wait until after your six-week checkup and do other abdominal and back-strengthening exercises to tone your muscles before trying this one.

   Do not do this exercise after cesarean delivery until given the okay. Start by placing several pillows behind your head and shoulders to lift you to a 45-degree angle.

   This exercise strengthens abdominal muscles.

1. Use the same position as in the reach-for-knees exercise, keeping your lower back flat on the floor.

Modified Sit-Ups

(A) Pelvic tilt with chin tucked. (B) Raise upper body.

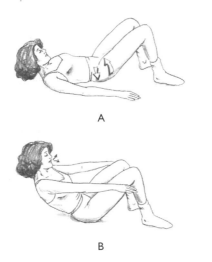

A

B

Straight Leg Raises

---

1. Lie on your back. Bend one knee, keeping the foot flat on the floor. The other leg is straight.
2. Lift the straight leg (Figure 14-14).
3. Lower to the count of 10.
4. Switch legs and repeat.

Work up (slowly) to 10 lifts on each leg.

Single Leg Roll

Wait until your abdominal muscles are strong before doing this one.

   Do not do this exercise after a cesarean birth until you are given permission by your care provider to exercise without restriction.

   When beginning this exercise after a cesarean, stop if it causes pain.

1. Lie on your back with your legs straight and your arms down at your sides (Figure 14-15A). Keep your shoulders flat on the floor.
2. Slowly lift your right leg (B) and bring it over until your right foot touches the floor on your left side (C).
3. Slowly bring the leg back up (D) and then lower it slowly to the floor (E).
4. Repeat with your left leg, touching the left foot to the floor on your right side.

Work up slowly to a set of 10.

2. Begin with a pelvic tilt (this reduces the stress to your lower back) and tuck your chin in toward your chest (Figure 14-13A).
3. Breathe out as you reach toward your knees with your arms and slowly raise your upper body until it is at a 45-degree angle from the floor (halfway between the floor and your knees). See Figure 14-13B.
4. Breathe in as you lower yourself back to the starting position.

Increase your repetitions slowly on this one. (You can also do this exercise reaching with both arms to the right of your legs, then next time to the left of your knees.)

Straight Leg Raises

Wait for your doctor's approval and until you have strengthened your abdominal and back muscles before doing this exercise.

   This exercise tones thigh muscles.

FIGURE 14-15

Single Leg Roll

(A) Starting position. (B) Lift leg. (C) Roll leg to opposite side. (D) Bring leg back up. (E) Lower leg to floor.

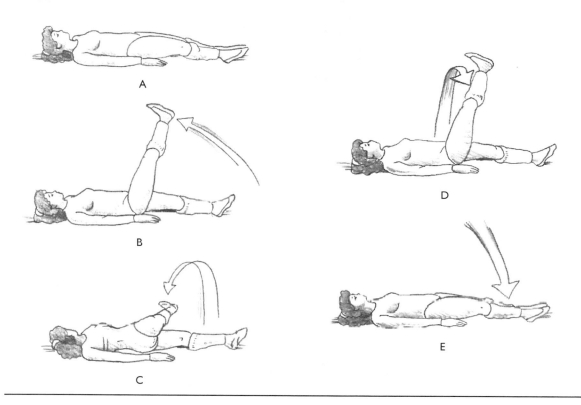

A

B

C

D

E

PART IV-

Baby Care

Your Newborn Has Arrived

From birth to age 21, your firstborn child gives you an initiation into all the ages, stages, and events of raising a child. I once called my 19-year-old at college and asked for what we call in our family an "erase." I said, "Craig, the letter I sent you contains things you do need to think about, but I regret the way I handled the situation, and I'd like to have the whole letter erased. As I've always said, you are my experiment, my firstborn, my trial and error! Hopefully I'll have parenting down pat for your brothers." We both laughed.

My point in telling this story is to help you understand that just as your child will make many mistakes in the course of growing up, you will make many mistakes along the road in raising your children. You and your child will live and flourish despite all the mistakes, as long as you do what you do with love.

I can now laugh about my first night home from the hospital with Craig. Since he could survive that night, I know he can survive anything! When my dear mother-in-law arrived the next morning, she found us both waiting at the door in tears. I can still hear the *enormous* sigh of relief he breathed when she took Craig into her arms. I will never forget the sound of that sigh! It sounded like, "Thank God, finally I'm in the arms of someone calm who knows what she is doing!" I had overfed, overchanged, and thoroughly exhausted the poor baby. Mom looked at me with very loving eyes and said, "Let's give him a sponge bath and get him settled for a nap. Then we can talk about what you might have done differently." (Notice she didn't say, "What you did wrong.") She gave Craig a sponge bath, and he slept for five hours without ever moving a muscle!

When Craig woke up refreshed, we got to start over anew. I hope this section of the book will help your first night at home with your new baby go a little more smoothly than my own. However, if you have problems despite all this preparation, then I hope my comments will help bring a smile to your face and help you to know that you will all survive the rough start.

Baby Care

251

Handling Advice

There is something totally fascinating about a pregnant woman and something totally irresistible about a baby. No matter how noninterfering your parents, in-laws, relatives, neighbors, and friends may be, it is *very difficult* for them to hold back advice when you are pregnant and *practically impossible* when an infant or a small child is involved. Even people who don't have children of their own can't resist offering words of encouragement and giving advice. Not all of this is bad—experience and wisdom are wonderful, and many bits of advice that you receive may be remembered at some point and help you through some discomfort or stage of pregnancy or some age, stage, or event in your child's life. But what about unwanted advice, or too much advice?

In regard to pregnancy advice, there are many old wives' tales. Those that are good advice you will hear from your practitioner or find in current books on pregnancy. Everything else needs to be handled in whatever way you are comfortable with. You can always say that you follow only your doctor's or midwife's advice and that you will run this idea by him or her. Or you don't have to say anything at all. Just walk away, with or without a smile—it's your call. **If some piece of advice makes you feel unsure and you now find yourself questioning something that you are doing or not doing, eating or not eating, ask your practitioner for an opinion. One of the reasons practitioners are there is to help you decide and do what is best for you and your baby.**

In regard to baby advice, it is important, first and foremost, for you to remember that you know your child better than anyone else. As parents, you are the two people spending the most time with this little person. So don't allow your confidence to be shaken by the fact that many people feel compelled to advise you. The majority of the people offering advice don't mean to imply that you are doing something totally wrong; they just think their way is better, easier, and so on.

Second, keep reassuring yourself that your instincts, your gut feelings, are worth a thousand words of advice. You can never be faulted for doing what your instinct says is best. (In fact, I told my teenagers that sometimes I would say no just because of a gut feeling. I explained to them that I wouldn't always be able to explain why I had this feeling and added that I didn't expect them to understand until they, too, were parents.) **The secret is to listen to advice, for it may be very wise and helpful, but make your own decision based on the information you have been given from your pediatrician (and other resource people), current literature, and your gut feeling.**

You really don't owe anyone an explanation for why you have chosen not to follow their advice. However, some people may push you for an explanation, or you may be more comfortable if you offer one. What worked well for me was, "I consulted my pediatrician about what we discussed (or what you suggested) and she would prefer that I do. . . ."

Don't lose sleep over unwanted advice. Get the facts from your resource people, and, with confidence in yourself, go forward.

The "Normal" Newborn

Your baby was surrounded by warm water for the nine months during your pregnancy, receiving oxygen and nourishment through the umbilical cord and placenta. At the moment of birth, everything changed. Your baby was exposed to air, atmospheric pressure, light, and a cooler environment. Openings in the baby's heart that were essential for proper oxygenation while oxygen was received from the mother through the placenta now, at birth, must begin to close as oxygen is received through the baby's lungs. The lungs, which have been filled with fluid, must clear with the first few breaths and begin oxygenating the baby's blood. At birth, the baby's kidneys and liver must begin to filter out many things that the placenta formerly sent to the mother for her kidneys and liver to handle.

When you understand the many adjustments that your baby's system goes through in the first few moments and days of life, you will better know what to expect. In addition, you will be better able to relax and enjoy this special time in your baby's life and in yours.

Let's begin by just *looking at your baby* and talking about *what is normal*. What should you expect?

Weight and Length

The average birth weight of a full-term newborn ranges from five and one-half pounds to nine pounds. The average length of a newborn is 19 to 20 inches, but lengths from 18 to 22 inches are not uncommon.

It is expected that your baby will lose 6 to 10 percent of his or her birth weight during the first week of life due to fluid loss. Let's say your baby weighed 7 pounds, 8 ounces, at birth. There are 16 ounces in a pound; therefore, 7 pounds × 16 = 112 ounces. So the weight of your baby is 112 ounces + 8 ounces = 120 ounces all together. Ten percent of 120 is 12 ounces. Therefore, your baby could lose 12 ounces (down to 6 pounds, 12 ounces), and this would be considered within the normal range for weight loss in the first week of life.

Your baby should begin to regain weight during the second week after birth. Your baby's weight will be evaluated by your pediatrician at the first newborn visit, usually scheduled for around two weeks of age. You do not need to be concerned about your baby's weight before the first newborn visit unless your infant is not eating well or is excessively fussy. ✐**In this case, you should notify your pediatrician of the difficulties as soon as you believe them to be a problem**.

Skin

Color: Be sure to review pages 185–187, "Seeing Your New Baby," in order to be prepared for what your baby may look like at the moment of birth. It is important for you to be prepared for the blood on your baby at birth, the possible skin markings, the enlarged genitals, and the head shape.

After the initial adjustment is made to life outside the uterus, your baby's color should be pink if he is Caucasian or the natural adult skin color of other races. Dark-skinned babies are often very light in color initially in all areas except the genitals. Within hours, however, the natural darker tones begin to appear.

Some babies also have fine hair covering their shoulders and back called *lanugo* or *downy hair*. It is most common on premature babies but can also be seen on full-term babies. It will disappear on its own.

Your baby's hands and feet may retain a slightly bluish color for a day or two. This happens because the vital organs are given top priority for blood circulation during this time. The hands and feet are given enough circulation not to be harmed, but not enough to be pink. This is normal, but during this adjustment phase the discoloration should be confined to the hands and feet only and should *not* include the legs or arms. ✐**Report to your pediatrician if your baby's skin is blue on the arms or legs or around the mouth. Extremely pale color should also be reported unless the parents are naturally very pale.**

Rashes: Normal newborn rash (erythema neonatorum) is often called "flea bite" inflammation of the skin. It got this nickname because it appears suddenly, anywhere on the body, and looks like flea bites. It is red and can be flat or raised. This rash does not contain fluid. It is not seen in premature infants but is common in infants at least 36 weeks in gestation and can be seen coming and going throughout the first three weeks of life. It can appear and disappear so quickly that by the time you get your pediatrician on the phone to describe the rash, it is gone! Although it may look serious, it is common, not harmful to your baby in any way, and requires no treatment.

(C) **If, however, a rash occurs on the face that looks like acne and does not come and go like normal newborn rash, please consult your pediatrician during normal office hours.** Some newborn facial rashes continue to produce increasing inflammation, which requires the use of special creams to reduce it.

Jaundice (Yellow Skin):   As our bodies produce new red blood cells, the old red cells are constantly being broken down. As this natural process occurs, *bilirubin*, a greenish yellow substance, is released into the bloodstream. During pregnancy, the placenta and the mother's liver remove the bilirubin from the baby's system. After birth, the baby's liver has the job of producing enzymes (chemicals) that break down the bilirubin in the bloodstream. Sometimes, the baby's liver initially has difficulty keeping up with this process. When that happens, the buildup of bilirubin in the baby's system can be seen as *jaundice*, a yellowish skin color. This is called physiological jaundice. It is not present at birth but begins to appear on the second to fourth day of life. Within several days, the liver is already more mature and more efficient at doing its job, so a mild jaundice will often resolve on its own. Other times, the blood bilirubin levels are too high, and the baby needs assistance in eliminating the bilirubin from his system.

Physiological Jaundice.   Jaundice that begins 48 to 72 hours after birth is called *physiological jaundice*. It is, in fact, seen to some degree in 85 percent of all newborns. It is seen first on the face as a yellow or lighter color around the ears, nose, mouth, and eyes, and then on the entire face. It then progresses downward to the chest, abdomen, and legs.

Here is one way you can tell if the skin is jaundiced. **When you push down on normal skin it blanches (becomes pale), and when the pressure is released the skin returns to its normal color within seconds. When jaundice is present, blanching with finger pressure is hardly evident. The skin just remains yellow before, during, and after pressure is applied.** As jaundice increases, the whites of the baby's eyes may become yellow.

(C) **At your *first* observation of jaundice, or the *first* increase over the amount of jaundice noticed and discussed with you in the hospital, notify your pediatrician. Do not wait to see if it will go away on its own. For your baby's safety, your pediatrician will need to assess the jaundice.**

You can help flush the bilirubin more quickly from baby's system by breastfeeding or bottle feeding more frequently. Bilirubin is eliminated from the body through the stools. If jaundice is present, breastfeed every two to three hours or, if bottle feeding, feed every three hours while jaundice is present. The more frequently your baby urinates and defecates, the more quickly the physiological jaundice will disappear.

Don't let the term *physiological* or *normal jaundice* make you lax in reporting jaundice to your pediatrician. It is called physiological because it results from the normal immaturity of the newborn's liver. However, high levels of bilirubin can be harmful to your baby's nervous system, especially to the brain. If they are dangerously high, your baby will be very jaundiced and also be sleepier than usual. He or she may also lack interest in feedings and being held and cuddled. A simple heel-stick blood test will tell your pediatrician whether your baby needs special light treatments to help bring the bilirubin down into the safe range more quickly. *(C)* **Report jaundice, excessive sleepiness, and lack of interest in feedings to your pediatrician promptly.**

Treatment for moderate levels of bilirubin can now be done in your home with a special blanket and machine. This treatment is covered by health insurance and is provided and monitored by a local Visiting Nurse Association or other contracted home health agency. It is easy to do and not at all painful to your baby. Treatment will continue until your baby's bilirubin levels begin to drop and your pediatrician is assured that the baby's liver can handle the breakdown and elimination of bilirubin.

If you are still in the hospital, or if your baby's bilirubin levels after discharge are very high, phototherapy will be started in the hospital nursery. Your infant will rest undressed, except for a small diaper and eye covers, under a special lamp. He will not be cold, because the lamp gives off heat. In addition, his temperature will be monitored closely. The baby must stay under this lamp at all times except for feedings. (The amount of time allowed out of the lamp light for feedings will be limited to approximately thirty minutes.) Often a special phototherapy blanket will be used in combination with the bili-light for double treatments. The blanket treatment can be continued while you are holding the baby for feedings.

Early and frequent feedings are especially important in both preventing and treating jaundice. The meconium stool formed in utero in your baby's bowel is very high in bilirubin. If this stool is not completely passed during the first two to three days of life, the bilirubin can be reabsorbed into the baby's system. Breastfeeding is especially helpful in preventing jaundice; when it is initiated early and done frequently, bilirubin levels in the baby usually rise only a small amount and decrease quickly. In addition, colostrum has a natural laxative effect on your baby's bowel, thus further promoting the quick passage of the meconium stool.

High levels of bilirubin can be partially a result of poor feedings (not frequent or not long enough). If you are breastfeeding, poor feeding may be a result of improper latching on by the baby or infrequent or insufficiently long feedings. If bottle feeding, you may not be feeding often enough or giving enough volume. Giving a baby water may also be adding to the problem because only about 2 percent of the bilirubin is excreted in the baby's urine, and drinking water may decrease the volume of breast milk or formula taken by the infant. Less breast milk or formula means less frequent stools.

What Is Breast Milk Jaundice? Breast milk jaundice is an unusual form of jaundice occurring five to seven days after birth and lasting from 10 days to up to 6 weeks. It occurs in about 2 percent of babies due to an abnormality of their mothers' breast milk. It is not known what the substance is in the breast milk of these few women that causes this form of jaundice. One suggested theory is that it is something that causes increased absorption of bilirubin from the baby's intestines. Other theories suggest a higher free fatty acid concentration or higher fat concentrations in the breast milk of these mothers.

Babies who have breast milk jaundice can usually continue breastfeeding. They are healthy and do continue to gain weight. If the bilirubin reaches very high levels, though, breastfeeding may be interrupted for one to three days and then initiated again, or supplemental feedings with formula may be suggested while breastfeeding is continued. In general, however, the interruption of breastfeeding is not usually required.

What Is Breastfeeding Jaundice? Another form of jaundice is called *breastfeeding jaundice*. It shows up about the third day of life in some breastfed infants. It has been proven that this form of jaundice is *not* due to a lack of breast milk on the part of the mother but is instead directly related to the frequency of nursing during the first three days of life. The more frequently the mother nurses during the first three days, the lower the bilirubin levels.

Colostrum is a natural laxative and promotes the passing of the remaining meconium stool in the baby's bowel more quickly, thus preventing the reabsorption of the bilirubin it contains back into the infant's system. When mothers nurse consistently eight or more times per day, spaced throughout both the day and night, their babies are much less likely to be affected by breastfeeding jaundice.

However, if nursing was not frequent in the first few days, or this form of jaundice develops despite frequent nursing, it is not necessary to stop nursing. Your pediatrician may ask you to supplement each nursing with formula until the bilirubin levels begin to fall in your baby. This is a short-term complication, and nursing without formula supplementation will be possible again

Baby Care

soon. (It is advisable to pump your breasts between feedings to make up for the volume the baby will be receiving from the bottle. This way, when the bilirubin levels begin to fall and you no longer need to supplement, your supply will already be equal to the new demand.)

What Is Erythroblastosis Fetalis?   There is another form of jaundice that can be present at birth. It is a blood disease called *erythroblastosis fetalis.* (This condition is rarely seen anymore since the advent of Rhogam. See Chapter 6, "Rh-Negative Mothers—Do I Need Rhogam?" pages 94–95.) The following is very detailed information that you do not need to read unless you are Rh negative and have *not* received Rhogam after every previous miscarriage or abortion, at 28 weeks of every pregnancy, and after every birth where the baby was then confirmed to be Rh positive.

Erythroblastosis fetalis is *only* seen in the newborn who is Rh positive and has an Rh-negative mother with the following additional special circumstances. In order for this form of jaundice to occur, an Rh-negative mother has to have had a previous pregnancy with an Rh-positive baby and become sensitized to and develop antibodies against the Rh-positive blood factor. (As explained above, the administration of Rhogam prevents this sensitization against the Rh positive factor from ever developing.) Once the mother becomes sensitized to the Rh-positive blood factor, it is possible that during another pregnancy with another Rh-positive baby, her system may send antibodies across the placenta to attack that baby's blood, causing the rapid destruction of the baby's red blood cells. (During this red blood cell destruction, bilirubin is given off, builds up in the baby's blood, and causes jaundiced—yellowed—skin in the fetus.) The fetus compensates for this by producing large numbers of immature red blood cells. In extreme cases the baby develops severe anemia and enlargement of the heart, liver, and spleen. Fetal death can occur, but intrauterine exchange blood transfusion through the PUBS method now prevents it in most cases.

(See page 89 for an illustration of the PUBS procedure.) **Again, this condition will never develop if the Rh-negative woman receives a Rhogam injection after every miscarriage or abortion, at 28 weeks of every pregnancy, and after every birth in which the baby is then confirmed to be Rh positive.**

What Is ABO Incompatibility?   Another form of jaundice in the newborn can occur if the mother has type O blood and the baby has A, B, or AB blood type. This is more common than the Rh incompatibility described above. Because mothers with type O blood already have antibodies in their blood against both A and B blood types (called anti-A and anti-B antibodies), this condition can occur during any pregnancy, even the first. The incompatibility occurs because the mother's anti-A and anti-B antibodies cross the placenta to the baby. (When this baby's cord blood is tested after birth, it will show a slightly positive result on a direct Coombs test, which tells the pediatrician and nurses to watch him very carefully for developing jaundice.) The jaundice that arises from ABO incompatibility rarely requires a blood transfusion and is treated with phototherapy (bili-lights).

Head Size and Shape

Head Size: Many people comment on the large size of their baby's head at birth. The size of an infant's head is, in fact, a greater percentage of its total length (25 percent) than an adult's head is (12.5 percent). Again, knowing what is normal prevents unnecessary concern.

Molding and Caput: Molding and caput of the head at birth are covered under "Seeing Your New Baby" in Chapter 10, pages 185–187.

Soft Spots: There are two soft spots (*fontanels*) on your baby's head. The largest, the *anterior fontanel,* is diamond-shaped and is located on the top of your baby's head. It usually closes between seven and nine months. The other soft spot is the *posterior fontanel.* You may not be able to find this one without help from an experienced hand because it is much smaller. It is shaped like a triangle and is located on the back of the head just above where the skull begins to taper inward toward the neck. It will close on its own by two months of age.

Don't be afraid to touch the soft spots—gentle touching or rubbing of the soft spots when shampooing will not harm the baby.

Eyes

All babies have blue-gray eyes at birth. This eye color usually changes to the permanent color by three months of age, but it may not change until later.

The newest research indicates that babies can see much better than we thought. They can see immediately, focusing best on objects about 12 inches away. Studies have proven that newborns show a definite visual preference for the human face, and newborns have even been shown to copy such repetitive actions of the face as rapidly sticking the tongue in and out of the mouth!

It is not uncommon or abnormal to see small areas of bleeding into the whites of the baby's eyes. This is caused by the birth process and will go away on its own within a few days. It is harmless to your baby.

Random eye movements are common during the first two months. However, during these early months, a baby should be able to fix and focus his eyes, at least for a brief period of time.

It is not uncommon for a baby's eyes to momentarily cross occasionally, but this condition should correct itself by six months. *If your baby's eyes cross most or all of the time, consult your pediatrician during normal office hours.*

Because of the way a baby's face is formed, the amount of white showing on the inner (nose) side of the eye is less than on the outer side. Also, a baby naturally crosses his eyes to focus on his hands. This happens naturally because babies' arms are so short. If you think your baby's eyes may be crossed, look at the reflection of a light in the baby's pupils.

If the reflection is located in the same place on each pupil, your baby's eyes are probably not crossed. However, mention your concerns to your pediatrician at your next regular well-child visit.

Many babies have a mild irritation of the eyelids for their first few days of life. The eyelids may appear slightly puffy and pink. This condition does not require any treatment. However, if your baby's eyelids appear red or develop a yellow or green discharge, or if the eyes tear excessively, treatment may be necessary. One or both eyes may develop dry "crusts" on the outer lids, especially noticeable after sleeping. *Please inform your pediatrician of these findings.* Meanwhile, to remove dry crusts that form on the eyes, use warm water on a cotton ball (a separate one for each eye), and gently wipe the outer lids from the inner to the outer sides, avoiding contact with the eyeballs themselves.

As mentioned earlier, if the whites of your baby's eyes appear yellow (jaundiced), call your pediatrician. Encouraging more frequent feedings to promote passing of stool helps eliminate jaundice; however, this is *not* sufficient treatment to prevent brain damage if the bilirubin level is excessively high. Your pediatrician *must assess* your baby and begin phototherapy if needed. A simple heel-stick blood test will determine whether phototherapy treatment of jaundice will be necessary. (See page 254 for further information on jaundice.)

Nose

During a prolonged pushing stage of labor, your baby's nose may become flattened or the end of the nose pushed off center. It will look much better even in a matter of hours and will correct itself completely in a very few days.

Mucus

Babies are nose breathers; they do not breath through their mouth. While your baby is developing inside your uterus, he or she drinks amniotic

Baby Care

fluid. A lot of mucus builds up in the esophagus (the food canal from the mouth to the stomach) and in the nasal passageways. Much of this mucus is gone before birth; however, your baby may sound stuffy and may sneeze often. This is not a cold—babies are very adept at clearing their nose and throat of what mucus remains.

Many babies, especially those born by cesarean delivery or with very short pushing stages, tend to be born with more mucus still present. It is as if the mucus didn't get squeezed out during the compression of a normal pushing stage during vaginal birth (although this has never been scientifically proven to be the reason that cesarean babies and babies born after less than 20 minutes of pushing tend to have excessive mucus).

If your baby has excessive mucus at birth, he will sneeze, cough, appear to be chewing, and gag occasionally until all the mucus is cleared. Until it is cleared, the baby may have difficulty sucking and swallowing, which is very disheartening and frustrating to many new parents. As soon as your baby spits up this mucus, however, he will begin to eat.

If your baby is having difficulty with excessive mucus, he will need to be watched carefully. Often when babies have mucus in the back of their throat, they stretch their mouth open and appear to be chewing. Remember, there is nothing solid in there for your baby to choke on. He just needs a little help getting rid of the thick mucus, so if he appears to be struggling with mucus or struggling to breathe, pick him up calmly (in order not to startle him into holding his breath) and put him into the *football hold.* Tilt him just *slightly,* with his head lower than his chest. Reach over with your free hand and pat his back gently—this puts gravity and vibration to work for your baby. Use your bulb syringe to remove secretions from the mouth and then the nose. (See pages 331–333 for further instructions and a picture.)

Breathing

A baby's normal breathing rate is much higher than that of an adult. It is *very important* for you to be aware of what is normal in this regard so that you will not be concerned when you find your baby breathing 50 times per minute (within the normal range) but you will know what to look for that may indicate respiratory distress or illness.

A quiet baby breathes 30 to 40 times per minute, and the pattern and rate are very irregular. The rate can go up to 60 when your baby is alert and crying and still be within normal limits. If you are counting the respiratory rate (number of breaths per minute), you must count for one full minute. Your baby may breathe 20 times in the first 15 seconds, and if you multiplied this by four, you would think that your baby was breathing 80 times in that minute. However, if you had continued to count, the number of breaths in the second 15 seconds may have been only seven. Remember, an irregular breathing pattern and rate are normal in the newborn. Count for *one full minute* to get the correct rate.

In an adult, chest expansion with breathing is obvious. In a newborn, it is the abdomen that goes in and out.

Occasional gasps in an otherwise quiet baby are common and normal. These often scare new parents. This is one reason why keeping the baby in the room with you can be useful. If you hear these gasps in the hospital, nurses are around to reassure you that they are of no concern. If you go home without knowing this, you may spend a sleepless night sitting and watching over your baby, certain that something is wrong. Then, after losing a night's sleep, you would find out from your pediatrician in the morning that these occasional gasps are nothing to worry about.

However, if your baby is coughing or choking during feedings, this could indicate a fistula (connection) between the trachea (wind pipe) and the esophagus (food canal). This is usually discovered with the initial few feedings. ☾**If your baby is coughing and choking *with the initial feedings,* notify a nurse immediately if you are in the hospital, or notify the pediatrician immediately if you are at home.**

Symptoms of respiratory distress are discussed on pages 363–364 in Chapter 19, "Identifying and Reporting Illness."

Temperature

Newborns are very susceptible to heat loss. Their immature system makes it difficult for them to regulate their body temperature. They do very well *maintaining* a normal temperature, but if they lose heat from getting chilled, they cannot bring their temperature up on their own, especially in the first week or two of life.

An environment that is too hot or too cold can be a problem for a newborn. Rooms should be draft free, and the baby should not be left to sleep directly next to a radiator, fan, or air conditioner. A good room temperature is 70 to 72 degrees. Humidity is also important—the room should not be too dry. Humidity between 35 and 65 percent is helpful to newborns.

If you need to use a humidifier to increase the humidity in your home, please follow the manufacturer's directions for disinfecting it *daily*, and use distilled, purified water. Check with your child's pediatrician about the advisability of using a humidifier.

Newborns need some clothing in the first week of life. Even on a hot summer day, your newborn needs a diaper, a cotton T-shirt or gown, and perhaps even a light blanket. In the winter, always cover the baby's head when outdoors—the head is the biggest surface of the newborn's body and therefore the greatest potential source for heat loss. If your baby is overdressed and therefore too warm, he or she will look flushed (have very red cheeks). Remove a layer of clothing.

It is not necessary to check your baby's temperature unless he or she feels cold or is acting ill. If you do take your baby's temperature, take it under the arm or in the rectum. (Take rectal temperatures *only* if your pediatrician requests this method.) Thermometers, how to take your baby's temperature, what to report, and fever as a symptom of illness are all covered in Chapter 19, "Identifying and Reporting Illness."

Umbilical Cord

The umbilical cord is the lifeline to your baby during pregnancy. It attaches to the inner surface of the placenta, the outer surface of which attaches to the uterine wall. The single vein in the cord brings oxygen and nourishment, obtained at the placental attachment site, from the mother to the baby. The two arteries in the umbilical cord return the waste products in the baby's circulation back to the placental attachment site, where they are passed to the mother for elimination. (This is opposite of the jobs of the veins and arteries in your body. Fetal circulation, and the adaptations made in order for the baby to receive oxygen and eliminate wastes through the placenta, is a fascinating and somewhat complicated study all in its own. It is worth looking this up in an anatomy book sometime!) The umbilical cord serves as the two-way road between the baby and the placental exchange with the mother.

The moist, bluish white-gray cord is clamped and cut at birth. Because there are no nerves in the cord, this can be done without an anesthetic. You will be instructed to clean the cord stump with alcohol wipes at each diaper change. Don't neglect the area where the cord attaches to the body. Gently push the surrounding skin away from the cord and clean well down into this area. Proper cleaning with alcohol helps prevent infection and promotes drying.

The cord stump will dry enough for the clamp to be removed within 24 to 36 hours, and it will now look black and yellow.

The stump will fall off, on average, between the 7th and the 10th days (a few days sooner or later is still normal). Continue to clean the area with alcohol after the cord has fallen off until the surrounding skin looks perfectly normal.

Breasts

In both male and female babies the breast tissue may be quite swollen at birth. This is because the mother's pregnancy hormones may cross the

Baby Care

placenta and enter the baby's system, thus stimulating the breast tissue. Female babies may even have a small amount of discharge from their nipples that looks like milk.

After birth, the baby is no longer receiving the hormones that stimulated and caused the breasts to swell, so the swelling disappears by two weeks after birth.

Genitals

Refer to "Seeing Your New Baby," page 187, for a description of your baby's enlarged genitals at birth and what causes this to occur. The small amount of bleeding that may occur in the diaper of a baby girl (sometime during the first week of life) is also explained.

The male foreskin covers the *glans* (end) of the penis. It is not retractable in infants. In the past, parents were told to retract the foreskin for cleaning, but this is no longer recommended, because it can lead to the formation of scar tissue: **do not force the foreskin back.** It will grow and retract naturally as your baby grows.

The testes can be felt in the scrotum in most cases. If a testicle is not descended (into the scrotum) at the time of birth, it will usually come down on its own during the first year and a half of life. If an undescended testicle does not come down on its own and the tip of the testicle can be felt by the physician, a surgical procedure is done through the scrotum. The testicle is brought down and secured inside the scrotum. If the tip of the testicle cannot be felt, the surgery is performed through a groin incision (in the lower abdomen on the side of the undescended testicle). The testicle is located and then brought down and secured into its proper position.

Circumcision and circumcision care are discussed on pages 341–342.

Urine

Nurses and the pediatrician check to be sure your baby urinates and passes stool in the first 24 hours of life. If you are being discharged early or have had a home or birthing center birth, please ask your nurse before you leave if your baby has urinated and passed stool and if this information is clearly documented on your newborn's record. *(?)***If your baby did not urinate and pass stool before leaving the hospital, notify your pediatrician if these functions have not occurred within 24 hours after birth.**

The first few times your baby passes urine, it may be dark (concentrated) and only a small amount. Because the urine is so concentrated at this time, it often leaves pinkish or brick-colored spots on the diaper. This is nothing to be concerned about: once your baby is taking more volume from the bottle or, if you are breastfeeding, once your milk comes in, your baby will urinate more often and in larger amounts, and the urine will become pale straw-colored.

A general rule to remember: six or more wet diapers a day indicate that your baby is getting enough volume from your breast milk or formula. However, it takes one week to get to this point. The first day a baby will urinate one time, the next day two times, and so on until urinating six or more times per day. When feedings are well established, most newborns will urinate at least six times per day, and some will urinate as much as 18 times per day.

Stools

I can't tell you how many new Moms and Dads have panicked at the sight of their baby's first stool. The stool that forms in the baby's intestine throughout development (during pregnancy) is a thick, sticky black substance that looks like oil. These first stools are called *meconium.* The number of meconium stools a baby passes per day varies; however, there should be at least one per day during the first two days of life.

Between the third and sixth day of life, the stools change in color and texture. These are called *transitional stools,* and they are thin and brownish green. During transition, the stools are slimy in texture, and your baby will stool five to six times per day (usually after every feeding).

After transitional stools, the breastfed baby's stools become loose in texture and golden in color. Sometimes they have a seedy appearance. There is no odor to this stool and it is generally not irritating to a baby's skin. By about two weeks of life the breastfed baby will have decreased the number of stools per day to about two. (However, it is not uncommon for breastfed babies to go several times per day due to the loose nature of this stool.)

After transitional stools, the bottle-fed baby's stools become formed but should still be soft. They are pale yellow to a light brownish color. They do have an odor and can be irritating to the infant's delicate skin. Bottle-fed babies should now pass stool one to two times per day.

The number of stools per day varies with each individual baby, and the number may vary from day to day. Therefore, if your baby is not passing stool at the frequency mentioned above, don't be alarmed. **You do, however, need to watch for and report both diarrhea and constipation.**

A baby that has hard, dry, difficult-to-pass stools is *constipated*. A baby that is excessively fussy and continually pulls his knees up or continually bears down without passing any stool may also be constipated. **Increase the amount of feedings and notify your pediatrician.** Do *not* add sugar to bottles or provide other home remedies—your pediatrician will advise you.

Many breastfeeding mothers call their pediatrician thinking that their baby is having diarrhea, because the stools can be loose enough to run out of the leg of a diaper. This is not diarrhea, it is the normal texture of a breastfed baby's stool. *Diarrhea* is forceful and usually very frequent episodes of watery stool. However, it can be either frequent small amounts or frequent or infrequent large volumes.

If you are concerned that what you are seeing may be diarrhea, please call your pediatrician. Dehydration from diarrhea can occur quickly in an infant. If you are uncer- **tain, it is better to err on the side of being cautious. Call and describe what you are seeing to your pediatrician for his or her assessment and advice.**

Nervous System (Reflexes)

It is amazing how neurologically intact babies are at birth. They can see, hear, grasp, breathe, suck, swallow, cough, sneeze, and cry, and they respond to light, sound, pain, and hunger.

There are several neurological tests doctors and nurses do at birth to evaluate your newborn. The Moro reflex (or startle reflex) is just one of the built-in responses they look for at birth. In response to a sudden movement or loud noise, your baby will extend his arms and legs and tilt his head slightly back (Figure 15-1); then the arms will be drawn up over the chest.

At birth, the nervous system is still immature in many ways. The short gasping or startled sounds a baby makes occasionally while sleeping are due to this immaturity. Your baby may also occasionally jerk suddenly, or startle in a way that, to an untrained eye, may look like a small convulsion or seizure. These *occasional* sudden jerks, lasting only one or two seconds, are seen in all stages of sleep and wakefulness and are *not* seizures. They

FIGURE 15-1

Moro Reflex

are just due to an immature nervous system, which will develop more fully on its own in a short amount of time.

*C)*You should report to your pediatrician any continuous jerking that is very frequent or lasts more than a few seconds. Also report any rolling back of the iris (the colored part of the eye). When this occurs, the colored part of the eye rolls up and disappears from view behind the upper eyelid. **Continuous jerking, frequent short jerks, and rolling back of the iris are symptoms of convulsion (seizure). Report these symptoms immediately to your pediatrician.**

Hepatitis B Vaccine

Please refer to page 98 for an explanation of hepatitis B. For the past several years, the United States Public Health Service has recommended that all infants be immunized against hepatitis B. In some states, the first of the three doses is offered in the hospital, usually free of charge. As with all vaccinations, it is hoped that aggressive vaccination programs will soon, at least by the next generation, wipe out the threat of this illness.

Your pediatrician (or the pediatrician covering your infant's hospital care) will discuss this vaccine with you and answer your questions. Your written informed consent must be obtained before the vaccine is administered. Once your written permission is obtained, the vaccine is given by injection into your baby's thigh. A vaccination record book, with this vaccination noted in it, will be given to you for your records.

Newborn Screening

State laws require that all newborns be screened for a number of disorders. These disorders are rare, but when they do occur they are associated with serious disabilities. However, in all of these disorders, if they are discovered early, intervention and treatment can be started that reduce and

in some cases prevent the serious disabilities. Thus, the importance of screening all infants for these disorders is clear.

Your baby will be screened for several metabolic disorders, including:

- ❏ Phenylketonuria (PKU), resulting from the body's inability to break down specific amino acids
- ❏ Hemoglobin disorders
- ❏ Congenital toxoplasmosis (an infection that may lead to retardation and blindness)
- ❏ Congenital hypothyroidism
- ❏ Congenital adrenal hyperplasia, a disorder in which an enzyme that is necessary to process hormones is lacking

Between 24 and 72 hours of age, a blood specimen is taken from a sterile heel stick on your infant. **Babies born outside of the hospital should also be tested.** If you deliver at a birthing center, most midwives will communicate with your pediatrician either by phone or through copies of your record sent home with you to give to your pediatrician. **In most cases, it is your responsibility to call to make the actual appointment.** Be certain that the receptionist who takes your call at the pediatrician's office realizes that the appointment you need is for newborn screening **that must be done within 24 to 72 hours of birth.**

*C)*If you had a home birth, it is your responsibility to call your pediatrician to make the appointment for newborn screening tests. They still must be done within 24 to 72 hours after birth.

Normal results are reported to the hospital where your baby was born or to your pediatrician, if you had a home birth. **You are not informed if the results are normal.**

If results indicate that retesting is necessary, the pediatrician listed on your newborn's chart (and also on the test slip itself) will be notified *both* by the lab doing the test and by the hospital receiving the test result.

Do not be alarmed if retesting is requested. Sometimes an inadequate quantity of blood was obtained to complete all the required screening tests. Positive test results only indicate that a disorder *may* be present. Premature babies or those with low birth weight sometimes have false positive test results on the first specimen, and repeat test results are normal.

If you object to testing on religious grounds, many states allow you to sign a form that relieves your hospital and doctor of any liability for damages that result from a disorder that would have been detectable by screening.

What to Report to Your Pediatrician

Please refer to the Emergency Call Box in Chapter 19, "Identifying and Reporting Illness," pages 368–369, for signs and symptoms of illness that should be reported to your pediatrician. This Emergency Call Box combines the information from both this chapter and the chapter on identifying and reporting illness.

Baby Care

16

Breastfeeding

Hospital downsizing of registered nursing staff and placing increased nonnursing responsibilities on nurses have taken their toll on patient teaching. In maternity nursing, the area most affected by these changes is breastfeeding teaching and support. It concerns me that, in many cases, mothers who wanted to breastfeed are not finding support and help available to them for a successful start in the hospital.

In the first 24 hours after birth, both mother and baby go through an adjustment period. It is not uncommon for a baby to sleep for long periods after birth and not be very aggressive about eating. In addition, the mother is so physically exhausted from labor she is often unable to absorb instructions during that first 24 hours after delivery. She can't keep her eyes open. The second day she may feel as if she is aboard the space shuttle with just 24 hours remaining to learn the controls before takeoff. Where does this leave breastfeeding? Pediatricians report a decrease in successful breastfeeding and an increase in switching to bottle feeding very soon after discharge.

The Art of Breastfeeding

Breastfeeding is an art. It is the rare mother and baby who have a successful feeding the first time with no assistance. Most mothers need instruction, assistance, and support to make it through the first few days of breastfeeding. New mothers beginning to breastfeed often feel as if they need another arm and another hand. There are so many things to remember and so many questions.

Your baby is also learning. Until she experiences a warm, full stomach, she does not know why you are placing your nipple in her mouth. Yes, there is an inborn instinct to suck, but the baby still does not *know* that something warm and tasty is coming! This is a two-way learning experience!

This chapter gives you a step-by-step guide to the process, developed over years of experience in working with new mothers. Read this chapter before you have your baby, and practice the positions with a teddy bear or doll. If you have practiced beforehand, you will feel less awkward when you are handed your baby to nurse for the first time. Understanding these basic principles should help you to have a smooth start in breastfeeding.

First, I would like to share a story with you about the experience that gave me the idea for this book. It speaks on a personal level about my experience and ability to help you succeed at breastfeeding. All I need from you to help you is a baby and a sincere desire to breastfeed!

Several years ago I was having dinner with some friends when our waitress came up to me and said, "Your name is Jerri, isn't it? I never got a chance to thank you. If it wasn't for you I would never have breastfed my son. You see, I was at the end of my rope. We had not had a successful feeding, my son was fussy, and I just didn't know what to do. I had already made up my mind to ask for a bottle at the next feeding. That's when you came in. You asked me to give you just 10 minutes to help me and said that, after your help, if I still wanted to switch, it was okay. But at least then we would both know we had tried our best. I agreed and you stayed with me, gave me lots of pointers, and then made sure my son latched on correctly. I successfully breastfed Jared for eight months, and I can't thank you enough."

What happened to this mother is not uncommon. In fact it happened to me the first time I breastfed. A nurse brought my son to me for his very first feeding and left the room. I hope this is less common today, now that most maternity nurses take pride in being advocates of breastfeeding, but I know it still happens. **If this happens to you, turn on your call light and ask for the nurse in charge.** Tell her what happened and ask her to please send you a nurse who supports breastfeeding and is a good teacher. You are paying for excellent maternity care–be an advocate for yourself and your baby, and get the help that you both deserve.

Every shift (every eight hours) you will have a new postpartum nurse, who may or may not have a lot of experience teaching breastfeeding. Certainly, give her a chance to assist you, but if she stays with you only a few minutes or leaves before your baby is latched on correctly, ask her to send in someone who has time to spend with you and loves to help breastfeeding mothers.

If it is time for you to be discharged and you still feel uncertain and uneasy about breastfeeding, again ask to see the nurse in charge, or the nursing manager if the nurse in charge does not help you. **You do not have to leave until your questions are answered or a first-day-home consultation is arranged for you.** This does not mean that you can get another night's stay. It just means that you don't have to be rushed out at nine in the morning. If you need instruction and have not been given that instruction, make sure you receive it before you leave.

A Step-by-Step Guide to Getting Started

There are three simple steps you need to think of each time you breastfeed, regardless of the position used. They are (1) your comfort, (2) your baby's body alignment, and (3) latching on correctly.

Step One: Your Comfort

Before sitting down to breastfeed, gather enough pillows to support your arm and your baby's back once he or she has latched on. Breastfeeding is a special time for you to relax and interact with your baby. You should never have a fatigued arm after breastfeeding from holding the weight of your baby.

An additional pointer: remember to pour yourself something healthy to drink. This is a good time to get in some of those extra fluids you need when breastfeeding!

Step Two: Your Baby's Body Alignment

Take your left hand and reach over your chest and hold your right shoulder. Turn your head until your chin points toward your left shoulder. Now try to swallow! Would you want to drink in this position? Would you be able to drink a full meal in this position?

Many frustrating breastfeeding attempts are caused by improper positioning of the baby. No matter which position you are using, for best results be sure you have remembered the following points *before* attempting to put your baby on the nipple:

❑ You and your baby should always be chest to chest and tummy to tummy (Figure 16-1).
❑ Your baby's neck and spine should be in straight alignment.

If you were to place a ruler along the baby's spine, it would touch from the back of the head to the bottom of the spine.

❑ Your baby's chin should be at a right angle to her body.

This means that your baby should not be looking up, down, or to the side. Straight neck—straight spine—looking straight ahead!

❑ Your baby's mouth should be directly in front of your nipple (Figure 16-2).

FIGURE 16-1

Position your baby chest to chest and tummy to tummy with you.

FIGURE 16-2

Position your baby's mouth directly in front of your nipple.

Be sure you have taken the previous steps before you do this. Once your baby is chest to chest with you and has a straight neck and back, you can use your arm, in the Madonna position, or pillows under the baby's bottom, in the football position, to bring your baby up to the level of your nipple.

Do not pull your breast up, down, or sideways to reach your baby's mouth. Bring the baby up until her mouth is directly in front of your nipple. Use pillows to help if needed.

❑ Your baby should have one hand on each side of your breast (Figure 16-3).

Again, imagine drinking with your arms crossed across your chest. Your baby will be more comfortable with one hand on each side of your breast.

Step Three: Latching on Correctly

Before we go any farther, let's clarify a few terms about the anatomy of your breast (Figure 16-4).

Baby Care

FIGURE 16-3

Be certain your baby has one hand on each side of your breast.

FIGURE 16-4

Anatomy of the Breast

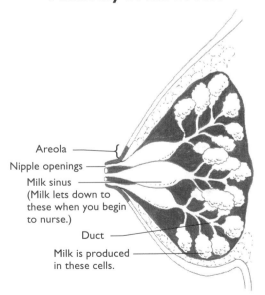

Areola
Nipple openings
Milk sinus
(Milk lets down to these when you begin to nurse.)
Duct
Milk is produced in these cells.

Your nipple consists of two parts: the *protruding* part of your nipple, which becomes hard and erect, and the *areola,* the brown or pink part of your nipple surrounding the protruding part.

The erect part of your nipple contains only the openings or passageways for the milk to get to the outside. No milk ducts or sinuses are located there; the milk sinuses that must be compressed in order for the milk to come out are under the areola, so the areola must be far enough inside the baby's mouth to be compressed by her sucking.

In order to suck effectively, your baby uses her tongue to compress the areola upward against her palate (the hard surface at the top of the mouth), which also compresses the milk sinuses. **The erect end of your nipple, when correctly placed well within the baby's mouth, has no pressure applied to it.**

For the baby to suck properly and effectively, a very large portion of the areola must be inside her mouth. When I assist mothers with latching on correctly, they often say, "But I feel like I am choking him." Breastfeeding takes getting used to. Once you see how rhythmically your baby sucks and how different it feels when she is latched on correctly, you will understand the importance of getting the areola well into your baby's mouth.

❏ Gently massage or pull out your nipple to make it erect.

Once your baby knows how to latch on and knows what your breast provides, she will be able to do this step on her own as she begins to suck. (Remember, during your first attempts your baby doesn't know what this is all about or what the breast is for. Why would she work hard for something without having any idea what she will get in return for her efforts?) By pulling your nipple out for your baby, you eliminate a step for her and make beginning easier.

❏ Gently stroke your nipple against your baby's lips to stimulate the rooting reflex.

It may take up to a couple of minutes, but stroking the baby's lips will cause the natural, inborn *rooting* (open-mouth) *reflex*. As you stroke the nipple across her lips, hold your baby far enough away to see the rooting reflex occur—be ready to act quickly!

❑ Pinch and shove.

Breastfeeding consultants generally recommend that the fingers cup the breast in a C formation (Figure 16-5). They will have you place your thumb on the upper surface of your breast and your fingers under and supporting the breast, close to your chest wall and ribs.

If your breasts are especially heavy, be sure to cup and lift your breast. A nursing bra acts like a third hand here—it helps prevent the weight of your breast from pulling the areola out of your baby's mouth once she latches on and you let go of your breast. A rolled face cloth placed under the breast can help support and lift a heavy breast.

In the *initial* stages of breastfeeding, while mother and infant are both learning, I teach what I call the "pinch and shove" method. Both this method and the C method are acceptable, and you should use whichever helps you best get your baby latched on properly.

For years, I have asked mothers to remember the expression "pinch and shove" as their baby opens the mouth wide. Let's look at and discuss each aspect of the process.

"Pinch."   With the padded underside of your thumb and index finger, gently pinch your breast *just behind (but not touching) the areola*. Your middle, ring, and little fingers remain under the breast, those entire fingers supporting its weight. **Be sure that your fingers and thumb are not touching the areola—they should be *directly* behind it.**

When you gently pinch the nipple, it should be angled slightly downward (Figure 16-6), not upward, and **your index finger and thumb should be aligned with your baby's nose and chin.** I have found that this helps to narrow the nipple where it needs to be narrow in order to be placed far enough into the baby's mouth. This will be discussed in detail in regard to *each* nursing position under "Breastfeeding Positions" (pages 270–276).

"Shove."   Stroke your nipple gently across your baby's lips. Sometimes the smell and taste of a drop of colostrum on the outside of your nipple helps your baby to get the idea to root! (The rooting reflex is seen when a baby opens his or her mouth to receive the nipple in response to the lips being stroked. See Figure 16-15 on page 275 for an illustration of the rooting reflex.)

FIGURE   16-5

C Hand Formation—Cupping the Breast

FIGURE   16-6

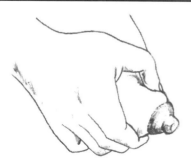

It may be helpful to narrow the nipple as shown here.

Baby Care

Once the rooting reflex occurs, you must act quickly to shove your nipple well into your baby's mouth. Two things will help. First, pull your baby's head inward toward you and hold it there. Second, use the end of your index (pointer) finger to stuff more of the areola into the baby's mouth. I'm serious! With an average-size areola, you should be able to see only a faint rim of the colored part outside of the baby's mouth. If your areola is more than two inches in diameter, you will see a little more rim. Be observant and get to know what proper latching on looks like for your nipples.

You must also be certain that your nipple is on top of your baby's tongue. Some babies put their tongue up against the roof of their mouth. It may be a struggle at first to get the tongue down, but with time and assistance, your baby will learn what to do. Once she gets the hang of nursing, you won't have to "pinch and shove" anymore! She will open her mouth wide enough and latch on correctly without any help.

The important thing right now, in the beginning, is that you teach your baby proper latching on. Babies can very quickly learn a good habit or a bad habit in sucking. A baby can suck vigorously for 15 minutes on both breasts and get very little volume if she is sucking only on the erect part of the nipple. The result: a sore, cracked, or bruised nipple and a baby who is still hungry. Why? Because *the milk sinuses are under the areola and they did not get compressed.*

We want the initial learning and sucking method to be correct. With the areola placed properly well within the baby's mouth, you will be sure that your baby will empty your breast more efficiently, and you will be preventing sore nipples at the same time. You will be well on your way to a successful breastfeeding experience.

It is also important to maintain proper latching on *throughout* the feeding. Do not allow the baby to slip down to the tip of your nipple. Use pillows or towel rolls to help support your arm and hold the baby's weight. This helps keep the baby close and well applied to the whole nipple and allows you to relax your arm. In addition,

do not allow your baby to turn her head toward one side. Even slight turning creates a tugging on the nipple, which can, over time, create a tender or bruised area on it.

Breastfeeding Positions

Before discussing breastfeeding positions, I want to emphasize the **importance of a nursing bra.** A nursing bra supports your breasts and actually acts like an additional hand. Many mothers, as they begin to breastfeed for the first time, have said to me, "I feel like I need extra hands." My response is always, "Put on a nursing bra; that's like one extra hand already."

A nursing bra holds the breast in position and prevents its weight from pulling the nipple out of the baby's mouth in any nursing position. **Bring your nursing bra with you to the hospital and put it on after delivery. Leave the bra flaps open to allow air to reach your nipples.**

There are three main positions for breastfeeding. Each position puts maximum sucking pressure on a different part of your nipple, so rotating positions with each feeding helps prevent sore nipples and localized blisters on the nipples. It also ensures that all the milk sinuses throughout the areola will be emptied adequately throughout the day, which helps to prevent *mastitis,* an inflammation of a milk duct that causes severe pain and fever.

Traditional Madonna Position

The following description shows how to use the Madonna position, with your baby on your *left breast.*

1. Choose a comfortable place to sit.

Whether you choose a chair, couch, or rocker, this is a good time to put your feet up, which helps reduce the swelling in your feet and legs that is common during pregnancy and after delivery. Be sure you have good back support and plenty of pillows available.

2. Position your baby (Figure 16-7).

Turn your baby toward you, chest to chest with you with her head on your left arm. Be sure that your baby has one hand on each side of your breast. Place your baby's head on the top of your left arm, directly over the bend in your elbow.

With the lower half of your left arm, reach behind your baby and support her back. Your left hand will be under your baby's bottom. After checking to be certain that your baby's back and neck are in straight alignment, comfortably adjust your left arm until your baby's mouth is directly in front of your left nipple.

3. Pinch and shove.

With your free hand (your right, if you are putting your baby on the left breast), reach *under* your left breast and place all four fingers on the far

FIGURE 16-7

Positioning Your Baby in the Traditional Madonna Position

outside of it. The underside pad of your right index finger will be directly behind the areola, which puts it in alignment with your baby's nose. Your thumb will now be on the inner side of your breast, directly behind the areola and in alignment with your baby's chin. **Be certain your fingers are directly behind the areola but not touching it.**

(Breast consultants may recommend the C hand position to cup the breast, illustrated in Figure 16-5 on page 269. You may use this technique if you prefer.)

Stroke your baby's mouth with your nipple to elicit the rooting reflex. When rooting occurs, use your left arm to pull your baby inward toward you as you put your nipple well into her mouth.

4. Check for proper latching on.

Is only the correct amount of areola (the amount normal for you) visible? When your baby is sucking, is her jaw moving, all the way up to and including her ear lobe?

5. Place pillows under your elbow, tucked up and against your arm for support (Figure 16-8).

FIGURE 16-8

Pillow Support in the Traditional Madonna Position

Baby Care

Relax and enjoy breastfeeding!

Modified Madonna Position

When you are first learning the Madonna position, you may find that this *modified Madonna* is easier and offers better control of your baby's head while you get her on the nipple. Again, for the sake of this instruction, I am describing positioning for nursing from your left breast.

1. With your *right* hand, reach across your baby's back, and hold her head securely. Move your right arm until your baby's mouth is directly in front of your nipple (Figure 16-9).
2. **Check for proper positioning of your baby.**

Check to be sure that your baby is on her side and turned chest to chest with you. Her head will be pointing toward your left breast. The baby's mouth should be directly in front of and level with your nipple. Also be sure that your baby has one hand on each side of your breast.

3. **Pinch and shove** (Figure 16-10).

FIGURE 16-9

Positioning Your Baby in the Modified Madonna Position

FIGURE 16-10

Pinch and Shove for the Modified Madonna Position

Use your *left* hand to support your left breast. Reach *under* the left breast with your left hand (wrist down, fingers up toward breast). Your thumb will be on the outside of the areola on the outer side of your left breast, in alignment with your baby's nose. Your index finger will be directly behind the areola on the inside of the left breast, in alignment with your baby's chin.

Pinch behind the areola to make it narrower for easier entry into the baby's mouth.

Stroke your baby's mouth with your nipple to bring on the rooting reflex. (See Figure 16-15 for a picture of the rooting reflex.) When your baby opens her mouth, pinch your breast and insert the nipple well inside it.

4. **Check for proper latching on.**

Be certain that the correct amount of areola is inside your baby's mouth.

When your baby is sucking, be sure that her whole jaw moves, up to and including the ear lobe.

5. **Use pillow supports.**

You may tuck pillows under your right arm for support, or move your arms to the traditional

Madonna position once the baby is latched on, if you find it more comfortable and relaxing.

Football Position

This is my favorite *initial* breastfeeding position to teach. In my opinion, the best view of the baby's entire mouth, your breast, and your hand positioning is found with the football position.

For the sake of illustration and teaching, I will describe here the position for nursing on the *right* breast.

1. Choose a comfortable place to sit.

Whether you choose a chair, couch, bed, or rocker, be sure you have good back support. This is a good time to put your feet up.

Place a thick, firm pillow with its long edge vertical behind your back (Figure 16-11). This brings you forward and creates extra space for your baby's legs in this position.

2. Position your baby.

For this position, when using the right breast, your baby will be on your right side. This position is similar to the football hold, but your baby will be in a more upright, sitting position (Figure 16-12).

You will need to place a pillow under your baby's bottom to bring her mouth up to the level of your right nipple.

Support your baby's back with your right arm, and hold her head securely in your right hand. Her feet should face the back of the chair. Do not allow your baby's back to curve outward (like a C) too much—the lower rib cage can compress her stomach and cause her to spit up.

Bring the baby up to your breast for nursing; do *not* lean forward into your baby.

3. Pinch and shove.

With your left hand, place your fingers under your right breast and your thumb on top.

Your thumb should be in alignment with your baby's nose, and your index finger with your baby's chin. Be certain that the undersides of your thumb and index finger are completely behind the areola. (You may wish to use the C hand position described on page 269 instead, to cup the breast.

Stroke your baby's mouth with your nipple to elicit the rooting reflex. When rooting occurs, use your right arm and hand to pull your baby inward

FIGURE 16-11

Place a thick, firm pillow behind your back when using the football position.

FIGURE 16-12

Football Hold Positioning—Upright

toward you as you put your nipple well into her mouth.

4. Check for proper latching on.

Is only the amount of areola that is normal for you visible around your baby's mouth? When your baby is sucking, is her jaw moving, all the way up to and including the ear lobe?

5. Use pillow supports.

Tuck a pillow against your right arm and hand to support your baby's weight.

In the football hold, the baby can be held as described above and shown in Figure 16-12 in an almost upright sitting position or angled more and brought in more from the side (as if wrapped around your side) as in Figure 16-13. Both ways are acceptable. In fact, alternating both angles helps to rotate the sucking position on your nipples even more.

FIGURE 16-13

Football Hold Positioning—Wraparound Side Pillow Support

Side-Lying Position

1. Choose a comfortable place to lie down.

A bed or wide couch is acceptable. Have two pillows under your head and one between your legs. A pillow tucked behind your back is also very comfortable. Have a towel roll available to use behind your baby's back and head.

2. Position your baby (Figure 16-14).

When you are lying on your side, place the baby on the mattress on her side, facing you. **In this position, your baby's head should be on the mattress, with her mouth directly in front of your nipple.** Do *not* put the baby's head on top of your arm.

You actually do not hold your baby in this position. She is lying on the mattress, and your lower arm is also on the mattress above her head and around her back. Stay directly on your side; *do not* roll partially toward your back.

3. Pinch and shove.

With your upper hand, pinch your breast behind the areola, in the same plane as your baby's nose and mouth. You may reach under your breast or over, whichever is more comfortable for you, but if you pinch the nipple from above, your view will be partially blocked. Be sure that your finger and thumb are directly behind the areola but not touching it.

Stroke your nipple against your baby's lips to elicit the rooting reflex (Figure 16-15). When rooting occurs, use your lower arm (the one against the mattress) to pull your baby in toward you (keeping your baby on her side), and put your nipple well into her mouth.

4. Check for proper latching on.

Is only the amount of areola that is normal for you visible around your baby's mouth? When your baby is sucking, is her whole jaw moving, up to and including the ear lobe?

5. Use pillow supports.

Use a towel roll behind your baby's back and head to keep her pulled in close to your breast.

FIGURE 16-14

Positioning Your Baby in the Side-Lying Position

FIGURE 16-15

Eliciting the Rooting Reflex

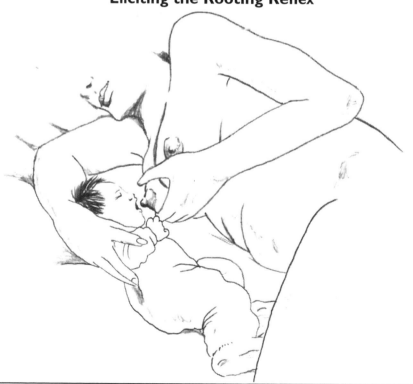

Baby Care

Nursing Positions for Twins

Feeding twins is certainly a challenge. By learning some basic techniques from women who have experienced multiple births, you can make this busy time a rewarding experience.

Keep in mind that you have many options, and you can choose a different one at each feeding. You can:

- ❑ Nurse both babies separately.
- ❑ Nurse both babies at the same time.
- ❑ Nurse one baby and bottle-feed the other baby previously pumped breast milk.
- ❑ Bottle-feed both babies separately.
- ❑ Nurse one baby all the time and bottle-feed the other baby all the time.
- ❑ At one feeding, nurse baby A and bottle-feed baby B, and at the next feeding, give baby A the bottle and nurse baby B.

Whatever you decide, it is a good idea to keep records to ensure that each baby is getting adequate feedings. You may feel as if "they" are eating all the time, when in fact one baby is the ravenous one. Records will help you and your doctor decide whether the baby demanding fewer feedings needs encouragement or not.

Remember that each baby is a unique individual. Eating patterns, likes and dislikes, and how easily each baby switches between breast and bottle will be different. Try to respect these differences.

If you are nursing twins, triplets, or more, follow the instructions for breastfeeding nutrition, but add approximately 200 to 500 healthy calories for each *additional* baby you nurse. You need extra protein and calcium in your diet to meet the additional demand of each nursing baby. Your pediatrician will be watching the weight gain of your babies carefully. She or he will help you decide whether their diet is adequate.

Whether you are nursing one baby or twins or triplets, fluids are essential. Women naturally feel thirsty when they are nursing. Do what your body is telling you to do! If your urine is pale yellow and you are not getting constipated, this is a good indication that you are drinking enough fluids.

If you have chosen to nurse both your babies, as previously mentioned, you do have some options. Although each baby needs its own private cuddling and feeding time, occasionally the mother's time is limited or both babies are very hungry at the same time. The three positions shown in Figure 16-16 will help you to nurse your twins simultaneously.

Special pillows are available to help a mother who needs to nurse both babies at the same time. Although these pillows are not necessary, their firm support does help you to lift and hold the infants in position with less effort. Using pillows also gives you that free hand you need if one baby comes off the nipple and needs help to latch on again.

It is usually easiest to position the less vigorous nurser first, while you have both hands free to assist her. Then put the more aggressive rooter and nurser on the other side. It is also advisable to alternate which breast is given to the most aggressive nurser in order that both breasts will receive equal stimulation.

If you decide to nurse your twins separately, you can choose to feed each baby on its own demand schedule or attempt to get both babies to eat on the same schedule.

Nutrition and Fluid Needs While Nursing

The nutritional information found in Chapter 2, "Living Healthy During Pregnancy and Beyond," will also be helpful during lactation. Breastfeeding success is directly related to your rest and nutrition. If you are excessively fatigued or undernourished, your breast milk supply will be affected.

If you are breastfeeding, you need extra fluids, calories, calcium, protein, minerals, and vitamins. These increases are necessary to produce breast milk, provide added nourishment for the baby, and meet your own needs for nourishment.

FIGURE 16-16

Three Positioning Options for Nursing Twins

Nutritional Needs

You need a well-balanced diet containing an extra 200 to 500 calories per day (per baby) to maintain good health for your infant and maintain your own body's reserves while you are nursing.

Within the first two weeks after delivery, you will naturally lose about 18 to 20 pounds. If you are nursing, this is not the time to diet. Your body needs proper nutrition right now in order to produce breast milk.

If you are a vegetarian and plan to nurse, consult your maternity care practitioner for supplements necessary to meet your nutritional requirements. It would be advisable for you to obtain information about your lactation diet during your prenatal visits, because there are many types of vegetarian diets, and your obstetrician may need time to consult a dietitian on your behalf.

Protein. Protein requirements increase to 60 to 65 grams daily during pregnancy and while you are lactating (breastfeeding). Protein can be obtained from milk, cheese, eggs, meats, beans, nuts, and grains. (See page 21 for more information about protein.)

Calcium. In order to not deplete your own calcium reserves while breastfeeding, the Dietary Reference Intake recommends 1300 milligrams of calcium daily while nursing. This is the same amount that was recommended during pregnancy. (See page 21 for more information about calcium and calcium sources.)

Vitamins. Vitamin requirements increase when you are breastfeeding. Your maternity practitioner may prescribe prenatal vitamins to be continued while you are breastfeeding to cover some of this need, but it is still very important to eat a wide variety of fruits and vegetables. Eating a balanced diet that includes foods from all levels of the Food Pyramid (Figure 2-1) is essential for proper nutrition.

Health food stores carry brewer's yeast (a natural source of all the B vitamins, iron, and protein) in a powdered form that mixes well with juice. However, brewer's yeast and large doses of vitamin C can cause fussiness in your baby.

Other Minerals. Mineral requirements for phosphorus, zinc, iodine, and magnesium are higher during pregnancy and lactation. However, if you are eating a well-balanced diet and obtaining the recommended increase in calories and protein, your mineral needs will be met.

Iron. Whether you continue additional iron supplements after delivery depends on the results of your post-delivery blood tests. The regular 18 milligrams of daily iron recommended for non-pregnant females is adequate while you are nursing, unless you are anemic. If your blood tests showed your hemoglobin and hematocrit to be low, additional iron will be ordered for you. (See page 22 for food sources high in iron.)

If you are required to take additional iron, be extra careful to avoid constipation. Eat bran, salads, and other foods containing fiber to help counteract the constipating side effect of iron.

Fluid Needs

Increase your fluid intake to approximately two quarts of fluid per day. Eight to nine 8-ounce glasses of fluid daily meets this requirement. The increase usually occurs naturally, because you will be more thirsty during the time when you are nursing.

If you are not drinking an adequate amount of fluids, your urine will be concentrated (dark yellow, or almost orange in color) and you may get constipated. If you see these signs, increase your fluid intake.

Foods You *May* Need to Avoid

There are no foods that you absolutely must avoid while nursing. Anything in moderation (except alcohol and smoking) is a good general rule. However, some foods *may* bother your baby. Some general guidelines follow.

Avoid caffeine—it is a stimulant and it does enter your breast milk. **When you eat chocolate or drink coffee, tea, or soda that contains caffeine, your baby may be fussy and seem unable to sleep.** Think of how charged you feel after consuming caffeine, and imagine that amount of caffeine packed into your small baby. No wonder you were up all night with a baby that wouldn't (couldn't) sleep!

The majority of mothers I have worked with over the years are unaware that **chocolate contains caffeine.** In addition to the stimulant effects,

a baby who nurses after a mother consumes large amounts of chocolate may show signs of an irritable bowel (gas, fussing, pulling up her legs). Of course, you may have one or two pieces of chocolate—anything in moderation—but be aware your baby and therefore you may both pay if you overdo it.

Any alcohol you drink also enters your breast milk. With the exception of an occasional alcoholic beverage to celebrate a special occasion, in your baby's best interest, **avoid alcohol while breastfeeding.**

Avoid nicotine—it, too, is a stimulant. In addition, research shows an increased number of cases of bronchitis and ear infections in infants who live in homes where smoking occurs. Smoking is also linked to increased risk of sudden infant death syndrome.

Some babies may fuss after their mothers have eaten garlic, onions, cabbage, broccoli, Brussels sprouts, cauliflower, or beans. A heavy intake of fruits has been known to cause indigestion and diarrhea in some breastfed infants.

If your baby is excessively fussy, can't seem to settle to sleep, or pulls her legs up with uncomfortable gas, it would be wise to make a record of what food you eat and when the fussy behavior or gas occurs in your baby. Often, when looking back over a few days of these records, you will discover caffeine, chocolate, or a specific food that may have triggered the upset. Be sure to look closely at foods that naturally tend to produce and cause gas: beans, corn, cauliflower, broccoli, cabbage, Brussels sprouts, onions, excessive sweets, fried foods, and spicy foods. You may need to eat these foods in smaller quantities or eliminate them completely if you discover they cause your baby discomfort.

Don't forget to consider chocolate as the possible cause if your baby is uncomfortable with gas or excessively wakeful and fussy. As mentioned above, chocolate contains caffeine and often causes stomach and gas discomfort in infants of breastfeeding mother. Some nursing mothers find that they also have to limit the amount of tomato sauce they eat because of its acidity.

Medications While Nursing

Do not take any medication while you are nursing without first checking with your obstetrician or pediatrician. This includes over-the-counter medications and previously prescribed medications for any chronic condition.

Frequently Asked Questions

Can I Nurse If I Begin to Take Birth Control Pills After Delivery?

Although breastfeeding suppresses ovulation, it has been found to *not* be a dependable method of birth control.

Estrogen has a negative effect on the production of breast milk, and there is some indication that it may have long-term health effects on the infant. Since estrogen is a major component of birth control pills, they are usually not prescribed if you are nursing. A new pill without estrogen is available. Consult your practitioner.

Because it is generally recommended that sexual intercourse, tampon use, and douching be delayed until after your six-week checkup, it is assumed that you will not need birth control until then. At your six-week checkup, discuss birth control with your practitioner, including the advantages and disadvantages of each method. Diaphragms must be refitted after every pregnancy, miscarriage, or abortion. If you choose the diaphragm as a birth control method, you should be fitted for one at your six-week checkup.

If you decide to have intercourse before your six-week checkup, you cannot assume that ovulation has not occurred. Another pregnancy can occur even at this early date.

What Should I Do If My Baby Cries When I Am Trying to Put Her to Breast?

Provide relaxed, quiet surroundings, including soft lights, possibly soft music, and gentle holding and rocking. Massage your breast before starting to nurse to stimulate and quicken the let-down response. If your breasts are engorged, express some breast milk to soften the firm areola; this makes latching on easier.

If you feel your baby is crying from hunger, hold your baby *gently* on the breast during crying if possible. Babies almost always suck immediately after crying—take advantage of that fact. Your baby may be crying because she is frustrated or impatient due to hunger. Removing your baby from your breast while she is crying, in this situation, only prolongs her frustration. Eating will solve the problem!

If the above measures fail, remove her from the breast, check her diaper, and comfort her until she settles down. Comfort comes in many forms, and what works one time may not work the next. Try singing softly or talking to her in a soft, relaxed voice. Sometimes nothing seems to help, and you just need to be there while the child slowly settles down. Don't hesitate to try lying the baby down to see if the absence of stimulation will comfort her. Of course, if the baby continues to cry, pick her up and try something else. (See pages 318–320, "Colic and Irritable Crying Spells," for more suggestions.)

Review your diet for foods that cause gas. Make a note of what those foods are and avoid them in the future.

Can My Baby Breathe While Nursing?

This has to be the most frequently asked question by nursing mothers. Look in the mirror at your own nose. You can see that the outer edges are rounded up slightly on the sides, so rest assured that your baby can still breathe even when the front of her nose is pressed against your breast.

Breathing is an instinct that takes priority over nursing. If your baby can't breathe, she will forcefully pull away from your breast.

Sucking and swallowing *cannot* occur without breathing. If your baby is nursing, she is breathing.

If you absolutely must push down on your breast to clear it away from your baby's nose, do so high up on the breast, at least half an inch above her nose, and press your breast tissue *inward*, into the breast. *Do not* pull the breast tissue upward away from the baby's nose, because doing so will pull on the nipple and change its angle inside your baby's mouth. (The erect part of the nipple may now hit the baby's upper gum with each suck, soon causing a bruised, sore, or cracked area on the nipple.) You should not tug or pull on the areola as you press downward on your breast to clear your baby's nose.

An alternative way to clear the baby's nose away from the breast, if you feel you must do so, is to reach under your breast (near your baby's chin) and on top of your breast (half an inch from your baby's nose) and pinch both sides of your breast. Pinching by this method avoids changing the angle of the nipple inside your baby's mouth.

Why Does My Baby Stop So Frequently for Rests?

Nursing occurs in rhythmic suck, swallow, and rest cycles. Each individual baby sets its own pattern. You will see 5 to 12 sucks, followed by a swallow that you can usually hear (once your milk is in). The baby takes short rests as needed.

As the richer hind milk lets down, the baby's sucking rate will slow and there will be fewer sucks before each swallow. (See page 286 for a further description of fore and hind milk.)

How Will I Know If I Have Enough of the Areola in My Baby's Mouth?

The easiest way is to look at your baby's jaw and ear while she is sucking. *If the jaw, all the way up to and including the earlobe, is moving, then enough areola is in the baby's mouth.*

Figure 16-17 shows improper latching on. If the baby's lips are closed around the erect part of the nipple and sucking movement is seen only around the mouth and lips, take the nipple out of your baby's mouth and try again. Dimpling of the baby's cheeks is also a sign of improper or poor latching on, which can cause nursing to be painful.

Figure 16-18 shows proper latching on: the baby's lips are open wide, covering the areola. The baby is held close, directly facing the nipple, and has one hand on each side of the breast. Proper sucking is rhythmic and powerful. The entire jaw is used, and the baby's nose and chin should be in contact with your breast.

What Is Colostrum and What Does It Look Like?

During your pregnancy, your body begins to get ready for breastfeeding. Mammary gland development is complete by midpregnancy, although milk production is inhibited by your high estrogen levels until after the delivery of your placenta. *Colostrum* is the initial breast fluid that precedes the development of breast milk.

A thin, clear, precolostrum fluid can be found in the breasts by the third month of pregnancy. This fluid thickens to the creamy yellow or white true colostrum at around 16 weeks. Toward the end of pregnancy, it becomes slightly paler in color. During pregnancy, colostrum may leak from your breasts by itself or during sexual excitement.

Colostrum contains water and a rich mixture of protein, minerals, and antibodies to protect your baby from disease. This pale yellow-white colostrum is present for your baby immediately after birth and is the only source of nourishment needed until your breast milk comes in.

FIGURE 16-17

Indications of Improper Latching On

FIGURE 16-18

Proper Latching On

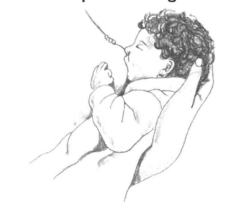

When Will My Breast Milk Come In?

Your breasts will begin to fill with breast milk two to four days after delivery. You will know when it happens because your breasts begin to feel firmer. This initial filling is called *engorgement*.

Initial breast milk is thinner than colostrum but still slightly yellow. After a week or two, your breast milk will be bluish white—it does not look like cow's milk.

Once your breast milk comes in, you should be able to hear your baby swallowing while nursing.

What Helps Relieve the Discomfort of Engorgement?

Initially, as your breast milk comes in, your breasts may feel swollen, full, firm, warm, and painful: this is engorgement. *Just before nursing,* warm compresses, warm showers, and massage will help the let-down reflex. Wearing a supportive nursing bra is important and helps relieve discomfort. Acetaminophen and ibuprofen may also be needed to relieve discomfort.

Nurse every two hours if possible during initial engorgement. After applying heat, massage the breasts and manually express or pump a little milk before nursing to soften the breasts and areola; this makes latching on less difficult. Use a breast pump to remove more milk for added relief if necessary after nursing. Fresh cabbage leaves wrapped around your breasts (and left there for twenty minutes) will help reduce swelling more quickly. Intermittent ice packs *after and between breastfeeding* will help reduce pain and swelling. (However, remember to use heat just prior to nursing.)

The discomfort of initial engorgement should pass in about 24 to 36 hours, but may linger for up to 72 hours. After this, the breasts will be softer and more comfortable even when full. The only time you will feel this degree of discomfort again is if you completely skip a feeding or if the baby takes only one side when the usual pattern is both sides per feeding. In both of these circumstances, pumping will relieve the engorgement.

What About a Swollen Lump in the Breast?

The sudden development of a hard, tender lump in your breast is usually one of two things: a plugged milk duct or a breast infection (mastitis).

In rare instances, breast cancer is detected during pregnancy. Because breast cancer is increasing among young women, no breast lump should be ignored. If a lump persists after the following treatment, biopsy may be necessary to rule out breast cancer.

When you detect a breast lump while nursing, begin treatment with heat applications, frequent nursing, and plenty of rest. ℓ**If you develop a fever, however, report it to your practitioner promptly.**

If not associated with fever, the lump is most likely a plugged milk duct. Because the milk can no longer flow through the duct, it backs up and causes a lump. Plugged ducts can be caused by delays between feedings, often a result of supplementation with formula or overuse of a pacifier (which can cause the baby to spend less time at the breast). Feeding delays can also occur when an infant suddenly starts sleeping through the night. The supply is still serving the previous demand, and yet the breasts are not being emptied.

Plugged ducts can also be caused by clothing or bras that are too tight around the breasts. I have seen plugged ducts many times in women who were indecisive about breastfeeding. They decided to delay purchasing a nursing bra until they were sure they wanted to continue nursing. Therefore they were pulling their regular bra (now much too small) up over or down under their breasts when nursing. This constriction, localized around the breast, most likely contributed to causing the plugged duct. If you do have a nursing bra and have developed a plugged duct, evaluate its size and purchase a larger size if it is too tight.

Plugged ducts can also be a sign that you are not getting enough rest. **An essential treatment of plugged ducts is rest.** At the very first sign of a tender spot in your breast, get into bed or, at the very least, get on the couch and put your feet up. **Wash the nipple with warm water to remove any dry secretions.** (Occasionally a plugged duct can be caused by dry secretions blocking the nipple opening and preventing the flow of milk from that one duct.) **Next apply either wet or dry heat to the area over the sore lump.** Wet heat is best, and can be applied by soaking in the bathtub three times a day with your breast underwater, taking warm showers, using a hot water bottle (covered with a towel to prevent skin burns), or putting warm, wet, small towels in a plastic bag covered with a dry cloth. Dry heat can be applied with a heating pad; be careful to check your skin frequently to prevent burns.

Gentle massage of the tender area after the heat treatment is very effective in getting the milk to begin flowing. **Follow massage with nursing, manual expression of milk, or pumping. It is essential to get the milk flowing to unplug the blocked duct.**

Continue to nurse your baby on the sore breast first, every two hours, until the symptoms are completely gone. Nursing on the sore side first ensures that this breast will be emptied at each feeding, an important part of treating plugged ducts. Be sure to review the section on proper latching on and rotation of nursing positions, pages 267 and 270. Improper latching on can cause plugged ducts, and inadequate and unequal emptying of milk ducts can occur when only one position is routinely used for nursing.

If a plugged duct is not treated promptly and correctly, it can develop into a breast infection. Therefore, begin the above measures immediately upon developing a sore or tender area on your breast.

Sometimes fever or other symptoms similar to those of the flu are present as the first symptom of the localized painful lump. ℓ**If you have a fever, headache, body or joint aches, or other flu-like symptoms associated with a tender lump in your breast, call your practitioner promptly.**

It is no longer recommended that you stop nursing on the infected breast. Your infection will go away much faster if you continue to nurse frequently. Your baby will not become ill from nursing while you have a breast infection (mastitis). The natural antibodies in your breast milk protect your baby from the infection. Antibiotics are generally ordered to treat mastitis. The antibiotic prescribed will be one safe for nursing mothers.

If an antibiotic is prescribed, follow the directions and finish the entire prescription. Do not stop taking the medication when you feel better in a day or two. Taking the full prescription is needed, both to kill the organism causing the infection and to prevent the organism from developing a resistance to antibiotic treatment. Often, several weeks after a full course of antibiotic treatment, the infection recurs and has to be hit a second time with another 10 full days of antibiotics. Be persistent: take the full treatment again. This is not uncommon and usually takes care of the breast infection once and for all.

Will I Feel My Milk Let Down?

The *let-down reflex* is a tingling or burning in the nipple felt as a feeding is started once your breast milk is in. It occurs as the milk comes down from the milk ducts toward the nipple and can be momentarily uncomfortable or even painful.

Although some women who successfully breastfeed never experience this reflex, it may be felt with the first few sucks as a feeding is started. Many women also experience it merely by thinking about their baby or hearing her cry.

If this reflex occurs at an inconvenient time, use the palms of your hands or your forearms to apply direct pressure to your nipples–this will stop the reflex.

How Will I Know When My Baby Wants to Nurse?

Crying is the most obvious clue that your baby wants to nurse. However, there are many other more subtle, early signs of readiness that occur before crying.

Watch for "readiness cues" that say, "I am ready to nurse." A baby in the early stages of wakefulness who is making facial grimaces, tongue thrusts, or sucking will often nurse very well.

Chewing or sucking on the hands or fingers, or merely putting the hands to the mouth, is often a sign of readiness to nurse. These signs may, of course, just be your baby's desire to suck. You will quickly learn what your baby is trying to tell you. However, if it has been two hours since the previous feeding, your baby will usually nurse if put to breast after you see these signs.

It won't take long for you to tell the difference between "I'm wet," "I want to be held," and "I'm hungry" cries. When a baby is mad and is punching the air with her fists and biting on her hands and fists between punches, you can be fairly certain that you are hearing the "I'm hungry" cry!

Should I Give My Breastfeeding Baby a Pacifier?

Breastfeeding consultants will often recommend not to use a pacifier right away (at least until nursing is well established). They are concerned not only about nipple confusion (the sucking technique is different) but also that the cues for the desire to nurse may be missed if a pacifier is overused.

Newborn babies often *cluster feed* in the beginning. This means that they may want to nurse every one to two hours for several feedings and then go five or six hours without showing any desire to feed. Do not expect any exact schedule—respond to the feeding cues of your baby. Understanding this normal pattern should help you to understand why nursing consultants fear that a pacifier may be overused if it leads to you missing your baby's pattern or readiness cues.

However, if you are desperate for sleep in those first few days home, a pacifier, offered after what seems to be an adequate feeding, just may allow you to get some much-needed sleep. Keep an open mind, and don't feel guilty if you *occasionally* use a pacifier for this purpose.

See page 378 for safety tips for using pacifiers.

Baby Care

How Will I Know If My Baby Is Getting Enough Colostrum and, Later on, Enough Breast Milk?

Before your baby is discharged from the hospital, she or he is seen by your pediatrician or the pediatrician temporarily assigned by the hospital, who will then inform you at what point after discharge you need to have an appointment. Breastfed babies are often seen by the pediatrician sooner than at the normal two-week point, often within two days of discharge from the hospital, especially if the mother and baby had a difficult start in breastfeeding. Your pediatrician needs to watch your baby's feedings and growth more closely if you are breastfeeding. (If an early checkup was not scheduled for your breastfeeding infant and you have concerns about poor feedings, call and request an appointment.)

There are ways for you to know if your infant is getting enough breast milk: during the first two days of life, your baby may have only one or two wet diapers and one or two black-colored meconium stools a day. The urine should be light yellow and not a dark rusty color. If you do notice dark, brick-colored urine, you should nurse more frequently to provide an increased fluid volume.

By the fourth day (which is also when your breast milk comes in), you should feel a fullness in your breasts between feedings and softness after nursing. Once the breast milk is in, you should hear the baby swallowing and you *may* experience leaking from your breasts. Your baby should be nursing about 8 to 12 times per day in his or her own unique pattern and should be content after nursing.

By the *end* of the first week, the best indicator of adequate fluid intake is noting at least six wet diapers in 24 hours. Also at this time, three to six stools per day are a good indication that adequate calories and nourishment are being received from your breast milk. (The frequency of stools may decrease to two per day after two weeks.)

A baby receiving adequate nutrition will have periods of restful sleep and will gain weight. After the initial normal weight loss of 10 percent in the first week of life, your baby should gain weight at a gradual rate.

*📞***If your baby is very fussy, is not wetting her diaper and moving her bowels as described above, or is not gaining weight, please notify your pediatrician.**

How Often Should I Nurse?

Every baby is an individual. There are no absolute rules to follow. *Breastfeeding on demand* means nursing when your baby shows signs of hunger. *Nurse your baby, not the clock.*

During the first two weeks of life, most breastfed infants will want to nurse 8 to 12 times in 24 hours (every two to three hours). However, because babies often cluster feed, they may nurse every hour to hour and a half several times and then take a longer break. Also, if you are overtired or not eating well, this affects milk production. Your baby will demand frequent feedings to build up your supply.

Several times during the first three months of life and then periodically throughout the first year, mothers call the pediatrician and say, "We were doing so well. I was nursing every two and a half to four hours and now all of a sudden my baby is screaming to nurse every hour. Do you think my milk has dried up?" **Remember, breast milk is produced according to your baby's demand. Although your baby's growth appears to be gradual, there are times when, especially in the long bones, it occurs more rapidly. When your baby is experiencing one of these growth spurts, she will suddenly begin demanding feedings at a much more frequent rate.** This will continue until your breasts produce enough milk to reach the new demand. Then the time between feedings will increase again, and you will return to the normal schedule that you had before. Growth spurts commonly occur at between one and two weeks, one to one and a half months, 10 weeks, three months, and six months, but can be any time.

What Should I Do If My Baby Seems Sleepy and Uninterested in Feeding?

During the first 24 hours of life, many babies have about a 12-hour "sleepy" time. It seems that no matter what you try, nothing works. I always remind mothers, "You can lead a horse to water, but you can't make it drink." Sleepiness in the first one or two days of life is not abnormal or unusual. Take comfort in the fact that babies do not starve themselves.

Watch for early signs of feeding readiness: sucking, putting hands to mouth, and so on. Babies will usually nurse very well if put to breast when these signs are present. If your baby's sleepiness is interfering with adequate frequency or length of nursing times, be vigorous in trying to keep her awake during a feeding. Unwrap your baby, rub her back, massage her feet, change her diaper, and wash her face with a cool cloth. Continue stimulating your sleepy baby during a feeding to encourage a longer feeding time.

✐Remember excessive sleepiness is a symptom of high bilirubin and low blood sugar. If you think your baby is jaundiced or jittery, and he or she is sluggish and sleepy, this needs to be reported promptly.

How Long Should I Nurse at Each Feeding?

You need to get to know your baby. On initial feedings, some babies nurse only 6 to 10 minutes (3 to 5 minutes on each breast), and others will nurse 10 to 15 minutes on each breast if allowed to do so. Do not interrupt a rhythmic nursing session.

How long you will nurse and how quickly you increase your nursing time should depend on the demands of your baby. **If you are experiencing pain or soreness in your nipples, ask for**

help. Sore nipples are an indication of improper latching on. Let a nurse experienced in teaching breastfeeding or a lactation consultant assist you.

Early in the breastfeeding experience, if you nurse more than 10 to 15 minutes on the first side, your baby may get tired before she gets a chance to stimulate the second breast and get colostrum from it. **Therefore, until your milk comes in and your breasts are soft again after engorgement, your breastfeeding goal is up to 10 to 15 minutes on the first breast and nursing until your baby is satisfied on the second breast.** You may or may not have to gradually build up to this point. **Let your baby be your guide** and get assistance in the beginning to be sure that your baby is latching on correctly right from the start.

If you had difficulty getting your baby started due to excessive sleepiness or fussiness, and she is now sucking well, don't interrupt her to switch sides just because the clock says it's been ten to fifteen minutes–that would be nursing the clock instead of your baby. In general, however, the goal is to give each breast the stimulation of nursing until your milk comes in.

Once your milk comes in and your breasts are soft again after engorgement, you will get to know your baby's usual length of nursing time. Average feedings run about 30 minutes, but you need to remember the importance of nursing your baby and not the clock.

On Which Breast Should I Begin? Should I Use Both Breasts at Each Feeding?

Until your milk comes in and your breasts and nipples are soft after engorgement, it is best to nurse from both breasts at each feeding. This provides milk-production stimulation to both breasts in the beginning.

It is not absolutely necessary to nurse from both breasts at each feeding. If your baby was fussy or had difficulty getting started, you may not want to interrupt her to switch breasts for fear she may get fussy again. Go with your gut feelings and let your baby be your guide!

If both breasts were used in the previous feeding, begin the next feeding on the breast you ended with on the last one. A good way to remember which breast to begin with at the next feeding is to mark your bra strap with a safety pin, piece of yarn, or other movable marker. Move the marker at the end of the feeding to the breast you ended with. At the next feeding, just begin on the breast with the marker! Of course, if your baby does not take both breasts at a feeding, move the marker to the unused breast and begin there the next time.

Once your milk is in and your breasts and nipples are soft again after engorgement, you may nurse on either one or both breasts per feeding. The one breast method provides a thin or slow weight gain baby with the benefit of the higher fat and calorie content of the hind milk. *Hind milk* is defined as the milk that continues to come down and be produced after the *fore milk,* or initial milk, is emptied. Research is showing that the hind milk has six to eight times more calories than the fore milk. You will know your baby is getting the hind milk when her sucking slows down and there are fewer sucks before each swallow. After 25 or 30 minutes (or when the baby seems to be finished nursing), burp your baby. Then, if she continues to show signs of hunger, put her on the other breast.

Nursing on one breast per feeding is not taught by all lactation consultants, and this technique will most likely not be how you are instructed by hospital nurses until the literature on hind milk is more circulated and the technique has been in practice for a while. **The traditional way of nursing using both breasts per feeding is certainly also acceptable.**

Since breast milk production is by supply and demand, your breasts get used to whatever method you use, one breast per feeding or both breasts. The choice is up to you—both methods work! However, if you are experiencing nipple soreness,

cracks, or blisters, please talk with a lactation consultant immediately. You will need further assistance with proper latching on and proper positioning to avoid maximum sucking pressure on the sore spot. A lactation consultant can best evaluate your situation and offer advice and suggestions.

If you are nursing twins, each baby should get one breast per feeding. You may want to alter which baby gets a particular breast at each feeding in case one breast produces more milk than the other.

How Do I Get My Baby to Begin Sucking Again If She Stops?

First, remember that babies will naturally take pauses to rest and take extra breaths. Be patient. Pat your baby's back gently or try other forms of gentle stimulation such as talking. If she does not resume sucking, **try these three techniques to stimulate her:**

1. Reach under the chin (avoiding the cheek). The bone under the chin forms a V shape. Move one finger off and behind this bone into the soft tissue and do a deep circular massage (Figure 16-19). This will usually cause sucking to resume.
2. Move your nipple around in your baby's mouth. If your baby thinks you are going to pull the nipple away, she will usually get the

FIGURE   16-19

Stimulate your baby to resume nursing by deep circular massage under the chin.

idea! This technique works best after a few successful feedings; in the beginning, your baby may not yet have learned what your breast delivers and therefore will not care much whether you take it away or not!

3. Unwrap your baby and flick her feet or rub her back. Breastfeeding is close, warm, and comfortable! Sometimes it takes being unwrapped and stimulated to get your baby going.

Oftentimes a nurse succeeds with the third technique when the parents have not, because nurses are more vigorous in unwrapping the baby, rubbing the baby's back, moving her around, and tapping or gently flicking those tiny feet! The goal is to wake your baby up! (If your child was 16, would you tiptoe into her room, very gently lay your hand on her head, and quietly whisper, "Sweetheart, the school bus will be here in five minutes?" This is the same principle, just a different stage in life!)

Now, after telling you to give it your best shot to wake your baby up to complete a feeding, I will counter with this: **Remember to allow your baby to be your guide. If stimulation does not succeed in waking her, then assume that she is full! Your baby is telling you the best and only way that she can that she is not hungry now. Wait until you see signs of readiness to feed (unless jaundice or illness is present, in which case you should report poor feedings to your pediatrician).**

Will My Breastfed Baby Need to Burp?

Breastfed babies seldom swallow much air while nursing. Therefore, the amount of "bubbling" or burping necessary is much less than for a bottle-fed baby. However, the need to burp after nursing is very variable.

It is a good idea to attempt to burp your baby between breasts if you are using both breasts at each feeding. When you are beginning breastfeeding, you may also want to try to burp her after the second breast.

If your baby does not commonly burp after nursing and is asleep after nursing from the second breast, you may put her down to sleep without burping. If she fusses within the first 20 minutes after being put down (pulls her legs up or cries), burp her and go back to burping after feedings for a while longer. It is a trial-and-error learning process as you get to know your baby's unique needs.

Once your milk is in and engorgement has passed, and if you have chosen to nurse from one breast per feeding, burp your baby after 25 or 30 minutes or when the baby indicates that the feeding is over.

See pages 309–311 for a description and illustrations of burping positions.

Does My Baby Need Additional Water?

No, it is not necessary and not recommended to give additional water to your breastfed baby, unless your doctor tells you to do so. Breast milk has all the water necessary to meet her normal daily fluid requirements.

How Can I Prevent Sore Nipples?

Prevention is the key word here! **The two most important points in prevention of sore nipples are proper latching on and rotating positions with each feeding.**

Proper Latching On: Be certain the areola is well within your baby's mouth. Refer to the section "Latching on Correctly," pages 267–270. Once your baby is latched on, support your arm with pillows or towel rolls to keep her close–do not allow her to work her way off to sucking directly on the erect part of the nipple only. Also do not allow your baby to turn her head to one side and thus tug and pull at the nipple at an angle.

Mild tenderness of the nipples is normal in the first five days of nursing. After that, if soreness occurs at any feeding, remove your baby

Baby Care

from the nipple and latch on again. If your baby is latched on properly, nursing should not be uncomfortable.

Rotate Positions with Each Feeding: Rotating positions places the maximum sucking pressure on different parts of the nipple at each feeding. Refer to "Breastfeeding Positions" on pages 270–276.

Other Important Ways to Prevent Sore Nipples

❑ **Express a drop of colostrum or breast milk and rub it into your nipple and areola.**

❑ **Wear a supportive nursing bra and keep the bra flaps open.** Keeping the flaps closed holds warmth and moisture next to your nipples, which can promote soreness.

❑ **Release the suction before you remove your baby from your breast.** Place your clean finger into the corner of your baby's mouth between her jaws. You will feel or hear the suction break. Pulling your baby off your nipple before breaking the suction is painful and can cause immediate soreness.

❑ **Do not allow your baby to sleep for long periods while latched on to your breast.** Babies often suck as they sleep. This intermittent sucking on the same spot of your nipple can lead to a tender or sore blistered area.

❑ **Limiting time at the breast has not been shown to prevent sore nipples.** Babies need to be satisfied when fed. If they become too hungry, they may nurse frantically and tug or pull on the nipple. This frantic improper suck may cause sore nipples and a poor feeding and can set up a vicious cycle of inadequate feedings, a frantic baby, sore nipples, and a mother frustrated with a frequent nursing schedule.

❑ **Do not wash your nipples with strong soaps.** Water is all you need to wash your nipples during your daily bath or shower.

❑ **Wear cotton clothing and cotton night-gowns.** Cotton fabric breathes and absorbs moisture if your nipples leak.

❑ **Do not use bra pads.** If you are going out and are concerned about leaking, bra pads can be worn for short periods of time *if* your nipples are not sore or cracked. Wearing a damp pad next to sore, cracked nipples is not recommended. Soft cotton handkerchiefs, cut to smaller size, can be used as a bra pad substitute when necessary. (Remember, you can stop the milk let-down reflex by pressing in on your nipples with your forearms, which should stop the leaking.)

What Should I Do If My Nipples Are Sore, Blistered, Cracked, or Bleeding?

Mild tenderness of the nipples in the first five days of breastfeeding is normal, but soreness beyond day five indicates a latching on problem. If you are experiencing more than *mild* discomfort during the first five days, you need prompt assistance.

*C***As soon as you see evidence of a developing problem with soreness, seek the advice and assistance of a lactation consultant.** (See "How Do I Reach a Lactation Consultant if I Need Assistance?" on page 290.) These individuals are specially trained to deal with specific problems. In most cases, they can successfully see you through this difficulty.

"Lansinoh" purified lanolin is being recommended by The Nursing Mothers' Council and the La Leche League for the treatment of cracked nipples. This lanolin is not only purified; it has had the alcohol removed. You do not have to wash Lansinoh off your nipples before feedings. If you cannot purchase or order Lansinoh at your drugstore, it is available through The Nursing Mothers' Council and the La Leche League, both of which are listed in phone books.

Do not stop nursing entirely on the blistered or cracked nipple. Doing so puts you at greater risk of breast infection. If your breast consultant feels that one nipple needs rest from nursing, she may provide you with a Madella electric breast pump to use on the breast you are temporarily not using for nursing. This pump has a cycle gentle enough to not irritate a sore, cracked nipple. **Your sore breast must continue to receive stimulation and be emptied in order to continue milk production and to prevent breast infection.**

Nurse on the side that is least sore first. Express a little milk before beginning, to stimulate the let-down reflex. Massage your breasts while nursing to stimulate the milk flow. Use deep breathing and relaxation music to help you relax while breastfeeding.

Use breast shields ("cuppies") for comfort and protection. Breast shields come not only with the piece to help "pull out" flat nipples, they also come with a piece for sore nipples. Wearing these keeps clothing off and away from the sore and tender nipple.

When using cuppies for treatment of sore nipples, attach the piece with the large hole to the vented dome (Figure 16-20). This opening should be large enough for your entire areola to fit through.

How Do I Know If I Have Flat or Inverted Nipples?

See page 84 in Chapter 5, "Prenatal Monitoring," for how to evaluate your nipples. Nipple assessment should be part of routine prenatal care. Figure 16-21A shows an inverted nipple retracting when the area around the areola is pinched.

Can I Nurse with Flat or Inverted Nipples?

Many women with flat or inverted nipples successfully breastfeed. If you have a strong desire to nurse and you seek assistance if needed, your chances of breastfeeding successfully are increased.

The best treatment for a flat or inverted nipple is the use of breast shields or shells, called "cuppies," designed specifically to draw the nipple out.

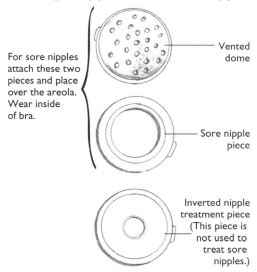

FIGURE 16-20

Using Cuppies for Sore Nipples

For sore nipples attach these two pieces and place over the areola. Wear inside of bra.

Vented dome

Sore nipple piece

Inverted nipple treatment piece (This piece is not used to treat sore nipples.)

Until recently it was recommended that you wear them as many hours as possible; however, this can lead to nipple irritation. **New research indicates that it is best to wear cuppies for half an hour prior to feeding and remove each individual shield just before putting the baby to breast on that side.** If you do not have cuppies when you come to the hospital, your nurse will provide them. It may also be helpful to use a battery operated or electric pump to help pull your nipple out before each feeding.

A breast shield, or cuppy, is a vented, two-piece, plastic device. When purchased, the unit comes with six pieces: two vented domes, two small-hole bottom pieces for treatment of inverted nipples, and two larger-hole bottom pieces used for the treatment of sore nipples. Figure 5-6, page 85, shows the pieces used for the treatment of inverted nipples. When these two pieces are snapped together and put over your nipple inside your bra, they both pull your nipple out and keep your bra off of it.

Wash and air dry your cuppies frequently, and discard all breast milk that leaks into them. Use only well-vented cuppies.

Baby Care

FIGURE 16-21A

An inverted nipple retracts when the area around the areola is pinched.

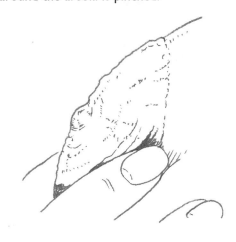

FIGURE 16-21B

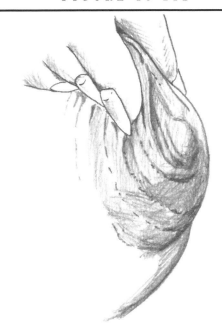

An inverted nipple may protrude somewhat if the outer skin is held and gently pulled at an angle.

Research has shown that most women with inverted nipples have adhesions behind the nipple that pull it in even farther when the area behind or on the areola is compressed for latching on. However, this same nipple may protrude somewhat if just the outer skin is held and gently pulled at an angle (Figure 16-21B). In this alternative technique for latching on with inverted nipples, you are actually holding the part of the areola that goes into the baby's mouth. Women with inverted nipples should try this technique for putting the nipple into the baby's mouth for latching on. Please ask a lactation consultant for assistance.

How Do I Reach a Lactation Consultant If I Need Assistance?

If you are still in the hospital, ask your nurse if there is a lactation consultant on staff. If not, most maternity units provide their patients with resource material before discharge, which should include the names and phone numbers of lactation consultants in the surrounding area. If you did not receive this material, look in your phone book under lactation consultants, breastfeeding consultants, La Leche League, or Nursing Mothers' Council.

Call your maternity care practitioner's office for referral information and phone numbers. If your area has an "ASK A NURSE" telephone service, they may be able to tell you how to reach a local lactation consultant.

Will I Need a Breast Pump?

The answer to this question will depend on your particular circumstances. If you are not planning to return to work or are planning to nurse for only a short period of time, you will probably not need to invest in a breast pump.

If you would like your husband or others to be able to feed your baby, a breast pump would be convenient. It would also be beneficial if you have inverted nipples, because it helps pull the nipple out before you begin a feeding.

See pages 292–297 for instructions on using breast pumps and pumping at work.

Supplemental Feedings

Adding Formula to Breastfeeding

There are special circumstances in which your pediatrician asks that a baby receive formula after each nursing. The most common reason is that the baby's blood sugar is very unstable and continually drops below safe levels, which can happen in premature babies, babies born to diabetic or gestational diabetic mothers, and in babies born at over nine pounds or under five and one-half pounds. This is a temporary treatment until the baby's blood sugar stabilizes. **Please follow your pediatrician's instructions to supplement with formula in special situations.**

Sometimes, when a breastfed baby is not gaining adequate weight, the pediatrician requests that each nursing session be followed by giving formula. This is not very common, but when it occurs, it is important to follow your pediatrician's advice. An additional suggestion for treating insufficient weight gain comes out of breastfeeding research: the newest studies indicate that nursing from only one breast at each feeding provides your infant with six to eight times more calories from the extra-rich hind milk than is contained in the fore milk (the initial milk secreted at each feeding when your milk lets down). Fore milk is higher in protein; hind milk is higher in fat and therefore higher in calories. Thus, if your breastfeeding baby is not gaining what your pediatrician considers a normal amount of weight at the proper rate, you may want to consider nursing from only one breast per feeding. Allowing the full 20- to 30-minute (or more) feeding on one breast gives the baby more hind milk, with its added fat and calories.

The remainder of this discussion is about supplementing breast milk with formula *by personal choice* for various reasons. **Again, it is important to understand and follow your pediatrician's instructions if told to supplement for a medical reason.**

It is best, of course, to avoid all supplemental feedings while you are beginning breastfeeding. It takes time for your breasts to build up their milk supply. If at all possible, wait at least three to four weeks before giving any supplemental feeding. Some professionals will recommend that you wait until your baby is two or three months old before offering supplements.

Once your breast milk is well established, you may personally choose to supplement with formula. However, you need to be aware that **sucking on a bottle is a different type of sucking than sucking on the breast and that nipple confusion may result.** In addition to nipple confusion, some babies rapidly develop a preference for the taste of formula, making it a struggle to return to breastfeeding.

Breast milk production is a supply-and-demand system. When you offer formula to your infant, your breasts do not "hear" that demand (or signal) from your baby for more volume, so your breast milk production does not increase. If you give formula during the initial few weeks of nursing, you will produce less breast milk. This sets up a catch-22. Because the breasts did not get the signal to produce more milk on the day the supplement was given, the next day the baby won't get more breast milk and may be fussy and again want more. If you keep giving formula, your breast milk volume will not increase to meet your baby's demand. When your baby is crying frantically in the middle of the night, you are trapped—you reach for formula again. The only way to stop this cycle is to nurse more frequently or pump between feedings until your supply reaches your baby's demand. If you want to succeed at breastfeeding, prevent this catch-22: don't offer supplements until your breast milk is well established.

Nipple Confusion

When supplemental feedings are started too early, *nipple confusion* can occur. Obtaining milk from a bottle is done with an easier and different sucking motion. The baby receives immediate gratification from the bottle and may show frustration when she then has to work harder at the breast.

Adding Solid Foods and Vitamin Supplements

Breast milk is considered the perfect food for the healthy full-term infant, at least for the first six months of life. Adding solid foods before this point will reduce your milk supply, and they are more likely to cause allergies. Please refer to pages 320–321 when your pediatrician does recommend the introduction of solid foods.

If you get adequate vitamins from your diet, with or without vitamin supplements, your baby will receive adequate vitamins in your breast milk. Your physician may suggest that you continue your prenatal vitamins while nursing.

Your pediatrician will discuss with you his or her feelings about vitamin and fluoride supplements for your baby.

Pumping Your Breasts

Breast pumping has many purposes:

❑ If your baby is premature or if nursing is delayed due to respiratory distress or other illness in your infant, your breasts will need to be pumped in order to receive the stimulation necessary to begin milk production.

❑ When you want to nurse but it is not possible due to special circumstances, you need to begin pumping within six hours after delivery. This ensures prompt stimulation of breast milk production. If properly pumped and stored, your breast milk can be used either for tube feedings (gavage feedings) or bottle feedings until nursing is possible.

❑ Pumping can be used to stimulate or maintain breast milk production when the mother is ill, temporarily unable to nurse, or temporarily on medication that is contraindicated when breastfeeding.

❑ Pumping can be used to relieve engorgement.

❑ Pumping is commonly used to help pull out a flat or inverted nipple before beginning a feeding.

❑ It can be used when added breast stimulation is needed to increase the milk supply (above what the baby has been able to do through added and longer nursings).

❑ Pumping allows the convenience of storing breast milk so that someone else can feed the infant.

❑ Pumping is necessary if a mother wants to continue nursing after returning to work. In this instance, pumping provides breast milk to be stored for later use and also provides relief from the engorgement that occurs when you suddenly skip feedings.

When to Begin Pumping

If you are nursing, it is best to wait three or four weeks before starting pumping, if possible. This allows your breasts time to get milk production well established and to meet the quantity demands of your baby before pumping begins. However, if you are going back to work, you may need to begin pumping sooner.

Manual Expression of Breast Milk

It is possible to manually express breast milk. You may choose manual expression if you are pumping only occasionally or temporarily or if you are pumping often but wish to avoid purchasing a pump. To manually express breast milk:

1. Wash your hands.

2. Always collect your breast milk in a thoroughly washed, rinsed, and air-dried bottle, or one washed in the dishwasher.

3. Before you begin, massage your breast from the outside downward in all four quadrants. (Follow the arrows in Figure 16-22A.) Next, massage around the areola in small circles.

4. Position your thumb above the nipple and two fingers below the nipple, behind the areola.

5. Push straight back into the breast tissue, then gently press your fingers together (compressing the milk ducts) and then bring your fingers forward toward the nipple. (See Figure 16-22B.) Fingers and thumb should move together. **Do not squeeze the breast or pull on the nipple.**

6. After completing these steps, rotate your thumb and index finger about one-fourth to one-half of an inch and repeat steps 4 and 5. Continue rotating your fingers around the areola until you have emptied all quadrants of the breast and therefore all of the milk ducts.

Types of Breast Pumps

There are three types of breast pumps: manual, battery operated, and electric. The pump that you choose should be easy and comfortable to use, efficient, affordable, and easy to clean. Many brands are available, and most large drugstores, maternity stores, discount department stores, and toy stores carry them.

Manual pumps are generally the least expensive, but they are practical only if you occasionally may want to pump your breasts, because they are tiring, time-consuming, and often awkward to use. They contain a manual plunger, like a syringe (Figure 16-23), or a bulb that is compressed to manually create suction. I suggest that you avoid the bulb style if possible. The baby's natural sucking motion is difficult to simulate with manual pumps. Read the directions before purchasing.

FIGURE 16-22A

Massaging the Breast Before Manual Pumping

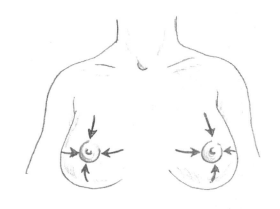

FIGURE 16-22B

Manual Expression of Breast Milk

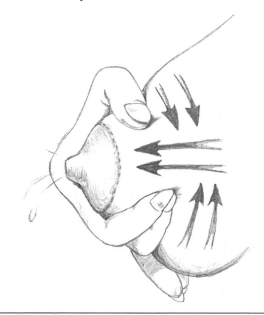

Baby Care

Battery-operated pumps are less expensive than electric pumps. They have a rhythmic suction that simulates an infant's sucking pattern. They are portable and can therefore be taken with you to work, but the batteries have to be replaced frequently. Look for a brand that allows the pressure to be adjusted for comfort. AC adapters are another nice option. Ask a lactation consultant from your area, or the nurses on your maternity unit, which brands available in your area have a reputation for patient satisfaction.

Electric pumps (Figure 16-24) can be rented or purchased in most large cities. They, too, have a rhythmic pumping that simulates a baby's sucking. They tend to be the most efficient and gentle pumps for long-term and frequent use. Some brands are small enough to be portable, and some have a double setup for pumping both breasts at once if time is limited.

Most maternity hospitals will provide you with information on electric breast pump rentals in your area. If this information is not available at your hospital, consult your obstetrician or pediatrician's nursing staff. The La Leche League, whose phone number can be found in most area phone books, will also have breast pump rental information available.

At What Time of Day Is It Best to Pump?

If you are unable to nurse immediately after giving birth, begin pumping within six hours if possible. This early breast stimulation is important for activating the receptors in the brain that trigger the breasts to begin milk production. Do not expect more than a few drops when you begin pumping soon after birth.

Once your milk comes in, pumping can be done before, during, or after feedings—experiment to see what timing schedule brings the most milk for you. Morning is generally a good time to obtain extra milk by pumping. Pumping after or between feedings usually works best be-

cause it assures that your baby receives the volume she demands before milk is obtained by pumping.

If you are working outside the home, you will need to pump on a schedule as close to your regular nursing pattern as possible; this will help prevent uncomfortable engorgement.

FIGURE 16-23

Plunger Type of Manual Breast Pump

FIGURE 16-24

Electric Breast Pump

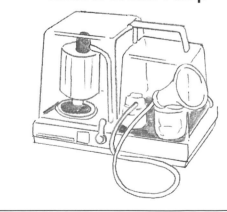

How to Use a Breast Pump

Read all the instructions on the use and cleaning of your pump before you use it. Wash the washable parts of the pump and wash your hands before you pump your breasts.

Use inserts (flanges of different sizes) provided with your pump to create a good fit between your nipple and the pump. If your breasts are small, you will need to use an insert in order to create suction. You may find that wetting your areola with a small amount of water helps maintain contact between your areola and the flange.

Place the erect part of your nipple directly into the opening on the flange. Always begin pumping with the lowest suction pressure available on your pump, and increase the pressure slowly. At no time should the suction be high enough to cause pain. Check your nipple to be certain it is centered in the flange and not being tugged against one side of it. Use the lowest suction that gets the milk flowing at a good rate. Massage your breasts on all four sides during pumping to help stimulate the let-down reflex.

Be certain to store your breast milk properly. (See "Proper Storage of Breast Milk," below.)

Wash and air dry all washable parts of the pump immediately after use. Certain parts of the tubing and filter system that do not touch milk cannot be washed. The parts that fit over your breast and come into contact with the breast milk may include a small filter that should be washed after feedings but must air dry before the pump is used again. Carefully follow the manufacturer's instructions with your unit for washing.

How Long Should Pumping Take?

Pumping time will vary depending on the type of pump used. Manual expression takes longer than battery or electric pumps. If your time is limited, an electric pump that can be used on both breasts at the same time is helpful.

Before your milk comes in, if your baby is unable to nurse for some reason, pump one breast at a time for five minutes, alternating every five minutes until both breasts have been pumped for 15 minutes each. Repeat every three hours while you are awake.

In general, once your milk comes in, if you must skip a feeding or your baby is unable to nurse for some reason, pump as long as you would expect your baby to nurse at that time. However, building up to a maximum of 10 to 15 minutes on each breast will usually be adequate. You should stop when the milk flow slows or stops. **Babies are able to obtain more milk by sucking than any pump. The amount of milk obtained by pumping is less than half the volume of what an infant would obtain if at breast.**

Proper Storage of Breast Milk

Human breast milk can be safely stored at room temperature for 6 to 10 hours because it has the ability to slow the growth of bacteria. It can be refrigerated for three to five days and can also be frozen for later use; however, as with any food, some nutritional value is lost in the freezing process. Fresh breast milk is always best. Breast milk can be frozen for only two weeks if you have a small freezer compartment inside your refrigerator. If your refrigerator has a freezer with a separate door above, below, or alongside the refrigerator section, breast milk can be kept there for as long as four months, even if the door is opened frequently. It is recommended, however, that you place the breast milk in the far rear section of the freezer. In a stand-alone freezer that maintains a constant temperature of 0°F, frozen milk can be stored for six months. Once the milk is thawed, however, it cannot be refrozen.

If you are collecting breast milk for a hospitalized baby, consult the nurse for any special precautions you must follow. Some hospitals provide sterile bottles for milk collection and storage.

Baby Care

When collecting breast milk, be sure to use bottles that have been thoroughly cleaned. You can sterilize bottles, caps, and bottle rings in the dishwasher on the hot setting or wash them in hot soapy water and rinse well. Either method is acceptable for collection, storage, and freezing of breast milk.

To freeze breast milk, follow these instructions carefully. The first supply, collected in a clean or sterilized bottle, with or without a nurser bag, can be labeled, dated, and placed directly in the freezer. **Before you add additional breast milk to this container to increase its volume, it must be cooled to refrigerator temperature.** Breast milk is at body temperature when obtained, and if added directly to the freezer supply it would cause thawing of the top layer of the frozen breast milk and therefore increase the potential of bacterial growth.

In addition to cooling the breast milk to refrigerator temperature, it is recommended that you add a smaller volume than the amount already frozen in that bottle or bag. This is another precaution to prevent thawing. When filling containers for freezing, allow room at the top of the container for expansion. Do not tighten caps until after the milk is completely frozen.

If you choose to use plastic nurser bags for breast milk storage, use double bags, both to prevent tearing and to protect against split seams on the inner bag. Squeeze out the air, fold the top of the bags down to within one inch of the milk, and tape closed. Store in the refrigerator or place in the *back* of your freezer. Set the bags in a container that holds them upright.

Either plastic or glass bottles can be used to store breast milk in the refrigerator or freezer. You will notice that the fat in the breast milk sticks to the sides of a bottle as it freezes and thaws. After thawing the milk, swirl the bottle well until the fat is mixed back into it.

If you work away from home and there is no refrigerator in which to store your breast milk, use a thermos or a small cooler. Put ice into the thermos in the morning to cool it, and then pour out the ice and add your breast milk as you collect it. If using a small cooler, you can keep ice packs in it and add containers of breast milk throughout the day.

To thaw your breast milk, follow these instructions. Breast milk should be thawed quickly under running water, beginning with cold water and gradually warming the water until the milk is warm. It should not be thawed at room temperature or on the stove or in a microwave oven. The microwave is not recommended because of uneven heating; the outside of the bottle may feel cool even though some milk inside may be scalding.

Loosen the cap and leave it on the bottle while warming the milk. Put the nipple on *after* warming–nipples expand when warmed, and the expansion could close off the hole, making it difficult for your baby to suck milk through it.

Breast milk separates when it stands for a while. Swirl it gently to mix before feeding your baby.

Returning to Work and Its Effect on Breastfeeding

You probably did some planning ahead for this big day while you were pregnant (as suggested on page 38). If you want to continue breastfeeding after you return to work, it certainly can be done, and it is being done by many women. If you do not plan to continue breastfeeding, you need to plan to wean your baby before you return to work.

Many women who continue to breastfeed after returning to work say that the special closeness of breastfeeding helps compensate for the time they must spend away from their baby.

Studies by Kathleen Auerbach, a lactation consultant and La Leche League leader, have shown that how soon a mother returns to work has more effect on the course of nursing than the numbers of hours she works. The mothers in

Auerbach's study who waited until 16 weeks after birth to return to work continued to nurse longer than those who returned to work prior to 16 weeks. These findings were attributed to the fact that mothers who have breastfed for 16 weeks are experienced and comfortable with nursing and their milk supply is well established by this time. The number of hours worked also does influence how long the mother continues to nurse. More of the women in the study who worked part-time continued to nurse for one year, longer than did those who worked full-time.

Pumping is another important factor in continuing to breastfeed successfully after returning to working. Mothers in Auerbach's study who pumped their breasts on a regular basis when away at work continued to nurse longer than those who did not pump. In addition, they experienced less engorgement, less leaking from their breasts, and fewer plugged ducts and breast infections.

It is best to pump your breasts every three hours when you are away from your baby or otherwise unable to nurse. See page 39 for other suggestions about nursing and the workplace.

Your determination to continue nursing and your dedication to the importance of breastfeeding both affect your success with nursing after returning to work. As suggested in Chapter 2, "Living Healthy During Pregnancy and Beyond," it is important to negotiate returning to work gradually after taking your full maternity leave and additional vacation time if possible. (Remember that statistics show that your chance of successfully continuing to breastfeed increase if you wait until after 16 weeks to return to work.) When you do return, a gradual reentry over several days is easier on you, your baby, and your breasts. Work part-time as long as possible and gradually increase your hours if your employer allows.

Be an advocate for yourself, your baby, breastfeeding, and working women in general. Seek to make changes in the workplace that put babies, families, and breastfeeding high on the priority list.

During pregnancy it was suggested that you purchase clothes that make pumping easier once you return to work. For example, a one-piece dress that opens in the back is not practical for pumping. You will need blouses or dresses that open in the front and a good supply of nursing bras and breast pads (to help prevent staining your clothes if your breasts leak). In addition, you will need a breast pump and a cooler for storage and transport of the breast milk.

Before purchasing a breast pump, be sure to explore your work environment to be sure there is a private area where you can use it. Also, before you buy an electrical pump, be sure to check for electrical outlets in the area where you plan to use it. **Consider purchasing a pump with a double set-up feature (allowing both breasts to be pumped at once) for added convenience and efficiency.**

Refer to the earlier sections of this chapter on pumping your breasts and safe storage of breast milk.

Giving Breast Milk from a Bottle

Many babies become upset if their mother tries to give them breast milk from a bottle but accept it from someone else, so it is usually best to have someone other than the mother give the first bottle feeding.

Weaning from Breast to Cup or Breast to Bottle

Weaning is the transition time when you decrease breastfeeding and introduce a bottle or cup in its place. There is no right or wrong time to wean your baby. Weaning can be initiated by the baby

Baby Care

who suddenly shows less interest in nursing or by the mother who wants to stop for any number of reasons. In addition, weaning may also be necessary due to a mother's illness, illness treatment (including medication not compatible with nursing), or changing job situation.

If your baby is younger than seven months, a bottle can be substituted for a nursing for one feeding during the day. Either breast milk or formula can be offered in the bottle for weaning. Some mothers find that the baby tolerates weaning to formula more easily if it is mixed half and half with breast milk. As mentioned earlier, babies will more readily accept a bottle from someone other than the mother because she reminds them of nursing.

If your baby is old enough to drink from a cup, usually around seven months, weaning can be done slowly, substituting a cup feeding for nursing at one feeding during the day. Either breast milk or formula can be offered in the cup. Once your baby is one year old, your pediatrician will likely allow you to offer her regular cow's milk.

Formula is generally used for weaning until 9 to 12 months of age, depending on your pediatrician and your allergy history. After this time, whole milk is allowed. **Consult your pediatrician before using whole milk to wean your baby; he or she knows your baby and the family allergy history and is therefore the best person to advise you as to what you should offer during the weaning process.**

If it is possible, weaning should be done slowly over weeks or months. This makes the process and transition easier for your baby and less uncomfortable for you. If nursing is stopped abruptly, or several feedings eliminated rapidly, painful engorgement will be a problem for you, and the sudden change may also be traumatic and difficult for your baby.

To begin weaning, choose one feeding per day. Do not begin with the first or the bedtime feeding. Your baby is extra hungry for the morning feeding and will be less willing to accept change at that time. Likewise, the bedtime nursing is a special time that helps to relax your baby and help her sleep. For most mothers, this is the last nursing time to be eliminated.

Remember that the older child often nurses for comfort; therefore she may not require a formula or milk feeding for every nursing time skipped, but she will require extra love, hugs, and attention for the closeness she will be missing.

If you do not need to wean quickly, it is best to skip only one nursing feeding until your breasts no longer feel full when the skip occurs and your baby does not seem to miss the breast-feeding. When you are both comfortable with the change, another nursing feeding can be eliminated.

17

Bottle Feeding and Adding Solid Foods

If you have chosen to bottle feed, your pediatrician will advise you on the formula she or he feels is best for your baby. Of course, you may indicate a preference if you have used a particular brand successfully in the past. Consult your chosen pediatrician on this subject prior to delivery—you will want to plan ahead and have supplies ready at home before the arrival of your baby.

If you are delivering at a hospital where your pediatrician does not have visiting privileges, a temporary pediatrician will be assigned to your baby. Be sure to inform the nursery of your formula choice immediately after birth. Otherwise, the standard formula of the temporary pediatrician will be started. It would not be a disaster to have to change formulas when you go home, but this switch can be avoided with preparation and communication.

In the past, people made formula with evaporated milk, corn syrup, and water. However, *you would never give your baby formula made from evaporated milk today.* It is no longer recommended because it does not meet the nutritional needs of infants.

Forms of Commercial Formula

Infant formula comes in three forms: ready-to-use liquid, concentrated liquid, and powder. **Always check the expiration date on the cans before purchasing and before opening them. In addition, once you have opened a can, label it with the date and time and follow the instructions on the can for storage and the**

299

length of time the formula can be used after the can has been opened.

Always be certain of the type of formula you have before preparing a bottle. It would be dangerous to give your baby concentrated formula without adding water, and adding water to ready-to-use formula would make it nutritionally deficient. You must know what you have and follow the directions carefully.

Prepared formulas without iron are available, but formulas with iron are generally recommended. Ask your pediatrician which formula brand he or she recommends and whether you should purchase the formula with or without added iron.

Ready-to-Use Liquid

You get a 24-hour supply of ready-to-use formula in a can, with no mixing required. Some companies also sell ready-to-use formula in individual eight-ounce cans or bottles, which are very expensive. They are, however, a nice convenience when you are away from home and chilling and warming of formula is a problem.

You would end up wasting a lot if you bought the 24-hour supply for a newborn, because a new baby cannot consume this volume in the time allowed after opening the can. If your water quality is an issue, though, ready-to-use formula is a good option.

Concentrated Liquid

Water must be added to concentrated liquid formula. The usual instructions require equal amounts of formula and water, but check your brand for specific instructions on the can or bottle. Although this usually costs slightly less than ready-to-use formula, there would still be waste if you use this for a newborn. Again, a new baby cannot consume a whole can in the time allowed after opening the can.

Powdered Formula

Water must be added to powdered formula, which comes with a scoop in the can. Most powdered formulas call for one unpacked scoop of formula per two ounces of water—check specific mixing instructions on the can.

Powdered formula has the same nutritional value as the ready-to-use and concentrated liquid forms, and it is especially convenient when you are traveling or shopping. Before leaving home, add water to a bottle that has been sterilized in the dishwasher or properly washed by hand. The water will come to room temperature, and the formula powder can be added at feeding time. Nothing needs to be kept chilled or warmed.

Powdered formula tends to be the least expensive formula. For a newborn, there is no waste when only small volumes are needed, and the powder has a longer shelf life than an open can of liquid formula.

Milk-Based Formulas

Prepared baby formulas are commonly made from cow's milk. To make them more like breast milk, the protein and salt content are reduced and lactose (milk sugar) is added to increase the sugar content. The butterfat is removed and replaced with vegetable oils, and vitamins A, C, and D are added.

Regular cow's milk should not be given to an infant, because an infant's digestive tract is not mature enough to handle cow's milk.

Milk-based formulas that are available in all three forms (ready-to-use, concentrated, and powder) include (in alphabetical order) Enfamil, Similac, and SMA. Carnation Good Start is also available in powder form, and Gerber Formula in concentrated form with or without iron.

Ready-to-use, milk-based formula must be refrigerated after being opened and must be used within 24 hours, whereas most concentrated milk-based formulas will last up to 48 hours after opening the can. Milk-based powdered formula, once mixed, must be used within 48 hours. Most powdered formulas can be kept in the covered can for one month after opening it.

Soy Formulas

Soy formulas are for babies who have a strong family history of allergies or who develop problems with regular milk-based formula. They use soy as their protein base and are milk-free and lactose-free. Do not begin with a soy formula unless your pediatrician instructs you to, and consult your pediatrician before switching to a soy formula.

Common nonmilk formulas with a soybean protein base include (in alphabetical order) Isomil, Nursoy, and ProSobee. Your pediatrician may recommend one of these if you have a strong family history of milk allergies or your baby did not tolerate regular baby formula well. Soy formulas come in ready-to-feed, concentrated, and powder forms. The instructions vary by brand as to whether the mixed bottle should be used within 24 or 48 hours. Follow your brand's instructions carefully.

Formula intolerance is manifested by stomach or intestinal symptoms, which may include frequent spitting up, stomach aches, excessive gas expelled both orally and rectally, fussiness, and pulling the knees up due to the discomfort. Allergy to a formula includes these symptoms and may also include all the symptoms of a true allergic reaction, such as a rash and wheezing.

If you had a previous baby who developed an intolerance or even a true allergic reaction to regular milk-based formula, most pediatricians will still suggest that you start your next baby on regular formula. They do not believe that you should assume an intolerance or allergy to milk-based formula. Other pediatricians will recommend that you begin with a soy formula if a real allergic reaction to regular formula occurred with a previous child. Under these conditions, some pediatricians will involve you in choosing a formula type.

Special Formulas

For babies with protein or lactose intolerance, special formulas are available. Do not begin with one of these formulas unless instructed to do so by your pediatrician. Also, please consult your pediatrician before switching to one of these special formulas.

In my research for this chapter, I found the following brands to be the most commonly available special-circumstance formulas. They are listed here in alphabetical order, with the description given on the side of the can.

Alimentum: Alimentum is a protein hydrolysate formula with iron, advertised as easy to digest. It is a hypoallergenic formula used for babies with protein sensitivity, food allergies, colic, and problems with digestion or fat absorption. It is available only in ready-to-use form in both quart and eight-ounce cans.

LactoFree: This is a milk-based, lactose-free formula, available in ready-to-use, concentrated, and powder forms. It is for babies with fussiness, gas, and diarrhea caused by a lactose sensitivity.

Nutramigen: Nutramigen is for babies with colic symptoms and other symptoms of protein allergies. It is hypoallergenic and lactose-free and is advertised as easy to digest. It is available in ready-to-use, concentrated, and powder forms.

Pregestimil: This is a hypoallergenic formula for protein allergies. It is lactose- and sucrose-free. This formula may be *ordered by a pediatrician* to feed infants and children with severe or intractable diarrhea, severe fat malabsorption, or cystic fibrosis. It is available in powder only.

Electrolyte Replacement Water for Babies

Be aware that these commercially bottled electrolyte waters for babies are for replacement of electrolytes lost through vomiting and diarrhea only. **You should not use electrolyte replacement water for the water in formula preparation unless directed to do so by your pediatrician.**

Electrolyte water is on the emergency medicine supply list to have on hand at all times (see Box 18-3, pages 328–329). When your baby has vomiting or diarrhea, your pediatrician may recommend this water until the severe vomiting or diarrhea has ended or been brought under control.

Keep a can on hand and replace it before it expires. You will be glad to have it if your pediatrician recommends it in the middle of the night. (Also follow storage and expiration instructions once the can has been opened.)

Common brand names in alphabetical order are Infalyte, Pedialyte (which also comes in freezer-pop form), Pediatric Electrolyte, and RevitalICE.

Opening and Storing Formula Cans

Always wash your hands before preparing a feeding or handling equipment that is used to prepare feedings. Proper technique should be followed in opening formula cans in order not to introduce contaminants (germs). Always wash the tops of cans with soap and water and rinse them well under running water before opening them. For ready-to-use and concentrated formula, shake well before opening or pouring. Use a clean pointed can opener to punch one full opening on the top of the can. Directly across from this opening, punch another, smaller hole for air to enter the can while you pour.

Cover the can with plastic wrap or a plastic cover sold to fit formula cans. If using a plastic cover, be sure it also is washed and rinsed well for each new can you use it on.

Store unused formula covered in the refrigerator. **Use within the time limits indicated on the can.** Some instructions say 24 hours, others 48 hours.

In the first few weeks, when your baby is eating small amounts, mark the date and time the can is opened on the side of each can. This will help remind you to throw away unused formula at the correct time. Eventually your baby will be taking the full amount in a one-day-supply can, and waste will not be such an issue. To avoid waste in the early weeks, use powdered formula, which can be mixed in small volumes.

Never use a formula that has been accidentally frozen or one that shows sediment or streaks after shaking. Unopened cans should be stored between 45° and 90°F. Refrigerate after opening. **When in doubt, throw it out!**

Powdered formulas should be covered with the lid provided and stored in a cool, dry place. Write the date that you open it on the side of each can. It is recommended that powdered formulas be used within a month after opening.

Warming Bottles

Bottles can be warmed by placing them in a few inches of warm water and shaking the formula occasionally for even warming. A commercially available bottle warmer can also be used. There are even bottle warmers available with adapters to use in the lighter outlet of your car. **Never heat bottles in a microwave.** The formula can become hot enough to cause severe burns to the mouth and esophagus (food tube), even when the outside of the bottle feels cool.

Before feeding your baby, test the formula temperature by shaking a few drops on your inner wrist. If it is at the right temperature, it should feel neutral (neither hot nor cold).

It is important to note that formula does not have to be warmed. **Babies get used to whatever they are served.** However, they do like consistency—if you usually warm a bottle and suddenly serve one cold, your baby will react. Likewise, if you normally give the bottle at room temperature or cold and one time decide to warm the bottle, he won't like that either!

Leftover Formula

Bacteria can grow very quickly in formula left over in the bottle after a feeding. It is best to play it safe and discard unused formula once a feeding has ended.

Traveling with Formula

Cold formula can be stored for short periods in insulated bags or kept in a cooler with ice. It can also be stored in plastic bags with an ice pack or ice cubes. The formula can be considered fresh as long as the ice cubes remain frozen.

Another travel option is to put water into bottles that have been washed in the dishwasher or bottles containing sterile plastic bottle bags and bring along powdered formula to mix with the water *at feeding time.* The water does not have to be kept cold, and the bottle will be at room temperature when prepared.

For longer trips, it is more convenient (although more expensive) to purchase ready-to-feed single-serving cans or bottles. They often need to be special-ordered, so plan ahead. If you are using cans, wash the tops before leaving home and take along a clean can opener. (Wash the can opener after each use.) Throw away unfinished formula in the single-serving can.

Bottle and Nipple Styles

Bottles and nipples come in many varied styles and shapes. You will have fun shopping for these items, but I am certain that you will also feel a bit overwhelmed by all your choices.

First you must decide whether you want to go with bottle liners or regular bottles. You do not have to make an either/or choice. You could choose one for use most of the time, and the other for travel (if one appears more convenient for that purpose).

Next you will need to decide on one nipple style (shape). Your baby may not like it if you use a short nipple at one feeding and a long nipple at another. Nipples range from the traditional long, narrow style to the short, almost square style to the orthodontic style. Hole size also varies: there are larger-holed nipples made especially for premature babies (due to their weak sucking), holes for newborns, holes for babies over six months, holes for juice, and so on. (I warned you that you may feel overwhelmed—just take it one step at a time!)

See Box 17-1 for a helpful list of equipment, other than formula, needed for bottle feeding.

Regular Bottles and Nipples

Once you have chosen a nipple style, pick out a bottle that you like. You will need to decide whether you want plastic or glass bottles. (Glass bottles are more difficult to find.) Again, there are many choices. There are even bottles on the market that are angled, which are advertised as helping to prevent your baby from ingesting air. Happy shopping!

Nursers with Disposable Sterile Bag Liners

These are sterile, plastic bottle bags that go inside a bottle, or liner holder, creating a sterile (germ-free) receptacle for the formula. If you choose this type of feeding system, you may want to purchase a starter kit first to ensure that you have bags and bottles (liner holders) from the same company. However, this is not absolutely necessary—most sterile bags are advertised as a universal fit. The sterile-bag bottle liners are marketed as "disposable bottles." Look for this name when purchasing replacement liners.

One advertised advantage to these bags is that they collapse as the baby drinks, thus reducing the amount of air ingested. Another advantage is the sterile environment created without effort. And last, but certainly not least, you will not have to scrub formula out of the inside of bottles! Just

Baby Care

throw the liner away, wash the liner holder and wash the nipples as usual.

The main complaint against the liners is that you can't judge the volume your baby has taken from one. If you can remind yourself to let your baby be the guide as to the amount of food he needs, not what the bottle says, this is not an issue.

The disadvantages of the bags are their expense and the added plastic waste in the environment.

Is Sterilization Necessary?

We need to break this issue down into parts: Is sterilization of formula necessary? What water source are you using? And, do bottles and nipples need to be sterilized?

Is It Necessary to Sterilize Formula?

No. Commercial formula, whether in the ready-to-use, concentrated, or powdered form, is already sterilized.

What Water Source Are You Using? Is It Necessary to Sterilize Water Before Adding It to Concentrated or Powdered Formula?

In doing the research for this chapter, I found many answers to this question. Basically, the

---

BOX 17-1

Equipment Needed for Bottle Feeding

Nurser starter set (if desired).

Disposable bottle liners and a hard plastic bottle made to hold your liners.

OR

9–12	eight-ounce plastic or glass bottles (fewer to begin with until you are sure you like this style and brand). Two or three are enough if you wash them between uses.
2	four-ounce plastic or glass bottles.
2	nipples (only 2 to begin with until you are sure you like this style and brand).
2	pacifiers (unless you choose not to use them). If you do choose to purchase a pacifier, get one that is recommended by orthodontists.
6	small round bibs or larger terrycloth bibs for drool and small spit-ups.
12	cloth diapers for burping cloths (prefolded are best because they are thicker).
1	one-quart measuring cup with ounce markings. A one-cup measuring cup would be convenient for smaller amounts but not absolutely necessary.
1	long-handled spoon for stirring.
1	whisk for mixing powdered formula.
1	sharp-pointed metal can opener.
1	bottle brush.
1	nipple brush.
1	bottle warmer (if desired).

answers depend on two things: what pediatrician you ask and what water source you use.

Many pediatricians today allow tap water directly from the faucet to be used with concentrated or powdered formula that requires the addition of water. They believe that if the water is safe for you, it is safe for your baby. Other pediatricians, unless they are already familiar with your town, want to see a recent report of the quality, mineral content, and fluoride level of your town's water. (This is available from your local water department.)

If you have been away on vacation, allow the tap water to run for a period of time before using it to clear the pipes of water that has been sitting there for a while.

If you have a private well, you may be asked by your pediatrician to have it tested for water quality and bacteria and fluoride content. Check your local phone book for a certified water analysis laboratory. Again, ask your pediatrician's opinion—what may be safe for an adult may not be safe for a baby.

If there is a concern about the quality of your water source, first consider ready-to-feed formula (because it does not require the addition of water). If this is out of the question due to its expense, your pediatrician may recommend using bottled water instead of boiling your water. The steam evaporation during boiling causes the minerals in the water to be concentrated. Although minerals are important in our water, over a long period of time a high mineral concentration caused by boiling water would not be good for your baby.

Do not purchase distilled water for babies. Distilling water removes minerals that he needs.

If your pediatrician recommends bottled water, he or she may ask you to find out the fluoride level in the bottled water you plan to purchase, because some brands have been found to be high in fluoride. (Check by calling the consumer number on the bottle.) Do this also if you have a home cooler and have water delivered to your home.

It is important to note that your pediatrician may be comfortable with your tap, well, or bottled water *without* checking the quality or fluoride levels. Over time, if no problems have been noted in your area, he or she may feel it is not necessary for you to obtain all this data.

Do Bottles and Nipples Need to Be Sterilized?

Again, the answer varies depending on the pediatrician asked and whether or not you have a dishwasher.

For many years everything that came in contact with a baby's mouth was rigorously sterilized. Special bottle sterilization units were sold, and formula and water were mixed and both sterilized together. Then commercial formulas that come already sterilized appeared on the scene; however, bottles, nipples, and water continued to be sterilized. For years now, many parents have been told that sterilization of any kind is unnecessary. Most pediatricians today only require that baby bottles and nipples be washed immediately after use in hot soapy water (using a bottle and nipple brush), rinsed well, and allowed to air dry. If you have a dishwasher, washing the bottles and rings in the dishwasher adequately sterilizes them (as long as you do not use the energy saver or no-heat cycle). The instructions on most brands of nipples say "Top rack dishwasher safe."

If you have a pet, your pediatrician may recommend sterilization of bottles and nipples to kill organisms that a pet can transmit to the infant. A pet can transmit organisms directly to a baby by sniffing his face or the bottle and nipple. Organisms can be transmitted from your pet to your infant indirectly if the bottle falls on the ground and the nipple is not washed before you give it back. In addition, you can transmit organisms from your animal to the baby if you do not wash your hands after touching your animal. If you are instructed to sterilize for this or another reason, and you do not have a dishwasher, see the next two pages for instructions.

Baby Care

In summary of our original question, no, sterilization is not necessary: the commercial formula comes presterilized, and it is no longer required that you sterilize bottles, nipples, or water, except in special circumstances when it is required by your pediatrician. Hot soapy water, a good rinse, and air drying are all that is needed. If you have a dishwasher, it goes even farther and sterilizes the bottles (and nipples in the top rack) if the energy-saving or no-heat buttons are not used.

Sterilizing Bottles, Bottle Caps, and Bottle Rings

If your pediatrician does instruct you to sterilize your bottles for any reason, or if you prefer to sterilize by choice and you do not have a dishwasher, refer to Box 17-2 for the necessary supplies and use the following instructions.

You can use an automatic sterilizer, but it is not mandatory. A kettle with a lid, large enough to hold eight bottles lying down, will be sufficient for the job. Fill the kettle with clean tap water. (If you have not run the tap water for some time, allow it to run for a bit before filling the kettle.)

Using a bottle brush, wash the insides of your bottles and rinse them thoroughly. Place the clean bottles on their sides in the kettle and allow them to fill with water. Place all bottle rings and flat caps in the kettle, too. Bring the water to a boil and boil for *20 minutes*.

Keep the kettle covered and allow the water to cool slightly. Pour most of the water out and use tongs to lift out the bottles, rings, and caps. Place a flat cap on each bottle, close loosely with a ring, and store in a clean place.

Use these bottles within approximately 24 hours. This does not mean that you have to boil a new supply if 24 hours is up, it is the middle of the night, and you have sterilized bottles on hand. What it means is that every morning you sterilize a new supply of bottles for that day and resterilize any bottles left over from the day before.

Sterilizing Nipples and Pacifiers

Wash nipples immediately after use in warm soapy water. Use your thumb or finger to squeeze soapy water through the nipple hole and rinse in the same manner. (Nipple brushes are available but not mandatory.)

Most nipple and pacifier brands come with washing instructions that say "top rack dishwasher safe." (Check the instructions on your brand.) However, because a dishwasher's heat cycle can dry out nipples and pacifiers, check them frequently and replace them before they become dry or cracked.

BOX 17-2

Equipment Needed for Sterilizing Bottles

(Necessary only if you are instructed to sterilize or you desire to do so and a dishwasher is not available)

- ❑ A large stainless steel kettle (big enough to hold eight bottles lying down) with a cover.
- ❑ A small covered kettle to boil nipples and pacifiers.
- ❑ A jar and lid that can also be sterilized to hold all the sterilized nipples.
- ❑ Tongs for picking up the sterile bottles and nipples after boiling.

If your pediatrician recommends sterilization of nipples and pacifiers, after you have cleaned them place them in a small covered kettle and cover them with cold, fresh water. Boil for the time recommended on the package they came in. This will vary from 2 to 10 minutes. Pour out the water and allow the nipples and pacifiers to cool. Store them in a jar that has been washed in the dishwasher or that you have washed well by hand and allowed to air dry.

To prevent burns, do not use a nipple or pacifier that has been boiled until it has fully cooled. Also, the rubber nipple material expands when heated, closing the holes in the nipple. The holes reopen as the nipple cools. If nipples or pacifiers are stained, soak them in baking soda and warm water.

Sterilizing Water

If you have been instructed to boil your water, for any reason, it is really very simple. However, remember that **it is not recommended that you use a water supply that will need to be boiled all the time. The steam evaporation causes the minerals to be overconcentrated, and in the long term this could be harmful.** To sterilize water, fill a clean, stainless steel kettle with cold water. Always run your tap water a short time to clear the pipes before filling your kettle. (Run it longer if you have been away for a day or more to push fresh water through the pipes.) Boil the water for *20 minutes* with the lid on. Allow the water to cool, with the lid on, to 100°F or less before mixing it with formula.

Store the water in the covered kettle in the refrigerator, or pour it into sterilized bottles in the amount required for the formula you will be using. Place a cap and ring on the bottles and store them in the refrigerator. Prepare a new supply of water every day.

Vicki Lansky offers a suggestion for storing bottles in the refrigerator in her book *Practical Parenting Tips* (see Bibliography). She suggests using empty six-pack bottle holders. What a great idea!

How to Bottle Feed Your Baby

Holding a Baby for Bottle Feeding

Hold your baby in your nondominant arm with his head in the bend of your elbow. Your baby should be facing up with his body inclined so that his head and shoulders are slightly higher than his waist (Figure 17-1). To prevent air ingestion, hold the bottle at enough of an angle so that formula fills the nipple completely.

If your baby tends to be very sleepy when feeding, try holding him in a less close position. Put your baby's bottom in your lap and support his back and head with your nondominant arm and hand. Hold his head out in front of you so that he will be looking at you (Figure 17-2). Do not use this position routinely—all babies, regardless of the feeding method, need close cuddling at feeding and other times.

FIGURE 17-1

How to Hold the Baby and Bottle When Bottle Feeding

Baby Care

FIGURE 17-2

If the baby tends to be sleepy during feedings, hold him or her in a less close position.

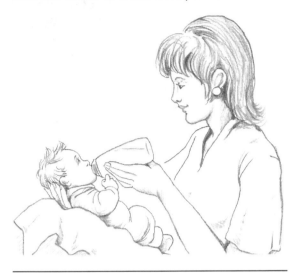

Putting the Nipple into the Mouth and Bottle Feeding

Stroke the nipple on your baby's mouth until he roots (opens his mouth). Put the nipple into his mouth, being careful to **place the nipple on top of the baby's tongue.** If your baby is hungry, he will take over from here!

Keep the bottle angled so that the nipple is always filled with liquid. This will help prevent the ingestion of air into the stomach, which causes the baby discomfort and gas.

Look for bubbles rising in the bottle. Nipples are designed with small holes in the outer rim that allow air into the bottle as formula is withdrawn. As we learned in science class, space must be taken up by something—when formula goes out, air must come in or a vacuum will occur and collapse the nipple. After a while, your baby will learn to pause and allow air to enter if too much of a vacuum is being created, making it difficult to withdraw formula.

You can also adjust this airflow with the ring of the bottle. If your baby appears to be sucking too hard to get formula or taking too long to finish a bottle, or you see few bubbles rising inside the bottle, loosen the ring slightly. If the formula appears to be coming too fast, try tightening the ring slightly (or try a nipple with a smaller hole).

Allow time for rest stops. Breathing takes priority over sucking and swallowing. Although your baby is breathing while drinking from the bottle, he will also take natural rest stops for additional breaths. Allow your baby to pace himself.

If your baby has excessive nasal congestion, your pediatrician may advise you to use a few drops of saline (sodium chloride) in each nostril before feeding. Saline nasal drops can be purchased over the counter at most drugstores. The usual instructions are to put one or two drops in a nostril, rub the outside of the nostril, and then use a bulb syringe to clear it. This procedure should not be done on a routine basis but only when the baby is unable to breathe through his nose and therefore is having difficulty feeding.

Burping

Will I Need to Burp My Baby?

Not all babies swallow enough air during feeding to cause them discomfort. Breastfed babies often do not require burping. Bottle-fed babies may burp a lot or very seldom; it is quite varied. You will get to know your baby's needs, although you may very well learn them in retrospect, as the following two paragraphs explain.

In the beginning, try to obtain a burp after every one-half to three-fourths of an ounce. Continue the feeding after your baby burps or, if your baby doesn't burp, when he cries for more. At the end of the feeding, attempt to burp for about three minutes (less, of course, if the burp occurs right away). If your baby doesn't burp within three minutes, you can assume (for now) that he isn't swallowing much air, and you can devote less time and effort to burping at the next feeding.

If you put your baby down to sleep after what you consider to be a good feeding for your baby, whether you have been successful in obtaining a burp or not, if he begins to fuss within 20 minutes, it is most likely a bubble causing the distress. Pick your baby up and attempt to get a burp. Now you have learned in retrospect to take more time to obtain a burp after future feedings.

How to Burp a Baby

There are several acceptable ways to properly burp, or "bubble," a baby. You will want to experiment and learn what technique works best with your baby.

Over-the-Shoulder and Chest Burping Positions: Putting the baby's head and arms over your shoulder (Figure 17-3A) is the most common method of burping. In this position, your baby is held in an upright position, which allows the gas bubble to rise up and come out. This puts the laws of science to use (gas rises to the top of a column of fluid). This upright burping position lifts the chest and straightens the back. It also gets your baby's head up over your shoulder, where you can easily hear his breathing and burping.

Support your baby's bottom with one hand, leaving your other hand free to gently pat or rub the baby's back. Continue until a burp is obtained or you decide there wasn't a burp there in the first place. (Three minutes is usually sufficient.)

You can also hold your baby upright against your chest and gently pat or rub his back (Figure 17-3B).

Putting a baby down flat and then returning him to the upright position will sometimes help a resistant bubble to rise up and come out.

If you have long hair, try to keep it away from your baby's mouth when burping and holding him.

Put a burping cloth over your shoulder or on your chest to keep your clothes from becoming soiled by a wet burp. (A small amount of spit-up comes up with the burp.) A clean burping cloth

also prevents germs from your clothing from getting near your baby's face and mouth.

Sitting Position for Burping: In this burping position, you cross your legs, creating a kind of chair out of them, or use one leg. Your baby sits on this "chair" with his legs hanging down (Figure

FIGURE 17-3

Upright Burping Positions

(A) Over the shoulder. (B) On the chest.

A

B

17-4A). With one hand, hold the angle of your baby's jaw *without* putting pressure on the front of his throat. (Your thumb and middle finger should be under each side of the jaw bone; see Figure 17-4B.) **In this burping position, you will want to be careful to keep your baby's back straight and not allow the baby's back to curve into a C.** The stomach is located directly under the lower edge of the rib cage on the left. If you allow your baby's back to curve too much, the end of the rib cage will compress his stomach. Your baby will spit up, not because he took too much formula or swallowed too much air, but because his back was allowed to curve too much.

Gently stretch your baby upward to keep his back straight, and then lean him slightly forward from the groin (Figure 17-4A). Use your other hand to support the baby's back and to gently pat and rub it.

It is common for babies in this position to arch their heads back—be prepared to use that free hand to support your baby's head and back when this happens. You may want to have a burping cloth in the hand you are using to hold your baby's jaw.

Over-the-Lap Burping Position: This seems to be a favorite position of babies suffering from colic. However, babies who are too full often resist this position because of the added pressure on their tummy.

Place your baby face down across your lap with his tummy over one leg and his head resting on the other. Put a burping cloth under his head to protect your clothes and to keep germs from your clothing away from your baby's face and mouth (Figure 17-5). Pat your baby's back gently.

Frequently Asked Questions About Bottle Feeding

What Formula Is Given for the First Feeding?

Many hospitals give glucose water to bottle-fed babies for the first feeding or at least the first few

sucks. The main reason this is done is to rule out any abnormalities in the esophagus (the food tube that connects the mouth to the stomach). One such abnormality is a rare fistula (canal opening) that allows food to enter the trachea

FIGURE 17-4

Sitting Positions for Burping

(A) Upright. (B) Lift up and forward at the groin.

A

B

FIGURE 17-5

Over-the-Lap Position for Burping, a Favorite with Colicky Babies

(windpipe). If this fistula were present, liquid taken at the first feeding would be aspirated into the lungs, and water would not cause as much distress to the lungs as formula. Once abnormalities are ruled out, formula is started. If your baby has a lot of mucus, half-strength formula may be used for the first few feedings to help thin out the mucus. (This is made by mixing equal amounts of formula and sterile glucose water.)

How Do I Know If the Nipple Hole Is the Right Size?

There are nipples that are designed specifically for newborns, premature babies, or older babies. There are also special nipples with larger holes for juice. Read the labels carefully when you make your purchase.

There are a couple of general rules for evaluating the nipple hole size. First, the nip-

ple hole is generally right for a young baby if, when you turn the bottle upside down, the milk comes out in a fine spray for about one to two seconds and then changes to drops. If the milk keeps spraying, the nipple hole is probably too big for a young baby. If the milk comes in slow drops from the beginning, the hole is probably too small. Second, it should take about 20 minutes of sucking time for your baby to empty a bottle.

If the nipple hole is too big, your baby may cough or choke from the formula coming too fast and may also suffer from indigestion. He will be more likely to eat more than needed because his body doesn't have time to signal his brain that "full" has been reached! In addition, your baby will get too little sucking time.

If the nipple hole is too small, you will have a very upset baby. He will be working very hard to obtain a small volume and probably tire out and fall asleep long before becoming full. Twenty minutes to an hour later, you may be wondering why your baby is crying for more formula again, when in fact the real problem was a nipple hole that was too small.

Warming a bottle with the nipple on can cause the nipple to expand, which results in the hole becoming partially or completely blocked. If your baby is working hard at sucking and then crying frantically, this may be the problem. If the nipple hole is partially blocked, you will not see the steady stream of bubbles rising in the bottle as you normally would with a nipple hole that is adequate. If the hole is completely blocked, there will be no bubbles rising when the baby is sucking.

In an emergency, when you cannot get to a drugstore to buy a nipple with a larger hole, you can enlarge a small hole by heating the sharp end of a sewing needle until it is red hot. Use a potholder to hold the other end of the needle, or tweezers held by a potholder or small cloth, to protect your hand from the metal needle, which will get very hot. Poke the red-hot tip of the needle only a short way into the nipple. You can enlarge the hole that is there or create a new one; add additional holes as needed. You can always make a hole bigger, but you can't make it smaller, so progress slowly and test the nipple as you go. (Wash the nipple before using and after enlarging the hole.)

Crosscut nipples can be purchased for when your baby is later taking juice with pulp. You can make a crosscut in a regular nipple using a new razor blade. (Do not use a used blade.) Squeeze the tip of the nipple and make about a one-fourth-inch cut along the top. Now squeeze the nipple again at a right angle to the first cut and make another one-fourth-inch cut. The edges of the cut do not open unless the baby sucks.

Should I Warm the Bottle?

Research has shown that babies do just as well regardless of the temperature of the feeding. Formula can be given cold, at room temperature, or warmed slightly. The important thing is to be consistent. A baby used to a warm bottle will probably balk at a cold bottle, and vice versa.

If you prefer room-temperature bottles, do not allow refrigerated formula to sit out to come to room temperature; this would take too long, and bacterial growth might occur. Instead, bottles can be warmed with a commercial warmer or allowed to sit in a small bowl containing a few inches of warm water for several minutes. Gently swirl the formula several times to allow even warming. You may have to add more warm water to the bowl if the water cools off before the bottle warms. Warming a bottle this way prevents overheating of the formula, and because it takes less than five minutes, does not allow enough time for bacterial growth to begin.

Never use the microwave to heat a bottle. The temperature of the formula can reach scalding temperatures even when the bottle feels cool on the outside. **(Be firm in your instructions to baby-sitters in this area: do not use the microwave to warm bottles!)**

What About Propping a Bottle?

Never prop a bottle. Bottle-fed babies need to be held and cuddled and talked to just like breast-fed babies. Propping bottles is also very dangerous because it can lead to choking.

What About Giving a Bottle in Bed?

For many years parents have been advised against giving a baby a bottle in bed. First, it is thought to promote early tooth decay (starting around 11 months that affects the primary teeth). Once the front teeth come in, it is thought that your baby is more likely to develop an overbite or "buck" front teeth if he bites down and holds the nipple in his mouth all night. In addition, ear infections are much more common in babies that take their bottles to bed. When a baby lies flat and sucks formula or juice, the ejecting liquid hits the back of his mouth, where the eustachian tubes are located. The eustachian tubes connect the ears to the back of the throat—they are what open and "pop" when you yawn to "open" your ears. This constant exposure to ejecting formula or juice causes many more ear infections than occur in babies who do not take bottles to bed.

There is presently a debate going on, however, about whether or not the issue of early tooth decay can be solely blamed on taking a bottle to bed. Dr. Norman Tinanoff, a pediatric dental specialist, wondered why 80 percent of American children sleep with an occasional bottle until they are two years old but only 10 percent of all children develop early tooth decay. He believes that there are three factors that cause early tooth decay: first, the organism *Streptococcus mutans*, which causes tooth decay and needs sugar to live, must be present in the baby's mouth. Second, what is in the bottle makes a difference. *Streptococcus mutans* cannot use lactose, found in formula or milk, to live—it needs sucrose. So taking bottles containing juice and sugary drinks (both high in sucrose) to bed is the second part of the cause of early tooth decay, in Dr. Tinanoff's opinion. Finally, the thickness of the baby's tooth enamel is also a contributing factor. According to Tinanoff, if the enamel is too thin, a baby is more at risk for early decay. (He warns that prenatal and infant nutrition, iron deficiency, and exposure to lead all affect how enamel develops.)

At any rate, as you can see, the issue of whether or not to allow your baby to take a bottle to bed is a complex one. Ask your pediatrician for advice. Don't forget, though, that bottle-fed babies need to be held and cuddled too. It is best to provide that holding and cuddling *before* bedtime, as the bottle is taken—then you can put your baby to bed. When you are ready to eliminate the bottle given just before bedtime from the feeding schedule (sometime between 9 and 18 months), your baby will already know how to go to sleep without a bottle. If your baby has always taken a bottle to bed, even a water bottle, he will be frantic and unable to fall asleep when you finally decide it is time to get rid of it.

Many pediatricians recommend that full-bottle weaning be completed by 18 months. Ask your pediatrician his or her opinion.

What About a Pacifier?

This is an area of personal choice and lots of opinions. First, let me assure you that your baby will not become attached to a pacifier if you use it during the first three months to help satisfy his tremendous sucking needs. Wean your baby from the pacifier by three months and you will not have to worry about having to do it when he is two years old, and very attached to it.

Purchase an orthodontic-style pacifier. (One common brand called Nuk is made by Gerber, but other companies make similar products.) These pacifiers are narrow where the gum rests on them and short and angled upward in the wider part. They are advertised as being better because they do not lead to future orthodontic problems. **Always be sure that your pacifier is safety-approved and made of one piece.**

Check the pacifier before each use for intactness and softness of the nipple. Replace pacifiers long before the nipple becomes brittle.

Never tie a pacifier around a baby's or child's neck. It could cause strangulation. **Never tie a pacifier (or a toy) to a high chair, car seat, playpen, and so on.** Again, the tie could become wrapped around your child's neck and cause strangulation.

Pacifiers fall out of the mouth frequently and are handled a lot. To prevent thrush (a yeast infection in the mouth) and other infections, it is advisable to wash them frequently. Also, boil pacifiers for 5 to 10 minutes before the first use and then occasionally. (Some brands are top rack dishwasher safe.) Watch them closely for deterioration. Both boiling and being run through the dishwasher can cause them to dry out, lose flexibility, and crack. At this point they would be a choking hazard, so replace them frequently.

Is It Necessary to Give Extra Water to Bottle-Fed Babies?

Formula contains all the water necessary for a baby's normal daily fluid requirements.

Water does not contain nutrients, and giving your baby water could prevent him from taking enough formula.

On a hot summer day, however, a *few sips* of water between feedings are okay. If your tap water has not been run for a period of time (for example, overnight or during a workday or a vacation), let it run first to clear the pipes to reduce the risk of lead exposure.

When your baby has a high temperature, vomiting, or diarrhea during an illness, a *special* electrolyte water may be ordered by your pediatrician. This special water replaces electrolytes, such as sodium and potassium, lost along with fluid during diarrhea and vomiting. (See pages 301–302, for more information about this special water given by doctors' order only.)

How Much Formula Should My Baby Take?

This is the big question—and there is no straight answer, because each baby is different! If you can just allow yourself to let your baby be the guide, and remember that no baby has ever starved himself, you will be much more relaxed.

The number of calories in an ounce of breast milk is about the same as in an ounce of formula, but we seldom see overweight breastfed babies. Breastfeeding mothers have no idea what volume their babies are taking. Breastfed babies seem to take as much, and only as much, as they need. **If you get too concerned with what the bottle reads, you may fall into the "finish-the-whole-bottle" syndrome.** Unless babies are ill, they tend to take what they require. They may take less than their usual amount for a few days and then eat ravenously for several days after that, increasing both the frequency and the amount of formula taken at each feeding.

The same thing goes for older children. When I was hung up on food issues with my first child, the nurse at my pediatrician's office told me something that helped me tremendously. She said, "From now until he grows up and leaves home, evaluate his diet by the week, not by the day." This was particularly helpful during the toddler and preschool years, when one day my son would eat mostly fruits and then another day mostly cereal and grains. It really did balance out over the week!

Your baby's weight will be monitored by your pediatrician. Some babies grow very quickly right from day one, and others just go along at a nice slow steady incline. As long as your child's growth increases on the growth chart (that is, it doesn't plateau or begin to drop), then he is growing at the rate that is preprogrammed by his metabolism. To fall into the "finish-the-bottle" syndrome may only lead to eating problems for your child in later life and go against the baby's natural inborn needs and metabolism.

Now after all that, I will offer you the benefit of what I consider average amounts in the first few days of life, based on my experience. I offer this *only* because I know that many of you have no experience with newborns and may not have any idea of the average volume they take in. Most babies do very well with one-half to one ounce at a time in the initial day or two of feeding, but some are content with less, one-third to three-fourths of an ounce per feeding. Other babies can tolerate one and one-half ounces; however, large spit-ups are common if this volume is given initially. There are a few babies who take two to three ounces on the first or second day, but this is a rare exception, and these ravenous babies very commonly are fussy after consuming such large volumes.

Feeding volume increases over the first few days of life. The rate of this increase is very variable. Some babies go home in two days still taking three-fourths to one ounce per feeding, and others do very well taking one and a half to two ounces per feeding. **By the end of the first week of life, if your baby has built up to six wet diapers per day, you can be assured that he is getting an adequate volume of formula.**

How Often Should I Feed My Baby?

Six feedings per 24 hours are sufficient. The times between these feedings will fluctuate between two and a half and five hours throughout the day. Unless your baby has feedings ordered for every three hours by your pediatrician there is no need to wake him at night for a feeding. Take advantage of the sleep time yourself! If you want that longer stretch between feedings to occur at night, do not allow your baby to go more than four hours between feedings during the day and evening, to reduce the chance that he will want to make up for feedings at night when you want and need sleep!

Your pediatrician may leave orders for your baby to be fed every three hours on a schedule. **It is important to follow these instructions—** there are reasons for this order of frequent and regular feedings. If your baby was under 37 weeks' gestation at birth or under five and a half pounds or over nine pounds at birth, he is at increased risk of having blood sugar levels so low that they would be dangerous. The regular and frequent (every three hours) feedings help counteract this tendency and keep your baby's blood sugar within the safe range. In addition, every-three-hour feedings may be ordered if your baby is jaundiced. (See pages 254–256 for an explanation of jaundice and why more frequent feedings are an important part of treating it.)

What About Poor Feedings the First Day of Life?

Many babies seem to require about a 12-hour period sometime in the first 24 hours of life to "regroup" and sleep after their birth experience. This is very common, but it does cause first-time parents concern. They attempt to wake their baby and are frustrated when he takes very little or nothing. Knowing that this is common should help you accept this slow start to what you had hoped would be a smooth eating routine. Also, it helps to remember that you can lead a horse to water, but you can't force it to drink. You offered, and that was your job. Your baby refused, and that was his answer *for now.* You will laugh looking back on your worry when you have a growing teenager and can't seem to keep the refrigerator stocked! You may not laugh, however, in a couple of days when

your baby goes through frequent feedings to catch up. It is amazing how suddenly this sleepy baby wakes up and looks at you and cries *at you* as if to say, "You have been staring at me for days and have never even *attempted* to give me something to eat! What have you been doing—sleeping?" **This is the beginning of your patience and flexibility training!**

Of course, if your baby is jaundiced during the first four days of life, you must rule out high bilirubin as the cause of sluggishness and poor feeding. See the section on newborn jaundice (page 254) for a review of this topic and what to report to your pediatrician.

What About Half-Finished Bottles?

Dr. Spock gives the best advice on this one: "If you let a baby stop when he feels like it and let him come to feel his own hunger, he will gradually become more eager for his feedings and take larger amounts." (*Dr. Spock's Baby and Child Care,* page 177.) Let your baby be the guide. (See "How Much Formula Should My Baby Take?" page 314.)

What Does It Mean If My Baby Falls Asleep After a Feeding Only to Wake Up in a Few Minutes Crying?

Do you remember my story about the first night home with my first child? Well, it was my response to my son's crying that started my baby's overtired, overfed, overchanged night! See Box 17-3 for help in avoiding my first-time mistakes.

What If My Baby Fusses as Soon as He Begins a Feeding?

First of all ask yourself, is it really time for a feeding? Did my baby demand this feeding, or was it just a convenient time for me? If you are certain that your baby is hungry, and he is showing signs of frustration early into the feeding, consider the possibility of a clogged nipple.

Baby Care

BOX 17-3

Checklist for a Crying Baby

- **Try changing the baby's position.** If your baby has taken an adequate feeding, even if the volume is several ounces less than the usual amount, and then wakes up crying *within* 20 minutes, hunger is probably not the cause. **Remember that a baby cannot move himself to a new position. Nor can he change position to move a painful gas bubble along.** Try gently turning your baby on his side, gently pat him on the back, and then gently put him back on his back.
- **Try burping the baby.** If your baby continues to cry, pick him up and try to "bubble" him. It may be a gas bubble that is causing the distress, in which case a burp may stop the crying.
- **Check the baby's diaper.** If burping your baby doesn't solve the problem, check his diaper. I list this as a third step, because changing a diaper will wake your baby more fully. Seldom will a sleeping baby wake up because of a wet or messy diaper (unless it is within the first few days after circumcision). Change the diaper if it is wet or soiled and put your baby back to bed.
- **Cuddle the baby and breastfeed (if you are nursing) or offer a pacifier (if you are bottle feeding).** If the above steps do not stop the crying, hold and cuddle your baby for a few minutes. Perhaps the comfort and the security of your touch are what is needed. Next, if you are nursing, offer your breast. Even if the baby only uses your breast for a few moments as a pacifier, if it stops the crying, it worked! If you are bottle feeding and you don't object to a pacifier, continue to hold your baby for a few minutes and offer him a pacifier. Perhaps he just has a need for sucking comfort.
- **Feed the baby.** If all else fails, and you feel the cry is truly that angry "I am hungry" cry, go ahead and offer a full breast or bottle feeding. Years of experience have shown me that a truly hungry baby can best be described as a "mad boxer." His cry is loud and angry, his arms are "boxing" the air, and in between the boxing, he is chewing and sucking on his hands. The hungry cry is much different from the gas-bubble or tummy-ache cry, which seems to show distress and a pulling up of the knees.

Did you warm the bottle with the nipple already on it? If you did, the rubber may have expanded from the heat and closed or narrowed the hole. Change the nipple.

Is the bottle ring screwed down so tightly that air cannot enter the bottle? If this is the case, a vacuum is being created as your baby sucks, making the nipple collapse and withdrawal of formula very difficult. If the ring is too tight, you will see very few, if any, bubbles rising while the baby is sucking. Loosen the ring slightly.

Is your baby old enough to need a nipple with a larger hole? When your baby is about six months old, it is usually time to purchase nipples for older babies. These nipples have larger holes. If you think this is the problem but do not have any larger-hole nipples on hand, you can enlarge the

hole in the nipple you have until you have time to purchase the new size (see page 312 for directions).

What If My Baby Falls Asleep as Soon as a Feeding Begins?

Again, first be sure that it is your *baby's* time for the feeding. Next, consider the above-mentioned problem of a nipple hole that is too small or clogged. Did your baby fall asleep from the fatigue of vigorous sucking that did not deliver formula? If you are absolutely certain that your baby just fell asleep from the comfort of being held and fed after fussing for some time, and it is over your baby's usual length of time between feedings, go ahead and stimulate him to wake up and complete the feeding.

In the first few weeks of life, you can wake a sleeping baby by holding him up in front of you and gently moving your fingers around. Babies have an inborn instability reflex that wakes them up if they do not feel secure. If this seems too drastic for you, unwrap your baby and rub his feet, back, and head. The cooler air and the touch stimulation usually work.

If your baby fell asleep soon after starting a feeding that was early for your baby's usual pattern, then food was probably not what your baby was looking for. Your comfort and attention met his need and now he wants to sleep.

Always keep in the back of your mind the thought that excessive fatigue, sleepiness, and inability to fully awaken and take a feeding can be due to dehydration, jaundice, or low blood sugar. *C*Consult your pediatrician if excessive sleepiness occurs so frequently that your baby is not wakeful enough to take adequate feedings.

What About Hiccups?

It is very common for a baby to develop hiccups after feeding. In fact, those rhythmic "jumps" you felt during pregnancy were hiccups! You really don't need to do anything except be sure that your baby doesn't need to be burped.

Hiccups can sometimes be stopped by giving your baby several swallows of water. However, this is not necessary because hiccups are harmless and will go away on their own.

What If My Baby Spits Up Most of His Feeding?

Spitting up causes a lot of worry for new parents. If you could just assure yourself that it is almost as common as messy diapers, you wouldn't lose so much sleep over it. Spitting up is so common that I always advise mothers to **have lots of burping cloths and a bulb syringe nearby during feedings for the first several weeks. (See page 332 for proper use of a bulb syringe.**

See page 333 for proper positioning to protect your baby's airway when he is spitting up or vomiting or when excessive mucus is present.)** If your baby loses a teaspoonful of formula when burping after feedings, this is not of concern. Also, if he spits up a large amount shortly after a feeding, don't despair! If your baby spits up a large volume again after the next feeding, then you've learned something: either your baby needs more frequent burping throughout a feeding, or the total volume taken at the next feeding needs to be reduced. (Reduce the next feeding by at least a half ounce from the feeding volume that just caused the large spit up.)

If your baby consistently spits up after each feeding, you should also think about your burping position. Did your baby spit up while burping? If yes, was his back arched in a C, causing his lower rib cage to compress his stomach? (See pages 309–310 for correct burping positioning.)

What has happened has not harmed your baby. He will make up the volume—trust me! *Babies do not starve themselves!* If your baby starts that "I'm hungry" cry shortly after spitting up what looked like almost the whole feeding, feed him again! This time try at least half an ounce less of total volume. Also, stop to burp him every one-half to three-fourths of an ounce during the feeding, and again at the end of the feeding.

On the other hand, if your baby seems content even after spitting up a large volume after a feeding, let him rest for awhile. Just plan on the fact that he probably won't go his usual amount of time before getting hungry again (because of losing part of the volume from this feeding). This is more of your flexibility training!

*C*A note of caution: spitting up *large volumes* after every meal or even most feedings is not normal. This symptom, as well as *forceful, projectile vomiting*, must be reported to your pediatrician promptly.** These are symptoms of a possible obstruction or narrowing between the stomach and the point at which it empties into the small intestine. If an obstruction or narrowing is present at birth, these symptoms may be observed during the initial

Emergency Call: Feeding Problems to Report to the Pediatrician

Help is available for all of the feeding problems listed below, so report them promptly to your pediatrician.

❑ **Forceful vomiting of every feeding, whether breast milk or formula.**

❑ **Spitting up of large volumes of undigested formula two or three hours after feedings on a regular basis.**

❑ **Constant fussing after feedings, persistent discomfort, or evidence of colic** (discussed below). If your baby constantly draws his knees up into his abdomen as if in pain or passes a lot of gas rectally, notify your pediatrician. If formula changes do not help, there are medication drops that reduce bowel irritability and decrease discomfort.

❑ **Any skin rash or skin blister.** Your pediatrician should evaluate rashes or blisters as possible signs of a developing milk allergy.

❑ **Frequent constipation problems.** Stools of formula-fed babies will be solid, but they should be soft. Your baby may have to hold his breath and push to pass stool. However, if he appears to be straining frequently without results, notify your pediatrician.

Formula with iron can make some babies constipated, but do not switch to a low-iron formula without consulting your pediatrician.

❑ **Diarrhea.** This can be a symptom of formula intolerance. Babies can develop intolerance or allergies to cow's-milk-based formula even if the formula has been well tolerated for some time.

feedings or later, when cereal is added and the food is therefore thicker.

When Will My Baby Want to Hold His Own Bottle?

Sometime around six or seven months of age, some babies show an interest in holding their own bottles. In order not to deprive your baby of being held and cuddled, it is probably best to begin the feeding by offering to hold and cuddle him as usual. Then, if he insists, allow him to hold his own bottle. You can still hold and cuddle him while he eats!

If your baby still resists and wants to sit upright, he should be allowed to do so. There is a special bottle attachment that consists of a straw-like device that runs from the nipple to the bottom of the bottle. This allows your baby to suck and obtain formula while in an upright position.

Other Feeding Issues

Colic and Irritable Crying Spells

There is probably nothing more disturbing to a parent than a baby who can't be soothed or quieted. A baby with colic may scream, pull his knees up into his tummy, and pass gas through his rectum. Sometimes you can even see that the abdomen is distended with gas.

Then there is the baby who has an irritable crying spell that lasts an hour or even several hours, often at the same time each day. This baby does not appear to be having gas pains but is crying nonetheless.

Although it doesn't seem to make the moment any easier to cope with, it is comforting to know that in most cases these babies flourish despite all the crying. The large majority of fussy babies continue to gain weight and grow. And perhaps most important, this difficult time for both parents and babies tends to pass at around three months of age. *There is light at the end of the tunnel!*

Any baby crying excessively should be under medical care. There are some things you can do at home to help yourself and your baby through this difficult time. However, when these methods fail to bring relief, medication can help.

When your baby cries, first go through the suggested checklist for a crying baby in Box 17-3. Next, feed your baby if you are convinced that he is hungry or it is close to the usual feeding time. Choose a quiet place that is free of noise and distractions.

If you are breastfeeding, eliminate cow's-milk products and gas-forming foods from your diet. If bottle feeding, call your pediatrician for a possible formula change. Burp your baby more frequently during feedings, and burp him well after feedings.

When none of the above works, consult your pediatrician again. There are also books specifically about colic, and getting suggestions from other parents who have been in your shoes is most helpful.

If crying continues, hold your baby. Colicky babies tend to be happiest while being held. Meeting this need will not spoil your baby—you are providing needed comfort and security at a difficult time for him.

Many babies with gas discomfort seem soothed when lying face down across your legs. The warmth of a *slightly warm* hot water bottle is also beneficial. Test the temperature of the outside of the warm water bottle with your wrist. It should feel slightly warm, not hot. (It is very important to never overheat a baby.) Place a towel between the warm water bottle and your baby. Do not over-fill the bottle. Place it under the waist and

abdomen of your baby while he is across your legs, as illustrated in Figure 17-5 on page 311. In this position, the warm bottle elevates your baby's bottom slightly, which helps the gas rise to the rectal opening, where it can be passed. (A warm towel, wrapped in plastic and covered with another towel, can be used if you do not have a traditional rubber hot water bottle.)

A warm bath is soothing to many crying babies, and a car ride (always in a car seat) puts many babies to sleep, even those without colic. It is worth a try when other things don't work.

Overhandling and overstimulation can lead to increased irritability. If you think that this is a possibility, put your baby down for 10 minutes. If he is still crying after 10 minutes, attempt to comfort him again.

Another well-proven suggestion is to try a soft carrier harness to hold and walk your fussy baby. The warmth of your body and your movement may help. In addition, a walk outside in a stroller (on an appropriate day) may help; fresh air calms many babies.

You may want to purchase a toy or tape with a recorded heartbeat sound, which is soothing to many babies.

Babies with colic and irritable crying spells seem to be comforted with pacifiers. This is not the time to worry about pacifier attachment—if it helps, use it. The crying spells tend to pass by three months, in plenty of time to wean your baby from the pacifier before attachment occurs.

Excessive crying is stressful for you, too. Plan sitters ahead of time so you can get away for a few hours now and then. However, think twice about leaving a colicky baby with a young sitter. This baby needs a person with self-confidence and mature methods of handling stress. If you don't have family support for baby care at this time, get out and away one parent at a time!

Continue to check back with your pediatrician for help. I repeat again, **any baby crying excessively should be under medical care. Also, ask for help yourself if you are feeling excessively stressed. There are support groups that may help you get through this**

Baby Care

difficult time. Refer to "Managing Frustration and Stress" (page 372) for additional suggestions. Above all, try to maintain your sense of humor. Keep telling yourself that future challenges will be easier to face after this experience!

Weaning to a Cup

Babies are not usually ready, physically or emotionally, to wean to a cup before seven months. Take your cues from your baby.

Begin slowly with a few sips at the beginning of a mid-day feeding. Your baby will be too hungry to try something new in the morning, and bedtime is not a good time because of fatigue and the importance of the bedtime routine to many babies.

Special two-handled cups are available that have a cover and drinking spout and make early learning easier. They also come with a weighted base to help prevent tipping and spilling. The lid can be removed once your baby has the idea.

Don't expect successive gulps until around one year of age—one sip at a time is all that your baby is capable of right now. At six to seven months, you are not using the cup for volume but simply introducing it. Your baby is getting accustomed to the fact that liquids can come in something other than a bottle.

Never give cow's milk to a baby under one year of age unless instructed to do so by your pediatrician.

Complete Weaning from the Bottle

Most pediatricians recommend full weaning from the bottle by one year (or 18 months at the latest). Weaning at this time prevents prolonged attachment to the bottle and keeps the baby's mouth free to develop talking and social skills. This is also the time when your baby will accept change without too much resistance—babies become much more stubborn by 18 months! Resistance to change lasts well into the twos, so do it now or plan on having a more difficult time later.

Adding Solid Foods

A newborn's digestive system is not ready for solid food, so this is not an issue in your initial adjustment to your newborn. The right time to add solid food is different for each baby. Your pediatrician will advise you in this area, taking into consideration the allergy history of both parents.

If the parents do not have a history of allergies, solid foods are often allowed at around four to six months if the parents wish to add them then. However, it is not necessary to add solid foods in the first six months for either breastfed or bottle-fed babies. With proper nutrition on the part of the mother, breastfed babies can go a year without added solids, but solids will be recommended before one year of age if you are bottle feeding.

Usually the first solid food recommended is a single-grain baby cereal (normally rice, oats, or barley) that is fortified with vitamins and iron. **Do not begin with multi-grain cereal**—if an intolerance develops, you will not know which grain caused the problem.

Once your baby is taking soft solid food well, and not having allergy problems, wheat cereal can be added. (Your pediatrician will advise you about when to add wheat.) Wheat and oatmeal are the best cereals for both protein and fiber.

New foods should be introduced one at a time for several days (four to five days) before adding another. If only one new thing at a time is added, you will know exactly what is or is not tolerated.

Babies are used to receiving their bottle or breast milk first. They will be more likely to resist if you attempt to introduce something new at the beginning of a feeding, when they are the most hungry. Initially, mix the new food with breast milk or formula for thinning. Once your baby becomes accustomed to solid foods, they can be given at the beginning of a feeding.

Use a small baby spoon (regular teaspoons are much too wide and big), and at first give only enough to cover one-fourth of the tiny spoon. Have a bib available! At first your baby will not know how to handle this solid food. He will do tongue thrusts, and the food will all come back out and drip down his chin! This is definitely a "Kodak moment"—have the camera ready!

Offer the new food only once a day for several days. If your baby shows a lot of resistance, wait another week or two and try again. It does more harm than good to force the new food on your baby.

Fruit is often the second food started; however, some pediatricians suggest that it be the first since so many babies love it. Begin with "apples, peaches, pears, apricots and prunes " (*Dr. Spock's Baby and Child Care,* page 192). All fruits should be stewed, except ripe bananas, which can be given mashed after other fruits have been introduced and are tolerated. Raw fruits are usually allowed in the latter part of the first year, with the exception of berries and seedless grapes, which are not recommended until your baby is two years old. Prunes and apricots are natural laxatives. As your child gets older, use them to your advantage (once a day) if he tends to be on the constipated side.

Apple juice is the first juice (usually added around four to six months). It should be given diluted with water at first. You can also give your baby diluted grape and cranberry juices. Orange juice is not recommended until after the first birthday.

Squash, string beans, peas, carrots, sweet potatoes, and beets can be added to your baby's diet once he is used to cereal and fruit. Again, proceed slowly. Only one new food at a time, for three or four days, at one feeding a day.

It is not uncommon for undigested vegetables to appear in your baby's stools. If this happens, give only small amounts and allow time for his digestive system to get used to them. Green vegetables color the stools green, and beets make the stools red. (It is helpful to know this ahead of time so that you don't think your baby is ill or bleeding).

Strained meats are added at varied times. Some pediatricians suggest that they be started at six months; others have you introduce them last. Beef, liver, veal, chicken, lamb, and pork are all acceptable.

Eggs can be added to the diet between 9 and 12 months. Although the yolk is a rich source of iron, we now know that the iron in egg yolks is poorly absorbed by babies. Because of this poor absorption and the high cholesterol in yolks, pediatricians are no longer in any hurry to introduce eggs. If allergies run in your family, whole milk and egg white are usually held back until after the first birthday.

If you are serving baby food from a jar, do not serve directly from the jar unless the last full serving in the jar and any remaining will be thrown away. Saliva introduced into the jar by the spoon can add bacteria to the food and cause it to spoil quickly. Leftover baby food in jars should be refrigerated. Fruits can be safely kept three days; all others should not be kept more than two days. Vegetables are especially prone to spoilage. (Check the jar labels for specific storage instructions).

Books are available to teach you how to make your own baby food. I used Sue Castle's book, *The Complete Guide to Preparing Baby Food at Home.* I especially loved the recipes given to make wholesome teething foods, and it was also helpful to have the storage charts showing how long certain foods could be kept when refrigerated or frozen.

Finger foods can be added between six and eight months, depending on your child's readiness. As your baby grows older, vegetables and strained meats can be combined. Junior foods, with coarser textures, can be introduced around seven or eight months.

Vitamin Supplements

Most pediatricians will prescribe liquid vitamin drops for babies at the first (or two-week) newborn visit. Follow your pediatrician's recommendation in this area.

Baby Care

Some babies become irritable due to a sensitivity to these drops. Inform your pediatrician if you see a major change in behavior when the drops are added or shortly thereafter.

Fluoride Supplements

As a result of the 1995 guidelines from the American Dental Association and the American Academy of Pediatrics, fluoride supplements are no longer given to babies under the age of six months.

WIC Program

Every state in the United States has a program called *WIC* (Women, Infants, and Children) to assist pregnant woman, infants, and children under five. Prenatal care, nutritional information, counseling, immunization screening and referrals, free formula, and financial assistance in obtaining nutritious food are some of the services available through WIC. Eligibility for these programs is based on total income. If you already receive AFDC, food stamps, or Medicaid, you are automatically eligible. Fathers, guardians, and foster parents may also apply for WIC for their children.

For more information or to set up an appointment, call the WIC program nearest you. The toll-free number for your state can be obtained by calling information.

18

Daily Care of Your Newborn

Planning Ahead for Needed Supplies

If this is your first baby, you're just beginning to discover how much special equipment these little people require! You'll find it helpful to have everything on hand *before* bringing baby home: clothes, bath and bottom supplies, and essential medications and safety items should be ready and waiting when you come home from the hospital. Even if this isn't your first baby, the checklists in this chapter can serve as handy reminders and help you avoid last-minute trips to the store.

Clothing Needs

When you have waited so long, it is hard to resist the temptation to buy every baby item on the market. Newborns do not want to wear fancy, tight-fitting outfits any more than you want to go to bed in a prom dress! Trust those of us who

have been there—you have years of clothes buying ahead of you. Unless you have money to burn, be thrifty and buy only the basics (Box 18-1).

Of course, you need to keep the season in mind when planning for the arrival of your baby, and remember to allow for hand-me-downs and gifts.

Boy or Girl? If you do not know the sex of your baby, don't buy everything in yellow and green. Not all babies look good in these colors. Purchase just what you need and then wait to see if you will be dressing a boy or a girl. Some stores will allow you to make up a girl list and a boy list of clothing items close to your delivery time. Then a friend or family member can pick up the correct order after you deliver and know the sex of your baby but before you come home from the hospital.

Laundry Facilities: Consider how often you will be able to do the laundry. If you have access to a washer and dryer, you will need a minimum number of items. If you or someone else will be

BOX 18-1

Basics for Baby at Home

The numbers of garments and supplies suggested are for those who have access to a washer and dryer. You will need a larger number if you will be washing only once a week.

Diapers

If you will be using disposable diapers, buy two boxes of newborn diapers and two boxes of the next-larger size. Don't buy too many diapers until you know the birth weight of your baby. Most newborn-size diapers only fit babies up to ten pounds.

If you will be using a diaper service, sign up for it a month or two in advance so that the company can plan and arrange to start service on your notification. Check to see what they use for laundering—avoid dyes, perfumes, and chlorine bleach if possible.

If you will be using cloth diapers, buy four or five dozen diapers, three or four waterproof plastic pants or plastic-alternative pants, and one package of diaper pins.

Clothing Needs

Three infant undershirts: The brands that open in the front are easiest to put on a newborn; however, they are not as smooth as pullovers. One-piece brands that snap at the crotch have the advantage of keeping the tummy well covered in cold weather and the disadvantage of often getting wet from a leaking diaper.

Three infant nightgowns: The brands that have a drawstring bottom are preferred. You will understand why after you see how many diaper checks and changes you will be doing in those first months of your baby's life! When your baby is old enough to lift his or her legs and pull on the drawstring, remove it for safety reasons.

Once your baby begins to move on his or her own, stretch sleepers with snap legs are more practical.

Two blanket sleepers: These will be needed only if your baby will be born during a cold-weather season. In infant sizes, blanket sleepers come in either a front- or bottom-opening bag style.

Stretch outfits with feet: Purchase three if your baby will be born during fall or winter, only one for a summer baby, and perhaps two for a spring baby. Consider the climate and temperature ranges where you live.

Three one-piece, short-sleeved outfits: These will be needed only if your baby is born in late spring or summer. If you rarely have a very hot day where you live, a diaper and T-shirt will get you through an unusually hot day without a special purchase.

Three pairs of socks: Infant-sized. Buy these for added warmth.

One pair of cloth booties: These will be needed to cover your baby's feet when he or she is not wearing a stretch outfit with feet. Socks would be sufficient for this purpose, except when you take the baby out on very cold days when both socks and booties are needed.

Four small washable *cloth* bibs: If you have a baby who spits up or drools a lot, these bibs will save many clothing changes.

Outerwear Needs

One or two lightweight sweaters: These will be needed for a summer baby.

One or two heavier sweaters: These will be needed for a winter baby.

One or two hats: For warm-weather babies, think about light weight and protection

BOX 18-1 (CONTINUED)

from the sun. For cold-weather babies, think about warmth and ear coverage.

One bunting, or snowsuit bag: This will be needed only if your baby is due in late fall or winter.

One 1-yard (36-inch) square blanket: This will be used on especially cool nights.

Three or four receiving blankets

Bed Linen Needs

Three fitted crib sheets

Three soft pillowcases: Remember that pillows are not allowed in the baby's bed. Soft pillowcases may fit a bassinet mattress or work as a cover for your carriage mattress.

Two or three quilted mattress pads: These provide extra warmth in the winter and are cooler in the summer than just

placing a sheet directly over a plastic mattress, which can cause your baby to sweat. Cotton mattress pads are cooler than synthetic pads.

Two or three waterproof pads: These will protect your crib, bassinet, and carriage. They are placed under the mattress pad to protect the mattress. If used directly under the sheet, they may cause sweating. **Never use a plastic bag for waterproof protection for a child of any age.**

Firm **bumper pads for crib**

Two washable crib, bassinet, or carriage blankets: Receiving blankets will do for summer, but heavier weights are needed for winter. Think safety when purchasing a blanket—avoid anything that dangles, including fringe.

taking clothes to a self-service laundry once a week, you will need extra items to make it through a whole week.

What Size? Purchase mostly six- to nine-month sizes. One or two three-month sizes are sufficient for those times you want the outfit to fit perfectly. Your baby will begin to fill out the bigger size very quickly.

Sizes are not true to age. Most six-month-old babies wear the 9–12-month size range, and many even wear 18-month sizes. Foreign company sizes vary greatly. Some run larger and some much smaller than U.S. clothing size ranges, so shop carefully.

Don't make the mistake of trying to guess your child's size a year from now in order to take advantage of a half-price sale. It's not a bargain if it doesn't fit when the season rolls around.

Recycled Baby Clothes: If you have a store near you that "recycles" used children's clothing,

check it out. You will better understand how quickly babies grow out of outfits when you see the like-new condition of the clothing in most of these stores.

Health and Environmental Awareness: Keep yourself informed on the latest research about dyes, perfumes, chlorine bleach, talc, food additives, and so on and their long-term health effects. A consumer informed about risks can make healthier decisions when purchasing supplies. If improvements are going to occur, we all must be both advocates and educators for the long-term health of all children.

Bath, Bottom, and Safety Items

Plan ahead for the supplies needed for your baby's bath, skin care, and care of your baby's bottom (see Box 18-2), and have on hand the essential medication and safety items listed in Box 18-3. Do *not* give your baby any medication without an order from the pediatrician.

Baby Care

Bath, Skin Care, and Bottom Care Supplies

Soap: There is nothing less expensive than good old soap and water. Choose a mild soap recommended for babies. Popular name brands in baby supplies are usually a good choice. Baby products containing fragrance, however, may be irritating and therefore may not be the best choice for a baby with sensitive skin. Some pediatricians also approve of mild unscented adult soaps. Ask your pediatrician for suggestions. Babies' skin is slightly acidic at birth (pH 5), so it is important to avoid alkaline soaps, which may alter its normal pH. Babies can also be bathed with plain warm water, with mild soap added only occasionally.

Shampoo: "No tears" brands are recommended. If you are using a liquid baby soap, most brands are also approved for use as a shampoo.

Washcloths: Small baby washcloths are extra soft. You'll need one for washing and one for rinsing during baths and several for face and bottom cleanups. (Purchase at least six washcloths for your baby, although only two are needed during a bath.)

Two water basins for sponge baths: One will be for the soapy water and one for the plain rinse water. (Any bowls will do.)

Infant bathtub: This is for use after the umbilical cord has come off (and the wound from circumcision, if it was done, has healed).

Two or three towels: Use soft terrycloth towels. Hooded baby towels are helpful in preventing heat loss through the head, but they are not a necessity.

Baby lotion: This is not routinely recommended. Your newborn baby's skin will naturally become dry and be replaced with soft, new skin. Lotions and oils can interfere with this natural process and are not necessary. If

you absolutely must use them, as a personal preference, choose a name-brand baby lotion *without* perfumes. Use only an amount the size of a pea for the baby's *entire* body.

Baby oil: This is not routinely recommended. Baby oils, like lotions, are not necessary, and they can clog the skin pores. Baby oil may be recommended for cradle cap but should not be used routinely. One tiny drop in the palm of your hand is enough for the whole body if you must have that traditional "baby smell!"

Comb and brush: It is important to have a fine-tooth baby comb on hand. When the scalp peels or flakes, a fine-tooth comb can be used along with shampoo to loosen and remove dead skin.

Sterile cotton balls (if required by your pediatrician): These *may* be recommended by your pediatrician for eye care. However, a clean washcloth used on the eyes before it is used anywhere else is what is most often recommended for eye care today.

Nail file: Using your fingers, peel your baby's nails or use a nail file. It is not recommended that they be cut with nail scissors in the first few weeks of life.

Baby nail scissors with rounded safety tips: These are for later use. See page 344 for a discussion of infant nail care.

Diapering

Diaper Wipes: Presoaked wipes are convenient to have on hand, especially for outings. Remember, however, that *if* the wipes contain soap or perfume and are used exclusively, they may irritate sensitive skin. When such wipes are used at home, sensitive skin will benefit from a once-over with a damp washcloth following the presoaked wipe. Think of what your skin would feel like if

BOX 18-2 (CONTINUED)

you washed with soap and perfume and never rinsed!

A mixture of one quart of water with one teaspoon of baking soda can be used as an alternative to diaper wipes. The organization Mothers and Others for a Livable Planet recommends storing this solution in a zip-lock bag along with soft flannel squares for wipes. Cotton balls can also be used to apply this solution, but they are small and don't go a long way when cleaning stool from the baby's bottom.

Cornstarch: Cornstarch is more absorbent and safer than powders containing talc.

I realize that baby powder smells wonderful and has been part of the traditional "baby smell" for many years. However, research is clearly showing that talc (found in powder) can reach the upper genital tract. It has been found in the ovarian tumors of women who use powder on their genitals, and this has raised the question about the safety and risk of using talc on infants. Further studies need to be done, but enough evidence is in for me. I no longer recommend the use of powder containing talc on babies.

Unlike powder, natural cornstarch does not contain talc or cake when it gets wet. It also does not contain perfumes.

Be sure to put the cornstarch in your hand first and then apply it to your baby's bottom. Avoid shaking it directly onto the baby— shaking cornstarch or powder creates airborne particles that can be inhaled.

Keep cornstarch out of your baby's reach on the changing table. If she picks it up and turns it upside down over her face, the baby may inhale the fine particles, causing respiratory distress.

Ointment for diaper rash: Petroleum jelly and ointments containing vitamins A and D are first-line defense ointments for *prevention* of diaper rash. Applied lightly after the bottom is washed and dried, they form a protective shield between the skin and the wet or soiled diaper.

There are many thick paste ointments containing zinc oxide on the market that are advertised specifically for *treatment* of diaper rash. Once diaper rash occurs, they provide a barrier between the wetness and organisms in a soiled diaper and the irritated, diaper-rash skin. Healing can then occur beneath the ointment.

Clothing for after bath

How Do I Hold This Little Person?

For years you have thought about this day. For nine months you have planned. Now this little person is in your arms. Why didn't they teach this course in high school or college? I hope you will find these instructions and hints helpful. My main goal is that through education and preparedness you will be more able to relax and truly enjoy this special time in your life and the life of your baby.

If you have experience holding babies, skip this section. I have included it because so many parents, especially dads, have a terrified expression when presented with their newborn. I can't even begin to count how many times I have gone over these step-by-step instructions with new parents inexperienced in holding a baby. You are not alone!

If you have little experience holding babies, borrow a doll or teddy bear that is close to life-size and practice the following holds before your baby is born. They take only seconds to master, and the practice will help you feel much more relaxed when "the real thing" is placed in your arms!

Baby Care

BOX 18-3

Essential Medications and Safety Items

No matter how careful you are, accidents and illnesses can happen. Don't be caught without what you need. Have these basic supplies on hand:

Liquid acetaminophen: One common brandname is Tylenol. Acetaminophen is an aspirin substitute. Aspirin is not recommended in infancy or childhood unless ordered by your pediatrician for a specific condition.

Calibrated spoon or dropper: For the administration of liquid medication.

Rubbing alcohol or alcohol wipes: For cord care and for cleaning thermometers.

Glass round-tip or digital thermometer: For taking your baby's temperature when necessary.

Rectal thermometer with a round tip (only if rectal temperatures are required by your pediatrician): Rectal thermometers have a rounded bulb for safety. They may also have the nice feature of a red marking at the opposite end from the bulb to remind you that this thermometer is for rectal use only.

Sunscreen for infants: Studies have shown that sunburns in infancy and childhood greatly increase the risk of skin cancer in later life. An infant can become sunburned at the beach by reflection of harmful sun rays off the sand and water even if shaded by an umbrella. These burns are usually not apparent while you are at the beach; therefore, you don't realize the damage until you are home.

In addition, babies dehydrate quickly if exposed to sun. Sunscreen may prevent a burn, but it doesn't prevent dehydration or exposure of the eyes to harmful sun rays. Protect babies from exposure to the sun.

Bulb syringe: Your hospital will provide one for your infant. It will be yours to take home. Buy another one, and keep one by the changing area and the other near your baby's sleeping area.

Electrolyte fluid: This is often *ordered by the pediatrician* if a baby has vomiting or diarrhea. Have one can of replacement electrolyte water on hand to give to your baby if recommended by your pediatrician. There is nothing worse than having to take an infant with these symptoms out in order to purchase this needed item or not having it available in the middle of the night. One can is enough to get you started until another family member can get you more—children with vomiting and diarrhea don't drink large volumes. These cans have expiration dates, so check them carefully. Do not use this without a doctor's order.

Ipecac Syrup: Have it on hand once your child can crawl or walk, **but do not give Ipecac Syrup without an order to do so, and keep all medicine cabinets locked.** If you suspect that your child has eaten a substance or plant that may be poisonous, call a poison control center at once and then notify your pediatrician. Inducing vomiting may not be advisable—the treatment depends on the substance that was ingested. The poison control center will instruct you in the proper action to take.

If vomiting needs to be induced, you will be instructed to give Ipecac Syrup, so having a bottle of it on hand is essential. The dosage for your child will be determined by the poison control center staff or your pediatrician. Record the expiration date of this medication on your calendar and replace it before it expires. Again, do not use Ipecac Syrup unless instructed to do so.

BOX 18-3 (CONTINUED)

There is follow-up care required after administering it—follow the instructions given to you carefully. (See pages 381–383 for information on preventing poisoning.)

List of poisonous plants: Many common houseplants and outdoor bushes are highly poisonous. (For example, even one berry from a yew bush can cause fatal irregular heart rhythms.) See the section on poisonous plants in Chapter 20 for further information on common poisonous indoor and outdoor plants (page 382).

Infant car seat—required by law: Do your research. Investigate many brands, and check to be sure they have passed federal safety standards. Then look for ease, safety, and speed in getting a child in and out of the seat.

Many infant car seats have a carrying arm as an added feature. Pick up the car seats and compare weights. Remember, you will be carrying it around with a baby in it!

Occasionally a company finds one of its infant care products to be defective in some way. (Recently the carrying handle on one brand of car seat was found to release). Either the item is recalled or a repair kit is sent to you free of charge. Notification is made through the media, the newspaper, and the offices of pediatricians. (Pediatricians post these warning in their offices—review them carefully whenever you are there). It is also important for you to send in the warranty registration card on all infant products. If you are registered with a company that later discovers a defect in the product you purchased, you will be notified.

Once your child is able to sit upright, look for raised car seats that allow him or her to see out of the car. Car behavior improves significantly when a child can see the world outside the car. Every ride becomes a "world" of education when a child can see out of the windows.

Always place the car seat in the back seat of the car. Infants have been killed by the force of expanding air bags when their car seats were in the front seat.

List of emergency phone numbers: Keep this list by every telephone in your house. If you have a speed dial feature on your phone, program them in and mark them clearly. When seconds count, you'll be glad you did.

> **Police and 911 (if available)**
> **Fire**
> **Pediatrician**
> **Poison control center**
> **Medical doctor for the adults in the house**

In addition, see page 385 for tips on keeping directions to the house (for baby-sitters' use) close to the phones and other suggestions.

For Older Children

Hydrogen peroxide for cleaning cuts.

Bacitracin, triple antibiotic, or neomycin ointment for minor cuts or scrapes.

Sterile adhesive bandages and gauze pads in various sizes and adhesive tape for securing gauze pads. Remember, infants and small children suck on their fingers and hands. Do not use an adhesive bandage on an infant's fingers or hands unless instructed to do so by your pediatrician.

Anti-itch cream or hydrocortisone cream (1/2 percent) for bug bites. Cortisone is a very potent medication and should not be used on babies for extended periods unless ordered by your pediatrician. **If your baby has a bothersome rash, consult your pediatrician for instructions.**

Baby Care

The Cradle Hold

If you are left-handed, place your baby with her head on top of your right arm. The right arm above the bent elbow supports your baby's head while your forearm holds your baby in close to your body and supports the baby's back. Your right hand ends up under the baby's bottom or legs (depending on the length of your arm). You are actually holding your baby with one arm (your right), but your other arm comes around and adds additional support (Figure 18-1).

Transferring the Baby to a New Position

When you are ready to transfer your baby to a new location, you will put that free right hand into use. If holding your baby with your left arm, place your right arm behind your baby's back and your right hand under her shoulders and neck, with your fingers extended to support the head (Figure 18-2A). Slowly bring your right hand and

FIGURE 18-1

The Traditional Cradle Hold

your baby's head out to the front of your body. As you do this, allow your left hand to slide up and support your baby's buttocks. Your baby will now be looking at you as she sits in your left hand with her head in your right hand (Figure 18-2B). You are now ready to transfer your baby to another person's arms or put her on the changing table or into bed.

Football Hold—A Must to Master

If your baby is spitting up, vomiting, or gagging on mucus, this position provides many advantages. First, and most important, your infant feels the comfort and support of your arms. Second, her head and chest can be lowered *slightly* to allow gravity to assist in getting things up and out of the mouth. Third, you have a free hand to reach over and *gently* pat her back. This free hand is also available to use a bulb syringe to help remove spit-up and mucus from the mouth and nose.

In addition, the football hold can be used (without lowering the head) anytime you want or need to be holding your baby but need a free hand. With your infant in this secure position, you can safely answer the phone, change linen in a bassinet, gather supplies, or give a hug to another child (Figure 18-3).

Picking Your Baby Up into the Football Hold: *If you are right-handed* and your baby is lying down, pick up the baby's shoulders, neck and head in your left hand, allowing your left forearm to support her back. Your right hand will be under her bottom. Turn the baby on her side facing you, and place her on your left hip. Your baby's tummy, chest, and legs are against your side, and your left arm encircles her with your elbow bend at the level of her buttocks, your forearm along her back, and your hand and fingers supporting her shoulders, neck, and head. Your dominant hand is now free. Of course, if you are left-handed, use the opposite hands in the above procedure.

In this position, your baby loves the normal swaying of your body. She is held close and secure and she knows it!

FIGURE 18-2

Changing from the Cradle Hold to Transferring Position

A

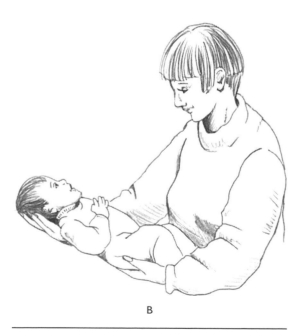

B

FIGURE 18-3

The Football Hold

Transferring Your Baby: To remove your baby from the football hold, take your free hand under your baby and place it under her bottom. Your left hand will already be in place to support the shoulders, neck, and head. Bring your baby out in front of you, and you are ready to transfer her to a new position or place.

When Your Baby Gags or Spits Up

If your baby is gagging on mucus or spitting up, she is as frightened as you are. You need to remember that there is nothing solid in your infant's airway. With gravity, gentle patting and a bulb syringe, the airway can be cleared. Your infant will not choke to death on a liquid. Keep this in mind and try hard not to panic—if you grab your infant in a panic, she will feel it and her normal reaction will be to hold her breath. This causes your baby to turn red or blue, making the whole situation appear worse than it is.

So, when your baby is gagging, pick her up gently and place her into the football hold as you

Baby Care

talk calmly to her. While your baby is in the football hold, lower her head and chest *slightly* below the level of her waist. If your hands are large, you may want to try tucking your *little finger* (of the hand supporting the head) under your baby's armpit. Some people feel more secure when lowering the baby's head slightly if this added technique is used. With your free hand, reach over your baby and gently pat her back. The gentle vibration and gravity can now go to work to help clear the airway.

Hopefully, you will have followed the rule to always keep the bulb syringe within reach of where your baby sleeps. With your free, dominant hand, you can now use the bulb syringe, first in the mouth and then in both nostrils. (See "Using a Bulb Syringe," below.) Since your baby is on her side facing you in the football hold, all secretions will drain down into her lower cheek. Clear all mouth secretions before doing the nostrils so that if your baby gasps when the nose is done, she will not suck secretions from the mouth back into her airway.

Using a Bulb Syringe

A bulb syringe (Figure 18-4) will be provided for your baby in the hospital. It is yours to take home. It is a good idea to purchase a second bulb syringe so that you will have two at home. (In drugstores they are sold as "ear syringes," but,

FIGURE 18-4

A Bulb Syringe

you will not be using them in the baby's ears.) **Keep one syringe near the diaper-changing area and the other near where your baby sleeps (or keep one upstairs and one downstairs).**

All babies have mucus at some time; however, cesarean section babies and babies born after a very short second stage of labor (the pushing stage) tend to have much more initial mucus in general. No one knows for certain why this is true. The following is generally thought to be a possible explanation, but it has never been scientifically proven. It is generally thought that most secretions are cleared from the baby during the pushing stage, when the baby is head-down and the chest and abdomen are compressed. During pregnancy, the baby drank amniotic fluid, which caused lots of mucus to form in the stomach and esophagus. Many people believe that if the pushing stage lasts a normal amount of time, most of these normal secretions are "squeezed out" before birth. However, if pushing is completed in less than 20 minutes or the baby is born by cesarean delivery, this mucus is not cleared as well and *may* cause coughing and gagging periodically during the first 24 hours after birth.

You will know that your baby is trying to get rid of mucus when she gags or begins to chew as if chewing on a big piece of bubble gum. In addition, babies with a great deal of mucus do not feed well and often spit up after swallowing. Although it is not fun to see your infant go through this, she must get this mucus up before she will be able to eat well. Sometimes babies continue to have difficulty with excessive initial mucus for one to two days; however, most infants will clear up this problem within the first 24 hours of life. Babies are very adept at taking care of this mucus problem. Be patient. Your infant will eat much better once she clears the mucus.

While holding your infant in the football hold, you can use the bulb syringe not only to help your infant clear the initial mucus after birth, but also to clear the remaining secretions from the mouth and nose after she spits up. Yes, you can use the same bulb syringe in both the mouth and nose. I know this goes against everything we try to teach our children later on in life, but it truly is okay! Bulb syringes can be easily washed and rinsed out well, but it is not necessary to do it after every use.

See Figure 18-5 for an illustration and Box 18-4 for step-by-step instructions for clearing secretions from your baby's mouth and nose.

Sleep Positions

Traditions change with the results from years of research. One such change is in the position recommended for infant sleep. Based on the latest research on sudden infant death syndrome (SIDS), pediatricians are no longer recommending placing infants on their abdomens or sides to sleep. **Although it is still not known what causes sudden infant death syndrome (SIDS), it is known that placing infants in the abdom-**

inal (tummy) and side sleep positions, smoking in the home, and overdressing infants increase the risk of SIDS. The American Academy of Pediatrics now recommends placing babies on their backs for sleep. This will be a hard one to explain to your baby's grandparents who swore that their babies slept longer and better on their tummies! However, just as with the issue of baby powder containing talc, you will have to help increase awareness of the health hazards involved in sticking with traditions that we now know are harmful.

The original SIDS studies were done in countries with the highest incidence of sudden infant death syndrome. These original studies showed up to a 50 percent reduction in the incidence of SIDS when the only thing changed was eliminating the abdominal position for sleeping, and more recent studies also eliminated the side position. **Place your infant on his or her back to sleep** (Figure 18-6).

When your baby is on her back, her head naturally turns to the side. Research has shown this

FIGURE 18-5

Clearing Secretions with a Bulb Syringe

FIGURE 18-6

The Back Sleeping Position

Baby Care

BOX 18-4

Clearing Secretions from the Mouth and Nose

1. **Hold your infant in the football hold.** This position makes your infant feel secure, gives you a free hand, and allows you to lower your infant's head and chest *slightly* to take advantage of gravity. If you are unfamiliar with the football hold, see the above section entitled, "Football Hold—A Must to Master."

2. **Pick up the bulb syringe and compress the bulb.**

3. **Place the tip of the syringe inside the baby's mouth.** If your baby is in the football hold, she will be on her side and secretions will accumulate in her lower cheek. Therefore, the tip of the syringe should be placed in the *lower* cheek.

4. **Release the compression on the bulb,** causing secretions to be sucked up into it. You may have to move the tip of the bulb around slightly while releasing your squeeze on it. If the tip is pressed firmly into the cheek, the cheek blocks the tip and the bulb can't extract the secretions. Once the bulb is again expanded, there is no further "power" to remove further secretions.

5. **Remove the bulb syringe from the baby's mouth and squeeze out all the secretions** on a burping cloth or tissue (or anywhere if your baby is still spitting up).

6. **Compress the bulb again and continue removing secretions from the mouth** until there are no further secretions being obtained. **Always suction the mouth before the nose.** When the nose is suctioned, the baby will often have a reflex gasp. Suctioning the mouth first *prevents* secretions from the mouth from being gasped into the airway.

7. **Suction the nostrils *if* secretions are visible or you can hear a lot of nasal congestion.** To do so, compress the bulb and insert it *gently* into one nostril. The bulb syringe is made to go in only as far as it should—don't push it in forcefully.

8. **Release the compression** and allow the suction to remove secretions from the nostril.

9. **Remove the bulb syringe from the nostril and squeeze it out to clear it of the secretions.**

10. **Repeat this procedure in the remaining nostril.**

to be a safe sleeping position. There has *not* been an increase in choking since parents have been asked to place their babies on their backs as a sleeping position.

This does not mean that if your baby has gas you cannot put her on her abdomen with the knees drawn up under the tummy, under your observation and for a short period of time, to help her pass the gas. In addition, there are special circumstances, such as when your baby has excessive mucus or excessive spitting up or vomiting, in which your pediatrician may discuss with you use of the side position, with a small towel roll for back support, as an alternative until these temporary conditions pass.

There has recently been some concern about head molding, or creating a flat spot, when the back sleeping positioning is used. Skull shape should be monitored both by the pediatrician and the parents. If you feel that a problem is developing, address your questions and concerns to your pediatrician for further assessment and suggestions.

The following are some things you can do to help keep your child safe while she or he sleeps:

❑ Use the back position for sleep.
❑ Use a firm mattress. Do *not* use a waterbed.
❑ Put no fluffy blankets in the sleep area.

❑ Use no pillows.

❑ Do *not* put sheepskin under your baby or anywhere in the sleep area.

❑ Put no soft stuffed toys in the crib.

❑ Crib rail pads should be firm, not soft and fluffy.

❑ Keep the room at a comfortable temperature.

❑ Do not overdress your infant.

❑ Keep your home smoke free.

❑ Have your baby seen by your pediatrician if he or she appears ill.

After a few months, when your baby begins to move around on her own, it won't matter which position you place her in—she will be able to move on her own. **Just be certain to always use a firm surface for sleeping, and never place pillows or large soft stuffed toys in the sleeping area. If your child can roll up against something soft like a pillow, stuffed toy, or very soft crib rail pads, she can suffocate.**

Taking Baby to Bed with You

At times you will comfort your fussy baby by taking her into bed with you. I am frequently asked how much is too much on this issue. At what point can a baby come to expect to be taken into bed with you?

First, we need to ask some other questions: What is causing the distress, and why aren't regular measures meeting this need? Is a referral to the pediatrician for assessment in order? Could there be a physical or medical reason for the baby's fussiness?

Any measure over time can become a habit or an expected standard. Certainly a baby does not start out thinking, "I prefer my parents' arms or their bed over my crib." If this preference develops, it is out of habit or because of what has been offered as the norm. In addition, before three months of age, a baby is generally less likely to develop a long-term behavioral habit than after

three months. Keeping these things in mind, make your decision about bringing baby into bed with you based on the individual situation. A crying baby needs to have his or her needs met and needs comforting. In addition, you should find out the cause of the fussiness that is constantly forcing you to consider bringing the baby to bed with you as a solution. Always bringing the baby into bed with you does not address the underlying problem and may not be the necessary solution.

However, in saying that, I will add that occasionally you may be desperate for sleep, and this solution may allow you to get some sleep on a given night. If you have tried everything else, this may bring needed peace. However, if this fussiness is an every-night thing, your pediatrician should be consulted long before bringing your baby to bed with you becomes a habit.

It is important that you always think of safety when deciding to bring an infant into your bed. Infants have been suffocated by adults who rolled over on them while sleeping. Placing pillows between your knees and a firm towel roll, or a firm toy that squeaks when compressed, against your abdomen or chest may help prevent such an accident.

There is also a risk that you might fall asleep when holding your infant for long periods while sitting in a chair. Use pillows or towel rolls to support your arms. Many infants have been dropped as adults fell asleep holding them.

Care of the Umbilical Cord Stump

The umbilical cord is bluish white at birth. Because there are no nerves in the cord, it can be cut without any need for a local anesthetic. The cord clamp applied at birth prevents blood loss from the baby. If the cord were cut without being clamped, the baby would hemorrhage from the open end of the cord. After birth, your nurse will be checking this clamp to be certain it is secure on the cord stump.

Baby Care

By the time your baby is 24 hours old, the umbilical cord will be partially dry and appear black and yellow. The clamp will be removed by a nurse between 24 and 36 hours after birth, when the cord is adequately dry and bleeding from the area is no longer a risk.

Your nurse will instruct you at the hospital in the protocol for cord care. Some hospitals initially apply an antiseptic to the cord that stains it a dark color; others do not. To aid drying and prevent infection, the most common treatment is to use alcohol prep pads that come individually wrapped. At each diaper change, the cord is wiped with a pad, starting at the base of the cord. Remember that the cord contains no nerves, so caring for this area does not hurt your baby. To treat the umbilical cord stump, gently pull the abdominal skin away from the base of the cord and swab with the alcohol wipe in this area, which will still be moist (Figure 18-7). Then progress up the cord, cleaning all edges and the top of the cord. Alcohol swab pads will be provided to you in the hospital and can be purchased in any drugstore for home use.

You may also use sterile cotton balls and rubbing alcohol for cord care. Put alcohol on a cotton ball and follow the same procedure as above. If you use cotton balls and alcohol, the treatment can be done two or three times a day instead of at every diaper change. The disadvantage to this form of treatment is that the alcohol drips on surrounding abdominal skin and can cause it to become excessively dry.

Normally the cord falls off between one and two weeks, with the average being 7 to 10 days. After the cord comes off, the skin will still appear red and moist. Continue to treat with alcohol until the belly button area looks like normal skin. Avoid one-piece tight outfits until the skin has healed.

(C)**Any time you see excessive redness around the cord area, report it promptly to your pediatrician. Also report bleeding or green or yellow discharge from around the cord.**

Special *newborn* diapers are available with a half-circle cut out to allow air to get to the cord. If you do not have these diapers, or if your newborn requires a larger size of diaper, fan-fold the diaper down below the cord.

1. Place the diaper under the baby with the tabs under the baby's bottom.
2. Bring the top edge up between the baby's legs and fold it down (on the outside of the diaper) about two inches (Figure 18-8A). The soft lining is against the baby's skin.
3. Bring the top edge (one inch) of this fold back up (Figure 18-8B). This allows the plastic to be on the outside to protect the baby's clothes from getting wet while allowing the soft inner lining to be against the baby's skin.
4. Secure the fan-folded area with the tabs.

FIGURE 18-7

Umbilical Cord Care

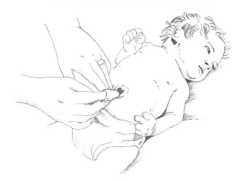

Bathing Your Baby

Bath time is a very special time for you to interact with your baby. It is your baby's main source of exercise during these early days of life. The lungs get good exercise (deep inflation) if your baby cries, and her muscles move to stretch and kick. Remember, exercise is healthy. Make bath time a fun time, and use it to your advantage!

FIGURE 18-8 A & B

Fan-Folding the Diaper Below the Umbilical Cord Stump

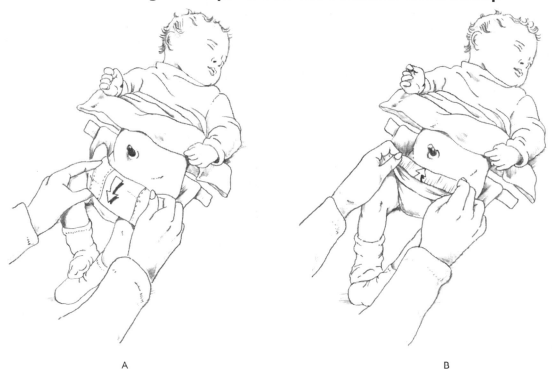

A

B

Bathing your baby requires special equipment and supplies, some of which are also used in diapering. See Box 18-2, page 326.

Safety First

Keep one hand in contact with your baby at all times during the bath. Accident prevention is another reason that gathering all necessary equipment before you begin is so important. If you must reach for something, have one hand in contact with your baby at all times while you reach. If the item is out of reach, pick your baby up and carry her with you. Infants learn very quickly how to scoot by pushing with their heels. **Always think accident *prevention*.**

If the phone rings during bath time, let it ring. Most of your callers will know that you have a newborn and will try calling back later. If you must answer the phone, wrap your baby in a towel and take her with you. Remember that wet babies are more susceptible to heat loss. Ask to call back after your baby's bath.

How Often Should I Bathe My Baby?

As long as you spot clean your baby's face after she eats or spits up and cleanse her bottom after each diaper change, total baths are not necessary every day. Until a baby begins to crawl, a bath two or three times a week is usually adequate.

A baby's skin pH is slightly acidic (pH 5), which allows the skin to inhibit the growth of bacteria. Too much washing or washing with an alkaline soap will change the natural pH of the skin, creating a more suitable skin environment for bacterial growth.

There are several other factors to take into consideration when deciding how often to bathe your baby. Does your baby enjoy or hate baths? Is bath time a fun time for you or an additional chore? Do you live in a hot, muggy climate? (In summer's heat, a bath gets rid of that sticky feeling and promotes relaxation.) Does your baby stop fussing and take her longest sleep after the natural exercise that comes with a bath?

What Time of Day Should the Bath Be Done?

Whatever time is convenient for you will be fine. It is best, however, to avoid bathing immediately after feeding.

When I mentioned using the bath to your advantage, this is what I meant. When my oldest son was born, he immediately got his days and nights reversed. At the end of the first week, I consulted the experienced nurse at my pediatrician's office. Her suggestion was so simple that I couldn't believe I hadn't thought of it myself. She asked: "What do you do with him right before he takes his longest nap?" I answered, "I give him a bath." Based on great wisdom and a lot of experience, she taught me the following trick.

Bathe your baby at night, but follow these rules first. Take your shower, and if you have other children, get baths and snacks completed—then do your baby's bath. After all that exercise and play time, wrap her up nice and warm and dry and feed her. Your baby will be down for the count, and you and your children will also be ready for bed! Everyone will be able to sleep the entire time the baby sleeps after her bath. Following this plan not only helped me to get the rest I needed; it helped my son learn the proper use of days and nights!

Sponge Bath or Infant Tub Bath?

Until the umbilical cord stump falls off and the underlying skin is completely healed, **you will give your baby sponge baths. If your son was circumcised, you will also give him sponge baths until the entire penis looks healed.** The reason sponge baths are used instead of infant tub baths is that the cord (and circumcision area) needs to be kept as dry and free of germs as possible. Once the belly button area and the circumcision look completely like normal skin, you can advance to bathing your baby in an infant tub.

Sponge Bathing from Head to Toe

The following is a step-by-step guide to giving a sponge bath:

Getting Ready to Sponge Bathe: Gather all necessary equipment and have it within arm's reach (Figure 18-9). See Box 18-2 for bath supplies, page 326.

Prevent heat loss by keeping your baby as warm as possible. Newborns do a good job maintaining a normal temperature, but they have a difficult time raising their temperature back up to normal if they become chilled. They are very

FIGURE 18-9

Put all bath supplies within reach.

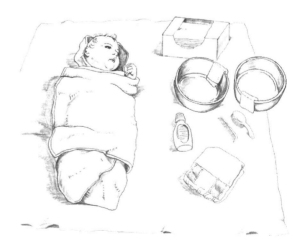

susceptible to heat loss during the first weeks of life until the heat regulating system in their brain has had time to adjust and mature.

Choose a room that is free of drafts and as warm as possible. Do not give a bath near a fan, air conditioner, or open window. A sponge bath is usually done on a changing table (with edges) or countertop.

Use towels to keep your infant covered during the sponge bath. The ends of the towels should be wrapped around your baby for warmth. I prefer to use a separate towel for drying. Only the face and the area being washed, rinsed, and dried should be exposed to the air (Figure 18-10).

There are infant tubs for *sponge* bathing that have a separate area for water and a seat that is at an angle (Figure 18-11). If you are using one, place a towel on the seat, put your baby on it, and wrap the ends of the towel around your baby for warmth.

If you have followed the above guidelines, you are now ready to begin.

Beginning the Bath: Put warm water and a washcloth into each of two bowls, one for wash water and one for rinse water. You may use your fingers for soaping instead of a washcloth if you prefer. The water in the bowls can be warmer than the water you will use when you later begin

FIGURE 18-10

Using Towels to Prevent Heat Loss During a Sponge Bath

FIGURE 18-11

Infant Tubs Designed for Sponge Baths

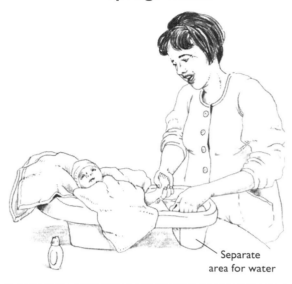

Separate area for water

using an infant tub, because washcloths cool off quickly. The water should feel warm but not hot.

Undress your baby and remove or check her diaper. If your baby has stooled, it is best to clean the diaper area now. It is not much fun to get done with the bath only to have a foot kicked in a soiled diaper! An unsoiled diaper can be left on until you reach the diaper area, or removed now. Just beware, especially parents of boys! There is something about cool air and the bath! You will get sprayed with urine if you don't keep something like a dry washcloth over the penis.

Wrap the towel ends over your baby, and expose only the area you are washing (as shown before in Figure 18-10). A hooded towel, if available, has the nice feature of covering the top of the baby's head for warmth (Figure 18-12).

Wash, rinse, dry, and cover each area as you go.

Begin with areas you need to keep extra clean (eyes and ears), and end with the area that is almost impossible to keep clean (the bottom)! This way your water and washcloth will remain clean and you will not bring germs from the bottom up

Baby Care

FIGURE 18-12

Hooded Bath Towel

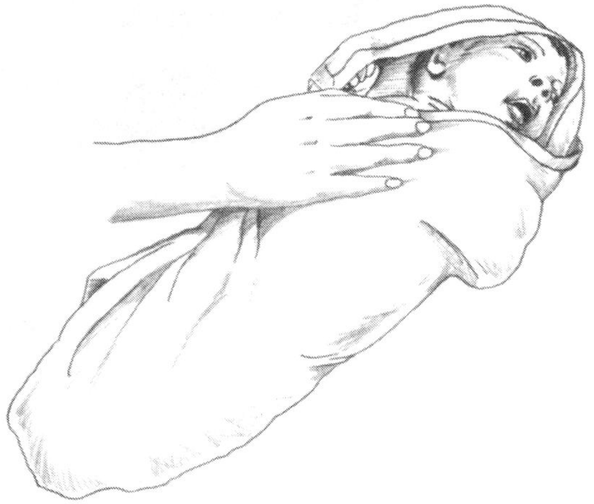

to the face. One exception: do the shampoo last, at the sink under running water. The head is the largest surface area on the baby, and the most heat can be lost through it. Once the baby's head is washed and well dried, you will need to dress your baby and wrap her up for warmth. For the first few weeks, after bathing her, include a cloth cap like the one she wore in the hospital nursery.

Eyes: Using a clean washcloth (or sterile cotton ball if preferred) moistened with warm water, gently clean the eyes from the nose (inside edge) outward. Do not use soap on the eyes. Use a different area of the clean washcloth, or a new cotton ball, for the other eye. Your purpose is to remove the sandy crusts on the *outsides* of the lids. Gently dry the eyes.

Ears: Clean the outer folds of the ears and behind the ears with water and just a dab of soap. Clean only what your finger can reach. *Never* use cotton swabs inside the ear canal. (Your pediatrician will check the ear canal at the first office visit. If there is a buildup of wax, which is rare, he or she will take care of that for you.) Rinse the ears with a damp washcloth, and dry them well.

Face: A baby's cheeks often get exposed to drool and the frequent, small secretions common after a burp. They need special attention. Wash the cheeks with water and a small amount of soap. Be careful to avoid getting soap into the baby's eyes. You may use plain water, without soap, if you prefer.

Don't Forget That Hidden Neck: As Ernie on Sesame Street reminds us, "Just because you can't see my neck doesn't mean it isn't there!" The many folds and creases on a baby need special attention. Secretions left unattended in the neck creases can cause serious skin irritation. Prevention is much easier than treatment! Wash, rinse, and dry the entire neck, front and back.

Arms: One at a time, wash, rinse, and dry each arm and tuck it back under the towel cover. Be sure to extend the arms to get into the elbow creases and open the fingers (by gently pressing on the baby's palms) in order to wash those tiny hands well.

Chest and Abdomen: Soap, rinse, and gently pat dry the chest and abdomen. Calling this a sponge bath doesn't mean you can't use lots of water. Sponge bathing prevents the umbilical cord (and unhealed circumcision) from *soaking* in water. If these areas get a little wet, don't panic—just pat them dry. Cover the chest and abdomen after drying.

Back: Roll your baby onto her side or place her on her tummy with her head to one side. Soap, rinse, and dry the back, and double-check those creases in the back of the neck.

Legs: Wash, rinse, and dry each leg separately. Don't forget to extend the leg to get to the area behind the knee. Also wash the groin area now. (The groin is the skin crease where the leg attaches to the front of the body.) Good diaper-rash prevention is important in the groin area. Cover the baby's legs after drying.

Diaper Area—Girls: With a clean washcloth and mild soap and water, or just plain water, gently spread the labia (folds) of the perineum and clean **from front to back** down the left side, down the right side, and down the middle. **Use a clean section of a fresh washcloth for *each* wipe.** After completing these wipes, wash the rectal area. Rinse by squeezing water over the entire area and pat dry.

Remember to only wipe and wash from front to back. This practice should be continued throughout life. If a woman or girl wipes in the reverse direction, she risks bringing contamination from the rectum into the vagina and urethra, which can cause urinary tract infections.

Diaper Area—Uncircumcised Boys: See Figure 18-13. The penis consists of the *shaft* and the *glans* (the wider part at the end of the penis). During infancy and for several years, the foreskin is attached to the glans of the penis. The open end of the foreskin is large enough for urine to pass through. Trying to retract the foreskin at this time can be harmful. It begins to separate from the glans as the baby begins to grow, but it takes several years for this process to be complete, so **don't try to retract the foreskin until the child reaches early school age.**

If the foreskin *naturally* retracts on its own as far as it can go, and you see a white substance on the head of the penis, do not be alarmed. This secretion is called *smegma* and is perfectly normal. It is secreted on the inside of the foreskin as a natural lubricant.

No special cleaning methods are required for the uncircumcised male. Merely wash the penis with soap and water, rinse, and dry. Be certain to lift the penis up and wash the under surface that rests on the scrotum. Collected urine crystals and the warmth and moisture under the penis can cause this area to become very irritated and red if not washed and dried adequately.

Wash the rectal area last. Rinse by squeezing water over the area, and pat dry.

Diaper Area—Circumcised Boys: In most hospitals it is the obstetrician who performs the *circumcision* (surgical removal of the foreskin of the penis; see Figure 18-14). Obstetricians are

FIGURE 18-13

Uncircumcised Penis

FIGURE 18-14

Circumcised Penis

surgically certified, whereas most pediatricians are not licensed for surgery.

Most surgeons want to see documented evidence that the baby has urinated before they will perform the circumcision procedure.

Immediately after circumcision, a dressing and tight pressure diaper will be applied by a nurse. This diaper will later be removed and the area checked by a nurse for bleeding. You will then receive instructions in circumcision care.

Always begin and end diaper changes by washing your hands. It is not necessary to wash the circumcision area after the baby urinates. In the first two days, the less irritation and touching the better. Avoid putting soap on the circumcision area. If the area becomes soiled with stool, drip warm water over the circumcision to clean the area of stool. Avoid all tub baths until both the circumcision and umbilical area have completely healed (until they look like normal skin).

For the first 24 hours, put a generous amount of petroleum jelly, or whatever ointment you are

Baby Care

instructed to use, on a sterile gauze three-by-three-inch or four-by-four-inch pad. From the outside of the pad, distribute the ointment over a large area of the gauze. (Do not spread it with your fingers.) Coat the entire circumcision area with the ointment, leaving the gauze in place over the penis, and apply a clean diaper.

The ointment-covered gauze should be changed each time you change the diaper for 24 hours. After 24 hours, your instructions may say that the gauze is no longer required. If so, clean and dry the diaper area, and apply a thin layer of petroleum jelly or the prescribed ointment to the penis using a sterile gauze pad or put petroleum jelly on the diaper in the area that will cover the penis and smear it around (using the diaper—not your finger). The petroleum jelly will prevent the baby's penis from sticking to the diaper.

To help prevent bleeding, hold your baby's feet during diaper changes—if he kicks his penis, it can cause bleeding in the circumcision area.

Wash the rectal area last to prevent contaminating the penis with germs from this area.

The circumcised glans will look red and raw for several days. During this time, there will be soreness and a burning after urination. A quick diaper change with the ointment you are instructed to use will bring immediate relief. As the area becomes less red, a soft yellow covering will form. This is actually a soft scab and is part of the healing process. (See Emergency Call—Circumcision Problems, page 343.)

Once the circumcision is healed, wash the penis with soap and water, rinse, and dry. Pay particular attention to cleaning the underside of the penis, which rests against the scrotum. Collected urine crystals and the warmth and moisture of this area can cause it to become red and irritated if not washed adequately.

Cord Care: See the earlier section on the care of the umbilical cord stump, page 335.

Shampoo: Like overall bathing, it is not necessary to shampoo every day. Two or three times a week is sufficient. Of course you will need to shampoo if your baby soils her hair by spitting up. Because the greatest amount of heat is lost from the head, always do the shampoo as the last step when giving your baby a sponge bath.

Wrap your baby in a dry towel and place her in the football hold (on the left side if you are right-handed). Go to a sink and adjust the water to a tepid temperature. (Water is considered tepid if you can't tell whether it's warm or cool when running it over your inner wrist.)

With your free hand, wet your baby's hair. Place a small amount of shampoo on the head and massage the scalp.

Test the water *again* for correct temperature by running it over the inside of your wrist (Figure 18-15A). The water should not feel hot or cold.

There are two ways to rinse your baby's hair after shampooing: use a cup to pour water over the hair, or if you are comfortable doing so, allow running water to flow over your baby's hair (Figure 18-15B). Place your finger over her ear to keep water out of it (Figure 18-15C).

Most infants love the feel and sound of the running water on their head. Enjoy the peaceful look that usually comes over them when their hair is rinsed this way!

FIGURE 18-15A

The Shampoo

Testing the water temperature.

If your baby's scalp is dry and flaky, gently comb through it with a fine-tooth comb during the shampoo (Figure 18-15D).

After rinsing, dry your baby's hair well.

Skin Care: As mentioned earlier, baby lotions and oils are not routinely recommended. If used excessively or in large amounts, they can block skin pores and alter the natural pH of the skin. If you are tempted to use baby oil on dry skin, one tiny drop in the palm of your hand is enough for the baby's entire body.

The Finish: Diaper, dress, wrap, and cuddle your baby!

Regular Bathing in an Infant Tub

After the umbilical cord has fallen off and the underlying skin is completely healed,

---

Emergency Call
Circumcision Problems
The area around the circumcision may spot very small amounts of blood for the first 24 hours. **While in the hospital, please report all bleeding to the nurse for assessment.**

If the circumcision bleeds more than the normal amount described above, and you are at home, **call your pediatrician immediately.**

Also report any of the following symptoms to your pediatrician:

- ❏ **Drainage from the circumcision area that is excessive or thick and green**
- ❏ **Swelling of the penis glans**
- ❏ **Fever and other symptoms of infection such as poor feeding and change in activity level**
- ❏ **Failure to urinate within 24 hours after circumcision**

Your baby should urinate within twenty-four hours after circumcision. If you are in the hospital, nurses will be certain to report to the doctor if urination is delayed. If you have already gone home, ✆**report by phone to the pediatrician if urination has not occurred within 24 hours after the procedure. This is very important.** If your baby cannot urinate due to swelling, pressure will build up in his kidneys and possibly damage them.

If unable to void on his own within 24 hours of the circumcision procedure, your baby will need to be further assessed by the pediatrician. Usually, through the pediatrician's assessment of the bladder, it is determined that the bladder is not distended (full) and that urination has actually occurred. More time can then be allowed for urination to occur and be visually verified (by a wet diaper). If the baby's bladder is distended, your pediatrician will insert a tiny sterile catheter through the opening in the penis and advance it to the bladder in order to empty the urine. Further assessment will then be done to determine the cause of the inability to urinate. After catheterization, the baby should be observed for urination again. Follow your pediatrician's instructions.

Baby Care

Rinsing the Hair

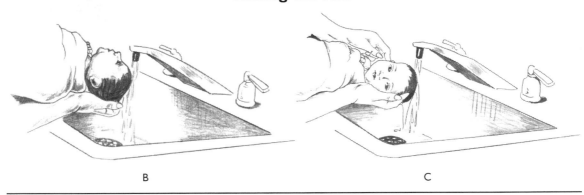

B   C

Using a Fine-Tooth Comb or Soft Brush During the Shampoo

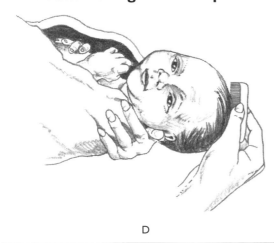

D

and the circumcision (if done) is completely healed, you may use an infant tub with an inch or two of warm water for the bath. Now your baby can be put directly in the warm water as you support her in a semi-reclining position.

Now that you are no longer sponge bathing, you can soap up and rinse a larger area at a time. Always begin with the face (the area where you want the cleanest water) and end with the bottom. The shampoo will be done last, at the sink. Be sure to avoid drafts when giving a bath.

Nail Care

In the first few weeks of life, if your baby's fingernails are long enough to scratch her face, they can be peeled away with your (clean) fingernails. (The tops of the nails are quite soft and rub off easily.) They can also be filed, but this is difficult because they are so soft. Do not use infant fingernail scissors for the first few weeks of life. Some T-shirt brands have hand covers to protect the infant from scratching herself. She may even "file" down her own nails on the insides of these hand covers.

Later you may use infant fingernail scissors (the ends are rounded for safety). When using infant scissors, pull the skin under the nail downward before clipping the nail. There is a thin layer of skin under the nails of infants that is difficult to see. If you are using infant scissors and a raw area develops, apply gentle pressure to stop bleeding. Do *not* put an adhesive bandage on a baby's fingers or hands; the baby may choke on it if it comes off when the baby sucks on her hands. Go back to peeling with your fingernails or filing the nails for another week or so, before using scissors again.

Diapering

Trust me: you will be able to perform this procedure in your sleep in a very short time!

Wash your hands before and after changing a diaper. This protects your baby from germs on your hands and protects you and others from the germs in a dirty diaper. If you are not at home, use a towelette or presoaked diaper wipe for your hands.

If traveling or shopping, remember to pack a clean surface to put your baby on for diaper changes. A cloth diaper or blanket will serve this purpose.

When Should I Change My Baby?

If you are using disposable diapers, you cannot use external wetness as your guide. By the time these diapers feel wet on the outside, much too much time has elapsed for good prevention of skin irritation.

Of course you will change a diaper when it is apparent that your baby has had a bowel movement or is very wet. A good time to change diapers is either before or after feeding. Many babies get added gas if you raise their legs immediately after feeding, however. If this is the case with your baby, try changing her before feedings unless she always stools while eating.

If your baby has not had a bowel movement and is not excessively wet, it is okay to skip the diaper change at the night feeding—for some babies, the stimulation of a diaper change at night makes it more difficult for them to get back to sleep.

Never wake a sleeping baby for a diaper change!

Disposable Diapers

Disposable diapers are certainly the most convenient, especially in the first few weeks, when parents need to conserve their energy. If you have chosen disposable diapers, buying them by the case when they are on sale cuts down on the expense. Watch your newspapers and magazines for coupons. Be careful to buy only a couple of newborn-size boxes; if your baby starts out at eight or nine pounds, they will be outgrown very quickly.

Folding the plastic top of a disposable diaper down *to the inside* prevents moisture inside the diaper from reaching baby's clothes. However, watch the skin that is in contact with the plastic for redness—some babies are sensitive to plastic. I prefer to fan-fold the top of the diaper outward and down two inches and then bring the top one inch of diaper back up to cover the exposed lining with plastic. In this way the plastic is the top layer, keeping moisture from the diaper lining off the baby's clothes, and the plastic does not touch the baby's skin. (See Figure 18-8, page 337.)

When removing a disposable diaper, open the tags and press them closed right away. If an open tag sticks to your baby's skin, it hurts when it is pulled away.

See "Diapering Hints," page 346, for more information on diapering.

For environmental health reasons, dispose of formed stool in the toilet before disposing of the diaper.

Cloth Diapers

Even if you are not using cloth diapers, it is great to have a dozen around as burping cloths. Cloth diapers can be purchased prefolded or flat. Prefolded diapers have extra layers sewn into the center panel so folding is not necessary. Flat diapers are long and of one thickness. They must be folded (usually in thirds) before you use them.

You will need plastic pants to put over cloth diapers. Plastic pants last longer and stay softer if they are air-dried after washing. If you are looking for an alternative to plastic, there are naturally water-repellent wool diaper covers available.

Purchase diaper pins, not safety pins. To prevent sticking your baby, always keep your fingers between the diaper and your baby's skin when putting in and removing diaper pins. Always insert diaper pins so that they point open to the outside. This is a safety precaution in case the pin inadvertently opens.

Store pins in a safe place—a bar of soap (with the paper left on) is convenient. The soap has the added benefit of helping the pin glide more easily through the cloth when you use it next. Never put the pins in your mouth during diaper changes—babies love to imitate!

You will need a diaper pail in which to store dirty diapers until they are washed. If you prefer not to use diaper pail deodorizer tablets, **an alternative is to soak the diapers in a mixture of borax and hot water to sanitize them and stop odors until you are able to wash them.**

Use a mild, unperfumed detergent for washing diapers and a small amount of nonchlorine bleach (also unperfumed) for disinfecting and whitening. **(A nonchlorine bleach substitute that brightens clothes is one-fourth cup of lemon juice or white vinegar added in the wash cycle.)** Rinse the diapers well. Double-rinsing helps if your baby has very sensitive skin. Fabric softeners are not necessary. Many babies develop skin irritation when fabric softeners are used routinely on their clothes and diapers.

Diaper Service

When you are looking at diapering options, be sure to price diaper services. Many people who prefer cloth diapers feel that a diaper service is not more expensive than washing their own diapers. If you will be washing your own cloth diapers, you must add in the expenses of diaper purchase and laundering costs (detergent, water, and electricity). **However, be certain to ask what products the company uses in the washing process, in order to avoid strong detergents, bleaching agents, dyes, and perfumes that might be irritating to your baby's skin.**

More Diapering Hints

I usually recommend to new moms that they use presoaked wipes on outings and use white, un- scented toilet paper, mild unperfumed soap, and water at home. If commercial wipes are always used at home, watch your baby's skin closely, because some brands may irritate it.

Choose toilet paper carefully. Extra-soft and perfumed papers are treated with chemicals that can be irritating to sensitive skin.

Your baby's first meconium stool is best wiped away with a *dry* wipe first. The oily nature of this first stool makes it smear if water is used for the first wipes.

When your baby has a bowel movement, the diaper can be used for the first wipe. Then fold the diaper in half, dirty side to the inside, and place it under the baby's bottom until cleaning is completed. This prevents stool or additional urine from soiling your changing area. If you are using toilet paper or presoaked wipes to clean the baby, tuck them inside the folded diaper and out of your way after use! (Using the diaper for this purpose also prevents soiling and contamination of the changing table or countertop from the used tissue or wipes.)

When diapering a baby boy, always cover his penis with a washcloth or your hand during a diaper change. There is something about that cold air—you will get a shower every time, if you don't heed this warning! Also, point the penis downward in the new diaper. This keeps the urine where the diaper has the greatest amount of padding for absorption.

Have age-appropriate toys available for distraction during diaper changes, especially as your baby gets older and more active.

Preventing Diaper Rash

Prevention of diaper rash is much easier than treatment! For daily prevention, first wash, rinse and dry the baby's bottom. (Remember, only wash from front to back on girls to prevent bringing germs from the rectal area into the vagina or urethra.) If your baby seems prone to irritation in the diaper area, use extra precaution. With your fingers, apply a thin layer of petroleum jelly or an ointment made for babies containing vitamins A and D. You can apply a small amount of cornstarch in addition if you like by putting a small amount in your hand and, from your hand, putting it on the baby's bottom. (This avoids shaking the container and prevents inhalation of fine particles.) Cornstarch is much more absorbent than powder and is safer. It does not contain talc, a known carcinogen, or perfumes, which can be irritating to sensitive skin.

Powders containing talc are no longer recommended for use on babies. Any kind of powder has very fine particles and can be irritating when inhaled, so do not shake powder near your baby.

Keep cornstarch containers out of the reach of your baby and other small children. If grabbed and turned over into the child's mouth, the fine particles can cause respiratory distress.

If a diaper rash develops, continue to follow the above prevention suggestions, and in addition, use an ointment made for babies that contains zinc oxide. Zinc oxide ointment is a thick white paste that forms a protective barrier between the wetness in the diaper and your baby's skin. During the day you can try placing a clean diaper under your baby or opening the one she is wearing to expose her bottom to air for short periods of time.

Always rediaper with a clean, dry diaper.

If the above methods do not bring the diaper rash under control, consult your pediatrician for assistance.

Keeping Your Baby Snug and Warm

Your newborn has emerged from nine months in a warm, soothing environment and needs to be kept snug and warm, *but not overheated,* in order to feel secure (and for easier handling!). Box 18-5 shows you three ways to wrap (bunt) a baby. Never bunt the arms straight down. Again, you can practice with a doll or teddy bear before you have the real thing.

BOX 18-5

How to Wrap (Bunt) a Baby

Bunting with a Receiving Blanket
1. Fold down one corner of the blanket. Place the baby's neck even with the folded edge. (See Figure 18-16A.)
2. Bring one side of the blanket over and tuck it in smoothly (Figure 18-16B). Bring over the shortest side first if the blanket is uneven.
3. Bring the bottom corner up (Figure 18-16C). If it is long, tuck the end over the baby's shoulder or fold it down below the chin.
4. Pull the remaining side snugly (but not too tightly) up and around the baby (Figure 18-16D).

Bunting and Creating a Hood
1. Fold down the upper corner. Place the top of the baby's head below the folded edge. (See Figure 18-17A.)
2. Create the hat (Figure 18-17B).
3. Fold over one edge and tuck it in smoothly (Figure 18-17C). Use the shortest edge, if the blanket is uneven.
4. Fold up the bottom edge (Figure 18-17D).
5. Snugly fold over the remaining side (Figure 18-17E). Do not pull this edge too tight.

Bunting with a Large Square Blanket:
If your blanket is a 36-inch square or larger, you can use this technique. This is especially useful if the blanket is bulky.
1. Place the baby on the blanket as shown in Figure 18-18A.
2. Fold over one edge of the blanket (Figure 18-18B). Cover the shoulder for extra warmth.
3. Bring over the other edge of the blanket (Figure 18-18C).
4. Open up the bottom two corners of the blanket (Figure 18-18D).
5. Bring up the bottom edge of the blanket as far as it will go, but not higher than the baby's neck (Figure 18-18E).
6. Wrap the edges around and to the back (Figure 18-18F).

Baby Care

FIGURE 18-16

Bunting with a Receiving Blanket

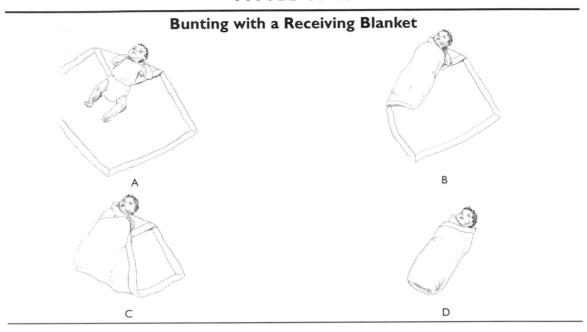

A

B

C

D

FIGURE 18-17

Bunting and Creating a Hood

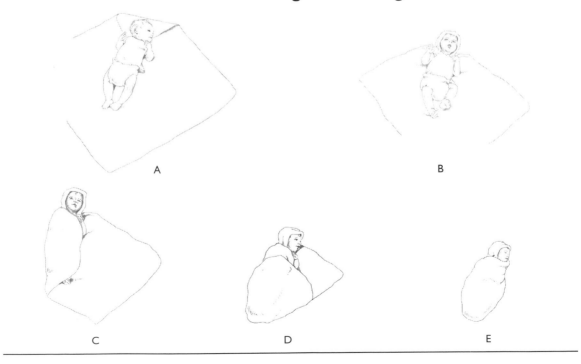

A

B

C

D

E

FIGURE 18-18

Bunting with a Large Square Blanket

A

B

C

D

E

F

Other Baby Care Issues

How to handle a fussy baby: see Box 17-3 "Checklist for a Crying Baby," page 316; "Colic and Irritable Crying Spells," page 318; and "Managing Frustration and Stress," page 372.

Breastfeeding or bottle feeding your baby: please see Chapters 16 and 17 which cover breastfeeding and bottle feeding, respectively.

Burping: see pages 308–311 for a step-by-step explanation of burping.

Pacifiers: see pages 283 and 313 for a discussion of pacifier use with breastfed and bottle-fed babies.

Feeding problems to report to your pediatrician: see the Call Box on page 318.

Weaning: see "Weaning to a Cup," page 320; "Complete Weaning from the Bottle," page 320; and "Weaning from Breast to Cup or Breast to Bottle," pages 297–298.

Adding solid foods: see pages 320–321 for a discussion of this issue.

Vitamin supplements: see page 321.

Fluoride supplements: see page 322.

WIC program: see page 322.

Other questions: refer to the index or the table of contents.

Low-Birth-Weight Infants

Any baby weighing less than the 10th percentile expected at term (approximately 5 pounds, 8 ounces) or falling two standard deviations or more below the mean weight for the gestational age is considered to be a low-birth-weight infant. Low-birth-weight infants are at greater risk of respiratory problems, meconium aspiration, low blood sugar after birth, and problems in maintaining a proper body temperature. Low birth weight can result from premature birth or intrauterine growth retardation (IUGR), both explained below.

Both low-birth-weight and premature babies are at risk for many health problems and complications during their early life. If your baby has one of these conditions, you will be working closely with your pediatrician to learn what you can do to help and care for your infant.

Intrauterine Growth Retardation

In IUGR, the placenta for some reason aged more quickly and is no longer able to provide for adequate exchange of nutrients. Without adequate nourishment, the baby either stops growing or growth is slowed dramatically. At birth, the baby's weight is below normal for gestation.

Premature Infants

A premature baby is any baby born before 37 weeks' gestation.

What Does a Premature Baby Look Like? You need to be prepared for what premature babies *are expected* to look like. Because they have not had the time to put down fat deposits, their skin is very transparent and you can actually see their veins right through their skin. The rib cage is very apparent for the same reason: lack of fat.

A premature baby's abdomen is very large in proportion to a full-term baby's. His or her genitals, depending on the length of gestation, may not be completely formed. The nervous system is immature and therefore the baby does not have the normal Moro reflex or the sucking and rooting reflexes of a full-term baby.

The premature infant faces tremendous respiratory challenges. Between 24 weeks and full term, more alveoli are being formed. (Alveoli are the many tiny air sacs throughout the lungs, where oxygen and carbon dioxide exchange will need to occur after birth.)

Surfactant is a substance secreted by the alveoli cells, coating the inside of the alveoli and preventing their collapse. Without this substance, the alveoli do not open and close properly. The biggest problem facing a premature newborn is the lack of surfactant covering the inside of the lungs' alveoli. It is not until 32 weeks that the alveoli are lined with enough surfactant to give a baby a better chance of survival. (This is why when a woman is in premature labor before 35 weeks gestation, her practitioner may want to administer a steroid medication by two injections to help the baby's lungs more rapidly develop surfactant.)

Premature infants often need their respiration to be assisted in some way after birth. They will be taken to the neonatal intensive care unit and placed under a warmer where they can be observed closely. Depending on the baby's gestational age at birth, if she is breathing on her own, she may only need a hood placed over her head that provides warm, moist oxygen support. If she is not breathing on her own, or if she is breathing but the alveoli are not opening and closing properly enough for the adequate exchange of oxygen and carbon dioxide, a tube will placed through her mouth into her airway. In addition to warm, moist oxygen, slight pressure will be delivered through this tube to assist in the opening of the air sacs. With all this necessary assistance, be prepared to see your premature infant hooked up to monitors that watch her heart, blood pressure, and oxygen saturation.

Many of the vital organs are not yet fully mature in their development. Premature babies lack the nutritional reserves stored in the bodies of full-term infants, and this can lead to many medical problems. The immaturity of all body systems in the preterm infant makes the transition to life outside the uterus much more difficult.

In addition to needing respiratory assistance at birth, the premature infant needs help maintaining her body's fluid volume and body temperature, getting adequate nutrition, and resisting infection.

With the advancements in neonatal intensive care units, the outlook for premature babies is continually improving.

Adapting to a Premature Infant: Parents of premature infants go through a period of grief that begins when they realize that they are going to deliver a premature infant and ends either with resolution of the loss if the baby dies or with relief when it becomes clear that the baby will live. These parents are grieving both the loss of the birthing experience they expected and the loss of the normal newborn they expected. This grief is normal and expected and needs the understanding and acceptance of all concerned.

Grief and depression may also occur because the parents may feel that it was their fault that they did not give birth to a full-term infant. They experience a sense of failure. In addition, the parents of the premature infants who spend a long period of time in the hospital after birth show a higher incidence of child abuse. This is probably due to the delay in bonding, as well as unresolved grief or anger. Knowing that you are at risk for these feelings may help you to promptly access the many resources available if you continue to feel depressed or angry. Therapy in these instances is very successful.

Bonding may be delayed for several reasons. First, because of the early birth, the parents were not psychologically ready for bonding. Second, they may feel both anger and grief over the situation. These feelings get in the way of bonding. Third, because the infant spends a lot of time away from the mother and father while in the neonatal intensive care unit, bonding is more difficult and can be delayed. The staff in neonatal intensive care units understand all of these issues and do everything possible to help you spend time with and touch your infant. However, this delay in attachment to the infant still occurs to some degree.

The parents need to learn new tasks that they didn't expect to have to learn, and this is stressful to some. They need to not only learn but also accept the specific needs of and expectations for

Baby Care

their child. At the same time, they are dealing with the stress of organizing their lives and schedules to meet the added time required at the hospital with their infant and the added time to learn to care for him or her. As if that is not enough, they may also be juggling the care and attention needs of other children.

The grief of grandparents and the questions of other siblings need to be dealt with and answered. Siblings may also be angry that this new baby is taking so much of their parent's time and energy. All of these issues require time, patience, attention, and love.

The parents and perhaps the grandparents need to learn and become comfortable with the skills necessary to take care of the premature infant when she is able to go home. You will be assisted through this process and given time to practice these skills with the help of the nursing staff before taking your baby home. Oftentimes follow-up home care is also scheduled through nursing home-care agencies.

You will be offered information on support groups to help you deal with this entire experience. *You are not alone.* Sometimes meeting with and talking to parents who have gone through this same experience can be a wonderful support. In addition, it may be just what the entire family needs to successfully adapt to your premature baby.

19

Identifying and Reporting Illness

Babies are very durable little people. They are born able to suck, digest, cry, breathe, cough, sneeze, and eliminate waste products. And, yes, they are born with the ability to survive and recover from colds and many illnesses.

Despite all your best care, your baby will at some time become ill. In fact, an occasional illness helps keep a child's immune system in good working order. Children who have never or seldom been sick in early childhood seem to be the ones who catch everything when they first go to school. So don't despair if your baby catches a cold. You and your baby will survive many illnesses between infancy and adulthood.

This chapter is not intended to frighten you. Instead, it is intended (as is the entire book) to help you *be prepared*. Most illnesses that affect newborns can be easily treated once they are identified. The goal of this chapter is to help you identify illness at its onset. Then, with your pediatrician's assistance, treatment can be started promptly.

Detecting Infections During Your First Days at Home

If you tested positive for vaginal group B streptococcus during pregnancy, had a fever in labor, had ruptured membranes for over 24 hours before delivery, or had thick meconium-stained amniotic fluid (or if the baby inhaled meconium-stained fluid into the lungs at birth), your baby is at higher risk for developing an infection after birth. The vast majority of babies born under the above circumstances do not develop infections, but it is important to know what symptoms would indicate that one is developing. Just like adults, babies who become ill are much quicker to respond to treatment when their symptoms are detected early in their infection and treatment is started promptly.

It is also important to note that *any baby,* not just those born in the special circumstances listed above, may suddenly develop an infection that

Baby Care

353

stems from pregnancy or birth. **Therefore, it is important for all parents to know what to report to their pediatricians promptly, even in the middle of the night, and what can be watched carefully for change and, if no change occurs, can wait to be reported in the morning.**

Further on in this chapter, I will extensively discuss how to evaluate your baby or child for illness. Using this detailed assessment, you will learn to notice even minor ailments. However, for the newborn, in the first few weeks at home, remembering a few simple things will ensure that you will detect serious infection in your baby, if it occurs.

Color Changes

Your baby may suddenly appear pale, or you may note a white or bluish ring around your baby's mouth. His nail beds may look a little blue instead of their normal pink color (after the initial blue in the hands and feet, which is normal immediately after birth, has gone away). Any sudden change in color should alert you to observe your baby closely for other symptoms of developing infection.

Behavior Changes

Many early infections have been detected by nurses or parents who have just sensed that something is wrong. A vigorous baby suddenly is listless or sluggish or just won't wake up enough for good feedings. Any sudden change in behavior like this should alert you to observe your baby more closely for other signs of developing infection and to call your pediatrician.

Breathing Changes

If you suspect that your baby is becoming ill, it is important to monitor his breathing for signs of respiratory distress. Pages 363–364 extensively cover breathing rate and other important information about respiration and signs of respiratory distress. Review this information carefully. Often an increase in the normal rate of respiration is the first sign of a developing infection.

Is your baby's nose stuffy, running, or producing a discharge of some kind? If there is a discharge coming from the baby's nose, you will need to describe its texture and color to the pediatrician (that is, thin, thick, watery, frothy, clear, white, yellow, green, and so on).

Does your baby have a cough? How frequent is the cough? Does your child cough only when active or also when quiet? Does he cough while sleeping? What does the cough sound like? Is it wet and loose, or is it a dry and hacking cough? Is there a honking or crowing sound to the cough? Having all this information helps in proper diagnosis of the cause of the cough and therefore the proper treatment. (Allergy coughs have a different sound and timing than illness coughs.)

Does the cough bring up any mucus? If so, describe the mucus to the pediatrician (thick, thin, watery, frothy, clear, white, yellow or green, and so on).

There are several viruses, including the common cold virus, that can make your baby's breathing sound raspy, croupy, or congested. ℓ**Whenever your baby appears to be working to breathe or is so congested that he is not eating or sleeping well, ask your pediatrician for assistance.**

Temperature Changes

Normal healthy newborns do a good job of maintaining a normal body temperature but have difficulty raising their body temperature on their own if they become chilled. A baby who is developing an infection often loses the ability to maintain a normal temperature. **Prior to a rise in temperature (fever), a baby who is developing an infection may experience a drop in temperature. During this period of developing illness, the baby may appear pale in color or have a pale or bluish ring around his mouth.**

When a baby's temperature drops, add an extra layer of clothing or an extra receiving blanket. In addition, a hat should be placed on the baby's head (babies lose the most heat from their heads). Hold the baby close to your warm body. If a baby has just been chilled, these interventions will be successful in getting his temperature back into the normal range within an hour. (The extra layer of clothes or extra blanket should now be removed.) However, in a baby who is developing an infection, either the above will not be successful or the temperature will come up, only to drop again in a short while.

In addition to persistent drops in temperature, **a fever is always a warning sign and should never be ignored.** See "Taking and Interpreting Temperatures," page 356, and Boxes 19-1, 19-2, and 19-3, which explain how to take underarm and rectal temperatures and what to report to your pediatrician.

Frequently Asked Questions About Using a Thermometer

What Type of Thermometer Should I Purchase?

There are many brands and types of thermometers available: strip thermometers that are placed on the forehead, strips for under the arm, battery-operated digital thermometers for oral, rectal, and underarm use, digital ear thermometers, and conventional glass thermometers. What you use will be determined by personal choice and the amount of money you feel you can afford to spend.

How Often Should I Take My Baby's Temperature?

It is really not necessary to check your baby's temperature at all under normal circumstances. This, of course, assumes that your home is kept at a reasonably warm temperature. If you live in a cold climate and never set your thermostat above 68°F, it

would be a good idea to check your baby's axillary temperature during the first few weeks at home to be certain that it has not dropped below 98°F.

Check your baby's temperature if

- ❑ You suspect that your baby is ill, or there is an overall change in your baby's color, behavior, or skin temperature to your touch.
- ❑ You see more shivering than the normal occasional shiver seen during the first few weeks of life.
- ❑ You see blue color return to the hands and feet once the initial, normal blue color in these extremities has resolved.
- ❑ Your baby appears pale in color or there is a pale or bluish area around his mouth.

How Do I Read a Thermometer?

Battery-operated digital thermometers will display the temperature. Strips come with their own specific directions for interpreting their results.

To read a glass thermometer, hold it under good light and rotate it between your fingers slowly until you can see the silver-colored mercury. The point where the mercury ends is the temperature reading. Markings are in large one-degree intervals with smaller markings every two-tenths of a degree. An arrow points to 98.6°F (see Figure 19-1), the normal oral temperature.

How Do I Care for a Digital Thermometer?

Read the literature that comes with the unit you have chosen. These thermometers need to be cleaned after use—follow the manufacturer's directions for proper cleaning and storage.

FIGURE 19-1

The mercury on this thermometer is at 99.8°F.

Baby Care

What Do I Look for When Purchasing a Glass Thermometer?

Unless you are clear in your understanding of the centigrade temperature scale and interpretation, be certain that you purchase a thermometer marked in the Fahrenheit scale. On the Fahrenheit scale, 98.6° is the normal temperature *when taken orally*. However, you will be taking axillary (under the arm) or rectal temperatures on babies and small children, and the normals are different in these areas. (See below for more information.)

If you have decided to use glass thermometers, you will need to have two: one for underarm use and a rectal one. Rectal thermometers are *always* rounded on the silver-colored bulb end for safety. They may be marked with red at the opposite end. The red color is there to identify this thermometer as a rectal thermometer *only*.

All Fahrenheit thermometers are marked with an arrow at 98.6°F for the normal oral temperature, but **never take the temperature of a baby or small child orally.** Axillary and rectal temperatures are used instead for babies and small children. For obvious safety reasons, most doctors do not recommend taking a temperature in the mouth until a child is four or five years old.

How Do I Care for a Glass Thermometer?

Cleaning: Before using a glass thermometer, wash it with soap and *cold* water. Hot water will make the mercury expand and may break or crack your thermometer. Before using it, wipe the thermometer with alcohol and then rinse all the alcohol off thoroughly.

After using the thermometer, store it in its case, filled with alcohol. If you do not have a plastic case for your thermometer, soak the thermometer in alcohol for 10 minutes before putting it away.

Shaking Down a Glass Thermometer: Before taking a temperature, you must be sure that the mercury level inside the thermometer is below 96° F. Do this by holding the end without the silver bulb and shaking the thermometer in a downward motion with several snaps of your wrist. Be careful to hold the thermometer securely and shake it down away from furniture and countertops. Mercury is highly toxic and has specific cleaning requirements that should be followed if the thermometer breaks. Check to be sure that the mercury has been shaken down below 96°F before using the thermometer.

If a Glass Thermometer Breaks: If you do break a glass thermometer, move away from the area, taking children and pets with you. Put on shoes (if you are not already wearing them). Remove your jewelry—mercury can damage precious metal. Without touching the mercury or glass with your fingers, and being careful not to get cut, use several layers of damp paper towels or cardboard to sweep up all glass and mercury carefully. (The mercury forms many tiny silver balls.) Do not turn the towel to expose a new area. (You may get cut in the process.) Instead, get a fresh handful of damp paper towels. Discard the glass and mercury in a trash bag. Vacuuming the area is not recommended for the initial picking up of glass and mercury. (The tiny, round, lightweight mercury balls may be pushed far away by the vacuum instead of being picked up. In addition, the glass may tear the vacuum bag. A moist paper towel is more efficient.) Go over the area once again with a new large handful of damp paper towels to be certain everything has been picked up. Discard the paper towels in the trash and remove the trash bag from the house. **It is important that children and pets do not touch or ingest the mercury.**

Taking and Interpreting Temperatures

You may be wondering, "Should I take my baby's temperature under the arm or in the rectum?" Some pediatricians require that you take your baby's temperature only by the axillary (underarm) method. Others would like to know the rectal temperature if your baby is showing signs of illness. **Ask your pediatrician for his or her preference on where the temperature should be taken.**

It is important to know how far the thermometer should be inserted into the rectum or how long it needs to be in place under the arm in order to obtain an accurate reading. It is equally important for you to know the normal temperature ranges in the rectum and under the arm. They are different, and you will not interpret the temperature reading properly if you do not know the normal ranges.

Box 19-1 explains how to take an underarm (axillary) temperature and the normal ranges of a temperature taken under the arm.

Box 19-2 explains how to take a rectal temperature and the normal ranges of a temperature taken in the rectum.

Box 19-3 offers general guidelines of what temperatures to report to your pediatrician. **These are guidelines only. Follow your pediatrician's specific instructions.**

Reporting the Temperature to the Pediatrician

Report the *exact* reading on the thermometer and whether you took the temperature under the arm or in the rectum. Your pediatrician will use this information to interpret the results.

Do not add a degree if you have taken the temperature in the cooler cavity (under the arm), or subtract a degree if you have taken it in the warmer cavity (the rectum). The doctor needs to know only the thermometer reading and whether the temperature was taken under the arm or rectally.

BOX 19-1

Underarm (Axillary) Temperatures

How to Take an Axillary Temperature

1. Properly clean and shake down your thermometer.
2. Place the silver-colored bulb end under the baby's arm. (The armpit should be dry.)
3. With your free hand, gently hold your baby's arm and elbow down against the chest wall.
4. Hold the thermometer in place for three to four minutes. Use distraction and or entertainment to help keep your baby still during this time.
5. Remove the thermometer and read the temperature.

All Fahrenheit thermometers are marked by an arrow at 98.6°F, the normal *oral* (mouth) temperature, but, of course, we never put a thermometer in a baby's mouth.

Interpreting Normal Underarm Temperatures: The axilla (underarm) is a cooler cavity than the mouth, so 97.6°F is normal in adults and children if a temperature is taken under the arm.

However, in newborns the desired underarm temperature is in the 98-degree range (98.0 to 98.9°F), with a normal variation range from 97.6° to 99°F.

It is important for you, however, to under-stand what a normal expected temperature is, based on where it is taken. Without this knowledge, you might think that a rectal temperature of 99.6°F means a fever, when in fact it is normal. Or you may miss a *possible* developing problem in a baby with an axillary temperature just above 99°F.

If you have determined that you need to check your baby's temperature, then obvi-ously you have other concerns that need to be discussed with your pediatrician or the pediatrician's nursing staff. You should not assume that everything is okay, based only on a normal temperature, when other symp-toms are present. ℭReport your observa-tions and let your pediatrician advise you. See Box 19-3, "Newborn Temperature Range (Guidelines) to Report to Your Pediatrician."

BOX 19-2

Rectal Temperatures

How to Take a Rectal Temperature

1. Properly clean a **round bulb rectal thermometer** by wiping it with alco-hol and rinsing all the alcohol off well.
2. Check to be sure the mercury is below 96°F. Shake down if necessary.
3. With your thumb and index finger, hold the thermometer half an inch from the rounded, silver-colored bulb end (Figure 19-2).

FIGURE 19-2

Correctly holding a rectal thermometer before inserting.

4. Lubricate the silver bulb end with petroleum jelly.
5. Protect the opposite end of the thermometer inside your palm. This prevents your infant from kicking the free end of the thermometer and pushing the ther-mometer farther into his rectum. (Again, see Figure 19-2)
6. Place your baby on his back and hold his feet up, or place him on his tummy across your lap and allow his legs to hang at a right angle.
7. Insert the bulb end of the thermometer into the rectum until your fingers (which are holding the thermometer half an inch from the end) touch the outside of the rectal opening (Figure 19-3).
8. Hold the thermometer in place for two minutes. Sing songs or use other forms of distraction to help your baby pass the time. (If your baby will not hold still and shows a lot of resistance, remove the thermometer and use an-other thermometer to take the temperature under his arm.)
9. Remove the thermometer after two minutes, set it aside, and re-dress your baby. The temperature reading stays the same until you shake the ther-mometer down—the mercury will not drop on its own.
10. Wipe the thermometer with a tissue.
11. Read the temperature.

FIGURE 19-3

Proper Insertion of a Rectal Thermometer

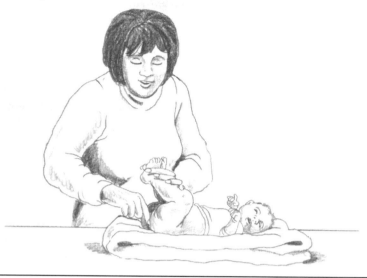

Interpreting Normal Rectal Temperatures: Remember, the arrow marking on the thermometer is at 98.6°F, which is the normal *oral* reading. **The rectum is a warmer cavity** than the mouth; the *normal* temperature when taken in the rectum is 99.6°F for newborns, children, and adults.

BOX 19-3

Newborn Temperature Range (Guidelines) to Report to Your Pediatrician

You should obtain from your pediatrician specific guidelines for what temperature ranges to report. If you have not received this information from him or her, report any elevation promptly the first time it occurs, and obtain specific range recommendations for the future at that time.

Refer to Boxes 19-1 and 19-2 for proper techniques in taking underarm and rectal temperatures.

It is important to remember that the baby can be ill without a temperature elevation. Therefore, do not rely on the temperature alone in making decisions about when to call your pediatrician.

If your baby has other symptoms of illness or is not taking feedings well, this also needs to be reported immediately.

Until you obtain specific guidelines from your pediatrician, use the following information as a general guideline:

Baby Care

BOX 19-3 (CONTINUED)

The American Academy of Pediatrics recommends that any rectal temperature of 100.2°F or above be reported to your pediatrician for evaluation.

Report any temperature above 99°F taken under the arm.

Report any rapid-onset, high fever.

Regarding low temperatures, report to your pediatrician if the measures described on page 355 fail to bring a low temperature up into the normal range. A low temperature can be a sign of a developing infection.

Treating Fevers

Medications

🄲Always attempt to reach your pediatrician before treating a newborn's fever with any medication.

Never use aspirin, or products containing aspirin, to treat fever (or any condition) in infants or children, unless told to do so by your pediatrician. It is now well known that giving aspirin to children with chickenpox or influenza (the flu) can cause a potentially fatal illness called Reye's syndrome. Certainly, aspirin has benefits over acetaminophen (a common brand of which is Tylenol) in certain illnesses, but your pediatrician should be the one making this decision based on the symptoms he or she observes. Do not ever give aspirin products to any child if a pediatrician has not told you to do so.

Likewise, ibuprofen (brand names Motrin and Advil) should not be used in children until you consult with your pediatrician.

In general, it is best not to give your baby any medication until you speak with your pediatrician. However, **if there is a delay in reaching your pediatrician, use liquid acetaminophen in the specific, infant-weight-related dosage specified on the bottle to treat high fevers until you are able to talk with your pediatrician or his or her nursing staff. Be certain to** use liquid acetaminophen for *infants* and check the correct dosage based on your baby's age and weight. Never use adult-strength dosages to treat children.

A fever is part of the body's normal defense against infection and illness, is helpful in fighting infection, and is safe at low levels, so some pediatricians do not recommend medication for fevers under a certain temperature. Ask your pediatrician his or her opinion.

Always encourage more frequent feedings in an infant who has an elevated temperature.

Sponge Bathing

Sponge bathing was once a routine treatment of fever. It is no longer used, however, unless fever-reducing medication is not working or your pediatrician recommends it. If told to sponge bathe, or to help a very feverish older child feel better, follow the method presented in Box 19-4.

Don'ts in Treating Fevers

Don't "starve a fever." Fevers increase caloric and fluid needs.

Don't give an enema. Enemas remove needed electrolytes from the system. *Never* give an enema unless told to do so by your pediatrician.

BOX 19-4

Correct Sponge Bathing of a Feverish Child

(if recommended by your pediatrician)

Use tepid or lukewarm water only. Never use alcohol for sponge bathing. Tepid water feels neither cool nor warm to your inner wrist; it feels neutral in temperature. Most children complain, however, that tepid water feels cold. They tend to prefer the water to be lukewarm, or just ever so slightly to the warm side of tepid. If it is too warm, though, it won't reduce the fever.

You can sponge bathe the child in a tub containing only a small amount of water, so that evaporation can occur off the unsubmerged skin, or give a true sponge bath in bed or standing at the sink. It is the evaporation of water off the skin that lowers the temperature of the body. Either way, be certain the room is warm and draft-free.

Your child should not feel chilled by the water. If the water temperature causes shivering, it is too cold. (Remember, shivering produces body heat and brings the temperature up. You defeat the purpose of the sponge bath if the child is crying vigorously or shivering.)

When sponge bathing, concentrate on the face, neck, underarms, and groin and the areas inside the elbows and behind the knees—circulation is closer to the surface in these areas. Gently rub the areas with a lukewarm washcloth (after wringing it out so it is not dripping), and allow the water to evaporate. If your child begins to shiver, cover the areas you are not sponging with a light covering (such as a cotton dish towel or other lightweight towel).

It takes 20 to 30 minutes to lower the temperature, so be patient and work slowly. Add warm water to the basin or tub if it drops below body (tepid) temperature. **Do not allow the child to become chilled.**

Try hard to make this a relaxing time for your baby. Talk, sing, and smile as you work to make your child more comfortable.

Don't overdress or overcover a baby or child who has a fever—this can cause overheating. Even though the child will feel cold when his fever is going up, keep the coverings light in weight.

Don't give any medication to treat fevers *under* 102°F taken in the rectum, or *under* 100°F taken under the arm, unless instructed to do so by your pediatrician.

Don't use ibuprofen (Motrin or Advil) unless it is ordered by your pediatrician.

Don't use aspirin to treat fevers without an order from your pediatrician. Instead, treat high fevers with liquid infant acetaminophen in the correct dose for the baby's

weight until you can reach your pediatrician for further advice.

Why Does One Feel Cold When Getting a Fever?

Why does a person feel cold when getting a fever and hot when breaking a fever? You would think it would be the opposite. To understand the answer, first think of the temperature-regulating part of your brain as being just like the thermostat in your home. When you turn the thermostat up in the house, it means you are feeling cold. The message sent to your furnace is, "You are too cold. You need to produce heat until the temperature in the house reaches the new setting."

When an illness resets the temperature-regulating "thermostat" in your brain, the same things happens. Let's say the virus or bacteria sets the thermostat setting in your brain at 101.5°F. Now your body, at its normal 98.6°F, says, "Wow, I'm cold. I'd better produce some heat." Shivering (the movement of your shivering muscles) produces heat. You continue to feel cold and produce heat by shivering until your temperature reaches the new setting.

While your temperature is going up, your hands and feet will usually feel cool or cold to the touch. This is because the vital organs (brain, heart, kidneys, and so on) take priority over the extremities (hands and feet) when it comes to blood supply and need for warmth, and in response to the stress of illness. Therefore, touching the hands and feet is not a good way to determine whether a person has a fever. The hands and feet may feel cool or even cold while the skin on the back feels burning hot.

When your illness has run its course and resets the brain thermostat back to normal, or fever-reducing medication resets the brain thermostat to a lower setting, suddenly you feel hot. Your temperature is still at 101.5°F and the new setting says you should be 98.6°F. Your brain says, "Wow, I'm hot. I'd better get to work cooling off." So you begin to sweat and the moisture evaporating from your skin cools your body. You continue to feel hot and to sweat until your body temperature is no longer hotter than the new setting.

Signs and Symptoms of Illness and What to Report to Your Pediatrician

There are signs and symptoms of illness that should be reported to your pediatrician, but do your homework before you call (unless, of course, it is a life-threatening emergency). Take notes, if necessary, so you don't forget anything you have observed. Follow this guide to assess your baby.

Parent's Intuition

I put this first because it should not be ignored. Oftentimes you cannot put your finger on anything specific, but your baby just doesn't seem right or the same to you. Go through the following checklist, and if you are still concerned, go ahead and call your pediatrician. **You are your baby's advocate, and your insight and intuition are important.** You may only need reassurance, but on the other hand, you may have detected something that needs treatment.

Fever

This is always a good starting point when checking for illness. However, remember that not all illnesses cause an elevated temperature. In addition, your child's activity level before you take the temperature, whether the child is overdressed or overwrapped, and the temperature of the room can all affect the reading to a small extent. However, your child won't have a 101°F temperature from just running around. Body temperature also varies with the time of day: it is lowest in the middle of the night and highest in the afternoon.

The temperatures of babies and children can go up very rapidly when they are ill, but they can also be ill and have a normal or below-normal temperature. In addition, it is possible for a child to run a low-grade temperature (in the 99° range) and not be ill. This may all seem confusing; however, it is meant to help you look at the total picture when evaluating for illness, instead of relying on the temperature alone.

(☞**Report any temperature above 99°F taken for three to four minutes under a dry arm (obtained twice, one hour apart, the second time after removing buntings, hats, or excessive clothing).**

Any rectal temperature of 100.2°F or above should be reported to your pediatrician for evaluation.

Regardless of the newborn's age, report a lower fever (lower than those just mentioned) if other symptoms of illness are present.

Report any rapid-onset, high fever.

Any temperature elevation that lasts for 24 hours should be reported. (Do not wait for 24 hours, though, if the temperature is within the report guidelines above or if other symptoms of illness are present.)

Report to your pediatrician if the measures described on page 355 fail to bring a low temperature up into the normal range.

Respiratory (Breathing) Symptoms

Count the rate of respirations per minute. A quiet baby breathes 30 to 40 times per minute, and the *pattern and rate are very irregular.* The rate can go up to 60 when the baby is alert and crying and still be within normal limits. If you are counting the respiratory rate (the number of breaths per minute) in a baby, you must count for *one full minute.* Your baby may breathe 20 times in the first 15 seconds—if you multiplied this number by 4, you would think that your baby was breathing 80 times per minute. However, if you continue to count for the full minute, because of the irregular breathing pattern normal in infants, the actual rate per full minute may turn out to be in the normal range, so be sure to **count for one full minute to obtain the breathing rate.**

*C***Call your pediatrician if your baby has difficulty breathing, appears to be working hard at breathing, or sounds congested or raspy; also call if the breathing rate for one full minute in a quiet baby is above 60, and a second count, done again in a few minutes, remains above 60.**

Observe the baby's nose during breathing. What doctors and nurses call *nasal flaring* is a sign of respiratory distress. If flaring is present, you will see the nostrils (nose openings) stretch open wider when the baby breathes in, and then go back to normal as he breathes out.

*C***Report flaring of the nostrils to your pediatrician immediately. Include your baby's respiratory rate and temperature in this report.**

Listen to the sound of your baby breathing. Although babies *occasionally* make noises while they sleep and breathe, generally their breathing is quiet. *Grunting* is a term doctors and nurses give to baby's breathing when *each breath or most breaths have a sound.* Usually this noise is made on *expiration* (breathing out) and sounds a little like a fast sigh. *C***Grunting is a sign of a developing respiratory problem. Consult your pediatrician immediately.**

Observe the baby's chest during breathing. The next and *most ominous sign* of respiratory distress is when the baby *puts his chest muscles to work to breathe.* In normal newborn breathing, the abdomen goes in and out gently with each breath, and very little chest movement can be seen. When the baby is fighting an infection in the lungs or having other difficulties, the chest muscles go to work and you observe what are called *chest retractions.*

*C***Chest retractions are a sign of severe respiratory distress that must be reported immediately to your pediatrician. If it is during office hours and you can get through to your pediatrician promptly, put in a call. If it is after hours or you cannot immediately reach your pediatrician (for example, if you get a busy signal) go to the emergency department of your hospital and notify your pediatrician from there.**

Chest retractions rarely occur in otherwise healthy infants. They are a symptom that normally develops well after an illness has progressed. However, parents need to know that this symptom calls for prompt attention and treatment.

There are two types of chest retractions: *substernal retractions* and *intercostal retractions.* Both types mean the baby is working so hard to breathe that he must use the chest muscles to get air in and out. Retractions can be very subtle in mild respiratory distress and extreme in severe respiratory distress.

In *substernal retractions* the bottom end of the sternum (the flat breast bone that goes down the middle of the chest) indents with each breath. The baby is using his chest muscles for

Baby Care

help in breathing, and in doing so pulls the lower end of the sternum inward into the chest with each breath. In severe cases, the indent or recessed area can be three-fourths of an inch deep.

The second form of chest retractions is called *intercostal retractions*. Intercostal means *between ribs*. Again, the chest muscles have been put to work to assist respiration. With each breath, the skin between the ribs is pulled in, giving the ribs a wavy appearance.

ⓒAll retractions require immediate intervention; subtle retractions will progress to more severe retractions with greater respiratory distress, so do not delay in seeking medical assistance. Take your child to the nearest emergency department if the symptoms are mild, or dial 911 for ambulance transport if retractions are severe.

If retractions occur during office hours and your insurance company requires prior approval by your baby's primary care doctor, notify your pediatrician if he or she can be reached *promptly*. If the line is busy, call a neighbor, friend, spouse, or anyone who can be reached immediately, and ask them to notify your pediatrician that you are on your way to the emergency department. Make certain that your message is clear about which hospital you are going to. Your pediatrician will then contact the hospital to let them know you are coming.

No insurance company requires prior physician notification for an emergency room visit in a life-threatening emergency. Severe chest retractions in a newborn are considered such an emergency. Therefore, do not waste time on the phone. You can notify your pediatrician once you have arrived at the emergency room **and** your child is safely under care.

This information is intended not to frighten you but to help you feel prepared as a parent. It is very rare that this serious form of respiratory distress would occur in an otherwise normal and healthy newborn. You have learned symptoms of respiratory distress to watch for (increased breathing rate and flaring of the nostrils) to detect breathing distress before it gets to the level of chest re-

tractions. Knowing what to look for can help increase your self-confidence. You can now properly assess for a *developing* respiratory problem.

Behavior Changes

In assessing your child for possible illness, ask yourself the following questions related to possible changes in your baby's normal behavior:

Is the baby suddenly very fussy? If so, are you able to console him? Does holding, rocking, or feeding seem to comfort the baby?

What is the timing of this fussiness? Is it constant or does it only last an hour after feedings? Does another feeding help?

Is your baby suddenly very tired, excessively sleepy, or unresponsive? Will he wake up to eat?

Is your baby not sleeping at all or very little? If you are nursing, has your diet changed? If you are nursing, are you consuming a lot of caffeine (in sodas, coffee, tea, or chocolate)?

Is your baby crying more than usual? What does the cry sound like? Is it normal sounding or high-pitched? When does the crying occur? Does it occur just after feedings? Does your baby draw his knees up as if he has a tummy ache when crying?

The answers to these questions will help your pediatrician get to the root of the problem. Try to think back to answer these questions, and then place your call.

Nervous System Symptoms

Do you see any chills or shivering? Newborns, in the first days of life, will have some quivering of the lips. These episodes, which look like shivering, are *short and infrequent* in occurrence. **ⓒFrequent shivering or frequent quivering in the lips or extremities should be reported.**

Is the baby having convulsions (seizures)? In the first few weeks of life, newborns will often make a noise and appear to jump in their sleep. These *infrequent, one-second-long* jerks are normal and are caused by their immature nervous systems.

*C*However, any jerking movements that are frequent or repetitive should be reported to the pediatrician for evaluation.

If you gently move the baby's chin toward his chest, does it seem to cause pain? Can your baby move all parts of his body normally?

*C*Report any abnormal symptoms promptly.

Changes in Eating Behavior

If your baby suddenly wants to eat more frequently, you can be pretty sure that a growth spurt is beginning—nothing to worry about. Babies eat on demand, and when they are going through growth spurts, their bodies demand more frequent feedings. This is true of both bottle-fed and breastfed infants.

If you are breastfeeding, expect surges in eating behavior periodically. Nursing more frequently for several days is your baby's way of telling your breast to produce more milk. When the supply increases to meet the demand of the growth spurt, your baby will go back to a more normal eating schedule again.

*C*If your baby is refusing to eat or is eating less food or less often than normal (or less often than the expected six to eight times in 24 hours), it is important to report this promptly to your pediatrician.

*C*Also report to your pediatrician if your baby is losing more than the expected 10 percent weight loss in the first week of life, or if he continues to lose weight or fails to gain weight during the second week of life.

Choking Spells

Initially, some babies have more mucus than others. These babies will chew as if they have gum in their mouth or stretch their mouth open fre-

quently. Eventually, the mucus will work its way up and the baby will gag and spit it out, ending the difficulty and helping the baby feed better.

There are some very rare conditions, though, in which babies will choke or gag repeatedly with feedings.

*C*Report repeated choking or gagging spells to your pediatrician. Also report any episode of choking that causes your baby to turn blue.

Vomiting and Diarrhea

Vomiting disgorges a larger volume and is more forceful than spitting up. Repeated vomiting can quickly dehydrate an infant, especially a newborn. If your baby has been vomiting, note the answers to the following questions before calling the pediatrician:

> What does the vomit look like? Breast milk or formula? Liquid or chunky? What is the color?
>
> Is there any blood in the vomit?
>
> How much is vomited?
>
> How frequently is this occurring?
>
> Does vomiting occur immediately after feedings, or is it unrelated to the timing of feedings?
>
> Is your baby vomiting undigested breast milk or formula two to three hours after a feeding?

Diarrhea also can be a serious problem for your baby, resulting in dehydration, as well as tenderness in the diaper area. It is important to note, however, that breastfed babies have very loose, yellow, and frequent stools. This is not diarrhea—diarrhea is forceful and usually very frequent episodes of watery stool. However, diarrhea can either be frequent small amounts or frequent or infrequent large volumes of watery stool.

*C*If your baby has diarrhea, note the answers to the following questions and call your pediatrician immediately:

Baby Care

How frequent is the diarrhea?

How much volume do you *estimate* each episode of diarrhea to produce? (i.e., two tablespoons each? One cup each?)

Is there mucus in the stool?

Is there blood in the stool? Blood can show up red or oily black. Remember, though, during the first 24 hours after birth the first stools, called meconium, are normally black and oily in appearance.

*C***Report vomiting and diarrhea promptly.** Dehydration can occur very rapidly in an infant.

***Electrolyte Water:* Your pediatrician may order** a *special* water designed to replace vital electrolytes that are lost during vomiting and diarrhea. This special water is *electrolyte water* and comes under several brand names.

Electrolyte water can be purchased at any drugstore and should be on hand in your medicine cabinet at all times (just in case your pediatrician tells you to give your baby this type of water and it is the middle of the night). There is an expiration date on the can, so check it and mark your calendar to replace it before it expires. Once opened, mark on the can the date it was opened, store as instructed on the can, and discard the remaining amount after the time recommended for keeping an open can.

Constipation

Although this is not an illness, it can be a problem. *C***Report to your pediatrician if your baby is not having at** *least one stool per day.* **Also report repeated, hard, difficult-to-pass stools.**

Urinary Symptoms

Is your baby wetting six diapers a day by the end of the first week after birth? *C***If not, report this to your doctor.**

Does the baby's urine look dark or have a different odor? Dark urine or urine with a strong odor means the urine is too concentrated and the

baby needs more fluids. *C***Report dark urine or urine with a strong odor to your pediatrician. In addition, if breastfeeding, breastfeed more frequently; if bottle feeding, increase the volume of formula given.**

Check your baby's fontanel (a soft spot). (See page 256 for the locations of soft spots and when they normally disappear.) A dehydrated baby (one that is not taking in enough fluids) may have a sunken fontanel. *C***Report a sunken fontanel to your pediatrician.**

Mouth and Throat Symptoms

Carefully inspect the inside of your baby's mouth. Use a penlight if necessary. Note the answers to the following questions before calling your pediatrician:

Are the gums swollen or red?

Are there white spots on the gums or tongue or anywhere else in the mouth? (These can be an indication of thrush, a fungus infection easily treated with medication in drops prescribed by your pediatrician.)

Is there excessive drooling?

Is your baby biting down on everything he can get into his mouth?

If you can see to the back of the throat, can you see redness or white patches?

*C***Report any abnormal findings.**

Eye and Ear Symptoms

Your child's eyes are windows to a world of information about his health. Before calling your pediatrician, note the answers to the following questions:

Do your baby's eyes appear sunken, glassy, or red?

Is there a discharge from the eyes? If so, describe it.

Is your baby pulling at one or both ears? Is there discharge from either ear?

Is your baby excessively fussy? Fussiness is often the first symptom of a developing ear infection and is often seen long before pulling at the ear or fever.

*C)*Report any abnormal findings.

Lymph Gland Swelling

Check above your baby's neck, above the collar bone, under the arms, and in the groin for any swollen glands. If there is a swollen gland, you will feel it as a soft lump.

If you find one small swollen lymph gland and your baby is not acting ill, don't panic. A swollen gland does not mean that your baby is seriously ill. The immune system is supposed to respond to a germ or organism by localizing the infection. The closest gland responds and will become swollen. (This often is caused by a bug or mosquito bite.) This means your baby's immune system is working. If only one small gland is swollen, and *your child is not acting ill,* just watch the gland for a few days. If it begins to reduce in size, your baby's immune system is doing its job and there is nothing to worry about.

*C)***Report one very large swollen gland or several swollen glands, regardless of size. If your child is acting ill, with or without a swollen gland, notify your pediatrician. Your baby may need the help of medication to fight the infection.**

Abdominal Symptoms

You look at your baby every day and have seen what his abdomen (the area between the belly button and the pubic bone) looks like, so a swollen, distended, or asymmetrical (lopsided) abdomen will be easy for you to spot.

Does your baby's abdomen appear swollen, distended, or not symmetrical?

When you press gently on the tummy, does this cause your baby pain?

If your baby has pain in the abdomen, does it seem to hurt more when touched in one spot than another (such as across the waist, in the right lower groin, and so on)?

*C)***Report pain or a swollen, distended, or asymmetrical abdomen to your pediatrician.**

Skin Changes

Be sure to review the section on the skin of a normal newborn in Chapter 15 (page 253), so you will know what *not* to be concerned about.

You have been looking at and feeling your baby's skin since birth. Before calling your pediatrician, note the answers to the following questions:

Has the skin changed in color or texture?

Is the skin dry and flaking, or cracked and bleeding?

Is your baby scratching his skin as if itching?

Is the skin red or flushed in appearance?

Are there any unusual skin rashes (not counting diaper rash)?.

Is the skin pale or gray?

Is the skin bluish at all?

Is there a white or bluish ring around your baby's mouth?

Is the skin wet, moist, warm, or sweaty?

Is the skin cool, cold, or clammy feeling?

Are there red, irritated-looking blotches of skin that appear inflamed?

Are there lesions (sores) anywhere on the skin? Are the sores open and oozing? How would you describe any discharge coming from the sores?

Are the nail beds blue (other than during the first 24 hours after birth)?

*C)***Call 911 immediately if your baby turns blue.**

*C)***If your baby turns pale or gray or has a bluish ring around his or her mouth, report this immediately to your pediatrician.** These symptoms can indicate dehydration, respiratory distress, or an infection.

Blue nail beds, other than during the first 24 hours of life, indicate poor oxygen levels in the hands or feet. *C)***If blue nail beds are** unresolved in 30 minutes with extra clothing, report them to your pediatrician.

_(C)_ With the exceptions of the normal dry and flaking skin soon after birth and normal newborn rash, skin changes should be reported to the pediatrician. Some newborn rashes require an anti-inflammatory cream to help bring them under control.

_(C)_ Sweaty or clammy skin can indicate fever. Check your baby's temperature and report abnormal findings. If fever is not present, continue to observe your baby carefully for a developing fever or illness.

Jaundice

Please refer to page 254 for an explanation of newborn jaundice, breast milk jaundice, and breastfeeding jaundice. It is your responsibility to observe your infant for jaundice. Pages 254–256 also describe how to tell if your baby is jaundiced, and, if so, what to do.

_(C)_ Report jaundice of the skin to your pediatrician for evaluation. If you happen to first notice jaundice in the middle of the night and it is only slight facial jaundice (not including the whites of the eyes), and your baby is taking feedings in adequate amounts at least every four hours, you do not have to call the pediatrician in the middle of the night. However, do call first thing in the morning even if it is a weekend or a holiday. In the meantime, feed your baby every three hours.

_(C)_ For jaundice that has progressed to the body, includes the whites of the eyes, or is accompanied by sleepiness or poor feedings, call your pediatrician immediately.

Emergency Call
What to Report to Your Pediatrician

Notify your pediatrician promptly if you notice any of the following signs and symptoms.

Parent's Intuition: If you feel that something is wrong with your baby, even though you can't quite put your finger on the problem, call your pediatrician. You know this baby better than anyone else.

Fever: See Box 19-3, page 359, for guidelines.

Respiratory System

More than 60 breaths per full minute (when the baby is not crying) on two separate countings taken a few minutes apart

Difficult breathing (raspy, croupy, congested)

Grunting noises

Nasal flaring

Chest retractions (substernal or intercostal)

Behavior

Any sudden change in behavior or unusual behavior

Tiredness, sleepiness, unresponsiveness

Inconsolable crying and drawing the legs up

Eating Behavior

Any sudden, unusual decrease in appetite

Weight loss of more than 10 percent of the birth weight in the first week of life, or continued weight loss beyond the first week of life

Failure to begin weight gain after the first week of life

Choking Spells

Repetitive choking spells

Emergency Call
What to Report to Your Pediatrician *(continued)*

Nervous System

Frequent chills or frequent shivering

Repetitive jerking movements

Apparent pain when head is gently inclined with the chin toward the chest

Abnormalities in movement, including the inability to move certain parts of the body in a particular direction (such as an inability to lift one arm; or a mouth drooping on one side)

High-pitched crying

Vomiting and Diarrhea

Frequent episodes of vomiting or diarrhea

Blood in the vomit

Mucus or blood in the stool

Bowel Movements and Constipation

Failure to pass stool within 24 hours after birth

Less than one stool per day

Urinary System

Failure to urinate within 24 hours after birth

Fewer than six wet diapers a day by the end of the first week of life

Dark-colored or odorous urine

A sunken fontanel (soft spot)

Failure to urinate within 24 hours after circumcision

Mouth and Throat

Swollen, red gums

White spots or patches, or redness anywhere in the mouth

Excessive drooling

Constant biting and chewing motions

White spots or patches that look like milk on the gum or tongue

Eyes and Ears

Sunken, glassy, or red eyes

Discharge from eyes or ears

Pulling at one or both ears

Excessive fussiness, even without pulling at the ear

Excessive rubbing of eyes

Yellowish color in the whites of the eyes

Lymph Glands

Any swollen glands in a child who is acting ill

More than one small, swollen gland in a child who is not acting ill

Any large swollen gland

Abdomen

Swelling, distention, or asymmetry (unevenness) of the abdomen

Apparent pain (possibly localized) when abdomen is pressed gently

Skin

Cracked and bleeding skin

Scratching

Redness or flushed appearance

Pale, gray, or bluish skin

White or bluish ring around the baby's mouth

Blue nail beds (after the first 24 hours)

Wet, moist, warm, or sweaty skin

Cool, cold, or clammy skin

Red, irritated-looking blotches

Lesions (sores) with or without discharge

Jaundiced (yellow) skin

Any unusual skin rash (not diaper rash)

Baby Care

20

Infant Safety
Preventing Accidents

Becoming a parent means making safety a priority wherever your child is: at home, in the homes of relatives and friends, in stores, at school, in the car, and everywhere. Injuries are the leading cause of death and disability in children. Many, if not most, injuries could be prevented by proper precautions including parental or other adult supervision of children's activities. This chapter can help prepare you and your partner to make your baby's environment safe and healthy.

Safety takes on new dimensions when your baby learns to roll, crawl, and, later, to walk. To properly assess hazards to your mobile child, get down on your hands and knees, at your child's eye level, and survey your home for hazards. Keep in mind that a child's natural curiosity and lack of knowledge about safety can lead him or her into dangerous, even deadly, situations. Preventing accidents is the key.

Learn CPR, the Heimlich Maneuver, and First Aid

The techniques for the Heimlich maneuver and CPR (cardiopulmonary resuscitation), are best learned in a classroom where there is a mannequin available for hands-on practice. **Learn CPR and how to assist a choking adult, child, or infant before you bring home your first baby.** Knowing and practicing these skills should help you feel better prepared in the event of an emergency. The actual hands-on practice is what comes to your mind and helps reduce your anxiety when you need to function in an actual emergency.

You need to stay up to date. The way CPR is taught changes slightly every few years as new research comes to light and old cases are reviewed.

371

Call your local Red Cross or American Heart Association. Ask for pamphlets and books on CPR (all CPR classes include how to assist the choking victim) and register for a class today.

Managing Frustration and Stress

Having an infant is wonderful in so many, many ways, but there are also times when it can be very frustrating. You are tired, your infant is fussy, and nothing you do seems to help. During these times, it is important to remember that your infant has no way to communicate with you except through crying. Perhaps she is wet or hungry—these needs are easy to meet quickly. On the other hand, perhaps she is having painful gas that takes some time to go away. Or she may be crying for what seems like no reason—babies do have fussy times when you just can't figure out what is wrong. These crying episodes can't be solved in a minute; they may go on for some time.

It is important to remember that your baby is *not* saying you are a terrible mother or father. This is *not* a reflection on you as a person or as a parent. It is just what it is—a fussy time for your baby. Even though you may not be able to do anything to stop the crying, your baby is glad that you are there. It may also be helpful to remember that long fussy spells usually pass by about three months of age.

Lately there has been a lot of attention focused on shaken baby syndrome. It is important to understand that **one out of four shaken babies dies. For those who survive, the outcome may include mental retardation, blindness, hearing loss, motor skill problems, or even a vegetative state.** Such severe effects occur from shaking because a baby's weak, flexible neck cannot support its large and heavy head. When the baby is shaken, the brain bangs first against the front and then against the back of the skull as the head flops back and forth. Blood vessels break and brain tissue is damaged as these

impacts on the brain inside the skull occur. To make matters even worse, if the brain tissue lacks oxygen during this injury, it swells. There is no space for swelling inside the skull, so death results. Even mild shaking can result in brain damage or death to an infant. **Never, ever shake a baby.**

The important thing is for you to control your frustrations. If you feel angry with your baby and can't seem to control this feeling, call someone to come help you or to give you a break. If this is not possible, and you know your baby is dry and not hungry, swaddle her snugly and put her in her crib for awhile. Take some time to cool down. Listen to soft music, take a shower, take some deep breaths. If you still feel that you may lose control, call a parental stress hotline. (Keep the number near your phone.) Trained staff are available 24 hours a day to give you support and helpful advice. Of course you can always call 911 if you need immediate help to control yourself and cannot find the proper resource.

If you tend to lose your temper easily or have difficulty handling stress, consider seeking counseling before your baby arrives. Prevent child abuse by learning about infant crying and learning new skills for dealing with stress. Prevention of child abuse through counseling, knowledge, and learning to handle stress is the best gift you can give yourself and your baby.

Car Safety

Car Seats and Seat Belts

Read the directions for your car seat carefully. Know how to use it, make adjustments for infant use, and practice setting it up before your baby arrives.

Be certain that your car seat is the appropriate size for your baby. **Your baby should not be slumped over in the car seat.** Her back needs to be straight enough (not rounded like a C) in order that her chin can be at a right angle to her body, *not* down near her chest. Infant car seat space fillers (Figure 20-1) are available to help ensure that your baby is in a good body posture in the car seat. It may not be necessary, however, to purchase a filler—rolled-up receiving blankets, rolled cloth diapers, or small towel rolls can be used along the sides of your infant to take up the extra side space if your baby has proper posture. However, if slumping is present, a space-filling pad will be needed.

Do not place anything under your infant's bottom to raise her up. Instead, adjust the arm straps to the lowest setting.

Do not place anything behind your infant's back. If your baby is too upright, recline the entire seat more. Car seats for infants should be reclined at least half-way back (to at least a 45-degree angle).

Shoulder straps should always be in the lower slots for infants. The harness should be adjusted to be snug, but not constricting.

FIGURE 20-1

Car Seat with Space-Filling Pad

If your car seat has a retainer clip, it should be across the baby's chest at the level of the armpits.

If your infant is less than 37 weeks' gestation at birth, or weighs less than five and one-half pounds, your hospital may do a car-seat test before your baby is discharged to ensure that your infant can breathe adequately in your car seat. Although most full-term infants can ride semireclined in a car seat, some premature babies (born more than three weeks early) have trouble breathing adequately in this position. You will be asked to bring in your car seat so that the baby's oxygen saturation can be tested over a 30-minute period while she is in the car seat that you plan to use. (The test is not invasive and does not hurt your infant in any way.) If your baby cannot breathe adequately in the car seat you have, and further adjustments in position do not improve her breathing, you will need to purchase a special flat bed made for use in the car until your baby is bigger.

If you have a premature baby, you will be given additional safety information for proper positioning and support when your baby is placed in a car seat. Follow your instructions carefully.

All car seats should be in the back seat.

Make it a habit for all of your children to "buckle up" for safety in the car. In most states wearing a seat belt is the law, but the law won't be there to remind your 16-year-old to buckle up—it must be an automatic habit by then. Begin on day one. **Make no exceptions, and remember that your actions speak louder than your words.**

When my children were young, I always carried a magazine in my car. If the children took off their seat belts, I pulled over and started reading. It didn't take long for them to get the idea! "If I want to get to my friend's house on time, I'd better buckle up. If I don't want to spend the entire day in this car doing these errands, I better put on my seat belt. This car goes nowhere unless belts are on."

This no-exceptions/make-it-a-habit policy paid off when our 16-year-old got into a bad car

Baby Care

accident. He lost control of the car, which wound up lying upside down. When he was asked if he had had his seat belt on, he said he wasn't sure—he didn't really remember putting it on. The emergency room confirmed seat belt use by the belt burn on his shoulder. The habit saved his life.

Before You Close the Car Doors

Little hands can be badly hurt if caught in a car door. One mother's solution for preventing such painful accidents was very simple. Before she closed and locked the car doors, she said: "Everybody put your hands over your ears." When her instructions were followed, she knew that little hands were out of harm's way.

When Emotions Erupt

If children are misbehaving, pull over to intervene. Safe driving demands your full attention; so does disciplining a child or separating squabbling siblings. Don't try to do both at once.

Don't Leave a Baby or Small Child Alone in a Car

Leaving a baby or small child alone in a car invites not only abduction but also death. Cars with closed windows overheat quickly in direct sunlight. Babies and animals can die from heatstroke in minutes in a closed-up car on a sunny day.

Don't leave your baby alone in a car with another child, even for a few minutes. An older child may be able to start the car or release the brake and cause a serious accident.

Don't Drink and Drive!

Set an example: never drive after drinking. From day one, set the example that you want your children to follow when they are teenagers and adults. They will grow up to remember. How can

you argue someday that it is okay for you to have two beers and drive, but it is not okay for them? Don't let your example today haunt you tomorrow.

Use designated drivers, and make it a point to tell your children who the designated driver is for the evening. My husband taught a great lesson to our oldest son when he hired him to pick him up out of town after an all-day golf tournament and dinner. He planned ahead—knowing he would have a few drinks, he got a ride to the tournament and booked his safe ride home in advance. This made a big impression on all three of our sons and their friends.

Have a written contract. Write up and sign a contract with your driving kids that ensures them a *hassle-free* and safe ride home if they call for a ride. Include in the contract a promise that you also will call for a ride if you have been drinking. The groundwork for the safety net is now in place—it is up to both of you to use it. Most high schools have these contracts in their SADD (Students Against Drunk Driving) programs.

Teach Safety from Day One

When your little children get into the car with Grandma or someone else you know, ask them before they get in, "Did you ask Mom or Dad if it is okay for you to go with _____?" When they say "Yes," say "Very good, then you may go." After a while, this question will be automatic, with strangers and *even with people they know.* It reinforces the important safety point that **either Mom or Dad must know about and approve of all rides in advance.** When school age is reached, talk to your neighbors and the parents of your child's friends, and let them know that your child will not accept a ride offer unless it is arranged in advance. Many parents agree today that a no-exception rule is more likely to be followed by a young child than one that has exceptions or allows for them to use their judgment.

Teach preparedness, starting at a very young age. Teach and encourage your older children (especially those in middle school, high school, and college) to always carry pocket change (and know their calling card number) when they go out. This way, if they find themselves in an unsafe situation, they can find a pay phone and call for a safe ride home. These lessons need to be taught when they are young and reinforced over and over again.

Having enough money to pay for a cab is also a good idea when you go out. I realize this is a book about babies, but teaching preparedness is important and it must be started young. The following story is worth sharing:

A young friend in her freshman year of college once told us that she was driven by a "friend" to a party about three miles from campus. When her friend started drinking along with everyone else at the party, she realized that she not only did not have a safe ride home, but she had no money for a cab. Since this was her first week away at college, there was no one else she knew well enough to call. The only thing she knew was which direction to start walking to find her campus (a parent's nightmare). Since it was 11 o'clock at night, she was lucky when she arrived at her dorm safely. She said she learned several valuable lessons from this experience: *I am responsible for myself, so I don't depend on anyone else. I always carry change and money with me. If I travel farther than a cab ride away from home, I have a credit card that can be used for a safe room in case I find myself in an unsafe or legally risky situation.*

Siblings

Never leave a baby alone in a room with a child under the age of five. They may put small objects into the mouth of the baby, leave a cover over the baby's head, or hug too hard, to name only a few of the possible dangers.

Involve other siblings in the baby's bath and changing times to help prevent resentment and

anger. Allow them to *feel included* in caring for their brother or sister.

Allow your other children opportunities to express their feelings about the new baby. Help them to understand that feeling jealous is normal—babies take lots of time to care for and demand a lot of your attention, too! Assure older children that they are still loved, special, and very important to the family. There are many good books on the market to help you help your children through this difficult time.

Animals

Even your most gentle pet can become jealous. Use common sense and prevention concerning where you leave your infant to sleep or play. Bassinets can easily be tipped over by an animal curious to see what is inside.

Baby-Sitters

Never leave a baby alone with a sitter who is young. I hesitate to put an age on "young," since different children mature at different ages. Generally, however, children under 13 or 14 are too young to care for infants.

Be sure that all your sitters have been trained in first aid and CPR. Most local schools have a list of trained sitters. They cannot give students' names to you, but they are able to give your name to students.

Ask for several references on all sitters. This is especially important if your child is too young to tell you about the care the sitter provides.

We have all seen separation anxiety in young children, but a child who is being harmed may be trying to tell us in his or her own way—with behavior, rigid body, facial expression, or white knuckles—that this is more than separation anxiety. Listen and watch carefully to what your child may be trying to tell you.

Baby Care

Keeping an Eye on Your Baby

❑ **Never leave a baby or small child alone, even for a minute.** This includes just running down the street to the mailbox.

❑ **Never leave a child alone in the car.**

❑ **Never take your eyes off your child in public places,** like stores, amusement parks, or parks.

❑ **If your baby or child is in a carriage or stroller, keep your hands on the stroller at all times.** Strollers make abductions easy—the child in a stroller is facing away from the person who is pushing it and therefore may not be aware for some time that it is not the parent who is pushing. By the same token, a parent distracted by shopping may momentarily fail to notice that the child has been snatched or replaced by some object of similar weight.

Preventing Falls and Head Injuries

❑ **Never leave a baby or child unattended.** When bathing or changing a baby, always keep one hand in contact with the baby when you reach for something. If you can't reach an object while touching your baby, pick your baby up and take her with you.

   Babies learn to roll and scoot very quickly. Be prepared. Don't leave a baby unattended.

❑ **Before your child begins to crawl, lock all cellar doors and install gates at the bottom and top of all stairways.**

❑ **Keep all upstairs windows locked.** If they must be opened, push the top windowpane down slightly, keeping the bottom window secure. All windows should have securely fitted screens to help prevent falls, as well as to keep out insects.

❑ Banister slats need to be close enough together that a child cannot get her head stuck between them. They should also be checked frequently to be certain nothing is loose.

❑ Most cellar stairs have a space between the steps and the hand rail that opens to the cement cellar floor far below. Before your baby begins to crawl, fill this space with one or two boards (Figure 20-2). **There should not be enough space anywhere between the steps and hand rail for a child to climb through and fall.**

❑ **Remove table covers that your baby can pull,** thereby bringing down lamps and other heavy items.

❑ **Don't use "jumping" devices that clamp-attach above doorways.** These devices have caused deaths when door frames too weak to hold the weight have come down on the child's head.

❑ **Do not leave children unattended near windows.**

FIGURE 20-2

Cellar Stair Safety

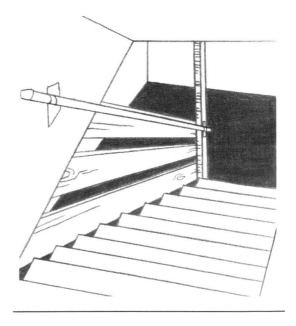

❏ **Do not leave children unattended in high-rise hotels.**

❏ Wipe up spills immediately. Put throw rugs in areas where floors (such as certain tiles) may become very slick if damp.

❏ Put the crib mattress on the lowest setting before your baby begins to pull herself to a standing position.

❏ Keep manual garage doors in good repair so that they don't become waterlogged and fall down. Keep small children away from garage doors.

❏ Purchase electric garage doors only if they have the built-in safety feature of stopping and going back up if something is in the way.

Bath Safety

❏ **Never, under any circumstances, leave a baby or small child alone in a bathtub.** Small children can drown in just inches of water. If the phone rings, let it ring, or wrap your child in a blanket and take her with you.

❏ **Be certain that your home hot water heater temperature is set no higher than 120°F.** In addition, while your children are young, **frequently check the temperature of hot water when it is running alone**—a small child may turn off the cold water or turn the hot dial up. The temperature of the hottest setting should not be hot enough to cause a burn. If it is scalding, turn down the water heater until a safe level is reached.

❏ Use nonslip bath mats.

❏ If your tub has a glass door, be certain it is safety glass.

Preventing Drowning

❏ Be certain that all swimming pools are secured with a fence that meets legal standards.

❏ Use a lock on your pool gate that prevents the gate from opening by merely pulling an outside cord.

❏ Lock all doors in your home leading to the pool area with a lock high enough to be out of the reach of children.

❏ Never leave a child unattended in the bathtub, not even for a moment.

❏ Keep toilet lids closed.

❏ If there is a stream or open pond near your home, invest in a fence to close in your yard. It is an investment that could save your child's life.

Preventing Strangulation and Smothering

❏ **Never use string, rope, or chains to tie toys to car seats, high chairs, cribs, or playpens.**

❏ **Never put a necklace of any kind on a baby or small child.** Make certain that ropes in clothing have large knots so that they cannot be removed through the loops that hold them in place.

❏ Cut long ties on crib bumper pads so that they are just long enough to tie the bumper to the crib rail.

❏ **Never use pillows; soft toys; large, soft stuffed animals; large bulky blankets; or soft, fluffy bumper pads in the crib or other sleeping or play area.**

❏ **Buy cribs that meet safety standards.** New cribs must meet the standards of the Consumer Product Safety Commission (CPSC)—check the labels.

❏ **Remove crib gyms as soon as your child can get on her hands and knees.** Falling forward onto a gym can cause strangulation.

❏ **If you borrow a crib or purchase a used crib, be certain that your baby or child cannot get his or her head caught between the crib slats** or in any woodwork

Baby Care

on the upper edge of the crib. Crib slats should have no more than two and three-eighths inches between them. In addition, be sure that an old crib does not contain lead paint.

❑ **Be certain that changing tables, high chairs, cribs, and playpens are placed well away from electrical cords, telephone cords and wires, and drapery or venetian blind cords.**

❑ Be certain that garage door controls are up high, out of reach. Children have inadvertently closed doors on other children. New electric garage doors have a safety feature that won't allow them to close if something is in the way.

❑ **Avoid all use of plastic bags.** Don't use plastic bags anywhere a baby or small child can get to them. Too often they have led to suffocation.

Do not protect mattresses with plastic bags. They easily slip out from under sheets, where little hands can find them. Clear plastic bags seem to hold special fascination for children, perhaps because they can be seen through. Many children see these bags as toys; thus, it is essential to **throw away all clear plastic bags *outside in covered trash cans or recycling bins* immediately.**

❑ **Toy chests should have**

Either no lids or lightweight or removable lids: If you have a toy chest with an attached lid, be certain that it has support hardware to keep the lid from closing on a child's head.

Smooth or rounded corners and edges (this goes for all furniture).

Holes for ventilation.

Absolutely no locks.

❑ **A stand-alone freezer should have a childproof lock.** When disposing of a refrigerator or freezer, remove the door.

Reducing the Risk of SIDS

For information on the recommended positioning of your baby for sleep and other ways to reduce the risk of sudden infant death syndrome, see "Sleep Positions," pages 333–335.

Preventing Choking

❑ Be certain that all toys are age appropriate.
❑ Avoid toys with small removable pieces.
❑ Specify one area of the house where the baby or small child does not play as the only place where an older child can play with toys that have small parts. These toys must be put away immediately after use.
❑ Do not leave small items sitting around the house.
❑ Do not leave pocket change sitting around the house or car.
❑ Teach older siblings never to feed the baby anything without asking you first.
❑ Test pacifiers before each use by pulling on the nipple to be certain it is not loose. Check it frequently for drying or cracking.
❑ Replace pacifiers every three months, or more frequently if they appear dry or cracked.

Safety at Play

Chemical-Free Toys

On September 17, 1997, Greenpeace distributed a press release on toxic toys. It informed the public that a scientific study had shown that toys made of a specific form of soft and flexible plastic contain toxic chemicals (phthalates, lead, and cadmium) that can leach from the product when sucked or chewed. Greenpeace makes it clear that there are other soft and flexible plastics that do not contain these harmful chemicals.

In addition, it provided shoppers with a list of specific toys that are made from safe alternative materials.

You can obtain a copy of this study and the list of toxic toys by accessing Greenpeace through one of the modes listed in Appendix D. After obtaining this information, you may want to help to educate, inform, and create change by sharing this material with neighbors, family, and friends. In addition, you may want to send copies of the study to your legislators and ask them to get involved in ensuring safe toys and products that are free of toxic chemicals.

Baby Walkers

Baby walkers can be hazardous. In recent years their safety hazards have become more evident. They result in many emergency room visits each year and cause injuries such as concussions, broken bones, burns, and skull fractures.

There is also a possible link between the overuse of walkers and late development of other motor skills such as sitting, crawling, and walking. Consult your pediatrician on this issue.

Toy Safety

Buy only *age-appropriate* toys by well-known manufacturers of children's toys.

If you have older children, allow toys unsafe for younger children *only* where the baby and small children will not be playing. Help older children feel they are taking part in ensuring that baby and toddlers are safe. Ask them to pick up unsafe toys and put them in a safe place immediately after use.

Avoid toys with small parts until your child no longer puts things into her mouth. Follow the age-appropriate safety recommendations on the boxes of all toys.

Never use string or rope to tie toys to car seats, high chairs, cribs, or playpens—strangulation can occur within minutes.

Safety Helmets

❏ All children being pulled in wagons and carts should wear helmets.

❏ **All children riding tricycles and bikes should wear safety helmets.** Be sure to check that the helmet you are purchasing meets the safety requirements for its intended use (for example, a bicycle helmet may not be safe enough for a moped).

❏ **Children should wear safety helmets and safety equipment when rollerblading.**

❏ **Set a good example: always wear a safety helmet and other proper safety equipment when biking or rollerblading.**

Preventing Electrical Injuries

❏ **Put safety covers over all electrical outlets.** This includes the ones above the kitchen and bathroom counters. Small children, unaware of the hazards of electrical shock, love to stick things into those tiny holes.

❏ **Remove, or put up a physical barrier around, any exposed electrical cords that could be chewed or pulled.** Remember, electrical cords provide a triple hazard: shocks (from minor shocks to electrocution), burns, and strangulation.

Shock and electrocution can occur from chewing the cord or touching a damaged section of it.

Shock can occur when a plug is pulled out *slightly* and those little fingers slip in and touch the metal prongs.

Severe mouth burns can result from chewing an electrical cord. Contact and exit burns result from touching the live metal prongs or a damaged area of the cord.

Pulling the cord, causing an appliance to fall off the counter and spill hot contents, can cause burns and head injuries.

Baby Care

Strangulation can result from entanglement in the cord.

Other Household Hazards

Electric Garbage Disposals

My second son was a very active climber. When he was two years old, I stepped out of the kitchen for one minute. In this short amount of time a disaster almost happened. He climbed up a breakfast bar stool onto the counter and crawled over to the sink. He became fascinated by the hole in the sink (the garbage disposal). I was understandably quite shaken when I found him with his arm well down into the disposal hole. The electric wall switch to turn it on was right within his reach.

Up until that moment, I had never thought of the dangers of an electric garbage disposal. We were blessed that he didn't find the switch that time. We eliminated the danger by putting a bypass switch under the sink and locking the cabinet to it.

Batch-feed garbage disposals turn on by turning a cover. The cover must be in place for them to run, but **electric garbage disposals do not require a cover to run.**

Guns, Knives, and Sharp Objects

Ten children are killed by handguns every day in the United States. According to the National Safety Council, accidental shootings are the fifth leading cause of death for children under five years of age. Some guns can be discharged by a child as young as two years of age.

❑ **Any guns kept in the home must be unloaded and secured in a locked area inaccessible to children. Bullets must be kept in a separate locked area.**

❑ **Knives, scissors, razors, sewing equipment, and other sharp objects must be secured out of children's reach** (on the top shelves in cabinets above the counter).

Items Containing Germs or Chemicals

❑ Toilet brushes and other brushes used for cleaning should be stored out of sight and out of reach.
❑ Dirty rags should be stored out of reach until washed.
❑ Dirty laundry should be in covered containers where it cannot be handled and placed in a child's mouth.

Radiators and Heating Vents

❑ Cover radiators with manufacturer-recommended covers to prevent burns.
❑ Cover the small holes of old metal floor heating vents with cheesecloth if needed.

Door Locks

❑ **Be certain that your child cannot unlock any door in your house and get outside.** If the child can, then it is time to add an additional lock higher up.
❑ If your deadbolt unlocks with a key, keep the key up high but near the door so it could easily be found in the dark or in the smoke of a fire.

Yard Gates

❑ Outdoor yard gates should all have child-resistant locks. This prevents a quick exit by your child and a quick entrance by an intruder from the outside.

Outdoor Gardening Tools, Equipment, and Chemicals

❑ Outdoor gardening tools and equipment should be stored safely out of reach. Be certain that large items cannot be pulled over.

❑ **As mentioned earlier, all chemicals, pesticides, fertilizers, and weed-killers should be on high shelves or, preferably, under lock and key.** Review the products you have on hand and consider whether there are nontoxic alternatives available that would pose no threat to you, your child, your pets, or the environment.

Preventing Poisoning

Box 20-1 has instructions to follow if you suspect that a child has ingested a poison, an inappropriate medicine, or a poisonous plant.

Medications

❑ **Keep all medications in a locked medicine cabinet and hide the key out of reach.**

❑ **Buy only medication with child safety caps.**

❑ **Never buy your children toys with "play pills."** Medications should never be associated with either toys or candy. (Advocate safety by voicing your objection in writing to companies that make candy pills.)

Lead Poisoning

Laws now prevent the use of lead paint in residential housing; on toys; on furniture; on cooking, eating, and drinking utensils; and on any interior or exterior surface or fixture of any dwelling. However, the laws vary by state. Call your state's Department of Public Health or Health and Human Services to obtain information about lead paint laws in your state.

If purchasing antique furniture or borrowing old items, think about this issue and rule out the presence of lead paint. **Remember, lead paint, even under layers of newer paint, is still a hazard if chewing occurs. Avoid any product with layers of paint or peeling or cracked paint. Avoid refinishing old furniture that may contain lead paint;** lead dust, when inhaled, also places you and your children at risk.

Many old homes have lead plumbing, as well as lead-based paint. Although the amount of lead allowed in paint was reduced after 1950, the amount allowed was later found to still pose a risk. Additional, more restrictive laws were not enacted until more than 20 years later. Homes built after January 1, 1978, had to abide by the laws banning all lead paint in residential homes.

Laws vary by state, but many states now have laws requiring every seller or real estate agent to provide all prospective buyers or leasers of property built before 1978 with a notification package about lead paint laws. This information must be provided before a purchase or lease agreement can be signed. The owner must also bring the building into compliance with lead paint laws if a child under age six will be living there. **If you are looking to rent or purchase a home built before 1978, get confirmation in writing that it does not contain lead paint.**

Toxic Chemicals

❑ **Keep all toxic chemicals such as drain cleaner, lighter fluid, and paint thinner (to name only a few) under lock and key.**

❑ Be certain that furniture you buy is not made from products that give off toxic fumes when they are burned.

❑ **Keep kitchen and bathroom lower cabinets locked if they contain soaps, scrub powders, or disinfectants.** When possible,

BOX 20-1

What to Do If You Suspect Your Child Has Ingested a Poison, Inappropriate Medicine, or Poisonous Plant

*©***First, call the poison control center.** Dial 911 or have the operator connect you if you do not know the number. Better yet, have the number posted on a list of emergency phone numbers by your phone.

Inducing vomiting is not always the treatment, especially if a toxic chemical has been ingested. Get advice from an expert.

If your child vomits, save all vomit for inspection. If pills, plants, or berries have been ingested, the doctors will want to analyze the vomit. **If your child has not yet vomited and you are instructed to go to a hospital emergency department, bring a bucket or kettle to save any vomit that may occur on the way to the hospital.**

Ipecac Syrup: **If you are instructed by the poison control center or your pediatrician to give Ipecac Syrup, remember the following important points:**

1. **Follow carefully the specific dose instructions given to you for your child.**
2. **If the child has not vomited within 10 minutes of the prescribed complete dose, take a bucket or kettle with you (to collect the vomit) and leave immediately for the hospital emergency department.**
3. **When you arrive at the emergency department, tell *a nurse* in the admitting area *immediately* that Ipecac Syrup has been given and *has not* induced vomiting. Ipecac Syrup must be pumped from the stomach before a specific amount of time has passed if vomiting has not occurred.**

Always keep Ipecac Syrup on hand in a locked cabinet. Mark the expiration date of your Ipecac Syrup on your calendar and replace it when needed.

keep these items up high in locked cabinets for double protection.

Poisonous Plants

❑ **Keep poisonous plants out of your child's reach.** Be sure to keep poisonous plants where dead leaves and berries won't fall where a child is playing.

When my first child was a toddler, I learned quite by chance that many indoor and outdoor plants are very poisonous. I ordered a pamphlet on the subject and was

shocked at what I discovered. **This is an area that needs more public education and publicity.** Some of the most common indoor plants such as philodendron, English ivy, poinsettia, holly, and mistletoe (especially the inviting white berries) are poisonous. Yew bushes, azalea, and mountain laurel are only a few of the common outdoor bushes that are poisonous. The ingestion of a poisonous plant can cause symptoms that vary from a burning sensation in the mouth to irregular heart rhythms, seizures, coma, and death.

The best thing to do is to go to your local library and check out an up-to-date book on the subject. Better yet, purchase a book or pamphlet with pictures as a home reference to help you identify poisonous plants and bushes (see Appendix D).

Preventing Burns and Scalds

❑ **Keep pan and kettle handles facing the back of the stove and out of your child's reach.** As your toddler grows, it's a good idea to check the height of her reach. Use only back burners if necessary.
❑ **Set your hot water thermostat no higher than 120°F.** Bath water that is too hot has caused many severe burns. When your toddler is old enough to reach up and change the amount of hot water coming from the bathtub or sink faucet, you may have to lower the thermostat even more. The hottest water at the faucet, with no cold water mixed, should not be able to cause a burn.
❑ **Be careful where you place your cup of hot coffee or tea.**
❑ **Limit candle use when children are around.** If candles are necessary, they should be up high and covered with a glass lamp chimney.
❑ **Keep matches out of sight and out of the reach of children.**
❑ **Keep electrical cords out of reach and out of sight.**
❑ **Keep crawling and walking children away from oven doors. Teach them that ovens can be hot.**

Fire Prevention and Safety

❑ **Install smoke detectors or fire alarms on all floors of your home.**

❑ **If you have electric fire alarms, have a battery-operated backup alarm near all sleeping areas.** (This precaution is needed in case of an electric storm, which can cause a home fire together with loss of electrical power, which eliminates your electrical alarm protection.)
❑ Mark your calendar in red to purchase a replacement battery for your battery alarm every six months. Have a second calendar reminder in red to remind yourself to actually put the new battery into the alarm. (This may sound like a ridiculous amount of reminders; however, I prefer to learn from the mistakes of others. How many times have you read about families who have died because the battery in their fire alarm was dead?)
❑ Vacuum fire alarms every six months (during battery changes). Dust can make the alarm go off in error or not go off at all.
❑ Have flashlights and battery lanterns available for use during power failures. This is especially important if you are leaving your children in the care of a baby-sitter.
❑ **Keep all matches and lighters in a locked cabinet.**
❑ **Keep all candles out of areas where small children can reach or climb to them. They should be out of reach and be covered with a glass cover when you are burning them.**
❑ **Keep small children away from outdoor grills and campfires.**
❑ **Keep a fire extinguisher in your home.** Learn how to use it properly and how to periodically check it to be sure the pressure is still adequate.
❑ Have an escape ladder if necessary for exiting upper floors in the event of a fire in your home.
❑ **If a key is needed to unlock your deadbolt from the inside, be certain that all older children know where the key is kept.** This key should never be moved or used for any purpose other than

an emergency. It should be near enough to the door that it can be easily found in a dark or smoky room (but not near enough for an intruder to break the door glass and reach the key). As part of your periodic fire drills, practice finding the key and opening the door in the dark.

❑ Have an escape plan and conduct practice fire drills at home.

❑ **Designate *one and only one* meeting place outside in case of fire and during practice drills.** This will avoid confusion and questions in the event of a real fire.

❑ Teach children emergency fire safety measures, such as dialing 911 if time allows; checking doors for heat before opening; stopping, dropping, and rolling if clothing is on fire; not opening windows, and why; staying low to avoid smoke inhalation when escaping; and meeting immediately outside in the designated area.

Smoking Hazards

Smoking during pregnancy is associated with miscarriage, stillbirth, low birth weight, premature birth, and high blood pressure (hypertension, with all of its related risks) in the mother.

Carbon monoxide from cigarettes crosses the placenta, decreasing the amount of oxygen available to the developing baby. Nicotine also crosses the placenta and causes its blood vessels to constrict, further reducing the amount of oxygen available to the baby. Constricted blood vessels in the placenta also mean decreased nourishment to the developing baby.

In the past several years, the risks of second-hand smoke have been recognized and well publicized. **Do not allow smoking in your home or car when children are present.**

There are more cases of asthma, bronchitis, and ear infections in children who come from homes where smoking occurs. The risk of sudden infant death syndrome doubles for those infants whose parents smoke. (Be sure to require no smoking while your child is in the care of care providers or baby-sitters.)

❑ **Do not allow smoking in your home or car when children are present.**

❑ **Do your best to set a no smoking example for your children.**

❑ **Keep all cigarettes out of the reach of children.** Lighted cigarettes are a burn and fire hazard to children.

❑ **Do not smoke when you are tired and may fall asleep. Never smoke in bed.**

❑ Do not throw lighted cigarettes out your car window.

Posting Emergency Numbers and Emergency Information

It is vital to have emergency phone numbers next to your phone, in open direct view. In an emergency, a person may be too nervous or upset to remember emergency numbers or find a number needed. The other important information listed below should also be included on the card to help emergency personnel reach your home quickly and give emergency department personnel important information.

Be certain that you point this emergency information card out to all baby-sitters and older children. Also instruct your baby-sitters to *give this card* to any emergency personnel who arrive at your home to give assistance and tape the number where you can be reached that day (or night) next to this card.

❑ **Include the following emergency numbers and emergency information:**

• **911** (Check with your local police to be certain that 911 is available and in service in your area.)

• **Police department**

- **Fire department**
- **Poison control center**
- Name and phone number of your pediatrician
- Name and phone number of parents' physician
- Parents' work numbers
- Parents' car phone or beeper number if one is available.

❑ **Include your family name, address, and directions to your home.** In an emergency, a baby-sitter may forget your last name. Few young people would be able to state your address or the directions to your home during the anxiety of an emergency.

❑ Include insurance information. Include subscriber name, subscriber number, and code numbers for each family member.

Also include the name of each family member's primary care physician and their phone number.

❑ Clearly mark the bottom of the card with the word *over* for more information.

❑ On the back, list a separate section for each family member. Include the following:

- Any special medical conditions the person may have (such as asthma, past heart attacks, diabetes, and so on)
- Any medication the person takes on a regular basis and why
- Any allergies to medications and the reactions caused by those medications
- Any food or seasonal allergies
- Any special needs the person may have (blindness, deafness, mental handicap, and so on)

Baby Care

Appendix A

Definitions of Common Maternal and Child Care Terminology

analgesia: The absence of the normal sense of pain without the loss of consciousness.

Braxton Hicks contractions: Irregular, mild contractions that begin around the 20th week of pregnancy. These contractions are a tightening of the uterus that progresses from the top of the uterus to the bottom. They last from 30 seconds to two minutes and are not usually painful, although in the ninth month they can be quite uncomfortable. These contractions are often called *false labor contractions* because they do not cause the cervix to dilate.

cervix: The narrow opening of the uterus, which dilates during labor.

dilatation of the cervix: The enlargement or opening up of the cervix during the first stage of labor.

effacement: The shortening, thinning, and softening of the cervix.

embryo: The products of conception from the time of conception to three months. After this, the developing baby is called a *fetus.*

engagement: The dropping of the presenting part of the fetus (normally the head) into the mother's pelvis. In your first pregnancy, engagement occurs two to four weeks before labor begins. In subsequent pregnancies, engagement of the presenting part usually does not occur until labor begins. Engagement is often nicknamed *lightening,* because there is now lighter pressure on the mother's stomach and diaphragm and therefore less heartburn and shortness of breath. (However, now there is more pressure on the bladder!)

episiotomy: An incision made by the doctor or midwife in the mother's perineum (the area between the vagina and the rectum) in order to enlarge the vaginal opening for delivery.

fetus: A developing baby inside the uterus from three months to birth. The term *fetal* refers to anything pertaining to the fetus. (A developing baby is called an *embryo* from conception to three months.)

fundus: The top curve of the uterus.

gravida: A pregnant woman.

induction: In this book, the use of medications to cause labor to occur.

intravenous (IV): Within a vein. In this book the term describes use of a special catheter to enter (or access) a vein. This catheter can be attached to fluids, making it an *intravenous line,* or capped off to provide a vein access point (with a device called a *heparin lock*).

lochia: Normal vaginal bleeding after delivery.

meconium: The first stools of a newborn. Meconium stool is greenish black and odorless and has a tar-like consistency.

multigravida: A woman who has been pregnant more than once. (*Multi* means many, and *gravida* means a pregnant woman.)

multipara, or multip: A woman who has completed two or more pregnancies to the stage of fetal viability (this term is often shortened to *multip*).

os: The mouth, or opening, of the cervix. Before effacement, the end of the cervix that opens into the uterus is called the internal os. The end of the cervix that opens into the vagina is called the external os.

oxytocin: The hormone that your body normally produces to begin and sustain labor. It is available as a medication (common brand name Pitocin) to be administered intravenously, to induce (begin) labor or augment (boost) labor when necessary. It is also used after delivery to help control bleeding.

parity: The number of a woman's *pregnancies* in which the fetus or fetuses have reached viability. Whether the fetus is born alive or stillborn after viability does not make a difference in parity.

PCA: An abbreviation often used for *patient-controlled analgesia,* or in other words patient-controlled pain medication. After cesarean sections and other operations, many doctors order an intravenous pain medication to be delivered through a controlled and programmed pump. The prescribed amounts, along with several safety features to prevent overdosing, are programmed into the pump. The patient then pushes a button to deliver his or her own medication when it is needed.

perineum: The skin-covered area between the vagina and the anus.

PIH: Pregnancy-induced hypertension. Hypertension means elevated blood pressure. In this complication of pregnancy, the elevated blood pressure is caused by pregnancy. A woman who has PIH did not have high blood pressure before pregnancy, and PIH usually goes away within 24 hours after delivery. To learn more about the symptoms of this serious pregnancy complication and what to report immediately to your obstetrician, see pages 108–110 and 122.

Pitocin: See **oxytocin.**

placenta: The oval structure that is attached on one side to the inside of the uterine wall and on the other side to the umbilical cord. This structure or "organ" acts as the exchange site where the developing baby receives its nourishment, oxygen, and antibodies from the mother. Also through the placenta, metabolic waste products from the baby are returned back to the mother, where her system eliminates them for the baby. The placenta is often called the *after-birth,* at the time it is delivered after the baby is born.

postpartum period: The six weeks from the birth of your baby to the time your reproductive organs return to their normal nonpregnant state. This period is also referred to as the *puerperium.*

presentation: The part of the fetus that enters the pelvis first.

primigravida: A woman who is pregnant for the first time.

primipara, or primip: A woman whose *first* pregnancy has now reached the point of fetal viability. This term is often shortened to *primip.* You may be described as a primip when you come into the hospital to have your first baby.

station: The level of the presenting part of the fetus in relationship to the ischial spines of the mother's pelvis. The station of the presenting part is determined by vaginal exam.

vernix: The thick white cheeselike substance covering the skin of the developing fetus. This substance covers the entire body until about 38 weeks gestation, when it begins to be absorbed. Therefore, premature babies will be covered in vernix, full-term babies will have vernix in the creases of the body, and overdue babies may not have any visible vernix remaining at all.

viability: The ability of the fetus to live outside the uterus. The point of viability is now generally accepted to be 24 weeks after the last menstrual period. This range changes as medical technology develops and improves and therefore increases the possibility for survival at earlier premature delivery dates. This term has become an issue in the abortion debates between people who believe that life begins at conception and those who believe that the point of viability must be considered.

Appendix B

Pregnant Patient's Bill of Rights

The Pregnant Patient has the right to participate in decisions involving her well-being and that of her unborn child, unless there is a clearcut medical emergency that prevents her participation. In addition to the rights set forth in the American Hospital Association's "Patient's Bill of Rights," the Pregnant Patient, because she represents *two* patients rather than one, should be recognized as having the additional rights listed below.

1. The Pregnant Patient has the right, prior to the administration of any drug or procedure, to be informed by the health professional caring for her of any potential direct or indirect effects, risks, or hazards to herself or her unborn or newborn infant which may result from the use of a drug or procedure prescribed for or administered to her during pregnancy, labor, birth, or lactation.

2. The Pregnant Patient has the right, prior to the proposed therapy, to be informed, not only of the benefits, risks, and hazards of the proposed therapy but also of known alternative therapy, such as available childbirth education classes which could help to prepare the Pregnant Patient physically and mentally to cope with the discomfort or stress of pregnancy and the experience of childbirth, thereby reducing or eliminating her need for drugs and obstetric intervention. She should be offered such information early in her pregnancy in order that she may make a reasoned decision.

3. The Pregnant Patient has the right, prior to the administration of any drug, to be informed by the health professional who is prescribing or administering the drug to her that any drug which she receives during pregnancy, labor, and birth, no matter how or when the drug is taken or administered, may adversely affect her unborn baby, directly or indirectly, and that there is no drug or chemical which has been proven safe for the unborn child.

4. The Pregnant Patient has the right if cesarean birth is anticipated, to be informed prior to the administration of any drug, and preferably prior to her hospitalization, that minimizing her and, in turn, her baby's intake of nonessential preoperative medicine will benefit her baby.

5. The Pregnant Patient has the right, prior to the administration of a drug or procedure, to be informed of the areas of uncertainty if there is *no* properly controlled follow-up research which has established the safety of the drug or procedure with regard to its direct and/or indirect effects on the physiological, mental, and neurological development of the child exposed, via the mother, to the drug or procedure during pregnancy, labor, birth, or lactation—(this would apply to virtually all drugs and the vast majority of obstetric procedures).

6. The Pregnant Patient has the right, prior to the administration of any drug, to be informed of the brand name and generic name of the drug in order that she may advise the health professional of any past adverse reaction to the drug.

7. The Pregnant Patient has the right to determine for herself, without pressure from her attendant, whether she will accept the risks inherent in the proposed therapy or refuse a drug or procedure.

Prepared by Doris Haire, Chair, Committee on Health Law and Regulation, International Education Association, Inc., Minneapolis, Minnesota. Used with permission of The International Childbirth Education Association (ICEA), Box 20048, Minneapolis, Minnesota 55420.

8. The Pregnant Patient has the right to know the name and qualifications of the individual administering a medication or procedure to her during labor or birth.

9. The Pregnant Patient has the right to be informed, prior to the administration of any procedure, whether that procedure is being administered to her for her or her baby's benefit (medically indicated) or as an elective procedure (for convenience, teaching purposes or research).

10. The Pregnant Patient has the right to be accompanied during the stress of labor and birth by someone she cares for, and to whom she looks for emotional comfort and encouragement.

11. The Pregnant Patient has the right after appropriate medical consultation to choose a position for labor and for birth which is least stressful to her baby and to herself.

12. The Obstetric Patient has the right to have her baby cared for at her bedside if her baby is normal, and to feed her baby according to her baby's needs rather than according to the hospital regimen.

13. The Obstetric Patient has the right to be informed in writing of the name of the person who actually delivered her baby and the professional qualifications of that person. This information should also be on the birth certificate.

14. The Obstetric Patient has the right to be informed if there is any known or indicated aspect of her or her baby's care or condition which may cause her or her baby later difficulty or problems.

15. The Obstetric Patient has the right to have her and her baby's hospital medical records complete, accurate, and legible and to have their records, including Nurses' Notes, retained by the hospital until the child reaches the age of majority, or to have the records offered to her before they are destroyed.

16. The Obstetric Patient, both during and after her hospital stay, has the right to have access to her complete medical records, including Nurses' Notes, and to receive a copy upon payment of a reasonable fee and without incurring the expense of retaining an attorney.

It is the obstetric patient and her baby, not the health professional, who must sustain any trauma or injury resulting from the use of a drug or obstetric procedure. The observation of the rights listed above will not only permit the obstetric patient to participate in the decisions involving her and her baby's health care, but will help to protect the health professional and the hospital against litigation arising from resentment or misunderstanding on the part of the mother.

Appendix C

What Happened and Why?
Miscarriage, Ectopic Pregnancy,
and Emergency Conditions

This appendix is mainly for those who are asking the above questions. If your pregnancy is progressing normally, be forewarned that reading this information may cause you needless worry. Other people, however, want to know all the possibilities, both happy and sad, that a pregnancy can bring.

In the many years that I have been a labor and delivery nurse, I have never seen a birth without having the sense of witnessing a miracle. It is one miracle that just nine months earlier, this baby was a tiny egg and a microscopic sperm joined together. It is another miracle that something doesn't go wrong more often.

Early Miscarriage
(Spontaneous Abortion)

Loss of pregnancy during the first three months is called an *early* miscarriage or *spontaneous abortion*. Approximately one in five pregnancies ends in miscarriage. Some authorities believe that this percentage is even higher, because some miscarriages occur even before the woman realizes she is pregnant.

About half of the women who have bleeding in the first three months of their pregnancy do not miscarry. Although you should report to your practitioner any bleeding and cramping during the first three months, most practitioners will not prescribe bed rest or medications. At this early stage, most authorities believe that unless you have suffered previous miscarriages and therefore might benefit from hormonal supplements, a pregnancy that for one reason or another is not "right" will abort itself, and a healthy pregnancy will maintain itself. It may help you psychologically to rest and put your feet up if you are experiencing bleeding; this way you can feel that you did everything that you could to maintain your pregnancy. However, the truth of the matter is that nature will take its course.

Although a miscarriage is difficult to accept, it helps to remember that it usually occurs because of a defective embryo, inadequate implantation in the uterine wall, some chemical or environmental factor, or a chance accident. Nature is actually doing what is best for this particular embryo. Do not feel guilty; you did nothing to cause this miscarriage. Unless tests have shown you to have hormonal deficiencies that make you unable to maintain pregnancy, you are *not* at greater risk of having another miscarriage. Each of your pregnancies will carry the normal 20 percent risk of miscarriage.

The most common symptom of an impending miscarriage is vaginal bleeding. Cramping is also a common symptom, as is pain around the area of the reproductive organs, with or without bleeding. The bleeding can be heavier than that of a menstrual period or merely spotting for several days. If you pass clots or tissue, it is a good idea to save them for examination.

Many times a woman expels the products of conception completely on her own. Other times, excessive bleeding or pain necessitate a dilation and curettage (D & C). A D & C is usually done under what is called *conscious sedation* at the hospital. An intravenous line is started to administer medication for sedation. Although usually you are not completely asleep, you will not remember the procedure. Your cervix is dilated, and any remaining fetal or placental tissue is scraped and suctioned out of the uterus. Cleaning out all remaining tissue helps control the bleeding to within normal limits and helps prevent further complications.

Late Miscarriage, Preterm Birth, and Stillbirth

A late miscarriage is a pregnancy that spontaneously aborts between the end of the first trimester (the first three months) and the 20th week. After the 20th week, pregnancy loss is called a *preterm birth* if the baby is born alive and a *stillbirth* if the baby is born dead.

(C)Any bleeding in late pregnancy needs prompt evaluation by your practitioner. Do not delay in reporting bleeding, severe or intermittent pain, or tenderness in your abdomen.

Ectopic Pregnancy

An *ectopic pregnancy* occurs when a fertilized egg implants before reaching the uterus, usually in the fallopian tube.

Symptoms: Severe cramps, intermittent pain, and tenderness to touch, usually on one side and radiating throughout the abdominal area, may be signs of an ectopic pregnancy. Light or heavy vaginal spotting or bleeding may occur days before the pain or cramps begin.

(C)An ectopic pregnancy is a serious condition. Therefore, it is important to immediately report pain, cramps, or bleeding to your practitioner. If the pregnancy is allowed to progress, the fallopian tube will rupture, leading to heavy bleeding and shock (dropping blood volume and pressure, causing a rapid weak pulse, cold, clammy, pale skin, and fainting).

Ultrasound and blood tests that measure the levels of human chorionic gonadotrophin are used to diagnose ectopic pregnancy.

Treatment: Removal of the ectopic pregnancy is usually done through laparoscopic surgery. Under general anesthesia, two very tiny incisions are made. One incision, hidden in the navel, is for insertion of the viewing instrument. The other incision, in the lower abdomen, is for insertion of the surgical instrument. If ectopic pregnancy is diagnosed and removed early, the fallopian tube can usually be saved, thus increasing the chances of a future successful pregnancy.

There are some new nonsurgical methods for treatment of ectopic pregnancy. These involve medications and *close* follow-up with your obstetrician.

Molar Pregnancy

A molar pregnancy, also called *hydatidiform mole,* occurs when the cells that normally develop into the placenta instead develop into many vesicles (grape-like, fluid-filled cells). The embryo stops developing because it lacks nourishment from a placenta.

Symptoms: The first symptom of molar pregnancy is usually a brownish vaginal discharge. Morning sickness is usually severe, and the uterus grows more rapidly than normal. The uterus feels soft instead of having the normal firmness. Some women actually pass a few vesicles from the vagina.

⚠**Report any of the above symptoms to your practitioner promptly.**

A tentative diagnosis is made after noting any of the above symptoms and finding no fetal heartbeat, and ultrasound will confirm the diagnosis.

Treatment: A D & C is done to evacuate the uterine contents. Careful follow-up is important because a repeat D & C may be necessary if the molar pregnancy continues to grow.

Although it rarely happens, a molar pregnancy can become malignant. If diagnosed early and treated with chemotherapy, however, this cancer (*choriocarcinoma*) is curable in most cases. Early diagnosis and treatment are essential to prevent spread (metastasis) of the cancer to other organs.

Abruptio Placentae

Premature separation of the placenta from the uterine wall is called *abruptio placentae* (see Figure C-1). This condition is potentially life threatening to both mother and baby.

Symptoms: As the placenta partially or completely separates from the uterine wall, the mother experiences *mild cramps or discomfort* (from a small, partial separation) to *severe and usually constant abdominal pain* (from a large partial or complete separation). In addition, in a large, partial separation or a complete separation of the placenta *the abdomen is very rigid and tender to the touch*. Although vaginal bleeding is usually seen with abruptio placentae, if the outer edges of the placenta remain attached to the uterus and only the inner margins separate, no vaginal bleeding

FIGURE C-1

Premature Separation of Placenta

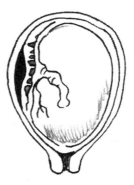

Partial separation (concealed hemorrhage)

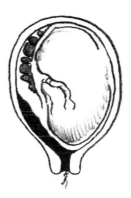

Partial separation (apparent hemorrhage)

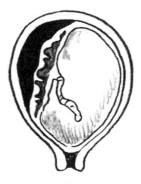

Complete separation (concealed hemorrhage)

Adapted from Ross Products Division, Abbott Laboratories, Columbus, OH 43216. Used with permission.

will be noted; however, the pain and rigid abdomen will be acutely present.

Ⓒ**Report any of the above symptoms immediately to your practitioner.**

Treatment: A small to moderate separation of the placenta usually responds to a few days' bed rest. Close supervision is essential for the rest of the pregnancy.

Immediate cesarean delivery is necessary for a severe or complete separation. With prompt diagnosis and the expert medical care available today, a large majority of babies and mothers survive this condition.

Uterine Rupture

Uterine rupture is a rare occurrence in pregnancy and labor and is generally related to a previous scar in the uterus. The scar can be from a previous cesarean delivery with a classical (vertical) incision, which is rarely used today, from other surgery to the uterus, or from bullet or knife wounds.

Rupture of the uterine wall can also occur with violent contractions that last a long time with little or no rest between the contractions. These severe contractions can occur spontaneously or after the administration of medication to induce or augment labor.

Rupture of the uterus is more common in women who have had five or more previous labors or extremely difficult labors. It is also more common in multiple births, in which the abdomen is excessively distended.

Shoulder dystocia (in which the shoulders become lodged on the pubic bone after delivery of the head) and mid-forceps delivery (in which forceps are used when the baby's head is only between zero and +2 station) increase the risk of a uterine rupture, as do abruptio placentae (premature separation of the placenta) and *placenta accreta* (in which the placenta imbeds itself deeply into the uterine wall).

Symptoms: The first sign of uterine tear or rupture is generally a severe pain in the abdomen that is described as a ripping, tearing, or coming-apart pain. This is followed by generalized pain and tenderness to touch throughout the abdomen. If the rupture occurred during the final minutes of delivery, hemorrhage and pain will follow immediately after delivery.

Treatment: Uterine rupture necessitates immediate cesarean delivery and uterine repair. If the damage to the uterus is too great for repair, a hysterectomy must be done.

In any uterine rupture, the outcome for the fetus will depend on the severity of the rupture and the severity of fetal distress it causes, as well as the amount of time from the rupture to the cesarean delivery.

Living Through the Loss of Your Baby

Recently I received writings from a couple whose full-term pregnancy had ended with a stillbirth. Their writings expressed many unanswered questions, conflicting feelings, and a deep soul-searching through their faith. On one hand, they were trying to deal with their anger and unanswered questions about why this had happened, and on the other hand, they had a strong belief that their faith would see them through the loss.

Lost Dreams

The couple described their lost dreams, their lost hope, and the lost future that they had wanted so much to experience with this son. I shared their pain at being denied the opportunity to know this little person whom they had grown to love over the nine months of waiting.

It is impossible to imagine any pain greater for a parent than losing a child. Whether the loss occurs during pregnancy, during labor, or after a short period of life, it is a child who has been lost. Studies have shown that recognizing a stillborn child as a son or daughter who has died helps the parents to begin the grieving process. Parents are strongly encouraged to touch, hold, and name their baby. At most hospitals, stillborn infants and those who die soon after birth are photographed; if parents do not take the photos home, many hospitals keep them, sometimes for many years, in case the parents change their mind about wanting to see what their baby looked like. In other hospitals, the undeveloped film is given to the parents, which allows them to develop it when they are ready. In studying parents who have suffered this devastating loss, researchers have found that seeing one's dead baby is far better than imagining what it may have looked like.

Autopsy and Burial

A discussion of autopsy and burial will be necessary, although it is difficult for everyone involved. Your practitioner will be able to advise you as to whether an autopsy may be helpful in determining why this happened and relieving fears about future pregnancies. Knowing what caused this death may help you to resolve the loss. However, an autopsy does not always find the cause of death.

If your baby dies after more than 20 weeks of gestation, you will be offered the option of letting the hospital dispose of the baby's remains or having a private burial. This is a difficult decision at a time of such intense personal pain. If you feel that having a permanent grave site would help you to deal with your loss but expenses are a concern, talk to the staff at your hospital. Most hospitals can refer you to funeral homes in the area that offer very reasonable rates to families who have lost a baby.

Grieving and Healing

Grieving must take place in order to resolve the loss and go forward with life. You cannot grieve someone who you deny existed. Holding and touching, naming, keeping locks of hair, hats, blankets, and footprints—all help you accept how real this little person was, how much you have lost. You will cry; you will need to cry, and so will your other children, your parents, your relatives,

and your friends. Through accepting and crying, resolution and peace can occur.

Grieving takes many forms. It is normal to feel depressed and sad for some time. Many people have nightmares or other forms of troubled sleep. Others continue to hear a baby cry for a while. Women often grieve differently than men. A man who feels that he must be strong for his wife often deprives himself of normal grieving, and unresolved grief may then show up in other forms such as difficulty in dealing with normal frustrations, poor temper control, suddenly poor work performance, or inappropriate behavior.

By all means, seek professional help if you are feeling guilty that something that you thought or did either in the past or during this pregnancy caused this terrible loss. This is an unnecessary burden to carry. The death of a baby should never be thought of as a punishment for your thoughts or deeds.

Your Children's Grief: Children grieve in their own special way, and it is most important that they be allowed to do it. They expected this baby too. Talk about your feelings openly and listen to their feelings. Make certain they know that if they felt unsure about wanting a baby in the house, their feelings did not cause this to happen.

Most hospital maternity units have books, other literature, and even coloring books available to help you talk to your other children about the loss of a baby.

Although this is a sad time, it is also an opportunity to teach your child how to find support within the family: how to grow and learn through an experience, how to make it through a disappointment, how to deal with death, and, most importantly, how one can go on to be happy after a sad experience. Cry together, and by all means talk to your practitioner about how you and all members of the family are feeling. Decide together whether professional help may be needed. You are not alone—there are many support services available to you. Seeking professional help, if needed, also teaches your other children another valuable lesson: there are helpful and caring professional people available to help us when we need them.

The above advice does not come only from doctors, nurses, and counselors. It is the advice of thousands of people who have experienced the loss of a baby. Researchers have studied many, many people who have suffered a stillbirth or the death of a young baby. Those who saw, touched, held, named, and cried and grieved deeply were able to resolve their grief and go on with life and feel happy again. Those who tried to deny that they had lost a baby and those who did not see and touch their baby had unresolved grief that left its mark for many, many years.

For doctors and nurses who experience the loss of a baby with their patients, our wish—our hope and our prayer, and the reason behind all that we do—is to help ensure that the couple and their other children will appropriately grieve this loss and will therefore soon be able to go on with their lives and feel happy again.

Appendix D

Resources

Books

Alber, Delores, and John Alber. *Baby-Safe House Plants and Cut Flowers: A Guide to Keeping Children and Plants Safely under the Same Roof.* Williamstown, Md.: Storey Communications, 1993.

Logan, Karen. *Clean House, Clean Planet: Clean Your House for Pennies a Day, the Nontoxic Way.* New York: Pocket Books, 1997.

Peterson, Roger. *Roger Peterson's Field Guides: Venomous Animals and Poisonous Plants.* Boston: Houghton Mifflin, 1994.

Steinman, David, and Samuel Epstein. *The Safe Shopper's Bible.* Indianapolis, Ind.: Macmillan, 1995.

Steinman, David and R. Michael Wisner. *Living Healthy in a Toxic World.* New York: Perigee Books, 1996.

Tauscher, Ellen. *Childcare Sourcebook.* Indianapolis, Ind.: Macmillan, 1996.

Organizations

Children's Health Environmental Coalition (CHEC)
P.O. Box 846
Malibu, CA 90265
(310) 573-9608
Fax: (310) 573-9688
E-mail: checnet.org

Environmental Protection Agency (EPA)
Public Information Center
Washington, DC 20460
(202) 382-7550

Greenpeace
1436 U Street NW
Washington, DC 20009
(800) 326-0959
http://www.greenpeaceusa.org

Healthy Mother, Healthy Babies Coalition
409 12th Street SW
Washington, DC 20024
(800) 424-8576

Mothers & Others for a Livable Planet
40 West 20th Street
New York, NY 10011-4211
(212) 242-0010
Fax: (212) 242-0545
http://www.mothers.org/mothers
E-mail: mothers@igc.apc.org

Safe Drinking Water Hotline, U.S. Environmental Protection Agency
(800) 426-4791

Services of Your State

Look in your yellow pages under "child" for various references. Look in your phone book or dial 1-(your area code)-555-1212 to obtain specific numbers for:

Child abuse and neglect

Consumer Protection Agency

Environmental management

Mental Health Department

Office for Children

Parental stress hotlines

Public Health Department, Lead Paint Division

Social services

Youth services

Childbirth Education

International Childbirth Education Association
  Box 20048
  Minneapolis, MN 55420
  (800) 624-4934

American Society for Psychoprophylaxis in Obstetrics (ASPO/Lamaze)
  (800) 368-4404

Courses

Consult your phone book for numbers of a local chapter:

  American Heart Association:

  CPR courses

  Health information

  Heart health

  Nutrition information

Red Cross:

  Babysitting courses

  CPR courses

  First aid course

Your Obstetrical Practitioner:

  Childbirth education classes

  Breastfeeding classes

  Child care classes

Breastfeeding Information and Assistance

La Leche League
  1400 N. Meacham Rd.
  Shaumburg, IL 60173
  (800) LALECHE, or (800) 525-3243 (24-hour line)

ILCA (International Lactation Consultant Association)
  4101 Lake Boone Trail
  Suite 201
  Raleigh, NC 27607
  (708) 560-7330
  Fax: (919) 787-4916
  E-mail: ILCA@erols.com

In addition, check your phone book for local lactation (breastfeeding) consultants:

La Leche League

Nursing Mothers' Council

Regional milk banks (often found in large hospitals)

ASK-A-NURSE

Other Resources

AIDS Network Hotline
  (800) 342-AIDS, or (800) 342-2437
  (800) 344-SIDA (Spanish)
  (800) AIDS-TTY (hearing impaired)

Alcohol and Drug Helpline
  (800) 821-4357

Alcoholics Anonymous
  Check your phone book for a local chapter.

America Belongs to Our Children
  (800) 783-6396

American Cleft Palate Association
  (800) 24-CLEFT, or (800) 242-5338

American Diabetes Association
  (800) 232-3472

American Red Cross
  430 17th St. NW
  Washington, DC 20006
  (202) 737-8300

American Sudden Infant Death Syndrome Institute
  (800) 232-7437

ASK-A-NURSE
Check your local phone book.

Association of Birth Defect Children
(800) 313-ABDC
(birth defect registry hotline)

CDC National STD Hotline
(sexually transmitted disease hotline)
(800) 227-8922

Centers for Disease Control and Prevention, Alliance of Genetic Support Groups
(800) 366-GENE, or (800) 366-4363

Cocaine Anonymous
(800) 347-8998

DES Action U.S.A.
1615 Broadway, Suite 510
Oakland, CA 94612
(510) 465-4011, or (800) DES-9288
E-mail: desact@well.com
http://www.desaction.org

Grief Recovery Helpline
(800) 445-4808

HIV/AIDS Treatment Information Services
(800) HIV-0440

Maternal and Child Health Center
(202) 625-8410

National Adoption Center
(800) 862-3678

National Association for Family Child Care
(800) 359-3817 (child care)
(800) 628-9163 (day care)

National Child Abuse Hotline
(800) 422-4453

National Coalition Against Domestic Violence
Hotline: (800) 333-SAFE, or (800) 333-7233
Check your phone book for the number of a local coalition.

National Cocaine Hotline
(800) COCAINE, or (800) 262-2463

National Council on Alcoholism
(800) NCA-CALL, or (800) 622-2255

National Down Syndrome Society Hotline
(800) 221-4602

National Easter Seal Society (rehabilitation services for the disabled)
(800) 221-6827

National Foundation/March of Dimes (Birth Defects Foundation)
1275 Mamaroneck Ave.
White Plains, NY 10605
(914) 428-7100
Access your local chapter through the phone book.

National Information Clearinghouse for Infants with Disabilities and Life-Threatening Conditions, Center for Developmental Disabilities
(800) 922-9234, ext. 201

National Institute on Drug Abuse
(800) 662-HELP

National Library of Medicine
8600 Rockville Pike
Bethesda, MD 20894

1-888-FIND NLM   Punch in 2 for research information on any topic (diseases, medications in pregnancy, cholesterol, and so on).

NLM home page: http://www.nlm.nih.gov/
This site offers assisted searching in Medline and other NLM databases over the World Wide Web.

Health hotlines: (301) 496-6308

http://www.ncbi.nlm.nih.gov/PubMed/   If you have an Internet account, Medline Series allows you to do your own journal research for a select service charge.

National Sudden Infant Death Syndrome Foundation
10500 Little Patuxent Parkway, Suite 420
Columbia, MD 21044
(310) 964-8000
(800) 221-7437

National Women's Health Network
(202) 347-1140
Fax: (202) 347-1168

Nutrition Information Service
(800) 231-DIET

Parents Without Partners
(800) 637-7974

Planned Parenthood Federation of America
(800) 829-7732 (national office)
(800) 230-7526 (for the nearest local office)

Spina Bifida Association of America
Washington, DC
(800) 621-3141

Appendix E

Bibliography

Alvarez, Manuel, and Karyn L. Feiden. *Recovering from a Cesarean Section*. New York: Harper Paperbacks, 1993.

American College of Obstetricians and Gynecologists. *Planning for Pregnancy, Birth and Beyond*. New York: Dutton, 1992.

Bobak-Jensen, Irene M. *Essentials of Maternity Nursing*, 3rd ed. St. Louis, Mo.: Mosby-Year Book, 1991.

Buckley, Kathleen, and Nancy W. Kulb, eds. *High Risk Maternity Nursing Manual*, 2nd ed. Baltimore, Md.: Williams and Wilkins, 1993.

Castle, Sue. *The Complete Guide to Preparing Baby Foods at Home*. New York: Doubleday, 1973.

Duyff, Roberta L. *The American Dietetic Association's Complete Food and Nutrition Guide*. Minneapolis, Minn.: Chronimed Publishing, 1996.

Gershoff, Stanley. *The Tufts University Guide to Total Nutrition*. New York: Harper & Row, 1990.

Hales, Dianne, and Timothy R. B. Johnson. *Intensive Caring: New Hope for High-Risk Pregnancy.* New York: Crown, 1990.

Heinowitz, Jack. *Pregnant Fathers: Entering Parenthood Together.* San Diego: Parents as Partners Press, 1995.

Huggins, Kathleen. *The Nursing Mother's Companion,* rev. ed. Boston: Harvard Common Press, 1990.

Jamroz, Deana. "Guide for Expectant Parents." *Parents Magazine,* 1993.

La Leche League International. *The Womanly Art of Breastfeeding,* 5th rev. ed. New York: Penguin Books, 1991.

Lane, Theresa, ed. *Foods That Harm, Foods That Heal.* New York: Reader's Digest, 1997.

Lansky, Vicki. *Practical Parenting Tips.* Deephaven, Minn.: Meadowbrook Press, 1982.

Lowdermilk, Deitra L., Shannon E. Perry, and Irene M. Bobak. *Maternity and Women's Health Care,* 6th ed. St. Louis, Mo.: Mosby-Year Book, 1997.

Mitchell, Anita, Norma Steffenson, Helen Hogan, and Sally Brooks. "Group B Streptococcus and Pregnancy: Update and Recommendations," *MCN (Maternal-Child Nursing),* vol. 22, September/October 1997.

The New England Regional Newborn Screening Program. *Frequently Asked Questions About Newborn Screening.* Jamaica Plain: State Lab Institute, August 1996.

Reuben, Carolyn. *The Healthy Baby Book.* Los Angeles: Putnam, 1992.

Spock, Benjamin, and Michael B. Rothenberg. *Dr. Spock's Baby and Child Care,* 6th ed. New York: Pocket Books, 1992.

Standing Committee on the Scientific Evaluation of Dietary Reference Intakes, Food and Nutrition Board, Institute of Medicine. *Dietary Reference Intakes: Calcium, Phosphorus, Magnesium, Vitamin D, and Fluoride.* Washington, DC: National Academy Press, 1997.

U.S. Department of Health and Human Services, Centers for Disease Control and Prevention/National Center for Infectious Disease. "Group B Streptococcal Infections." Brochure. January 1996.

"The Whole Grain Guide." *Nutrition Action Health Letter,* vol. 24, no. 2, March 1997, pp. 7–13.

Index